AMERICAN COLLEGE OF DENTISTS

# ETHICS REPORT

## THE NEW PROFESSIONALISM

David W. Chambers

*For the Officers and Regents of the*
*American College of Dentists*

ISBN: 978-1-7353254-0-8
eBook ISBN: 978-1-7353254-2-2
Kindle ISBN: 978-1-7353254-1-5
First Printing: August 2020

American College of Dentists:
839-J Quince Orchard Boulevard, Gaithersburg, MD 20878
office@acd.org
301-977-3223
www.acd.org

*Book and cover design: Annette Krammer, Forty-two Pacific (42pacific.com)*
*Cover graphic: © 2020 George Peters, istockphoto.com*

# Dedication

This report is dedicated to Dr. Jerome B. Miller (1942-2019),
a past president of the American College of Dentists and stalwart
advocate of every aspect of its mission to advance the standards
of oral health. The idea of a systematic study of where the
dental profession stands with respect to ethics was largely Jerry's.
He always reminded us that talk is fine, but if we want to make
a difference, we must have some "skin in the game."
We welcome all who would walk with Jerry toward the
opportunity for a "new professionalism."

# Contents

# Appendices

# American College of Dentists Ethics Report: The New Professionalism

## The Pamphlet

### The Main Points

In 2015 the Board of Regents authorized the *American College of Dentists Ethics Report: New Professionalism*. The model for this project is the 1926 Carnegie Foundation study of dental education in the United States and Canada conducted by the assistant secretary and editor of the college, William Gies. The distinguishing features of both reports include extensive collection of data as opposed to expert opinion, attention to defining the issue and its causes rather than advancing solutions, and abstaining from making recommendations regarding what others should do. The report is 520 pages in length, comprising 18 chapters and 14 appendices that present empirical work. Comments were gathered from dentists, patients, and opinion leaders, in small settings, and from surveys and tests. Information was provided by more than 2,000 participants. The relevant literature on ethics; dentistry; dental, business, and professional ethics; and social psychology was consulted. The project was compiled by David W. Chambers, the editor of the college, and monitored and approved by the Board of Regents of the college.

The major themes to emerge in this study include:

A. Dentistry and society are both changing. To remain ethical, the relationship must be constantly rebalanced.

B. Sustainable mutual understandings about ethics must meet the needs of all involved. No one group will be able to control the message or dictate the standards. Thus listening and discussion (engagement) are indispensable for sound ethics.

C. Organizations as well as individuals function as ethical agents, both in their own right and as context that promotes or hinders the ethical behavior of others. Both are indispensable for sound ethics.

D. We cannot talk people into being ethical. We must show them how they can thrive being ethical in the world we leave for them. Learning the language of ethics is different from habitually acting ethically.

E. It is more effective to change the conditions that control behavior than to change individuals who must then work against group norms.

F. Care should be taken to avoid the appeal of "ethical substitutes." These include the use of power, selective information, money, political pressure, and the like to force others to conform to values those in power favor. Ethical substitutes also include the use of ethical language, either in an abstract and theoretical fashion or as rationalization, without actually acting morally.

G. The major challenges facing the profession include: (a) individualism; (b) commercialism; (c) fragmentation of the profession; and (d) privileging technology over service.

The major findings to emerge in this study include:

1. Patients, dentists, and leaders in the profession and public policy share the following concerns as the leading ethical issues currently facing dentistry.
   (a) Dentists practice independently, using private standards.
   (b) Commercialism and overtreatment are increasing.
   (c) Greater leadership is needed to reinforce the ethical dimension in dentistry.

2. Dentistry is both a profession (by virtue of training and shared values of service) and a commercial practice (by virtue of licensure). Dentists identify with the values and regulations of multiple groups.

The number of such reference groups is increasing and their ethical standards are becoming diverse. This makes it more difficult for dentists to craft their professional identities. The dominant view of professionalism, embodied by membership in the American Dental Association, is eroding.

3. Historically, the business model of dentistry has been the professional service firm, where value is delivered on a customized and as-needed basis to individuals by highly trained professionals. This model is softening as more care is delivered to those with the least need by individuals with narrowing focus using mass technologies and commercial delivery models. The unequal adoption or adjustment to this trend is fragmenting the profession along the ethical dimension.

4. Most "unethical" behavior is small transgressions committed by people who regard themselves as fundamentally ethical. Many of these small missteps are regarded as "excusable" under the circumstances. Paying attention only to gross transgressions is dysfunctional because the costs of enforcement here are too large to activate effective effort. Small, mass change is also difficult because that would involve all of us.

5. About five dentists in a thousand have disciplined licenses (extreme ethical failure). Roughly one-third each are because of poor dental work (mostly inadequate records), fraud and overtreatment, and personal problems such as alcoholism. The average age of discipline is 57, and young practitioners are conspicuously underrepresented among dentists with disciplined licenses. Dentists avoid accepting responsibility for engaging colleagues whom they recognize as practicing below the standard of care. There is a proportion of bad actors the profession is willing to "accept."

6. The ethics of judgment assumes that one's view of what is right should be endorsed and exemplified by all others. It is often used to cloak political or economic interests or to demonstrate one's standing among one's peers.

7. The ethics of justification assumes that any behavior that is consistent with a principle is ethical. Although popular in bioethics, philosophers of ethics find this approach to be "expedient" and indefensible because of inconsistencies among principles. The ethics of judgment and the ethics of justification share the shortcoming that they do not alter the level of unethical behavior because they address the symptoms rather than the root causes and are likely to engage only those already highly ethical.

8.  The ethics of engagement requires that all affected by policies and action have a voice in determining the mutually most sustainable path forward. Otherwise it is power masquerading as ethics. Power is an "ethics substitute" and can be imposed on others—ethics cannot.

9.  It is always possible to reach a moral understanding that no party to the engagement would wish were different under the circumstances. Such arrangements optimize community thriving, and no external inspection or enforcement is needed. Regulation and lack of transparency are signals that ethics has failed.

10. The ethics of leadership leverages the power of organizations to create conditions where individuals can more easily act ethically. It goes beyond the traditional approaches of role modeling, coaching, and mentoring to include organizational change. The focus of the ethics of leadership is systemic ethical improvement.

11. The ethical core is the place from which our behavior is guided. Public description often differs from the true core. Codes of ethics have a mixed record for guiding action and sometimes function as *post hoc* justifications and public relations. The average score on a test of the American Dental Association's Principles of Ethics and Code of Professional Conduct is under 50%. Among dentists, the core is centered on private values and assumptions about what colleagues would approve. Ethical codes and experts, such as teachers and ethicists, are not consulted as authoritative. Codes for members are more common than are codes that place ethical expectations on the organization itself.

12. Dentists place highest value on technical prowess, followed closely by income. Ethics and oral health outcomes are regarded as having considerably less value. Technical skill and income are "opportunities," in the sense of being open-ended at the top. Ethics and oral health results are "obligations," in the sense of there being an acceptable minimum above which additional effort has small reward. On standardized value tests dentists score lower than the general public on caring and justice and higher on respect for authority and sense of who is entitled to benefits. Younger dentists are more accurate in judging the value of others in the profession than are older practitioners.

13. Ethics is a group activity where others exert subtle but pervasive influence on what individuals do.

14. Organizations protect members who behave unethically and sometimes excuse their (the organizations') bad behavior as the work of

a few bad actors. Organizations engage in types of unethical behavior that is uncommon among individuals, such as ethical shifting, moral bleaching, and especially moral distress where members are forced to choose between acting ethically and forfeiting some benefits of group membership.

15. Attention to dental ethics in schools is minimal, but dental students show good moral habits compared with other professions or previous generations of dentists. Ethics presentations in schools involve fewer hours than a dentist practices in a typical week. The true "teachers" of ethics to new members of the profession are senior practitioners. There is no evidence that educational debt is associated with good or bad ethical behavior. But it is clear that the shift to easy private loans has increased the number of graduates and put pressure on the overall economics of practice.

16. Some of the elements likely to be found in the new professionalism include: (a) diminished attention to "teaching abstract rules;" (b) building positive contexts; (c) engaging all affected; (d) moving at the accelerating pace of change found in society in general; and (e) building leadership for ethics.

17. Dental organizations and their leaders are the key drivers of creating a new professionalism built on ethics.

# Chapter 1

# Ethics Starts with Listening

*"Don't tell me what to do. Since this situation matters to both of us, let's talk about it and see whether we can help each other find a better way forward so neither of us would feel disrespected, cheated, or coerced."*

Let us begin with an assumption that those reading this report and organizations that represent the profession are ethical. There are many reasons to believe this, and this report is grounded in that conviction. There is no inconsistency between starting here and the evidence to be presented that a new and more ethical profession is needed. The world around dentistry is changing. Dentistry needs to change just to retain the positive reputation it has earned. The public perception that dentists are becoming more commercial and are not serving all those who need oral health care merits attention. The organized profession is showing signs of increasing fragmentation. Technology may be a boon, but also may allow others to intrude. Leadership in the profession speaks less often and less strongly in favor of ethics, sometimes turning a blind eye to the bad actors among us and sometimes measuring hoped-for impact in other dimensions such as power and "success."

Ethics matters. But maybe it does not matter as much as some of the other yardsticks dentists use. Perhaps we can retain the language of professionalism while emphasizing the kind of success others enjoy. After all, dentistry is both a profession and a business. But we would be fooling ourselves if we diminished professionalism. We will not fool the public and others such as the government and those industries that interact with dentistry. For them, they are doing business with a profession. That is part of their understanding of dentistry, and no group can dictate to others where they are to look for value. No group can long talk professionalism without delivering as expected by others.

For many it may be an open question whether the growing gap between professionalism and commercialism is really that much of a problem. Some would say the new range of options for defining success is a blessing. It opens up options for dentists to find their proper place along a continuum. Perhaps the public has come to accept that some dentists have paper-thin ethical standards. Perhaps there are just a few bad actors and the odor in some quarters will not contaminate everyone. Maybe there is alarmism. It might even be that this could all be scrubbed clean with the right kind of media campaign. Perhaps it would be enough to require ethics courses for students or for those practitioners who cross the line in some egregious fashion. That would demonstrate that ethics is a serious matter. We could point with some satisfaction to ethics codes. Even if they are imperfectly understood or weak guides to action, at the very least they demonstrate that the leadership understands the importance of ethics. If matters become ugly, we could say that the public needs to stand aside and let the profession define what is professional. And in the end, ethics is fundamentally a personal matter, is it not?

This report is built on a different set of assumptions. Ethics is not a private matter. A professional is a member of a profession in the collective and best sense. It is believed that the behavior of all practitioners who call themselves dentists affects the relationship of the profession with society. It is an ethical obligation to engage all members of the profession, including those who have lost their way. Even, perhaps especially, if society is changing, the relationship with the profession must be reconsidered. That will require leadership, not judgment of those who "should have known better." That will require systemic change to create ethical cultures.

This report will not lay out standards that one small group in the profession thinks everyone else, including society at large, should follow. It is a call, supported by a large amount of evidence, that the best way forward is engagement with all those affected by dentistry and all whose actions affect the profession. Fear of talking about our opportunities to do better, or not knowing how to have these conversations, may be the greatest ethical challenge we face.

## How the Project Began

The Carnegie Foundation for the Advancement of Teaching published its Bulletin Number 19 in 1926. Titled *Dental Education in the United States and Canada*, the bulletin was written by William J. Gies and was a companion piece to the earlier landmark report on medicine written by Abraham Flexner and several studies of legal education authored by Alfred Reed. The *Gies Report* contained 241 pages of text and 249 pages of appendix material. Although the title correctly conveys the fact that Gies focused on formal, predoctoral dental education, there were chapters devoted to the evolution of the profession, statutory requirements for practicing dentistry, distribution of dentists, access to care, control of education by the profession, and research—together accounting for about 40% of the text.

Gies found a profession a century ago struggling to advance beyond its origins as a trade practiced by inadequately prepared individuals in isolation from each other and one lacking a unifying set of shared values. Dentistry was heavily influenced by outside, commercial interests and watched over but imperfectly improved by licensure and regulations.

The *Gies Report* did not contain recommendations in the sense we are used to seeing them today. In their place were observations about the most important problems to be addressed. These were offered in trust that professionals of good will would work together to advance dentistry. What needed attention, in the opinion of Gies, included: (a) focusing on improving oral health through prevention (rather than repairing disease); (b) agreeing on and implementing common standards for treatment based on outcomes; (c) freeing practice from the influence of advertising and commercial concerns; (d) creating an education system to make dentists the peers of physicians; (e) promoting independent disciplined inquiry (research) in schools and in practice; and (f) making dental education affordable.

Leaders in organized dentistry, dental education, and the American College of Dentists (ACD) took Gies seriously and started discussing his report. (Gies was assistant secretary of the ACD and then editor of the *Journal of the American College of Dentists*, as well as the *Journal of Dental Research*.) Over the next few decades educational standards were strengthened, particularly with respect to clinical training, through the cooperation of the Commission on Dental Accreditation and the state boards of dental examiners working with schools. Dental schools were required to become part of universities, especially research-intensive ones. The dental literature was wrestled away from commercial interests, and advertising and self-promotion were suppressed. Some states passed regulations prohibiting individuals with commercial interests from being present at state meetings. Membership in the American Dental Association (ADA) rose to over 90%. Dentistry shook its public image as a craft repairing defects through painful and often crude interventions. Research became the dominant outside influence. Practitioners moved toward shared values of professionalism.

The changes that took place during the period between 1920 and 1980, when dentistry became a respected profession, had little to do with talk about ethics. The term appeared infrequently in the *Gies Report* or in professional conversations. What did change was the profession and its response to the world around it. "Professionalism" was created as an alternative to independent practice motivated by profit and influenced by external, commercial forces.

There is concern today that dentistry is drifting back toward the habits of a century ago. The ACD has commissioned this report to gather information bearing on this unfortunate prospect.

This first chapter in the report is concerned with starting a conversation about the role of ethics in dentistry; some of the challenges to probing in this area; a sketch of the methods used to develop this report; a sampling of what dentists, patients, and others say about dental ethics; and opening the discussion about which matters fall in the domain of ethics.

## Beginning the Discussion

Even those who are most proud of the profession acknowledge that there are problems. Often it is thought that dentists were more "professional" a generation or so in the past. This is a feeling, but one held by many so strongly that it approaches a given. Despite the absence of good data that signal a historical direction, let alone a glimpse into the underlying dynamics, certain solutions are commonly mentioned. One hears it said that we could get the profession back on the right path if some or all these steps were taken: (a) getting rid of or disciplining the few bad actors that have recently entered the profession; (b) teaching everyone the codes and principles of ethics; (c) curbing the influence of insurance, government, and others interfering with the historical ideals of dentistry; and (d) protecting the success potential of practitioners while keeping the pecuniary interests of corporate structures at bay. For reasons that will be elaborated in this report, this may be wishful thinking.

The problems are deep and have many interconnected parts. They involve the relationship between the profession and its social context. Both society and dentistry are evolving.

A new professionalism will require work at the systemic level, without preconceptions regarding the best way forward. What is needed is an open, multiparty discussion.

One of the giants of social psychology, Kurt Lewin, famously remarked that the reason change is difficult and short-lasting is too much focus on change itself rather than on the conditions that govern change (Lewin, 1946/2008). Too often one repair is replaced in quick succession by the next, as small groups of influential individuals offer solutions that appear attractive in the moment and to a narrow group. According to Lewin, there must first be a broad recognition that change is possible and worth the effort. He proposed a three-stage model. First there is "unfreezing" or building a case that change is necessary and that certain kinds of change are possible. The "change process," the second stage, is guided by the diagnosis of the real problems and identification of the working levers. "Refreezing," the third stage, requires that the change moves matters to a new, stable position. Too often change fades quickly or depends on the flagging sustaining energies of a few leaders because it failed to establish a new equilibrium. That leads to much effort on a treadmill of change or, more commonly, to half-hearted acceptance of change or just talking about how difficult it might be.

This is a report primarily about the "unfreezing" part of the change process. It is not a blueprint for what one group thinks others should do. It is clear to many that dentistry is drifting in various ways back to its former condition as a trade practiced by individuals who judge their success in financial terms. There are reasons for that, and making the right course correction requires that we understand those reasons. The following pages will contain quite a bit of empirical work and analysis. Some of this will focus on basic human nature, but there is little to hope for in the direction of changing that. Much of the analysis will be about the systemic, institutional, and cultural shifts of the past half-century and how dentistry and dentists have responded.

Unfreezing is difficult because it necessarily involves pointing out gaps in our better nature. It can hardly be otherwise. But there is a special problem here because those most concerned with making improvements are exactly the ones least likely to engage in questionable ethical practices. It may even appear offensive to mention problems the profession as a whole tolerates when those who are called on to fix the problems are not the ones who created them. It will be proposed that the ethical leaders in the profession have something special to contribute as "unfreezing" agents who highlight the problem and lay the foundation for solving it.

Lewin was quick to note that, up to a point, increasing pressure to make changes will activate proportional defensive resistance. So pushback can be counted as an indication that progress is being made. Once the unfreezing is accomplished, a tipping point is reached, and significant growth is possible. But improved ethics will not be had for nothing. There is a cost to be paid, and regrettably this cost is too often disproportionally borne by those with the highest personal ethical standards. Stepping up for the profession is the ethical thing to do. There will be repeated calls in this report that dentists should consider going beyond "just not breaking any rules." The need now is for ethical leaders. These are dentists who will work individually and through their organizations to lay the foundations for their colleagues to be more ethical. This report is not written for all dentists as a handbook for being "ethical enough." It is a challenge to the leadership to make it easier for all dentists to be part of a thriving profession. At his testimonial dinner in 1937 when William Gies retired from his active role in the ACD, he made a point of underscoring his faith in dentistry. He said that if dentists sat down and talked frankly about how the practice of oral health care could be renewed, we would create a new professionalism. This report is an invitation to renew that conversation.

## The Project

The ACD historically has been recognized for its role in calling for the best in the dental profession, with particular emphasis on ethical conduct. The college engages dentists through its publications, ethics summits, and affiliation with groups such as the American Society for Dental Ethics and the Student Ethics and Professionalism Association. Almost 150,000 free, online ethics courses have been taken as of 2019, with continuing education credit provided to practicing dentists. Scholarships have been given to dentists seeking advanced training in ethics, and hands-on ethics workshops are a regular feature at convocations. The primary effect has been on individuals, through awareness or knowledge of ethical issues and approaches. The response has been positive, but necessarily limited in scope and impact because these programs have been of short duration and without follow-up. Multiplying the effort a hundredfold would still leave the majority of dentists in the country untouched by the message.

The ACD Board of Regents felt that the current problems in dentistry are of a more systemic nature. They involve organizations as moral agents and the interaction between the various parts of the profession and between the profession and its changing environment. Further, limited numbers of individual dentists (usually those already exhibiting high ethical standards) may acquire facility with the language of ethics at the same time they face challenges in living up to these ideals in environments that loudly proclaim contrary values.

In 2015 the board of regents commissioned a study of ethics in the dental profession. It was understood that this would be a multiyear project designed to produce a report to stimulate discussion among the broadest possible range of constituencies in oral health care. From the beginning, it was assumed that the report would follow the pattern of William Gies's original work by being based on empirical investigation rather than expert opinion. It was also assumed that, like the original *Gies Report*, the outcome would be fact-based discussion rather than a list of recommendations for others to implement.

This project is consistent with the mission statement of the college expressed in its articles of incorporation, including to: (a) foster and maintain the honor and integrity of the profession; (b) study, improve, and facilitate the delivery of health services; (c) promote research and continuing education; (d) promote suitable standards for research, education, communication, and delivery of health services; and especially (e) to cause to be published and to distribute addresses, reports, treatises, and other literary works on dental subjects.

The report is based on the results of gathering data from several thousand dentists, patients, and opinion leaders regarding their perceptions of the profession, their personal values, and their behavior. It follows the method described by Lee Schulman in his preface to the 2010 report of the Carnegie Foundation Flexner study of medicine as *ambulando discimus*: looking for the data where it exists (Cooke et al, 2010). The report contains 18 chapters summarizing findings from the empirical work. More detailed analyses of the surveys, tests, and behavioral analyses are contained in 14 appendices. Each appendix item is presented in the form of a published journal article, most of which have appeared separately in the *Journal of the American College of Dentists*.

## In Their Own Voice

This introductory chapter will illustrate the empirical approach used throughout the report and highlight three major findings of the project. In particular 182 dentists and patients, in 18 focus groups in five states, were asked, "What do you think of ethics in dentistry?" Participants responded to this open-ended question in front of their peers and interacted with each other to elaborate various perspectives in sessions that lasted from 45 to 90 minutes. Verbatim remarks were captured in written and voice-recorded format and in detailed summaries by Dr. David Chambers and by an organization contracted for this purpose—the Citizen Advocacy Center, a nonprofit association representing members of health boards such as dental state boards. In addition, written answers to the question about the perceived importance of ethics in dentistry were obtained from an age-stratified sample of 237 graduates of one dental school. All records were analyzed using standard methodology for qualitative research, including summarizing verbatim comments, then summarizing the summaries, at each step grouping similar remarks while preserving original content and avoiding interpretation (Charmaz, 2006).

The full project and extensive remarks are described in detail in Appendix A. What follows is a summary of the stories about ethics in dentistry as told by patients, practitioners, leaders in the profession, and public policy experts. The place to begin answering the question "Does ethics matter in dentistry?" is with those affected. We start by listening as they discuss the matter in their own voices.

## The Practitioners' Story

Dentistry has become fragmented, with each practitioner functioning independently. Patients are being taken advantage of, but this is overlooked. Dentists do not communicate about standards, and they compete for patients.

- "Afraid of conflict; must go on tip-toes when discussing values in dentistry."
- "Dentists just don't talk much with each other about what they have in common, except for common 'enemies' such as insurance, understood in the sense of common excuses."
- "'Standard of care' is a term with unclear and often private or expedient meaning."

- "We are a profession of self-appointed experts."
- "Sense of professionalism seems to be declining. Dentists are withdrawing into their own offices."

Profit-driven treatment planning is leading to overtreatment. Patients are manipulated by advertising and inadequate informed consent, and care is piecemeal.
- "In the competition between ethics and business, business usually wins."
- "Treatment options given or preferred may be ones with highest profit margin."
- "Dentists just tell patients enough to get them to go along with what the dentist wants to do."
- "Dentistry is becoming a job rather than a profession."

Organized dentistry is losing its stature as standing for high standards and representing the profession.
- "The ADA is 'toothless.'"
- "The way it is now, a smaller and smaller number of dentists are carrying the water for a larger and larger number of those who are getting a free ride. Not sustainable."
- "Organized dentistry's voice is getting weaker."
- "Do not see the payoff for lobbying."

## The Story from Leaders in the Profession

Solo practices cause lack of collegiality. As long as dentists can make enough money they can afford to practice as they see fit. Colleagues are seen as competitors.
- "Patients are confused, and consequently, trust in the profession is eroded."
- "Neither patients nor colleagues have a voice in quality or type of care provided."
- "Every dentist can do whatever he wants as long as he can talk enough patients into it."
- "Overtreatment comes from a feeling of competitive need."

Overtreatment is a big issue. Bad dentistry, cutting corners, doing part of the job, and other erosions of quality are also growing concerns. This seems to be driven by seeking profits from those who are not in a position to evaluate quality—patients.

- "The new standards are money, technology, and egotism."
- "Patients and insurance companies are putting downward pressure on dentists' ability to maximize treatment offered."
- "Patients are 'customers' rather than individuals needing professional care. Dentistry is now something to 'sell'; treating teeth instead of patients."
- "Rebranding (anti-aging dentistry), smiles, brand named technologies disguise what oral health is really about."
- "In the corporate model we are seeing 'diagnosis' at the front desk."
- "Treating to insurance."
- "Dentists blame government and insurers for not putting enough money into the system."
- "Patients do not hear same story from all dentists."
- "Getting too close to commercial organizations, advertisers. The benefits of membership [in organized dentistry] are no longer obvious."

Organized dentistry is no longer setting the standards. The values of other groups, often commercial, are being allowed to intrude. Benefits companies and marketers are calling the tune.

- "We are aware of the problem [confusion and miscommunication leading to reduced trust], and we talk about it. But organized dentistry really cannot do anything about the problem."
- "There is no common place to discuss ethics or the alternatives to the way dentistry is trending."
- "Enforcement is spotty. State boards no longer involved except in most outrageous cases or cases where dentist does not put up a fight."
- "Organized dentistry focuses on legal and regulatory action rather than dealing directly with influential others."
- "The most questionable dentists are probably not members of organized dentistry, so we have no influence over them."
- "The ADA has become a bureaucracy that does not represent individual practitioners."
- "Organized dentistry is prevented by law from interfering in individual dentist's commercial activities."
- "The [ADA] code of ethics is aspirational and not enforceable." [This is not an accurate statement: See Appendix G—Editor's note.]

- "Practice is increasingly being steered by marketing values."
- "Benefits companies will not pay for all work dentists want to provide."

## The Patients' Story

Cost is the major concern, and patients sense that they are being sold unnecessary treatment.

- "Dentists want it both ways. They sell as much as they can, so insurance picks up some and the patient gets stuck with the rest. Those without insurance are just out of luck."
- "This 'full amount up front and then we'll see what we can squeeze out of the insurance company' attitude makes me think they [dentists] are in it for the money."
- "Way too expensive."
- "I'm missing two teeth because I couldn't pay for what I needed.... I'd still have these teeth if they'd given me a payment arrangement."
- "[Even with insurance], it's still too much. From my experience, I feel like a lot of dental offices charge extra because they know it's covered."
- "We should reduce cost by having dentists take home less money."
- "It's like going to get your oil changed, then the sales guy comes in with a list of things that 'really need to be taken care of' even though I didn't know they were a problem."

Competence of a dentist is assumed, but patients have no way of confirming that. They look to referrals from friends and appraise the dentist's communication style, but do not trust advertising. There is no way to hold a bad dentist accountable, so dissatisfied patients just move on to the next one.

- "Good is not having to go back or to hassle the encounter."
- "I think most of the dentists have competence. It really boils down to their personality. Do they make you feel at ease?"
- "It [dental license] doesn't differentiate any of them from each other because they all have it."
- "I want to steer away from the people with the new technology and stuff because, I mean, like, you're going to be doing fillings and root canals and things like that just like everybody else and you're going to have to charge three times as much for all your new machinery and it doesn't necessarily make you a better dentist."

- "I am beginning not to trust [some] dentists. But I trust lawyers and the government even less. I hope dentists don't become like lawyers or big business retailing."
- "Is there a dentists' association that a patient could go to?"

Prevention and hygienists get high marks.
- "The hygienist will come in and explain what she's doing and what she found. The dentist comes in and agrees with her assessment. Then I go to the front desk."
- "To me, the hygienists—they are the face of the practice. They are the ones you're going to work with."
- "The dentist is playing a smaller and smaller part in the system, just the technical stuff."
- "For basic cleaning it would be better to make an appointment directly with the hygienist and have it be cheaper and easier. All the dentist does is go over and look at it for 30 seconds and you have to spend however much money just for that."
- "I go to the hygienist; they have a dentist there too."

### Health Policy Leaders' Story

Dentistry is practiced on patients, not for them. Individual practitioners function independently from each other and organized dentistry functions independently from the rest of health care.
- "How can the profession tell the public that oral health is part of total health and then isolate itself from the rest of the healthcare system?"
- "Patients are not drawn to dentists; feel they cannot escape."
- "I was put off by the dentist taking a doctrinaire attitude that he should save every one of my teeth. The standard should be effect on health."
- "Dentists protect each other, so they cannot be trusted to do this job. Government is no good because it cannot get the data."
- "No transparency."
- "When I asked DC society of dentists, they would not say [anything about a suspected case of mistreatment]. Checked online, but that stuff is unbelievable. Everybody can't be that good."
- "The perception of the public and policy makers is that dentists are refusing to discuss costs and access."

- "I have been successful as a well-educated and well-connected individual in negotiating price adjustments with dentists; as a representative of groups of patients, I cannot get a hearing on this."
- "Patients are not respected. They have no voice."

Cost is an issue for patients and managed differently in dentistry—each provider negotiates independently.
- "Insurance reimbursement rates have not kept pace with inflation at the same time that dental fees have outstripped inflation." [Data from the ADA support this assertion (Vujicic, 2012; 2014)—Editor's note.]
- "Cost is becoming a factor in patient decisions regarding care. The well-off are consuming optional care and the poor are postponing or declining any."
- "Smart patients handle oversell by going to another dentist."
- "Dentists are pricing patients, government safety net schemes, and even insurance companies out of the market."

## Survey of 237 New and Established Practitioners

Many senior dentists (40%) saw the major ethical issue facing the profession as overtreatment, malpractice, and fraud. This is followed by concern over low reimbursement rates from insurance and corporate practices competing at the low-quality end. Together, 85% define ethics in terms of money, or inadequacy thereof. Of those in practice fewer than ten years, half are concerned over economic issues, but primarily debt load.
- "Every dentist knows the 'best' way to do things. He thinks that they are correct & that every other dentist is wrong. Public goes to 3 diff dentists and gets 3 diff answers. Dentists used to be a trusted profession. Dentistry lives in the dark ages."
- "The current state of the economy both globally and locally and its negative impact on the ability to deliver optimal dental care in a private practice setting. Inflation, rising cost of supplies and salary, educational debt, etc. require higher fees and more procedures and costs to patients."
- "How do we justify the cost of doing business in private practice?"
- "We place way too much faith in latest and greatest technique or technology."
- "We are losing our soul to corporate dentistry and our associations are not addressing the loss of the solo practitioner."

- "Eliminate the moral code of self-sacrifice and teach the alternative of rational egoism." [Ayn Rand's *Atlas Shrugged* philosophy that the strong deserve everything they get—Editor's note.]

The ethical issue is how dentists respond to a changing world. The most frequent reaction (20%) is to maintain personal standards without engaging other dentists or organized dentistry. This is followed (also 20%) by "do nothing." Talking to colleagues is slightly more common than talking with patients. Declining to participate in insurance plans was only considered an option by established practitioners.

- "Clear communication with patients regarding the need for the work regardless of insurance reimbursement."
- "Declining to take patients from insurance companies that don't reimburse adequately."
- "I can't change other people, so I do my best to serve my patients and community according to my values."
- "I retired, didn't want to deal with the stress anymore."
- "Keep educating my patients of the abuse [of insurance companies]."
- "Not much, other than pay my ADA, CDA, and local dental society dues. One person can't do much."

Established practitioners (20%) expect organized dentistry to fight for higher reimbursement rates on their behalf. A further 20% look to organized dentistry to establish and enforce standards, curb the impact of corporate practice, and educate the public. Established practitioners favor adding ethics education to the dental school curriculum. [This has existed as an accreditation requirement for almost 20 years—Editor's note.] One in five dentists said either that organized dentistry and state boards were ineffective in establishing or maintaining standards or that they did not expect them to do so. No young dentists expressed negative views regarding organized dentistry.

- "Making sure the dental field is not in a race to the bottom for affordable dentistry. There will come a point where reimbursements will be so low that it would not make financial sense to do clinically acceptable dentistry. Dentistry will always be practiced, but quality dentistry may fade."
- "Good luck on that one; organized dentistry is avoiding getting involved."
- "I am too old to worry about this."

- "Many dentists have to sacrifice patients' care to maintain their profits by spending less time, recommending unnecessary treatment."
- "The intrusion of govt, insurance, & corporate into our noble profession is disconcerting. Integrity is being compromised and yet we wonder why. Unbelievable. [Too many] people from other countries not growing up with basics of unbendable ethics of right from wrong. Get rid of the Democrats."

## What Did We Just Hear?

The dentists and patients have spoken, but they are saying things we may not have expected and have not been talking much about. The questions asked to stimulate the focus groups were not judgmental or leading. At no time was it asked "What is wrong with dentistry?" or "What is praiseworthy?" Panel members were asked to react spontaneously to putting the words "ethics" and "dentistry" together. The responses reported were not cherry picked (as can be seen by comparing the comments above with the full set of verbatim remarks in Appendix A). There is noticeable consistency across groups. The results are consistent with a previously published survey showing that practitioners and patients see the same ethical issues in dentistry (Chambers, 2010). (See Appendix B.)

It will be difficult for some to listen to this. It would have been more comforting to hear that dentistry is nobler than others give it credit for. But there is no division between the concerns of the practicing profession, its leadership, and those it serves.

It is difficult to hear that there are gaps in the ethical tone of a profession, and it is especially challenging when a prominent one of these gaps is a perception that the profession is not listening.

The center of concern is money. Dentistry is becoming dollar-denominated, much as it was a century ago. Patients feel cost is the primary impediment to their oral health. This fact has been confirmed in surveys by the ADA and the U.S. government (American Dental Association, 2016; Vujicic, 2016). Fifty-nine percent of Americans list cost as a reason for avoiding the dentist, as evidenced by not having attended in the previous 12 months. Another 22% say they are "afraid of the dentist," signaling that visits are unpleasant, perhaps due to pain or to being given unwelcome news about needed care.

Dentists are also concerned over cost, but in a different way. First, the money in dental benefits programs has not risen as fast as the rate of inflation-adjusted dental consumer price index has risen (Chambers, 2014b). This means that dentists are raising their fees faster than the incomes in America are increasing. The impact appears to be a combination of slower growth in dentists' incomes, escalating costs that keep increasing numbers of patients away, and selling treatment that formerly would have been optional or is plainly overtreatment. The first of these is not an ethical issue; the second is an issue of social justice; and the third is clearly an issue of professional ethics. Until about 15 years ago, money had not been the number-one concern for patients and dentists at any time in the last hundred years.

The second theme that cuts across the image of the profession—for all groups—is the independence of dentists. Each is substantially his or her own standard. This concern was the opening comment at the first panel discussion in this study, in 2016 when meeting with young leaders in dentistry in Ohio. The moderator acknowledged the remark politely but a bit dismissively, asking for real "ethical" issues instead. The room erupted in multiple voices arguing that this is central to ethics. Multiple standards mean that patients hear diverse stories and come to distrust the profession, that dentists disagree over evidence or whether evidence matters, that bad actors and even sketchy ones with strong personalities are not answerable to their colleagues, and that the very concept of "organized" dentistry is weakened.

Such behavior was expected when dentistry was a trade in which dentists, as small business owners, "recruited" paying customers. As the scientific and professional foundation was laid from the 1920s to the 1980s, individual practitioners absorbed these advances in their own offices, to the benefit of patients and dentists alike. The model of independent practice is still appropriate for real estate agents and Uber drivers where low entry-level skills suffice, minimal technology is required, direct customer contact is key, and little need for collaboration exists among specialized co-professionals.

The third common theme heard in the focus groups also has a historical trajectory. The organizations that represent and that oversee the profession are regarded as being less effective than they need to be and are becoming even less so. Practitioners voiced concern that organized dentistry is letting them down. Leaders in the profession voiced "helplessness" over the ability to influence how dentists practice, and the fall in ADA membership from the mid-90% range in the 1970s to the current 65% is evidence of this drift (American Dental Association, various dates). Policy experts see dentistry as self-isolated from the rest of the health professions and as ineffectively combative with other constituencies such as government and benefits carriers. Even the public is troubled, not even recognizing that there are groups responsible for enforcing professional standards. As one member of a focus group in San Francisco stated, "I sure wish there were something like peer review in California, or at least someone we could turn to if we have problems with a particular dentist." There is peer review, of course, but not for all patients and only for members of the California Dental Association.

## But Are These Really Ethical Issues?

The various codes in the profession are generally silent on matters of money and fair incomes for practitioners, independence of practice, service of professional organizations to their constituents, and interactions among organizations. With a few exceptions in the case of commercialism as an invasive value, these topics are not taught in the ethics programs now required in dental schools. There are no bioethical principles or major schools of philosophical thought that take positions on these topics. We just do not run dilemma discussions on cases like this. There are editorials complaining that somebody else is misbehaving and they should "get ethical."

The concerns expressed in the focus groups are in fact ethical issues, and important ones besides. The confusion lies in the current conceptions of dental ethics theory. We have borrowed from bioethics a thin version of ethics that focuses on identifying and naming issues rather than addressing them. We have also accepted the view that ethics is an individual responsibility and that failures are due in large part to a small number of individuals who either lack character because of their backgrounds or could be corrected by taking a few hours of instruction from the right people. There is no discipline of dental ethics in the sense of a cumulative body of verified knowledge that is unique to this profession. Dental ethics has become something we talk about using bioethics language.

How then do the commercialization of the profession, allowing each practitioner to be his or her own standard, and a weak organizational or common core become true ethical issues?

It will help when reading this report if one keeps in mind the perspective that ethics is the behavior that makes it possible for two or more moral agents (individuals or groups and organizations) to find the most beneficial mutual way forward. An ethical relationship is one reasonably informed and uncoerced parties would not seek to change, given the actual circumstances (Chambers, 2016c). This does not mean everyone gets what he or she wants or that we "owe" something to everyone (above the satisfaction of living in a flourishing society). That is expecting others to join the world we imagine is ideal. It means instead that we treat others as though they have the natural capacity to affect us in just the same way we are capable of affecting them. There is no such thing as "private ethics," and principle ethics that only works when others agree to the same principles is just "club ethics" under a high-tone name.

Money *per se* is not an ethical issue. The commercialization of dentistry, however, is a significant one as it can distort who receives oral health care and can affect whether there is a just distribution of costs and benefits and whether some cheat by appearing to act professionally while taking advantage of patients who are not in a position to defend themselves. Every dentist being his or her own standard is by definition an ethical issue because it guts the common core of professionalism. Allowing an individual to determine what is right and good on a case-by-case basis, to the exclusion of those they serve and one's colleagues who are serving similar others, damages the ethical core. Lack of trust in one's colleagues or weak support for the profession and ineffectiveness of the organizations that serve the profession are ethical matters when they crimp or forgo the opportunity for everyone to thrive together.

## Summary

The *American College of Dentists Ethics Report* was commissioned by the college in 2015 and conceived in the tradition of William Gies's work on dental education at the beginning of the twentieth century. At that time, contemporaneous with the founding of the ACD, dentistry was largely a commercially driven trade with little sense of shared professional responsibility. Over a period of more than half a century, dentistry worked to become a highly respected profession. A sense that we are slipping back toward a model that existed a hundred years ago motivated the current study, and the report is intended to open a conversation about creating a new spirit of professionalism. The report's fact-based approach aims to identify the multiple factors that are gripping the profession and pulling it away from its ethical moorings. "Unfreezing" the danger of tolerated unethical practices is the first step, involving extensive discussions among the many concerned constituencies and the training of ethics leaders. This is not a set of recommendations for how others should behave; it is an invitation to open the discussion. Verbatim comments from dentists and patients who participated in focus groups suggest that the conversation could well begin with the ethical issues associated with commercialism, a sense that dentists are not part of a common profession, and an understanding that organized dentistry and all groups in the profession could have a stronger role to play in creating a new sense of professionalism.

# Chapter 2

# Does Dental Ethics Matter?

Treating others as moral agents would be an appropriate response to all the concerns expressed in the focus groups of patients, dentists, and others. This is the standard:

Act so that no one involved in or affected by our actions, including ourselves, would be motivated to act differently. This assumes that all involved have not been misled or coerced.

The rule does not say that anyone, including us, is entitled to everything desired or even all that can be justified by a standard chosen to support the hoped-for outcome. The aim is a more modest one of agreeing on the foundation for a world where everyone thrives to one's potential, but not at the expense of others. It is respect for others elevated to the point where others are regarded as our moral equivalents. Unlike ethical substitutes such as power, economics, and the legal system, this standard is self-enforcing. No one will resist or try to undermine what they agree is the common good. There are no inspections or enforcement costs and no intrusive others. We all thrive together. That is the blessing of grounding our relations with others on ethics. No other way of relating to others can make such claims.

Is that not the very standard for optimal oral health care—the best for patients and dentists together? Is this not the relationship we wish to have with our peers, with the community? If we cannot answer in the affirmative, there is a strong likelihood that some other devious self-interest is working and we will need to continually fight for what we want with the resources at our disposal. We can be sure that our momentary wins will carry continuing costs to protect against half-hearted conformity and counterattacks. If we signal that we have not taken self-interest off the table, it would be reasonable to expect all others will be planning a similar strategy. The prospect of temporary victories through power is a significant obstacle to ethics. Its worst manifestation is the hypocrisy of wearing an ethical disguise while making what is right for us the ultimate standard.

This report advocates an ethics of engagement rather than judgment or justification. This view shuts the door on the American College of Dentists or any other group or individual telling others what they should do. At the same time, it establishes an ethical imperative to sit down and talk with all others who are affected by our actions. Ethics begins with listening, and then it moves to honest exchange of ideas. The only "recommendation" in this report is that we talk frankly with all those who have the potential to influence oral health care. Talking only with those who see it our way undermines the ethical stature of others. We should not make it a precondition for these conversations that only those who already agree with us can have a place at the table.

Conducting focus groups with dentists, dental leaders, patients, and health-policy experts is not the only way to bring out what matters to the ethical future of the profession. Many other sources of information were consulted in preparing this report. Each will be introduced in its own chapter and supplemented in the appendices. What follows below is a preview of the highlights of the full report. At this level, the claims will be painted with very broad brush strokes. Each topic will be unpacked and documented in detail in following chapters.

This chapter is concerned with establishing the boundaries of dental ethics and providing perspective on the overall project. The report considers ethics to be the actions of individual dentists and dental organizations and places the concept of practice in the center. It scans and compares various approaches to ethics, examines dentists' core values, considers organizations as ethical agents, and identifies some challenges that might be on the agenda for future conversations about enhancing ethics in dentistry.

## Dental Practice

There is an ethics of dentistry that is different from the ethics of building inspectors, mining companies, those who use the Internet, or the unemployed.

There is something distinctive and unique called "dental ethics," which flows from an understanding of dental practice. If we borrow the clothes of bioethics or academic philosophy or police officers or government bureaucrats, we should not be surprised to find they do not fit.

Some of the awkward feeling of talking past others in dental ethics comes from a confusion over what it means to be an oral healthcare professional. There is something more expected of dentists than that they be good technically or be assets to their communities. One must be an ethical dentist in the full sense. The expectations for ethical dental behavior are set by the public, professional colleagues, the government, industry, and others. These are the norms of good dental behavior, and norms are expected to be action-guiding as well as action-justifying. A "corrective reaction" can be expected from involved others if the norms are discovered to be abridged.

Practice necessarily entails standards, and these can be private only up to a point. In America today what it means to the public to be "a professional" is becoming too fuzzy to be useful (Sullivan, 2005) and is even resented (Nichols, 2017). The traditional notion of specialized knowledge and service is being replaced by an acceptance of any group that has some control over membership, is good at what it does, uses the latest technology, and generally commands good remuneration. Belief in the myth that professionalism is an implied contract between the public and a group of individuals who have the privilege of deciding what is well done has all but been absorbed in good lawyering over favorable monopolistic regulations. Now professional means "well paid," as in the *U.S. News & World Report* rankings. Another myth—that there is a single organization that represents an entire profession or can speak for everyone—is also beginning to show holes. Dentists legitimately owe allegiance to multiple groups within the profession and some external ones, such as family and religious or political organizations. It is also a myth to conflate professionalism and licensure. The latter is a commercial warrant permitting market access to a public not in a position to judge quality of services. Licenses are granted and regulated by branches of state governments, not by professions.

The "ethical codes" of professions are written by members to express the behavior expected of other members and are not a negotiated agreement between the agents of the profession, individually or collectively, and the agents they serve or interact with. The definition of oral health has always been problematic in dentistry. Too often the process of treatment has been accepted as a proxy for health outcomes rather than honoring the outcomes themselves. Processes are easier to monetize. For most of the past century, dental practice has followed a model known as the "professional service firm," or PSF (not to be confused with the professional service organization, or PSO). In a PSF (Maister, 1993; Maister et al, 2000), the work is customized, highly expert, and delivered on demand. Mass purchasing, building inventory, and standardized products are impractical. Dentistry has been a cottage industry of necessity, with the only means of increasing profits being to use more auxiliaries, to focus care on high-end procedures for cash-paying customers, and to defend monopoly status. Those conditions may be changing with corporate models and large-scale technology.

## Bad Actors

Here is a paradox: Most unethical behavior is committed by ethical people ...just ask them. Questionable ethics is not a character flaw so much as an opportunity for arguable small adjustments in our relationships with others. The statistics are impressive, with 90% of Americans admitting on surveys that they have broken the law and more than half cheating on their taxes (Rhode, 2018). Some would steal small supplies at work while others would misrepresent a business proposition for an economic advantage. But they would each say the other is unethical (Hartshorne & May, 1928). Because all of us feel that we are good most of the time, we also feel entitled to a little slack (Ariely, 2012).

It is human nature to overestimate the proportion of others who share our views. We are more apt to take credit for successes and excuse ourselves on the ground of bad breaks when things go south. But we are ready to blame others for flubs and chalk it up to circumstances when others succeed. Those in power cheat more, but we can improve ethical tone by setting positive expectations.

Every group has precisely the number of bad actors it is willing to tolerate, and many groups find it convenient to live with a tolerable proportion rather than invest resources in trying to drive down the ratio. The number-one reason people give for dishonest behavior is that "others are doing it" (Gabor, 1994). There is a "sweet spot" in community dishonesty where the bad behavior of a few outrageous individuals serves as cover for the small transgressions by the rest of us. There is actually a stigma attached to those who make too big a deal out of enforcing the rules.

Records of actions taken against dentists' licenses show that about four to six per thousand practitioners are disciplined each year. Of these, approximately equal numbers are for faulty dentistry in the technical sense (mostly inadequate records), for malpractice (including overtreatment, fraudulent billing, patient abandonment, and the like), and for personal reasons (such as driving under the influence, drug abuse, assault, and other crimes). Most disciplined licenses occur when dentists are in their forties through sixties, with young practitioners conspicuously underrepresented among the bad folks. Justifiable criticism of colleagues for gross or continual faulty treatment almost never occurs. Dentists are afraid to talk with colleagues about standards and usually find ways to rationalize problems they see or place the burden on patients for finding a solution.

## Alternative Approaches to Ethics

In everyday conversations, the term "ethics" is used loosely, almost as a synonym for "what I like." Sometimes "That would be unethical" means "That is not what I would have expected or hoped for." On other occasions, being ethical is equated with being able to ground behavior in principles or codes or other justifications. Ethics, in a third sense, means working with others we recognize as moral agents to find a way forward that no one would want to change, given the true circumstances. Finally, there is an ethics of leadership where the goal is to help others become more ethical.

Judgment ethics is little more than griping. The judgments are invariably about others, as in, "They should know better than to do that." Often there is a reference to a supposed character defect in those who do not share our values. Usually it is implied that no explicit standard is needed. Others "just don't get it." Part of the ethics of judgment is based on an assumption that one's own position is superior or even objectively ordained. The ethics of judgment functions to shut the door on discussion rather than invite mutual exploration of alternatives. Paternalism, assuming that one's superior knowledge about part of a problem justifies deciding what is best for others, is a dignified form of the ethics of judgment. Charity, although laudable, is not equivalent to ethics. Helping others is good as long as others are asked what help they most need and their moral agency is not compromised, and as long as we are not too selective in who we choose to help.

We are most familiar with the ethics of justification. This is a matter of linking the behavior we favor to principles or codes. Some of the shortcomings associated with this approach include: (a) different groups have different sets of principles, so it is arbitrary to pick one principle over others; (b) many behaviors are acceptable under one principle and unacceptable under others; (c) dilemmas are, by definition, a mixed bag of attractive and unattractive alternatives, and thus admit of alternative justifiable actions; (d) there are always cases where legitimate differences exist over which principles are dominant; (e) knowing what is right does not ensure right behavior; (f) and justifications are often *post hoc* — they are manufactured after the behavior and sometimes adjusted to suit diverse audiences. The evidence that principles, ethics codes, and honor codes improve ethical behavior is equivocal.

The ethics of engagement is based on treating others as moral agents. It is a process theory as opposed to a content theory of ethics. The notion is "Act to optimize morality." (Content theories work the other way: "Follow the rules.") The ethics of judgment begins with the assumption that "I am right." The ethics of justification begins with the assumption that "I am consistent with a few principles I endorse." The ethics of engagement asks a question instead: "Can't we talk about your needs and mine and find common ground that maximally satisfies both our concerns?" The operative pronouns in alternative ethical approaches shift from "I" (for judgment) to "it" or "they" (for justification) and then to "we" (for engagement). Ethics should not fear transparency and should reduce the need for regulations and monitors and sanctions external to dentistry.

Leadership ethics means working to build moral capacity in others. The assumption is that one will thrive more consistently in an environment where others act ethically. Ethical leaders work to some extent to build the ability in individual colleagues, but primarily they stimulate organizations to create the conditions where it is natural for members to behave ethically.

Recent neurobiological evidence shows that humans have the first three of these ethical systems (judgment, justification, and engagement) wired into our mental apparatus. Each system resides in a different region of the brain and comes online developmentally in the order mentioned here. The capacity for the ethics of engagement arrives only in the mid- to late-teens, the age of legal independence in most cultures. A pathological few never attain the capacity for the ethics of engagement. Leadership ethics is far too uncommon.

## The Ethical Core

Dentists center their ethics in principles, touchstones, practice goals, values, and practice norms. Each of these was measured empirically as part of this study.

Of these, principles seem to have the weakest impact. A test on the American Dental Association *Principles of Ethics and Code of Conduct* taken by hundreds of members of the association produced an average score under 50%. It is possible that the traditional principles of patient autonomy, nonmaleficence, beneficence, justice, and veracity serve primarily as a vocabulary for discussion in theoretical circumstances such as dental school, continuing education courses, or ethics columns. The codes of state associations and other oral health groups often use different principles.

When asked about "touchstones"—the most trusted sources of ethical guidance—dentists list in order from most to least trusted: (a) themselves (without consulting others); (b) colleagues; (c) engagement with involved others; (d) codes; and finally (e) experts such as lawyers and ethicists or the state board. This continuum moves from preferring ethics one controls to declining interest in the ethics of others, especially those who might have a legitimate claim on the dentist's behavior.

Practice goals were measured using a methodology that eliminated social-desirability response bias. The dominant professional goal is technical excellence, followed by income. These are not inconsistent with the focus of optimizing practice and they represent opportunities in the eyes of dentists. Of much less value are the goals of being ethical and achieving excellent oral health outcomes. These latter can be regarded as obligations. The difference is that opportunities are open-ended at the top, while obligations have a minimum threshold. One can be "ethical enough."

Dentists' values were measured with a widely used standardized instrument, the Moral Foundations Questionnaire (Haidt, 2012). The rank ordering of young and experienced practitioners was identical, ranging from a high for caring, then fairness, purity, authority, and loyalty, to a low for individuality. Compared with the general public, however, both young and experienced dentists scored lower on caring and justice and higher on authority, individuality, and not relating to those who are seen as unworthy of respect. Although young and experienced practitioners have similar value profiles, they diverge noticeably in what values they attribute to each other. The public sees "professional values in action" much as young practitioners do.

The teaching cases used in dentistry, nursing, journalism, and business programs were compared. By contrast with the other professions, dental cases emphasized hypotheticals in a controlled environment where the individual practitioner is the sole determiner and judge of right and good in the dental office. For the dental dilemmas in particular there are several alternatives available and equally justifiable based on personal choice and principles.

## Organizations as Moral Agents

Multiple organizations serve as both the context in which individuals behave ethically and as agents themselves in their interactions with other organizations. Power casts its shadow wherever ethics is a viable dimension of the way humans treat each other. It is often a substitute that blocks recognition of the need for treating each other as morally equal. Organizations more easily than individuals can pass costs on to others, hide questionable practices, and shift ethical responsibilities to others. Moral hazard occurs when group actions intended to facilitate fairness actually promote unethical behavior. Free riding occurs when members of groups claim more benefits than they are entitled to or shirk their fair contributions. Decoupling is a form of organizational hypocrisy where abstract, publicly praiseworthy ideals are proclaimed, but actions that would bring about these changes, especially if they have costs attached, are slow-walked. When leaders claim reward for short-term success in an organization and exit before the costs come due, this is called "milking." Moral bleaching involves converting a moral abuse into an economic issue and then buying off the obligation, usually with organization members' money, and walking away with no moral sanctions or public shame. Gifting creates implied obligations and is often frowned on in professional communities. A hidden ethical issue here is that organizations seek to deny influence from other groups by placing limitations on gifts their members can receive from others. Moral shifting is simply trying to blame others for one's failures. Moral distress exists when groups place their members in ethically untenable circumstances and then blame them for being unethical. Young dentists complain of moral distress in one-shot initial licensure examinations by testing agencies and corporate practices. Experienced dentists complain of moral distress in their dealings with benefits providers.

Although many organizations have ethics codes covering the actions of their members, very few have codes that set standards for how the organization itself should behave with respect to its members or in interactions with other organizations and constituencies. A conspicuous exception is dental schools, which in order to meet accreditation standards must have an ethical code for the school itself and must produce evidence that they are adhering to their own humanistic standards.

## Ethics Education

Since the late 1990s, dental schools have had an accreditation requirement for graduating students competent in applying ethical principles. The typical curriculum involves lectures, sometimes by individuals other than faculty members, supplemented by small-group case work. The anticipated outcome is awareness of principles and reasoning about their potential application in hypothetical "dilemma" situations. The average total time devoted to ethics instruction is 23 hours, with a wide range from more than 100 hours to "none reported." Some schools say that ethics is "handled as part of instruction generally." There are no full-time, formally trained dental ethics educators, and the content of dental ethics is largely borrowed from bioethics or practice acts. The time devoted to ethics and the number of peer-reviewed ethics publications have been declining for the past 15 years. Attention to academic integrity (the euphemism for cheating) may be overemphasized because it is so easy to conduct studies in schools, in contrast to studying practices. The rate of self-reported cheating in dental school is comparable to percentages found in other professional education generally, and in the public. The highest reported level of cheating in dental schools was reported in 1980.

Most habits of ethical behavior are learned after graduation and formed by probing to see what actions are accepted by patients, colleagues, and the commercial licensure mechanism of the state boards. A strong source of "real ethics" is senior dentists, associateship relationships, and corporate and clinical practice models (Fischman et al, 2004). It has yet to be demonstrated in the court of peer-reviewed science that one-shot initial licensure is valid or ethical, or even necessary.

## Challenges Facing the Profession

Four dysfunctional features in dentistry represent emerging challenges the profession must negotiate. These include individualism, commercialism, fragmentation, and technology.

Individual independence was at one time a strength in dentistry and is still a major attraction for those entering the profession. But dentists are increasingly seeing each other as strangers or competitors. This includes cross-generational suspicions. The solo practice setting places dentists in the questionable position of requiring knowledge of and effective control over a dramatically increasing science-based knowledge, technology, and complex health delivery and finance systems. At the same time individual dentists are expected to both make the decisions and judge whether the decisions are right for all concerned. Codes that once were broad enough to fit all seem to fit most rather loosely now. Regulations are the public's answer to this problem. But regulations are resented by the profession, and along with them, any form of external standards or inspection. This naturally creates a resistance to the ethics of engagement.

Commercialism is the movement away from personal relationships between dentists and patients based largely on trust, on the one hand, to dentistry as a bundle of economic transactions, on the other. Transactions are suited to monetizing the profession and permit the intrusion of external values, such as those of lawyers, outside financial interests, and marketing people. This trend is working to destroy individualization in dentistry, but it may not be an attractive substitute. Practices with fictitious business names or multiple offices have a much higher rate of disciplined licenses, for example.

The profession is fragmenting. Membership in the American Dental Association is declining at the rate of 1% per year, with the largest drops occurring among general practitioners in their forties and fifties. This corresponds with shifts in the association, as reflected by the content in the *ADA News*, away from direct participation by members (now handled by professional staff) and a dramatic increase in advertising, especially advertising to members. The income of dentists has flattened since 2006, but the range of incomes continues to increase. There are, for the first time in decades, some dentists earning less in real dollars than they did ten years previously. At the same time, there are dentists who are earning more than four times the average in the profession. It will be an increasing challenge for any organization to speak for all dentists when dentists are becoming less like each other.

Technology is emerging as a defining dimension in all professions. For years, advances in technology were small enough to be controlled by dentists in their offices and to drive both increased quality and productivity. The new technologies are more expensive to finance and justify in solo offices. Some technology is direct-to-customer, and this trend will continue, eventually moving some parts of dentistry out of the solo office. As the profession drifts toward defining itself in terms of technology rather than service, scalable technology, controlled by others, will put pressure on the traditional professional service firm model.

## A New Professionalism

It is fair to ask whether we really need to work on improving dental ethics now. Perhaps it is sufficient to mount an advertising campaign reaffirming dentistry's traditional values and to hope to see changes in a few bad actors, the government, the values of the public, and benefits carriers. Maybe targeting some of the more interested practitioners with continuing education programs centered on short ethical dilemmas or adding this as a licensure renewal requirement will be satisfactory. Perhaps it is sufficient to advertise our concern for being ethical. This report casts doubt on the wisdom of this non-strategy.

Dentistry has evolved since the days when it was a trade. It grew in impact and status by incorporating and adjusting to changes in patient expectations, techniques, research, specialties, and reimbursement systems. Today the external context of dentistry is evolving faster than dentistry is responding, and the borders between dentistry and society and our economic system are becoming more porous. The ethical task for dentistry is centered on how the profession interacts with and remains relevant to major social trends. It is necessary but not enough to salvage what remains of the noble behavior of former generations. The profession cannot dictate or resist change; it must participate.

Very likely the new professionalism will involve some combination of the following elements: (a) toning down the public relations and academic dimensions of ethics talk; (b) creating conditions where it is easier for dentists to do the right thing rather than telling them to do it; (c) engaging in ethical discussions with fellow dentists and fellow organizations and the public; (d) embracing a level of flexibility at least as great as the society around the profession; (e) paying attention to the more rapid rate of change and modifying overly long leadership paths and response times; and (f) rewarding leaders—those who challenge the status quo and make those around them more ethical. The ethical leaders from various stakeholder groups can come together and identify parts of the new professionalism most vital to their constituencies and support each other in specific action plans to engage and make it easier for all to be ethical in a changing world.

## Summary

Ethics is acting with others to bring about the best we can become together. In an ethical community there is limited need for either external inspection or enforcement. Ethics substitutes, such as power, money, political influence, and deception, should be taken off the table. This chapter is a preview of the material developed in detail in the rest of the report.

The classical model of dentistry as providing customized service to those who need it when they need it is wrapped in a professional and licensure context that is showing signs of unraveling. Occasional and "minor" personal ethical indiscretion is part of human nature, as is our tendency to excuse it in ourselves and our friends. Ethics work is some combination of the following: (a) judging what others do; (b) justifying our own actions; (c) engaging others in working for the common good; and (d) leadership in building communities where others can be more ethical. Individual dentists' ethical behavior is built on an imperfect understanding of principles, reference to touchstones that tend toward the individual rather than the public, and values that emphasize technical skill and income rather than ethics or oral health outcomes. Organizations can be ethical agents, acting toward their members and other organizations in ways based on ethics or alternatives. Great opportunity exists for organized dentistry and dental education in these areas.

Among the ethical challenges facing the profession are individualism, commercialism, fragmentation, and technology. These are not the result of a decay in the ethical core of the profession; they are tears in the fabric attributable to society changing at a different pace or in divergent direction from the growth that naturally characterizes a dynamic profession. The American College of Dentists does not offer a set of recommendations that "somebody" needs to put into action as the most appropriate way to bring about the needed new professionalism. It does seem inescapable, however, that there should be a wide-ranging conversation involving all those affected and effective in bringing about ethical change.

# Chapter 3

# The Profession and the License

Dentists share ethical obligations with all humankind and those standards most cherished in their communities. These general norms include not harming or misleading others; hospitality and reciprocating kindnesses; confidentiality; respect for civil discourse; being clean; not using or destroying what is not one's own; contributing a reasonable amount to the common good; helping others when we can; keeping one's promises; being fair or at least not conspicuously inconsistent; tolerating others' differences if no one is damaged in the process; not grabbing more than one's share of common resources; and abstaining from torture or bullying. And there are more. Thomas Donaldson and Thomas W. Dunfee made a brave attempt to enumerate the top worldwide ethical ideals (Donaldson & Dunfee, 1999). Robert Fulghum's 1986 blockbuster *All I Really Need to Know I Learned in Kindergarten* is more readable, and he boils it down to what kids can recognize as good and right without having to take a course in philosophy or study a code. None of this means that we actually act ethically. That comes separately.

This chapter is concerned with establishing the need for a unique dental ethics, one based on dental practice in the context of collegial professionalism and the profession's role in society, the evolving concept of professionalism, the underdeveloped definition of oral health, and the distinction between licensure and professionalism.

The norms mentioned above are general, but not universal. Each has exceptions. Circumstances dictate deviations, as in killing for self-defense or shading the truth to protect a friend's feelings. With so many norms, there are bound to be collisions. Perhaps it is appropriate to underplay a treatment alternative if it violates other deeply help convictions. Catholic hospitals not performing abortions comes to mind. Nobody is ethical because he or she follows all the cultural norms all the time. Religions emphasize seeking over attaining perfection and wisely combine that with forgiveness. In the civil domain, there are minimum standards that everyone must almost always follow. But the honors for reaching for very high ethical status are haphazard. There are supererogatory opportunities: we may go above and beyond what is required if we are in a position to do so. But we are usually not faulted for sometimes taking a pass here.

Self-help books on ethics are a multimillion-dollar industry. A few on the shelf behind where this report is being written include: Dan Ariely's *The (Honest) Truth about Dishonesty: How We Lie to Everyone – Especially Ourselves*; Annette Baier's *Moral Prejudices*; Simon Baron-Cohen's *The Science of Evil: On Empathy and the Origins of Cruelty*; Zygmunt Bauman's *Does Ethics Have a Chance in a World of Consumers?*; Max Bazerman and Ann Tenbrunsel's *Blind Spots: Why We Fail to Do What's Right and What to Do about It*; Sissela Bok's *Lying: Moral Choice in Public and Private Life*; Niall Ferguson's *The Great Degeneration: How Institutions Decay and Economies Die*; Gray Fradin's *Moral Hazard in American Healthcare: Why We Can't Control our Medical Expenses*; Thomas Gabor's *Everybody Does It! Crime by the Public*; Joshua Greene's *Moral Tribes: Emotion, Reason, and the Gap Between Us and Them*; Jonathan Haidt's *The Righteous Mind: Why Good People Are Divided by Politics and Religion*; Stan Haski's *The Arrogance of Distance*; Robert Jackall's *Moral Mazes: The World of Corporate Managers*; Larry Johnson and Bob Phillips's *Absolute Honesty*; Muel Kaptein's *Workplace Morality: Behavioral Ethics in Organizations*; Steven Pinker's *The Better Angels of Our Nature: Why Violence Has Declined*; Deborah Rhode's *Cheating: Ethics in Everyday Life*; Douglas Rushkoff's *Coercion*; and *Ethical Norms, Particular Cases* by James Wallace. This is only a sample, but two features stand out. First, most of this genre focuses on one dimension of ethics or another; not ethics *per se*. Lying, crime, evil, or coercion and other evils are taken up individually. Second, most of the attention is on how others are misbehaving and the implication that we are victims of someone else's bad behavior.

The academic literature on the subject is quite different. There are more than 30 journals devoted to papers on moral behavior and ethical theory generally in the professional fields alone, many that specialize on issues in context, such as nursing or management of public resources. These are technical and often define the problem to be solved so narrowly that the hoped-for solution emerges naturally. But few would ever be in exactly such a situation or have the time to work through the nuances before having to act. Dentistry is the only profession that does not have a peer-reviewed journal devoted to ethics.

There is also a classical literature, mostly in the form of books by dead people, that works out general approaches to ethics. Aristotle's virtue ethics (1935), Bentham's utilitarianism (1780/1909), and Kant's duty ethics (1785/1948) are the best-known examples. The academic field of ethics is divided between applied ethics and metaethics. In the former, the context is narrowly defined and a specific rule proposed. By contrast, in metaethics, philosophers are concerned with abstracting general approaches that work across all, or nearly all, cases. "Lying is immoral" is a general principle that comes from metaethical theory. Submitting a false insurance claim is applied ethics. The latter concerns which general rules apply.

To the extent possible, this report will avoid the popular literature, broad ethical theory, and prescriptive lists of what should be done in well-defined situations. The popular press is choppy and sensationalistic. Metaethics operates at 30,000 feet and is subject to diverse personal interpretation when a practical decision needs to be made. Applied ethics is such a large and loose collection of issues that it often ends by being a discussion of available alternatives from which one may choose what matches one's personal interpretation of the currently most relevant features.

My favorite example of ethics on stilts (to borrow Jeremy Bentham's apt phrase) is the rather large literature known as the "trolley problem" (Thomson, 1976). Readers are asked to imagine that they are on an overpass and notice below a rapidly approaching trolley that is bound to run over and kill three folks tied on the track. You are in a leg cast and cannot jump onto the track to save the three unfortunates. As luck would have it, standing next to you is a 350-pound drunk degenerate who for some reason is trying to climb onto the railing of the overpass. The ethical question is whether to "nudge" the large person and thus trade three lives for one. Or closer to home, should an emergency physician assist the speedy demise of an accident victim with a donor card that would afford transplants for three patients who would otherwise expire? As presented in the literature, these are contrived dilemmas, intentionally constructed to block natural and direct resolutions and force trade-offs. They are nice for extended discussions in hypothetical situations. The odds of anyone studying this voluminous literature before deciding what to do in an actual situation, or even reflecting for more than a moment, are very small. Acting the right way most of the time is what people do; talking about it is what ethicists do.

Perhaps the field of academic philosophy will be able to provide only indirect guidance on current issues in dental ethics.

## Dental Ethics

Are there not moral obligations that are unique to dentists? Informed consent is expected to compensate for asymmetries in knowledge. But this standard is uncommon in a grocery store. A very high standard of cleanliness in a dental office is expected because of possible exposure to saliva and blood. Because patients must reveal personal information on their health histories, confidentiality is mandatory. Because oral disease is a process and not an event, dentists are expected to engage patients in a continuous and comprehensive relationship. By contrast, we go to a big-box store to buy replacement filters for our furnace until the furnace fails; then we go to a specialist. A high level of technical skill backed up by trust compensates for patients' inability to judge quality of treatment. Dentists have obligations to their staff for providing a fair and safe work environment. Overtreatment, improper billing, and sloppy records are unprofessional.

The nature of dental practice and the unique relationship between dentists and patients impose a special set of ethical requirements. There are strong ethical dimensions to the relationship between dentists and staff and dentists and third parties such as benefits carriers, commercial organizations, and regulators. The relationship among dentists themselves will get special attention in this report.

The character of dentistry creates a set of ethical expectations that no one else has. Thus it is necessary to understand the nature of dentistry to fully appreciate dental ethics. Context matters. This chapter is about what makes dentistry different from virtually all other human relationships. Dental ethics must fit within the context of dental practice.

It is natural to think in terms of dental ethics as the chair-side choices dentists make. It is more complex than that. Some patients and even some staff members are unethical. Others besides the dentist have ethical capacity. Further, groups of dentists acting in a collective sense adopt policies and engage in behavior that is ethical (or not), sometimes to the surprise of their members. Certainly regulatory, commercial, reimbursement, and related professional organizations engage in behavior that is deemed ethical (or otherwise). If a dentist acts outside the generally accepted social standards or contrary to what dentistry stands for, the dentist is often considered to be unethical. If dentistry as a profession strays from what the public accepts as appropriate, embraces the values of commercial groups, or fails to respond to the changing context in which the profession is practiced, the profession is off base ethically as well.

## Professionalism

Dentistry, medicine, law, pharmacy, nursing, and others speak positively about professionalism. So do first responders, phlebotomists, occupational therapists, race-car drivers, and diplomats. It is not so much the status these groups are seeking as the freedom to chart their own way. An excellent resource on dental professionalism is Jos Welie's 2004 three-part series of articles in the *Journal of the Canadian Dental Association*. Collections of papers on the topic have also appeared in the *Journal of the American College of Dentists*, in 1996 and 2000.

There is broad agreement that professions are occupations defined by three characteristics: "Specialized training in a field of codified knowledge, usually acquired by formal education and apprenticeship; public recognition of a certain autonomy on the part of the community of practitioners to regulate their own standards of practice; and a commitment to provide service to the public that goes beyond the economic welfare of the practitioner" (Sullivan, 2005, p. 36).

William Sullivan of the Carnegie Foundation for the Advancement of Teaching, who was just quoted, led an effort in the late 2000s to replicate the earlier studies of Flexner, Gies, and others. Five book-length reports have been produced describing medicine, nursing, engineering, the clergy, and law. The newest Carnegie reports (Benner et al, 2010; Cooke et al, 2010; Foster et al, 2006; Sheppard et al, 2008; Sullivan et al, 2007) focused on education, not practice. The greatest deficit across professions was lack of teaching ethics, what the Carnegie Foundation writers called "failure of professional identity formation."

The classic professions were the clergy, medicine, and law (Chambers, 2004b). They were formerly open only to the elite of society, essentially to those who had no need for earning a living by practice. Cicero, the famous

Roman lawyer, was prohibited, as were all lawyers then, from accepting a fee for services. Medicine was, until a few hundred years ago, an avocation for gentlemen and was dominated by second sons who lost out on primogeniture. The Hippocratic Oath would not have recognized dentists as professionals because it very specifically forbids doctors from cutting tissue. That, until recently, was the domain of an inferior class of tradesmen called "surgeons." The clergy was also throughout the Enlightenment the sinecure of second or third sons, and the relationship was with a community devoted to God and not primarily a set of interactions in a community of individuals who chose their professional.

Specialized training and skill are marks of professionalism. Add to this set some personal characteristics and connection if one wants to be a professional athlete or actor or an influential lawyer or dentist to the stars. Normally completion of formal, accredited training is accepted as adequate demonstration of professional status. Professionalism is seldom judged by actual practice performance unless it is so outrageously bad that the public can recognize incompetence. As will be discussed in detail later, determination of continued competency is usually left to patients and regulatory agencies rather than colleagues in the dental profession.

Paradoxically, completion of accredited training is not accepted as sufficient evidence for licensure in dentistry in any state. Demonstrated knowledge of certain regulations is also expected, as is the lack of a criminal record. Dentistry is nearly unique in also requiring a one-off demonstration of a small sample of performance. There are licensure requirements for some privileges such as conscious sedation, but not for specialization generally. No state requires, through a performance test on patients or selective review of records, that dentists demonstrate current competence (American College of Dentists, 2012).

Most professional codes of ethics began life as "codes of professional etiquette." They described the behavior of a professional, especially with respect to one's colleagues. For example, the original American Dental Association code required that dentists engage in price fixing (American Dental Association, 1866). This was phrased as consulting and conforming to the prevailing fees charged by other dentists in one's area. Of the 32 standards in the current American Dental Association code, 19 speak primarily to the relationships among dentists, not those between dentists and patients. Item 1.A in the code is an example of the ambiguity between whether a dentist would act as other dentists expect the dentist to act or as society would expect. "The dentist should inform the patient of the proposed treatment, and any reasonable alternative, in a manner that allows the patient to become involved in treatment decisions." Patients in the United States have the right by law not only to participate, but to make the final decision on all matters concerning their bodies. A superstructure was added to the American Dental Association code in the 1990s referencing the standards in the code to four ethical principles advocated by the bioethics community. A fifth category, veracity, was added to accommodate about 40% of the standards that do not fall into the classical categories recognized by the bioethics community. (See Appendix G.)

It is not known whether there is any professional code that was created with input from patients or clients. Codes of ethics are aspirational: codes of professional conduct are enforceable. Professional codes can be interpreted as defining memberships when they contain provisions for sanctioning or expelling members. This is a difficult matter because the U.S. government, through the Federal Trade Commission, only allows such a provision for voluntary organizations, such as trade groups. A dentist can belong to multiple professional organizations, each with only partially overlapping codes.

There is a strong case to be made for professionalism as an essential part of ethics. Professionalism moves the criteria for what is good and right for dentists away from the individual dentist to a collective responsibility of one's peers. That is right and useful because it clearly identifies a profession as a collective moral agent. An entire profession can be a force for ethical integrity. Most likely a profession, like any other group in society, sometimes shines ethically and sometimes not so much. But it is useful to broaden our inquiry to include what individual dentists do for the public good and what they do as well when acting collectively. Organized dentistry has the collective responsibility, not for providing care to the public, but for creating a context in which individual dentists can do so ethically.

Professionalism and ethics have much in common for raising the level of oral health care, but they are not quite the same thing. Among the important differences are who participates in creating the norms, who they apply to, and how they are communicated. Professionalism refers to a set of standards expected of all members of a group. Their norms lay out a minimum and standard list of expected behavior for every group member. These are often codified and published, and they help define who belongs to the group. Professional standards are determined formally and by a representative small group within the profession. In the example of dentistry, other entities the profession interacts with (benefits carriers, the government, and patients) do not participate in the creation, interpretation, or modification of the standards. Professions do, however, go to lengths to tell others about their professionalism. It is an important group asset.

Professions increasingly advertise that they are ethical. This does not always mean, however, that they are informing the public about how to protect their oral health. Advertising that a group is especially ethical has a certain unpleasant character or even a bit of competitiveness in implying that others are not as ethical as the public assumes all professionals are.

There is a difference between an organization of professionals and an organization for professionals. Membership does not define professionalism, and it is awkward for an organization to represent itself as speaking on behalf of an entire profession as opposed to speaking for its members, when some number of those in the profession are not members of one professional group or another.

There are reasonable concerns in society today that the professions have retained the forms of specialized knowledge, skill, self-regulation, and service, but are gradually altering the balance between self-regulation and service. This will be a central theme in this report. We see, across all professions, greater effort being devoted at the organizational level to seeking partnerships with commercial and regulatory interests for protection of markets and less attention on ensuring ethical behavior. The professional group is becoming a corporate entity, working with other corporate interests on behalf of its members. Quoting Sullivan again: "The problem is that the whole notion of the conscientious discharge of one's function, traditionally described as an ethic of vocation, seems to be breaking down. At the same time, the ever more Byzantine elaboration of rules fails to satisfactorily replace it." (Sullivan 2005, p. 259).

## Oral Health

Although professionalism has characteristics that partially define how dentists interact with the public, it does not present a complete picture. It has yet to be explained what the fundamental interaction is between dentists and patients. Why do we need dentists in the first place? How, for example, does a dentist add value to a patient's life? How do we know when an individual is better off for having gone to a dentist or dental hygienist, or used fluoridated drinking water, or exercised effective personal oral home care?

Some current definitions of oral health sponsored by organized dentistry, as listed on their websites, favor the approach of defining ideal patient conditions.

World Health Organization definition: "Health is a state of complete physical, mental, and social well-being and not merely the absence of disease or infirmity."

American Dental Association definition: "Oral health is a functional, structural, aesthetic, physiologic, and psychosocial state of well-being and is essential to an individual's general health and quality of life."

World Dental Federation definition: "Oral health is multifaceted and includes the ability to speak, smile, smell, taste, touch, chew, swallow, and convey a range of emotions through facial expressions with confidence and without pain, discomfort and disease of the craniofacial complex."

This opens the prospect that dentistry can define its role as anything that closes for a particular individual the gap between current oral status and ideal. This is a very broad remit. Almost certainly some of the features of psychological and psychosocial rehabilitation claimed in the definitions are beyond the training of dentists. Speaking and some other functions may be entirely in the domain of other disciplines or only incidentally dental. Certainly it is assumed that this broad field is shared with other professionals and, to a very large extent, with patients and even society at large. The definitions are also broad enough to allow situations where most of the profession crowds in one corner of the field defined by attractive opportunity while leaving some concerns under-attended to. On a definition of ethics that focuses only on individuals, this might be defensible. Viewing a profession as a collective moral entity, the case becomes noticeably weaker.

These definitions also fail to account for maintainability. Two patients may be objectively in optimal oral health after treatment but face very different futures. One may be able to maintain the condition achieved and the other incapable of doing so, even to the point of facing accelerating decline. The reasons are many and include financial condition, access to care, age, natural biological development, motivation, and the patients' understanding of their own roles. Some would hold that this is all assumed in the standard definitions of optimal oral health. It would be wiser to explicitly state this and to quantify the relative contributions of various factors in maintaining oral health. Reimbursement based on standardized fees per procedure type do not match any of the definitions of oral health listed above for moving patients closer to sustainable oral health.

Perhaps a more robust definition would be oral health as resilience: the capacity to resist and recover from both current and anticipated future environmental insults. The patient whose oral health will remain strong five years from now is healthier than another patient who starts from the same objective point but faces known barriers to maintaining the treatment given. The current system of marketing treatment and reimbursing for services presupposes a definition of oral health that is open to question. Society and groups such as benefits carriers and the government may force this consideration into future discussions.

Defining oral health as resilience is explicit in identifying overtreatment, unnecessary treatment, or treatment that cannot be maintained as unethical. This definition also calls out more clearly undertreatment, missed diagnosis, and failure to work with the patient's life situation as being ethically suspect. Finally, the definition shows that oral health cannot be defined outside the context of the existing conditions and the most likely future progression of the patient. Defining optimal oral health as a dentist restoring function and esthetics in the best way possible at the moment seems to be too narrow a view.

The point being made here is the difference between dental treatment (a procedure) and promoting oral health (an outcome). As will be seen in Chapter 11 and Appendices B and L, dentists naturally orient toward the former and patients and the public focus on the latter. That is an ethical issue.

There were three schools of medicine in ancient Greece (Chambers, 2001). The Hippocratic School believed that the role of the healer was to restore balance in normal human functioning. The Cnidians (the C is silent), who flourished on what is now the mainland of Turkey across from the Hippocratic base on the island of Cos, intended to create health by direct intervention, even enhancement. The Asclepiad schools, which were based at oracle sites throughout mainland Greece, favored palliative measures, such as dream interpretation and healthy stays at resorts. The palliative view of medicine dominated Western practice for centuries because cure and prevention were poorly understood. This approach was the province of women (herbalists) and mechanics (surgeons). Today, the Asclepiad approach is seen in spa dentistry or other approaches to managing symptoms and enriching the care experience. It is also associated with "esthetic enhancements" that have questionable basis in patient health. The rise of science in the Arab world in the tenth century and in Europe in the eighteenth tipped the scales in favor of the Cnidian view. Disease was found to be caused by germs, funguses, or trauma, so medicine was the elimination of the causes and repair of the damage that had resulted. The Hippocratic approach gained some respect at the turn of the last century with public health initiatives and a view of health as involving the entire individual in context. Since the 1960s there has been some rebound under the flag of individualistic holistic medicine (Nuland, 1988).

Contemporary dentistry inclines very strongly in the Cnidian direction, with individual overtones of the Hippocratic and Asclepiad approaches. Dentists find it natural to hold an image of optimal oral health and see their responsibility as moving patients toward that ideal by direct intervention of the dentist. Environmental and personal factors, such as the availability of sugared soft drinks or home-care habits, are given some consideration by dentists, but usually as they support the direct treatment interaction between the dentist and the patient. The definition of ideal oral health may even be framed so as to justify favored dental treatment patterns, as in defining target markets. One could only hope that the voice of organized dentistry on issues such as public water fluoridation or sugared drinks would be as strong as the positions on reimbursement or scope of practice.

Efforts have been made to define health as a capacity rather than a state. Norman Daniels's work (1985) is a well-known example, and Martha Nussbaum and Amartya Sen (1993) edited a volume on the topic sponsored by the World Institute for Development Economic Research of the United Nations University. The issue was discussed directly in the oral health area in Marita Inglehart and Robert Bagramian's 2002 work *Oral Health-related Quality of Life*. There is a rich empirical literature in this field. Regrettably, it has been dominated by quarrels over measurement methodology. It is both a characteristic of human nature and a fact of logic that "optimal states" are fuzzy, cannot be consistently rank ordered, tend to be resisted when suggested by others, rapidly become contradictory as the number of descriptive adjectives is increased, and are more likely to be decided on political or commercial grounds than scientific ones.

## Licensure

Licenses are granted by states to permit participation in various activities about which the public has an interest. We have marriage licenses and driver's licenses. Pest control businesses and liquor stores have licenses. But a license does not make one a professional. Licenses are intended to protect the public in interactions where parties are unequal in their knowledge and power in specific transactions. They attempt to establish nothing more than minimal, common standards, while permitting maximum commercial opportunity.

A dental license is granted by the state as a permit to engage in business. There are requirements for obtaining a license and for maintaining one. Regulations relative to commercial activity of dentists and exclusion of others from engaging in commerce where dentists have monopolistic privileges are determined by state legislatures and interpreted by administrative agencies. There are often differences across states in licensure requirements for the same trades. There is also a national overlay of a general sort administered by the Federal Trade Commission.

Management, investigation, and sanctions are administered by a branch of the state government, usually in the Department of Consumer Affairs or a similarly named entity. It is mistakenly believed by some that the recent U.S. Supreme Court decision involving the Dental Board in North Carolina placed limitations on dentists serving as board members (American College of Dentists, 2017b). There is no language in the ruling bearing on that point. (The Court Decision Syllabus in this case can be obtained at www.supremecourt.gov/opinion/14pdf/13-534_19m2.pdf.) What the court affirmed was that board members, regardless of their occupation, all serve as public members who can only act through the various state regulations and executive offices. They are not agents of the profession, but agents of the commercial functions of the state. The court ruling noted that the dental profession has various ethical codes for some of its members and urged that these be adhered to.

It may be true that the public attempts to protect itself from the failures of professionalism by piling on regulations. It would, however, be a tragic mistake to confound licensure and professionalism and expect that the ethics of professionalism can be enforced through the commercial mechanism of licensure. Overtreatment and the health distortions caused by very high costs for dental care, for example, cannot be effectively managed by state administrative departments. It appears questionable whether a short lecture on ethics as a continuing education requirement for relicensure will be more than well-intended camouflage when placed in the commercial rather than professional environment. There is wisdom in the saying that one cannot legislate morality. But one can be drawn away from the real business of enhancing professional ethics by trying to do so.

## Summary

The field of ethics generally offers some suggestions about ways of looking at how dentists should treat patients, each other, and the public. But it is also necessary to focus on dental ethics—what it means to be an ethical dentist or an ethical professional organization. The focus of this report is on professionalism—how individual dentists practice in the context of how all dentists practice. It also includes the collective agency behavior of various organizations, such as group practices; component, state, and national organizations; and specialty, ethnic, honorary, and other groups that claim to represent segments of the profession.

Oral health, as the common professed goal of dentistry, has yet to be clarified as a defined concept. Some confusion seems to exist between the goals of providing dental treatment and enhancing oral health. Differences in expectations leave open the possibility for ethical misunderstandings. Licensure should not be conflated with professionalism. Some individuals who are licensed to practice dentistry are unethical and probably not good examples of professionalism. Because licensure is framed in terms of minimal standards, an ethical profession must look higher.

# Chapter 4

# The Practice and the Office

The previous chapter looked at the macro context of dental ethics: professionalism, oral health as a reason for the profession's existence, and licensure as state permission to engage in commercial activity. This chapter is focused on ethics in the dental office. What are the defining characteristics of the practice of dentistry and what are the features of the dominant solo or group practice model? The premise is that any viable ethics must fit the way dentistry is actually practiced. In later chapters, this theme will reemerge in the form of two challenges: (a) If the practice of dentistry is changing, must its ethics also change? and (b) Who should have a voice in deciding how dentistry is practiced?

Here we are concerned with defining the notion of a practice and the traditional single-office dental model, known as the professional service firm (PSF). The universality of both concepts is being questioned and new alternatives are appearing. The ethical question is whether dentistry will resist or participate in discussions of the best paths forward.

## Dental Practice

Consider the thought experiment of a conversation among four folks who are carpooling. Abel says, "Boy, I have had this most awful intermittent pain in my jaw. Five or six days. Comes and goes, but sometimes it is really distracting." Baker says, "You should lay off the sugary stuff. I always say, 'You are what you eat.'" Charlie adds, "Nothing much you can do about things like that. My wife had a problem. It cost us a bundle and she lost the tooth anyway." The fourth passenger, a dentist, was silent.

Baker and Charlie gave bad advice, but they were not unethical. The dentist was. All those who accept the privileges of professional status have a moral obligation to help others where that expertise is needed. A suggestion to have the problem looked at in a timely fashion by a professional and a referral would be the minimum expected response. Dentistry is a characteristic of the relationship between special people (dentists) and others; practice is the name for this relationship. It is not the name of a place with lots of scary equipment.

The contemporary philosopher Alasdair MacIntyre says, "A practice involves standards of excellence and obedience to as well as the achievement of goods. To enter into practice is to accept the authority of those standards and the inadequacy of [one's] own performance as judged by them. It is to subject [one's] own attitudes, choices, preferences, and tastes to the standards which currently and partially define the practice" (MacIntyre, 1981, p. 178).

The case is being made that no dentist is his or her own standard. If one expects the benefits associated with being a dentist, one will be judged by the standards common to all dentists. Even more to the point, dentistry is not a transaction where the dentist gets something and the patient gets something in exchange, and that is the end of the matter. It is a relationship that affects both parties into the future as well as others. This relationship extends to include all dentists and the community. Both dentists and patients can add a little something to the exchange that carries over in a positive way or they can steal from the profession's collective reputation. Dentists who attempt to skirt the norms of practice are unethical. That is true regardless of whether they think they can define what an ethical practice is. We may be unclear on how to define ethics, but no one can escape the responsibility of behaving by an actual operational definition of ethics.

MacIntyre even goes so far as to invoke the prevailing norms common across the professions and the heritage and traditions of the professions. "To enter into practice is to enter into a relationship not only with its contemporary practitioners, also with those who have preceded us in the practice, particularly those whose achievements expanded the reach of the practice to its present point" (MacIntyre, 1981, p. 181).

There is a saying, "A professional practices on the basis of his or her skills and the reputation of his or her colleagues." If dentists seek to give credence only to the first, the inevitable result will be fragmentation of the profession.

Dentistry, like all professional practice, is custom work. Cases that fall in a certain diagnostic range may nevertheless require different interactions. Those that fall outside the range must be referred. But within the range of treatment options for any case, only some approaches would be ethical. These are the ones that are recognized by one's colleagues. Donald Schön's work on the "reflective practitioner" is clear on this point: professionals do custom work, but only within the range acceptable to their peers (Schön, 1983; 1987).

In his classic studies of practice in engineering, architecture, management, psychotherapy, and town planning, Schön discovered that all professionals experiment with approaches, seeking better ways by various client and personal standards. But there are limits to the range of what can be tried or what becomes customary practice. Range should never be confused with standard of care. Differences in treatment approach are normal in any profession. It is a separate question whether all of these approaches are above the standard of care. Wide diversity of top-quality outcomes is fine. A narrow range where some of the work is unnecessary or poorly done is not.

Schön lays out an extensive line of research showing that ethical professionals learn continuously on the job, but always within parameters established by their colleagues. Except in trivial matters, professionals start with an observed gap between what they encounter as the problem and the solution they believe their colleagues would approve. Then they go back and forth between the goal and the emerging effect of interventions, making those changes deemed most appropriate. This is known as "reflection in practice." Professional practice is often continuous problem solving. "Reflection on practice" is another matter. After the work has been completed, professionals sometimes think back on what might have been a better approach.

Dentists may also confuse the notion of practice with that of scope of practice. Certainly scope of practice is an ethical issue, but at the organization level. Dentists may be allowed to perform surgery in the sinus area in one state but not in another, regardless of their qualifications and technical skills. State legislatures determine scope of practice through statute, and the dental profession and other professional and public interest groups assist the legislature in defining what dentists can legally do and what they are prohibited from doing. They also assist in the interpretation of practices that may or may not fall on one side or the other of the scope of practice line. When dentists perform or allow staff to perform work not authorized by the state's practice act, that is both unethical and unlawful. When dentists perform procedures they are entitled to perform, but do it in a gross or continuously faulty fashion, that is an ethical violation and may also be unlawful. This topic will be explored in much greater detail in Chapter 6.

Standard of care is not determined by statute but by the accumulation of individual court cases under various circumstances. Whereas practice acts (scope of practice) are codified in writing, standard of care is found in the interpretation of scattered court documents. It flows from case law, with lawyers and witnesses presenting alternative claims about what patients are legally entitled to expect based on how communities of dentists practice and what research substantiates. Generally, the dental and other professions pool resources in the form of malpractice insurance to provide protection for borderline cases that are simply bad outcomes as opposed to wanton breaches of standards of care. This is a professional responsibility since large groups of dentists can take advantage of this protection for a rate that is the same for all.

It is unethical to practice in opposition to either scope of practice or standard of care, knowingly or in circumstances where one should have known better. It is also illegal in most cases. Practice contrary to scope of practice exposes dentists to legal sanctions. Practice contrary to standard of care exposes dentists to monetary sanctions. Violators may not always feel shame or guilt, which are the traditional accompaniments of violating ethical norms. But their colleagues usually do in an indirect way. This often leads to unnecessary regulation and higher costs for everyone, including those who have been acting ethically. Thus bad practice cannot be contained in legal or monetary terms. It spills over, causing ethical issues for colleagues.

## Professional Service Firms

Most dentists serve the public under the professional service firm (PSF) business model. (This is something entirely different from a dental service organization, or DSO.) This section draws heavily on the work of David Maister (1993) and his colleagues (Maister et al, 2000).

In extraction economies, such as oil drilling or farming, value accrues naturally or with certain help and it is economically feasible to harvest this value, provided that externalities such as environmental degradation will be accepted by the extractor or the public. In manufacturing, the value of assembled parts exceeds the cost of the individual parts plus the labor and distribution costs. In sales, value is added by making products or services available to consumers at a price less than what they would otherwise pay in finding and getting the goods themselves. Employees are reimbursed for time in a job grade. Innovative technology discovers new combinations of things and behavior that can be used, licensed, or sold to others who in turn improve their efficiency.

By contrast, a PSF provides customized, specialized services to customers on an as-needed basis. Dental care is provided one patient at a time, usually only when a patient needs it. The work is highly individualized, and although there are similarities across all Class II amalgam restorations for example, every patient expects to have a personalized treatment plan. There is no inventory of finished goods. Neither patients nor dentists can stockpile procedures and they are only useful when they are needed. Two prophies in the first week of January and none for the rest of the year makes no sense but two pairs of socks can be sold on this plan. The delivery of services is almost always face to face, unlike those socks that can be ordered online. There are minimal economies of scale. PSFs are usually reimbursed on a fee-for-service-when-rendered basis, but sometimes on a retainer basis or even as employees. For the most part, performing four quadrants of root planing on different patients requires four times as much chair time as performing one.

The value of one service compared to another in a PSF is almost entirely a function of the skill level of the person providing it. This fact is dangerously underappreciated in dentistry. One could easily form an impression by reading the commercial as well as the research literature that better dentistry is a function of better materials, techniques, or equipment and nothing else. There is an implication in evidence-based dentistry that better dentistry is a matter of proving that one independent variable is superior to another and that among the factors that "cause" good dentistry, the operator is somehow controlled out of the process. There are no journals that compare one dentist against another. In fact, the American Dental Association Principles of Ethics and Code of Professional Conduct discourages comparisons. In all professional service organizations, the skill and judgment of the person providing the service is a critical component and cannot be assumed to be uniform.

The classical professions are all PSFs. So are investment counselors, building contractors, chiropractors, optometrists, personal trainers, appraisers, social workers, therapists of all types, and plumbers. There is almost an exact correspondence between PSF agents and those who are licensed. Because the interaction between those in a PSF and the public is direct and of consequence that the consumer is incapable of fully evaluating, each state has an elaborate system for qualifying individuals in PSFs. The state retains the prerogative of establishing qualifications, regulations, and disciplinary oversight of PSFs independent of the profession or trade group representing its members.

Because of the kind of value added by PSFs, they tend strongly toward being reparative in orientation and to charge based on time and labor, plus supplies. Almost always, PSFs are in the "fix a problem" business. Sometimes a lawyer or financial planner is consulted for business or estate planning in a preventive fashion and may work in part on a retainer basis. Optometrists occasionally, plumbers almost never. This means that the value relationship between PSFs and consumers is different from the relationship with a hotel in Hawaii, a Broadway musical, or a restaurant. Usually the best thing that can be said about a visit to a PSF is that nothing happened. We seldom introduce our visits for varicose vein treatment in social conversations. By contrast, the value added by buying a new product or receiving a desired service is a net positive. And we do brag about our Rhine cruise, but not our endo. PSFs add value in a different fashion than do other segments of the economy. Consumers' standards for judging value they receive differ as well. Many products and services are sought as positive enhancements; PSF work tends to be a "necessary disruption."

In Chapter 12, a distinction will be introduced between obligation and opportunity. Both can prompt action, but they do so in a different fashion. Obligations are put off as long as possible and we tend to curb our effort once a minimum satisfactory level has been reached. We are always looking for opportunities, and we do not stop with just a little. For patients, dental care tends toward being an obligation. The same act, seen from the dentist's perspective, is usually regarded as an opportunity. When dentists complain that patients do not seem to value oral health the same way they do, there may actually be two different value sets involved in such a mismatched comparison. In the later chapter, the discussion will pick up the topic of whether ethics is an obligation or an opportunity.

There is an ethical implication to the difference in how value is determined for PSFs and other kinds of business. In the eyes of the public, patients, and regulators, the issue is to ensure safety rather than to promote the public good. States concern themselves with protecting the public from common abuses and harms and not with elevating the level of care or increasing the availability of services. Licensing jurisdictions and patients usually think in terms of "good enough or safe enough." And those in PSFs are obligated to meet minimal standards. The public falls back on proxies such as friendliness, convenience, or cost while assuming that the state guarantees safety and minimal quality. This means that the ethical standards in dentistry are different in nature than those in other markets. Of course the comments in this paragraph must be qualified when considering elective dentistry.

Those in PSFs are less apt to think in terms of minimums and more likely to try to maximize quality, volume, or profit. There are unique ways profitability can be increased in PSFs. Economies of scale, inventory control, distribution channel managements, advertising, and innovation make small differences and can be easily copied by competitors.

Delegation is an effective strategy for PSFs. Lawyers use legal aides, contractors use subcontractors, pharmacists use technicians. Much of what highly trained professionals do, such as paperwork, can be handled by properly trained and supervised helpers with no loss of quality. The savings achieved by good work design and delegation can be passed on to customers or retained as profits, as the owner's ethical inclinations suggest. ADA figures (Beazoglou et al, 2012; Guay & Lazar, 2012) report that 70% of the difference in net income across dentists is a function of the number of auxiliaries they employ.

The second way PSFs can become profitable is by serving better clients. It is well understood in business that products migrate upstream over time (Christensen & Raynor, 2003). Additional features are added, and the strategy of extending low-margin services and products to a larger market is avoided. It is a common refrain among continuing education experts that services to high-end patients pay well. In the study of dentists with disciplined licenses in Appendix C, the zip codes of 138 dentists in California selected at random were recorded. An analysis using software that reports the median household income of individuals by zip code revealed that the median household income in the zip codes where dentists practice was $79,095 while the average median household income in California (in 2016) was $61,888. Dentists practice in communities that are about 25% wealthier than average. One county in the state had no dentists and several had fewer than ten. There is an ethical issue associated with providing more services to those patients who need them less. As will be discussed in Chapter 6, there is evidence that patients with lower incomes receive poorer quality care. The ethical issue of selectively underserving those with high oral health needs but low incomes is built into the PSF model. It is more than dentists avoiding public assistance patients; it is also dentists seeking high-end customers over the general population because that is part of the business model of PSFs.

The third way that PSFs thrive is by obtaining monopoly status or securing regulations that are favorable to their form of practice. The ADA spends large, but undisclosed, amounts of members' dues each year to secure a playing field favorable to PSFs. This is in addition to what is spent by various state associations. The strategy works. Since the mid-1980s, dentists have worked on average fewer hours per week but their net inflation-adjusted incomes have increased by an average 56%, compared with the rise in average household income of 3%. The consumer price index (CPI) for dental services has risen twice as fast as the general CPI (meaning that the cost of dental care to patients is increasing at double the rate of what it costs to buy a car, feed a family, or go out to eat). Dentists are now in the top 3% of income earners in the country (Chambers, 2014b).

## Is the PSF Model Sustainable?

The PSF model has been so solidly identified with dentistry that it is often accepted as being *prima facie* ethical. Or at the very least we hold up the lens of traditional dental practice as a standard for judging whether emerging alternatives are ethical. It is perfectly fair to contrast commercialism, third-party payers, government standards for safety and privacy, and corporate ownership to the dominant PSF dental model. All the above are businesses, but dentistry functions on a different business model. There are only two parties in the traditional dental practice model: dentists and patients. Today, practices are part of more complex systems, and the system includes entities that have different business models. One frequently voiced concern in focus groups was that insurance does not give full credit to the way dentists would like to practice. This was flagged as an ethical issue, occasionally with a bit of righteous indignation, as an example of the ethics of judgment presented in Chapter 7. Others in the focus groups complained that some of their colleagues were trying to have it both ways: claiming professional status while engaging in questionable commercial strategies. They called for enforcement of clear rules, along the lines of the ethics of justification to be presented in Chapter 8. Regardless, it is obvious that the boundaries between the PSF business model and the rapidly evolving and increasingly encroaching context in which dentistry finds itself stand in need of renegotiation. That is the ethics of engagement, and that will get full attention in Chapter 9.

Instinctively, many dentists see any change from the PSF model as a threat to be counterattacked. Certainly the past decades have justified this approach by placing dentists in an enviable economic, social, and political position. There are recent signs, however, that new models of practice are attractive to outside businesses, expected by patients, and welcomed by some dentists. PSF is a good model, but it just may be that society will find alternatives more to their liking or at least make room for several competing models. That is an ethical matter of the first importance since practice models reflect the values of dentists. It is unlikely that the profession can long ignore such changes, and it would be a doubtful strategy to avoid discussing the matter.

In 2006, shortly before the Great Recession, dentists' incomes went flat and have remained so since (Vujicic, 2014). There are multiple explanations, including an oversupply of dentists, more aggressive posture by benefits carriers, declining attendance by adults, conservative states reducing Medicaid benefits, and commercial ownership models that compete on price in an effort to secure a market share large enough to amortize capital investments. Educational debt has been overrated as a factor in this equation since that has increased at a constant rate for decades and only shows up in a negative fashion because practitioners' ability to service the debt from income has recently declined (Chambers, 2014b).

The PSF model is subject to several vulnerabilities. It is unlikely that dentistry can prevent these changes, but options are possible regarding how the changes are navigated. Certainly, the capacity to alter the course of changing practice models in the future will not be entirely in the hands of individual dentists. Perhaps not even the organized profession will be able to dictate the terms of this evolution.

Consumerism will drive patient behavior toward cost considerations. For some time now the dominant concern of patients has been cost of dental care (Vujicic, 2016). In surveys this shows up as more than twice the level of concern of the nearest other disincentive and figured prominently in the focus groups studied for this report. Recall that in the PSF model, clients are not seeking a positive value in dental care; they are seeking to minimize a negative situation. That means there will be a limit on how much value can be added by dentists. The business model of "corporate" practice is not to augment the product, but to drive down cost by standardization, consolidation of back-office functions, volume purchasing, and aggressive marketing. This is a price-driven strategy, and traditional offices will be forced to compete unfavorably on price, compete for a limited pool of high-end customers, or work at an economic disadvantage in rural and inner-city areas where corporate practices do not choose to locate.

Although we are waiting to see what the next "boom" will be to replace esthetics from the early 2000s, there are still voices urging dentists to concentrate on the upper end of the market. This may work for some, but costly or elective dentistry is too narrow a market to support more than a segment of the profession. The limited size of the upscale market may be a contributing factor to the growing gap between the most and least financially successful dentists that is beginning to emerge. (See Chapter 17.) There is also a cautionary view in the business community generally. Clayton Christensen has argued persuasively that the strategy of moving up-market by continually adding features that few customers understand or feel they need creates an opening for disruptive markets (Christensen, 1997; Christensen & Raynor, 2003). To do so without leaving patients a low-cost, but acceptable, alternative becomes an ethical issue. Disruptors that service those who cannot afford "the best" will come in with basic products and services at a price point where consumers say, "I did not need all that stuff anyway; I am satisfied with a less expensive but basically adequate service." This progression has been observed predictably in many markets and is especially likely to be in play where unmet need exists and cost is a barrier. Dentistry has long maintained that there is substantial unmet need and that cost is a clear issue.

Price competition is not the only threat to the traditional model of dental care delivery. Technology is moving forward at a very rapid pace. This will be considered in detail in Chapter 17, but the preview is that imaging, diagnostic, treatment, and management technology is already having an impact on changing how dental care is delivered. To the extent that patients will pay for the improvements in speed and quality that technology affords and that dentists can maintain a monopoly over the distribution channel, it will benefit those dentists who have the capital to invest in expensive and rapidly obsolete technology. To the extent that technology makes it possible for patients to move from dentist to dentist or move around the dentist, they will do so if the cost is reasonable. Dentists may argue that the quality of do-it-yourself dental care is inferior to dentist-provided care, but patients have always been poor judges of quality. The argument holds as long as there are no alternatives.

Patient needs are also changing. There is a shift away from reparative dentistry toward prevention and maintenance. According to the Centers for Disease Control and Prevention website, 85% of dental visits are asymptomatic. Because the procedures most in demand now require less training and because technology is lending a hand, such work will increasingly be passed to ancillary staff or even to patients themselves. Because dental benefits organizations support a significant proportion of patients and they deal in groups rather than individuals, they will increasingly seek to work with group practices. This will reduce the traditional role of the dentist as the chief "decider" guiding those patients who can afford it to high-end, customized treatment. If dentists turn to web designers, marketing services, incentives, and success merchants, this will further erode the dentist-patient relationship that is the foundation of the traditional PSF model.

Perhaps all of these forecast changes will not take place; perhaps they will roll out differently. And it is even possible that a few major market disruptions will appear that no one has foreseen. The smart money is betting that there will be big shifts that bump the traditional model off its course. The ethical issue is how the profession responds. Ignoring or denying these trends seems unwise. Resisting them is overly optimistic. Letting dentists face the challenge on their own is a betrayal of dentists by their profession. Looking around and getting into the conversation with the big players seems like the wisest way forward. The ethical challenge will be for dentistry to find a way of engaging with others that does not begin with the assumption that dentistry is the ultimate decider in all matters.

## Summary

Dentistry is a practice. That is true in the technical sense of custom work delivered using approaches endorsed by one's professional colleagues. The understanding challenges the notion that dentists are free to do as they see fit and are not answerable to their colleagues. Practice has an inescapable ethical dimension because it matters what others—patients, colleagues, and the public—want. Scope of practice is a statutory minimum and standard of care is a legal minimum. Practice is a community, ethical ideal. The traditional model of practice is the PSF, where a few staff and the dentist provide individualized care directly when needed. The economic options in the model are normally limited to delegation, segmenting the market to serve the high end, and protecting monopoly status. There are signs that corporate and other commercial models; government involvement for safety, privacy, and access; and patient concerns over cost are putting pressure on the traditional model. Technology and marketing may undercut the high-end strategy that has served dentistry over the past half-century or more. These threats should not be ignored. A conversation should be started with all concerned.

# Chapter 5

# Bad People

Most unethical behavior is done by folks who consider themselves to be fundamentally ethical. Criminologist Thomas Gabor (1994) notes that we overestimate the level of violent, physical crime and underestimate the small missteps of many of us. For example, many times the number of deaths are caused annually by drunk driving or driving over the speed limit than are the result of terrorist acts or school shootings. It is 60 times more likely that a dentist's license will be disciplined than that an American will die of an overdose from any drug. We think of the bad as remote and large. Muel Kaptein's *Workplace Morality* (2013), Sissela Bok's *Lying* (1978), Douglas Rushkoff's *Coercion* (1999), and Deborah Rhode's *Cheating* (2018) talk about human moral failings as though they were commonplace. They are. Max Bazerman and Ann Tenbrunsel's *Blind Spots* (2011) and Robert Jackall's *Moral Mazes* (2010) argue that organizations are often far from morally pure, and this on a wholesale basis.

Here are a few more references to add to one's schadenfreude bookshelf: Carol Tavris and Elliot Aronson's *Mistakes Were Made (But Not By Me): Why We Justify Foolish Beliefs, Bad Decisions, and Hurtful Acts*, Robert Trivers's *Deceit and Self-deception*, and Robert Kurzban's *Why Everyone (Else) Is a Hypocrite: Evolution and the Modular Mind*.

What we think of unethical acts that damage others depends on the perspective from which we view them. Robert Baumeister and colleagues (1990) created scripts describing hurtful events and asked subjects to take either the role of perpetrator or victim in describing what had happened. Victims imagine that there is a long history of grievances but nothing in their own nature that would warrant an unethical attack. The attack was regarded as a reflection of the malevolent personality of the attacker, and the harm caused was judged to be irreparable. Perpetrators described the same set of events differently. They started with the act itself, which they described as small or insignificant, and certainly warranted by the nature of the victim. Nothing more, they thought, needed to be said and the whole matter should be dropped. The point is that the prospects of improving the moral character of the profession by telling dentists what they should do or feel is unlikely to get us very far.

The first step in better ethics is to locate the problem correctly. It is mostly a lot of small transgressions, widely distributed and often only grumbled about. Because the likelihood of making substantial changes in human nature is small, the better strategy will be to look at the circumstances in which people shine and work to enhance the conditions that promote the most desirable behavior.

This chapter will address why most of us act less ethically than we think of ourselves as being. There are some easy fixes, and because they are easy to implement, this kind of work has great potential. The following chapter will apply these ideas specifically in the dental context. Chapter 14 considers organizations as ethical entities and as context in which dentists find it easier or more difficult to act ethically. We are dealing with deep human nature, and previous attempts to change character have been disappointing (Sparks, 2010).

## We All Say We Are Ethical

We think of ourselves as being ethical, even when in our honest moments we can recall a time or two when we bent the rules. (See Chapters 11 and 12 and Appendices E, H, and L for discussions of how dentists actually interpret their basic values.) The problem here is in the way the question is phrased. There is a conflating of a general characterization and particular actions. Einstein played the violin. He did not do it all the time, but he was still a violin player. We are the same about ethics.

We can be systematically ethical at the same time we are situationally unethical. We are generally most ethical when thinking in theoretical terms and when we are not confronted with specific temptations. In a certain sense it is accurate to say we honor patients' wishes and give them full informed consent, even when there are a few situations where that was not exactly so. We uphold 4.C in the American Dental Association Code of Professional Conduct, which requires us to report instances of continuous or gross faulty treatment, even when we have never actually reported anything. We intend to take steps to uphold the standards of the profession if we are certain that the pattern of abuse that is emerging regarding a colleague "really" is a pattern. We want to behave ethically and we describe ourselves as doing so in the past and for sure in the future, and the few counterexamples just prove the generalization.

Figure 5.1. **Our ethical self-concept.**

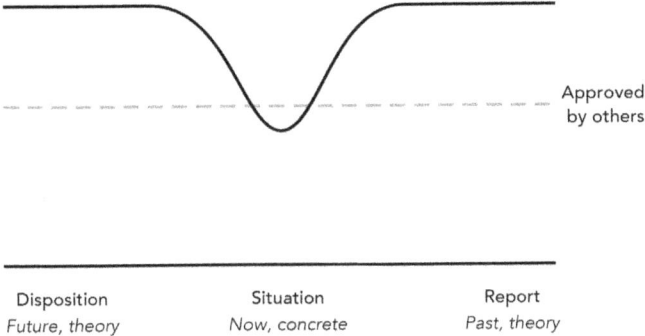

| Disposition | Situation | Report |
|:-:|:-:|:-:|
| Future, theory | Now, concrete | Past, theory |

Figure 5.1 diagrams general ethical behavior in schematic form. The curved line at the top is moral behavior. Higher levels represent "better ethics." In the natural resting position it is at a high level, one that qualifies us as a member in good standing in our community. Generally it is well above the heavy line at the bottom that represents the threshold for illegal actions or behavior that would draw substantial public disapproval. There is also a dashed line near the dip where situations call for "justifiable adjustments." This is the "fudge line" that will be explained below.

This schema is general and varies widely across individuals and situations. An off-the-cuff estimate by Thomas Gabor (1994), who made it his life's work to study these things, is widely quoted. He said that roughly 10% of people are scrupulously ethical and "never" deviate. Five percent cross the line of what is moral so often or egregiously that they are just waiting to get caught. The remaining 85% give themselves an occasional pass for what they consider small or excusable exceptions in certain cases. Some of the highly virtuous 10% will be interested in providing leadership for the slackers. The 5% will not be interested in this report. That leaves the vast majority of us who could help each other stay consistently above the fudge line.

## Fudge, Engagement, and Priming

We stumble over the threshold, not the fence. The problem we have to explain is whether these small ethical missteps are common, where they come from, and why they persist. Then we must consider what might be done about it.

### Others Are Doing It

The evidence is overwhelming that ethical indiscretions are everywhere (Levitt & Dubner, 2005). A self-report survey found that 99% of Americans admit to at least one crime during their life, with malicious mischief, disorderly conduct, and larceny all over 80% and tax evasion at 50% (Wallerstein & Wyle, 1947). Two-thirds of garages, 64% of radio repair shops, and 40% of watch-repair shops charged for repairs that were not made (Riis, 1941). Estimates are that between 15% and 25% of federal expenses for health care are fraudulent (York, 1987). The U.S. Internal Revenue Service's own website estimates that 17% of returns are underreported (www. forbes.com/sites/ashleaebeling/2012/01/06/new-irs-tax-gap-report-cheating-still-rampant/#79c271c25043). Evidence shows that this is wishful thinking. Self-reports of tax cheating are usually three times as high (Carroll, 1992; Feige & Cebula, 2011; Slemrod & Bakija, 2006) and often exceed the proportion of the American population that votes. The references cited in the first paragraph of this chapter are catalogues of ethical misconduct on a small but pervasive scale. One reason we feel we are making such slow progress on ethics is that we tend to overlook the huge number of small problems we could do something about personally at the same time we complain about the ineffectiveness of those to whom we have delegated the dirty work of controlling the relatively rare gross criminality. The point is not to make us feel bad about ethical missteps. But perhaps we should feel bad about not doing much to fix these common and individually undramatic bad judgments.

The reasons for lots of little missteps have been well researched. To begin with, there are just plain differences in interpretation of how situations stand and which codes have priority. Some cheat just for the thrill of getting away with something (Ruedfy et al, 2013). Human beings are limited rational thinkers, and we often make approximations to ethical decisions rather than working them through, especially in complex cases. That leads to inconsistency and bad choices (Chugh et al, 2005). Ethical fortitude varies across contexts and by how much stress we are under. We are less ethical when tired or hungry or threatened (Baumeister & Vohs, 2004; Gino et al, 2011; Hagger et al, 2010; Killgore et al, 2007; Mead et al, 2009; Muraven & Baumeister, 2000). People are more willing to cheat to get ahead than out of fear of loss (Kern & Chugh, 2009). Strong role models—for good and otherwise—color what we pay attention to and how we interpret it (Brief et al, 2001; Callahan, 2004; Gunia et al, 2010; Kish-Gephart et al, 2010). Power is also a good predictor of rule bending and will get its own section at the end of this chapter. Culture, the unstated assumptions about what a group is willing to accept, exerts such emphasis that it will be given a whole chapter (Chapter 10).

But we can explain most of this away. This is complicated by the way individuals interpret their own ethical responses and what they think about how others behave (Minor, 1981). Who does not justify their behavior even, or especially, when it is a close call? "Everybody is doing it" is a good defense because it is often true (McCabe et al, 2001). It is also rational: most people are willing to be ethical as long as others are (Fehr & Gächter, 2000; Fehr & Schmidt, 1999). But there is so much evidence that justifies being suspicious that we are being played for a fool. Failing to cut the common corners is a sure recipe for being left behind. No one wants to be on the low end of an uneven playing field. It is nice to be noble, but often expensive. We "balance the books" ethically by excusing a little slip in one direction justified by our doing extra, unrecognized good in some other circumstance (Merrit et al, 2010). We sometimes engage in a little sleight of hand regarding which role we are playing. The early sixteenth-century Italian Baldesar Castiglione wrote in *The Book of the Courtier*, "Beware the gentleman who is the most chivalrous courtier in the army camp and also the bravest soldier at court" (1507/1967).

It is even expected that we will cite justificatory principles to cover questionable cases. There will be a chapter on that as well (Chapter 8). The justificatory principle need not be the only or even the most important reason for our action. It just needs to be believable enough so others will stop looking so hard at our unexpected behavior. Of course, humans rationalize (invent *post hoc* reasons for what we have already done). Studies show that we rationalize over ethics, even to the extent of moral hypocrisy (Batson,

1997; Batson et al, 1999; Batson, 2011). Max Bazerman has a paper titled "Negotiation with yourself and losing" showing that cheating yourself is not always effective (Bazerman et al, 1998). Dog owners who do not pick up after their pets expect sympathy by complaining that "there are too many rules" (Webley & Siviter, 2000). When all else fails, forget it. Those who cheat have more difficulty remembering the rules that govern the situation (Shu & Gino, 2012).

There is a temporal dimension to the amount of credit we take for our ethical acts. As Ann Tenbrunsel and her colleagues phrase it, "We forget how unethical we have been in the past and overestimate how ethical we will be in the future" (Tenbrunsel et al, 2010, p. 156). The default position is that we are certainly ethical, and others may be as well, based on the presumption of being innocent until proven otherwise. It is also easier to claim the ethical high ground farther out after the concrete situation in question. Empirical work shows that cheating is less problematic after we have decided to do it (Batson et al, 1999) or when we can do so indirectly (Airley, 2009; Palmer, 2012).

## Fudging

The area in the diagram at the head of this chapter where behavior dips slightly below the threshold for completely acceptable behavior is known as "fudge." It is too close a call for others to get involved and perhaps can be excused as necessary under current circumstances or "due" to an otherwise ethically upstanding individual. Many small adjustments represent one of the two great opportunities for enhancing the ethical tone of the dental profession. (The other is organizations showing leadership in building positive ethical cultures.) Nina Mazar and colleagues have a theory, and data to back it up, that we all seek to maintain a positive self-image about how ethical we are (Leavitt & Sluss, 2015; Mazar & Ariely, 2006; Mazar et al, 2008).

The fudge zone is entirely personal. Some play it close; others allow themselves more room. John Carreyrou (2018) describes the virtually boundless fudge of Elizabeth Holmes, who sold a half-billion-dollar bill of goods to venture capitalists who backed a nonfunctioning portable blood-testing device. Some people fudge in one area but not in others. Building an addition on one's house without a building permit could be independent of cheating on one's spouse, for example (Hartshorne & May, 1928).

One thing we can count on is that people understate their own fudge and believe that they fudge less than others do (Ross et al, 1977). (See

Appendix N.) Some people get pretty righteous over these things. The most troublesome ones are those who allow themselves a lot more fudge than they permit others around them. Fudge will tend to accumulate near individuals and organizations that value "independence," avoid transparency, and work to control the message.

## No Fudge Snitching

It is bad form to fudge in public. It is also questionable to call others out on fudging. Even a knowing look could be regarded as bad manners. Questioning a colleague's treatment plans is often enough to get a "mind your own business" and an approving nod from the other dentist's friends. Rude drivers are tolerated, dirty political tricks and misstatements only justify snickers among friends, but not public criticism. Most fudgers have carefully calculated the limits of what they can get away with, and they count on the cost and embarrassment of potential complainers to be greater than their benefit of speaking up. Famous fudgers can be counted on to have a justification at hand: "This is a private affair," "You do not understand the whole situation," "Somebody or something made me do it," or as a wimpy last resort "Oops, my mistake." Buddies even cover for fudgers of similar stripe: "We don't snitch on classmates" and "There may be a few bad apples in the group, but it is unfair of you to point them out because most of us are above the line." Herrmann and associates (2008) have demonstrated that some rule breakers even work to discredit the upright who are minding their own business as a way to provide future protective cover.

Based on computer pattern matching, benefits carriers know better than professional colleagues or state boards who is engaged in insurance fraud. They tend to let the small stuff go and do not turn most offenders in to the authorities, preferring to negotiate for lower levels of reimbursement in exchange for lower levels of fudge.

Snitching does not work because it makes a situation others thought was private into a public one and thus there must be a public defense. J.P. Morgan famously said, "Every man has two reasons for doing something. The reason he gives and the real one." When a member of a group is questioned, the challenged individual will fight for his or her reputation and the group will have to choose between distancing itself from the fudger or distancing itself from the snitcher. This usually depends on the company one is keeping. Mostly we distance ourselves from the entire situation.

## Engagement

But it is wrong to let fudging go if it is damaging to oneself or if one has a position or role where there is a reasonable expectation that one stands for the public good. It is easier, for example, to overlook an uncalled-for public insult to somebody else. It is expected that a patient will more often overlook bad dentistry than will a state board member. In such cases, calling out the bad behavior may be necessary, but only after discussion. It will be a central tenet of this report that discussion is indispensable to ethics. This theme will be developed at length in the three chapters on ethics as judgment, ethics as justification, and ethics as engagement. The underlying idea is that ethical rumpuses are rough sport when individuals or groups need information from each other. The first move should be to share those differences and determine whether there is a common way forward.

Engagement might look like this. "I see that you are parking in the handicapped space but you do not have a placard. Is there something I need to know?" Or: "Usually we do not talk about a candidate's family life in these elections. Is there something special about this case you need to tell me?" Or: "I have had two referrals for second opinions from your patients over treatment plans that I am not able to fully explain to them. Let's have breakfast and share our approaches to big cases."

Notice that none of these little scripts is judgmental. None requires that the other provide a justification. They only invite an exchange of perspectives. The goal of engagement is for both parties to understand the effect of their behavior on others, allowing them the maximum amount of flexibility for fixing the problem, given how the other is likely to react. The goal is always to fix the problem, not fix the blame. Of course, there is always the possibility of your being dissatisfied with the response and taking your better understanding of it to others (Chambers, 2009).

What is at stake here is elevating the dashed line in the figure above. Individuals crossing the heavy one at the bottom signal serious misconduct, either one-time very bad things or repeated violations of social norms. Society as a whole should care, and it normally designates some people with special powers—such as police or investigators with state boards—to look into these matters and take action. The dashed line is everyone's concern. Steven Pinker (2011) has amassed evidence to show that having a common understanding that public authorities will handle serious breaches works better than trying to take matters into vigilante hands. But this is only true where those who know about big missteps speak up. And by speaking up when fudge begins to get out of hand, we are likely to be successful and are apt to prevent the dashed line from descending toward the bottom.

## Priming

Fudge can be manipulated. A series of experiments by Dan Ariely and his colleagues (Ariely, 2009; 2012) demonstrated that people tend to be about as ethical as we expect them to be. This is called "ethical priming." A prototypical study involved asking college students to take a test on numerical puzzle solving. Subjects self-scored their efforts and received a cash reward when turning in their papers based on the number of correct answers they claimed. Although the study was camouflaged so subjects expected their scores and their actual performance could not be matched—there was a big shredder in plain sight—a system was in place to connect actual responses with reported scores while still preserving anonymity. Fudge was widespread, but the amount was usually not more than 10% or 20%.

Subjects are primed in a typical fudge study by being asked to engage in a purposeful activity prior to performing. For example, some subjects are asked to name as many songs as they can remember that were popular when they were in high school (neutral priming). Others are asked to list as many as they can of the Ten Commandments (ethical priming). The first thing these studies demonstrate is that very few of us know the Ten Commandments. (In actual fact, very few Americans (13%) endorse all of the ten commandments [Patterson & Kim, 1991].) The second point is that just trying to recall these moral rules significantly cuts the fudge rate (Mazar et al, 2008).

Ethical priming has been demonstrated for healthcare professionals (Leavitt et al, 2012). Army medics have two identities: military and health care. The priming in this case involved medics giving opinions about ethical issues in either of two circumstances. In one condition they were wearing their uniforms in a room decorated with military insignia. In the other, they were in scrubs in a room furnished with medical equipment. Medics were asked to make decisions balancing financial expenses versus ethical fairness in setting the dollar amount of compensation to families of soldiers killed in combat. Those primed to activate their medical moral template did in fact demonstrate more ethical opinions than the same individuals did when they were primed to think of themselves as soldiers.

Priming has been studied directly with respect to dental ethics. Chambers (2016c) demonstrated the effect of context on ethical outlook in a sample of regents and officers of the American College of Dentists. (See Appendix D.) The regents and officers completed a modification of Jonathan Haidt's Moral Foundations Questionnaire (2012). Embedded within the questionnaire were three additional items designed to measure pro-moral attitudes: (a) "Copayments should not be waived;" (b) "Colleagues working below the standard of care should be reported when justified;" and (c) "Commercialism undermines dental professionalism." High scores on these items were taken to represent a greater moral commitment to the standards of the profession. Board members completed the same survey twice: once at the board meeting of the college and then again about one month later where they were primed to take the role of a practicing dentist. Respondents served as their own controls. The scores for commitment to professional ethical standards of the board members on the survey were higher when opinions were taken in the context of a meeting where ethics was a conspicuous part of the culture than in the practice setting. It is encouraging that such a simple effort as assembling as a group where ethics comes up in the conversation can raise the salience of ethical values. It is cautionary that commitments to ethics made in meetings tend to fade in practice. Context matters in ethics (LeBoeuf et al, 2009).

## False Consensus, Ethical Attribution Effect, and Power

We are all a bit biased in how we score ourselves ethically. No surprise: we often simply do not take into account how others view situations where ethics is at stake. And when we do think of how others might see the situation, several well-understood biases creep in. Three important dimensions of this fuzzy view are false consensus, fundamental attribution error, and the blindness of power. These effects are like a moral black hole, making it difficult to escape the force of our personal views of ethics.

### False Consensus

In their classic study, Ross, Greene, and House (1977) asked a large group of individuals how appropriate various kinds of behavior were (say, making exaggerated claims to enhance one's reputation or coming to an event late or dramatically informally dressed). Respondents were also asked how likely they thought others would be to engage in similar behavior. Invariably, respondents overestimated the proportion of others who saw things the way they did (Gilovich, 1990; Krueger & Clement, 1994; Marks & Miller, 1987). Politicians routinely overestimate how much support they have in the public. Enthusiasm for innovations in dentistry is similarly overly optimistic. Perhaps those who announce ethical standards for the profession overestimate how widely these norms are shared. Evidence for the large role of false consensus in dental ethics is contained in Appendix E.

## Ethical Attribution Effect

A close relative of false consensus is the human tendency to attribute different explanations to our behavior and to the behavior of others, depending on how this affects us. This is called the "fundamental attribution error" in the psychology literature (Jones & Harris, 1967; Ross, 1977). Consider the example of a patient who declines an implant in favor of a removable partial. Is that because the patient fails to properly value oral health or is it because of financial circumstances? Another patient goes out of her way to tell all her friends what a wonderful dentist she has just found (you). Is that because you merit that respect or because this new patient is by nature gullible and generous? What about situations involving a dentist's behavior? Is it because of poor technique or lack of attention that a restoration fails or is it just bad luck on a heroic effort? What is responsible when an office turns in the best month of production by far in the past several years—dentist leadership, staff effort, or a random up-tick in the economy?

Naturally there will be many ways to answer these questions, but the evidence is pretty clear that our successes and others' failures will be attributed to personality characteristics and our failures and others' successes will get counted in the "circumstances" column. It is a fundamental error to attribute motives or causes to ourselves and to others in a fashion that always makes us look like the most skillful and ethical agent in the room.

Research findings on the role of what might better be called the "ethical attribution effect" among dentists is found in Appendices E, H, and L. Appendix N provides data showing the dramatic effect of this bias specific to dentistry. Mentioning the fundamental attribution error is not an appeal for greater humility. It is, however, an appeal for discussing how we got to where we are and where we might go with others who have a stake in the matter. Going off on our own without consulting others is risky; telling others what their true motives should be is pretty much a nonstarter. As discussed in Chapter 16, Learning Ethics, changing circumstances is more promising than changing human nature.

## The Liability of Power

Some individuals are more apt to take into consideration the effects of their behavior on others—in other words, to frame situations as ethical. Power in its various forms, such as expertise, money, and political influence, is an "ethics substitute." It is an attempt to change others' behavior just because one can. There is no need to negotiate over who is "right."

There is a body of research in the business literature studying who is likely to reveal full information in a transaction (showing ethical respect) and who is likely to withhold it for personal gain (Aquino, 1998). The analogue in dentistry would be informed consent. Questionable behaviors such as taking more than one's fair share and imposing policies that present a hardship on others have also been studied (Ashforth et al, 2008). Those who have natural positions of power (who are generally not answerable to others) are most likely to act unethically (Hegarty & Sims, 1978). In something like a priming effect, unethical behavior associated with power can be artificially induced. In a typical study, individuals in groups are first given a "test of leadership ethics." Those who believe they have done well on the test are more likely to abuse their peers in the subsequent role-playing exercises. This is true despite the fact that the reported high scores are phony, assigned at random. In a clever study, researchers (Kabanoff, 1991) recorded traffic behavior at an intersection. In particular the issue was minor law breaking, such as running a red light and violating right of way. Make and year of the vehicles involved were recorded. Drivers of late-model expensive cars, such as BMWs and Mercedes, were significantly less ethical. They were also ruder (Diekmann et al, 1996). High-IQ children lie more often than others (Lewis & Saarni, 1993) and professional students seeking admission to graduate programs are more likely to cheat (McCabe et al, 2001).

That does not mean that all successful people bend the rules just because they can. It is just more likely to be the case that power short-circuits ethics. It has been reasonably established, however, that those who enjoy power "adjust" their view of ethics. "The more power people have the more they condemn the unethical behavior of others.... At the same time, it was shown that the more power people have the less they disapprove of their own unethical behavior" (Lammers et al, 2010, p. 742). Those in positions of power are less likely to recognize its role in ethical matters, and conversations about ethics among those with differing levels of power are inherently difficult. Those whose power is insecure are especially likely to resort to ethical double standards (Fast & Chen, 2009).

In an early paper (Chambers & Eng, 1994), dentists in their first 12 years of practice were asked to identify the most troublesome aspects of practice and how they handle them. Technical issues did not rise to the level of concern. The most prominent problems were uncooperative staff and patients and unethical senior dentists. But the response to these problems is what is of interest. Patient and staff problems were addressed by explaining to others how the dentist expected things to be managed. Arguably, this works because of the power differential. Difficulties with other dentists, especially owner dentists, were handled by tentative negotiation, probing for a fair engagement. Problems that could be managed with power were judged to be easier to solve than those requiring ethical give and take. Evidence for the fact that dentists create environments that sustain their personal ethical views is presented in Appendix F.

## Summary

The purpose of this chapter is to discuss bad acting in general. We must begin by recognizing that the large part of ethical problems is widespread small abuses that we excuse and others overlook . Complaining about "someone" not addressing the outrageous abuse of a tiny number presents an attractive camouflage of the problem that is in everyone's power to correct.

Often when we think we see bad people, we are really looking at fundamentally good people (people much like ourselves) who simply do not know how to be better in the prevailing circumstances. It would be a fool's errand to chase every instance of individual indiscretion or every policy of organizations that overlook small deviations from the proclaimed standards. That is not an apology for bad ethics. It is a suggestion that we focus on the conditions that prompt misconduct and avoid the mistaken belief that there are a few others who are causing all the problems. It is a theme of this report that if the community organizes to promote general good ethical conduct it will be better positioned than if it attempts to get others to attack a few cases or tells others what we would regard as ethical behavior on their part. Ethics is everyone's problem. The evidence supports this approach.

# Chapter 6

# Bad Dentists

As a thought experiment, consider this very unusual dentist. By a flip of the coin we will make him male and will call him Dr. Noggin. A noggin is a cup or vessel that is too small to hold what it is intended for and by extension, sometimes a person's head that has the same characteristic.

Dr. Noggin is well trained, professional, and is active in the dental community. He worries that patients do not place enough value on oral health. He would prefer a world where benefits providers and the government made it possible for more patients to receive care with less interference in dentists' treatment decisions. He believes that high educational debt is causing younger practitioners to engage in overtreatment. He has a small "academy," the Noggin Elite for Real Dentistry, of like-minded colleagues whose motto is "First do no harm." Sometimes they are called Noggins, or more familiarly by the initials of the organization.

But Dr. Noggin has never actually treated anyone. He is an "expert." He talks about the highest standards in dentistry—for both specific patients and for the profession as a whole—and it all starts with people just doing the right thing. He has a five-star rating on nonmaleficence. He is ethical, but could he be called an ethical *dentist*?

Reread the immediately preceding paragraphs and change the references from "dentistry" to "ethics." Is it enough to accurately diagnose dilemmas, to express concern using the correct language, to criticize those who are clearly off base, to assemble a club of like-minded professionals? Is ethics not something one actually does? Can ethics be a default position where one is presumed ethical without doing anything to prove it? The author's father used to say, "Just because a person talks a lot about ethics doesn't mean it's safe to stand beside them."

What has been on offer as dental ethics has tended toward the academic or how very good individuals should behave according to one or another ethical principle. Dentists, like all humans, come equipped with diverse and often conflicting and imperfectly worked-out life goals, ways of seeing the world, and habits and behavior patterns that have been found to work in experience. They should not be required to surrender who they are as a precondition for being welcomed into the ethical community. Ethics should be for everyone, not just the elite, and it should start where people are, not where some imagine others ought to be.

Neither do dentists practice in a vacuum. And the circumstances and reward incentives and penalties built into the system are an inevitable part of how dentists practice. We should look into making the changes that are possible. We should bring about better contexts that promote, or at least do not erode, the natural impulses of dentists to do what is good. That part of the ethics business has received little attention.

Estimating how many dentists are bad actors and knowing what to do about them depends on how a "bad actor" is defined. One way to see the profession as being "adequately" ethical is to dodge the problems. The better question is "What is the proportion we could reasonably make some improvement in?" That could be a low but achievable bar, which would matter a lot. Dentists have been heard telling students in ethics courses that there is never a situation where a dentist should refer a colleague for disciplinary action. On several occasions in preparing for this report, the author asked groups to estimate the proportion of dentists who have overtreated or overcharged patients during the past several months. The estimates range from 20% to 30%. Not to quibble over numbers, but it would certainly be a worthwhile goal to cut this in half. The Gallup poll of trust in the professions regularly puts the proportion of dentists trusted by the public to have their best interests in mind at around 60% [news.gallup.com/poll/1654/honesty-ethics-professions.aspx]. That leaves a substantial number who have doubts, some large enough to cause patients to stay away from offices or to switch to different ones. Reducing by half the number of Americans undecided about trusting their dentist would be a worthy pursuit. Dentist Marvin J. Schissel (1970), under the pseudonym Paul Revere, wrote *Dentistry and Its Victims* in 1970. The book was an unusual combination of a few chapters about how, in his opinion, organized dentistry avoids discussion of poor quality work and many chapters explaining in understandable lay language why dentistry is important and how to identify high-quality care. That was 50 years ago.

This chapter will be about those who are arguably the greatest concern, those dentists who have disciplined licenses and who engage in gross or continual faulty treatment. This will lead naturally to the questions of what could be done about this and how much dentistry is concerned to raise all its colleagues above ethical reproach.

## Disciplined Licenses

Licenses, as commercial permits, are disciplined for violations of the law or of statutes. Absence of discipline does not mean that a dentist is ethical, but it is a workable position to use disciplinary action as a marker for being caught engaging in very obvious unethical behavior. Issuing, monitoring, and disciplining of licenses is managed through branches of state government. About 20% of complaints lodged with medical boards are investigated and about 1% result in disciplinary action (aspe.hhs.gov/basic-report/state-discipline-physicians-assessing-state-medical-boards-through-case-studies). Among dentists, from 2 to 8 in 1,000 practitioners are sanctioned each year, with consistent large discrepancies from state to state. Although disciplinary actions of state regulatory boards are public record, differences also exist in how easily one can access these records.

As part of this project, a study was made of disciplined licenses. The detailed report is found in Appendix C and is summarized here. A paper based on this work was published in the *Journal of the American College of Dentists* (Chambers, 2018).

Records were obtained for 255 dentists for whom disciplinary action was taken between September 2015 and July 2017 in four states: California, North Carolina, Ohio, and Oklahoma. These records were read several times and information about the nature of the behavior that led to the sanction, date on which licensure was granted, the nature of sanctions imposed, practice location, and other demographic information were coded.

The types of behavior that resulted in disciplinary action fell into three categories, with roughly equal numbers in each. These are characterized in Table 6.1.

## Table 6.1. Characteristics of disciplined licenses by type of inappropriate behavior.

| Behavior | Technical | Practice Management | Personal |
|---|---|---|---|
| N | 86 | 98 | 71 |
| | % | % | % |
| Diagnosis | 64 | 27 | 4 |
| Treatment | 65 | 25 | 4 |
| Overtreatment | 9 | 38 | 3 |
| Case management | 24 | 20 | 0 |
| Incomplete records | 42 | 26 | 3 |
| Informed consent | 27 | 16 | 1 |
| Overbilling | 7 | 39 | 6 |
| Abandonment | 0 | 6 | 1 |
| Unlicensed practice | 1 | 20 | 1 |
| Overprescribing | 0 | 13 | 7 |
| DUI | 0 | 1 | 18 |
| Drugs | 0 | 4 | 32 |
| Cognitive impairment | 0 | 0 | 17 |
| Sexual misconduct | 0 | 1 | 13 |
| CE/Paper work | 1 | 4 | 20 |
| Other crimes | 0 | 3 | 14 |
| Deaths | 7 | 1 | 0 |
| Multiple patients | 17 | 33 | 11 |
| Court records | 0 | 18 | 38 |
| Out-of-state | 1 | 0 | 10 |
| Repeat offenders | 7 | 10 | 25 |
| ADA membership | 40 | 37 | 35 |

*Percentages in this table do not necessarily total to 100% because a license can be disciplined for more than one reason.*

"Technical" problems included failure to diagnose, poor quality treatment, inadequate records, lack of informed consent, and improper case management (usually performing treatments out of sequence). The second category, "practice management," involved overbilling, overtreating, issues of diagnosis and treatment quality, patient abandonment, and use of unlicensed staff. About a third of these problems involved mismanagement of multiple patients. The third category was labeled "personal" because it included patient care only indirectly. In this group were DUI, drug use, cognitive impairment, sexual misconduct, and civil crimes. Many of the cases in the latter category (and always those involving patient death) are automatically referred to the board from other state agencies. There was a single incident of trouble with a technical procedure, an overhang, of the type tested on one-shot initial licensure examinations. One state only disciplined cases of personal drug use.

There were significant predictors of sanctioned practice, such as multiple offices, fictitious business names, type of patient treated, and so forth.

One characteristic that was strongly associated with bad acting was age of the practitioner. In the table below, age distribution of dentists sanctioned for inappropriate patient management (overtreatment, overbilling, treating out of sequence, and other abuses of patients) are represented by the columns in age categories. There is a bimodal pattern, with most incidents occurring among dentists in their forties and late fifties. This corresponds with previously reported findings that the average age of physicians with disciplined licenses is in the mid- to upper-fifties (Papadakis et al, 2008). The dashed line in the graph represents the proportion of all practicing dentists in the United States by age. Younger dentists are conspicuously underrepresented among those with disciplined licenses. The graphs for disciplined licenses for technical reasons and for personal reasons are reported in Appendix C. They are similar, and problems with alcohol and drug abuse are even more skewed toward older practitioners.

Figure 6.1. Practice management difficulties by age.

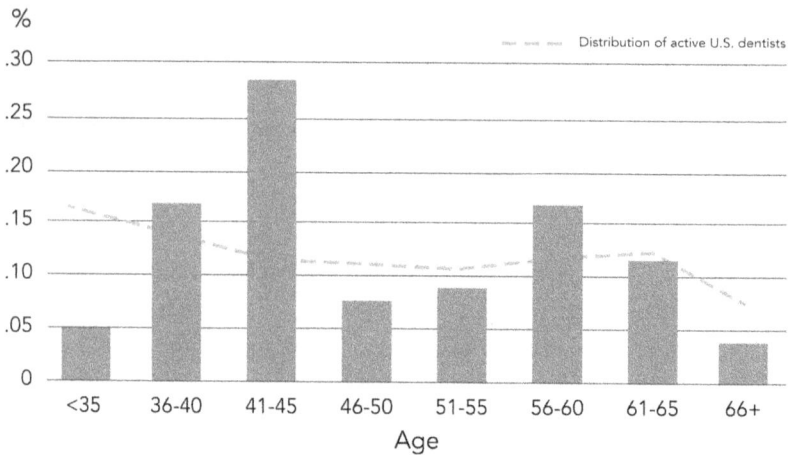

These findings give the lie to claims sometimes heard that new dentists abuse their patients because of their high debt load. It also offers insight into the nature of unethical behavior. A case can be made that unethical practice is a habit rather than an event. It seems to take some time for patterns of poor practice to establish themselves. Probably, there is a small and tentative misstep at the beginning. This might be a probe of the fudge line introduced in the previous chapter. If it is left unchecked, either by untoward consequences or by intervention from professional colleagues, stepping over the line multiplies in frequency and magnitude. The fudge line of what one is entitled to drifts down toward the grossly unacceptable level. The habit of unethical behavior continues until it can no longer be ignored and is reported, usually by patients. The proportion of such behavior that is identified and disciplined, versus that which continues undetected or unreported, is unknown.

## Justifiable Criticism

Justifiable criticism does not mean offering constructive comments to a colleague about how he or she could become a better dentist. That would be an opportunity to make dentistry better. Instead it is an obligation imposed by the American Dental Association (ADA) under penalty of losing one's membership to report suspected instances of gross or continual faulty treatment to a third party that has the authority to sanction the concerned dentist. It is correct that there is language in the supporting Advisory Opinion in the American Dental Association code explaining how the Council on Ethics, Bylaws and Judicial Affairs might interpret failure to report a colleague or reporting a colleague. It is noted that it would be appropriate under some circumstances to consult the previous treating dentist if there is a question regarding the conditions under which care was provided and that irresponsible criticism is unwarranted. But there is no positive obligation in the ADA code to help one's colleagues. (See also Appendix G for information about how well the ADA code in general is understood by practicing dentists.)

A series of studies was undertaken in order to better understand how dentists interpret their professional obligation with respect to bad actors who are their peers. This included polls of both dentists and patients regarding a common situation involving a "third opinion;" a survey of dentists about how "reportable" they felt certain mistreatment might be; videotaping of 21 dentists working through a series of situations where gross or continual faulty treatment from a single practitioner seemed to be present; and a survey of patients regarding the severity they attach to certain untoward outcomes. The full report was published in the *Journal of the American College of Dentists* (Chambers, 2017b) and appears as Appendix G.

As shown in the graph below, patients are more likely than dentists are to expect that their current dentist will become involved in addressing work performed by a previous treating dentist when a problem is identified.

**Figure 6.2. Likelihood patients and dentists favor reporting dentist for gross or continuous faulty treatment.**

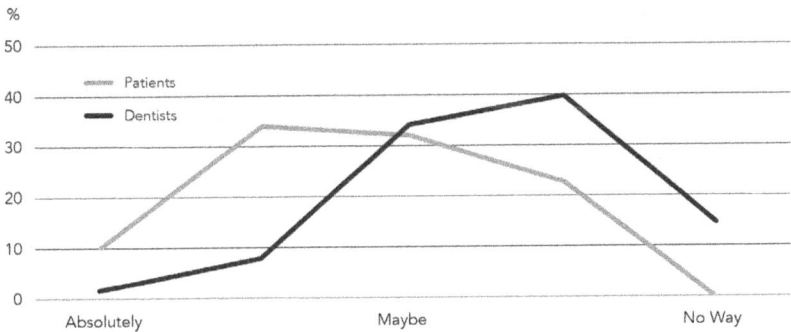

A survey of 68 patients found differences between patients and dentists (who were surveyed in a separate study). But there were also differences with respect to information expected from the consulting dentist and expectations for the relationship that exists among dentists. Dentists were twice as likely to let an incident pass without involving either the patient or the treating dentist as were patients (40% versus 20%). Both dentists and patients wanted the treating dentist to play a role, but with substantial differences in the extent to which patients were to be informed. Dentists chose to engage patients about 40% of the time, but patients expected to be informed and to participate in decisions about correcting the problem in 80% of the cases. In the American Dental Association Code of Professional Conduct, 1.A, this is supposed to happen 100% of the time. At issue here is whether the patient is informed of his or her present oral condition and what needs to be done about it. Dentists seem to prefer that this remain a matter kept to the current dentist, or perhaps mentioned to the previously treating dentist. Less desirable would be engaging both the patient and the previously treating dentist. The least attractive response would be to report cases of gross or continual faulty treatment to the proper authorities. Most dentists considered a case involving previous poor work to be a new case, needing attention that they (the new dentist) would be willing to treat if they felt it could be done without difficulty.

This order of preferred means of handling the problem of poor work by colleagues is consistent with a further study (see Appendix H) where it was found that dentists seek to minimize the number of others involved in solving ethical issues. The results were also similar to findings from a videotaped simulation study where a specialist observed a pattern of continual faulty treatment by a single referring general practitioner. In those exercises, dentists who constituted the experimental sample were more likely to engage the previous treating dentist than the patient. Few referred the matter to the state board or other agency, often commenting that the previous dentist may be incompetent, but not in an actionable way, even based on as many as ten substandard cases in a row. Some stated that such a string does not necessarily constitute evidence of "a pattern."

The reasons respondents offered for their behavior are summarized below. The incidents ranged from a large overhang or an open margin to prepping anteriors that were periodontally unstable for veneers and leaving an endo file in the patient's sinus without informing the patient of the condition.

1. *Alerting the treating dentist is sufficient.* When an action was taken by the consulting dentist it was most often first and entirely a matter

of informing the treating dentist of the presence of a condition that might be considered below the standard of care.

"I think he is aware now that I have mentioned the open margin. I trust him."

2. *Patients are informed tenuously.* Patients were often informed of the existence of a compromising condition, although that information may have been ambiguous, and consulting dentists resisted responding to patients regarding matters other than the technical nature of their clinical condition.

"Now I'm just going to retreat this [poorly done endo] and not say anything to the patient. If he asks me whether that is because Dr. X did not do it right, I'll just make up something about new circumstances requiring special additional care."

3. *Reframing the situation as convenient hypotheticals.* Consulting dentists reinterpreted the presenting case as either so underdefined as to excuse involvement or by imagining additional facts that excused the need to become involved.

"The important thing is to resolve these matters ethically, and to do the right thing. These things need to be handled right and resolved peacefully, I mean without entanglements. I'm not sure specifically what I would do."

4. *Patterns and general conclusions are avoided.* Individual cases tended to be considered separately; the dominant context was the current clinical situation, and elements of comprehensive care and generalizations about the treating dentist were suppressed.

"There's no line that separates competent from incompetent."

5. *Responsibility for corrective action rests with the patient.* The consulting dentist was seen as responsible for addressing the referral (if indicated), the treating dentist was responsible for restoring the patient to prior clinical standard, and the patient was responsible for everything else, including action against the treating dentist for general incompetence.

"I would not report this matter myself. I would refer the patient with the complaint to peer review."

6. *There is no sense of general professional responsivity.* There was no "we" in these cases; treating dentist, consulting dentist, and patient had separate interests that were confined to individual treatments and they did not work together for a general resolution of difficulties or a general elevation of the profession.

"If the guy doesn't respond [to my feedback], I'd just let it lie. Pretty soon something really bad will happen and then maybe somebody will do something."

In a separate study of 62 dentists, the same set of incidents suggestive of poor quality treatment from the videotape study were judged in terms of severity, as measured by willingness to refer the case for possible disciplinary action. As a further variable of interest, the dentist who was associated with the poor treatment was described as either a senior dentist in the community, a new member of the profession, or a candidate on a one-shot initial licensure examination. Although there was a slight tendency to judge the licensure candidate more harshly for the same outcome, the major determinant of propensity to refer for discipline was each reviewing dentist's own personal standards. Eighty-five percent of the variance in likelihood of referral was due to the reviewing dentist's own values, not features of the previous treating dentist or nature of the faulty treatment. The likelihood of referring for the same type of incident ranged from 6% to 92%. The type of problem (overhang versus file in the sinus, for example) accounted for only 10% of the variance. The experience and community involvement of the previous treating dentists was of little concern, accounting for only 5% of the variance. This finding that dentists use a wide range of personal standards when considering whether to become involved is consistent with evidence reported from the focus groups summarized in Chapter 1 and other empirical findings reported in Appendices A, E, H, and J.

The extent to which one decides to become involved in correcting the low end of care or raising the performance of one's colleagues is a personal choice. The range of concern with better dentistry is enormous, and it does not appear to be related to either who is causing the problem or the objective nature of the conditions. Dentists seem to set their individual standards for participating in the good of the profession. Some are capable of insulating themselves in that "good enough, so I do not have to become involved" category both by choice and because they practice independently.

Ethicist Joshua Greene summarized the general findings of research in this area. Groups that draw strength from letting each member be his or her own standard stay clear of judging each other. True professionalism requires looking after each other. "Societies in which people are most cooperative are also the societies in which people are most willing to punish people who are not cooperative" (Greene, 2013, p. 72). Perhaps reluctance to criticize colleagues is loyalty to a system that shields all from external scrutiny rather than loyalty to one's colleagues.

## Stable Professional Communities Include Bad Actors

All dentists are ethical actors in two ways: they behave ethically (or not), and their behavior becomes a reference point for their colleagues. This includes bad actors, who both engage in damaging practices and lower the standard of the profession. Devious dentists hurt patients and they also signal their peers. Good dentists can choose to engage unethical colleagues or ignore or even take steps not to notice the misconduct. In any case, they are also making an ethical decision and sending a message about how the profession should behave. The habit of being ethically uninvolved is contagious.

For this reason, it makes little sense to approach ethics on the assumption that all professionals are isolated, interchangeable individuals. The job of building a strong profession includes more than reaching as many dentists as possible and inoculating them ethically before placing them back into the environment. If the environment is not supportive of the new behavior, old habits will reemerge. It is much too expensive to go at it this way. Many are uninterested, and the treatment is unlikely to hold.

One approach to studying systemic ethics is to use the methods of modern systems dynamics or computer simulation. A study by Chambers (2014a) is the only example of this approach in professional ethics. (See Appendix I.) The key to this study was to consider the relationships among ethical actors rather than the character of the actors themselves. For example, when a bad actor in dentistry practices in the same community as a typical practitioner, it works slightly to the benefit of the devious dentist and slightly to the detriment of the good dentist. If this condition continues because it is not worth the effort to make an issue out of it, there will be an increase in the number of dentists who overtreat, advertise in a deceptive fashion, keep shabby records, and ignore comprehensive patient care. A few of the good dentists will be tempted to gravitate in this direction. We could also imagine a community with a few ethical leaders who are willing to confront the bad actors, as is expected by the American Dental Association Code of Professional Conduct (4.C). These interactions most likely will cause a slight curbing of the devious dentists' behavior, but at a personal cost to the ethical leaders. We can also imagine an interaction between a bad actor and an enforcer agent such as a state dental board. Generally, these confrontations go rather poorly for the bad guy and are slightly to the benefit of the enforcer (after all that is why they exist and receive funding). Erving Goffman (1959) has pointed out a paradox with respect to interactions among fraudsters: they naturally limit their own numbers. A con artist depends on there being enough honest folks to make their false actions credible. There are a dozen other relationships, such as ethical dentists taking one another for granted and dental boards supporting each other.

Consider a 4 x 4 matrix for the possible effects of: (a) bad actors; (b) ethical but passive dentists; (c) dentists who are ethical leaders; and (d) enforcers. No one knows in detail what the true values are that belong in this matrix, but anything outside a very narrow range of common sense will cause the system to collapse, so extreme values can be ignored. For example, bad actors cannot go unchecked to some degree or the whole world would turn bad. In the research reported by Chambers, the values were set initially by taking a survey of officers and regents of the American College of Dentists (ACD). Baseline values, how many of each type of agent are present to begin with, also need to be estimated. As it turns out, the 4 x 4 matrix of interactions is critical and the baseline matters little. In the published study, it was assumed initially that about two-thirds of dentists were good but passive professionals and about one-third were ethical leaders who were willing to take steps to ensure the ethical tone of the profession. The system was stocked at the beginning with 1% enforcers and .01% bad folks. The ACD board members thought this number of devious dentists was too low, placing the estimate at about 20% (an estimate confirmed by later polling).

The computer model used for the study, a Markov replicator, runs on an Excel spreadsheet. The basic logic is that during the first time period, all agents interact with all others (or with their impression of what others are like) and the results of these interactions are carried forward to the second time period as potential adjustments to what the real values are in the community. The system drifts toward having more of the kind of agents that are rewarded in the system. Figure 6.3 shows what happens over the first 1,000 iterations with a typical set of assumptions.

It is obvious that the network of dentists stabilizes fairly quickly. Each type of agent settles at a more or less fixed proportion of the population. This is determined by the relationship among the agents and not by characteristics of the agents. To demonstrate this point, consider the deflection for bad actors in the center of the graph. At this point the computer program was adjusted so that 90% of all devious dentists would be converted to good dentists, or even leaders in a few cases. This might be thought of as a massive continuing education effort where every single bad actor was trained and nine out of ten of the training sessions was so successful that these misguided individuals became good practitioners, indistinguishable from those who had always been good. The very quick reversion to the status quo ante after the education stopped reflects the relative strength of the norms in the practice community over the lessons in educational programs (Treviño & Youngblood, 1990). Perhaps there is even a hint of "revenge," as a dentist with a disciplined license might feel when required to take ethics courses as a condition for staying the judgment. (See Chapter 15 on Teaching Ethics.)

**Figure 6.3. How a community adjusts to its own norms over time.**

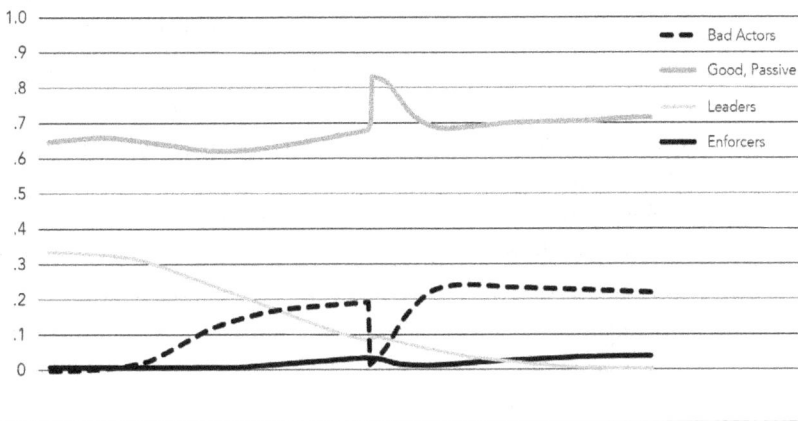

The system is sensitive to assumptions about how the various agents interact with each other. Typically, jiggering the relationships within a narrow range produces slight changes in outcomes, but when certain thresholds are exceeded, it becomes nonsense. This is very Darwinian: most combinations, including some that look good in theory, either cause the system to crash or are quickly corrected by reality. There are several lessons to be drawn from this simulation.

- Systems establish stable patterns based on the interactions among their members.
- Each system will have exactly the proportion of bad actors that it tolerates.
- The number of bad actors has a greater influence on increasing the number of enforcers than does the number of enforcers have on decreasing the number of bad actors.
- The proportion of bad actors increases at the expense of the leaders, not the good but passive dentists.

The picture suggested by this simulation contains some surprising suggestions. First, there will always be a certain number of bad actors. Talk of ridding the profession of them is hyperbole. The system is designed for a certain amount of unethical behavior. Some communities can be created that have a smaller proportion. Second, the bad behavior of some dentists will not be an especially grave concern to most dentists. It is apparent in the trend lines in the figure that the proportion of passive dentists, those who just take reasonable good behavior as a given, remains constant as the proportion of bad folks works up toward a stable point, and after that it does not matter. The ones who suffer are the ethical leaders, and of course the public. The single factor that has the greatest influence on the proportion of bad actors is, surprisingly, the relationship between ethical leaders and passive, good dentists. This can be determined by adjusting the relationship. The most powerful force to reduce bad actors is how the leadership works with the passive members. It is foolish to try to punish the bad folks out of dentistry or to educate the whole profession in good standards. What matters is leaders narrowing the fudge and creating the priming environment that raises the entire level of the system. (See Chapter 5.) The conversation among the active and passive parts of the ethical dental community is critical. The rebound following massive, effective education is hardly a recommendation for mandatory continuing education on ethics. What matters most is the general ethical climate created by all dentists.

## Summary

Because of the nature of dental practice, dentists can create worlds where they insulate themselves from being noticed or influenced by colleagues or the public. There is ample room for fudge and self-priming. Power and a system with a large cushion for "good enough" encourages a passive response from the most ethical. Bad actors are an expression of systemic considerations. The easiest way to change the proportion of bad actors is to change the system.

Doing something about ethics will remain a low-priority issue until the context in which dentists practice changes. As that is beginning to happen now (see Chapters 4, 16, and 17 for discussions of the emerging pressures on the traditional model of dental practice), we might anticipate that the profession will fight against change rather than become involved in negotiating the best possible improvements (Festinger, 1959; Lewin, 1946/2008). The profession as a whole will not register a significant change in its ethical tone by doubling the small number of dentists who learn about ethics in a formal setting or by our improving the quality of that instruction.

It is a worthy effort to improve the quality of very short-term theoretical ethics presentations to a small number of dentists and to write motivating editorials. But systemically changing how dentists relate to each other and to patients will require a deeper commitment.

# Chapter 7

# The Ethics of Judgment

*Beaucoup condemner c'est peu comprendre*—
to condemn much is to understand little.

There are multiple lenses through which to look at ethics. Each brings into focus certain aspects of what is good and right about dentistry and what needs to be improved. At the same time, that makes other views more obscure. Four meanings of ethics are presented in this and the three following chapters. They are not competing schools of philosophy, such as utilitarianism, bioethics, virtue ethics, or care ethics. Nor are they three failed models for how we should treat each other and one grand solution. All four are our natural inheritance and together represent the suite of ethical equipment we need for a very demanding job. We use at least the first two daily. The danger is in thinking that there is just one right way to act and that everyone sees this as clearly as we do (or they should). There is also a risk of overusing one favored approach and thus needlessly narrowing what it means to be ethical.

There is a literal sense in which we grow into our ethics and build moral communities. A child is incapable of understanding, let alone finding, the optimal behavior in this confusing world of competing expectations. A philosopher may be good at theory and stumble at putting it into practice.

Ethics is hard work and not so much brilliant insight or faith in the right dogma. It is certainly more than learning the names of some rules.

There are probably other ways to cut the pie, but the four ways of being ethical that figure in this report are the following:

- the ethics of judgment—identifying what one thinks is best and challenging others to behave accordingly
- the ethics of justification—grounding one's actions in general principles
- the ethics of engagement—treating others as our ethical counterparts and searching for a better way forward together
- the ethics of leadership—building communities as group ethical agents through leadership

Most of the material in these few chapters is new. It is a synthesis of classical philosophy, social theory, neurobiology, systems dynamics, and social psychology. Traditionally, dental ethics has borrowed heavily from the field of bioethics. That will be mentioned in the next chapter.

The current chapter will explore the human tendency to look at ethics from our own point of view. It is instinctive to start with what matters most to us. That has a biological base. The ethical challenge becomes acting consistently on our own beliefs (including paternalism, the Golden Rule, and charity) while still allowing others to be ethical.

## It Feels Good to Judge Others

Many people believe they are being ethical when they wag their finger at others and say, "You know you really should not do that." An opinion column in the 21 August 2017 *ADA News* takes third-party payers to task over a policy decision the writer finds objectionable. The piece and its title, "They should know better," reflect the ethics of judgment, sometimes called "righteousness." It might actually be better for dentistry if third-party payers followed the advice of the letter writer, but branding them as unethical and stupid in the bargain seems to lack promise as a starter for constructive conversation. Quite possibly, this approach will shine the light of ethics only as far as those who already share the writer's perspective can see. Although we seldom succeed in shaming others into acting ethically, it provides a certain sense of satisfaction.

No one should doubt that there are occasions when it is necessary to speak from a sincere and deep conviction about fundamental beliefs. It takes courage to tell others their behavior is unwelcome. It is beyond doubt as well that this will often cause others to ignore us or push back based on their moral sentiments. Being right may be necessary for moral change, but it is not sufficient.

There is a bridge between awareness of one's personal sense of what is right and wrong and getting others to work on behalf of that vision. That bridge should not be burned for dramatic effect. The basic structure is that A comes to believe that a certain type of behavior by "the bad guys" is unethical. A tells B that the bad guys are acting unethically. Perhaps more typically, this is an internal conversation where we imagine how we would fix things if we had a mind to. The ethics of judgment becomes public in editorials where something smelly is pointed out and somebody, actor C, is admonished to "shape up." This is popular as a format for continuing education courses on ethics built around showing examples of how others have screwed up.

It is satisfying for A and B to agree that they are better than C, especially when we do not have to say so to the bad guys' faces. It is usually assumed that A and B have done their ethical duty by agreeing that others are out of bounds and somebody ought to do something about it. In the study of justifiable criticism reported in Chapter 6 and Appendix J, many dentists said something to the effect: "I have done enough by pointing out the gross or continuous faulty work. It is up to others to do the right thing now and fix it." Often, the person expected to rectify the situation is the patient or the government. Ethical conversations where we or our friends are the misguided ones are rare and tender conversations.

Harvard professor Steven Pinker says, perhaps a bit unsympathetically, "Most applications of the moral sense are not particularly moral but rather tribal, authoritarian, or puritanical, and it is reason that tells us which of the other applications we should entrench as norms" (Pinker, 2011, p. 669).

### Ethics as an Expression of Basic Instincts

The ethics of judgment serves three functions, all basic to survival. First, it makes clear where we stand and what matters most to us. It defines our personal sense of the right and the good. Second, it is fair warning to others about our convictions. Third, public stands on what is right and good mark our membership in like-minded communities. This is a powerful ethical action since groups function as ethical agents to provide personal protection. The ethics of groups will figure prominently in Chapter 13 on Three-party Morality and Chapter 14 on Organizations as Moral Agents.

A common pattern in the ethics of judgment is that ethics does not come up as a topic without first assuming that others are "wrong." Judgment ethics is the most fundamental kind. It is the basic tool kit, issued at birth, and can fairly be called "human nature." In fact, the urge to respond this way is instinctual and instantaneous (Damasio, 1999; Decety & Wheatley, 2015; Greene, 2013). Jonathan Haidt (2012) has studied what he calls the "righteous mind" in thousands of cases, across age groups and cultures. (See Appendix E for evidence regarding what these foundational beliefs are among dentists.) He argues that certain moral judgments are wired in. We are disgusted by behavior that is cruel, dirty, contrary to our sensibilities, or otherwise "unnatural." Most people cannot articulate a rational argument why unmarried brothers and sisters of legal age should not have consensual, protected sex with each other. It is just "wrong." Religious taboos also come to mind. Children react negatively to mean behavior well before they can talk (Hamlin, 2013). But mean behavior is not universally condemned. Lynch mobs and fanatic cliques surprise themselves by doing as a group what none would do individually (Curriden & Phillips, 1999). There is an elevated sense of group identity if we can be clear about who the "enemy" is and mark their unethical conduct (Atran, 2010; Keen, 1986). The ethics of judgment has personal and group survival value.

We do not need to be taught it, but often those who believe they have authority attempt to do so. This is the way we first learn our ethics. As children or as new members of a group, we are just told what to do. There is no presumption that we will understand why we are expected to behave as instructed. After all, it is said, there may not be time to explain everything and everyone needs to do the right thing regardless of whether they have the capacity to understand why. If everything is submitted to reason, novitiates might wiggle out from the need to conform to authority. Sometimes our early training comes with a message, "That is what good little boys or girls are supposed to do" or "Members of this organization are expected to adhere to certain standards of conduct." These are not ethical justifications; they are reminders that remaining on good terms with a powerful person or being a member in good standing or a viable candidate for honors requires conformity to norms. A popular line of scholarship posits that until the age of about eight years most of us use an ethics of conformity to those who have the capacity for making our lives easy or difficult (Colby et al, 1987; Rest et al, 1999). The ethics of judgment is learning what the alpha-group does.

The speed of ethical judgment decisions and actions—on the order of a couple hundred milliseconds—and its self-protective character suggests that it is located in part in the limbic system (Light & Zahn-Waxler, 2012). As Joshua Greene (2008) noted, information about a favored political candidate's hypocrisy activates centers in the brain that control emotional but not cognitive responses.

We never outgrow this basic level of ethical functioning. We use it as a default system and add additional layers of ethical criteria on top of it as we mature and as these are necessary. There are two additional layers of moral development that supplement this foundation. These depend on certain neural centers in the brain coming online in the preteens and in early adolescence. These higher-order ethical skills will be discussed in the next two chapters. They help us override the primitive ethics of judgment. Some people, such as sociopaths and narcissists, never or incompletely develop the overlay of ethical maturity. For all their life they burst out with blaming others for things they do not like.

When armchair ethicists say that folks learn their ethics before they get to college or dental school they are correct in a certain sense. Such statements are best understood as referring to the ethics of judgment. They are entirely autobiographical. The misleading part of this statement is that there are also new parts of ethics that are normally added as we grow up.

## The Golden Rule and Paternalism

The unflattering side of the ethics of judgment is when it cuts others off from functioning as their own independent moral agents. We want others to freely choose at least an ethical position that is compatible with our own. Starting from the position that "the other" is morally defective for not seeing things fundamentally as we do sets up an ethically uneven relationship. If only one party gets to use the ethical equipment, the other is somehow less human. For some people, the important thing about being ethical is to be right.

There is a more upstanding side to the ethics of judgment. It seems fair to share personal ethical views as an invitation to start a conversation, to clarify where one is coming from, and as something more than "my way or the highway." According to Roger Fisher, an expert on negotiation (1971, p. 113): "An attempt to point out to an adversary that he ought to make a decision where the 'oughtness' is based on our ideas of fairness, history, principle, or morality is at best a diversion from the immediate task at hand; at worst it is destructive of the result we want.... We have to appeal to their sense of right and wrong." Allowing others the courtesy of judging us if we intend to judge them on ethical grounds opens the possibility of stronger ethical communities. It increases the chances of coming to a mutual agreement everyone can live with.

What usually happens in the ethics of judgment is that we convince ourselves that we, but not others, are on ethically sound ground. Then we use nonethical means, such as position and expertise, economic pressure, or other forms of coercion, to try to get our way. That is power pretending to be ethical.

In this section, we will take up three levels of the ethics of judgment:

- deciding for others
- deciding as we think others might decide
- deciding with others

In the health professions, deciding for others is usually known as paternalism (Dworkin, 1972). The logic is that the professional, because of his or her superior knowledge in health matters, should determine what is best for others, or at least have the dominant voice. The assumption in the dental profession is that patients have no other legitimate values than optimal oral health.

Informed consent is in place as a check on paternalism. The legal requirement is that patients must be given sufficient information so they can understand enough to make a free and informed decision, incorporating matters of personal values, finances, and other considerations that may be unknown to the dentist. Patients make the ultimate decision about how they want to be treated. They do not participate: they decide. Informed consent is sometimes confused with "hold harmless" language or exculpatory wording that forces patients to waive some of their rights. Sometimes informed consent is rendered practically useless because of the circumstances in which patients are asked to give it, under stress and burdened with pages of fine print. Sometimes dentists, because of paternalism with the best of intentions, shade the information given to tip the decision in a direction that they would choose if making the decision from their own value perspective. In the end, whether justified by the Golden Rule or not, the ethics of health decisions always cautions against deciding for others (Buchanan & Brock, 1990).

The Golden Rule is a venerable guide to human conduct. Some version of it exists in all religious traditions. It is a good place to start when seeking to get along with others because it moves us to deciding as we think others might decide. There are two parts to the familiar ethical maxim: (a) parity of standards for the actor and those acted upon; and (b) grounding of the standard in the individual values of the actor. "Do unto others as you would have them do unto you" means there is a single standard for the good and the right and not one for me and a different one for others. It is antihypocrisy medicine. One could not use the rule to justify getting one's way at the expense of others, for example. (Of course, that gets a little dicey if one places great value on altruism and charity and frowns on those who are not so enthusiastic about self-sacrifice.) The downside of the maxim is that it privileges the view of ethics favored by the actor. Making one's views of ethics the standard for everyone is "self-sealing." There is no position outside one's own ethical framework from which to test whether any other system might be better. "As I would have others do" pretty clearly defines whose set of standards will dominate.

It has sometimes been suggested that the Golden Rule could be improved if reworded to say, "Do unto others as they would like to be done by." This is essentially altruism said otherwise. It is not really an improvement on letting the professional decide what is right for others. It is just reversing the roles of who gets to make the rules. But there is something here worth following up on. We might use a formula such as this: "Do unto others only in situations where you would be willing, if required to do so, to trade positions." This comes close to the position of the eighteenth-century philosopher Immanuel Kant (Kant, 1785/1948) and the late John Rawls (1971), who wrote 200 years later. This "are you willing to trade positions" perspective does have the advantage of insisting that all those we deal with be treated as moral agents. That will be important in the discussion below of charity. Kant famously insisted that ethics requires that all be treated not merely as means to our ends, but as ends in themselves.

Perhaps a better ethical rule for deciding how dentists should treat patients and others would be dual decision making (Chambers, 2011b). This is deciding with others. This approach is gaining respect in the health professions (Djulbegovic et al, 2012; Helfrich et al, 2018). On this view, both professionals and those they serve are interdependent ethical agents, and both have to independently agree before an action is taken that affects them both. This means that dentists, as much as patients, have a right to refuse to pursue certain treatment approaches. When dentists decline, because they feel it violates their personal (not the patient's) values, that option can be taken off the table. Only those treatments that both parties agree to are ethically acceptable. Because of a historical accident, the American Dental Association Principles of Ethics includes only patient autonomy (self-governance or uncoerced choice). There is a good argument that it should include dentist autonomy as well.

## Charity

Dentists are generous. The American Dental Association estimates the value of donated dental services at approximately 5% of billed services (Forsberg et al, 2004). Some dentists give much more. But about half give nothing (Kramer, 2012). There may be a slight tendency among the nongivers to temper the situation, but write-offs and taking Medicare patients do not count. The Internal Revenue Service is very clear that one cannot deduct for the presumed difference between what one could "really" charge and what is actually charged. True professional altruism takes the form of volunteering for a Mission of Mercy event, accepting a number of poverty patients as part of a program such as Donated Dental Services, mission trips in the developing world, and days out of the office to serve on committees in organized dentistry.

Charity is the positive side of the ethics of judgment. Some would go so far as to place charity among the highest of virtues: everyone should always be altruistic. That, of course, is nonsense, or as Herbert Spenser said more than a hundred years ago, it is suicide (Spencer, 1887/1978). Charity is selective. If charity were a universal ethical imperative, we would be forced to admit that all of us are unethical on a wholesale basis. At best it is something special and not part of our daily routine. What needs to be explained is why charity is valuable when practiced for and by some and not others.

In the first place, not all acts of giving deserve to be labeled charity. Citizens in a state may prioritize scarce public funds so that mental health and substance abuse treatment rank higher than oral health. Organized dentistry might campaign for resources going in the latter direction on the grounds of promoting the charitable benefit of dentistry. Sometimes this shades off into corporate paternalism. We should help others. What needs to be worked out is how we decide to help some and not all and why we do not give 100% (Singer, 2016).

Giving to others is not a universal good. There are individuals who claim a tax deduction for charitable contributions to organizations and causes that others take strong exception to. Terrorists sometimes make the ultimate sacrifice for a cause they believe in. Individuals drop their memberships in organizations because they cannot support some of the initiatives or policy positions their dues money is going for. The point here is that charity also serves the needs of the giver. When an action can be explained by reference to more than one benefit, the analysis becomes complicated. For sure, however, it is suspicious to claim only the publicly laudable part of the motive.

Charity is selective in another sense. Every generous person is not liberal to all comers and all causes. They pick and choose. Every generous person does not show unlimited beneficence. There are rare examples, often in history, of those who have given away everything. Altruism, by definition, means giving to others at one's own expense. It is a transfer of resources without expectation of compensation. If everybody did it all the time the world would be no better than it would be if everyone always pursued their own self-interest; it would just be turned on its head. (See Chambers, 2016c, for a mathematical proof of this point.) Charity is seldom uniformly distributed. Sometimes the selectivity is just a form of self-interest dressed up in fashionable apparel.

There is smart charity and a not-so-smart kind. The questionable variety is just using power and propaganda to advance a favored cause while denying the intelligence, capability, and moral agency of others and claiming an honor for doing so. America has a history of isolating rather than reaching out to those who are struggling to fit into society. This took the form of poorhouses that isolated those who could not keep up in the nineteenth century and is evident today in the homeless crisis (Eubanks, 2017). Good charity strengthens one's community rather than segmenting it.

## Judgment Alone Is Not Enough

Judgment ethics is insufficient. Mother Nature realized that and gave us empathy, rationality, and the capacity to create moral communities by mutual consent. Of course it feels good to tee-off on a soft target, and if we can do so in the presence of an admiring crowd of those who share our values, so much the better. It is said by some that young members of the profession are unethical because of their educational debt burden, their indulgence in the digital world, and the fact that so many of them were born in other countries. Perhaps there is real evidence to support these associations, but such evidence has not been made public. It is not necessary, however, to vilify others to make a point. Usually, a positive message, accompanied with a promise to become personally engaged, works best. If nothing personal and positive comes to mind, that might signal either that the issue has not been well worked out or that it is not worth more than a little strutting and a discreet exit.

Here are some of the benefits of the ethics of judgment:
- serves as an alarm signal for oneself and one's group, warning that something may be amiss

- makes one feel good, especially if eloquent emotion is unleashed
- marks one as a member of a group, perhaps a high-status member
- warns others that they should work up some defenses

Here are some of the downside features of the ethics of judgment:
- unlikely to produce the desired effect in others (except one's friends)
- blocks one from seeing one's own role in the ethical situation
- divides groups, pushes people away
- may really be about getting our own way by power disguised in ethical language

Garrett Hardin wrote perhaps the most frequently cited essay in social theory, "The Tragedy of the Commons," 50 years ago. In his related book *The Limits of Altruism: An Ecologist's View of Survival* (1977), he cautions against thinking the job of ethics is finished once the problem has been pointed out to others: "Don't count on others to solve your problem if doing so means acting against their own best interests" (Hardin, 1977, p. 26). Positive personal action typically works better. If others make ethical missteps or take unknowing or ill-advised action, we should work with them not against them.

## Summary

The ethics of judgment turns on telling others what we think is right and good and expecting them to bring their behavior in line with our views. The first part of that proposition is strong; the second part is questionable, both ethically and practically. We are born with a basic neurobiological system that helps us survive as individuals and differentiates us from others as group members. This is our first, instinctive system of ethics. The Golden Rule is a positive expression of ethics at this level because it honors parity between our behavior and what we expect of others. But it privileges our personal system of ethics and leads to paternalistic choices and charity that compromise the moral agency of others. There are alternatives, such as dual decision making (the ethics of engagement), that move to higher systems of ethics.

# Chapter 8

# The Ethics of Justification

The ethics of judgment, understood as calling on others to do the right thing, is the private or group default position. If necessary we supply reasons to justify our views as being more than personal preferences. When necessary we can all do this in virtually any case. Every organization has a code with well-reasoned principles. Dilemma training in dental schools and ethics continuing education programs are usually built on a set of principles. The "Ethical Moment" column that has appeared for many years in the *Journal of the American Dental Association* invariably references exactly five principles. We are more comfortable in our ethical positions when we can justify them.

The ethics of judgment is the ethics of emotion. Justification gives space for our rational side. We consider ourselves social creatures, so we need a common way of talking about ethical choices. We are not capricious. Others can count on us. We value being able to ground the way we act in language that appeals to others. The ethics of judgment is about the way we interpret rules. Those we treat do not have to agree with the principles we use, but those in our reference group should grant them at least *prima facie* credibility. Others' values do not override our principles, so we can disagree and still be reasonable. The ethics of justification is about our doing the right thing relative to our own norms. The late bioethicist Berny Gert (1998) put it rather starkly when he proposed that "anything that is justifiable is ethical."

This chapter is concerned with showing the broad range of ethical principles that underlie justification. That is followed by a handful of questions that seem unanswered when grounding behavior in principles. Finally, the neurobiological evidence for the ethics of justification is presented.

## Principlism and Codes

This is essentially where dental ethics is today. We are learning the language of bioethics and adapting it to dental situations. It is a "new catechism" required of dental students, maybe the necessary first step. Those who convert to new religions or systems of thought begin by matching new names to important behaviors and observing the routines and honoring the ceremonial symbols of others who serve as guides. Dentistry has been in this phase for perhaps a quarter-century, and it is now comfortable to talk about ethical principles.

Dentists who have studied the language of bioethics and practiced the skills of analyzing cases should be proud of these skills. One of the themes of this report will be that this has been valuable and useful. But it is time to go beyond that or risk losing interest in the topic. There is already evidence, presented in Chapter 15, that the didactic approach to biomedically based ethics is losing momentum.

Academic philosophers have lively discussions about norms (sentences that contain words like "should" and "ought"). They are trying to figure out how to express norms in clear terms, how they relate to the objective world (if at all), and whether there can be any reason for saying that some are better than others (Wallace, 1996; Wedgwood, 2007). Although there are minor technical differences, the words "principles," "norms," "codes," "ethical rules and standards," and "maxims" will be used interchangeably in this report. Generally, the academics do not pay much attention to the particular individual principles, assuming that this is the business of various communities or professional groups. Philosophers have delegated questions about how and whether norms actually get translated into behavior to the psychologists. Philosophers have focused their attention on the really big and general questions, and they have been at this business of metaethics for about 2,500 years. They have produced a rich menu of norms from which to choose, so there is little urgency about reading the literature in hopes of finding the definitive set.

Principlism, or the development of rules and codes for businesses and professions, came into fashion in the 1950s with the rise of the subdiscipline of bioethics and the professionalization of America (Toulmin, 1950). The Nuremberg trials shocked the world with revelations of the inhuman things done by Nazi doctors, justified in the name of science (Arendt, 1963). But there were dark secrets closer to home. The U.S. Public Health Service had for years conducted experiments on prisoners in Tuskegee, Alabama, randomizing mostly African Americans with syphilis to either receive or not receive penicillin. The experiments continued after it was obvious that subjects were needlessly dying because they were denied medication. In response to this and related abuses, the U.S. Department of Health and Human Services, through the National Commission for the Protection of Human Subjects of Biomedical and Behavioral Research, formed a working group of ethicists that met in Belmont, Maryland. In 1978 guidelines for the ethical conduct of research involving human subjects were issued. Known today as the *Belmont Report*, this was the foundation for the creation of federal regulations governing all research involving humans. The central portion of the report is known as "the common rule" and can be found online at 45 CFR 46, in the Consolidated Federal Record. The report and its resulting regulations are based on three principles: (a) respect for persons, from which informed consent is derived; (b) beneficence, which supports the notion of not involving individuals in greater risk than necessary or warranted by expected gains; and (c) justice, or the rule that one group should not suffer excessive cost for the benefit of others.

The incubator of the bioethics movement was Georgetown University in Washington, DC, and its Kennedy Center for the Study of Bioethics. The *locum classicum* of this field is Tom Beauchamp and James Childress's *Principles of Biomedical Ethics*, now in its fifth edition (2009). With some renaming and splitting the effect on individuals into a positive side and a negative side, bioethics had its four classic principles of bioethics: (a) respect for autonomy; (b) nonmaleficence; (c) beneficence; and (d) justice.

Bioethicists as a general group have flourished because those associated with hospitals can bill for their services and those who train other bioethicists in university programs draw a salary. Ethicists working in specific professions that are not hospital-based often work in isolation and draw their content from other fields. The health professions borrowed liberally from the Georgetown work. Medicine has nine principles and a book-length code. Dental hygiene has six core values, occupational therapy six, and so forth. The principles are not the same across the professions.

In 2016 the American Dental Association celebrated the hundredth anniversary of its code. Although the various versions in the early years were called "codes of ethics," they were properly examples of professional etiquette, focused on the relation of one dentist to others. For example, for many years the code admonished dentists to consult with colleagues to ensure that fees were fixed. Today, of course, that is illegal. In the 1990s the association appointed a committee to update the code of professional conduct. Consultants were brought in from Georgetown. It was decided that a superstructure of ethical principles would be erected to surround the code of conduct without changing the code itself. But almost half of the items in the code could not be fitted to the conventional bioethics principles. A new principle, veracity, was added to accommodate this shortcoming.

History matters with respect to detail. The Belmont principle of "respect for persons" was changed at Georgetown to "respect for autonomy" and then by the American Dental Association to "patient autonomy." Georgetown may have been right to emphasize that all people have a right to self-governance (that is the literal translation of the original Greek from which our term *auto* [self] *nomy* [rule] is based) as a corrective to implied paternalism. But the association's limitation of self-determination only for patients is an unhappy restriction. Not all people in need of oral health care are patients (Chambers, 2015a). A patient is one who has agreed to the conditions offered by a provider. Thus only those who agree to a dentist's terms are covered by the principle. Although the code states that dentists should not deny services to individuals based exclusively on certain personal characteristics such as race, it states (oddly enough under the principle of justice) that dentists "in serving the public may exercise reasonable discretion in selecting patients for their practices." Further, the phrasing of the American Dental Association code excludes autonomy for dentists. It will be explained in the next chapter that ethics loses much of its power when all parties to a relationship do not have the same status as moral agents, especially equal autonomy.

As the official name indicates, the current American Dental Association code is a three-part structure of: (a) Principles of Ethics (which occupy a small portion of the document and are aspirational in nature); (b) a Code of Professional Conduct (of which there are 27 items, all of them enforceable through sanctions on members); and (c) Advisory Opinions that are intended to clarify interpretation of the elements of the Code of Professional Conduct.

The American Dental Association code is "owned" by the House of Delegates. It cannot be amended except by vote of that entire body. It is administered by the Council on Ethics, Bylaws and Judicial Affairs, which is responsible to circulate the code, may suggest changes, and can discipline members who are in violation of the code. Similar structures, both in terms of various content in the code and in terms of promulgating and enforcing it, exist in virtually every state, for ethnic and specialty groups, and for commercial enterprises in dentistry such as the Association of Dental Support Organizations. This pattern is repeated for other professional associations. For example, hospitals where dentists may have privileges or corporate entities for which dentists work usually have codes. It is possible that a dentist who belongs to an organization can violate that organization's code while attempting to honor the code of another organization or be excused by one from doing what another deems mandatory. As examples, the statement on autonomy in the California Dental Association Code of Ethics is different from that found in the American Dental Association document, and the American Dental Association code is not in harmony with the American Medical Association code, as seen in how each handles the waiving of copayments.

A distinction between aspirational and enforceable codes is useful. Aspirational codes tell others what an organization expects of its members. They are identity-guiding documents. Enforceable codes prescribe or prohibit certain kinds of behavior on penalty of being sanctioned or removed from the organization. The latter assume a reporting and enforcement mechanism, and usually a due process disciplinary procedure. They imply to the public that all members of the group always adhere to the standards of the group and that those who do not will be remediated or removed. These are action-guiding documents.

There is a tension between licensure as an authorization to engage in a commercial activity and enforceable professional codes. That is that codes and laws are not the same. It is illegal to exclude individuals for violating an organization's codes if that act also deprives them of the opportunity to practice based on a license. Enforceable codes are limited to organizations with voluntary membership and only govern membership in the organization, not behavior itself. No organization can use its code to impose its vision of professional practice on members of the profession as a whole or control the public understanding of what is appropriate ethical behavior in the profession.

Commercial organizations, religions, and social groups have codes and sets of principles as well, and for the same reasons professional groups do. They focus the behavior of members and suggest an image to the public.

There can be conflicts among codes for various groups. Birth control counseling in Catholic hospitals is an example. Dentists working in some commercial practices or hygienists may experience difficulty harmonizing codes for various professional groups. State dental association codes, but not state practice acts, often have principles that preclude use of unearned "degrees" (such as fellowships in "institutes") in announcements of continuing education programs, but they seldom enforce them. In another case, the author was personally involved with a fellow of the American College of Dentists who retained an advertising agency to promote a commercial innovation of his devising. He had referenced his induction in the college as an endorsement of this commercial product. This is a violation of the American College of Dentists Code of Professional Conduct. The dentist did not respond when asked to talk about this, but representatives of the marketing firm certainly did. They stated in rather forceful terms that no standards in *their* industry had been breached.

Codes do not automatically lead to detection or enforcement of violations. Enron developed a 46-page code that was sweeping in scope and detailed in prescribing enforcement. (It can be viewed online.) Evidence for the effectiveness of codes so far involves only commercial organizations, and the results are mixed. But the general conclusion is that organizations with codes of ethics are prosecuted for crimes against the community at about the same rate as organizations that do not have codes (Brief et al, 1996; Kaptein & Schwartz, 2008).

Principles are customarily associated with organizations rather than individuals. It is natural for dental hygienists to speak of trust or respect for all human beings, as these are elements in their code. But we may not be overly impressed if a dental hygienist said, "My personal code of ethics emphasizes the principle of reciprocity." It happens that reciprocity is arguably the most widely recognized moral principle in the world (Donaldson & Dunfee, 1999), but one that would not fit comfortably in a relationship such as dentistry that is built on a very steep power gradient. This may be part of the reason principles are popular among the professions but not so much so in ethics generally.

Organizations choose their principles carefully to reflect values that characterize the group. They tend to reflect behavior of the most powerful group members. They embody the habits that have allowed the most successful to thrive. They describe the habits that the organization's leaders would not be happy to see changed. They are naturally conservative (see Chapter 11 and Appendix E).

## Some Concerns About Principles

Principles and codes are helpful if not misused. They are an easy introduction to thinking about what is right and good. They are somewhat common language within the groups that use them and attractive things to say to others. Generally, however, they cannot do the heavy lifting required of professional ethics. If they remain general suggestions and slogans, they have a useful, but limited, role to play. If they are offered as common guides for how we should all behave all the time or standards that we can use to judge others, they trail off into abstractions.

Consider these six problems: (a) there are too many principles; (b) they are often misapplied; (c) they are inconsistent; (d) they leave questions undecided; (e) they do not reliably guide action; and (f) they justify too much.

### Incommensurability

That is a fancy but useful word meaning that principles in one system cannot be adequately mapped into other systems. Ethical principles get trapped in the groups that endorse them and they do not necessarily travel well to other groups. In fact, there is no general agreement on what the universal ethical principles are. Philosophers have been at this for more than two millennia, and in each generation we discover the flaws in the previous candidates. Various groups working in the same field or similar ones craft different sets of principles, and they change them from time to time, usually in committees or by vote. The fact that we have not yet agreed on the touchstones suggests that this may not be exactly the right project.

### Interpretation

Principles are generalizations. They require interpretation. Various individuals who strongly and honestly endorse a given principle may nevertheless pursue contradictory behaviors.

A typical principle in professional codes is "beneficence." This means acts of charity, mercy, and doing good for others. The word implies moral obligation for doing the right thing. The problem is that it characterizes the motive but does not define what the "right thing" is. Professionals can legitimately claim to be acting beneficently while engaged in contradictory behavior, perhaps even the kind of acts that their patients are not especially interested in. One dentist may say, "I am beneficent because I have given the patient the veneers she wanted," while another says, "I am beneficent because

I talked her out of unnecessary treatment." This is most obvious when an action is chosen and the principle of beneficence is later attached to it as a justification (Boudes & Laroche, 2009).

*Primum non nocere* is Latin for "first do no harm." It is often identified with the principle of nonmaleficence and with the Hippocratic Oath. Both are unfortunate partial truths. One way to avoid harm is to refuse to be involved in treatment, as Dr. Noggin did in Chapter 6. That would hardly be a good position for healthcare professionals. The quick retort, and there is some validity to it, is that by failing to become involved, we are *letting* harm happen. Ethicists still debate the difference between causing harm and allowing it, and thus the debates over just distribution of limited health resources will keep bioethicists in business for generations. But as soon as the trade-off is framed as one between harms and benefits, the distinction between beneficence and non-maleficence becomes shaky. The *Belmont Report* was anchored in the requirement that anticipated benefits should exceed anticipated harms and by as large a margin as possible. If that standard is applied, healthcare professionals need to ground their treatments on what care is best for the patient or the community (say fluoride) and not on whether the preferred treatment will provide a specific benefit.

The Latin in the phrase for "first do no harm" probably dates from the early middle ages, so it would not have appeared in the Hippocratic corpus, which was Greek, fourth century BCE. The actual wording in the oath can be translated, "Use your talents for the benefit of mankind and not for evil." What the School at Cos was concerned about was poisons and giving medications that would cause abortions. The Hippocratic Oath is also very clear that doctors should not cut tissue—hardly a welcome aspiration for dentists.

Philosophers have long known that the use of principles in ethics is a matter of rational syllogistic reasoning (MacIntyre, 1988). The principle is the major premise. For example, "It is unethical to waive copayment" (5.B.1 in the American Dental Association code). There is a minor premise, such as "Dr. X did not bill the patient for anything although the particular insurance plan states that it will only cover 80% of the usual, customary, and reasonable fee." We apply a little logic here: A is unethical, Dr. X did A, therefore "Dr. X is unethical."

It does not require a college course in logic to know how to retain both the major and minor premises and at the same time avoid the conclusion. The usual process is to introduce additional minor premises. "The insurance company has often overlooked these cases in the past." "The insurance company has been gouging me, so here is an easy way to even the score." "The patient has been paying top dollar in the past and has just fallen on hard times so it is either this or leave the patient with an unmanageable condition." Or, "The dentist's primary obligation is service to the patient and the public-at-large" (from Section 3 of the American Dental Association code). The addition of any or several such premises justifies a conclusion that the dentist is ethical when waiving copayments at the same time it does not alter or invalidate the principle.

Principles operate at the abstract level and there are multiple ladders for climbing down to reality. All ladders do not end in the same place despite beginning with a single principle. There is a relationship here between situational and systemic self-perceptions of ethics developed in Chapter 5 on "Bad People."

## Inconsistencies

There is a classic case, involving a commonly encountered ethical dilemma, discussed in virtually every dental school ethics course. The patient needs to bring his or her periodontal health under control before the restorative work can begin. The patient refuses any care other than cosmetic restorative treatment. The principles of beneficence and patient autonomy are in conflict. The usual advice is that the dentist needs to "educate" the patient about doing what the dentist knows is right (the ethics of judgment). But this is not an ethical solution; it is a psychological escape that cancels the dilemma. What if the dentist is not a satisfactory teacher?

Ethics education is often described as dilemma training. Teaching cases such as this are well suited to practicing abstract reasoning skills. A lemma is a partial proof. (In math or engineering or computer science, a commonly encountered problem has a conventional solution called a "lemma.") In the working out of large problems, lemmas are inserted by name where needed, and it is assumed that the proof goes through without having to be specific about the details. A "polylemma" is a problem that involves multiple lemmas. (By convention, we just refer to cases with more than one potential justification as "dilemmas.")

But sometimes the lemmas point in contradictory directions, as in the case of beneficence and patient autonomy mentioned above. The introduction to the American Dental Association code is explicit about this: "Principles can overlap each other as well as compete with each other." Beauchamp and Childress (2009) admit that this is a problem common throughout bioethics, and they urge that conflicting principles be managed in a "balanced" fashion. That is magical thinking since balance is undefined and is certainly not offered as a "superprinciple." People claim that the solution they favor at the moment is always a "balanced" one. Dilemmas play a significant role in ethics education precisely because they offer individual practitioners an escape from having to conform to a principle that is inconvenient. They can all be "balanced" by giving greater weight to the principle that justifies the preferred outcome. The different role ethics cases play in dentistry compared with other professions is detailed in Appendix F.

Fortunately, ethical dilemmas are extremely rare in actual dental practice. In most ethical challenges, there is a clear right and wrong. Overtreatment, overbilling, cherry picking treatment, incomplete diagnosis, failure of informed consent, patient abandonment, and sexual improprieties are not dilemmas. The issue is not which principles apply or the need to find a rational justification; it is having the courage to do what is clearly right.

## Indeterminacy

The fourteenth-century philosopher Jean Buridan is remembered today for his ass. He imagined the animal of that name exactly equidistant between two piles of hay and starving to death because it could not decide which way to go. This is unlikely to happen in the healthcare environment, except in academic discussion in schools, contrived ethics case reports, or political debates over policy. When that is a danger, it is because there are too many parties to the discussion and too many alternatives to satisfy the requirements for a rational resolution.

Kenneth Arrow received the Nobel Prize in 1984 for his work on what is known as the social welfare problem (Arrow, 1951). Why can we not agree, for example, on the proper level of state funding for dental Medicare? Given several possible applications of resources and several reasonable people who have ideas about the best allocation, should there not be a rational, ethical solution? Yes, there always is if there are fewer than three alternatives and fewer than four decision makers. Otherwise, the problem is insoluble. Arrow demonstrated that this is more than being just difficult, but possible to pull off. It is indeterminate—period. Everyone who has participated in policy debates knows the grip of Arrow's conclusion and how such matters are typically managed with a little politics and by otherwise relaxing the requirement to be completely rational. The rooms where such debates take place always have a door clearly marked "politics."

It happens that there are three easy ways out of the embarrassment of the indeterminate social welfare problem. The first is to loosen the requirement for consistency in one's preferences. One hears, for example, arguments such as this: "The most important function of the state board is to ensure patient safety and also the most important function is to protect maximum practitioner independence. Issues have to be decided on a case-by-case basis." Another common escape from Arrow's constraint is to empower a dictator or supreme committee that brings about a power solution. It is usually also required that the solution have a plausible justification, even though other actions are also justifiable. That is the ethics of judgment. Finally, such ethical challenges can be "dissolved" rather than resolved. The issue is broken into parts, and each of several groups crafts a solution satisfactory to its interests and then declares that others solved the wrong problem. There is nothing inherently wrong with any of the ways of sneaking around Arrow's ethical indeterminacy...except for the phony claim that these dodges are ethical. They are not. They are ways of shifting a problem out of the domain of ethics.

It is always possible, in principle, to make an ethical problem insoluble if one brings in enough experts or creates a forum the purpose of which is to debate multiple issues, in principle. It is also always possible to get a clear solution if each dentist is the framer of the problem and the decider of the validity of the solution. Chapter 15 shows that this is the most common form of ethics teaching cases in dentistry.

## Incontinence

There is a gap between figuring out what is the most ethical thing to do in a situation and actually doing it. Philosophers call this "incontinence"—when one balks at doing what one knows "ought" to be done. There is usually a significant gap between codes and conduct (Dawson, 1994). Dental school, continuing education programs, and professional endorsements of codes have elevated reflection on principles while largely paying too little attention to the matter of seeing ethical problems in the first place or taking action to meet the needs of the situation. The literature is dominated by case reports that name the principles that are in play. The cases come to us plucked out of the blooming, buzzing confusion of practice, usually crafted to make them more complicated than they really are so that one principle can be played off against another. After the analysis, very little.

James Rest was a physiologist interested in ethics who accumulated a large body of research on how people, especially professionals, address ethical issues. He developed a four-component model that is respected in many disciplines (Rest et al, 1999; Rest & Narvaez, 1994). Managing an ethical situation begins by identifying that there is a problem. Ethical sensitivity differs from one individual to another and across contexts. As the British ethicist Simon Blackburn noted (2001, p. 203), "The big problem is not that people are unethical, they are morally blind." A good way to have an easy conscience about ethics is to avoid looking for problems or only be on the lookout for those that embarrass others.

Rest's second component is moral reflection. This is the rational work of naming the principles, identifying whose interests are at stake, and identifying and weighing or "balancing" the possible outcomes of each. This chapter has been all about moral reflection. There have been a few hints about why this is inherently a sloppy and incomplete substitute for taking on the full ethical challenge.

The third component is moral character or integrity. Some people care about ethics and others have accepted that this is not a big part of their lives. Some dental students can walk, with a clean conscience, out of a seminar on ethics and minutes later collaborate with a clinical faculty member on an expedient treatment plan that puts the patient at risk. Other students would say, "That is not the kind of person I am." Some faculty members do not know the school has an ethics seminar. Some practicing dentists have not read the American Dental Association code. Appendix G presents evidence that the code is very poorly understood, so likely not intentionally followed. Integrity is about who one is.

Moral courage, the fourth component, is improperly named. The idea is that awareness, analysis, and character have to be turned into action. Otherwise they are academic. Recently a dentist came at the last minute to sign in for continuing education credit and left immediately from a seminar the author was presenting. The program he skipped but claimed credit for was on ethics. For the most part this is not about "courage" but about interpersonal skills, political connections, and going to the right place at the right time. This is the essence of ethical leadership that will figure prominently throughout the rest of this book.

The American College of Dentists had on its website at one time a short, self-scoring test that anyone could take to determine which of the four components in Rest's model are individual strengths and which areas might be in need of further attention. Research using this instrument (Chambers, 2011c) revealed an unexpected finding. A group of students reported their relative strengths on Rest's components and also nominated classmates who were recognized as being moral leaders. Three of the components were significantly predictive of recognized ethical impact in their community. The only one that was not was moral reflection—the very skill that depends on facility with principles and that is the backbone of current thinking and teaching in dental ethics. Chapter 15 explores ethics instruction in dental schools in detail.

## Post hoc

Not all justifications are formed before an ethical decision is taken, nor do they necessarily figure in determining the decision. Often the theoretical explanation, the appeal to principle, comes after the fact. We sometimes rationally justify our emotional judgments. Joshua Greene (2013) has assembled a large body of research evidence on this aspect of human nature and argues that it is determined by systemic or group needs, not individual ones. Sometimes two or three versions of a justification are tested before the one that best suits the expectations of one's friends is found; sometimes a few justifications are needed, different ones from different sets of friends.

Justifications are rare unless they are requested by others. A justification is just that: a rational framework placed around an action. Its function is to preserve the actor's place among rational members of a group.

William Jennings Bryan was successful in the Scopes Trial. He argued that evolution is bunk and he won. Bryan is also credited with saying, "It is a pretty poor mind that can't gin up some reason for doing whatever you want."

## Slow Ethics

The hot topic in ethics these days is whether moral behavior can be reduced to facts about the brain. Currently neurobiologists and systems theorists seem to be making significant gains in the territory formerly thought to be the exclusive domain of philosophers (Churchland, 2011; Kelso, 1995; Thagard, 2012).

The ethics of justification or ethics grounded in principles represents an evolutionary advance over the ethics of judgment. Children cannot use the higher skills of ethics. They lack the mental apparatus to make abstract judgments, especially conditional and counterfactual comparisons (Bogdon, 2010). The necessary neurology comes online in the early preteens when regions in the prefrontal cortex are myelinated (LeDoux, 1996; Schwartz & Begley, 2002). Myelin is the "white matter" that sheaths long-haul neurons and greatly accelerates their transmission speed. This makes it possible to bring information from diverse brain regions into a particular processing center for comparisons. That is the function of the ventrolateral regions of the prefrontal cortex (Damasio, 1994). This is an interactive process, with the region sometimes recognizing that information is missing or that "something is not quite right." Processing time is on the order of seconds instead of milliseconds, as in the like-it-or-not snap decisions of the judgment system. Because memory is involved here, moral decisions can be reviewed and spun out over minutes, days, and longer. The justification almost always comes after the decision, and awareness of the decision is certainly a few hundred milliseconds after the decision is initiated (Libet, 2004). Awareness that things are not quite right with the ethics of judgment triggers reflection. When it is recognized that a justification is needed for the action taken, further reflection is needed. But justification always comes after the decision to act has taken place, although sometimes by a fraction of a second. Typically, the rational ethics of justification is triggered when it is recognized that the ethics of judgment is not working as expected or when multiple explanations are needed for multiple audiences.

Rest calls this second, group-rationality level of ethical work the "conventional stage" (Rest et al, 1999). We are motivated to ground our ethics in the conventions of the important groups around us. We care about the norms of those we identify with. The important thing is not so much to follow the principles of the groups as not to be seen violating them. This is the business of justifying our actions.

There is a "close enough" argument here. There is substantial wisdom in taking a practical view of the problems identified with the ethics of justification in the paragraphs above. There may be Nobel Prize-winning proofs that normative ethics is inconsistent or incomplete. It may be the case that organizations place more emphasis on norms as general goals and publicity planks than on enforcement. It may even be the case that the link is weak between knowing what is right and following through in action. But are we not better off with these approximations than we would be without them? Even if we sometimes get carried away and claim certainty for an approach that is short of being certain, is this not close enough to be of value? Of course it is. No one is campaigning to ditch normativity. There are, however, two points worth making. First, we should not claim more for principles than they can deliver. A good approach often draws suspicion when it is peddled as being so perfect that others have no place to stand. Second, there may be other approaches that are also close enough to warrant use in selective circumstances. The ethics book is not closed. It is foolhardy to have read the first few chapters and jump to the conclusion.

## Summary

The ethics of justification goes beyond personal views of the good and the right and seeks to ground action in norms. Norms, principles, and other such terms refer to external rational standards shared in various communities we might belong to. They can work to ensure our membership in these groups. Codes have histories, they may be inconsistent with each other, and there is little evidence that they make members or organizations ethical. The study of principles of ethics is long and deep, and several unresolved issues remain. These include: (a) difficulties translating across alternative systems multiple interpretations of single principle; (b) inconsistency across multiple principles; (c) indeterminacy or the impossibility of creating workable consistent systems; (d) the frequent failure of principles to translate into action; (e) principles coming in after the fact to justify previous actions; and (f) sometimes different justifications for the same action being offered to different audiences. The neurobiology necessary to support the ethics of justification does not become available until about age eight.

# Chapter 9

# The Ethics of Engagement

The Greek philosopher Aristippus had an interesting take on the relationship between ethical theory and moral behavior. Basically he said there was none. "When all the laws are finally just and fully enforced, the true philosopher is the one whose behavior has not changed." Confucius had pretty much the same point in mind when he said, "First put words into practice; then say what has been done accordingly."

This chapter pivots from the personal views of ethics as judgment and justification to look at the ethics of two morally equivalent agents engaged in finding the best common way forward. Engagement is the move from ethical theory to moral action.

## Moral Behavior

Consider this case. Mr. Buckum drove trucks on an on-again-off-again basis in order to keep his family just above the poverty line. He resented those who "lorded it over him and his family." The family dentist had suggested that Buckum's daughter, 11-year-old Anne, would benefit from braces. Mrs. Buckum was optimistic. She had been bullied in school when she was a teenager because of her crooked teeth, but her family had been too poor to afford treatment. On the first visit to Dr. Straight's office, Anne was told that she had a classic Class II malocclusion that could be easily corrected. There were no obvious skeletal and dental complications and no contributing health issues. A fee of $5,500 was mentioned, but it was said that very generous and long-term arrangements could be worked out. As the mother and daughter were leaving the office, the patient care coordinator asked when Anne and her mother would like to schedule the CBCT scan at an independent imaging lab in which Dr. Straight owned an interest. The fee would be an additional $700 up front. Mrs. Buckum demurred, saying she did not think she would be able to afford that. The nature of the scan was explained and it was stated that all of Dr. Straight's patients should receive this service.

After an explosive conversation with her husband, Mrs. Buckum phoned the office very apologetically, saying that they could not afford the cost of the treatment if it involved an extra fee for the CBCT scan. The orthodontist would either have to proceed with treatment without the scan or Anne might go elsewhere or go without braces. She hoped the office would understand their situation and change their mind. The office manager phoned back and explained in a very matter-of-fact manner that Dr. Straight had established this policy for all patients in order to provide the highest level of care and to protect against unforeseen complications. It would be impossible to treat Anne without the CBCT. She hoped the family would reconsider and make sure their daughter received the best care to which she was entitled.

It is not obvious that there is a normative principle of ethics that universally dictates the correct ethical solution here. However, the American Association of Orthodontics issued a white paper in 2019 recommending against the routine use of CBCT scans (www1.aaoinfo.org/wp-content/uploads/2019/03/sleep-apnea-white-paper-amended-March-2019.pdf). In moving from the past two chapters that focused on one-party ethics (the ethics of judgment and the ethics of justification), we are now facing two-agent ethics. Those who see the problem from the patient's perspective have several principles they could use to defend their position. The same is true for the office. Is it possible in this case to act morally without first establishing the preeminence of one set of principles and then forcing both parties to accept that guidance? Is agreement on principle a precondition for acting morally? Of course if it is, we are in for interminable battles over whose principles are the right ones. We also create a world of ethical winners and losers, or ethical and unethical people. This kind of ethics often divides people rather than uniting them in a common way forward.

Look again at the case and note the following.

- There are two parties who have to make a moral choice (the Buckums and Dr. Straight).
- Both parties are focused on the kind of future they prefer (the amount of money that will change hands and the probability of altering treatment protocol based on test results).
- The futures that will come to pass depend on the mutual actions of both parties, neither one alone can decide the outcome.
- There are four different ways the case could go (no CBCT and no care, care without CBCT, CBCT without care, and care with CBCT).
- There is no guarantee that there will be a Win-Win solution, so one party or both may have to accommodate.
- Even when none of the possible futures is ideal, some are better than others.

Morality can be defined as choosing the mutually best available alternative future in collaboration with informed and uncoerced other moral agents.

It would automatically be immoral to force others to act against their self-interest if or to the extent that it is unnecessary. It would automatically be immoral to fail to recognize others as having a free choice in their future. It would automatically be immoral to make decisions affecting others that were not grounded in an honest understanding of one's own motives and values and the best understanding possible of the other's motives and values.

The language has shifted slightly here from the two previous chapters. The ethics of engagement is associated with the term morality. That is intended to signal a change in perspective from the theoretical to the actual. The dictionary definition of ethics is the study of right and wrong, good and bad. Morality is not a study, it is a set of habits: the actual pattern of behavior one engages in. The movement up from the ethics of judgment to the ethics of justification and then to engagement in morality is a change in perspective from self-centered blaming of others to rational justification of one's behavior based on principles to mutual interaction with others to produce a better future world, given the situations that actually exist at any moment. The model is presented in full detail in Chambers's *Building the Moral Community* (2016b).

## Moral Choice

The ethics of judgment is easy: we know what we do not like and our job is to say so. It is also pretty easy to do ethics as justification: find a principle among the large number that are available to warrant what one wants to do. There is no role for others to play in either. Moral choice is harder. First, it requires complete honesty. Second, it requires a working awareness of what others are prepared to do. Third, there are a few cases where the calculations needed to find the best mutual path forward are difficult; however, in most cases it is clear how to proceed. There are books that explain how to find the best mutual pair of paths for oneself and others and convenient rules of thumb (Rapoport et al, 1976). But common sense handles most of the cases. The fourth, and most challenging, difficulty in the ethics of engagement is that we cannot determine in advance that we will get things our way or even that we will be able to walk away in righteous indignation if others "don't get it." Ethics is not always winning.

### Win-Win

Win-Win cases are those where the best choice for one agent coincides with the best choice for the other. Dentistry is based on the assumption that patients are better off receiving good care and that dentists are better off giving it. Virtually all the problems mentioned by the panels of dentists and patients in Chapter 1 were complaints about distortions of this basic engagement. Dentists were getting good reimbursement, but patients were getting inadequate or unnecessary care; or patients were staying away and not getting the care they needed and dentists were not professionally employed in the fullest sense.

Most of life is Win-Win, and as a result we underestimate how moral we are most of the time. It would be immoral when Win-Win is on the table to attempt to extract a penalty from others. Revenge and teaching others a lesson fall into this category. Some are even willing to make personal sacrifices if they can hurt others. It is immoral to seek any other solution when Win-Win is available. There was no Win-Win for Dr. Straight and the Buckum family, nor is there for many who need dental care. That is a moral fact.

### Next Best

Another commonly encountered engagement goes by the name of Next Best. One agent can get his or her first choice while the other settles for second best. It may still be ethical to forgo the ideal if Next Best is the most attractive available alternative. Sometimes circumstances simply dictate against the ideal. It is easy enough to imagine that Dr. Straight generally prefers to have CBCT scans as a matter of policy and that Mr. Buckum is adamantly opposed to anything that appears to be an unnecessary expense forced on the poor by those perceived to be in positions of power. The rule for Next Best engagements is that the one with the most to lose should yield. Mr. Buckum is very unlikely to pay for the scan because his pride is right up there with his daughter's appearance, so Dr. Straight should choose between, on the one hand, not having the 3D images but having a patient and, on the other, having neither the images nor the patient.

The Next Best example often encounters two objections. First, some champions for the logic of "the one in the most favored position calls the shots" hold that patients are ignorant of what is in their interest so doctors have the privilege of position and ethical responsibility to insist on the highest standards. That collapses to the ethics of judgment and substituting one's own preferences for those of others. As long as there are enough who accept this view, paternalism is defensible—but not exactly on ethical grounds. Maintaining one's own standards at the expense of the ethical standards and personal needs of others is a thin view of ethics. A second objection commonly heard is that principles may have to be bent. The Buckum-Straight case seems to be about nothing more than how people should treat each other and somebody is going to have to trim their principles. But that is exactly what ethics is. Morality matters even when big principles cannot decide the matter.

Our days are filled with an endless stream of opportunities to treat others well or poorly. We respond so much by habit, and usually for the good, that we dramatically underappreciate the role morality plays in daily life. The methods of the ethics of engagement can be applied to any situation where there are two agents, each of whom has two alternatives. This would include all ethical dilemmas, except those where one agent overlooks or denies that others may have different views and are free to act on them.

## Compromise

A third type of moral engagement is called Balanced Compromise. These are cases where if one agent gets everything he or she wants, the other must settle for third best. (This is different from Next Best where the agent in the least favorable position gets second best.) Typically, in such cases the problem looks the same from the perspective of either party, so the best way forward would be for both to accept second best. Such cases seldom occur in reality because perfectly balanced situations are inherently unstable and some folks try to game the situation by bringing in extraneous precedents. When folks reject compromise "on principle," we should be suspicious that they want you to believe that they have the upper hand. If there is no Win-Win or Next Best, the smart thing to do is negotiate in hopes of achieving that kind of engagement.

## Other Cases

There are degraded versions of these three prototype models where circumstances simply preclude anyone doing well. Disaster recovery, crime, war, domestic abuse, cheating, and patients who have neglected their mouth so long that they present with awful alternatives are engagements where the circumstances on the ground have blocked all the winning moves. But even when there is no ideal alternative, there is still always a best one possible, provided the problems are justly shared. In all there are 78 possible ways two parties can arrange their order of preference across two mutually interacting alternatives (Chambers, 2016b; Rapoport et al, 1976). More than half of them can be solved using the first three rules above, and another 15% are near approximations. There are some stinkers, such as the famous Prisoners' Dilemma (Poundstone, 1992). But in most of these rare and contrived confrontations, the mutually best outcome—the situation that is best for both parties—is to negotiate for all you're worth.

## Making Engagement Work

Getting good at the morality of mutual engagements requires a heavy dose of honesty. Agents need to make lists of the benefits (to them) if the outcome of mutual action comes to pass. For example, for the outcome of having paying patients with CBCT scans Dr. Straight's office could list a greater financial return, a more complete diagnostic database, standardization of treatment protocols, and possibly a relationship with an imaging company or owning such equipment. A list of disadvantages might include losing or alienating patients. The Buckum family could make a similar list. On Buckum's inventory would be not being pushed around by the elite, having more cash, and minimizing hassle. Note that the items on the lists are future states and not ethical principles. Further, the advantages are not the same or even mirror images for what the other moral agent values. Dentists and patients and dentists and third parties use different value dimensions, not opposing ends of the same dimensions.

No great mathematical logic is required to convert the lists into the right moral choice. The four alternative outcomes are simply ranked 4 (best) to 1 (worst), and the choices mentioned above are exercised. The reflective exercise of honest and comprehensive understanding of what is at stake in various courses of action is what matters. When available, pick the 4 and 4 options (Win-Win). If that is not among the available alternatives, go for 4 and 3 (Next Best). The Compromise of 3 and 3 might be necessary. Otherwise negotiate to see whether the apparent mutual solution can be reframed. Avoid any option that requires either party to be forced into their third choice. (For example, Mr. Buckum would rank treatment without CBCT 4 and no CBCT and no care 3. So Dr. Straight insisting on a CBCT would be forcing Mr. Buckum into an unethical situation, one ranked 2 or 1, where he would likely escape by finding another orthodontist or denying his daughter treatment.) By strict definition, any insistence where others must take a 1 (the worst alternative) or that you must do so is inherently unethical. There is always an ethical mutual way of avoiding this. This is most likely to come about as a result of a revenge motive or outrageous self-interest. Understanding both one's own and another's hopes for a better future matter because both are moral agents, capable of acting to bring about their desired future.

## Perspective Matters

There is one little subtlety that should not be overlooked. The approach to morality is based on the engagement of two agents, each with two choices. It is not a calculus based on the rank preferences for two agents made by some omniscient bystander or by either agent denying that the other's views matter. Dr. Straight's choice is not determined by comparing his and Mr. Buckum's priorities; it is based on Dr. Straight's own preferences and his assumptions about what Mr. Buckum values. Morality requires honesty and empathy (Decety, 2012). Morality also leaves both agents with an ethical responsibility since they are making their own choices.

## Principles Do Matter

Principles count, however, and absolutely nothing of the ethics of justification is scarified by moving to the higher level. Principles are all given full weight in proportion to how willing the ethical decision maker is to act on them.

Dr. Straight may hold nonmaleficence as theoretical principle but give it relatively low weight in terms of influencing his behavior. Instead he might say, "I would feel badly if something unanticipated and negative happened because I failed to have a complete diagnostic database." Only the principles we are prepared to act on—and only to the extent that we will make sacrifices to honor them—matter in ethical decision making. It is not the principles that count. It is their power to direct our actions. If a principle is applicable in theory, but it is not strongly action-guiding, it does not really enter the ethical deliberation. Notice that this is much more powerful than simply referencing a norm. The ethics of engagement approach is stronger than the ethics of justification because it weighs each ethical principle by the power it has over our behavior. Different individuals wear their principles differently. Sometimes they do not actually enter moral decisions and sometimes they are a minor consideration.

## Situations Matter

The ethics of engagement makes allowance for the situation on the ground. There are circumstances where it is not possible to optimize. The way to treat an honorable colleague is not the same as the ethical way to treat a reprobate. Besides making the best of situations and realizing that circumstances change, the ethics of engagement also allows for improving one's moral life. We can, and in many cases should in the ethical sense, negotiate with others with a view toward reframing the engagement in the mutually most advantageous fashion. There is no rule that says ethical problems have to be solved as one finds them. A further advantage in negotiating is that we can improve our understanding of the true values of involved others. We may even come to understand our own assumptions and values better in the process. Trying a few mutual small steps often opens new doors. Notice that the type of negotiation suggested here concerns perhaps changing the situation rather than changing the other's personal values. (See Appendix N.)

## An Example

Following is a brief example of an ethical situation worked out in detail using the system of the ethics of engagement. A patient of record but with irregular home care and attendance habits phones with a complaint of a throbbing tooth, #14, that has persisted for several days. The patient is worked in during the slot reserved for these emergencies just before noon on the day of the call. The general practitioner confirms that there is evidence of necrotized pulp based on percussion and in response to both hot and cold. There is a large three-surface amalgam restoration on the tooth, but no sign of an open margin. The general dentist has largely discontinued doing molar endodontics but is prepared to do an initial access opening to relieve the pain. The patient could not be happier. But on an impulse, a call is placed to the endodontist who is in the same building and who sees many referrals from this office. The specialist has a cancellation and could see the patient soon. After a short conference, the patient chooses to return "in a while" to the endodontist.

The general dentist could intuitively and quickly see that there is a fourfold matrix of outcomes, depending on the commitment of the patient to follow through on care and the dentist's management of the case. If the dentist recommends referral to the specialist for both access and treatment, it is expected that the patient will follow through and will receive appropriate care, but the general dentist will lose a billable procedure. If a referral is recommended but not followed through on, the patient will likely very quickly reverse course and may reappear at an inconvenient time. But this is still within appropriate standards for patient management. A third possibility is to perform the access and expect to perform the root canal later in the general dentist's office. Very likely the patient would agree, but there is a chance that such a patient with a poor pattern of care seeking would not follow up in a timely fashion if relieved of immediate pain. If the dentist does the work while the patient would have preferred to see a specialist, the patient will likely say nothing but may resent the appearance of the dentist trying to retain all billable treatments. Of course, if the case goes poorly, even for unforeseen reasons, the patient will be upset. Assume that the dentist ranks the four outcomes as shown in Table 9.1; the dentist's priorities are the first numbers in each cell, with 4 as the most desired outcome and 1 as the least. The dentist's list could be made much longer, but there is no need for that as additional items would have very little chance of changing the rankings.

Table 9.1. **Finding the stable moral solution.**

|  |  | Patient Referral | |
|---|---|---|---|
|  |  | Yes | No |
| Generalist | Yes | [3 3] | [1 2] |
|  | No | [4 4] | [2 1] |

The dentist will also make some assumptions about how the patient will see the case. One appointment with the specialist seems like the obvious most preferred future. Declining treatment while in the chair (for some imagined reason) would be a very poor outcome and should be labeled 1 for last choice. Declining the appointment by the specialist would also be awful, but a bit less publicly so. The second-best solution would be the two-appointment path, but part of the work being done by a known professional who perhaps inspires a bit less credibility in the field is a downside. The ranks for the patient are shown on the right in each cell in Table 9.1.

Tables like the one above can be submitted to formal analysis and will always identify the best mutual outcome. It is clear, however, that this is a Win-Win situation [4 4] and an afternoon one-visit appointment with the specialist is the most ethical course of action. Some may imagine a slightly different rank ordering of potential outcomes. They would use exactly the same logic of locating the best way forward in the ethics of engagement based on their assessment of the relative desirability of the outcomes. They are allowed to do so because they honor ethical principles in a different, but personally defensible, fashion.

All of this will most likely be obvious to both the dentist and the patient at a glance. No fancy calculations or stepping through a protocol for solving cases is necessary. Cases that stand out as bad outcomes can be understood as violating this logic. Dentists probably engage in hundreds of such cases in a day at the office. It would be unusual to call this an ethical "dilemma," although principles could be artificially added if needed to make it one. It is just the morally right thing to do. Overtreatment is morally indefensible because it always forces the patient to take a 1, whether they suspect it or not.

## Moral Outcomes

Academic ethicists will point out that the difference between the ethics of justification and the ethics of engagement turns on the distinction between content theories of ethics and process theories (Shafer-Landau & Cuneo, 2007). The normative approaches focus on which map or GPS we should be using. They are usually silent on how one goes about getting to the goal or even whether there is any energy behind movement in the right direction. Process theories emphasize the actions that are most appropriate. These tend to be "best" alternative approaches rather than requirements for perfection. The logic is that those communities that generally and consistently act to promote mutual benefits will gradually thrive. This is known as meliorism—the faith that working together ethically will bring about a better world.

Morality, or the ethics of engagement, will have the following effects.

- There will always be an identifiable best (but not necessarily perfect) mutual outcome in ethical situations that both agents can agree to.
- There is no need for external enforcement in morality because, per definition, both agents are acting on what they regard as the best approach.
- Communities that practice the ethics of engagement will thrive to a greater extent than those that use any other approach.

Kenneth Arrow received a Nobel Prize for proving that the ethics of justification, structured as a principles approach to the social welfare problem, will always be indeterminate in realistic situations (Arrow, 1951). John Nash received a Nobel Prize for proving that the two-agent, two-alternative framing of the ethics of engagement just described will always produce a best solution. His seminal publication also appeared in 1951. (Sometimes there are three solutions, two good ones and a weak contender, and sometimes there is only a rule for randomly varying approaches in a predetermined ratio, but those are the exceptions.) The Nash criterion for an optimal solution is a pair of actions that neither agent would want to have otherwise. This does not mean that participants in ethical engagements get everything they want, just that they see that they are not entitled to expect anything better. Patients, for example, want optimal oral health and low or no cost, but that does not mean they are entitled to it. Dentists, on the other hand, want willing patients with challenging cases and ready cash, but that does not mean they are entitled to it. Society as a collective whole may recognize the humane and economic advantages of general oral health, but be unwilling to rank this high compared with other uses of public money. Even if it is not ideal, there is always a dynamic equilibrium with a local best available. Any deviation from that is ethically suspect because it works by expecting others to abandon their legitimate self-interests.

Sometimes one determines that the best possible mutual path forward is good but less than perfect. There is a temptation to abandon the approach based on engagement and go for the best personal win. A little deception, perhaps some velvet-gloved power, maybe economic or legal threats, might do the trick. This is nothing more than removing the situation from the ethical realm. It is not unethical. It is amoral.

## No Private Deals

It happens often that two agents go over to the side and cut a private deal that damages the community as a whole. A dentist and an unqualified employee may agree to improper delegation. That is why two-by-two ethical engagements are nested with local ones fitting within more general ones. A bad actor in the eyes of the profession may have reached an agreement with patients (often through misleading them) that colleagues consider objectionable. Quacks and charlatans hurt the profession as well as patients, and thus the profession has a legitimate ethical stake in curbing their activities. Whether anything comes of this will depend on how the ethical part of the profession, as a collective agent with the options of engagement or looking the other way, chooses to engage with the deviant dentist. The options include challenging the bad practice or hiding it. Multiple levels of nesting are typical in a profession such as dentistry, but the "rules of engagement" are the same all the way up. Each interaction and all potential-but-ignored interactions are moral encounters.

In every situation, across levels and regardless of whether framed as conscious ethical issues, the ethics of engagement permeate the profession. There is always at least one right thing to do in every case and several poor choices. And the right thing does not depend on the interpretation or personal preferences of individuals or groups. It can be unambiguously identified. The most common moral failing of groups and organizations is doing nothing because they do not recognize that they are moral agents. The second most common failing is to say that ethics is a private matter between individuals and their conscience.

## Freedom from Outside Interference

Because the ethics of engagement comes to rest when neither agent has any reason to want to make changes, it is self-enforcing. There is no need for regulations, inspections, external review, or sanctions when parties to an arrangement have no incentive to change the pattern of interaction. That is the point Aristippus made centuries ago. Even when this does not carry completely into practice (as when circumstances change or one or both parties come to believe they have been misled), all approximations can be regarded as saving cost and increasing trust. A predictable consequence of winning a confrontation in a fashion other parties feel is unfair is that they will be always on the lookout for ways to even the score. That will be true regardless of how justified winners' actions are in their own minds.

Sometimes the cost of maintaining a victory can be large and long-lasting, eating up all the prize. The existence of rules and the need for enforcers is *prima facie* evidence that the community harbors unethical practices. A sure signal that ethics has been muffed is the metastasis of regulations.

The ethics of engagement does not dictate specific behavior. Two pairs of individuals facing identical circumstances may nevertheless settle on different behavior, but both are ethical. One pair may be seeking to provide high-end care to patients who can afford and appreciate it. The other pair is providing the best care possible for those who otherwise would do without. One argues for an investment in a program that might strengthen the profession generally, and a colleague resists on grounds of fiscal conservatism. There are many ways of being moral. This is not ethical relativism. Each must be as ethical as possible given the circumstances they find themselves in. Naturally that will be strange to those who expect to impose a universal standard (their own) on everybody.

It may appear to some that the ethics of justification provides more secure anchors for desirable behavior than does the ethics of engagement. From within a closed ethical system built on principles there are at least theoretical absolutes. From the wider perspective, justification schemes are just relativism to which those in the systems are blind. By contrast, the ethics of engagement offers a number of firm procedural rules for finding the best options. The only absolute is that it is more ethical to engage with other moral agents than to use any other means of getting one's way.

It would automatically be immoral to:

- leave others with only the worst of all alternatives; first or second best is almost always possible
- force others to act against their self-interest if or to the extent that it is unnecessary
- fail to recognize others as having a free choice in their future
- make ethical decisions that are not grounded in an honest understanding of one's own motives and values and the best understanding possible of others' motives and values
- attempt to extract a penalty from others in a Win-Win situation
- settle for any resolution that one party would have a strong interest in resisting or changing

The ethics of engagement can be easily summarized: have a conversation with involved others before deciding what to do. One cannot be ethical alone.

## The Biological Basis for Morality

The ethics of engagement is built on two features that uniquely characterize *Homo sapiens*. We are the preeminent social animal. Morality should tilt human interactions in the social direction. The days of the hermits of the desert earning their way into heaven by turning their backs on their fellows have long passed. It can be demonstrated that communities that use the ethics of engagement enjoy a higher level of general personal thriving than those that avoid interactions or base their interactions on principles (Chambers, 2016b; Young & Saxe, 2009). It is also the case that this approach performs better in the long run than self-interest, cheating, reneging, coercion, or contempt. Morality is self-correcting and self-optimizing.

Morality is also dynamic. On reflection, it is obvious that norms change across history. Slavery was once accepted on principle. The role of women is changing. Some among us still treat others atrociously, but that is now on the decline (Pinker, 2011). The good doctor who a few centuries ago oversaw palliative care in the hopeless face of most diseases would now be regarded as engaging in malpractice. An ethical code that is fixed or one that requires constant outlays of attention may very well indicate that society has moved on and that those once in power are clinging to outdated norms to protect their position.

Just as the ethics of judgment and the ethics of justification develop at different stages of human growth and are controlled by different centers in the brain, the ethics of engagement continues this pattern. Among the last regions of the brain to myelinate is the right temporoparietal junction (Bzdok et al, 2012; Decety & Lamm, 2007; Koster-Hale et al, 2012). Located in the very center of the cortex, it is uniquely connected with hot lines to virtually all of the brain. The prefrontal cortex gives humans the capacity to project how others feel. The temporoparietal junction gives us the capacity to project how others, acting as uncoerced agents, might affect us. This new capability is necessary for morality as it underlies the two-way calculus of the ethics of engagement. This brain region becomes fully active at about age 16, the age of legal adulthood and moral responsibility in most cultures. In a few individuals, more often males than females, this development is interrupted and we witness schizophrenia, sociopathic behavior, and other social-ethical dysfunctions.

## Summary

Two honest people who begin from different principles are more likely to agree in a mutually productive way than are those who insist on their own way, who are deceptive, who seek to impose their views by power or economic means, who fail to recognize that opportunities exist, or who simply walk away. But that requires engagement.

The ethics of engagement is about the way individuals treat each other rather than what they say. There is only one rule: Engage with others as moral equals in an effort to find and follow the mutually best way forward. Often power and coercion are cloaked in righteousness and normative justifications that accentuate human differences rather than our shared human nature. Joint actions that are seen as the best possible under the circumstances are in no need of further justification, nor do they require inspection, monitoring, regulations, or sanctions. They are self-enforcing. It has been proven by a Nobel laureate that there is always such a solution on the table and that often these can be made even more attractive by honest negotiations. The ethics of engagement may be resisted by those for whom power, coercion, or deception appears to offer at least a temporary better deal. This is not "bad ethics." It is a denial of the role of ethics in human interaction. The neurobiological structures needed to support the ethics of engagement do not come online until mid- to late-adolescence.

# Chapter 10

# The Ethics of Leadership

P art of this story really happened. The general plot is universal. One of the most beautiful places in the world is the sea coast at Point Reyes National Park, a triangular 111-square-mile range of mountains, tidal marshes, and seashore an hour north of San Francisco. It is separated from the rest of the state by a sliver-like bay and set of rivers along the San Andreas Fault, and the mass is gradually moving to the north. Hiking out to the shore offers a spectacular view of the Farallon Islands outside the Golden Gate to the south and Drake's Bay to the north.

Imagine a fellow walking on the beach to restore his peace of mind and heading back toward the distant parking lot. There in the path was a beer can. All the way back to the car, the hiker wondered at the insensitivity of whoever left this trash. As he started to drive away, he was already rehearsing a pretty bold letter to the editor that somebody should send. This was certainly an ethical breach. And the reaction was to activate the ethics of judgment.

A few miles on, it occurred to the hiker that his response was short of the ideal. He drove back, walked back out toward the shore, and picked up the can. It still seemed to have some content. The can was emptied and put in the trunk of the car to be disposed of at home. That felt so much better. It was the ethics of justification. The hiker had done the right thing. Somewhere there must be an ethical principle about beer cans.

Judgment and justification are low-budget ethics. But the best guess about the extent of ethical shortcomings after we judge and justify is that things will be the same in the future. Several years later, the nature lover realized the inadequacy of the whole business. He and his wife retraced this path to watch the sun set on their anniversary. There on the path was another beer can. If many were visibly angered by this behavior and the careless took notice and cared perhaps some good would come of this kind of emotional response. But, the direct force of judgment and justification is dominantly internal.

What would have happened if the hiker had seen the irresponsible person drop the beer can? Would he have engaged, perhaps by comment? "Oops. I think you dropped something." That might have made a difference, for that one can and maybe even for some in the future. The suggestion might have been ignored or even drawn some pushback. That is the price of engagement. Venture a little in hopes of changing the future behavior of others. The more those who leave bad deposits identify with us the more likely they are to come into line with standards, if we let them know what the standards are and that someone cares. The more obvious it is that we are engaging because ethics is a community activity, the wider we make the community. The idea of offering a course on the ethics of picking up after yourself, perhaps making it a requirement for park entrance, seems only attractive to those who would like to present such courses.

The ethics of engagement is hard work. We end by paying a small price over and over again. There are too many willing to litter the landscape of professionalism for this to be the long-term general solution unless it becomes a widespread habit. We need something systemic, something that will make it easier for others to do the right thing. Would it not have been a good thing if there had been a trash can right there on the path near the picnic tables? That is the ethics of leadership. We change the conditions on the ground so that others find it more convenient to act ethically.

This chapter explores four models of direct leadership (guidance, role modeling, mentoring, and coaching) and indirect leadership through building organizations with the culture to affect many individuals for the good.

## Direct Effect on Others

Leaders change others, usually collectively. There are many positive ways of encouraging others in ethical behavior. We should use all of them, and some will come more naturally to one person and some will be more comfortable or appropriate for other cases. First we look at direct influence, one person to another or to a group. Power, manipulation, threats, bribes, and straightforward *quid pro quo* transactions will be skipped. Usually they kick the relationship out of the ethical domain right from the start. Teaching, in the sense of telling others about ethics, will be addressed later, in Chapter 15.

## Guidance

Helping others find their way in difficult situations is guidance. It involves sharing how one has connected the dots in one's own life in hopes that the dots in others' lives are laid out much the same way. Guides offer advice. And they need to be seen as credible and to be offering something of value. Some guides, such as psychoanalysts, accountants, and web designers, charge for their services. Others provide services for the personal satisfaction it brings and the prospect of making the world a better place.

For a period of time, the American Dental Association offered ethical guidance in the form of an "Ethics Hotline." Dentists phoned in problems and the calls were triaged to members of the Council on Ethics, Bylaws and Judicial Affairs and others to make replies. Most of the calls concerned legal matters and inquired about the extent of the caller's obligations. The program has been discontinued. Many organizations in dentistry provide program content for guiding dental students. The American Dental Association has a Success Program that makes trained speakers with prepared slide material available to schools. State associations and component societies do the same, as do ethical organizations, recognized and self-proclaimed specialty groups, corporate enterprises, and individual practitioners.

Typically guidance of this sort takes the form of suggestions for how one should practice to do well. They are recruiting opportunities for the groups presenting. Guidance has generally been focused on students rather than established practitioners, and student organizations are pleased to have such speakers to fill their programs.

## Role Models

Role models are those who are imitated. The activity is passive on the model's part, with those copying the behavior choosing whom to emulate and which parts of their model's many characteristics are best to try. When four-handed, sit-down dentistry was being introduced through continuing education programs, one study found, by going to participants' offices, that the objectives of the presenter were often misunderstood. One participant enthusiastically stated that the course had changed his practice. He had noticed that the slides used by the presenter showed light blue walls in the operatory, and he thought that was comforting to patients so he repainted his office (Chambers et al, 1976). Some of us are models without realizing it, and we have little control over what is imitated.

We know from a solid literature that conspicuous behavior is more likely to be copied (Bandura, 1977; 1986). Bold and unexpected action is imitated. So is violent behavior and any action that leads directly to results. In fact, imitators are more apt to mimic behavior the more likely and directly the behavior is to lead to success in the imitator's eyes. It is the behavior that is imitated, not the motives. Imitated behavior is classed by psychologists as superstitious behavior, meaning that there is no necessary connection between prominent features of the model's actions and what caused the results. "Cargo cults" sprang up on small Pacific islands during and after the Second World War. The indigenous people observed that Japanese and American soldiers built flat, straight places for planes to land. And they did, with loads of marvelous abundance. Lots of runways were built by natives.

Experts on the lecture circuit often describe novel features of their practices, such as a marketing program or an approach to improving treatment plan acceptance, and mention that they have been very successful. Sometimes the success is an accident like a new employer in town or the component society launching a patient education campaign. Because the former are more "conspicuous," they will be imitated. Ethical conduct, especially the quiet excellence that is a natural way of preventing problems in the first place, is unlikely to be imitated.

Combining these characteristics urges some caution in placing high hopes on role modeling for ethics. "Bad" role models get the attention, including those who make overblown claims for novel but questionable schemes (Bandura, 1999). Of course it is wonderfully rewarding and worth remembering when one learns, often years later, that someone was inspired by something we said or did. But role modeling is a strategy for improving ethics only when there are a lot of ethical role models. One could not organize a campaign built around it. Being good and not being ashamed of it is the right thing to do. But it is too passive and fails to account for the fact that there are many bad role models, and everyone is free to choose.

## Mentoring

While Odysseus was absent from Ithaca at the ten-year Trojan War and wandered for years on his way home, he left his son, Telemachus, in the custody of an aged and close friend. The boy was raised as the absent father would have wished. The trusted advisor was named Mentor. Interest in mentoring, especially in business organizations and research laboratories, has waxed and waned (Chambers, 2006; Johnson & Riley, 2004; Zachary, 2000).

Mentors have a more established relationship with those they influence than do givers of advice and a more active relationship than do role models. In fact, a characteristic of mentorship is an explicit power relationship. Usually mentoring takes place in the context of a hierarchical organizational and professional structure. A junior executive become the protégé of a senior member of the firm who introduces the junior to the right people, arranges access to important assignments, and makes certain the accomplishments of the protégé are brought to the attention of those who make decisions. A senior researcher gives special help to the most promising post-doc, for example. The junior partner in a mentorship gets access to opportunity. The senior member gets prestige and often a chance at a better job for having trained up a talented replacement. Such relationships generally last one to three years, until the work structure changes. In dentistry, the quintessential mentor relationship is the associateship.

The track record for mentorship is not impressive. Usually half or more dissolve naturally within a few months or linger on in name only. Organizations that have experimented with assigning mentors find that this seldom works, even when supported by mentorship training (Johnson & Riley, 2004). Dental schools and state dental associations have experimented with mentorship, with varying degrees of longevity. Most such programs are lists of recent graduates matched with dentists, usually those looking for an associate. These are often accompanied with an annual picnic or gathering at a sporting event.

## Coaching

A coach is someone dedicated to bringing out the potential in another through a combination of advice, feedback, and arranging for learning experiences (Brounstein, 2000; Peltier, 2010). There are dental coaches and several well-respected firms that provide management systems, personal advisors, data analysis, and feedback systems. Usually the coaching is in the area of the business operations of a practice, and the coach is often a former hygienist or assistant who has worked at the front desk. A defining characteristic of a coach, in contrast to a mentor, is that the person being helped does not want to become the person who is helping. Another feature of coaches is that they often focus on improving the performance of a team rather than an individual. Practice consultant coaches consider the office to be their client rather than the dentist. Dental schools often use a person trained in ethics to both advise individual students and coach the clinic, the administration, or other aspects of the school. Firms in the dental industry, such as Proctor & Gamble, have chief ethics officers. Typically, dental organizations do not have such a role.

The most famous name in basketball in North Carolina, and perhaps in the United States in the second decade of the twentieth century, is Krzyzewski. Although he coached his teams to a record number of NCAA basketball titles, he could not now make even the junior varsity at Duke.

## Leading Dental Organizations

Dentistry should welcome all the advice, role modeling, mentoring, and coaching that can be mustered, provided it comes from the right places and points practitioners to the emerging future. But more is needed by way of leadership. And more is possible. The essence of leadership is helping groups thrive. Leaders change organizations and organizations affect people's lives.

Too often we take a needlessly narrow view of leadership, equating it with filling a position in a fixed hierarchy of positions one can be selected for. The opportunities to make a difference in the communities we belong to are much broader. The opportunities for leading from within—from a personal ethical core and from wherever one is in the organization—are large. The sign of leadership is not a title or set of privileges. The surest place to discover it is in the behavior of members of the community. If individuals are more fulfilled through participation in the group than they would be otherwise, the group is being well led.

### The Need for Strong Organizations

It is obvious that powerful organizations can go to bat for their members—lobbying, sharing collective wisdom, advertising, consolidating economic leverage, and bargaining for a playing field more to the advantage of members. None of these are ethical matters, however. Where organizations shine for their members in moral terms is by making it easier for members to be ethical. This takes three forms.

Organizations define identity. They establish the boundaries for who belongs, who is outside, and who wants in. Dental organizations are the custodians of what it means to be a dentist. Increasingly there are plural images and alternative voices. But surprisingly, none of the hundreds of patients and dentists who took part in the focus groups across the country for this study expressed any difficulty with the questions "What are dentists like?" or, for dentists, "What is organized dentistry like?" These are general constructs that are part of the persona of every dentist. Every dentist is, in the eyes of others, partly an individual and partly a professional. To the extent that dentistry builds a positive identity for the profession, it creates a positive image for all dentists. If the image of the profession has a strong ethical foundation, that makes it easier for all dentists to behave ethically. Organizations pretty much get the level of ethical behavior they allow.

Organizations function as picture frames. We look there to find ourselves and our friends. When the Newsletter comes, we often skip the president's message and thumb to the spread on the bar-b-que to look for ourselves. In this day of selfies, the organization as image enhancer is losing impact. When organizations feature outsiders, such as advertisers, interest declines. (See the section below on Reading the Dynamics of an Organization.)

Second, organizations are holding companies for group behavior. Very simply, individuals can do things as members of a group that they cannot do on their own. Sometimes this underlies silly or worse behavior, as when a college student pulls pranks at a frat party that he would be too ashamed to do on his own. Usually it calls forth noble community effort, as in community health fairs, fundraising for local causes, and relief in natural disasters. Fraternal organizations such as Rotary and the Kiwanis often sponsor health causes. A professional community allows individuals to be ethical in ways that they could not do alone.

Organizations act like goodwill banks. Not every deposit is guaranteed to return more than it is worth. But in general and over time and across individuals we all thrive because we are part of groups that spread risk and reward. That is the very reason we join groups. It is also the reason why we leave them or switch to others when they fail to give us a good return on our ethical investment (Sober & Wilson, 1998). This is the flywheel effect. Group behavior maintains momentum and, as a result, tends to be a few years behind the optimal point for course correction. That is an advantage for those members who prefer to move in the company of colleagues in directions that have already proven effective.

Finally, organizations can engage other organizations on equal ethical footing in ways that individuals cannot. Organizations are collective moral agents. They have the same ethical standing as individuals, with a right to uncoerced action with a goal of maximizing their futures, subject to granting the same privileges to other individuals and organizations. Some organizations are bad actors, asking more of their members than they collectively give back and not keeping faith with other organizations with which they share common interests. Often they see members as customers and the other organizations as competitors.

Organizations function like gyroscopes. As long as its internal momentum can be maintained, an organization is stable. It can function as a viable moral agent, capable of engaging the world on behalf of its members. United States law recognizes public entities as "persons." That means they have moral status and can benefit from collective action and, at least to some limited extent, bear collective responsibility when they cause damage.

Being a leader means optimizing the functions of identity, compounding the efforts of members, and interacting with other organizations to improve mutual benefit. Being an ethical leader means ensuring that these goals are achieved by ethical means rather than otherwise. There is a style of "positional leaders," those who are chosen to fill predetermined structural positions because they reflect the current values of the organization. They serve *ex officio*. Research shows that this contributes to the decline of organizations (Goldstein et al, 2010). All closed systems run down to entropy, which is a state of sameness unresponsive to changing environments. True leaders have one foot in the organization and one outside. They provide just the right amount of external energy to maintain the vitality of the organization. Although they represent the organization to the world that swirls around it, they also represent the emerging environment to the organization. Ethical leaders know that they cannot always call the tune for the rest of the world just because it is a strong value of the organization.

## Reading the Dynamics of an Organization

Here is an example of how an organization changes over time as a function of its relationship with its members. A study was undertaken of the relationship between membership in the American Dental Association and the image the organization projects of itself. The *ADA News* was studied for the manner in which it reflected the image of the organization. A content analysis methodology was used in which subject matter of various types was quantified by the amount of attention it received. Content importance was measured as the proportion of space allotted various matters in the publication. The *ADA News* was first published in 1975; four issues were analyzed for that year, as were four issues per year at ten-year intervals until 2015. (See Appendix K.)

Two patterns emerged relating attention of the organization to declining membership numbers. These included advertising and coverage of member-generated or member-focused content. The early issues of *ADA News* were heavy with letters to the editor, sometimes being as much as 15% of the entire publication, and with features telling stories about individual dentists with unusual accomplishments or especially those who had contributed to the profession. As the proportion of attention given to these matters declined, so did ADA membership. The correspondence was almost exactly one to one: 1% less member-generated content = 1% fewer members.

**Figure 10.1. Association between featuring members' letters and membership rate on association membership.**

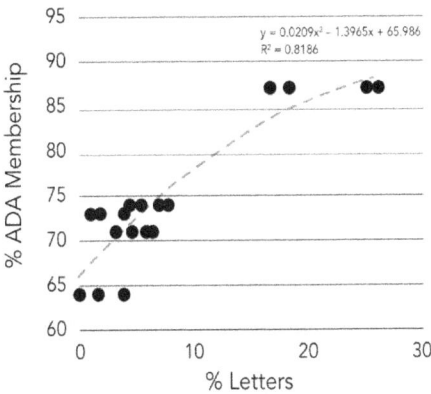

$$y = 0.0209x^2 - 1.3965x + 65.986$$
$$R^2 = 0.8186$$

Advertising over this period rose from about 20% to 65% in a pattern that also very closely paralleled declining membership. The correlation coefficient relating advertising space to decreasing membership was $r = 0.875$. More advertising is associated with lower membership proportions. Almost nonexistent in the early years, but rising significantly, was a special form of advertising directed from the association to its members. Members were urged, in addition to their dues, to take advantage of material available for sale from the American Dental Association and to participate in commercial programs for which the association received a percentage of sales. Again there is a parallel between more internal marketing and lower membership rates. One could get the impression that the organization viewed dentists as customers as well as members.

**Figure 10.2. Association between shout-outs of members' accomplishments and membership rate.**

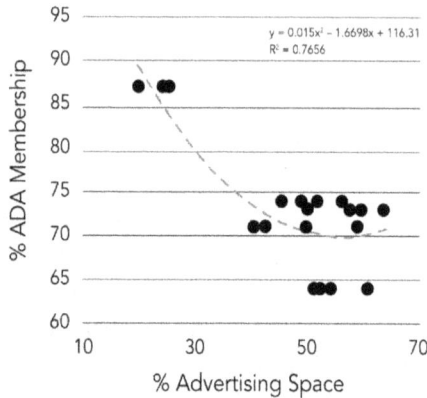

Of course, correlation is not causation. It is actually reasonable to speculate that lower membership caused less attention to the accomplishments of its members and magnified the need for more advertising revenue.

As Robert Putnam (2000) mentioned in *Bowling Alone*, the decline in organization membership, especially in professional organizations, has led to a professional double identity. The members of the profession (dentists) used to play larger roles in their organizations. Now their participation is increasingly of the checkbook variety, with the operation of the organization being managed by another class of professionals: lawyers, public relations experts, sponsors, and vendors. Increasingly these services are now being contracted out, sometimes to the same people and organizations that staff other professional organizations that are pulling members away in the first place.

### Becoming an Ethical Leader

There are three kinds of leaders. The nominal ones fill established positions and function more as managers, maintaining the functions of an organization. They look good in front of a group. Strong leaders challenge and inspire enthusiasm among the members by their presence. We are glad they are here because their positive energy keeps us going the right way.

The disappointing aspect of these leaders is that when they step down, the organization loses energy or direction. The very best leaders are those who leave a lasting change. They "show us how to fish," as the saying goes. They build organizations that raise the moral tone of large numbers of people in ways that are self-sustaining. The ancient Chinese wisdom of the *Tao Te Ching* says, "When his [the leader's] task is accomplished and his work done the people all say, 'It happened to us naturally.'" The famous and indispensable leader is a contradiction in terms.

The number of bestselling books on how to become a leader is now overwhelming. There is one for everybody and every occasion. The old style (Bennis, 1989; Covey, 1990), which counseled that leaders have certain characteristics and act certain ways, have not sold well recently. The rage for reading leadership strength by reverse transcription from those firms that had done well over time (Collins, 2001; Peters & Waterman, 1982) has tapered off as new evidence shows that even the winners of a few years ago cannot stay on top (Pfeffer & Sutton, 2006; Rosenzweig, 2007). Some are even saying today that only organizations that are nimble enough to change as fast as society is changing will avoid obsolescence and that leaders must change their own styles as quickly and as often as needed (Christensen & Raynor, 2003; Goldstein et al, 2010; Satell, 2017).

As detailed in Chapter 1 and Appendix A, two of the three dominant dental ethical issues in the minds of the profession, its leadership, the public, and opinion leaders in the public are independence of dentists in their own offices and overtreatment and commercialism. Neither of these will likely be responsive to the ethics of judgment or justification, nor is it likely that much headway can be made by role modeling, mentoring, or coaching by the right-minded. Much of the difficulty stems from the nature of the problems with dental ethics in the first place. If dentists practice in isolation and consult their own consciences above all else (as in Chapters 1, 6, 11, and 12 and Appendices A, B, E, F, H, and I), they will tend to orient toward those voices that offer them opportunity and success. Until recently, economics and technological advances have provided a cushion. Now that there is less security due to income pressure and rapidly changing technology and market conditions, the profession is looking for a new kind of guidance and leadership. The historic model and dentists' voices are not as strong as they once were in this rapidly changing world. As shown in the first chapter, many in the profession are looking for leadership.

This is not a report on how to be a leader. There are so many ways of succeeding at that and the demand is huge. But the analysis so far and what will be presented in following chapters makes the case that ethics should be one of the levers for change in any organization. America has crowded toward considering only short-term economic gain as the yardstick by which the health of an organization is measured. It would be a shame if dentistry, either in the individual office or in the various groups that represent the profession, were to follow. The literature on steward leadership (Block, 1993) and social entrepreneurship (Chahine, 2016) are encouraging places to find needed new models. Regardless of the organization or the leadership style, the standard should always be the same: Has the leadership of the organization made it easier for its members and those it does business with to be more moral?

None of these issues is likely to be well managed entirely by guidance, role modeling, mentoring, or even coaching. The solutions also require changes in the system generally. If left to each dentist, solutions may come at the expense of one's colleagues and thus fragment the profession. To the extent that it becomes a game of each dentist for himself or herself, the profession loses even the potential to reverse declining ethical fortunes.

Systemic leadership is not the only way to strengthen ethics in dentistry, but it is a powerful means and one that should not be overlooked for growing, encouraging, and welcoming leaders who can use the entire apparatus of the dental community to lift the whole community.

## Summary

Ethical leaders establish the conditions under which others can become ethical. This is done directly through guidance, role modeling, mentoring, and coaching. Although each is worthy, they are not known to be predictably effective techniques and they reach only a few at a time. An alternative, indirect form of ethical leadership is to promote practices in organizations that make it easier for members and for other organizations with which there is regular interaction to function more ethically. At the very least, there should not be such heavy emphasis in an organization on power, money, and political influence that ethics is given second consideration. Organizations define identity, serve as mutual benefits holding companies, and engage other organizations as moral agents. A case study was presented showing the effect of not giving sufficient emphasis to the ethical dimensions of a member organization. Training to become an ethical leader of an organization is especially challenging where the external environment changes rapidly.

# Chapter 11

# Core Ethical Norms

This is the first of two chapters about how dentists center themselves morally. Nothing will be said about how they *should* do this. There are excellent guides for several approaches to working through previously structured cases (Graskemper, 2011; Ozar & Sokol, 1994; Rule & Veatch, 2004). The American College of Dentists offers a rich array of practical, online ethics training material at www.dentalethics.org. The benefit of having methods for systematic and comprehensive reflection in regularly occurring situations is obvious.

The question is what norms dentists actually use to guide their behavior. It remains the case that given a common set of circumstances and using a common analytical approach, dentists reach divergent assessments regarding what should be done in their offices. Dentists bring much to the table that is personal, and although that may be difficult to channel, it cannot and should not be left out. The present chapter looks at the wide range of ethical touchstones. Where do dentists look for what matters most in their personal choices? Who do they trust as ethical guides? The subsequent chapter will open a discussion of what dentists value and seek to promote and how the range of values works into their moral choices. If ethics reflects our better natures, it is fair to ask about how we understand our better natures.

This chapter is concerned with how dentists actually use ethics codes to guide behavior and where else they look for help in moral matters.

## Identifying the Core

The ethical core is the base position, what we expect of ourselves at our best and what others can reasonably expect of us. Morality is selecting the shortest distance to where we should go in this chaotic world. Where we want to go (values) matters, and so does where we look for guidance on the journey (touchstones). The core cannot be ordered online or given a test run on the convention floor. A few hours in an ethics course would surely be desirable, but not all such courses are habit forming. If we only hear about ethics from others who remind us of our obligations, as they see them, it will eventually become a burden we would willingly stash someplace unnoticed. Bad acting is mostly inappropriate responses to those around us because we are not centered on our personal ethical core. Ethical ventriloquism is mouthing someone else's values, and it is for dummies.

It is customary to talk ethics in terms of principles. In order for this to be the center it will be necessary to show that dentistry has unique principles, that dentists know what they are, and that these principles, once known, are consistently action-guiding. Alternatively, we might look for the core in dentists' values. Values are what one is aiming for. They might be a better way to characterize how dentists make ethical decisions, and they will be taken up in the next chapter. These are the good things one is trying to optimize when making choices. They are what we want in unforced situations. Finally, there has to be some discussion of the question whether ethics is a matter of individual character or a matter of responding appropriately to others in changing contexts. Very likely any of these perspectives would give a useful insight into how dentists think of themselves and how others think of dentists as being moral. Several of them might be combined.

The great danger to guard against is acting from one source and using another set of standards as justification. Today the term hypocrisy is used in the hard sense of being judgmental of others who say one thing and do something else. If we fail to ground our behavior in our ethical core it may still be hypocritical if we paint over it with false public rationalizations, especially if we mislead others about who we really are.

Consider this case, which will be looked at from different perspectives in this chapter and the next. You are walking through the hotel corridors between sessions at the state meeting and see four of your acquaintances engaged in pretty animated conversation. You approach the group, get a few nods of recognition, but the conversation continues without interruption. One dentist is describing a system he read about in an online dental chatroom that neatly gets around some restrictions on insurance claims. It promises to increase reimbursement noticeably above what these types of policies are intended to pay out and would be a competitive advantage to those who use the loophole. Perhaps it is not exactly fraud. Another member of the group is cautiously interested in the idea. She volunteers, "Well, I can see a certain advantage here in leveling the playing field. This might be a way to balance the years of under-reimbursement and unfairly restrictive regulations we have endured." One other keeps interrupting to share other schemes, some actual and some potential. Some have been tried and known to fail, others are clearly fraudulent. After a few minutes, the fourth dentist, who has been scowling through the whole conversation, walks away without acknowledgement, as if to say, "Go for it if you want. I'm having nothing to do with this." The question to consider is what should *you* do right now in the hotel hallway?

## Ethics Codes

Ethical principles are general statements of characteristics of the good and the right. A fiduciary relationship, one built on trust, is a relationship one wants. Integrity and caring are also the kinds of adjectives we like to attach to the behavior of those we admire. Loyalty, charity, sustainability, hospitality to strangers, favoring members of one's group over outsiders, reciprocity, continual striving for excellence, and contributing one's fair share and not taking more than is appropriate from the common good are also commonly endorsed ethical norms. None of these are publicly proclaimed in writing by organized dentistry. Although principles are often used to describe someone or an act felt to be ethically praiseworthy, it would be going too far to expect that the ethical person could be defined by a list of principles. Some corrupt politicians are lavish in their charity. The Little League coach may beat his wife. Ken Lay of Enron and Bernard Ebbers of WorldCom, both leaders of rotten firms that bilked Americans out of billions of dollars, began their executive committee meetings with prayers (Rhode, 2018). This is not a criticism of prayer; it is criticism of the abuse of prayer by individuals who wanted to cover bad behavior with good principles. Principles work well in theory, but are clumsy for doing ethical work. They do not qualify in themselves as a sufficient moral core. (See Chapter 8.)

In order for principles to play an effective role in the ethics of a profession they must meet at least two conditions: principles must be known and they must be action-guiding. A principled dentist should be able to say, "I see that this principle is the one I should be applying here and that is sufficient motivation for my behavior."

## Knowledge of the American Dental Association Principles of Ethics and Code of Professional Conduct

In a 2014 survey of 285 dentists, Reid and his colleagues (2014) found a substantial gap between the ideals practitioners professed and their reported behavior. More recently, in this project, familiarity with the American Dental Association Principles of Ethics and Code of Professional Conduct was assessed with a 16-item test given to 232 individuals in four groups. (See Appendix G.) The test had good internal consistency and each question had three distractors, so the "chance" score was 25%. Fifty-four dental students took the test. The largest group tested was 139 fellows and candidates for fellowship in the American College of Dentists, all of whom are members of the American Dental Association and were selected in part for their high ethical standards. A group of more typical dentists, 23 in number, was tested when they participated in a continuing education program. Sixteen additional respondents identified themselves as Canadian or as dental hygienists. Those in the latter group were marked separately, but they scored on average as high as the others. The highest-scoring group, statistically so, was the students who were just beginning their ethics training and had not yet been exposed to the code.

The average score on the test across all groups was 46.5%. This raises a question about how well the American Dental Association code is understood and thus to what extent it figures in dentists' ethical decisions. Because forced-choice tests are sometimes criticized as "not allowing respondents to tell all they know," an open-ended question was asked at the beginning of the test for practicing dentists. Respondents were invited to identify the single element in the code they felt had the greatest significance to them. Three-quarters of respondents left the question unanswered. Of those who did mention an item, one-half of the suggestions were not actually part of the American Dental Association code. Several confessed to never having read the code or to preferring their own conscience as a guide.

## Are Codes Action-Guiding?

The other criterion that principles must meet in order to serve as ethical touchstones is that they must be action-guiding. They must consistently motivate ethical behavior in the absence of other incentives. The specificity of the association between choices of ethical action and reasons for these choices was studied previously (Chambers, 2015b) and is reported in Appendix B. A common set of eight ethics cases was presented to 91 dentists and 54 patients. For each case, respondents were asked to rate the likelihood of taking various actions from among sets ranging from four to seven alternatives, depending on the case. The actions were not mutually exclusive. For example, a dentist could remove a patient from the practice for sexually inappropriate remarks to the hygienist and also discuss the matter with the staff. Respondents further rated the importance of 47 reasons (justifications) in sets appropriate to each case. The issue here is the relationship between the moral actions and the ethical justifications.

About one-third of actions were undertaken with no identifiable reason given. In about a quarter of the cases, there was a connection between a specific action and a specific reason. In the remaining cases, multiple reasons were given. There was no particular pattern relating the reasons to the actions, and large variation was observed from respondent to respondent. Some dentists would do A for reason X and others would do A for reason Y. Some who held reason X would do A and others B. Fifty-five percent of the actions and 68% of the reasons were chosen by someone in both the highest and the lowest categories possible, thus showing extreme variation. The modal choices were never more than 50%, meaning that whatever either a dentist or patient decided to do or what reason they gave for it, at least half of their colleagues would disagree. But even in those cases where there was a singular connection between action and reason, it was not the same pairing for every respondent. The correlation between action and reason was $r = 0.104$.

These results are consistent with the general literature on whether principles or codes of ethics have a positive impact on the behavior of members of an organization (Brief et al, 1996; Kaptein & Schwartz, 2008). The rate of government actions against firms is comparable for those with and without codes of ethics. There are publications touting the benefits of honor codes in reducing cheating, and there are well-known cases of cheating despite such codes (Cizek, 1999; McCabe, 2001; 2005; McCabe et al, 2006; Puka, 2005; Treviño & Victor, 1992). One study of this type, reported by Rhode (2018), may be instructive for how codes operate. Some students at the Massachusetts Institute of Technology and Harvard were tested after signing a pledge to abide by their school's honor codes and others similarly tested without signing such a pledge. There was less cheating among those who agreed to abide by the honor code. The problem is that neither school has an honor code. This certainly raises the prospect that it is not the existence of a code itself that is action-guiding but the gentle reminder that someone else cares how you will behave in the next few minutes that promotes good behavior. (See the discussion of ethical priming in Chapter 5, Bad People.)

## Codes as Public Relations

Codes and sets of principles may serve purposes other than or in addition to providing informed action guidance. They can be reminders that others care. They also occasionally serve as anchor points around which valuable discussions are held. This is especially the case when core values are being debated before their adoption or modification and when initiates are being educated into the culture of an organization or profession. These are valuable activities, but they are typically brief in duration, often presented outside actual practice settings, and seldom reinforced.

Codes also serve a public function, announcing that an organization has paid attention to ethics. The public is seldom told the details of what these ethical norms are or how they were crafted or are enforced. There is always the danger when using ethics as a public relations tool of getting caught off base. Enron famously had T-shirts, coffee mugs, and other corporate ware emblazoned with the initials RICE for "Respect, Integrity, Community, and Excellence"—the company's core values. These were sold on eBay after the firm's collapse amid ethical corruption with the tag line, "Like new, never used."

## Codes as Justification

Probably the most powerful use of codes is as justification for action. In order to be action-guiding, principles must be closely linked with the action *before* it starts and must *motivate* it. They are private. A justification takes place after the action has been selected and is not exclusively determinative of the action. Justifications are what is said to make the action acceptable to others. Justifications make us look good in others' eyes and seldom make their appearance unless our behavior might be challenged in public.

As explained in Chapter 8, the problem with justification, and with the normative approach in general, is that there are so many ways to justify any action. Insurance fraud is illegal, but could be defended on grounds that it gives more patients access to dental care and thus enhances beneficence. Limiting who can provide care can be justified on the grounds of quality of services (nonmaleficence) and criticized because it limits care to those more well-off (a violation of the principle of justice). When considering justifications, we must distinguish between the motivating set of reasons and the justifications offered to get others to go along. A state legislator recently said she had never seen a proposed regulation that did not claim to promote public safety (a justification). All of them also involved benefits to the sponsor, thus compromising the criterion of guidance by ethical norms. Testing ethical touchstones by asking whether the behavior would flow from it in the absence of any other benefit is an easy way to smoke out ethical hypocrisy.

## Codes for Members and Codes for Organizations

There is a difference between the ethical codes of the Department of Justice and Starbucks versus those of the American College of Dentists, the Academy of General Dentistry, or the Association of Dental Support Organizations. In the former case, the elements of the codes describe what can be expected of the organization. By contrast, member organizations have codes for what is expected of individuals belonging to the organization. The latter are normally offered as aspirations or general characterizations of member behavior. In the case of the American Dental Association and the American College of Dentists, the code of professional conduct, not the principles of ethics, sets the requirements for membership. These codes are typically written by the most active members of the organization and never with the input of patients or those served by the members. They do not address the relationship between the public and the organization or the ethical relationships between organizations.

There is no reason why professional organizations cannot have two codes: one for members, the other for the organization itself. After all, organizations are moral agents, capable of taking action intended to influence others—members, business partners, government agencies, and the public. Much of a member organization's communications are aimed at influencing outsiders on behalf of the membership in general. Not being specific about this intent leaves an ethical gap. Professional organizations could write norm-based codes containing elements such as: (a) the set of outcomes it would pursue as an organization at the expense of other outcomes; (b) stewardship of resources; (c) assurance of full opportunities for all members to participate in policy discussions; and (d) a policy on transparency.

In the Commission on Dental Accreditation requirements for dental schools there is a standard for what students should learn regarding ethics. Standard 2.20 states: "Graduates must be competent in the application of the principles of ethical decision making and professional responsibility." Thus, dental education privileges the principles approach to ethics, and students are deemed ethically competent if they can name the five American Dental Association principles and give examples.

But there is a much more powerful accreditation standard for schools, one that requires them to represent an ethical environment. Standard 1-3: "The dental education program must have a stated commitment to a humanistic culture and learning environment that is regularly evaluated. Intent: The dental education program should ensure collaboration, mutual respect, cooperation, and harmonious relationships between and among administrators, faculty, students, staff, and alumni. The program should also support and cultivate the development of professionalism and ethical behavior by fostering diversity of faculty, students, and staff, open communication, leadership, and scholarship." In other words, dental schools, as organizations, are required to be ethical.

The case of the opportunistic insurance loophole presented at the beginning of this chapter would strike most as containing some element of ethical challenge. Something seems not quite right, despite the possibility that the legal issues might be equivocated. But it is difficult to name a principle that should guide behavior. There is no issue of respect for patients, nonmaleficence, beneficence, justice, or veracity on the table, although we could certainly imagine unstated elements to make this into a dilemma. Dentists, as professional colleagues joining a hall conversation, have no obligation under the American Dental Association Code of Professional Conduct to offer justifiable criticism since that concerns only dental treatment not business practices.

## Touchstones

Where do dentists turn for guidance when faced with an ethical challenge? Are some sources of information, advice, or ready standards more action-guiding than others? In the example of the hall conversation regarding "creative" insurance billing, would one mentally or actually consult the American Dental Association code, a trusted colleague, or the benefits provider, or perhaps even join the conversation to hear what colleagues think? It turns out that the most typical behavior is none of these.

Two hundred sixty-five dentists in several samples from across the country completed a short survey that asked where they would seek help in making ethical decisions. The study is reported in detail in Appendix H. The survey described six scenarios: (a) detected faulty treatment by a colleague; (b) use of an insurance reimbursement loophole; (c) sales of one's practice to a dentist with a shaky reputation; (d) dealing with a patient trying to avoid payment; (e) taking on very large and complex cases and untested procedures; and (f) treating Medicaid patients. The same question was asked of these six situations: Who would one turn to for advice on making a decision? Each of five potential ethical touchstones was rated on a scale from 5 ("Almost in every case") to 1 ("Very rarely").

Figure 11.1. **Ethical touchstones.**

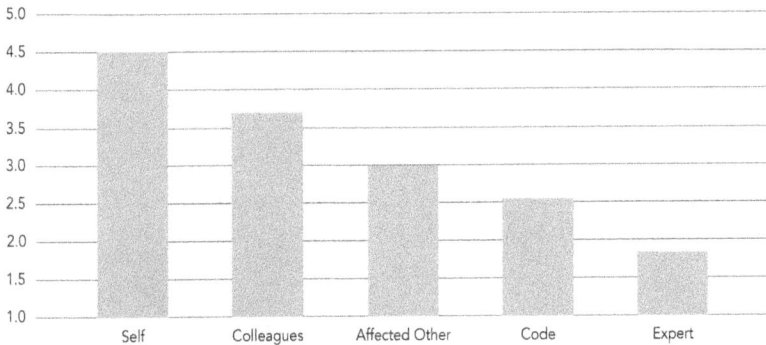

The results are shown in Figure 11.1. The most likely standard is each dentist's personal sense of what is appropriate and what is not. The advice of colleagues and trusted friends would also be looked to. Codes, laws, and other professional standards would be consulted in fewer than half the cases. In last place, one would speak with a lawyer, ethicist, or peer review or law enforcement, someone with authority to act or advise from a position of expertise. A test was performed showing that all of these differences between pairs of sources were statistically significant. For example, respondents were reliably more likely to consult a code (something that could be interpreted privately) than to consult an expert (a source that actively interprets the situation and has power to act independently). Codes and experts, formal standards for right and wrong, are relatively unlikely to be consulted. Dentists prefer to retain freedom of control in how or whether to act on ethical matters.

The unusual touchstone in this study is "affected other." The respondents selecting this alternative signaled a willingness to engage others affected by the decision or with the power to affect the decision. This is an endorsement of the ethics of engagement. For example, they might discuss with a scofflaw patient their concerns and listen to how the patient framed the issue. Talking with a colleague suspected of rendering substandard care would be another example. This type of response is different from consulting oneself or codes because it suggests that affected others are moral agents who have a role in determining how an ethical conflict should be handled. This concept will feature prominently in discussions later in this report as we move toward considering ways of strengthening the ethical tone of the profession. In the current survey, respondents indicated that they would consider sharing the ethical issues with affected others in half the cases or that half of the dentists would consider such an approach.

Respondents were also asked to rate each of the six challenges in terms of how important the issue was seen to be. High scores reflected those challenges deemed most troublesome to the dentist. The three challenges having to do with dentists' incomes (insurance, sales of practice, and big or novel treatment) were statistically significantly more apt to be considered important challenges than the other three.

## Private Standards

The fact that dentists first consult their own sense of what is ethical has important implications for professionalism in dentistry. At the very least, this means that dentists' moral compasses may not be calibrated at the beginning. The influence of codes and experts will be filtered through each dentist's personal standards. Because of the relative weight of these sources of ethical standards, we would anticipate that the most influential sources of guidance will be what already meets with one's existing beliefs.

Confronted with a discrepancy between personal sense of right and wrong and what "outside" sources say is right and wrong is likely to cause dissonance (Festinger, 1959). The most likely response in such situations is to acknowledge the public standards and privately act on one's own beliefs. As will be discussed in Chapter 14, when organizations do this it is called ethical "decoupling." Such a bifurcation of what one espouses and what one does can only be maintained when circumstances permit acting largely unobserved by others. Holding a private standard and proclaiming a public one also works when dealing with those who do not understand what is at stake or are relatively powerless to challenge those in authority. The dominance of private ethical standards is a large source of concern in light of how prominently it featured in the discussion of both dentist and patient focus groups reported in Chapter 1.

Dentists practice in circumstances that allow private ethical standards, as will be discussed in the next chapter. A potential balancing effect of private ethics is the opinion of colleagues. This does, according to the respondents in this survey, matter. As will be emphasized in the final chapter of this report, collegiality is an important lever for raising the standard of ethics in the profession.

We can now predict how ethical touchstones might influence the hall conversation about taking advantage of a potential reimbursement loophole. This scenario was actually tested as part of the study reported in Appendix H. Rank ordering of guidance on this ambivalent business practice challenge followed exactly the general pattern in the research study. Making up one's own mind was the most likely response to the survey question about potential insurance fraud. Attractiveness of alternative touchstones went down in likelihood from talking with colleagues, talking with the insurance company, and consulting a code or in this case a contract. Speaking with a lawyer, accountant, or other expert was equally likely with consulting a code or a contract. The issue of "fudging" on reimbursement received a high score for being an important ethical challenge. (See Chapter 5 and Appendix D.)

## Summary

The ethical core is what practitioners consult when making moral choices. It includes values and principles and touchstones such as the sources of guidance regularly consulted. In order to be effective, principles of ethics must be generally known and they must be action-guiding. Evidence suggests that neither condition is broadly met in dentistry or in the general public. In order of importance, dentists report the following touchstones: (a) their own conscience; (b) their colleagues; (c) affected others; (d) codes; and least important (e) experts. The gradient here moves from personal control to less-favored engagement with others.

# Chapter 12

# Core Ethical Values

This is the second chapter focusing on the individuality of dentists in the moral decision process. The previous one looked at which guides dentists prefer to accompany them on their ethical journey. Now it is time to look at which directions dentists see as attractive. This chapter will be concerned with identifying the most important values of dentists, both as practitioners and as human individuals. Evidence will also be presented that ethics is heavily influenced by the situation and that dentistry has unique situational characteristics.

## Measuring Values

Dentists want to be known for having good ethics. It is difficult to imagine dentists saying they do not really care that much about what is right and wrong. It would be a sign of gross cynicism if dentists said it would be good for others to be ethical so they could take advantage of those suckers. As noted in Chapter 5 the evidence is overwhelming that virtually all unethical behavior is committed by individuals who consider themselves to be basically ethical. So what value would there be in asking dentists to report how ethical they are? Probably very little, since no dentists can be expected to answer a question about whether they value ethics with anything less than a very positive response.

## Stripping Off Social Desirability in Reporting

It is possible and important to test the relative weight dentists place on ethics compared with other goals, such as financial success. But the problem remains of finding a way to overcome reporting bias. It is human nature to shade expressed opinion in the direction of socially acceptable responses (Baron, 2013; Ross & Nisbett, 2011). And dentists are probably smarter in this regard than the run of the general population.

A study was undertaken to determine the relative importance of ethics and other practice goals using a bit of bias jujitsu. (See Appendix L.) The phenomenon of attention bias—something different from reporting bias—is well documented (Pfabigan & Tran, 2015). We pay more attention to those sources of information that confirm our favored positions than to objective facts and we avoid sources of information that promise disappointing news. It would be surprising, for example, to find left-leaning liberals to be regular viewers of television known for having a strongly conservative slant. We want to be reassured that the world is as we would like to find it. So we attend more to sources that report good news about what we consider good and to sources that report bad news about what we regard as bad.

This logic can be turned on its head. The information about what people attend to reveals their underlying values. Those who look for good news about X or bad news about the absence of X can be said to value X.

In an eight-item survey completed by 265 practitioners, respondents were given a list of descriptive titles to hypothetical journal articles and asked how interested they would be in reading each. The titles appeared in random order but were paired. There was one positive and one negative title having to do with ethics ("Surveys show patients trust dentists" and "Dentists disagree on reporting incompetent colleagues," for example). Although respondents were somewhat interested in reading both articles, there was slightly more interest in the negative one. There were also paired titles having to do with technique innovations, financial success, and oral health outcomes. "Characteristics of top income earners" and "Dentists' incomes predicted to be flat" were examples of the items used for financial success. In this case there was a strong preference for reading the good news, signaling a pro-income value bias.

The results of this survey are displayed in the chart below. It is apparent (and confirmed by statistical analysis) that dentists in this sample were especially interested in values having to do with technique and income and relatively less interested in ethics and oral health outcomes of patients, individually or generally. Dentists like to do dentistry and to be rewarded for doing it. These study results are consistent with reports from dental students about why they entered the profession (Wanchek et al, 2018). The same pattern is apparent in continuing education offerings and in the published literature.

When a small sample of "patients" (randomly selected individuals approached outside any dental context) was given examples of these four motives, they ordered them the same way. Patients thought dentists oriented more toward technique and income and less toward ethics and oral health outcomes.

**Figure 12.1. Level of concern (value) regarding dental issues.**

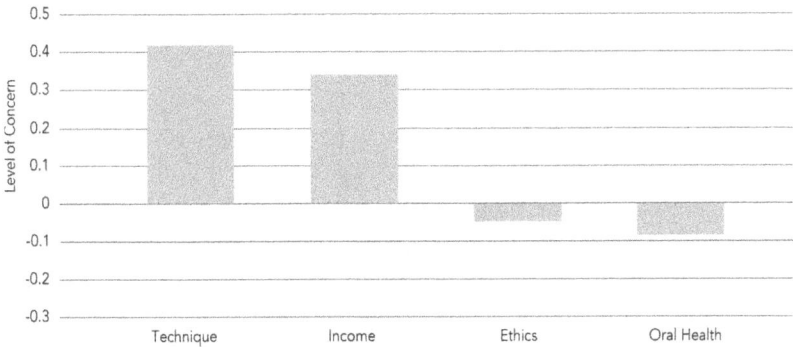

## Opportunity versus Obligation

Although it is not obvious in Figure 12.1, there are two characteristics of the value orientation of dentists reflected here. Height of the bars shows the overall interest (positive or negative) in each value. Whether the bar is above or below the neutral line signals an orientation toward each. Bars above the line for technique and income mean that dentists view these as opportunities. Bars below the line show obligations for ethics and oral health outcomes.

There is a difference in kind between opportunities and obligations. They do not necessarily balance each other and they work differently as driving forces. An opportunity has an open-ended upper range. Dentists seldom say, "Gold foil and alginate were good enough, and those who want to be technically at the top of their game are wasting their time" or "I am satisfied with what I am earning." Of course there are examples to the contrary, and opportunities are a game of diminishing returns (Tversky & Kahneman, 1981), but dentists rarely place limits on technical quality or financial goals. By contrast, ethics and oral health outcomes have a "good enough" standard. Performance below the threshold is a matter of concern, but once minimal acceptable performance is achieved, effort will be diverted to other matters, such as faster, cheaper, better technology or financial rewards.

The distinction between opportunities and obligations and the "good enough" ceiling on obligations was first introduced by Frederik Herzberg (1968) 50 years ago.

In dentistry, and in general, ethical concerns cluster on probing the boundary between the barely ethical and the unethical, and it would be rare indeed for someone to seek out an ethicist and ask for tips on how to be more ethical. For sure, there are a number of dentists who donate their time and talent to charity work. But the "standard of care" is the bright red line of acceptable oral health outcomes not the goal to be sought. "Access," as one measure of quality of oral health outcomes, has a slightly tainted connotation.

There is a different logic to enhancing technology and income than the logic of enhancing ethics and concern for oral health outcomes. These do not compete for practitioners' attention; they compete for how they are influenced. Dentists will respond as appropriate if shown "how" to take advantage of the opportunities for new technology and better financial success. The same may not be true for ethics and oral health outcomes. It is quite reasonable to assume that dentists already know how to do better in these areas. What is lacking is the opportunity or the culture and systemic reward structure that calls out the application of what dentists already know how to do. Leadership could create more opportunities for ethics.

Based on what has been presented in this section, we should anticipate that the hall conversation about a potential loophole in an insurance reimbursement system, introduced in the previous chapter, will proceed along these lines: "Yes, but is it legal?" "Perhaps not, we are uncertain." "Okay, but I don't see how anyone is hurt by this. If insurance companies take a hit, that is only just since they have been taking advantage of us for years." "So if there is no real issue over ethics or public safety, why not maximize what our families deserve?"

## General Value Structure

To this point we have considered only matters of ethical standards particular to dentists. In this and the next section, attention will be directed to how dentists' values compare with the values of populations at large.

The literature on dentist values is thin and somewhat inconsistent. Most studies are dated and report findings from dental students, not practitioners. On standardized psychological tests, students and dentists express a preference for concert or practical thinking over abstract and theoretical framing of issues (Kirk et al, 1963; Linn, 1968; Manhold et al, 1963; More, 1961; Mozer et al, 1988; Schwartz & Shenoy, 1994). However, a few studies report a preference for theoretical thinking among dentists (Cain et al, 1983; Heist, 1960; Silberman, 1976). There are studies reporting dentists' orientation toward economic values (Cain et al, 1983; Heist, 1960; Manhold et al, 1963; McDaniel et al, 1985) and toward technical topics (Schwartz & Shenoy, 1994).

## Moral Factors Questionnaire

One standardized value survey in wide use today is Jonathan Haidt's Moral Foundations Questionnaire (MFQ) (Graham et al, 2011; Haidt, 2012). It contains value dimensions that have been identified in many thousands of individuals from many countries. The six value dimensions include:

| | |
|---|---|
| Caring | Protecting others, especially the helpless, concern for other's safety and well-being, compassion and kindness |
| Fairness | Justice as the best distribution of rewards and benefits, cooperation, absence of cheating, fidelity and trustworthiness |
| Loyalty | In-group cohesion, pride and defense of distinctive features of the group, patriotism, not questioning or betraying what the group says it stands for |
| Authority | Seeing the world as hierarchically ordered, respect for those in high positions, obedience |
| Purity | Order and cleanliness, avoiding unclean things and people, ritual, observance of taboos, distancing oneself from "unworthy" situations and people |
| Individuality | Each makes his or her own way, keep what we earn, minimal answering to others for what we think is right |

Working with Haidt's group, a modified version of the MFQ was developed, uniquely customized for dentists. A seventh value dimension was added concerning technical excellence. For most of the groups tested in this study, respondents were asked to report their own values and to report their understanding of the values of one other group. For example, dentists were invited to self-report and to offer their opinion regarding the values of their dental peers. The survey instrument had good internal consistency across the value dimensions. The survey instrument and a more detailed description of the study and conclusions that can be drawn from it are found in Appendix E.

The survey has been completed by 141 individuals, including 118 dentists and 23 "patients," defined as individuals not engaged in the dental field or tested in a dental context. Haidt's international norms were also available. The dentist sample was divided for the sake of some analyses into a cohort of "new" dentists who were 40 years of age or younger or who did not own a practice and a cohort of "established" dentists.

General results are shown in Figure 12.2. Both dentists and the public, using Haidt's norms, are similar in the rank ordering of values. But there are differences in the relative strengths of these values across groups. Compared to dentists, the public places higher value on caring and justice. Dentists score significantly higher than the general public on authority (deference to experts), purity (avoiding "unclean" conditions and people), and individuality (deserving what one earns). They also place highest value on technical excellence, consistent with findings reported earlier in this chapter.

Figure 12.2. **Value structure of dentists and general population.**

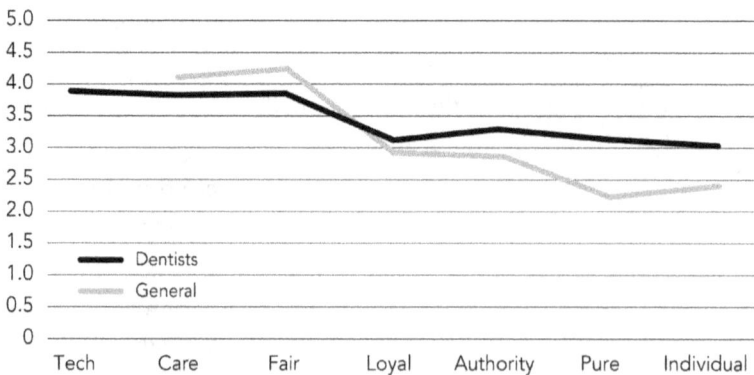

## Generational Differences in Moral Values

Much has been made recently by senior dentists regarding the value structure of their younger colleagues (California Dental Association, 2018). Often one hears that millennials are wanting of the traditional values upon which the profession has been founded. Sometimes these opinions carry the implication that younger dentists are value-deficient. To date there is no published research showing that this is the case.

The study of values using the MFQ revealed a somewhat different picture. As reported in Appendix E, the self-reported value profiles of young and established dentists are virtually identical. Statistical tests failed to detect any difference on any of the seven measured dimensions. Young and senior dentists self-reported the same values.

The challenge is to reconcile this finding with the reports that older dentists see their younger colleagues as not honoring what they honor. Respondents' self-reports on each value dimension were compared with their projection of the values they ascribed to members of their own age cohort and to those in the opposite age cohort. Figure 12.3 shows what established dentists thought of themselves and of other established dentists and what new dentists thought of established dentists. Values above the zero line represent inflated self-image. For example, established dentists considered themselves to be about two points higher, on a five-point scale, than their peers pretty much across the board. By contrast, new dentists judged themselves to be especially caring, but otherwise much as they felt their seniors valued all other dimensions.

There are several possible explanations for these findings. A straightforward interpretation is that senior dentists view themselves as defending a value profile that other dentists of all ages have weakened or abandoned. They seem to extend this projection in particular to the motives of their young colleagues. This interpretation is consistent with the finding reported in Chapter 1 and Appendix A that a dominant ethical issue in dentistry is that dentists do not trust their colleagues. Younger members of the profession and the public at large do not share this bifurcated view of the values in the profession.

Attributing motives to others is always a risky business. The social psychology literature warns of two dangers. A well-established trait in human nature is known as false consensus (Marks & Miller, 1987; Ross et al, 1977). We overestimate the proportion of others who see things as we do. If we enjoy skiing, we think lots of others do as well. If we like a technique or material, we overestimate the number of our colleagues who use them. That should make professionals think twice about paternalism (choosing or steering others toward care alternatives one thinks are in a patient's best interest) and make us all think twice about the Golden Rule. The second proven danger in judging others' motives is called the fundamental attribution error (Jones & Harris, 1967; Ross, 1977). It is somewhat complex. Undesirable outcomes of our actions and good outcomes in others' actions tend to be attributed to chance and external factors. Positive personal results are attributed to our own character, and others' negative outcomes are thought to be reflections of their deficient character. (See Appendix N.) The results of the value study using the MFQ are consistent with both of these established theories.

Figure 12.3. **Relative perception of established dentists' values by new and established dentists.**

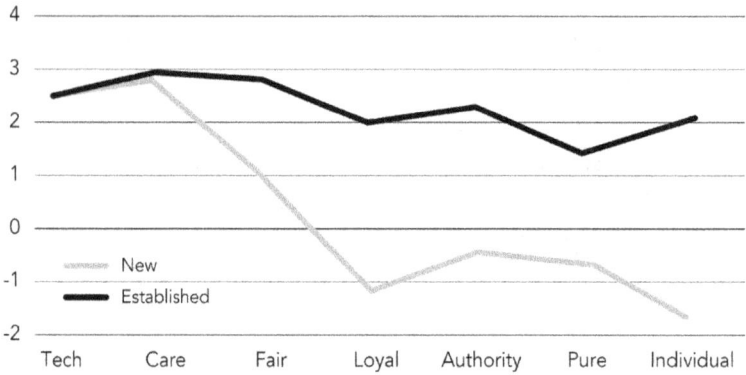

## The Situation Matters

It has been demonstrated pretty convincingly by research that ethical behavior is situational (Fletcher, 1966). There may be an interaction between individual ethical character traits and context, but the preponderance of weight seems to be on the environment. Kaptein's (2013) and Rhode's (2018) summaries are extensive catalogues of situations, each supported by research evidence, where individuals chose different ethical courses depending on how the context is structured. Russ Shafer-Landau (2007) devotes an entire section of his anthology, widely used in introductory college ethics courses, to constructivism. This is the view that we assemble our ethical perspectives out of some combination of norms, personal values, and our reading of the present situation.

To the extent that dentists follow the general pattern of expressing ethical behavior as a matter of character filtered through the situations at hand, we would expect to see wide variations in ethical practices in the profession, even among dentists who have similar public value structures. There would probably be something like a positively skewed normal distribution with a few individuals reaching for very high levels of ethical performance, even under trying circumstances. There would also be a bit of a bulge around the "good enough" point. A few would be testing the lower boundary of what is ethically acceptable. The informal summary of the American Dental Association's ethics hotline found that many of the inquiries took the general form of "Do I really have to do this?" Variations on the theme included "Isn't it unethical for others to treat me this way?" and "What is my obligation?" but not "What are my opportunities?"

The difference between the top and the bottom of the distribution on ethical behavior in the profession is probably narrow, perhaps narrower than the spread of income or technical skill. A few practitioners fall under the line. Those who miscalculate mostly do so momentarily and just a bit. Those who no longer care will drift further and further from the norm and continue to do so as long as no one stops them.

### The Ethical Environment of Dental Practice

Dentists do not work in the same ethical space that others do, even other professionals. They largely practice in isolation from their colleagues and do not evaluate each other's work or consult on the joint care of patients to the extent that physicians, nurses, physical therapists, or other healthcare professionals do. Dentistry as an organized profession, despite claiming that the mouth is vital to total health, has distanced itself from collaboration with other parts of the healthcare delivery system. (The recent trend toward interprofessional practice has so far largely penetrated only the schools.) In dental practices there is usually only one authority figure. The dentist has the advantage over patients in understanding what is at issue and being in a unique position to fix it and has authority over office staff to hire and fire and assign work schedules and decide policies. Dentists are rich and powerful, two characteristics routinely associated with a propensity to cut ethical corners. (See Chapter 5.)

There are virtually no studies of ethics in practice. Absent a good body of data on which problems rise to the level of ethical awareness and how dentists deal with them in practice, some help might be gained by looking to what dental ethicists focus on. There are case books of dental ethical issues that are at least a face-valid list of common problems. These teaching cases underrepresent the obvious problems, such as practicing impaired, charging patients for work not performed, or perforating root canals, much more often than one's colleges do. But cases can still be read as offering a useful glimpse of what ethics means in the office. A study was undertaken of the ethics cases in dentistry and three other professions. (See Appendix F.)

Two widely used dental ethics texts were studied: Ozar and Sokol (1994) and Rule and Veatch (2004). Comparison ethics case books were chosen in journalism (Patterson & Wilkens, 2014), business (Lewis, 2014), and nursing (Fry et al, 2011). In all, 358 cases were read and classified in terms of: (a) whether the case was meant to illustrate a matter that had already gone well or poorly or one that challenged the readers with a situation that might go either way depending on what the reader decided to do; (b) whether the reader was to assume the role of an actor deciding the ethically right action or to assume the role of external commentator; (c) whether the reader could imagine himself or herself having complete authority to act or could only advise or reflect; and (d) whether the issue at hand concerned a specific action that would only affect one person (the patient or client) or whether a matter of policy was at stake.

Dental cases were predominantly hypotheticals (constructed imaginary situations with fictitious names), with no intent to illustrate behavior widely recognized as exemplary or blameworthy. The reader was expected to assume the role of initiator of action and could imagine having complete authority to do so. We generally call such cases "dilemmas," as readers are supposed to project what they might do given a situation where each course of action has some advantages and some disadvantages. Because they are hypothetical situations, there is usually no right or wrong answer. In fact dental dilemmas are normally constructed to encourage discussion, so they have the potential for multiple interpretations built into them. They allow participants to defend a variety of alternatives, but there is no forced choice of a single action. Usually when teaching with ethics cases, there is no intent to arrive at a consensus among participants, so dentists can carry the case forward as an example of how they might behave. As dental offices are often under the control of the individual practitioner, this approach is sufficient.

By contrast, the journalism cases tended to be documentations of real incidents that had occurred, and readers were invited to determine how they would evaluate and frame general policy that involved cooperation with others. Business cases were also retellings of actual, historical situations, but usually accompanied by information about the good and bad consequences of what actually happened. Readers in these professions usually work in teams, arriving at a proposed general policy solution. Nursing cases were hypothetical, like the dental ones, but the reader was normally expected to comment on the appropriateness of others' actions rather than take personal initiative. This is realistic given the context in which nursing is practiced.

The differences in the structure and use of cases across several disciplines reflect an expectation about the ethical context in which different professionals practice. By contrast with other disciplines, dentistry intends to teach future practitioners that they have large control over behavior in hypothetical situations and that multiple interpretations are defensible. Thus a variety of actions are ethical and the dentist is primarily responsible for acting independently, provided that an appropriate justification can be framed. The use of dilemmas, where multiple principles are understood to apply, creates an expectation that private standards or private interpretations of them are acceptable. That conclusion is consistent with the evidence presented throughout this chapter. It is identified in Chapter 1 as a significant concern.

The model for what it means for dentists to be ethical in practice may be at variance with what it means to be ethical generally or in other professions.

The hall conversation regarding the ethics of reimbursement loopholes introduced in the previous chapter is most likely to end something like this. The speakers will continue to talk for as long as they believe others are listening to the opinions they are expressing. After that, the dentists will drift away and decide what they want to do independently, as it fits the needs of their particular practices. They will not know what others have done. Independently, the benefits carriers will monitor irregularities in this area. If the loss of business exceeds the cost of taking corrective action, new standards for compliance will be introduced that tighten the loophole. These standards will force a small number of devious practitioners to hide their increasingly dubious behavior or look for alternative ways to game the system. In the meantime, dentists who have been unaware of the potential loophole or who knew of it but avoided compromising their ethical standards will be burdened with new reporting requirements or other constraints on their practice. They would be justified in complaining about intrusions into their practice that are unnecessary because they would behave appropriately anyway. But they would be mistaken to blame the carrier for instituting these intrusions. Either the profession will monitor the ethical behavior of its members or someone else will. It is a privilege of professions to be given first rights of refusal in most such matters of professional ethics.

## Summary

Among those concerned with raising the ethical tone in the profession, there are many who believe that ethics is a matter of character and that the job of making improvements, which is largely assumed to be the responsibility of dental schools, is to change human nature or, failing that, to weed out those who lack the integrity to be dentists. Perhaps a greater number have pinned their hopes on teaching students, and sometimes practitioners, about ethics. This approach is based on the notion that dentists do not know the difference between right and wrong and that if they only knew, in some intellectual sense, the names of the right things to do, they would do them. Some, quite regrettably, either think the task is too large to tackle or just do not care too much about it. The evidence presented in these two chapters, and generally throughout this report, takes the view that across the range of character and integrity that represent the men and women in the profession, the critical factor is to create environments where it is easier to do the right thing. That is the ethical responsibility of the professional collectively, as well as of individual members.

# Chapter 13

# Three-party Morality

D odo birds probably thought Darwin was biased. From their point of view, they were arguably the best dodo birds around. This sort of thing is all a matter of perspective. From a real "bird's-eye" point of view, adaptation to context really matters. When context changes, survival depends on an appropriate adaptation. This is true for individuals and also true for groups and organizations.

In theory, ethics can be a self-contained and complete system. In practice, it is a set of shifting approximations. We only need to satisfy ourselves that we are following the right rules in single-party ethics, but not as groups. That is why it is natural to retreat into a world of private ethics instead of dealing with difficult others.

Unpredictability in our ethical world is brought under some control by engaging with others who have an effect on us as we search for mutually satisfactory working relationships. This is two-party ethics as presented in Chapter 9. Those we interact with are part of our context. The fundamental idea is that dialogue changes the world that seemed at first to be "wrong" for us into the best possible, sustainable future.

But that is still not good enough. Moral behavior takes place in context. Others who are not directly involved legitimately care how we resolve our ethical difficulties. It is appropriate for the profession as a whole to care whether practitioners overpromise, under-deliver, or steal patients from each other. The decision to enter corporate practice affects many: the practitioner, the corporation, patients, other dentists in the area, and the profession as a whole. Organized dentistry educates the public, influences regulations, promotes science, and rehabilitates and disciplines members because it is inescapably involved in all, not just selective, aspects of oral health care. There are always third-party ethical agents. There are very few private ethics or side deals.

It is far beyond the scope of this report to identify all relevant moral agents, their multiple and shifting values, and the almost endless array of combinations of possible interactions. Two general points matter, however. First, the community, the profession, organized dentistry, the commercial marketplace, and others are the context in which moral behavior is evaluated. Second, these third parties are themselves moral agents. Some of the things they do promote moral behavior among members or other organizations and some make it more difficult for members to be ethical. Systemic ethics matters.

This and the next chapter are about morality in community. Organizations are moral agents in their own right, over and above the typical moral behavior of their employees or members. The morality of individuals is influenced by the organizations they belong to and the roles they play in them. A partnership of three dentists can enter into contracts, establish protocol for the office, be sued, enrich the community by its charitable work, and so forth. In fact, the partnership can engage in every kind of behavior that is called good or bad ethical conduct. It can suffer consequences of its actions just as an individual can. This applies to study clubs, benefits carriers, academic departments in a school, component societies, the Alaska Native Tribal Health Consortium, off-shore dental labs, the American Dental Association, and the Centers for Medicare & Medicaid Services.

This requires some broadening of the ethics business. We saw in Chapters 9 and 10 that there are advantages in going beyond ethics as the relationship of independent individuals and their interpretation of the principles they aspire to live by. In every interesting ethical situation there are at least two agents who make informed and uncoerced commitments to acting together for their mutual benefit in ways that neither has any reason to wish were different. In this chapter that logic is extended to include those cases where there are three or more parties. This includes the two who are creating a relationship and interested and affected others. A dentist and patient may think it fine to waive a copayment, but the benefits carrier usually has a determining opinion. Dentists may want to advertise procedures they are not qualified to perform and patients would be none the wiser in many cases. But the profession would not and should not stand for this. It will not work to say that "some group" sanctions what I want to do. It has to be the right one for the circumstances.

In Chapter 8 it was noted that the ethics of one person standing under the favorable light of a principle is a bit theoretical. When our behavior affects no one else, it is academic whether to struggle with an ethical analysis. It will turn out now that we can count on the ethical dyad having an audience. We have not tended to think of three-person or systemic ethics, the ethics that involves organizations, as part of what we ought to do to make things go better. That oversight has left a whole part of the field unexplored.

In this chapter, the concern will be with identifying which third parties have a legitimate interest in the ethical arrangements individuals and side groups make.

## Nesting

Dentists are not the final word on ethics in their practices. There is nested oversight in the form of the entire office and community where a practice is located, component and state societies, state practice acts, and numerous national entities, professional, commercial, societal, and governmental. These groups normally sit passively on the sidelines when everything is running smoothly. But they can or should be counted on to become actively engaged when innocent others are damaged.

An ethics that focuses too much on individual dentists or dentists and their abstract principles is incomplete. It is also shortsighted to the extent that it imagines that changes taking place in society do not matter to dental ethics. There are books about the ethics of individual dentists at chairside, but none yet about the ethical dental office. The American College of Dentists does have an online program that engages the entire office in a month's-long practice assessment and development program centered around ethics (www.dentalethics.org/pead/). There are ethics seminars for dentists, but one for dental organizations would be a novelty. Dentists who violate a practice act are often mandated to take ethics courses. Members of the board of an organization are sometimes given individual training on how to function in that role. But conversations about how boards should function in the public's interest are usually thought of as political rather than ethical matters.

The naïve view is that it is sufficient to give members of a group ethical education and that is enough to make organizations ethical as well. This is the approach of raising the average, one individual at a time. We often take people out of context, give them a few hours of instruction, and reinsert them into an environment that may or may not support the values emphasized in the instruction. In doing so, we assume they will function ethically in the familiar, unsupportive setting or perhaps even raise the general level for the group. Of course that happens...sometimes on a small scale for a short period of time. (See Appendix I.) It is equally the case that the reality of the context overwhelms teaching that is episodic and not presented as practical activity in environments where it will be used. (See Chapter 15 on Teaching Ethics.) Often good teaching is wasted.

The defendants at the Nuremberg Trials certainly felt they had done nothing wrong (Arendt, 1963). They had simply chosen to place greater value on loyalty and authority than on caring and justice, to use the concepts of the previous chapter. Had the military outcome of the war been different, these individuals would have been honored rather than put on trial. Harriet Beecher Stowe's *Uncle Tom's Cabin* has an almost incomprehensible scene where a domestic slave in New Orleans who was a bit sassy needed to be whipped so she understood her place. She was given a note and small amount of cash and told to get herself to the local establishment that administered such punishments and to return with a receipt. These stories illustrate three points: individual ethical behavior is context specific, individuals and small groups receive "ethical correction" from superordinate groups, and ethical norms are not fixed in time.

Our court system is a good illustration of how, at least in the legal area, decisions at one level are nested in higher-order decisions. A personal decision is subject to review at the level of group expectations or organizational policy, then it might go to administrative or regulatory review, followed by lower-level courts, and possibly all the way to the U.S. Supreme Court. Each level claims the prerogative of reviewing the actions of lower levels. The same happens, but less formally, for nested ethical decisions. What is fine among friends may be judged unacceptable in a local group such as a school or dental society. Larger organizations act as stabilizing forces, maintaining big-picture consistency, and so on even to society as a whole. Sometimes there are superordinate groups that hold conflicting views of moral reviews. This causes jurisdictional battles and legitimizes the competing principles that give rise to "dilemmas." Conflicts at higher-level nesting also underwrite the cultural wars that are tearing this country apart at the moment, with some claiming the right to tell others how they should behave in private.

## Moral Behavior In Groups

Individuals often behave differently in groups than they do when alone. Thus it is problematic to assume that the behavior of organizations is the sum of the actions of its members. Some dentists bridle at having to wait at the DMV but routinely schedule their own offices so patients wait needlessly. Each of us becomes part of the ethical context of others who are trying to fit into their contexts. A magnet message on the author's refrigerator proclaims: "Most of my problems are caused by other people successfully solving theirs."

There are also some dynamics that operate in groups independent of the internal structure or personal characteristics of group members. We do not act the same way in every group. We tend to sport a little in crowds of our friends and remain cautious among strangers. We certainly dress differently for occasions and at home. We are even suspicious of those who seem to preserve private standards.

The larger the group, the more its interactions are dominated by emotion. The author was raised on a sheep farm and vividly remembers his father shooting packs of dogs that were mauling sheep. The saddest part of the experience was that the dogs belonged to neighbors who were outraged when my father brought back the dead bodies. "My pet is naturally good and would never attack innocent sheep," they said with scorn. Individually that was true. Collectively it was not. It is a poor guide to human nature to assume that all folks are good because we are or that we will be equally praiseworthy when reflecting rationally and when going along with the crowd.

It must be borne in mind that each of us is influenced by the norms of the multiple groups we belong to at the same time we contribute to creating those norms (Reay et al, 2017). We are simultaneously guided toward what others think is right and good and we guide others. Good behavior in a group is a complex topic, one that has been largely passed over because it cannot be understood with the old tools of investigation.

Arguably the most influential book written on ethics in the past century is John Rawls's *A Theory of Justice* (1971). His thesis is simple: it is futile to forgo the benefit of groups when defining ethics. Groups contribute to make us all more ethical, but not always the same way.

## Who Does the Organization Serve?

The use of power, justified by private principles, is an alluring alternative for those individuals or organizations that believe they can manage it. A famous teaching case in business schools involves Ford Motor Company's handling of problems with the design of the Pinto model sold during the 1970s (Gilbert, 2012). The gas tank was positioned so that accidents involving rear impact often triggered explosions, fires, and ultimately 27 fatalities. Management at Ford performed an analysis of the costs of settling lawsuits (about $49M) versus redesigning the car (about $137M). It was clear that the less expensive option was to pay damages, as return to shareholders is a paramount principle in any organization that handles money. So Ford used lawyers rather than engineers to solve its problem. The flaw in the logic was that the moral analysis included only the two parties directly affected by the decision (Ford and victims). Public outrage over Ford's solution to the moral problem on its own terms eventually forced discontinuation of the Pinto line and damaged Ford's overall profits. Ford came up with the correct solution to the wrong question because it treated the public as "customers" rather than moral agents in their own right and ignored the third-party moral audience.

Organizations persist in substituting power for morality when they can pass costs on to others. For example, taxpayers carry the burden for bad dentistry and practice. Enforcement of state dental practice acts is the responsibility of boards that are not funded by the profession. Civil suits to stop practices by organizations such as benefits carriers or corporate entities are adjudicated in the public courts. States have reduced their support of professional education because private loans rather than the previous system of government-sponsored loans has passed the burden on to individuals. Good dentists subsidize the cost of malpractice insurance for bad practitioners. Organizations often invest substantial amounts in lobbying or other attempts to make the playing field advantageous to their interests.

The costs of ethical bad acting subsidized by those who are acting ethically is technically known as an externality (Buchanan & Stubblebine, 1962). Firms that design obsolescence into their products, overuse the highways, or expect the government to manage polluting byproducts create externalities. The bankruptcy laws that discount what is owed others for mismanagement and even, perhaps, emergency room dental care and Medicaid are externalities. We see ethical externalities wherever burdens are unjustly shifted to third parties.

A century ago, the relationship between industry in dentistry—called "supply houses"—and the profession was openly acrimonious. The profession complained loudly that manufacturers were intruding on the prerogatives of treatment decisions and research information through control of journalism (Johnson et al, 1932) in much the same way organized dentistry views benefits carriers today. By the 1940s, several states had created regulations barring individuals from supply houses from attending, let alone participating in, state dental association meetings. There was a strongly supported movement that all journals must have a sponsor that was either organized dentistry, a school, a dental specialty, or an honorary. That antipathy collapsed because it was recognized that the profession and industry have mutual interests that outweigh the advantages each might enjoy working independently or antagonistically. Perhaps the same is the case for the relationship between organized dentistry and professional groups representing hygienists, recognized and unrecognized specialties, and benefits carriers and closed panels. Commercial ownership of dental practices and recognition of independent auxiliaries are current widely debated topics in the area of relationships among groups in dentistry today.

## "Right-Sizing" Organizations

System dynamics thinkers and anthropologists have worked out the nature of these relationships (Holland, 1998; Miller & Page, 2007; Waldrop, 1992). Humans, as the quintessential social creature, must live in community. They must also protect themselves from hostile groups. These two dynamics can be worked out mathematically to determine the optimal size for various groups needed to provide mutual support and protection from others. Declining membership in organizations may represent the perfectly appropriate response to a changing world. Digital communication has made it easy for many small groups to flourish simultaneously. As one's needs become complex, multiple groups are needed and membership in some falls off. It is not always the case that the optimal size of an organization is "everyone." Some organizations are too large for current conditions.

Understanding the moral calculus of the benefits and costs of moving with a group helps to explain the size of the group. To the extent that potential members face common threats that are easier to manage as a group and to the extent that individuals are incapable of putting together on their own a collection of resources to address their unique concerns, membership in groups will grow. Large groups face the burden of divided interests, and when an individual can satisfy his or her particular needs by joining several groups that uniquely match the temporary needs better than one large group that imperfectly approximates them, the larger group will experience loss of membership. In what has been claimed to be the most often-cited publication in the management literature, Ronald Coase (1937) argued, in "The Nature of the Firm," that the size of an organization is determined by its utility. Utility is relative and determined by the characteristics of all available organizations, not just the one whose size is in question. Often it is smart to spin off independent support groups or negotiate with others who have unique resources. Otherwise there would only be one large organization in the world. It is not the relationship between the organization and its members that matters. It is the ability of the organization to negotiate mutually beneficial engagements between members with diverse needs and the changing environment. Biology and systems dynamics scholars have extended this logic as a rule that applies to all living systems (Holland, 1995; Ostrom, 1990; Sober & Wilson, 1998). Appendix I of this report demonstrates that size must change when functional relationships with others change.

Stacking one agent or community of agents inside another is the same sort of logic that is at work when multiple public entities vie for the attention of legislators who are ultimately responsible for the massive burden of regulation that exists today. It is a sign of moral failure. Rather than working out the best stable direct relationship, we use power to entangle government to hamper others on our behalf.

Just as there is a moral dimension to the relationship among organizations, there is also an ethical aspect of the relationships between organizations and their members. Each member is like a group in the larger American society. Their portfolios of interests and values are not identical, but they share the common feature that together on an informed and uncoerced basis they will thrive by cooperating. We join because we are stronger together than we would be otherwise (Putnam, 2000; Stiglitz, 2013). In some cases, the anticipated reward from stable or self-enforcing mutual action exceeds the expectations from going along and saving the cost of joining. That is not always so, however. As discussed in the final chapters of this report, changes in society generally can alter the calculus of joining and alter the organizational landscape.

The fact that members join groups for various reasons raises the issue of joint action. Complete satisfaction of everyone's hopes all the time is out of the question. *Consensus* is achieved when *all* members agree that moving forward in a particular direction is better than doing nothing. *Majority* rule is achieved when *most* members agree. When a *minority*, either through deceit or partitioning and manipulating rules or gerrymandering rules for access to power positions, circumvents the interests of most members, this is called *abuse of power*.

Most organizations have formal rules for ensuring at least majority rule. These procedures are usually codified in bylaws. Although there are exceptions, the fundamental understanding is moral in nature. Members have a choice between going along with the will of the majority or leaving the group. Trends in membership are a vivid indicator of the moral character of an organization.

Normally, there is a precaution designed to protect against the "tyranny of the majority." Parliamentary procedure is a bit off-putting these days because a few have violated the ethical intent by using arcane procedure to gain power or to "show off." There is really only one tenet in the process. As Alice Sturgis states in *The Standard Code of Parliamentary Procedure*: "By the act of joining a group, a member agrees to be governed by the vote of the majority. Until the vote on a question is announced, every member has an equal right to voice opposition or approval and to seek to persuade others. After the vote is announced, the decision of the majority becomes the decision of every member of the organization. It is the duty of every member to accept and to abide by this decision" (Sturgis, 1988, p. 8). Most organizations manage fine as long as they stay close to this moral principle even if they brutalize the fine points of rules.

## Ethical Hazard

Rules sometimes work against the interests of morality. That is not obvious when considering only the behavior of one dentist and one principle. But when some dentists follow the rules and others do not, it can damage the ethical ones. This is known as ethical hazard.

Occupational Health and Safety Administration regulations and insurance contract requirements have been put in place to protect the public from the abuses of a few practitioners who are either not very smart or somewhat devious. That is a direct transfer of cost—measured in compliance time, restrictions on freedom of action, and out-of-pocket expenses—from those who would abuse the system to those who are ethical. The system is further burdened with enforcement costs that are borne, for the most part, by the public.

But that is not the full extent of ethical hazard caused by building ethics on rules. Rules, including ethical principles, are minimal standards. One meets his or her ethical obligation by being ethical enough and gets no particular credit for excelling on any dimension. Voluntarily going beyond what is expected counts for the good, but at a much discounted rate compared with not coming up to standards. The technical name for this is supererogatory behavior. Corporations have tried to protect themselves from the buffeting of greed, monopoly, legal corner cutting, and bullying by public relations work. But what is above the line is weighed differently from what goes on under the table. The formalization of rules often works to drive natural behavior down toward the minimum. In this sense, ethical principles can actually discourage good behavior. Making the ethical line brighter or placing it low enough to avoid false negatives can have substantial aggregate negative impact.

Occasionally "ethical" dentists count on unethical ones to give them cover for questionable practices. A little up-coding does not seem so objectionable if it is widely believed that there are a few bad actors who abuse the system wholesale. Malpractice insurance premium rates would be lower for everyone if there were not a number of practitioners who are pushing the upper limits of what they can get away with. There being a very wide range of what dentists would consider appropriate care in a single case may not be regarded negatively. Such wiggle room affords freedom for probing the boundaries. Appendix I contains a published paper showing that up to a certain (actually a rather large) proportion, bad actors may benefit and certainly do not harm dentists who intend to follow the rules. The combination of bad actors taking advantage of the rules and passive practitioners who wink at this works largely to the disadvantage of those in the profession who would promote an across-the-board improvement in the ethical tone of the profession.

There is one more layer of ethical hazard that is even more pernicious. Even (especially) when the rules are clear, there will always be a range of conformance. Some will allow a wide buffer of ethical compliance, while others are willing to risk having their transgressions undetected or are prepared to fight it out. There will always be folks on both sides of the line, regardless of where the line is drawn. The really bad effect of too many rules is that good dentists will follow them and bad ones will work around them. Not only do the bad actors profit from cutting corners, they also rob ethical dentists of their just benefit by luring away patients and by running operations at a lower cost point (Goffman, 1959).

The solution to ethical hazard is not more rules. It is enforcement of the underlying moral understanding by communities. Self-enforcement is uncommon when others (patients and the public) can be left wondering. Ethical hazard is the price ethical practitioners are willing to pay to avoid having to confront their slippery colleagues.

## Summary

Ethical solitaire, where one sits alone and imagines how things should be, is not really ethics at all. It is a reflection about ethics. Engagement with others to find the best, sustainable way forward is actual moral behavior. But it is still not the full story. Others are watching. They have a stake in the ethical engagements others work out. In nested situations, bosses, judges, officers, and others in positions of authority have a legitimate say in ensuring that the private deals we make are consistent with the norms of the wider communities. Sometimes others might be part of the solution or be affected by it so they would want to participate. It can even be the case that agreements that are mutually rewarding shift costs onto others. The latter are probably not ethical at all, but many are willing to pay the cost of shifting the burden to others. Many moral practitioners are willing to pay this "ethics tax" rather than try to fix the problem.

# Chapter 14

# Organizations as Moral Agents

Organizations are powerful and all-pervasive moral forces. Their impact cannot be gauged by looking only at the behavior of individuals within the organizations. Organizations have a responsibility to act ethically, over and above what their members do. Organizations exist to influence others. That makes them moral agents. Morality is still the informed and uncoerced mutual thriving of those whose futures are affected by others. Naturally, they touch base with their own deepest values. But when that is all they do, and when they try to impose their values on others, the behavior is ethically questionable. Some organizations are dominated by the ethics of judgment and the ethics of justification. The very best pursue the ethics of engagement and leadership.

Organizations as collective entities, for example, sometimes cheat and they may endorse cultures that promote or protect members' cheating. In a two-year period in the late 1970s, the federal government charged two-thirds of the Fortune 500 corporations with law violations, half of them of a serious nature. It was estimated that the cost of these crimes was $200B, compared with $8B for street crimes committed by individuals (Clinard & Yeager, 1980). Economic losses from white-collar crime amount to 250 times the losses from robbery. At the same time, the number of arrests for burglary, larceny, and motor vehicle theft are 133 times greater than the number of arrests for embezzlement (Reiman, 1979). As a rule, systemic ethical failures are more damaging to society than are individual ones.

Although organizations and individuals are both moral to the extent that they engage others as moral agents, there is an important difference. Organizations are collative agents. It is not always easy to know where to find their conscience. Their complexity means they must answer to multiple interests. Because they have greater scope and power than individuals, and because each component unit has personal standards, their left hand often acts independently of their right. In the extreme, organizations can have departments pursuing aggressive self-interests and departments charged with covering this exact behavior with positive public relations. Because they "invest" the moral capital of their members, there are special moral dangers that organizations face.

This chapter will identify and explain a set of moral challenges confronting organizations that are not normally concerns for individuals.

## Unethical Behavior Within Organizations

The typical organization loses an estimated 5% of its revenues each year to fraud, amounting to a global total of some $3.7T annually (Association of Certified Fraud Examiners, 2014). One-third to one-half of employees report having observed dishonesty at work, usually engaged in by otherwise upstanding colleagues who do not see themselves as being unethical.

Unethical behavior takes place within organizations for three reasons: (a) members of the organization feel it owes them something; (b) organizations are lax in establishing and enforcing standards; and (c) leaders within the organization pressure members to engage in unethical behavior on behalf of other goals valued by the organization.

### The Organization Owes Me

A sense of small entitlement because one's contributions are not fully appreciated is the rationale for loafing, using the office copy machines for personal matters, and padding the expense account. Taking season tickets to the local sports team as a business expense also falls in this category (Vaughan, 1983). Having policies against this sort of behavior without enforcing them increases bad behavior by giving cover. If it is "policy" that misconduct is unimportantly small, each member can be a little unethical in confidence that this does not matter to the organization. Members are less likely to cheat on ethical organizations but no less likely to cheat on organizations with unenforced or irregularly enforced rules.

## The Organization Does Not Seem to Care

Weak and intrusive compliance systems tend to be ineffective, except for forcing devious behavior underground and building resentment (Sims & Brinkmann, 2003). Across-the-board inspections to block minor indiscretions backfire, prompting resentment and system gaming (Gneezy & Rustichini, 2000; Tenbrunsel & Messick, 2002). Research has not established that either ethics training or codes improves matters (Treviño & Victor, 1992). Ethical indiscretion tends to creep in by small increments and is difficult to trace to single individuals (Mayer et al, 2013). Whistle-blowing has an uneven record of changing organizational culture (Mesmer-Magnus & Viswesvaran, 2005; Miethe, 1999). Disparities in penalty promote certain kinds of abuses. For example, perpetrators of Medicaid fraud are less than half as likely to get jail time as those who commit blue-color crime, but losses are ten times as great (Tillman & Pontell, 1988).

## Leadership Models Unethical Behavior

A major cause of unethical behavior in organizations is pressure from the top to show profit or other forms of organizationally defined success (Rosoff et al, 1998; Shulman, 2007). It is the day-to-day behavior of leaders that is imitated, not their policy pronouncements (Mayer et al, 2010). In some cases leaders keep their hands clean by delegating the dirty work to subordinates (Paharia et al, 2009). There is an urban legend that a Cherokee elder gave the following advice to a young man troubled by his conscience: "Your trouble is caused by the fact that you have two wolves in you. One is good and will earn great respect. The other evil and will harm many." The young man said, "If that is true, please tell me which wolf will prosper." "That depends on which one you feed."

## *Moral Hazard and Free Riding*

Moral hazard and free riding are related phenomena that erode the moral tone of group activity (Dembe & Boden, 2000; Hardin, 1968). They only exist in community. They affect others in the group, who do not have a chance to participate.

Moral hazard is a dirty trick played on society when it tries to help those in need. The community attempts to correct a deficiency, and in the process magnifies the problem. The common example is insurance. If a family has health insurance or fire coverage, they are more likely to engage in practices such as smoking in bed. Sometimes writing a dues check to an organization that works on behalf of a professional is considered sufficient to fulfill one's professional obligations. "The professional lawyers, lobbyists, and public relations folks are at work on my behalf, so I can take it easy." Pooling risk lessens an individual's sense of personal responsibility. Organizations that depend heavily on "professional" staff rather than volunteers are buying moral hazard (Fraser & Simkins, 2010; Haski, 2005). (See Appendix K.)

Moral hazard is a self-reinforcing, dynamic process (Axelrod & Cohen, 2000). All of us from time to time have felt we should only "pay for what we use." This is not an ethical principle, but it does have moral consequences. If some are allowed to opt out on the grounds that they are unlikely to benefit as much as others do, that will increase the resources of those who opt out. It will also increase the cost to those remaining in the pool. The increased cost to those favoring shared protection will cause additional members to perform the personal calculation and leave the community. In many cases this process destroys the benefits that can be achieved from pooling risk. There are natural differences among individuals in terms of how generally they favor provisions for sharing risk within a community, and these play out in political affiliations. Organizations that start on the slope of declining membership face a substantial challenge in overcoming the "I've got mine" force that erodes group moral strength. Professions whose ethical members look the other way when some cut corners because it is not worth the cost to engage the bad actors eventually lose their status as professions.

Another way of expressing moral hazard is the effect known as "bounce off." As organizations mature and as the environments around them shift, different types of members receive the maximal reward from belonging. A church, to use one example, may become established in a new community and strongly meet the needs of young families who are seeking affordable housing in the suburbs. It thrives and grows. But as housing costs increase, fewer new families replace the gently aging congregants. The church begins to emphasize general social causes, and donations pay for "professionals" who organize volunteer events or the money is "sent to national." Eventually, the church becomes a support system for those who are losing spouses and friends.

It would be understandable, but wrong, to wonder why such a church has difficulty replicating the success of its early growth years. A young couple with every need identical to those who were the strength of the church in its early years would look at the mature church and not see their counterparts. It is not that they are made to feel unwelcome or even that young folks have different values now. The organization has just grown up to the point where it no longer reflects the needs of those it once attracted. The new potential members "bounce off" and find a better fit elsewhere. The best remedy is to place new arrivals in top leadership positions following a very short internship. But few who have been waiting their turn with their hand on the tiller are enthusiastic about this. Bounce off is most commonly seen in organizations where the path through the leadership chairs is longer than the response time needed by the organization to make adjustments to a changing environment.

The related concept of free riding is also grounded in the tension between individual and group cost and benefit. Free riding means taking more of the common resources than one is entitled to or contributing less than one's fair share. It is an expected characteristic of groups when the amount withdrawn from the community is smaller than the cost to the community of correcting the abuse. Think of up-coding. An example of this practice is submitting an insurance claim for an impaction rather than a simple extraction since the case was "difficult" anyway. This is worth perhaps $100 to the immoral dentist. The benefits carriers might have to spend more than that amount to block this practice across the boards or to prosecute every offender. The result is that insurance premiums are passed along to all plan purchasers, and the upright members of the profession bridle at gestures by insurance to put measures in place to curb the abuse generally. The cost of sustaining a few bad actors is passed on to the public and the rest of the profession. This is a systemic moral problem more so than an individual ethical one.

Free riding is natural and inevitable. Every community, every profession, has its characteristic level of free riding (Geuss, 2001; Miller & Page, 2007; Sober & Wilson, 1998; Waldrop, 1992). This can be worked out mathematically, as demonstrated in Chapter 8 and Appendix I. As the benefit of taking a little extra or skimping on the contribution to the common good increases and as the costs of detection and enforcement go up, the level of free riding also increases. State boards, for example, will more likely take action against a dentist convicted in the public courts of a minor drug offense than against a corporate entity with many lawyers that has damaged many patients through questionable staffing patterns. Prosecution of dental students who cheat is often determined by the legal policies of the parent university.

Organizations are most apt to complain about free-riding members and members are most apt to complain about organizations that place them in positions of moral hazard. An organization can free ride, as some "big box chains" have been accused of doing with their low wage scale and lack of health benefits, expecting that tax-supported safety nets will pick up the slack.

## Let Someone Else Mind the Shop

There is a rich body of literature showing that the level of free riding is most sensitive to the willingness of one's peers to make small sacrifices to protect the community (Fehr & Gächter, 2000; Fehr & Schmidt, 1999). (See the discussion elsewhere in this report on justifiable criticism, Chapter 6 and Appendix J.) This literature can be explained with a simplified example of what is known as the Common Good Game. Individuals are given a stake, say $25, and can invest up to $5 in each round by putting money in the common pool. Let's assume that there are six players. A benevolent banker multiplies the total investment by a fixed amount, perhaps 44%. That means that if the initial pot was $25 from each of five players who participated at $5 each, the investment would grow to $36 (25 x 1.44). The investment is returned after each round to the participants, all of whom get an even distribution regardless of what they put in. In this example, each of the five contributors earned a dollar and the free rider earned $6. Professionals are like this. The best result across the boards will follow from everyone putting in his or her best and sharing the mutual benefit. But sometimes there are those who ride on their colleagues' coattails.

The results from research on this situation are predictable. After a few rounds, no one is investing. Free riders sap the vitality out of group effort. Among the many variations on the Common Good Game that have been studied, one is particularly relevant here. Sometimes the banker offers to enforce a penalty on free riders. Anyone can purchase the opportunity to penalize a fellow player by paying the banker a service fee, perhaps $1. Those who pay can nominate who is to be penalized, and the amount might be nominal, such as $2 for each dissatisfied colleague who contributes to the penalty fund. The effect is spectacular. A few players "invest" in cleaning up the game, and by the third or fourth round after the penalty is imposed, free riders have become contributors and all players are doing many times better than in the early rounds. The need to continue the sanctions is only occasional. It would be misleading to consider the Common Good Game as an excuse for punishing others. Imposing sanctions in a group is typically done reluctantly and selectively. The point is to reinforce a common rule from which the group benefits. The plan does not extend to the ethics where an individual personally benefits from having a rule imposed and then clamors for enforcement. Neither does it extend to a group making rules that benefit members at the expense of others. Protecting the common good is an ethical imperative only for those who are moral agents within the group. As Steven Pinker notes: "Our fitness depends not just on our own fortunes but on the fortunes of the bands, villages, and tribes we find ourselves in and which are bound together by real or fictive kinship, networks or reciprocity, and commitment to public goods, including group defense" (Pinker, 2011, p. 522).

The Common Good Game is an apt metaphor for dentistry. The profession is a positive-sum game. That means that there are plentiful Win-Win opportunities, and generally the more dentistry that is done the better for dentists, patients, support industries such as benefits providers and industry, and society at large. The dispute is over dividing the pie: who pays and who benefits. No part—the profession, the public, or any other— should be allowed to ride free. Penalizing free riders is effective in raising the rewards of everybody. It is useless to wait for others to sacrifice to do the penalizing. A little bit from everyone affected up front is the best approach. Morality in community is not an entitlement. It is an investment. Or to use the distinction introduced in Chapter 10, morality switches from being an obligation to being an opportunity, but only when viewed in the context of community rather than one individual acting alone.

## Moral Decoupling

When a website says, "Dr. Kind will always be there for you," but there is no provision for emergency services or they are inadequate, this is called hypocrisy. When you phone the organization and are greeted with the reassuring message "Your call is important to us" and then wait three minutes while a series of public relations and internal sales messages is cycled, that is called decoupling. (Same concept as hypocrisy, better euphemism.)

The term refers to an organization's simultaneously affirming its commitment to ethical standards but dragging its feet on any action related to meeting those standards (Weaver et al, 1999). This differs from the individual case of hypocrisy because one involves an obvious inconsistency by a single individual and the other is often hidden in "collective bureaucracy" and tangled policy. The organizations can separate responsibility (decouple) so some send the public one message and different parts of the organization send a different message or stonewall. There can even be units of an organization assigned to perpetuate the questionable practice while others are working to correct it. The ethical problem is that organizations that decouple put the financial advantage of bad practice in one pocket while getting public relations credit in the other for making happy claims. Sometimes advertisements simply add, as a marketing ploy, the term "ethical" to practices that are entirely matters of self-interest. This is doubly unethical because it devalues the very concept of ethics.

A week's watching the evening news is apt to turn up an example or two of decoupling. A 2017 interview with the president of Volkswagen, held after revelations that the company was gaming smog tests, began with the claim that "Volkswagen is committed to the highest level of regulatory standards." In California, Pacific Gas and Electric was being sued in 2019 for improper maintenance of its power lines, which sparked widespread fires. That launched a massive ad campaign around the theme that "PG&E places highest priority on community safety." The company may spend more on public relations than on clearing brush from power lines.

Research shows that decoupling follows a predictable pattern where positive public messages affirm generalities while concrete corrective measures are late and partial (Crilly et al, 2012; Heese et al, 2016). The closer the corrective action is to the organization's financial bottom line, the slower and more incomplete the corrective response. This is essentially the same pattern that was described in Chapter 5 on Bad People, where good folks do questionable things that are easier to justify the farther one is from the event. In the organizational context, this can be compressed in time by assigning different goals to different parts of the organization.

Decoupling is often associated with lack of transparency. In commercial settings, this is justified by appeal to proprietary interests—the capacity to make money as long as others do not know how it is being done. The proprietary argument is even used by not-for-profit organizations on the grounds that their non-dues revenues must be protected. Sometimes information is blocked from public view by regulation or legal precedent or the threat of lawsuits. Sometimes organizations simply and needlessly obscure a clear view of what they are doing in order to reduce hassle. In rare cases, lack of transparency covers ethically questionable practices or, at the least, makes it difficult for other moral agents to know what is at stake in the engagement.

In 2018 when investigative journalism uncovered the fraud of Theranos, which was marketing unreliable blood testing technology (Carreyrou, 2018), the pattern of decoupling was clear. The firm's support for the *principles* of federal testing standards was widely circulated public relations work, while the compliance records (really evidence of noncompliance) on actual testing was a carefully guarded trade secret. A nondisclosure agreement is a signal that one is in a commercial business, not a healthcare practice.

It is said from time to time that schools bury ethical violations in order to cover irregular or uncertain due process procedures or to avoid potential legal action. This is normally associated with discussions of "academic integrity"—the euphemism for discussions of cheating (Andrews et al, 2007). State dental boards tout their role of "protecting the public." They certainly do accomplish this to an extent, but the public is left without any clear means of knowing what that extent is. (See Chapter 15 and Appendix M.) It is a legal requirement that the names of practitioners with disciplined licenses be made available to the public. (See Chapter 6 and Appendix C.) While that is done in every state, getting the names is easy in some states and not so easy in others. The proportion of licenses disciplined varies from state to state, with some states having less than half the national average. In such cases, it appears that the only prosecutions are for patient death, driving under the influence, or narcotics violations—all of which are already public records. Based on data from medical boards, less than 1% of confirmed patient complaints are investigated and result in disciplinary action. Conversations with state dental boards suggest that the issue is limited state funding. This follows the pattern of decoupling by virtue of pronouncements about protecting the public that do not match the level of action necessary to bring this about covered up with murky transparency. Naturally, there are privacy concerns, but matters of public record and discussions of procedures and standards are not private.

## Moral Bleaching

Also called ethical fading (Tenbrunsel & Messick, 2002), this practice resembles decoupling in that both individuals and organizations can engage in it, but it is more common in groups, especially those that are legally recognized as persons. Here is an example: A large dental corporation settles a suit with the U.S. government over using unlicensed employees to deliver patient care for which they are not qualified by state regulation. There is a reputed large, but undisclosed, monetary penalty. The public does not know the details of the matter or whether their health has been compromised and the company admits no wrongdoing. The last part is the critical element in moral bleaching. Legally, the shield of no admission or finding of wrongdoing protects the firm from having this behavior introduced in subsequent legal action over new misconduct. Smart legal and economic maneuvering is used to limit a firm's liability.

But there is something more going on here. A moral abuse has been reclassified from the ethical to the legal or commercial sphere. A price is placed on bad behavior, and those who can afford it pay the price, thus discharging the ethical obligation in the same stroke used to buy off the financial one. The moral matter has been bleached out of existence, or bought off. Obviously fading is more common among the rich and powerful and in larger organizations because they can afford it. It is a common enough trope in fiction and history where the scion of a wealthy family is caught with his pants down and the female servant is discharged with a tidy wad of cash.

Central to morality has been the notion that bad acting alters one's relationship with the community. One becomes untrustworthy by lying, feared for using coercion, and disrespected for violating social norms (Bandura, 1999). Normally, one regains acceptance by a slow process of repentance and good behavior that demonstrate both understanding of what is right and a willingness to change one's ways. This is usually reinforced by internal feelings of guilt and shame. Guilt is awareness of having done wrong and acceptance of the community's right to hold a disrespectful attitude. Shame is the internalization of this attitude in the form of self-recrimination that tends to reinforce corrective behavior. In moral bleaching, there is no need for reworking the relationship with the community or of experiencing shame or guilt. The conscience is disabled. The debt is converted to legal-commercial currency, paid off, and that is the end of it. It is not immoral. It is a denial that morality is a valid concern.

Here is another example. There is a dental honorary organization that announces on its web page that it welcomes commercial memberships as partners in its mission. The benefits to commercial partners are enumerated, including the amount of mention in the honorary's material and the number of minutes of face time with fellows for each level of donation. That is a clear example of moral bleaching, even so blatant as to place an announced price on the dignity of that group.

The second book of the ancient Chinese text on ethics, the *Tao Te Ching*, contains this lesson (loosely translated): "When virtue is lost, there are customs (principles) particular to one's group; when these are lost, there are laws; when laws fail, there is war." The point of this ancient wisdom is to establish a hierarchy in the way people treat each other. Virtue or morality is the highest and most natural way. The consequence of failure to follow morality or of trying to short-circuit it begins a cascade of increasingly less desirable and effective ways of conducting our relations. It is often remarked that the ethical and the legal are different. It is the view of the American College of Dentists that ethics stands higher.

## Gifting

By definition a gift is something given with no expectation of reciprocation. If it is expected or implied that what is given creates an obligation for some future consideration—a *quid pro quo*—it is not a gift, it is a transaction (Rodwin, 1993).

Despite this, it remains the case that most professional organizations have policies prohibiting "gift" receiving by their members. Often this is limited to a specific dollar amount. For example, occupational therapists are expected to refuse a gift in excess of $25. There are federal regulations now in place requiring the reporting of certain gifts from pharmaceutical firms to physicians. These transactions must be reported online so that the public can see them. The management of intangibles such as positive Yelp postings, even though they may be of great value, is so far exempt from being considered a "gift." Journals and convention sponsors have sought to separate themselves from the taint of gift giving. They require that endorsements and commercial conflicts of interest be disclosed, thereby transferring responsibility to the consumer. Australia's code of ethics and Canada's code, when it had one, specifically prohibited endorsements.

The morality of gift giving looks different when considered as a two-party relationship or when viewed as involving a wider community. The first would be a straightforward ethical transaction involving the concerned agents. What makes it a moral concern is the valid interests of others who are also affected. A dentist may be very willing to accept a Caribbean cruise sponsored by an equipment manufacturer; it is one's colleagues and patients who are looking sideways. For this reason, such "educational opportunities" are kept quiet. And naturally, sponsors want exclusive rights. Organized dentistry is proud of the service it gives to members. They would benefit if the influence of outside interests could be restricted. Placing barriers in the way of outside agents by limiting their gifts accomplishes that purpose. Industry has recognized this fact and directs much of its resources going to the profession through dental organizations in the form of advertisements and collaborative programs, thus co-opting those who want to control access to members.

## Moral Shifting, Milking, and Moral Distress

In moral fading, an organization, or occasionally an individual, pays for the opportunity to get rid of a moral misstep. In moral shifting it sells off assets with questionable moral odor for cash. It profits by getting rid of questionable practices, but the bad acting remains or may even grow. The Internal Revenue Service licenses collection agents for both economic reasons and to avoid a negative public perception. Dental conventions do not market commercial products to dentists. They rent commercial space to vendors who do and collect fees from them. The less-attractive patient interactions such as financial arrangements and nagging about home care are often delegated to staff. Commercial-sounding activities such as advertising and bad-debt collection are outsourced entirely by practices.

Nonprofits spin off for-profit subsidiaries, partly for matters of efficiency, but always because the relevant laws and the ethical standards are different. For example, the U.S. government cannot market drugs developed by its researchers or those on government grants. But universities that develop patentable innovations based on federal grants can under the Bayh-Dole Act of 1980. And they usually do. The majority of medical device innovations are ideas from physicians (von Hipple, 1976), but medical doctors are not renowned for their entrepreneurial skills, although they may take an active role in promoting innovations they have a financial interest in when these are marketed by others (Katila et al, 2017). Dentists may feel "ethically uneasy" about pitching standardized high-end treatment plans to all patients, including those they have known for years and believe cannot afford them. But they might be okay with working on a commission basis for a corporation that does this, since their obligation is now limited to providing only the best quality technical care in their capability (one pocket) while the compensation has already been received (in the other pocket).

Moral shifting is most common in organizations since they deal in products and services that can be compartmentalized and sold off piecemeal. The practice is most often observed in organizations that have invested heavily in building a recognized brand that would be tarnished by association with questionable practices. It is no accident that the hangman of old wore a mask.

Soenen and colleagues (2017) have studied this practice. In one complex example of moral shifting, a well-known pharmaceutical firm arranged with a generic manufacturer to have the latter illegally begin marketing a drug generically a few years before the patent was due to expire. As agreed in advance the firm with the high-end image sued the generic drug maker and a settlement was reached that permitted the "illegal" product to be sold out-of-patent. The settlement amount, also agreed in advance, was essentially an indemnification of the industry leader's position as marketing only new and patentable drugs. It further had the advantage of being a court-sanctioned sale of a license to violate the law. This amounted to a Win-Win for the two firms and a blow to the public and the justice system. There are currently attempts to rewrite law to prevent this practice, known as "pay for delay," as selling one's good name is a growing practice.

Another example concerns the choice by patients between generic and patented medications. Physicians may feel bound to advise patients of both alternatives and the benefits carriers have been locked into agreed prices and copays for the more expensive drugs. The physician cannot ethically waive the copay or exaggerate the severity of patients' conditions to increase reimbursement rates (although surveys [Wynia et al, 2000] say that this is quite common). The manufacturers of the more expensive drugs have found a way around this. They offer to reimburse patients an amount equal to the copayment if they request the more expensive drug. The amount of reimbursement is smaller than the markup of the drug. Thus the benefit is shifted to the manufacturer and the burden is shifted to the public in the form of higher costs for insurance coverage.

A related moral trap that works better in organizations than for individuals is called "milking" (Jackall, 1988). Here the shift of responsibility is temporal rather than from one organization to another. A leadership team runs an organization into the ground by underinvesting in maintenance and development. Because the bottom line looks good in the short run, the leadership is rewarded. If the "milkers" are able to exit at the right time, they will leave their successor with no way to continue the high level of returns stakeholders had grown used to. The bad actors get a free lunch and get out before the check comes due. In dentistry, this can occur when a high-value practice is sold and it is later discovered that the dentist was cherry picking the most lucrative treatment plans and leaving a backlog of untreated need (Jabr, 2019).

Moral distress is one of the nastiest ways organizations abuse ethics. The practice works like this: Rules are put in place requiring that members or those doing business with the organization must choose between leaving the relationship and violating their own moral integrity. Individuals must choose between remaining in good standing in the organization and violating their ethical standards. The literature is best developed in the nursing field (Austin et al, 2005; Corley, 2002; Hamric et al, 2006; McCarthy & Deady, 2008). Nurses are sometimes called on to perform duties, at the doctor's orders or as hospital policy, that are contrary to their own best judgment. Dentists may feel that benefits carriers place them in such "take it or leave it" situations. These are forced trade-offs between ethical action and other standards, such as employment, income level, or even getting a license. As such they are tests of how much one's ethics are worth. What makes moral distress so disgusting is that organizations that engage in it delegate unethical actions to others over whom they exercise economic, political, or other power. So it is a trade of power for ethics.

## In Loco Parentis

This is a Latin phrase that means organizations can create some of their own rules and thus avoid having to conform to broader societal rules. Universities have their own police forces and an internal discipline system. Companies that have "ethics officers" receive lighter penalties in the U.S. Uniform Sentencing Guidelines when they do violate the law of the land. The courts look to expert witnesses to determine whether dentists are guilty of malpractice.

People are more likely to cheat when earning money on behalf of organizations than on their own (Jordan & Monin, 2008; Khan & Dhar, 2006; Monin & Miller, 2001). Firms that use ethics-related terms such as "ethics" and "corporate responsibility" in their 10-K reports are more likely to be associated with "sin" stocks, or publicly traded companies involved in producing alcohol, tobacco, and gaming. They are also more likely to be the object of class-action lawsuits and to score poorly on corporate governance measures (Loughran et al, 2008). More cheating occurs when we can rationalize that others benefit from it, such as in waiving copayments (Wiltermuth, 2011). Many corporate ethics codes contain verbatim copied sections or sentences from other companies—plagiarism. Max Bazerman notes that "an organization may espouse ethical values, require ethical training, and even have an ethics 'hotline,' yet such symbolic moves may have relatively little impact on ethical behavior" (Bazerman & Tenbrunsel, 2011, p. 160). People will cut corners on behalf of groups they identify with (Dukerich et al, 1998) and are reluctant to cause problems for colleagues at work (Jackall, 2010). In some cases this will be due to altruism; in others it is not wanting to sacrifice the advantages of membership in a group that gives social benefits or in a group that may be willing to look the other way on the potential snitches' indiscretions. (See Appendix E on dentists' ranking of loyalty as a professional value.)

There are two questions involved with the *in loco parentis* system of organizational ethics. Do organizations and their members benefit from letting the organization make and enforce some of its own rules, and do other organizations and the public benefit from this system? The answer to the first question seems pretty clearly to be in the affirmative.

## Summary

All of the examples in this and the preceding chapter move beyond the simple ethical logic of individuals conforming their actions to a personal principle or of two individuals working in harmony toward an agreed mutually satisfactory future. They involve at least three parties or nested groups. There are many moral issues in dentistry that would otherwise remain undetected and undiscussed without allowing that morality often, indeed regularly, involves more than two parties and that organizations are moral agents. Common examples of moral problems most likely to arise when individuals or organizations can shift issues among parties include moral hazard, free riding, failure to punish, decoupling, bleaching, gifting, shifting, milking, moral distress, and *in loco parentis*.

# Chapter 15

# Teaching Ethics

Each door in a building can have two signs. The one on the outside says "entrance." The one on the inside says "exit." It all depends on where you want to be, not on the door. Education is similarly two processes: teaching and learning. The first is about what teachers do, the second can only be done by students. Naturally, the two activities are related, but never as tightly as teachers might hope. In fact, most of what we learn in life has not been taught to us. We just adjust to new situations based on how things seem to be working out, and we stick with it until something better comes along. If others tell us things that do not work well when we try them, it cannot fairly be said that we learned anything from that.

This double focus is certainly true for ethics. Confusing teaching with learning would suggest a doubtful conclusion that dentists trained before the 1990s are less ethical than are the newer generations. Twenty years ago the Commission on Dental Education began requiring that dental schools *teach* the principles of ethics. So by this suspect logic, one could argue that younger dentists are more ethical because it is finally being taught in a formal fashion. Perhaps the "naturally good" dentists have signed up for continuing education programs that corrected this oversight. There is a vanishingly small probability that the big offenders in the profession will have their lives changed by requiring that they take 30 or so hours of mandated courses to keep their licenses current.

The focus of this chapter is on the changing landscape of teaching ethics in dental schools, cheating, and the emerging movement for students and young dentists to make ethics their own responsibility.

## Is There Enough Ethics Teaching?

Consider where we have come in dental ethics education, especially in the dental schools. It was only in 1997 that the Commission on Dental Accreditation instituted Standard 2.21 requiring that "Graduates must be competent in the application of the principles of ethical decision making and professionalism." (Appendices F and M, Ethics Cases and Survey of Dental Ethics Educators, present a picture of the state of the art in dental ethics education.) Most schools now have formal courses, and about half of them include experiences in three or all four years. The standard format for ethics courses includes case work where students discuss hypothetical dilemmas and reflect on the application of ethical principles. There are White Coat Ceremonies and guest speakers from organized dentistry. Several excellent textbooks have been written, and some are in their second or third editions. Both the American Dental Education Association and the American Student Dental Association have codes of ethics. The American Dental Association has sponsored conferences and working groups to look into lack of academic integrity in schools and annually offers a prize for student video skits on ethics. We have the American Society for Dental Ethics; the American Society of Law, Medicine and Ethics; the Academy of Professionalism in Health Care; the Association for Practical and Professional Ethics; the Student Professionalism and Ethics Association; the International Dental Ethics and Law Society; and special-interest groups on dental ethics of the American Dental Education Association and the American Bioethics and Humanities Association. Dentists with disciplined licenses are often required to pay for remedial ethics instruction as a condition for a stay on enforcement actions. Online and meeting-based ethics courses, usually based around dilemmas, are available, but not common at state or regional conventions. Scholarships are available through the American College of Dentists for dentists seeking formal training in ethics.

### The Optimistic View
Surely if teaching were the answer, wobbly dental professionalism would no longer be much of a concern. There are a very few cynics who hold that

one's character, presumably including their own, is fixed before college by one's family and cultural background. But a more encouraging view is that the years of dental education are a prime opportunity to influence young professionals, and the schools will be able to set beginning dentists on the right path. Certainly, it is the time when sufficient resources should be made available to train all those who have the ethical potential to be strong professionals and to gently steer those who do not into other lines of work. If the job is done right, it should be sufficient to last an entire professional career and be immune from erosion by commercial and other negative pressures in practice.

This view can be called the ethics teaching model. The fundamental assumption is that individuals can be made as ethical as necessary when told what is expected of them. Apples that have rotten cores can be discovered and dealt with. Knowing what is right is both necessary and sufficient to ensure good behavior, and it can be taught, and a few hours in dental school should be all that is needed.

The teaching model is on shaky ground generally as well as in dentistry. Beginning in 2009, the Bill & Melinda Gates Foundation spent $575M on teacher hiring and training to improve educational outcomes in targeted schools. Susan Moore Johnson, in her book *Where Teachers Thrive: Organizing Schools for Success* (2019), concluded that this seven-year effort failed to improve academic achievement or graduation rates. The effects of teaching were swamped by societal forces.

### The Reality

We know pretty clearly what dental school ethics teaching consists of. The average hours of instruction is approximately 23 over the entire curriculum. The typical dentist now works 36 hours per week, year round for an entire career. The ratio of formal to informal opportunities to learn dental ethics varies by the length of a practice career.

There are no full-time dental ethics educators. About half of those who teach the topic are not dentists. Four out of five of these teachers report that they started to inform themselves about dental ethics *after* they agreed to be responsible for the program.

The American Dental Education Association Survey of Seniors (Wanchek et al, 2018) reports that only the biomedical sciences are viewed by students as being more excessive in curriculum time than is ethics.

Membership in the many professional ethics associations is small and overlapping, and the numbers are falling. The number of hours devoted to ethics in dental schools and the number of published journal articles in the field have both been declining since about 2000.

Many students and practicing dentists have an imprecise understanding of the American Dental Association code. (See Appendix G.) Educators and students both point to the "realities" of competing practice environments as undermining ethical theory. There is no evidence that the ethical tone of the profession has been elevated since Standard 2.21 was introduced 20 years ago. The rate of disciplined licenses remains about four to six per thousand dentists. (See Appendix C.) Some senior practitioners believe that young dental professionals are not as ethical as they were and neither are their same-aged peers. (See Appendix E.)

The point of this chapter will be to show that the effort to bend the course of dental ethics in the schools has been small and the results largely unnoticeable. The reason is that the ethics teaching model is incomplete. This is not a counsel of despair. It is a suggestion that we have been looking in the wrong place for the right answers. Dental ethics is how one practices, not what one has been told. Changing the conditions of practice holds promise for making more ethical dentists, and that will be addressed in the next chapter.

## Are Schools Responsible for the Ethics of the Profession?

Over a period of several months in 1991, in a small hospital in England, four children died and nine were seriously injured on a single ward. An investigation eventually revealed that a nurse, Beverly Allitt, had been giving injections of insulin and other drugs that caused the harm. The hospital had been suspicious that something was amiss, but the connection and conviction were made by police. A national inquiry was called, and almost two years of deliberations were consumed in fixing the blame. Nurse Allitt was sentenced to prison. The hospital was exonerated because it had policies of high standards in place and because so many government regulations had been imposed on hospitals that they could not follow through everywhere. The physicians who treated the patients were similarly excused because they had extended professional courtesy in assuming the integrity of their colleagues or those who worked for them. Eventually the blame was fixed principally on a part-time nursing program Ms. Allitt had attended years previously. A note was found in her file stating that she had exhibited unusual behavior and in particular had not accepted offered help. It is natural to want to move garbage away from one's front porch. It is not always helpful, however, to place it where it probably makes no difference and remote from those most directly responsible (Chambers, 2017a).

Closer to home are the papers of Maxine Papadakis, widely read in the early 2000s, showing a connection between questionable conduct while in medical training and eventual disciplinary actions by state medical boards (Papadakis et al, 2004; 2005; 2008). Some argued that this research demonstrated a failure on the part of schools to teach ethics or to identify and screen out those who were known or could have been known to be future bad actors. The data do not lie, but they do not tell the whole story either. Documentation of school behavior was drawn from the files and included nervousness on the admissions interview, questioning faculty, needing reminders, and a few cases of illegal or unethical actions involving patients. The research is suggestive, but did not really answer the right question (Chambers, 2016a). It was not reported how many who have been disciplined raised no concerns while in school. The percentage of greater interest is the proportion of practicing physicians who are unethical who have not had their licenses disciplined. That number is unknown. (See Appendix C: Disciplined Licenses.)

In both of these cases it was assumed that bad acting was a personality trait of the individual and not the circumstances in which the individual practiced. Allitt had practiced for many years before her horrendous behavior emerged, and physicians in the Papadakis studies were on average in their mid-fifties when disciplined. Either it takes some time for doctors and dentists to drift into reportable unethical behavior or the system for managing these abuses is imperfectly insensitive. Yet in both cases there was an attempt to reach back and say that schools should have said something that would override faulty character. At the least, they should have detected problems and barred suspicious people from becoming professionals. Dental schools in the United States do in fact do this at the rate of about 2% or 3% per year, which is about the same as the rate for initial licensure examinations (Chambers, 2004a). State dental boards also have this responsibility, but they have a standard that is not as strict as the one used by schools.

### Ethics Within the Academic Community

We know very little for certain about how ethical practicing professionals are. For the most part, we simply have not looked. The definition of "unethical" is open to wide interpretation and professions are reluctant to get too specific about these things. This extends to declining to participate in research studies. (See Appendix J: Justifiable Criticism.) An exception is self-reported cheating behavior among students in professional programs, a hot topic among researchers from 1990 to 2010 (Cizek, 1999; McCabe, 2001; 2005; McCabe et al, 2006; Puka, 2005; Treviño & Victor, 1992). The customary approach to studying this phenomenon is to ask students to report anonymously whether they have ever cheated on a test. Typically between 70% and 80% say they have. This kind of project has been carried out in dentistry as well, with similar results (Andrews et al, 2007; Beemsterboer et al, 2000; Graham et al, 2016; Nath et al, 2006). The year with the highest percentage of cheating in dental schools was 1979 at more than 90% (Fuller & Killip, 1979). There has been less reported cheating in recent years.

Among dental students, cheating on examinations is about ten times as likely to be the cause of a disciplinary action as is any transgression involving a patient, such as forging a faculty signature (Graham et al, 2016). Fortunately, practicing dentists take very few examinations, and it is unlikely that any have had their licenses disciplined for cheating on written tests. Cheating in dental schools is similar to the rate in other professions, despite the fact that more than 90% of dental programs have honor codes and orientation lectures on academic integrity for students. Those students who are most apt to cheat are near the top of their class and interested in getting into graduate programs. A "success" motivation is a good predictor of cheating (Dweck, 2006; Murdock & Anderman, 2006). The justification most often cited is "others are doing it." The strongest deterrent is perceived likelihood of being detected. It is often done simply because it is frustrating not to look good (Chambers, 2007b). Chambers also reports that the reasons students fail to report incidents of suspected cheating by their classmates is the expectation that no action will be taken by the administration. The reason most often given by faculty for failing to report cheating is wanting to manage the matter personally. Faculty seem to avoid the uncertainty of engagement if they cannot control the outcome. These excuses for not becoming involved in academic integrity should be compared with the reasons practitioners offer for sidestepping justifiable criticism. (See Appendix J.)

De Los Reyes and colleagues (2017) make the case that the ethics of students in business schools is a function of the climate that the schools' leadership creates rather than of the character of individual students (see also McCabe & Treviño, 1997; Rettinger & Kramer, 2009). It is unclear whether it is the honor code or its enforcement that has an effect on cheating (Jendrek, 1992; McCabe, 2001), but there is evidence that unenforced honor codes breed contempt for the system (McCabe et al, 2001). This generalization aligns well with the extensive literature showing that employees conform their moral behavior to the behavior demonstrated by leadership, especially what leaders will allow without comment, and not to the professed norms of the organization (Kalshoven et al, 2012; Mayer et al, 2009; Thoms, 2008; Toor & Ofori, 2009).

It is not an easy matter to interpret the evidence on academic integrity in dental schools. Certainly it is not the case that 70% of graduates from dental schools (or larger numbers in previous years) are so ethically flawed that they should not practice dentistry. There is evidence that students anonymously over-self-report questionable behavior such as plagiarism and drinking in order to give themselves an excuse in case they need it (Prentice & Miller, 1993). This would be consistent with the research reported on the false consensus effect in Appendix E (Marks & Miller, 1987). We overestimate how common questionable behavior is in general in order to provide cover in the form of "everyone is doing it" in case we need to bend the rules a bit ourselves.

There is a natural response to the "it's pretty common, and dental students are actually not so bad" argument in the preceding paragraph. Some would say, "Any amount of cheating or other form of dishonesty in a profession is too much. We might as well begin with the schools and fix this problem instead of offering excuses about what others say they do." Although often well-intended, this is mostly good rhetoric. The true question is "Isn't any inaction on the part of the *profession* for cleaning up this problem wherever it exists an evasion of responsibility, and isn't it too easy to shine the light someplace not so close to home?" It would be appropriate for the profession to provide learning opportunities for ethics at every point in dentists' careers and in every context in which dentistry is practiced.

## Educational Debt

Much has been speculated regarding the effect of educational debt on dental practice. It is understood that the combination of practice purchase and educational debt has risen at the same time there is increasing concern over the ethical tone of the profession. But that association does not mean that the first is causing the second. There is good reason to argue that the causal arrow points from commercialism to debt. The issue is complex.

For the past half-century, dental school educational debt has risen at a constant linear rate, approximately 1.7 times inflation (Chambers, 2014b). Until about ten years ago, both net income of general practitioners and dental school debt were increasing in parallel and debt plus interest was a constant 70% to 80% of one year's earnings. Three things changed about 2006 that altered the *perception* of debt. Most importantly, dental incomes have been flat since then while debt continues to grow. This has made the servicing of debt more difficult. Second, the absolute size of debt repayment has delayed practice purchases. The practices that sell well now are those with very large volumes that generate sufficient income to make monthly debt payments. Third, it is taking longer for recent graduates to establish a personal economic equilibrium. More of them are spending the first years out of school driving from office to office for part-time opportunities and working in commercial operations. It is increasingly difficult for older dentists to sell practices, especially traditional family- or community-oriented ones of the professional services firm type described in Chapter 4. Arrangements that use dentists as productivity units, in both a corporate and a dentist owner with associate form, are changing the nature of dental practice.

There is little discussion of the systemic unethical nature of educational and practice debt. More typically the conversation is about young dentists being individually unethical in providing poor quality and unnecessary care because they owe so much. There is no published evidence that this is the case. The only study that attempted to validate this rumored effect found no difference in quality of care provided as a function of educational or personal debt (Chambers et al, 2002). Young dentists are underrepresented among those with disciplined licenses and overrepresented as members in organized dentistry. Cheating in dental school has declined in recent years.

The dynamics of how educational debt affects the profession are more nuanced and more serious. It is a case of excess liquidity causing a realignment of parties having an influence on the profession. In the 1980s and early 1990s academic deans sat with student affairs officers on a quarterly basis to review students on government-backed loans. Only expenses necessary for education of students with reasonable prospects of graduation were approved. That changed with the Federal Student Loan Reform Act of 1993. A substantial influx of money was stimulated by allowing private lenders to make loans directly to students instead of the government loaning to institutions. It has become more common for parents of means to have their children borrow for normal or "augmented" living expenses to get favorable student rates. Limitations on allowable amounts and types of expenses were liberalized, and legislation was enacted that prohibited borrowers from discharging educational debt through bankruptcy. The increased supply of money was good for banks and attractive to candidates for the profession.

It also had an effect on dental schools. Suddenly there were more individuals wanting a dental degree, and they had the money to pay for it. More than a dozen new dental schools were created in the decade following passage of the Student Loan Reform Act. Funding for state schools was cut dramatically, sometimes in half. The downward pressure on tuition was removed as schools became indirect borrowers.

There have been several effects of the commercialization of financing of dental education through privatizing funding. Most noticeably, the number of dentists has gone up at the same time that patients are attending the dentist less frequently and pass-through funding for care in the form of benefits programs is getting tighter (Vujicic, 2014). That simply means that the incomes of practitioners are flattened. It is also economically more difficult to begin a traditional practice. In order to maintain the stability of this system with greater numbers of practitioners with larger debt, a new mechanism was created that allowed recent graduates to manage their early debt by working it off in commercial settings. Twenty years ago the economics of dentistry would not support the corporate practice model. Now it is almost a necessity.

The effects on dental education are not as obvious, but are nonetheless real. The cost of education has continued to rise at two to three times the rate of inflation and faithfully tracks the supply of loan money available (Hersh & Merrow, 2005). Because students and their parents are now the authors of schools' survival or growth, they have a greater say in how students are taught. Some see the dental license as a receipt showing payment for the educational experience. Tom Nichols, in *The Death of Expertise* (2017), offers a strong critique of how students showing up with money distorts what it means to be educated. Schools that continue the practice of basing graduation on a requirement system to boost their clinical income are thereby training new graduates for corporate practice that use this system as well.

There is validity to the argument that student debt is eroding the professional status of dentistry. But it is a systemic effect rather than a direct connection between recent graduates cutting corners in patient care to make their loan payments. Organized dentistry is aware of this problem and offers advice and services to make recent graduates "successful." The deeper problem is that the system is misaligned. This includes the intrusion of three new players—banks, those offering marketing shortcuts, and corporate practices and senior dentists who employ multiple young practitioners—that alter the value structure of dentistry. These institutional forces are influencing schools, dentists, and the profession in troubling ways. This is an example of moral distress. The rules have been adjusted to increase the ethical demands on part of one group for the benefit of others who are excused from having to make these kinds of difficult ethical decisions. (See Chapters 2 and 14.)

## Student Professionalism and Ethics Association

SPEA, the Student Professionalism and Ethics Association, deserves its own section in this chapter. First, it is by far the largest dental ethics organization, with several times more members than all other dental ethics groups combined. But more to the point, it is the only group that defines its responsibility to include all those participating in the organization. SPEA is a national, student-driven association that was established to promote and support students' lifelong commitment to ethical behavior in order to benefit the patients they serve and to further the dental profession.

The objectives of the association are to act as a support system for students in strengthening their personal and professional ethics values by: (a) providing a resource for ethics education and professional development; (b) fostering a non-punitive, open-forum environment for ethics communication; (c) promoting awareness of ethics standards and related issues within dentistry; and (d) collaborating with leadership of the dental profession to effectively advocate for its members. Note the emphasis on inclusiveness, communication, and creating a positive environment.

The founding of SPEA at the University of Southern California dental school in 2007 is a story that must be told repeatedly. A group of students met with Dr. Al Rosenblum, a faculty member known for his concern over ethical matters. The students described several situations in the school they felt were unethical. Dr. Rosenblum listened sympathetically and promised to take care of these matters with the faculty and administration. The students said, "No, we appreciate everything that others are doing, but we want this to be a student concern. At some level, this is our issue, and unless we are involved in making the needed changes, we lose an important element of responsibility." There are now SPEA chapters at about 80% of U.S. dental schools, and SPEA has a place at the table with the American College of Dentists' Board of Regents.

There is a famous teaching study used in business schools, known as the Hovey-Beard Case, that is relevant here (www.chegg.com/homework-help/part-1the-hovey-beard-company-manufactured-variety-wooden-to-chapter-6-problem-1cq-solution-9780078029462-exc). The case is based on an actual incident where employees of a toy manufacture and painting company created their own standards that substantially improved morale and productivity. But these more effective work standards were rejected by management. Involved employees were fired despite the better outcomes. The fault was that the solution had not come from the right source: the top. When management imposed their solution, both productivity and morale at the firm tanked (Chambers, 2007a).

The practice of bringing dentists into schools to explain what they expect of new graduates may not be as useful to students as it is to the guest speakers. Teaching, even the best teaching, should not be mistaken for learning.

## Summary

Teaching is what people say or demonstrate for others. Learning is how others experience that and what changes they make in their lives. It has been difficult to demonstrate a clear relationship between teaching of ethics and changes in moral habits. Evidence suggests that dental students are more ethical than in previous years and are also more ethical than the general population. Assuming that dentists only learn ethics during a four-year window and only from those with the mantle as ethics teachers is unrealistically optimistic. Resources devoted to teaching ethics in dental schools have been very thin. Although they increased between 1980 and 2000, they are now in decline.

# Chapter 16

# Learning Ethics

I t happens all the time: we get mixed up and equate teaching with learning. We even forget that we can learn without being taught and that sometimes we can do what the teacher is talking about before the teacher arrives. Here is an easy way to keep this straight. Learning is the behavior of learners; teaching is the behavior of teachers. Performance is how students demonstrate what they know; learning is change in performance. The organizational training consultants Robert Mager and Peter Pipe summarized it this way: "Unless a person is unable to do the right thing when their life depends on it, you do not have a training problem" (Mager & Pipe, 1983).

This chapter will focus on how individuals learn, placing emphasis on "teacherless learning" and learning in practice and from experience. The key distinction is between building better ethics by changing human nature or by changing the circumstances in which dentists practice. Some attention will be given to determining whether the right kind of learning has taken place.

## What Is Learning?

Of the many possible definitions of learning, this one highlights the key features discussed in the chapter: Learning is *all* the relatively permanent changes in behavior resulting from the learner's experiences.

Very few students show up in dental school knowing how to place an implant in the maxillary arch. Most both value benefiting others and know many ways to do it. Learning only occurs when there is a change in performance. Sometimes the only learning that results from a lecture on ethics is that students realize the lecturer also values doing what is right and good. Being lectured to should not be mistaken for changing behavior. It is certainly not a necessary condition. King Leopold of Belgium famously advised his grown daughter that she should give serious thought to being taller.

The "relatively permanent" part of the above definition is meant to insist that others can count on a general pattern of appropriate behavior, not just a one-off performance as often happens for exams and licensure tests. But learning also leaves open the expectation that students will update their repertoire when appropriate.

Students do not learn from what their teacher does. They learn from what they experience, including how they interpret what potential mentors appear to be doing. That is why one teacher can get different outcomes from different students. Students who sleep through class and borrow their classmate's notes learn how to pass the course. It does not matter that the student's and the teacher's goals differ. The only way to ensure that students learn what teachers know is to give students the same or comparable experiences that the teachers had. Students are very good at the process of "I saw that Dr. X said Y, thus I know enough in the relevant circumstances to say that 'Dr. X said Y.'" We admit students to dental school who are usually very skilled at this. If we make the relevant performance that of being able to report or demonstrate what the teacher did, students will learn to do that. Case teaching is intended to place learners in situations where they experience reflection on competing priorities. The method is most effective when teachers remain silent. (See Appendix F for a discussion of case teaching in ethics.)

These comments apply equally to the experiences of practicing dentists reading articles about ethics, attending ethics seminars, or serving on peer-review or other professional ethics bodies.

Too often we overlook the word "all" in the definition of learning. Teachers have to accept that students learn a variety of things from their (the student's) experience. In an interview with medical students who had just completed a course on medical ethics, one student reported, "This was insulting. The presenter talked down to us to the point where I began to question his integrity. If our professional seniors have so little respect for us, I want nothing to do with anyone on the ethics circuit" (Glicksman, 2016;

Sheehan et al, 1990). Other students may have learned other things and the teacher certainly was hoping for something different. But that is what this student experienced, so that is what the student learned. Likely there was no change in the kind of behavior the faculty member was looking for. But there was learning. Teachers cannot pick and choose, taking credit for the changes they like and distancing themselves from all the rest. Making ethics continuing education a requirement for relicensure or a probation requirement for those with disciplined licenses may be sending exactly the wrong kind of message about ethics.

## What Kind of Fish Is Learning Ethics?

The ancient Greeks had three words for what we signify by the term "to know." "Techné" meant "know-how," and this is the root of our term "technique"— the ability to consistently produce a tangible result of acceptable quality under the right circumstances. Much of dental education and most of dental practice is this kind of knowing. "Know-that" was a different idea. The Greeks called this "episteme," from which we get the word "epistemology." Knowing that the HIV virus causes AIDS and knowing that the American Dental Association rules about advertising fall under the principle of veracity are examples. The third kind of Greek knowledge was "phronesis." We have no linguistic descendant, but it roughly means wisdom or even common sense. This is good judgment or "know-whether," as in knowing whether to honor a pregnant teen's request to skip radiographs or to involve the parents or to avoid getting involved at all.

Ethical theory is episteme. Moral behavior is phronesis or applied wisdom. A dentist may know *that* a badly decayed tooth could be extracted to make other restorations easier, know *how* to remove the tooth, but remain uncertain *whether* to perform the procedure. Perhaps the patient had not consented to or expected this treatment before being sedated. A dentist may know that the benefits carrier is likely to pay for an up-coded procedure if proper documentation can be provided and know how to get the necessary records. But there is still a question of whether that is the right thing to do.

Too often we make the educational mistake of confounding *knowing that* this or that is ethical without managing the necessary accompanying *know-how* and *know-whether*. It is unwise and occasionally dangerous to assume that teaching dentists to say, when asked, that certain behavior is unethical is the same thing as teaching them how to express that behavior and whether they should do so. Often know-that and know-whether fail to bring about moral conduct because of a lack of know-how. (See Chapter 9.) Multiplying know-that is not sufficient for creating know-whether. It is compounding the error to further assume that hearing a wise person say they "know that" something is the case means that students or practitioners will be changed in an ethically meaningful fashion (Moberg, 2006).

### Unsupervised Learning

Most learning is "teacherless." Who taught us how to kiss, or whom to kiss? Who taught the "cappers" that there is money to be made by sending vans around in poor neighborhoods to bring in individuals with Medicaid coverage for the needed 28 occlusal fillings? Who pointed out the best procedures to be billed without having done the work? Where did some organizations learn to misrepresent the benefits of legislation that would favor their economic interests?

For the most part, we just figure out what to do on our own. It is trial and error, and we keep the patterns that turn out well when matching the circumstances. When we realize that things might not be headed in the right direction, we pull back and reflect (Schön, 1983) so we can find a better way forward the next time. In fact, it is a definition of being stupid to persist in the same behavior when it produces undesirable outcomes. And it is still stupid to persist when someone told us this worked for them, but it does not work for us. We move to and stick with what gives us the results we are looking for. This is unsupervised learning. Although other people may be involved, they do not play the role of teacher. What controls and changes our behavior is how we react to the results.

Change the environment and smart people learn to adapt. Some environments are such that we adapt in a positive fashion. We are invited by a friend to a component society meeting and meet some fantastic people. We spend time with them and become better dentists. We have a nervous mother and a frightened child in the chair. Instead of rushing, we explain what is happening and make it possible for them to take some responsibility in a challenging situation. When done often enough, we have learned to treat patients better.

Not all environments, however, predispose learners to adopt ethical habits. The major complaint of those who teach ethics in dental schools is that the clinic is often structured to make it difficult to implement what was taught in ethics courses. Clinical faculty are usually excused from attending ethics courses and sometimes directly contradict what has been taught.

The comments by dentists in the focus groups reported in Chapter 1 and Appendix A are monotonous in complaining that "circumstances" make it hard to be ethical.

Consider the (actual) case of a dental student who was taught in the ethics program that ethical dentists place the patients' interests first and was instructed in the clinic that school policy forbade making adjustments on partials unless the partial was fabricated in the school. The student in this situation learned four things: He got an A in the ethics course for saying that patients' interests come first; he got an A in clinic for following policy that might have been different; he found out that such behavior is a good way to avoid inconvenient patients; and he learned that circumstances play a large role in how ethical one can be. Because the patient was dismissed without care, consistent with American Dental Association Code of Professional Conduct item 4.A, it is arguable that the patient's interests had in fact been placed first.

## Ethical Attribution Effect

There is a rich research tradition in social psychology probing the question whether outcomes such as good or questionable moral behavior should be attributed to the character of the actor or to circumstances (Gawronski, 2004; Jones & Harris, 1967; Malle, 2006; Sabini & Silver, 1983). The results are clear: "It depends." This matters for how we approach elevating the ethical tone of the profession. There could be circumstances where the smart move would be changing the dispositions or value structure of dentists by "educating them." There could be other situations where the best results would be elevated by placing dentists in ethically favorable circumstances or working to build a stronger general ethical culture for the profession.

A research project was undertaken to explore this well-known phe-nomenon, called the "fundamental attribution error." This research focused specifically on dentistry and moral behavior. (The full details are presented in Appendix N.) A survey was prepared containing eight incidents, such as volunteering for a health fair or practicing in a setting that emphasized volume on quotas over quality. Respondents were asked to indicate the degree to which they felt such behavior was attributable to the character of the actor or to circumstances. Half of the incidents depicted generally pro-ethical behavior and half depicted questionable behavior. This was confirmed by pilot testing. There was no clear preference for attributing the moral behavior, good or bad, to character or to circumstances. There were two forms of the survey. In one, half of the incidents were attributed to the person completing the survey. ("If you were working in a 'quota' clinic" vs. "Someone you know is working in a 'quota' clinic.") Again, there were no differences in attribution to character or circumstances based on self-reporting or reporting on others. These findings are consistent with what has been reported in the literature.

Also consistent with previous research was the finding that there is a dramatic interaction between who performed the behavior and whether the behavior was considered morally sound or questionable. As shown in Figure 16.1, we attribute our own praiseworthy moral acts to our character while believing that our questionable behavior was heavily influenced by circumstances beyond our control. As documented in detail in Chapter 5, we deal ourselves a personally flattering hand in ethical matters.

Also consistent with the literature, the survey results show that we reverse the attribution for others. Good ethical behavior is ascribed to circumstances when others perform it. At the same time, their bad acts are attributed to their character flaws.

**Figure 16.1. Ethical attribution.**

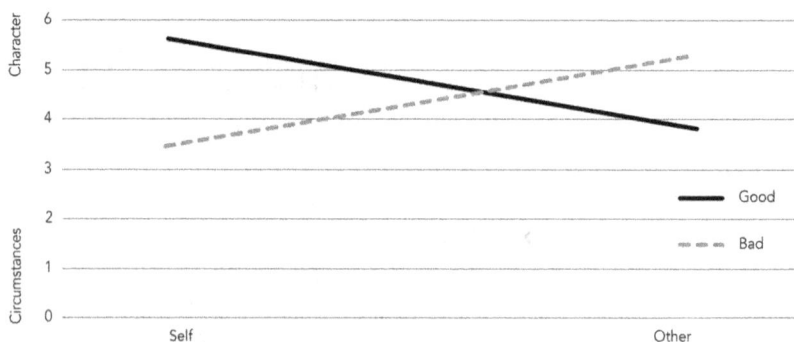

This research explains two trends in current efforts to raise ethical standards in dentists. First, our reflex is to tell others what they should do to become more ethical (the ethics of judgment). Their character needs a little fixing. Thus we will try to teach ethics. On the other hand, we will likely be resistant to learning ethics, at least as others teach it. We largely assume that we are ethical, and the major reason others fail to recognize this is that unfortunate circumstances have clouded the issue. Of course that is exactly the perspective of those we are trying to "teach." Learners will be more receptive to changes in circumstances that promote ethical behavior than to efforts to change their human nature.

The best way to manage the self/other and positive/negative interaction on moral behavior is to allow others the same moral status that we expect of ourselves (the ethics of engagement). The best way to promote pro-ethical circumstances is the ethics of leadership.

Leaders in the profession are responsible for everything students and practitioners learn about ethics, even when the learning is unintended and the leader is not present. Any situation one has control over that tends predictably to change the way others behave is the responsibility of the person in charge of the circumstances. (See Chapter 10.) Leaders educate by establishing conditions that encourage ethical behavior, or not. Any individual or organization that claims credit for starting a program, adjusting incentives, involving others, or otherwise creating opportunities for success must also bear equal responsibility for creating or allowing conditions to exist, if it is within their power to change them, where others naturally respond in dysfunctional ways.

It is unethical to create circumstances that promote others doing bad things. This is a hard rule and one that many in positions of authority try to play only on the side that brings them credit. Individuals or organizations, including the administration in dental schools and organized dentistry, as well as practice owners who are dentists and those who are not, can delegate authority for teaching but they cannot delegate responsibility for the learning that results. We cannot escape responsibility for creating or allowing circumstances where our colleagues learn unethical behavior. What we say in front of others may be another matter entirely.

Sometimes there is an antagonism between what leaders say about ethical behavior and the environments they foster or permit. In such circumstances, learners generally learn better by seeing what works than by attending to the rhetoric (Chreim et al, 2007; Fotaki & Hyde, 2015; Hollensbe et al, 2008; MacLean, 2008; Schaubroeck et al, 2012; Voronov & Yorks, 2015). Sometimes we attempt to move responsibility for awkward ethical situations. This was discussed in Chapter 14 on organizations as moral agents, especially under the heading of "ethical shifting."

## What Is Learned: Who Learns?

It is natural to confuse teaching ethics with teaching students or practitioners. Is it the theory of ethics that needs to be passed on like a family manual for good conduct or is it predictable positive behavior patterns—the family's reputation in the community? The safe answer is "both." But that is the wrong answer. It is correct that we speak informally of some colleagues as being ethical and others as unethical. But that is just a shorthand way of saying, "For the most part, the behavior I have seen in those I admire has been admirable, and the others have crossed the line more often or in dangerous ways."

In their classic study of boys cheating over an extended period of time, Hugh Hartshorne and Mark May (1928) found that 90% were dishonest, but they were inconsistently dishonest. One who stole the teacher's pencil might be repulsed at the thought of swiping a classmate's lunch. What was considered unacceptable varied from day to day and situation to situation. The work of Hartshorne and May has been widely interpreted to mean that there is little evidence dishonesty is a character trait and good reason to consider it to be habits, situationally determined and idiosyncratically defined. This is part of the reason why it is so difficult to make any headway managing ethics with generalizations or for one person to talk another into doing things the way the "ethics experts" think everyone should do them.

## The Necessity of Unlearning

Sometimes the challenge in ethics is to get professionals to stop doing the wrong sorts of things. Who shows alcoholics how to cover up their habit? A dentist continues to perform endodontic procedures after he or she has lost current knowledge or adequate manual skill and despite the fact that two excellent specialists have moved into the community. Another shouts at staff. It is well known that there is an affair going on with one of the married patients. This kind of behavior needs to be unlearned.

Instructing a dentist to stop these behaviors is likely to meet with even less success than a lecture from an association officer telling dental students about 2.G in the American Dental Association Code of Professional Conduct.

It is usually more difficult to get rid of undesirable ethical habits than it is to build sound ones. The reason is that we mistakenly try to punish them out of existence. The correct method is to reverse the process that works so effectively in unsupervised learning. We learn and we confirm the things experts tell us by trying them for ourselves and noting whether the results are encouraging. If we like the outcomes, we keep the behavior. If nothing good happens, if something unpleasant occurs, or if it is just too much effort, we stop trying. The wisdom of unsupervised learning is to make it easy to do good things and difficult to do bad ones. We can actually combine these two methods for even faster results. Known as counterconditioning (Pearce & Dickinson, 1975), the approach is to teach and reward positive habits that contradict undesirable ones. The goal is to create conditions where people are so busy doing what is right that they are less apt to behave badly. Unfortunately, this positive approach to ethics is handicapped by a view that ethics is an obligation. The "good enough" view of ethics was explained in Chapter 11. If a staff member is brusque with patients, the right approach is to reward him or her for being considerate. If whistleblowers are rewarded and publicly praised, knowledge of corrosive environments will not be turned into low morale and sabotage. If a dentist advertises ethically, the chances are reduced that he or she also advertises unethically (Miceli & Near, 2002).

Punishment is not the opposite of rewarding good behavior and it does not have the opposite effect. Punishment drives bad acting underground. It usually multiplies devious behavior with a goal of covering up the unethical behavior. Lying, cheating, aggression designed as a distraction, and withdrawing from contact with those who can help are the typical consequences of a punishment strategy. Once the threat of punishment is remote, the bad acting will return. Lack of transparency is a telltale symptom of questionable ethics. There is no evidence that increasing severity of penalties is related to reducing likelihood of unethical behavior (Aronson & Carlsmith, 1963; Dunegan, 1996; Kahan, 2000; Small & Loewenstein, 2005). Monitoring and administering punishment is also expensive and sows dissension within groups.

## One-Shot, Commercial Initial Licensure

William Gies devoted an entire chapter to state dental boards in his report. Much of the material was historical, tracing the need for protection of the public as dentistry freed itself from being a trade and became a profession. He was frank in calling boards to work with others to set high standards and a bit harsh on them for the way they conducted patient-based exams. He called for national licensure, and he focused his attention on the schools as the ultimate arbiters of competency to practice. In the closing section of his chapter on the boards, headed "Important opportunities open to the National Association of Dental Examiners to effect improvements," he stated: "With the rapid elimination of commercialism from dental education, and the impending extinction of unacceptable dental schools, the prevailing statutory requirement of reputability has lost its original practical importance, for all of the schools will soon be reputable" (Gies, 1926, p. 69).

That was 1926. There was good reason for independent testing by dental boards of graduates of the proprietary schools of the time. Owners of those programs made money by cutting corners and advertising that they could get a young man "practice ready" in a short period of time. The educational standards of the day were weak and not uniform. Such conditions have long passed. Today it is more likely that an established practitioner will have to hustle to keep up with a rapidly growing profession. Today the proprietary interests are with the individuals and organizations that maintain commercial continuing education, convention businesses, and profit-making testing agencies and not with the schools.

Certainly initial licensure testing is an economic, political, and measurement issue. It is also an ethical one. There is no evidence that the various states with alternatives to a patient-based, one-shot performance examination on a sample of what dentists do in practice have a higher rate of bad treatment by dentists in practice. But there are ethical concerns. The use of patients in situations that are not part of a system that provides continuous care or corrective treatment if needed as a result of the testing is inconsistent with current standards of care. Schools accept this responsibility for their students while they are enrolled, but commercial testing agencies do not accept this ethical responsibility when testing candidates. They pass the burden back to schools or to candidates. This is a form of moral shifting as explained in Chapter 14. Another ethical concern is the temptation for candidates to alter the natural treatment sequence of their clinical patients so that the "right kind of lesion" is present on testing days. The third frequently voiced ethical concern is the brokering of board patients. It is understood that patient selection is critical to board success (but discouraged in the American Dental Association Code of Professional Conduct, 4.A). "Ideal" board patients can command large fees, and this fact has created a market for individuals who broker such patients.

Commercial testing agencies deny ethical responsibility for any of these ethical issues. This is known in ethical theory as "moral distress." (See Chapters 2 and 14.) The notion is to pass ethical responsibility to individuals who must make a choice between bending the rules or performing at a disadvantage because they lack the power to create a more equitable and just framing of the ethical issue. These are several examples where a commercial agency, testing boards, profit economically by shifting moral responsibility to others. And this is accepted by the organized profession.

Another ethical issue associated with one-shot initial licensure examinations is lack of demonstrated validity. Commercial testing agencies say they have evidence of reliability and validity, but this usually is not made public to the standards expected for peer-reviewed publishable research. It is said several examiners will agree with each other when they look at a single procedure completed by a candidate on a particular patient. That is one form of reliability, but not the kind that is needed (Chambers, 2004a). The correct question is whether a candidate can perform competently across multiple patients in the various disciplines and skills needed to begin practice. In one naturally occurring experiment where candidates took two boards within a single month, the correlation between scores for periodontal performance for the same candidate on multiple boards showed no reliability—in fact the correlation was negative (Chambers, 2011a).

A decision is valid when reasonable additional data would not change it. The narrow sample of behavior tested in initial licensure examinations should be a concern in this respect. The fact that dentists have their licenses disciplined (see Chapter 6 and Appendix C) after having passed the initial test raises validity concerns. It is fair to say that a one-shot performance test does in fact identify candidates who failed on that day with that patient. The ethical argument is whether this was the most useful evaluation that could have been undertaken and whether this is the same standard that the profession applies to all practitioners on all occasions throughout their careers.

## Summary

Dental schools play an important role in influencing the ethical habits of students. But it is only for four years, or a few more counting residency or specialty training. Most of the effect on ethics is due to the culture of dental education, the unsupervised learning that comes from experimenting and discovering which ways of behaving work best, and how much latitude one is given when ethical norms seem inconvenient. Of course, while in schools there will be situations where people tell students what they ought to do. But the hours devoted to this sort of thing are very few, and often the advice comes from nondentists or dentists who are not part of the school's clinical culture. On the whole, a strong case can be made that dental students learn to be ethical students. After graduation they learn to become ethical dentists. Most learning is under the control of senior dentists and the general culture of professionalism accepted by dentistry.

The profession would probably not benefit from imitating the brief lectures and hypothetical dilemma instructional format now used in the schools as a way of teaching ethics. Leadership in the profession in arranging practice conditions that make it easy for dentists to do the right thing seems to offer more. And to the extent that ethics can be based on positive interactions rather than punishment or name calling, it will continue to grow.

# Chapter 17

# Ethical Challenges Facing Dentistry

The following are among the myths surrounding ethics.

- (Myth) Most of the objectionable odor comes from a few bad actors.
  (Truth) The cumulative burden of questionable ethics is the result of a little bad in many places. This means the potential for improvement is vast.
- (Myth) There are ethical people and unethical ones, and bad acting is a character flaw.
  (Truth) It is natural to think that our positive behavior and others' questionable behavior flow from character. But circumstances, including those that can be made better, play a dominant role.
- (Myth) Being ethical means following the rules (or one's conscience).
  (Truth) Ethics is a mutually beneficial relationship between ourselves and those we affect and those who affect us. All others have a right to follow their rules. Otherwise it is just power dressed up in justificatory language.
- (Myth) Only individuals have ethical responsibilities.
  (Truth) Organizations and communities that have members and interact with each other are ethical agents to the extent that they create

policy and reward systems that enhance or damage their own members or others.

- (Myth) We can talk people into being ethical.
  (Truth) Individuals compare what they are told with what works in practice. It is more effective to create conditions where practice is ethical.
- (Myth) Sometimes we have to use power, selective information, legal or regulatory means, sanctions and penalties, and advertising to get others to behave ethically.
  (Truth) This is using coercion to get our own way and covering it with high-sounding language that appeals to those who have the same values we do.

There is a lot more going on here than agreeing on the rules, telling others about them, and staying away from those who behave badly. Ethics is working with others toward policies and habits where all parties can sustain mutually beneficial behavior. The system has to be made better.

The result of keeping these myths in play is that organizations will seek to take credit for talking about ethics while maintaining silence regarding endemic features that hold us back. They will blame a few rogue colleagues and organizations that have different ideals. In the end, very little will change. We will float at the whims of broader currents and continue to call for help, claiming the victim status. Some will propose "if only they would..." solutions, but few will go so far as to take action to remove the "if" in this formula or step into the role of "I" or "we" instead of "they." We are too often content with "they should have known better."

Most of us, most of the time, are ethically neutral—not so much unethical as a-ethical. Most of the time, our interests and those of others are the same or close enough not to cause concern. Where there are differences, the instinctive response is to use power—our momentary or informational advantage over others—rather than the ethics of engagement. Commenting on those we cannot change sometimes becomes a group spectator sport. Ethical heroes, those who stand up in public and show what they are willing to stand for, are admirable, but scarce. Ethical leaders, those who organize groups to work collaboratively to create conditions where many find it natural to act ethically, are also to be highly respected. They too are few in number. But their impact, through a multiplier effect and through engaging groups as well as individuals as moral agents, offers the best prospect for advancing ethics in dentistry. A profession that has a single and imperative message in a diverse environment runs the risk of speaking to a decreasing audience.

This chapter looks at the ethical challenges created by the fact that the dental environment is changing rapidly. Four challenges will be given consideration: (a) individualism; (b) commercialism; (c) fragmentation; and (d) technology.

## Speaking Ethics to Power

Ethics is about more than good and bad types of behavior. It is about relationships, especially relationships across multiple levels of complex systems. The most obvious of these relationships with ethical implications is that between the profession and the public it serves. There was a time when this could have been expressed as the relationship where one dentist with a small staff served a stable family of patients. The entire profession could be understood by multiplying this fundamental unit by the number of dentists in the country. The one-size-fits-all model of professionalism began to fade in the 1950s. Ethics by learning the playbook from that period has become an increasingly wobbly ideal.

A substantial part of the problem stems from the fact that society is changing around dentistry faster than the profession is responding to these changes. This creates dislocations in values and expectations. Throughout much of human history, life work was unchanged from generation to generation. For much of the twentieth century, a career was approximately the same length as one's lifespan. We simply moved up in a fixed progression and one organization was sufficient as our home base. Increasingly, we will need to reinvent ourselves several times across a professional career. And we will customize our reference standards from multiple sources.

This opens the door to plurality among ethical norms. There is uncertainty over how to manage relationships with others who see the world differently. And these ethical dislocations are pulling at the dental profession because some parts of the field are adapting to some social changes and others are reacting to different ones. Overall, the pace of adjustment is faster in some places than in others, and even reactionary in spots. A half-century ago, dentists could be pretty confident that any other dentist looked like him and expressed professionalism the same way. Now, even when dentists share the values of service, excellence of work, integrity, and continuous improvement, they may express them differently. All of them are still true professionals. But they do not show professionalism the same way. This is a new professionalism, but no one person or group gets to define it for everyone else.

This situation angers some dentists. It is understandable that it should. But anger is not an ethical principle. Building a strong profession that responds in a timely fashion to the community around it is an ethical ideal. Perhaps this is the ethical imperative of organized dentistry. Some believe, and see no reason why they are not justified in believing, that professional ethics consists of vigorously advocating the values they spent a lifetime honing. Others are thought obliged to follow their lead. An alternative view is that the profession is better served having a discussion among all its own members, especially those young enough to see the future effects of engaging in change. Some feel that it would be wise to engage all constituencies in creating mutually sustainable policy prior to announcing the group's consensus. It is a certainty that the traditional forces in dentistry will be unsuccessful in dictating their version of how others should behave toward their colleagues going into the future.

New forces, including some dentistry will struggle to control, are certain to come up. Whether they are threats or opportunities will depend on the conversations the profession has about them. These conversations will involve both those who are driving the changes and those who are affected by them (Habermas, 1993). Ethics is a relationship with others that neither party would wish were different made in full recognition that others affect us just as we affect them.

The integrity of dentistry is not vulnerable because it has developed some strange ethical disease that is eating the core of its membership. Human nature does not change that quickly. The problem is that the profession is embedded in a social complex that has its own notions about how things should be moving or remaining unmoved. Certainly we must control what we can for the good. But we must also work with others where control is not possible. There will be more of the latter in the future than there has been in the past. Former successes are not all assets in such a case. Speaking with one voice to others is a liability in a complex and evolving world, not always a strength. If we do not trust our colleagues, we need to go to breakfast with those who are different from us and get to know each other better.

## Individualism

Many choose a career in dentistry in order to be their own boss (Wanchek et al, 2018). This is especially true of the children of immigrants who seek to avoid dependence on others for job assignments and promotions. A hundred years ago, there were few barriers (economic or otherwise) to establishing oneself in the profession (trade). Gradually, state licensure entities developed minimal education and work sample demonstration requirements to obtain entrance into the market. But the profession has resisted other requirements, leaving the determination of whether things are going as they should to the discretion of the individual dentists and their patients. In the world of dentistry as individual practices, the dentist normally has the final say regarding what is appropriate. This is in contrast to physicians whose work more typically is seen by colleagues and who cooperate in care to a much greater extent. In the hospital setting, frequent handoffs in care require agreement on treatment protocols. Nurses, pharmacists, hygienists, social workers, occupational therapists, and others regularly work for or with colleagues.

The profession has ethical standards for its members. These are clear and appropriate. But they are based on a limited conception of what it means to be an ethical professional. There is one code for members of the American Dental Association, another for various specialties or researchers, one for students, and various others for different groups. If there were a single standard for what it meant to be a dentist, in ethical terms, there would be one code. The American Dental Association code applies to only two-thirds of practitioners, and that code is explicit in stating that its principles can be contradictory. Association members belong to other organizations that have their own codes. Thus, individual dentists are left to select from elements in the various available ethical standards.

On the other hand, organizations that propose codes make an assumption that a single ethical standard fits all. Uniform ethical standards presume that all dentists are good in the same way. That may be an ideal in the abstract. But codes often get into the details. There are large areas of commonality, but some of us are also good in special ways. And implementation is always an issue. Ethics necessarily involves sharing values and the effort of ensuring conformance. When this becomes expensive, that leaves exhortation.

This project found repeatedly that the major ethical issue in dentistry is dentists who fail to practice by the standards their colleagues would expect of them. Practitioners may generally endorse the existing picture of ethics, as long as there is sufficient latitude in interpreting the principles or freedom from others checking too closely. Dentists take advantage of the individuality of practice to carve for themselves considerable personal interpretation of the common standards espoused by the profession. Better principles, better taught, will have limited impact in improving the ethical tone of dentistry. Closer monitoring in offices, more regulations, and firmer sanctions are resisted, and probably they should be.

Current concerns over dental ethics are only minimally a consequence of declining adherence to codes. They result from the fact that trying to unify a profession on a single standard for isolated offices driven by a professional service motive that prevailed several decades ago is losing its influence as the universally proper model. The implicitly trusted professionals who put their hands on individuals to get them out of pain are giving way to a new sort, those who arrive after a prophy to see whether there is anything that is treatable. They look like the pictures on the office web page promising quite a bit that their predecessors would have felt embarrassed to imply. Dentistry is not only becoming a business, it is a big business, with porous boundaries that let in other interests and values. Values of individualism in a world that depends on multiple transactions seem to be like clothes of the wrong size.

Compounding the problem is the fact that the profession sees ethics as the collective behavior of individual dentists without recognizing that the profession as a whole, as a legal entity, has an ethical role distinct from the sum of the behavior of its members. The profession can take positions on opioids, care for special populations, or charity care. But these positions may be independent from the positions of many of its members. It can also advocate for monopoly status, freedom from regulations, reimbursement rates, and other causes that are not the consensus of its members' interests. These positions have ethical implications.

Dentistry needs to have a discussion with dentists about the role ethics is expected to play in both the conduct of individual practitioners and various organized groups within the profession. Too often, ethical standards have been set by the leaders of various groups reflecting their personal paths to previous success. The conversation we need would be larger and probably lengthy. Initially, substantial benefits would come from listening to one's colleagues.

Some issues include the following.

- What role do ethical norms play in the daily lives of dentists?
- What do dentists value and where have these values come from?
- What ethical issues do dentists talk about in public and which do they hide? What are they tempted to do when they see colleagues behave in ways they think are ethically questionable?
- Why do dentists who can name principles fail to recognize ethically challenging situations or fail to act on them?
- Can we build ethical codes beginning with what dentists and patients think the real problems are rather than from abstract philosophical theories (bottom up rather than top down)?

- Is there evidence that ethics in the dental office meets dentists' needs?
- What do individual practitioners need from professional organizations to make it easier to act ethically?
- Why do dentists behave differently in different organizational contexts?
- Can individuals make organizations more ethical? Can organizations make individuals more ethical?
- What is the best path forward for all concerned? What doubling down and what changes will result in the fewest attempts to resist or change the new model?
- Is there any way to monitor emerging practices to know whether further course corrections are necessary?

## Commercialism

People used to go to the dentist. Strange to say, increasingly people are going to the hygienist, or to a clinic, or even to the same office their parents went to, but now it sports a happier name, a large and rotating staff, and a newsletter, and it seems somehow more interested in smiles than health care. One survey (Chambers, 2010) placed the proportion of offices with fictitious business names at 44%, but just 60% of these were registered with the state dental board as required by the practice act.

The problem here is not the separation of the front and back offices or ownership of practices by nondentists. It is the separation of the patient from the dentist. Or at the least it is a growing trend to fragment care and deliver it piecemeal, either on customer demand or to get patients to come to the office for non-restorative procedures. Currently between 80% and 85% of office visits are asymptomatic (Vujicic, 2014). That would be something to be proud of if the caries burden in America had declined in a parallel fashion. It has not (Vujicic, 2016).

### Transactions Replacing Relationships

The relevant distinction here is between relationships and transactions. A patient of record is a relationship; a billable procedure is a transaction. A transaction is the mutually beneficial exchange of things valued as governed by a market. Transactions are one-off affairs. Each transaction is judged on its merits at the moment, with little thought to future transactions. (There is hot competition in American marketing generally to reverse this through customer loyalty campaigns. Ever notice how everyone wants your e-mail address as a required part of any economic exchange?) The focus of transactions is each party seeking to maximize his or her self-interest. The value of a practice that is built on transactions can be read in the Current Dental Terminology codes and the income statement. That is how practice sales are priced.

Relationships, like transactions, are built on exchanges. It is not the deal that matters, but one's sense of worth. The value proposition is slightly different. In a transaction, success is measured as the excess of reward to expense. In a relationship, success is measured in terms of whether the world one lives in tomorrow is more like the one we want to live in. Relationships tend to be positive and furnish the basis for personal growth. They are open. No one has ever heard of a role for a "closer" in relationships. They extend over time and across settings.

Of course, dentistry must be concerned at some basic level with the efficiency of transactions. To the extent that oral health care is seen as attending to a predominantly chronic set of conditions where continuity of comprehensive care and trust are important, the correct arrangement will be built on relationships. That said, there are advantages to dentistry as transactions. Patients need not commit to a professionally guided comprehensive program of self-care. They can seek care when necessary or visit the hygienist as a habit, much like going to the gym. They can also shop more effectively for price. Dentists who view their practices as bundles of transactions can more readily segment patient types and procedures to focus on those transactions with the largest margins and can delegate more effectively. A transaction approach erases distinctions between dentists based on skill and oral health impact, making dentists production units that can be hired out. When a practice is being considered for sale, volume of transactions usually nudges the price up and health of the patients usually nudges it down.

Transaction dentistry is not a result of corporate models. It is the necessary first step that makes them economically feasible. And transaction dentistry is not limited to organizations owned by investors who are not dentists. There are no reports of any private practice relationships where the associate is paid based on oral health outcomes of those patients assigned or where a hygienist is compensated exclusively or partially for reducing the number of patients the dentist has to provide reparative care to. There is no obvious reason why corporate dental care or dentists employing other professionals is unethical. It is the relationship with the patient, the repackaging of a person in need of oral health care as a bundle of potential transactions, that should be raising concerns.

The great strength of the profession has been the many dentists who cherish the practice model build on relationships and the quality of long-term oral health outcomes. But inadvertently some are sending a message to the public that contradicts this goal. The public is growing increasingly used to online ordering and instant shipping based on superficial web searches and limited-time offers. It is tempting for dentists to follow this trend. Often they end by filling their practices with "shoppers and bargain hunters." But competition is fierce. To even say so is an admission that economics is a more important criterion for success than is ethics.

## "Professionalization"

Dentistry is welcoming new partners into the practice. It is true that the group practice model has increased slightly over the past decade and will likely continue to do so (Vujicic, 2017). The professionalization at issue here, however, is the acceptance into the practice of web designers, business consultants, those running marketing schemes, and of course benefits providers. At the organizational level, this includes lawyers, public relations specialists, lobbyists, and contract work for many activities formerly done in-house. The days of a dentist focusing almost exclusively on personally delivering care are behind us. The organizations that represent the profession rely less and less on volunteer member participation.

Naturally there is an argument to be made in favor of efficiency and effectiveness gained by contracting with specialists. And even when this is cost-effective—perhaps especially when it is cost-effective—there is a danger. The ethics of a helping professional such as a dentist is not necessarily the ethics of other service providers. When a dentist or dental organization works with others, there is some accommodation to the value systems of the new partners. Eventually we accept the habits of those we associate with.

Every fall the Gallup organization surveys the public with this question: "Do you trust the members of this profession or line of work to have your best interests at heart?" The results are reported online as the proportion who answer "Very strongly agree" or "Agree." Dentistry has been surveyed about every three years for the past few decades. Figures 17.1 and 17.2 show the relative status and trends for several occupations.

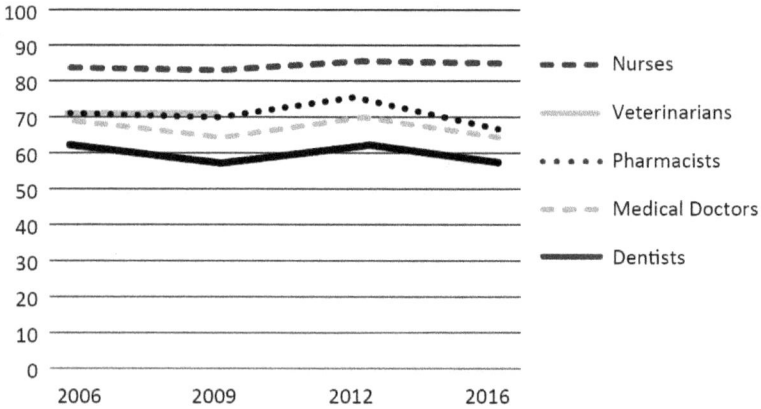

Figure 17.1. Gallup Survey of public trust in health professions.

Nurses
Veterinarians
Pharmacists
Medical Doctors
Dentists

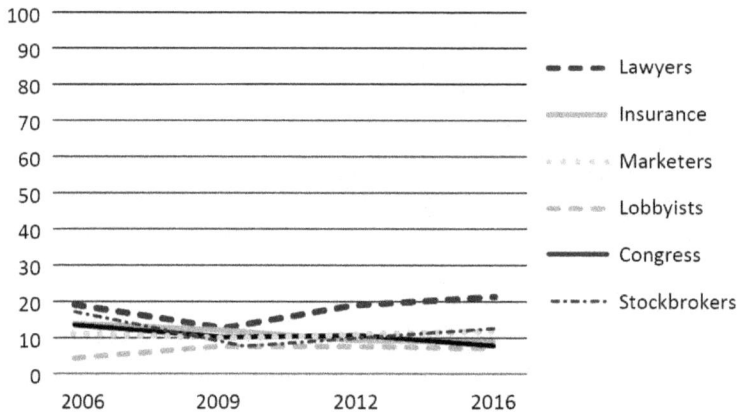

Figure 17.2. Gallup Survey of public trust in dental associates.

Lawyers
Insurance
Marketers
Lobbyists
Congress
Stockbrokers

In Figure 17.1, it shows that dentistry is the least trusted of the health professions surveyed. Forty percent of the public did not say they trusted dentists, and the proportion has tended to fluctuate. Among the least-trusted actors in Figure 17.2 are the usual suspects: lawyers, politicians, marketers, and lobbyists. These are exactly the types of people dentistry is increasingly turning to in order to promote its image. These are the "professions" dentists are paying to shape their values.

There is direct evidence that commercialism is bad for patients' oral health. As shown in Appendix C, dentists who have had their licenses disciplined because of practices such as overtreatment and patient abandonment are 2.6 times as likely to have multiple offices and 2.6 times as likely to practice behind a fictitious business name as are dentists without such board actions. This effect is age-related. Young practitioners are less likely to announce that they engage in transaction-based dentistry. Associates and contract dentists in corporations are more likely to be on a transaction quota system, although they do not announce themselves as such. Others do that for them as a form of moral shifting.

Dentistry needs to engage in conversation with some of its important constituencies over how commercialism will affect its future. It is unlikely that we will see a change in the level of competition in the profession or the public's toleration of superficial exchanges not guided by trusted advisors. Benefits carriers and government policy makers seem reluctant to accept more risk for long-term contractual commitment based on outcomes. This report takes a fundamental position that open conversations are needed now more than retreat behind historical positions or demands on others. The ethical obligation here is to engage with others to seek solutions.

Some issues that need discussion include the following.

- What are the consequences, and to whom, of various forms of commercialism (dental care based on transactions rather than relationships)?
- What are the forces that push toward or resist transaction-based oral health care, and what is the likely trajectory of these forces?
- What models exist or could likely be brought into existence that could address these needs, and could more than one model function side by side?
- Who would benefit from and who would be harmed by these models?
- What more does everyone need to know before making a good decision?
- What is the best path forward for all concerned? What doubling down and what changes will result in the fewest attempts to resist or change the new model?
- Is there any way to monitor emerging impacts to know whether further course corrections are necessary?

## Fragmentation

Dentistry is functioning in a world of increasing diversity, plurality of values, and information overload. This is causing compensatory selectivity of what matters and how it is pursued. Dentists were more similar to one another even a few decades ago. Some respond more quickly to an environment in flux than do others. A larger proportion of the population is choosing whether or not to go to the dentist at a particular time, rather than responding to needs that cannot be ignored. So today's dentists face more demands to position themselves as offering something special that other dentists do not provide. Just like all Americans, dentists have been told and seem to realize that they cannot do it all. And the message everywhere is "Try this new way of expressing your uniqueness." There is less worry about being different, partially because practitioners are looking more to various segments of the population to define who they are and less to their colleagues. With so many opportunities, there is less pressure to belong and more pressure to entertain multiple identities and to move from one to another after a year or so. The process is supported in society both by creating new "professions" such as real estate agents and acupuncturists and creating certifications and multiple leadership opportunities for traditional professions.

It is unlikely that this trend will reverse itself or even slow any time soon. Harvard sociologist Robert Putnam (2000) chronicled the nearly across-the-board decline in joining in his classic study *Bowling Alone*. The case of churches is illustrative of what is going on below the surface. Membership and participation in churches has declined, but only a small amount. It has mostly been a matter of redistribution. Establishment churches are being raided by churches of conscience. The former are those supported as national churches such as the Anglicans in England, the Lutherans in Sweden, and the Catholics in Spain, and the main-line denominations such as Presbyterians and Methodists in the United States. Evangelical denominations are doing well, as are liberation theology religious communities in South America and "church substitutes" such as Qigong, New Age spirituality, and wicca.

It is helpful to observe a distinction between participation, membership, and belonging. Individuals participate because they have an interest that matches an opportunity at this exact moment, and there is a very low barrier to entry. Participation is active, but often multiple, episodic, and short term. There is some evidence that Gen-Xers and millennials value participation (Myers & Sadaghiani, 2010). Membership, by contrast, is long-term and tends to be passive, except for an elite core who commit to moving through a multiyear leadership process. There is no necessary relationship between participation and membership. Belonging, the third way of relating to organizations, is a special form of membership. When one belongs to an organization, there are expectations about support for the organization and identification with its values. At a minimum, this usually involves paying dues and allowing the organization direct contact for internal marketing. Some members of organizations regard it as an ethical obligation for others to belong.

As shown in Figure 17.3, the trend in American Dental Association membership follows a pattern that would be predicted by knowing the context in which this organization functions in American society.

**Figure 17.3. Historical trend in American Dental Association membership.**

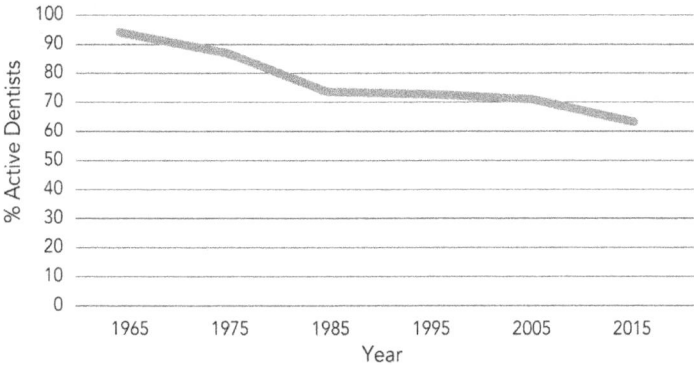

Although some professions, such as nursing and law, have not suffered declines, dentistry is losing about 1% of its membership each year (American Dental Association, various reports; Putnam, 2000). It is unknown whether dentists are shifting membership from the "established organization" to a variety of other "organizations of conscience" that serve more narrowly focused concerns or whether participation is falling at the same rate that membership is. What is known is that membership in organized dentistry is a function of age and type of practice (American Dental Association, 2016). Membership is highest among young dentists, among specialists, and among dental educators. We know for certain that these three groups belong to other groups, so the hypothesis of "membership fatigue" appears weak. The largest declines are among general practitioners with established practices.

The American Dental Association is aware of its declining membership. The current and recent strategic plans place increasing membership numbers as their highest value objectives. Various initiatives have been tried to stabilize membership. But these approaches have tended to focus on the relationship between individual dentists and the organization rather than various three-way relationships that include other societal changes. Especially absent is a robust discussion of dentists' relationships with other influential parties or the possibility that membership changes are a function of changes in the association itself.

## Dentists' Incomes

Another example of the fragmentation of the dental profession resulting from failure to participate in large social changes is diagrammed in Figure 17.4. This shows annual incomes and debt in inflation-adjusted dollars for the past 50 years. The solid line in the middle of the graph represents the average annual income of general practice dentists. This has risen smartly compared with the average household income of Americans over the same period (the gray line at the bottom of the graph). This means that, compared with the typical American, dentists would be able to buy two cars for the price of one or pay half-cost for pizzas compared with their parents who were dentists. General dentists are now in the top 2% to 3% of income earners. Although there were high fives when *U.S. News & World Report* announced in 2018 that dentistry was the #1 job in America, some were shocked to learn that dentistry is now a job and not a profession. Others were not.

---

**Figure 17.4. Economic trends in dentistry (in thousands of dollars adjusted for inflation).**

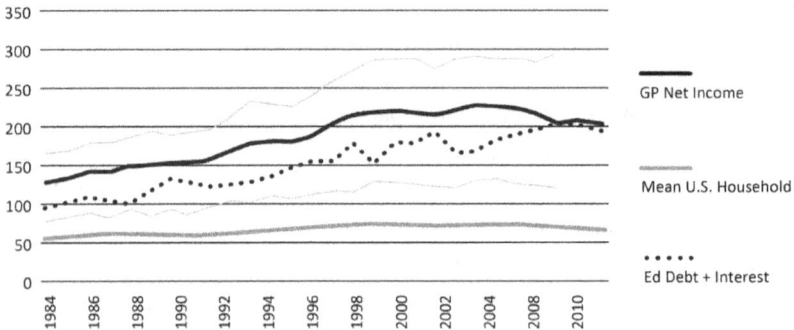

---

There are two dark spots in the income numbers in the graph. The thin lines surrounding the income curve represent standard deviation bands. It is clear that the spread in incomes is growing faster than income itself. This means that about one in seven dentists is earning five times as much as the typical American and the same proportion are earning a bit less than twice as much. About 15% of the profession is earning less in real dollars than it did five years ago. It is reasonable to expect that the practice world and what it represents for dentists is not the same across the profession. With this kind of diversity, it is difficult for the profession to speak with one voice.

The second troubling trend in these data concerns average income and educational debt. Beginning shortly before the recession in 2006, dentists' incomes hit a flat spot and have not recovered their former momentum. Although there are minor effects of dentists practicing more years and government insurance picking up the slack from private carriers, the major driver of stagnant incomes has been the very large and sudden increase in the number of dental school graduates. Between 1998 and 2005 the number of patients per dentist was 1,904; from 2005 to 2015 it dropped to 1,652 [www.ada.org/en/science-research/health-policy-institute/dental-statistics/workforce]. That is a 15% decrease in an almost step-wise fashion that can only be made up by increasing prices if dentists' incomes are to remain constant.

This is related to educational debt. From 1985 to 1996, the average total educational debt plus interest was approximately three-quarters of a typical dentist's annual income. This is shown in the line composed of dots above. The ratio changed about a decade ago, but not because of a bend in the cost of the educational debt curve. Debt is growing while earnings are stagnant. The length of time a recent graduate is in debt is what is changing. The reasons for this effect of debt on the health of the entire profession are explained in Chapter 15.

This is a complicated picture, but most systems such as oral health are. The message is that the profession cannot control important aspects of its future through unilateral action. The American Dental Association Foundation, to its great credit, launched a campaign a decade or more ago to head off this cycle of loans and pressure on private practice. The aim was to enlist the entire profession in stabilizing income disparities. This was not a success.

Dentistry needs to engage in conversation with some of its important constituencies over fragmentation. It appears less likely that organized dentistry will be able to exert complete influence over who participates, directly and indirectly, in the profession and how. Making a firm stand that the traditional relationships must remain unchanged while the practice context is changing may not work. There is also a real risk of missing opportunities for becoming a partner in emerging realities. In the less-connected world of former times, the professions could enlist the participation of all concerned members and send a unison message because there were nearly universal needs among members. Today, when dentists interact with complex worlds in complex ways, support for organized dentistry needs to be as complex and fast moving as its environment (Ashby, 1958). It needs to work with all or at least most of the partners that its members engage with. Participation may be the true goal rather than membership numbers.

Some issues that could be rethought include the following.

- What is the range and the natural pattern of practitioners' needs?
- Where are these needs being met, and what are the characteristics of the most popular resources?
- What are the needs that are not being met, and can organized dentistry do so effectively?
- What kinds of partnerships could organized dentistry engage in that assist all dentists beyond retaining current members or boosting non-dues income?
- Does organized dentistry have a role as partner, as catalyst?
- What is the best path forward for all concerned? What doubling down and what changes will result in the fewest attempts to resist or change the new model?
- Is there any way to monitor emerging impacts to know whether course corrections are necessary?

## Technology

The ethical elephant in the room is technology. Not technology *per se*, but how it will be managed and how it will change the profession. The analogy is not novel with this report. The psychologist-ethicist Jonathan Haidt (2012) used the metaphor of ethics as the rider whose job it is to steer the elephant of emotion he or she is riding. Without proper guidance, technology can take us someplace we would rather not be.

Technology often redistributes resources because it changes who participates and how (Chambers, 2019). Blacksmiths were not thrilled with automobiles. The railroads did not welcome air travel. Physicians in some states have been successful in passing legislation requiring that medical doctors be part of all telemedicine transactions. Coffee, the printing press, margarine, farm tractors, electrification, home refrigeration, and transgenic crops were all bitterly opposed, and often by less-than-honest public campaigns (Juma, 2016). Some technology change raises inherent ethical tension because it changes the balance of power (Jasanoff, 2016). When those who control existing technology offer its established clients more powerful or less expensive technology, everyone wins. When a new party enters with a novel technology that is better or more accessible, clients gain but there is resistance from the incumbent masters of technology. Sometimes the fighting gets dirty.

The received view is that technology is the handmaiden of the dentist. It has helped dentistry move from a trade to a profession precisely because the craft model was never abandoned, just augmented. The delivery of dental care is basically similar to what was done a century ago, except for the fact that dentists have better tools and know how to use them. Most of the dramatic increase in dentists' incomes in the 40 years prior to 2005 was due to higher fees and the use of more auxiliaries (Guay & Lazar, 2012). But much gain also came from better technology that permitted more high-fee procedures and less chair time. (Dentists actually work fewer hours per week than formerly.)

## Technology as Useful Stuff

The joke is that dentists love gadgets and have a garage full of old ones to prove it. Dentists advertise on the web often touting some of the technology they use, such as sleep dentistry, CAD-CAM, and cone beam computed tomography, for example. As mentioned in Chapter 12 and Appendix L, the foremost value for dentists, even above income, is technology. This is confirmed by floor space and hours at conventions and by a professional literature dominated in promotional literature extolling "faster, cheaper, and better" things. In the scientific literature randomized control trials and evidence-based dentistry studies make technology the independent variable (the purpose of the research).

But we may have reached a point where the model of dentists' control of technology is not the only one in play. First, technology is becoming expensive. A cone bean computed tomography unit is a significant investment. It will either eat into the dentist's income or require that more images be taken in order to pass the cost to patients. Dentists who have purchased CEREC units tend to make CEREC crowns, routinely. Dentists in small towns with low patient volume simply may not be able to justify such investments or may have to postpone them. The same can be said of practitioners nearing the ends of their careers who are cutting back on days worked. But dental offices with high capitalization will have an advantage.

That means large loans with consequent interest payments requiring higher volume. There is also pressure toward pooling resources. Multiple dentist offices and offices with investment capital in high-traffic communities, especially chains, can more easily justify the cost. Technology is changing who can practice dentistry, where it is practiced, and who receives dental care, as well as how it is practiced.

There is danger in partnering with those offering to extend our power through new technology. It allows a new voice and potentially foreign values into the profession. A web designer's thoughts about what is a professional claim for potential new patients may be quite different from a dentist's. An investment banker's notion of acceptable risk in launching a new clinic model will often deviate from prudent notions of what it means to service a community with health care. Those who develop the technology have an opportunity to influence how it is used, through licensing agreements and covenants in the sales contract. The greatest impact, however, is usually subtle. It can take the form of expectations for success by commercial standards rather than the standards of the profession. Of course, some dentists welcome this opportunity to broaden the range of values beyond those traditional in dentistry. Their colleagues and patients may not, and therein lies the ethical tension.

The effect of technology is even more profound. Although it is natural to talk of technology as things, gizmos, and stuff one can buy, that is an off-center use of the term. Technically, technology is how work is done—all aspects of how it is done, including training and skills, process flow, rules for performance and standards, supply of material (including availability of the "right kind of" patients), and sometimes new equipment (Satell, 2017). Operating microscopes would be poor technology in an orthodontist's office; CAD-CAM is dubious in a pediatric dental practice. In the 1970s, computers as word processors failed to make substantial improvements in typing pools. It was not until the workflow and personnel involved changed, essentially eliminating the typing pool, that digital text work revolutionized communication.

Technology usually changes how things are done and often who does them and where. It is becoming increasingly clear that technology does more than allow dentists to do what they always did at a higher level, more quickly, and with more predictable outcomes. It also changes what is done. It allows staff to do new procedures better as well, resulting in increased profit and sometimes in preferences for different treatment plans. Ultrasonic cleaning technology for hygienists is a humble example.

But technology may move some aspects of dentistry out of the dentist's office entirely. Imaging centers come to mind. "Invisible" orthodontic aligners are another. The firms that manufacture these devices do not really sell them to dentists so much as use dentists as part of their distribution chain for the firm's products and services. Any technology that is leased has some elements of this model of shared control between the creator and those interfacing with the end client. There is now technology for the cell phone that permits orthodontic patients to send images to the dentist, just as dentists send images to radiologists. Teledentistry appears to be a technically viable emerging technology that will certainly alter the location, type of care, and personnel delivering it. The Dental Board of North Carolina unsuccessfully sought to block nondentists from taking tooth whitening technology directly to the patient (Parker, 2015).

### Disruptive Technology

When the "stuff" of technology changes the delivery path, this is usually referred to as disruptive technology. That means something much more specific than innovations that shake up the market. Clayton Christensen (1997; 2003), who popularized the idea, had something particular in mind. In the first part of the twentieth century Austrian economist Joseph Schumpeter (1934/1983) noted that as markets mature they drive out profit. The first pocket calculators were priced at more than $100. The profit in that business was obvious and attracted firms that were happy to sell the same device for $50 because there was still some profit there. As new suppliers were drawn in by the remaining profits, better manufacturing processes and larger markets drove the cost even lower. Now instead of bragging that one owns a Texas Instruments calculator, your real estate agent gives them away, made by "somebody somewhere" as promotionals with a business card on the back.

There are two ways to protect against the inevitability of profit erosion. The obvious move is regulation. All the health professions see this as the first and most effective line of defense. The other approach is called "feature creep," and this is the standard in the free-market economy. New features are continually added to the base model and the price stays up. Customers may have no need for the new features, but the "new and improved" model replaces the old one. Most people use only a fraction of the capability of their electronic devices. But the provider continues to innovate in order to maintain the profit margin. In dentistry, we see new products coming on the market before long-term research can prove that the old one was effective. Sometimes the "improvement" is too vague to evaluate. Dentists do this to patients as well, insisting that all patients either have the best or nothing.

But eventually another firm will find its way into the market with a basic model that satisfies the essential requirements of a large enough market segment that is sensitive to price. This is the true meaning of disruptive technology. It is changes in the rules of the market. It only works, however, where there is unmet need caused by high prices. That certainly is the condition that is emerging in oral health care today. The fights in the profession for the next few decades will be over whether the public will continue to allow monopoly status to professions to protect them from disruption in their markets. That is an ethical issue.

## Scalability

Another feature of technology that is just becoming apparent is scalability. Dentists have traditionally done custom work. One of the characteristics of better dentists was that they could perform procedures that more closely matched each patient's unique needs than could others, given the equipment and materials commonly available. When the physical technology was limited by what solo dentists could purchase on a credit card and deploy in their office, the true "technological impact" was the skill and professional standards of each practitioner. That has been the traditional view of dentistry and the ground for its ethical foundation for many decades.

Scalable, as a technical term, means that the unit cost of doing a procedure decreases to the point where it is profitable to obtain and deploy the technology. A digital imaging system for taking impressions would be prohibitively expensive if used only a few times per week. When the cost can be amortized over many patients it will drive down the cost of dental care to patients or increase the profits to dentists. Who benefits from scalability is clearly an ethical question of some significance.

Currently there is a ceiling on the impact of technology in dentistry. It has traditionally been limited to what can be managed by a single dentist with limited capital, serving a small number of patients seeking customized care. (See Chapter 4.) Standardization shifts the metric for "good quality" away from private standards based on "the procedures I use" to aggregate oral health outcomes. It is a change of emphasis from procedures to outcomes. Scalability changes the way we judge what is good. It allows more individuals to have a say in what is desirable. It means that others besides those who do the work will have a voice in whether care has been well provided. That is an ethical challenge in determining both what is good and who gets to participate in that discussion. The past few decades have seen dentists, researchers, and groups that promote consensus policy focus on standardizing the "what" part of this question. Less attention has been paid to the "to what effect" and "from whose perspective" parts of the question.

Another ethical issue to work through in scalability is the trade-off between individual versus public benefit. There is merit in the argument that all dentistry is custom work to the highest standard achievable. But scalability requires standardization. There are alternative dimensions on which to ground the standardization. An obvious one is minimal acceptable care that a sufficient number of patients will purchase. Another is minimal scale that justifies innovation favored by innovative practitioners. Yet another is maximizing aggregate oral health outcomes taken across all individuals who have a need for oral health care. Each of these standards would lead to a different dental profession. The voice of dentistry should probably have a place at the table in deciding which future is better. Absent such policy input, the choice will be left to outside, commercial interests and perhaps a few dentists motivated by entrepreneurial spirit. Dominant practice forms will put pressure on all dental offices, depending on how closely they are able to follow technological innovation. Typically this pressure is negative for late adaptors (Rogers, 1995). So all of dentistry is affected by the rate of technological change, regardless of interest in participating.

Technology will create multiple delivery channels, and the issue will increasingly draw public debate over whether oral health care can remain a monopoly for professionals. That is an ethical issue the profession cannot avoid. But it may not be one the profession will have exclusive control over. The point should not be overlooked that crowns and television sets are not the same. One is often regarded as a fundamental human need and the other is seen as an enhancement. Western liberal thought has generally taken the position that the provision of fundamental human needs can and perhaps should be protected by monopoly status. But some in the public are confused by the profession's recent campaigns that dentistry is more than basic health. Can both parts of the market be protected by monopoly status? Some in the public hear clearly that oral health is a fundamental right and the monopoly should go to the government. This report takes no position on these issues...other than to affirm that these are ethical issues and that dentistry is vulnerable to the extent that they are ignored.

## Technology Redefining What It Means to Be a Professional

William Sullivan, formerly of the Carnegie Foundation for the Advancement of Teaching, has argued that the greatest threat currently facing all professions—from the clergy to medicine—is technology (Sullivan, 2018). His argument goes something like this: Professionals increasingly define their special place in society in terms of their control of technology. This has spawned the emergence of new professionals and pseudoprofessions. The status of professions in the market is protected by certification, regulation, and special access to delivery systems such as hospitals that grant privileged use of advanced and expensive technology. Increasingly both the old and the new professions define themselves in terms of the equipment they use rather than the benefit they provide others. To open a market or protect an existing one, it is now necessary to control access to its technology. In the end, this will lead to the erosion of the traditional professions as others will gain key technology and use it in ways that were not intended, but ways that the public may welcome. When professions define themselves by their technology, anyone who gains access to less expensive or more convenient substitute technology will undermine a profession.

Dentistry needs to engage in conversations with some of its important constituencies over how oral health care is provided in the future. Changes are beginning to occur that are challenging what it means to be a dentist and even what it means to be a patient. It seems unrealistic that the profession would pull up the technology drawbridge and defend the moat. Others will simply move around any position fortified in this fashion. The masters of technology are powerful and have already established working relationships with the public. They know folks in the legislature. It is time to talk as partners with a common interest.

Some issues that could be on the table are the following.

- Are there other criteria, in addition to profit, for what technology should be developed or funded during development?
- What is the best delivery system, including patient contact, personnel, and delivery process, for each type of technology?
- Who bears the investment cost, risk, and rewards of technology?
- Is there a necessary role for third parties in technology deployment?
- How do we measure the impact of technology?
- Are there standards for the effectiveness and safety of various technologies, and can any system that meets these be accepted?
- What is the best path forward for all concerned and what doubling

down and what changes will result in the fewest attempts to resist or change the new model?

- Is there any way to monitor emerging impacts to know whether course corrections are necessary?

## Summary

Each of the threats mentioned in this chapter—individualism, commercialism, fragmentation, and technology—presents dentistry with a common ethical challenge. Essentially, the problem of dental ethics is no longer entirely internal to the profession. And it will not be solved with ethical principles, short-term ethics seminars or online activities, by editorials, or by disciplining a tiny fraction of the profession. The challenge is to renegotiate the relationship between the profession and the society that is changing quickly around it. This is not an ethical issue that the profession can handle on its own. Nor is it reasonable to expect that this can be left to individual dentists to manage if they would just "do the right thing."

# Chapter 18

# A New Professionalism

The question raised in this report has never been "What is wrong with dentistry?" The focus is "What are the current best opportunities to extend the dramatic century-long evaluation of the profession?" Dentistry has thrived by adapting to a changing world. The materials and techniques dentists command today would astound colleagues at the turn of the twentieth century. The range of conditions that can be prevented and treated is much larger. The results are more predictable. The oral health of the population is clearly better, although perhaps not evenly so. The public image of a dentist has gone from the carnival tooth puller, to the inflictor of pain to relieve pain, to the trusted family healthcare doctor, and sometimes to one provider of personal services among many in an increasingly commercial world.

Continued evolution of the profession is not an option. The problems facing us include: (a) identifying only those changes that are ethical; (b) making changes consistent with society as a whole to avoid becoming out of date; (c) working in collaboration with key partners; (d) responding at the quicker pace and interconnectivity now governing society; (e) being smart about what change is possible and avoiding the illusion of change; and most importantly, (f) updating dental professionalism. The foundation of this report is that a strong ethical core is the surest guide to dentistry's building a new professionalism for the immediate future. There is no alternative but to unite the maximum number of dentists in a common mission to enhance the oral health of the public. This must take a form the public will embrace. And it must be done in partnership with the dental support industry, reimbursement carriers, the government, regulators, those selling services to dentists, and policy people. But this new conversation must never be engaged in only on political, economic, propaganda, and power terms. The unique strength dentistry brings to the table is its ethical foundation.

New times call for a new sense of professionalism. The one unifying theme—the common thread that ensures identity and influence in the world—is ethics.

This report was not designed to provide rules dentists should follow or to tell those who interact with the profession what they should do. The intent has been to explore what it means to be an ethical profession. We have looked at how people act ethically, what ethical opportunities are closest at hand, and how we might establish a stable ethical equilibrium in a changing world. No one has said that good ethics is mastering theory or demanding change of others. The difficult work of bringing out the ethical potential in dentistry is before us.

This chapter looks back at what has been found regarding how ethics actually works in a professional context. Some of the multiple available approaches to raising the standards are discussed as examples.

## Do We Really Need to Do Anything About Ethics?

This report has been about the need for renewed professionalism, the unique relationship dentists have with patients and colleagues, and the way organizations and companies acting as moral agents interact with their constituencies. There is growing concern that dentists and dentistry consider their relationships with others in ways that leave out ethics altogether. There is a big market these days for ethics substitutes.

One last research study to clarify this point. Uri Gneezy and Aldo Rustichini (2000) explored the thinking of parents who used a daycare center in Haifa, Israel. The problem was that parents were often late in picking up their children. In an effort to promote more responsible behavior, a fine was imposed, gradually increasing as the pickups became tardier. To everyone's surprise, the result was that parents picked up their children even later. Parents felt they were purchasing additional daycare. They had traded money for responsibility. This is an example of moral bleaching (see Chapter 14).

A moral obligation owed others was transformed to an economic concern and then bought off by those who could afford it. The great concern in oral health is that dentists will see ethics issues of professional responsibility in terms of power, money, lobbying, or political influence. Ethics will become invisible. It will be relegated to an academic exercise or something to complain about in others.

The evidence paints a picture of dentistry as a profession in need of renewal. It is drifting away from its historical grounding as a calling of highly skilled service that is also rewarding in so many ways to practitioners. Increasingly, there are signs that commercial success is an ascendant value. Ethics is often something we now talk about, as in something that needs to be paid attention to. Too many practitioners are seen orienting toward income and technical prowess, overtreatment, fragmented care, and isolated practice. Dentists have an arm's-length relationship with each other, and the center is losing its former cohesion. That is a view shared by dentists, patients, and leaders in the profession. It is also a shift commercial interests are pleased to see. Practitioners are becoming a marketing opportunity for outsiders. Dentistry may be a top "job," but it is losing stature as a profession.

Many new voices are calling for dentists' attention. Dentists are expected to be independent leaders of a small team with little daily contact with colleagues. Some even in the profession regard dentists as employees, valued for their productivity potential. They are licensed by state boards using trade standards, and some abusers of the system vigorously defend these minimums and occasionally even less. At the same time, the profession collectively speaks of high standards. It would be a tragedy if that balance tips any farther in the commercial direction.

Other interests, such as "success" consultants, are intruding new "values" into dentistry. The traditional model of a professional service firm providing customized service directly to a small family of patients is being challenged by other systems. Many of these are based on transactions rather than relationships. The fundamental unit of dentistry (the dentist-patient relationship) is being rethought—or being undermined without thought. This sometimes aggressive, redefining force is predominantly outside the profession and should not be let in. Commercialism, legal maneuvering, money, and prestige are ethics substitutes. They work, and may even be necessary, in some sense. But absent ethics, they are dangerous.

The chapters on bad acting made the case that dentists are much like everyone else. Disappointing ethical conduct is not limited to a small number of individuals who have character flaws. Neither can these bad actors be spotted early and talked out of their unprofessional habits. For the most part, we know this already and those who have chosen to cozy up to the line or occasionally step over it are unlikely to be influenced much by their good colleagues wringing their hands. Financial gain and technical prowess are widely seen as opportunities by dentists. If we can see, even a little, that ethics is also an opportunity and not merely an obligation, many will benefit. We can prime this by publicly expecting it of ourselves and of our colleagues. Viewing others as bad by nature and ourselves as good in all circumstances will freeze the most valuable asset for renewal (the best dentists) in inaction.

The four levels of ethics—judgment, justification, engagement, and leadership—are all in play as the profession determines how it will raise its ethical tone. But there is a hierarchy here. As we move from blaming others to creating systems to enhance ethics across the profession, the likelihood of making a positive difference increases. Naturally the personal costs go up as we become more engaged. It is unlikely that ethics can be had on the cheap. But evidence from other areas where it has worked shows that it is worth the investment. For many, a question remains whether this is an important enough project to justify collective and coordinated effort. If ethics is seen as an opportunity, the findings of this report will be a rich field for raising dentistry to the stature it has historically merited. If viewed as an obligation, this will come as unpleasant news, often ignored or denied.

Focus on the technical aspects of dentistry and financial success are dominant values, perhaps more so than in previous years. Dentists consult themselves and their beliefs about how colleagues might act. They are less apt to consult professional codes (indeed, they are somewhat sketchy on what is in such codes) and are least likely to consult an ethicist or other expert who might have independent opinions. Dentists are caring people who favor justice. But these values are not as strong as they are in the general public, and other values such as authority, loyalty, avoiding the undeserving, and independence are strong among practitioners. Dentists tend to think of themselves as having more positive personal values than do their colleagues. Established dentists in particular are not especially accurate in their views of younger colleagues. That may not be the right place to start.

Dentists, as do all humans, behave somewhat differently in groups than independently. Organizations provide identity and serve as collective "bankers" for ethics and the public trust. Historically, organized dentistry has been a commanding voice for the common professionalism the public expects. Organizations can also engage as moral agents with other groups in their own right. But organizations are prone to some special ethical "diseases" such as moral hazard, free riding, shifting, decoupling, and bleaching. A special danger that groups sometimes allow is setting rules that force members and others to choose between being ethical and working against their own interests—moral distress.

It would be unrealistic to expect that dental schools will substantially redirect the ethical growth of professionals. The average curriculum is less than a single average work week of a practicing dentist. By contrast, the moral climate created by the practicing community is pervasive and powerful. Its effects for good or otherwise have just not been studied. Dentists can be fairly said to learn ethics from what they see their senior colleagues do and what passes as acceptable. Sometimes what is not commented on is taken as ethical guidance.

Generally the challenges the profession faces do not come from an erosion in the core of the profession. Instead they are the result of the profession not responding quickly enough to changes in its environment. Or perhaps more accurately, some in the profession are moving more quickly in various directions than are others, and there is increasing division on what is the best response. That is pulling the profession apart and signals a strong need for discussion. Individualism, commercialism, fragmentation, and uneven adoption of technology are challenges that only the profession, acting as a whole, can address. In a 1999 National Public Radio interview, cyberfuturist William Gibson said, "The future is already here—it's just not very evenly distributed."

Ethics is not (just) a short course, a code, or a policy. Neither is it something we are born with (or without). Ethics is fundamentally a collective habit and a culture. This chapter will mention a few conversations we might want to have about ethics in dentistry.

## Ethics As Relationship

Relationships that depend on economic pressure, regulations, and power are expensive, come unraveled over time, and are resented. They signal that ethics has failed, or perhaps that there has not even been an attempt to be ethical.

Ethics is more about our relationships with others than what we say about these relationships. None of us, individually, professionally, or as parts of any other community, has complete control over our lives. It is well enough understood that economic exchanges are give and take, are often competitive, but often under the best of circumstances may be Win-Win. The same is true for social relationships such as marriage, community involvement, and professional relationships. Politics, at least until recently, has been understood as negotiating over what is needed by all in order to remain part of the group and being willing to go along. But this is not how all people view ethics. Too often it is seen as a matter of one person or group deciding how things should be and letting others know how they should behave. To negotiate over ethics seems somehow self-contradictory to them. "What's right is right—and all that remains to be considered is whose definition will we use and how we can get others to toe the line." There is not a human alive who has not felt or said at least a few times "the matter is self-evident." That is a quick exit from potential relationships. In Chinese culture it is tantamount to conceding the argument.

The alternative perspective explored in this report is that everyone is entitled to his or her understanding of what is ethical, at least as a starting point. But we are interconnected. The importance of private values depends on how others will respond to them. This is a symmetrical and mutually influential relationship. To ignore what matters morally to others will ultimately limit how ethical we can be. Think, for example, of conversations with patients about what should be done for their oral health. This is a champion ethical question. Turning away a patient who cannot afford "the best" because that is what you place highest value on seems less than fully satisfying. Doing substandard work that will have to be redone also seems wrong. *Pro bono* is sometimes an option, but is suicidal if over-practiced. Talking patients into the kind of care you feel good about with technical argot, half explanations, and a bit of fear, and in the process making them feel they have been "sold," is ethical compromise.

It makes sense to think through such situations in advance and have repertoires of skill habits regarding which approaches fit. There is no way to know in advance what is ethically ideal in every particular case. Fortunately, human nature allows for trying alternatives and making adjustments if sufficient trust exists. The same is true with respect to which communities need a dentist, which new techniques should be used, the right mix of reimbursement mechanisms, overlapping scope of practice with medicine, types and duties of auxiliary, and so on down a long list. The range of issues to be negotiated between dentists and others is almost limitless. Regardless of the role of power in these negotiations, ethics establishes the ground rules for how these exchanges should be conducted. It is ethical to talk about money. It is not ethical to use money to squelch or distort or hide honest ethical talk.

To refuse to negotiate, including over ethical values, may have the appeal of principled martyrdom. Even when one stands firm on ethical ground, there is a danger of being run over for other reasons. To abandon or, more typically, to pay loose attention to ethics is equally irresponsible. It is unfair to oneself and one's colleagues, and it is confusing to others.

Negotiating on political grounds has rules. For example, there are standards for who gets to decide matters and some have voice and some less voice. There are rules in economics as well. No bait and switch, enforcement of contracts, and issues with fraud and violating licensure agreements are examples. Ethics is no different. Regardless of the subject over which one is reflecting, the following rules can be used to identify who is trying to be ethical.

- Each party is regarded as a free agent with the capacity to affect the future of other agents (mutual agency rule).
- There is always a mutual pair of actions that both parties have no reasons to deviate from. Find it (best solution rule).
- Mutually agreed best solutions require no external enforcement (self-enforcement rule).
- Failure to inform others of all one's relevant motives or to learn from others their relevant motives creates bogus ethical understanding (full communication rule).
- When circumstances change, it may be necessary to renegotiate the ethical agreement (current circumstances rule).
- Others besides the contracting ethical parties, such as colleagues or society at large, may have a legitimate stake in our ethical practice (all affected count rule).

In Chapter 1, evidence was presented that patients, dentists, and leaders in the profession are worried about overtreatment, dentists acting independent of common values, and the need for leadership in the profession. If we apply the view of ethics in the preceding paragraph we come to the following conclusions.

- Overtreatment is unethical—period.
- Practicing independently of one's colleagues undermines the ethics of the profession because it allows questionable behavior by some.
- Leadership in discussing ways to address these problems would strengthen the profession.

Think again about the central ethical relationship in oral health: the treatment alliance between a dentist and patient. Patients can affect dentists, for example, by attending or not, in their choice of treatment plans, through noncompliance with therapeutic suggestions, or spreading positive or negative opinions. Some treatment options are better than others for the dentist, some are preferred by the patient. The optimal treatment is the one neither dentist nor patient would want to change, given the circumstances. The mutually best treatment stands on its own merits. It does not require external inspection or outside enforcement. If the dentist deceives the patient, through incomplete informed consent for example, the relationship may unravel. If the patient deceives the dentist, by not disclosing pertinent health history or weaseling on payment, the relationship may also fail. Perhaps the patient cannot maintain his or her treatment or a reconstruction case grows in unanticipated ways. The ethical arrangement must be renegotiated. That is not because someone was unethical, but because the relevant circumstances have changed. Others care about what dentists and patients decide. Bad acting damages the reputation of all members of the profession (that should be part of the code). Benefits carriers have opinions about which care has been purchased on behalf of various patients. The state will revoke a dental license when work is performed by unauthorized personnel, regardless of the success of the treatment or the patient's satisfaction with the outcome. This is the definition of ethical treatment developed in this report.

The same standards for ethical conduct apply to organizations. States establish Medicaid reimbursement levels and eligibility criteria, including those for dentistry. It matters to the disadvantaged, to taxpayers, and to dentists where these levels are set. This affects their behavior and what these groups do matters to others (mutual agency). Obviously the conditions prohibit there being an optimal situation—everyone cannot have everything desired. But there is always a best solution, a compromise that both parties would accept as better than the alternatives. Forcing others into an untenable position or bargaining in bad faith may appear attractive in the short run, but will come undone at the first good opportunity. The best solution should be self-policing. Satisfied patients will be welcomed in a practice because that is a Win-Win. Because they work, honest relationships between dentists and benefits providers or dentists and staff need no recourse to law enforcement or monitoring by government bodies.

Where there is a lot of talk or complaining about monitoring, reporting, and enforcement, this signals trouble in the ethics department. As the budget for lawyers and lobbyists goes up, the ethical tone of the profession declines proportionally. When one wonders where all the regulation in America is coming from, the answer is obvious: We are going for political and economic solutions to problems that could be better addressed by ethics. The simple rule is: More ethics, less regulation.

Positive solutions that come apart are usually a result of each party mistaking the other's motives. There are two explanations for mishandled ethical issues. Sometimes the fault is in not listening or not wanting to hear what the other is saying. Sometimes this is caused by deception or lack of transparency. Regardless of the reason, failure to establish full communication will have both parties back at the table soon enough or grousing to sympathetic ears or, most commonly, resorting to political or economic campaigns rather than ethical ones.

The most pernicious abuse of ethical rules is when groups claim to be speaking on behalf of the interests of others. Each concerned agent speaks for itself. That is how it is supposed to be. Agents should not claim to be speaking for the good of others. Being honest about one's own interests is difficult enough. It is also the most stable foundation for moral engagement (Reay et al, 2017).

Dentistry, like most professions, has historically embraced the content approach to ethics. The focus is on getting the right results, at least those thought best from one's point of view. This is often a two-step process. The ethics of justification is used to figure out a solution. Then power and other ethics substitutes are used to get others to go along with the solution. There is motive here: Content approaches drive searches for justification, they lead to bold claims and undercut transparency, and they turn others into obstacles rather than potential partners. This approach comes more naturally to individuals or organizations that believe they have the power to back themselves up or who are in fear of losing the power they once enjoyed.

The alternative is to emphasize process. Commit first to the ethical method. The results will follow. This does not mean we assume or make it a prerequisite that others are ethical. It means that it is unethical on our part to ignore their nature as agents capable of ethical action. The view promoted here is that when moral agents honestly engage with each other, the agreement will be fair and self-sustaining.

## A New Ethics for Dentists and Dental Organizations

The Carnegie Foundation for the Advancement of Teaching has conducted a hundred years of in-depth studies documenting and in some cases influencing the professions in changing social circumstances (Benner et al, 2010; Cooke et al, 2010; Foster et al, 2006; Sheppard et al, 2008; Sullivan et al, 2007). Bulletin Number 9, the *Flexner Report* of 1909, challenged the for-profit model of teaching medicine. Medical education was controlled by entrepreneurial tradesmen who clubbed together to use the apprenticeship model in what was called proprietary professional education. Lecturing was featured because it was cheaper than lab training or clinical supervision. When, in the late nineteenth century, licensing boards were calling for two years instead of the then-standard one, some medical and dental schools just repeated the one-year lecture series on the grounds that students could use a refresher. Clinical faculty were usually compensated by having patients pay the faculty members directly, and students often took their clinical training in the faculty member's private practice. Flexner suggested to the profession that cheap education was flooding the market with underqualified individuals. The profession agreed and raised the standards, cutting the number of physicians dramatically.

The *Gies Report* of 1926, Bulletin Number 19, was also well received by the profession. It advanced the concept that dentistry should be a distinct profession from medicine. But in order to ensure its status, dental education should prioritize prevention and take place in research-intensive universities to guarantee a scientific base. Generally the profession and the forward-thinking schools could get behind that change. Health care was beginning to move from the palliative to the restorative model and greater levels of training and access to better technology were a recognized need. Prevention has received uneven emphasis at various points in the past century.

The *Reed Reports* on law, in 1922 and 1928, were not as successful. Reed argued for night and weekend programs to supplement the traditional full-time elite programs. There was a growing need for lawyers, particularly those representing individual clients rather than large corporations. Reed's timing was off. In the 1920s America was anti-immigrant and the professions recognized that "some of the wrong sorts of folks" would be able to take advantage of this more accessible education and thus provide services to a broader range of Americans. The kinds of reform Reed envisioned did not begin to emerge until the 1960s. We can see in the Reed reform the interplay between the values of a profession and the values of society. It is necessary to coordinate the timing of professional and societal change.

Another example of synchrony between professional and societal evolution concerns the relationship between dentistry and commercial influences. As dentistry was emerging from its status as a trade about the time of the founding of the American College of Dentists in 1920, the public voice for scientific practice was industry, what was then called "supply houses." The dominant journal, *Dental Cosmos*, was published by S.S. White and was very widely read and highly respected. The American College of

Dentists, led by William Gies, studied this situation in the early 1930s and issued a report, *The Status of Dental Journalism in the United States: Report of the Commission on Journalism of the American College of Dentists 1928-1931* (1932). This led to among other things the virtual extinction of proprietary dental journalism, the creation of the American Association of Dental Editors, and barring of trade representatives from schools and dental conventions. [See entire issue of the *Journal of the American College of Dentists* 2017 (4).] Dentistry's assuming nearly complete control over commercial access to practitioners may have played a role in moving dentistry away from being a trade toward being a profession. The trend has almost completely reversed itself now, however.

At the beginning of this century the Carnegie Foundation commissioned a series of five studies, one each in medicine, nursing, engineering, law, and the clergy. The book-length reports from panels of experts who visited many schools were quite similar to each other. They found that training in the mechanics of the professions (its technology) was excellent and not in danger of falling behind emerging trends. They found that students were troubled by an apparent lack of opportunity to learn the actual practice of the profession. For the most part, this was left to the established professions or others to socialize new members into the profession. Apprenticeships are reemerging, sometimes with a clear motive of using beginning professionals to respond to the burden of service to segments of society their established seniors prefer not to treat. Increasingly, beginning professionals are expected to work for or buy the practices of older colleagues.

What the Carnegie studies discovered was missing, and largely unnoticed, was a sense of ethics. The reports are unanimous that across the professions, there is insufficient attention paid to what the researchers termed "professional identity formation." Professionals first function as students, then as apprentices. In both cases they do not participate as equal partners in discussions of professional standards and practices. They get to try out what their seniors have determined worked best previously. But guidance among professional colleagues is less common. This retards the growth of the profession.

## How the Dental Profession Fits Society Today and Tomorrow

Dentistry, as a profession, has changed dramatically in the past 100 years. When it was a trade, the professionalism that was most in need meant establishing common standards so the public could distinguish between quality practitioners and those entrepreneurs who traded on the good name of those following higher standards. The early versions of the American Dental Association Code of Ethics strongly emphasized collegiality and upholding the integrity and image of the profession. Perhaps unwittingly, the current Code of Professional Conduct stresses what individual dentists are entitled to do on their own. It could be read as defining what is permissible.

The early efforts of the American College of Dentists were directed toward promoting graduate dental education and common standards for licensure and education. We no longer pay as much attention to these dimensions of professionalism because of the tremendous progress that has been made. In the mid-twentieth century, professionalism in dentistry meant membership in the organized profession so dentistry could speak with a united voice on behalf of independent journalism, economic security, lobbying for protective regulations and defense against insurance and medicine, and better research and technology. These were the foci of the college during those years. Membership and participation in organized dentistry were nearly universal.

The identity and the common strength of the profession have now been ensured. The emerging challenge of professionalism is to establish the place of dentistry in health care and society generally.

## What Does Society Need from Dentistry?

- America is struggling with issues of distribution of resources, particularly a growing gap between the well-off and the 20% living below the poverty line. That is not a problem that dentistry created, but society cares about what dentistry intends to do about it.
- America is struggling with multiculturalism. The clashes between "I can do whatever I want" and "You have to behave the way we do around here" are real and damaging. They exist within dentistry and between dentistry and the rest of the country.
- America is struggling with the rules of engagement. We are turning increasingly to regulations, litigation, and mega-funding in an effort to tilt the playing field to our advantage. The two-party relationship between the dentist and the patient is being replaced by a three-party relationship involving external arbiters of care. This has led in a few cases to a "faux professionalism" where dentists are speaking through lawyers, lobbyists, and other specialists who are not dentists.
- America is struggling to manage a new commercialism. Markets

have become amazingly complex. The former model of a long-term relationship where irregularities were worked out personally has given way to the multiparty chain of transactions. New "professions" are trying to make a living in the gaps previously worked out informally. Insurance is the obvious example where the two-party relationship between a dentist and a patient now often involves five players: plan purchasers (companies and labor groups), benefits carriers, and the government, in addition to the dentist and the patient.

- America is struggling as more interests try to ride each exchange. The value in many contemporary dental offices cannot be understood today without taking into account industry (especially bundled services on contracts and large capital technology such as cone beam computed tomography), consultants and continuing education experts on the convention circuit, back-office dental services organizations, and web designers. These "new partners" in dental practice have easier access now because of digital technology and business-to-business relationships forming outside of dentistry. So-called corporate dentistry is just one manifestation of these trends. It is in the early and uncertain stages of development, but common features seem to include: (a) capital formation that permits market fragmentation; (b) lawyering and mass marketing; (c) provider-level segmentation; and (d) economies of scale on supplies, equipment, and marketing.

- America is struggling to control a technology feeding frenzy. Things are doing the work that people once did. That changes how people relate to each other, and as new things arrive at an ever-increasing pace, relationships change more quickly. Our sense of time and who we are is less and less under our control.

Like the sorcerer's apprentice, dentistry may be mistaken in believing that it can control technology or its effect on how dentistry is practiced. It certainly cannot control the other problems society is scrambling to manage.

## A Place at the Table

All of these societal changes involve interactions with dentistry that were small or not particularly influential decades ago. The solutions the profession used so successfully in the past—common standards for practitioners and control of the market—may not be successful in the future. Doubling down on the successes of the past might work, but might also be exactly the wrong sort of solution. It is more likely that dentistry will have to redefine what it means to be professional. That is why this report uses the subtitle "New Professionalism." This redefinition could take various forms. Most likely any successful response will include better defining the relationship with patients and society so we can begin discussions with others as partners sharing a common future. That means dentistry will not be the only voice for determining what is ethical. Others are also moral agents whose choices about what is right and good have the same kinds of effects on the profession that dentists' choices have on them.

There is an argument that says, "Granted, social reality evolves over centuries and even decades, but ethics is eternal. What is good and right is our constant pole star. Human nature does not change. The fundamental values of dentistry should never change either."

That position is exactly right, but not very helpful. Human nature changes at a millennial pace. The core of dentistry is service. What does change is how these values are expressed. It would have been helpful to a patient 100 years ago to pull a painful tooth. Today our first thought would be endodontics and perhaps a crown. Same goal, different method of attaining it. Those who are grounded in the fundamentals of professionalism can participate from an advantageous position in the ethical discussions we need. But they are not excused from sitting at the table.

It is equally indefensible for others to embrace an "anything goes as long as some justification can be ginned up" style of ethical relativism. Those individuals who are completely satisfied with their ethics because it serves them well are not excused from the conversation either. Nor are organizations that have historically enjoyed success on terms that are no longer on offer.

## Moral Leadership

Dentistry needs moral leaders. Of course moral leaders must behave ethically in the personal sense. But that is not the extent of their responsibilities. Moral leadership means creating the conditions for others to act ethically as well. Part of that might involve sharing experiences. But the great contribution will come through making organizations ethical, negotiating relationships with other groups, and steering colleagues toward actions that are mutually self-reinforcing for the common good. Ethical leaders arrange things so it is natural for dentists to behave morally.

It is always a winner to call for more ethics, especially if the appeal is general in nature and costs are not mentioned. Often such calls are understood as campaign promises that "someone" will finally "do something" about those "others who don't get it." Of course we all think we know who the bad actors are. It begins to get ticklish when we inquire about who the "someone" is who is supposed to handle this and what precisely it means to "do something." And if the needed changes come close to us, there will often be calls for "further study." Common experience, history, and research all confirm that we would often prefer to live with a little "fast and loose" than impose rules that might limit our own freedom or require us to get involved with limiting what professionals can do.

The "somebody ought to do something" approach to ethics typically plays itself out formally in publicizing general principles and organizing teaching opportunities. Informally, it shows up as grousing and editorializing and in dental boards, as arms of the state, disciplining a small proportion of practitioners whom others (patients and law enforcement generally) call to attention for behavior unbecoming a professional.

This is exactly why ethical leadership is so hard. It would be wrong to be silent on ethics in the dental profession. It might also be unwise to be too vocal. Trying to help others is sometimes misunderstood as having an undertone of implying that others could benefit from a little help.

There are two problems with the "we are ethical enough given the current circumstances" approach.

First, there is little evidence that it is working. As far as anyone knows, no dentist has ever lost membership in organized dentistry for failing to turn in a colleague engaged in gross or continual faulty treatment. Being able to put a technical name to a questionable practice and finding a justification for some that colleagues raise their eyebrows over is something that can be taught in an hour in the schools. Honor codes and organizational codes of ethics seem to have mixed influence. We are spending less time teaching ethics than we did a decade ago, and the literature (other than opinion pieces) has dried up. Dentists are leaving organized dentistry because it does not represent the values they feel are core in professionalism. Those who teach ethics and those who serve on judicial councils and dental boards deserve our respect. But it would come as a surprise to many to hear discussions about increasing dental school tuition or membership dues as a way of assembling the resources needed to raise the ethical tone of the profession. There is no funding to document that current efforts are effective in changing professional behavior in a way the public would notice.

Second, it is not clear that telling individual dentists how they should behave is the right project. It was a compelling vision a century ago. Speaking to government and industry in unison was a very effective strategy in the

1950s and 1960s. We must continue to do so, but this is no longer sufficient. Times have changed, and with them what it means to be a professional. It is no longer possible to get all dentists to act the same way in every ethically ambiguous situation. Even if it were, this would not be enough to meet the issues facing the profession today. The challenges are no longer entirely within the profession. They are now substantially matters that involve the relationship between the profession and the rest of society.

### The Parable of the Hot Rock

Let's assume you are interested in heating the deep end of a small swimming pool and you have a very hot rock in a small container with a handle. There would be very little to expect by waving it a few feet above the deep end and urging the water to heat up, or else. There would be even less to expect by waving it over the shallow end because that is more convenient. But, using the handle, one could submerge the rock in the shallow end, for example, as a form of engagement. Some warming would be expected there, but probably only a minimal effect at the other end of the pool. Perhaps if several hot rocks were placed in the shallow end they would warm the water there and that would spread by contagion throughout the pool. The whole pool would not heat up because of a few hot rocks at one end. One would have to count on the warmed water at the shallow end affecting the cooler water next to it. Now haul the formerly hot rock out after a few minutes and feel it. It will be cooler. It is going to cost something to heat this pool.

The parable has these features. It does little good to gesture about ethics. One has to engage, at least on issues that matter. Perhaps the water really "wants" to be warmer, but that does not matter, nor does showing it some really hot stuff. Most of the effect is the spread from water to water. A hot rock cannot heat the whole pool, but it can get a chain reaction going. Finally, it is going to cost something. Otherwise it is just a story.

### Bringing About the New Professionalism

This report has held faith with the work of William Gies nearly a century ago. Dentistry at the time was trying to figure out what it meant to be a profession. Most dentists had uneven training and skills, an inadequate scientific foundation, and deep financial motivation. Gies began his work by surveying in detail the conditions on the ground at the time. He was sometimes critical of various practices, but always placed these inadequacies side-by-side with better alternatives. In the end, his report was a picture of what the profession could be and, to a large extent, what it has become. It was not a set of recommendations in normative form: "Government should do this, insurance should do that, or organized dentistry needs to be more respected." It was an invitation to wide-ranging conversations to see how multiple constituencies could work together to build a new profession for the early twentieth century.

A new round of discussions seems to be in order today. The evidence presented in this report suggests that we can in fact do better. The following are not recommendations; they are themes for conversations.

First: How can we tone down the current approach of telling dentists that they should follow a common set of rules? This can be overdone and cause some to avoid the issue. Too much of it points us in the wrong direction and may even encourage cynicism among those who notice too large a gap between what is preached as an ideal and what is commonly observed.

Second: How can we make it easier for dentists to do the right thing? What will happen as we remove economic barriers to ethical practice (especially for those entering the profession), publish information so dentists understand their real alternatives, mentor rather than use new members of the profession, listen to colleagues we may not understand, and tell lots of small moral rather than financial success stories in detail rather than big ones in generalities? Are lack of transparency or use of double messaging benefitting the conversation?

Third: How can we fail to engage others who matter? Dentistry is becoming increasingly an interaction with other healthcare services, government, industry, the research community, consumerism, politics, and even alternative delivery systems. Although it might be resisted, that trend is unlikely to abate. In fact, it is likely to define what professionalism means in dentistry during the next few decades. Isolation and resistance are possible responses. The smart money, however, is on sitting down and working out mutually satisfactory approaches. That will require treating others as moral agents, not as antagonists or clients.

Fourth: How can we make differences an asset rather than a source of unease? The context in which dentistry functions is diverse and getting more so every day. The strategy of confronting it with one voice may be exactly the wrong way to go. Systems theorists have proven that an individual, an organization, or any system must be nimble enough to engage with a complex environment or it will die. Some diversity is a distraction or even a burden to the established order. Some is essential to its survival. The problem is, we cannot always pick what kind of variation will be the winning strategy in the future (Cohen et al, 1972). All we can know for pretty sure is that perfecting the way it used to be will not be the winner.

Fifth: Timing matters. Change takes time, especially big change. The proprietary model of health professions education had about a 70-year run until the 1920s. Extreme makeovers were popular in dentistry for about a decade. Direct reimbursement was no longer a viable option by the time the profession was gearing up for it. Problems emerge, solutions emerge, but each has its own pace that is determined by an interaction between internal and external dynamics. Not only is the pace of change increasing, the complexity of interactions is creating discontinuities and friction at the borders between rapidly changing organizations. Organizations that grow and respond at different paces are hard to align. Sometimes organizations react too quickly for the conditions emerging around them. Usually they react too slowly. What is the right pace for change in dentistry? No one person knows, but it is reasonable that we can come closer to finding the right answer with many at the table.

Sixth: Is it time to expand our definition of leadership? Models of professional ethics are always inspiring, mentors are encouraging. Both are admired and valuable to the extent that conditions are the same now as they were when the models and mentors made the tough choices and showed the pioneering way. In a dynamic world, we need other kinds of leaders as well. We need those who can bring out the best in others without necessarily having been through the same circumstances. Coaches are respected because of the potential they release in others. Would there be an advantage in creating multiple leadership paths, including some very short ones and a more active role for those who have already passed through the chairs? Is there anything that can be done to multiply leadership opportunities?

## Summary

The American College of Dentists Ethics Project began by listening to small groups of patients, dentists, and leaders in the profession. They were frank about the need for correcting the drift of dentistry toward commercialism and the softening of the collaborative center. In fact, despite the diversity of those expressing their concerns, the message was the same: Dentistry is adopting the standards of business and political power offered by those outside the profession. Society is changing, but that does not mean that dentistry is faced with only the alternatives of going commercial or becoming fragmented by holding onto a previous image of the profession.

This project has made one cycle. It began by listening, and it heard a similar message from diverse groups. Weaknesses in the system were complained about and defenses offered. There were many messages of judgment and justification. This report has assembled the evidence about ethical behavior in the public and the professions in general and about its manifestations in dentistry. It suggests something about what is possible.

Perhaps now is the time for a new round of listening. But this time all those involved—all those who are affected by dentistry and all those who have the potential to affect dentistry—should be in the room together. Now might be the time to pivot to the ethics of engagement and leadership.

# Appendix A

# Focus Group Results

Published as Chambers, D. W. (2020). Focus Group Results. *Journal of the American College of Dentists, 87* (1), 4-17.

## Abstract

One hundred eighty-two dentists and patients participated in 18 focus groups across the United States in approximately one-hour discussions of the perception of ethical issues facing the dental profession. Additionally, 237 dentists completed an open-ended survey on dental ethics. All data gathering was unguided. Written and oral comments were recorded. Results of this "listening" are reported here, grouped by type of respondent. The findings are reported as frequency of common responses and verbatim remarks. No attempt has been made to interpret these comments or to connect them to positions or opinions regarding approaches to addressing ethical concerns.

There is value in listening to what patients and dentists say about ethics in dentistry. If anyone knows how ethics "feels" rather than what it "should" be, they would be the first ones to say. A reasonably large sample should give a true picture, one richer than theory or statistics.

## The Sample

Small groups of dentists, leaders in the profession, patients, and those involved in healthcare policy contributed their opinions. Eight focus groups were conducted among 86 patients in the states of California, North Carolina, Ohio, and Oklahoma. Six of the focus groups were organized and conducted by the Citizen Advocacy Center (CAC), a Washington, DC, nonprofit that represents members who serve on state health boards. Two groups were conducted by Dr. David W. Chambers. Patient groups were recruited by professional polling agencies or from church groups in an effort to sample the range of the public. All sessions were recorded, and written summaries were made immediately following the sessions. Dr. Chambers reviewed all tapes and was present at four of the panels.

Thirty-seven dentists in the practitioner cohort participated in four groups, two each in Maryland and North Carolina. By show of hands, approximately two-thirds of those participating identified themselves as American Dental Association (ADA) members. These sessions were conducted by Dr. Chambers. He also conducted four focus groups with leaders in the profession. These included nine officers of the California Dental Association (CDA), 13 members of the CDA Judicial Council, 20 "young dental leaders" identified by the Ohio Dental Association, and 17 officers in the Oklahoma Dental Association. All of these participants were assumed to be members of the ADA.

The CAC conducted a session for healthcare policy experts in Washington, DC. Those participating on this panel included former staffers of AARP, a representative of a state dental board, and policy analysts and lobbyists. There were nine participants as well as three representatives from the CAC and Dr. Chambers present.

The final such *viva voce* source was an anonymous survey completed by 237 graduates of one dental school as part of the school's annual survey of graduates. Written comments regarding ethical issues in dentistry were provided in response to open-ended questions.

## The Stimulus

For all cases, respondents were invited to address questions regarding ethics based on their personal experience. Most groups answered three questions: "What is the greatest current ethical issue regarding the relationship among dentists?" "What is the greatest ethical issue regarding the relationship between dentists and patients?" and "What is the greatest ethical issue regarding the relationship between dentists and organizations?" Respondents usually answered these questions by writing short phrases on personal but anonymous response forms, followed by public discussion. Both written remarks and group contributions were recorded verbatim and counted in common categories. The discussion sessions were mature and candid, with no steering by the facilitators. Usually no comment was made by the facilitators other than to ask the major questions. Participants did not make frivolous remarks since they were commenting in public in front of their peers.

## Summarizing the Data

Conventional standards were followed in analyzing such qualitative data (Charmaz, 2006; Corbin & Strauss, 2008; Denzin & Lincoln, 2003). Recordings and written records were preserved. These were summarized separately for each panel or set of related panels. Naturally occurring clusters of comments were identified in each group independently of what other focus groups reported. The number of mentions of each topic was recorded, and illustrative verbatim comments were recorded [shown below in square brackets]. These numbers may be interpreted as reflecting the extent of concern over various themes. At the third level of analysis, data was aggregated (but not modified) for each of the types of panels: practitioners, leaders, patients, policy experts, and alumni. The final level of analysis involved highlighting, but not further synthesizing, trends for each of the five respondent groups. This final level was called the "story according to..."

This Appendix reports the summary data at the third level: combined summaries for each of the five data sources.

## Results

### Practitioner Focus Groups

Fifteen practitioners in two sessions in North Carolina; 22 in two sessions in Maryland. Approximately 66% ADA members. Written notes were completed by participants prior to open discussion.

**Dentist-to-Dentist Ethical Issues**

*[N = 18]* Differences of opinion among dentists is an ethical issue.

- "There's a dentist in our area who pays people a 'finder's fee' to get referrals. I don't know what to do about that. There's no point in going to the board."

- "Afraid of conflict; must go on tip-toes when discussing values in dentistry."
- "Mostly when there is bad dentistry that comes to my attention I try to smooth it over. But if it is serious I suggest that the patient contact the state board—it is ultimately the patient's problem."
- "When I see something that should not have happened in a patient's mouth I am angry with my colleague. But I don't know what to say to him or what to say to the patient."
- "Dentists just don't talk much with each other about what they have in common, except for common 'enemies' such as insurance, understood in the sense of common excuses."
- "ADA Code requirement to report improper behavior is generally ignored."
- "Everybody knows we have problems and challenges, but we are afraid to talk about it. There is no forum for communication and there seems to be a tacit understanding that even talking about differences is an insult to professional integrity."
- "Most differences of opinion among dentists are about very small differences; often just preferred habits."
- "The best way to manage patients' problems caused by other dentists is to keep the discussion at the descriptive and technical level. Stick to the facts."
- "Most problems about the poor work colleagues have done is really about money—who is going to pay to make it right. And the insurance companies keep out of these things, saying they have 'already paid for the treatment.'"
- "I just do not know what to say to my colleagues, especially those who have a different idea about dentistry."
- "Problem patients are passed from one dentist to another."

*[N = 13]* Each has his or her own standard; dentists mistrust each other; cannot communicate
- "There is diversity of opinion regarding standards in the profession."
- "'Standard of care' is a term with unclear and often private or expedient meaning."
- "We are a profession of self-appointed experts."
- "Differences in professional opinions are about ego and money."
- "Dentists do not always share information about their patients."

*[N = 10]* Competition among dentists
- "Criticize others' work in effort to steal patients."
- "Not commenting on the consistent bad work of colleagues creates an environment where standards other than quality of treatment are acceptable or even come to define the profession."
- "Sense of professionalism seems to be declining. Dentists are withdrawing into their own offices."
- "Dentists competing for insurance contracts drives down the reimbursement rates for everyone."
- "There are too many dentists."
- "Dentistry is becoming a job rather than a profession."

*[N = 9]* General practitioners (GPs) and specialists competing for patients
- "Fewer referrals. More GPs trying to do all the work to avoid losing the patient."
- "Specialists are now doing general dentistry."
- "Sometimes specialists cherry pick care provided."
- "Turf or scope of practice conflicts in dentistry: specialists want regulations that favor them; generalists want to do traditional specialty treatment."
- "The whole business of the relationship between GPs and specialists is murky; it goes differently in different situations."

*[N = 4]* Misleading advertising
- "Marketing has gotten out of hand. The claims dentists are making to patients have nothing to do with dentistry. They are about price and convenience and smiles."
- "Some make promises about treatment outcomes that are impossible without seeing the patient."
- "Internet marketing is not about quality of dental care."
- "Voluntary restraint on advertising only penalizes the good dentist."

*[N = 4]* Questionable business practices, kickbacks, pay for referrals
- "Unethical business practices are becoming the norm: 'everybody is doing it' becomes the justification."
- "I know a dentist who has for years kept two sets of books."

*[N = 2]* Fear of having own work evaluated [not mentioned in the general discussion]

*[N = 2]* Pseudo credentials and specialties

*[N = 2]* Quota dentistry displacing quality dentistry in schools and in corporate model
- "If parts of the profession are moving to judging success as production, the rest of the profession has an excuse to follow."

**Dentist-to-Patient Ethical Issues**
*[N = 20]* Overtreatment: Profit-driven treatment planning
- "In the competition between ethics and business, business usually wins."
- "Treatment options given or preferred may be ones with highest profit margin."
- "Patient selection by ability to pay."
- "Here patients are written up for the most expensive treatment options plausible on the grounds that it is easier to forgive planned treatment than to break the news that more is needed."

*[N = 17]* Inadequate informed consent, "steering" patients; breaches of confidentiality
- "Who should decide when there are alternative treatment options?"
- "Dentists just tell patients enough to get them to go along with what the dentist wants to do."

*[N = 7]* Piecemeal treatment, not comprehensive care

*[N = 5]* Eroded trust; conflicting opinions
- "Dentistry is no longer about the dentist and the patient and oral health needs; it is about money and outside interests. The patient is the one who is being used."
- "Patients hear different stories from different dentists and so they lose faith in the profession as a whole."
- "The *Readers' Digest* story was fully to be expected: each of the alternative treatments could be justified."
- "Patients just go from one dentist to another until they find one they can trust."

*[N = 4]* Misleading advertising
- "Advertising is creating unrealistic expectations."

*[N = 4]* Use of unproven technology, bad science
- "New technologies seem to be profit driven and are often untested."
- "EBD [evidence-based dentistry] does not help in this area because techniques are evaluated in isolation and because there is so little actual data."

*[N = 2]* Faulty or improper care

*[N = 2]* Patient self-determination
- "Don't try to stand in the way of patient who wants a second opinion."
- "Patients want to be heard; to know that the dentist has their best interests in mind."

*[N = 2]* Not current on CE

### Dentist-to-Organization Ethical Issues
*[N = 8]* Organized dentistry less valuable, declining membership and participation
- "Does anybody know why the membership in the ADA is declining?"
- "The ADA is 'toothless.'"
- "The way it is now, a smaller and smaller number of dentists is carrying the water for a larger and larger number of those who are getting a free ride. Not sustainable."
- "Organized dentistry's voice is getting weaker while Kellogg and Macy and others is getting stronger."
- "The ADA does not even seem to be aware of what EBD is or whether it matters."

*[N = 8]* Organized dentistry no longer represents the profession, controlled by the few, lost trust
- "The ADA gives too much attention to specialties."

*[N = 6]* Insurance
- "PPOs [preferred provider organizations] and managed care are taking control away from the practitioner."
- "Insurance is intruding on diagnosis, treatment planning, and dentist-patient relationship."
- "Insurance limits treatment options. Patients perceive that insurance undermines patient confidence in the dentist."

- "It is impossible to standardize the correct reimbursement for any procedures because of differences in clinicians' skills, lab costs, front desk and other practice characteristics."
- "Insurance industry has failed in the role of standardizing and raising level of care: only concerned with its own bottom line."
- "Dentistry needs to involve the employer and government and those who ultimately pay for dental health, not just the insurance companies."
- "Insurance companies are profiling dentists' claims, ostensibly to detect abusers, but perhaps to lower benefits generally."
- "Capitation doesn't work for dentists because each office is like a private hospital and we do surgery, not comprehensive and long-range care."

*[N = 6]* Lack of transparency
- "Corporate hides what is really going on behind nondisclosure."
- "There is no forum for discussing our concerns."

*[N = 5]* Organized dentistry is too focused on political action committees and lobbyists, own structure, and survival
- "The ADA is too far away and seems to want to relate in terms of money and advertising. Real participation is at the local level."
- "The ADA's primary objective is to stay in business."

*[N = 4]* Corporate entities are taking advantage of student debt to intrude commercial values in place of professional ones.

*[N = 4]* Dentists cheat on insurance.
- "Waiving copays is common because patients ask for it."

*[N = 4]* Live patients on initial licensure exams.
- "Such tests are out of context and invalid because they do not measure comprehensive care."
- "Would like to see nationally standardized licensure."

*[N = 3]* Intrusions into treatment and dentist-patient relationship from various sources
- "Beginning practitioners cannot start their own practices so they have to start as associates or employees and pick up the business habits of their profit-oriented bosses."

- "Younger members aren't joining organized dentistry." [Fact: They are overrepresented compared to general dentists in their mature years.]

*[N = 3]* Tech companies, suppliers influencing treatment decisions
- "Massive advertising in professional journals, at trade shows, and in 'throw-aways' distort true professional values."
- "Gurus hype major productivity; what's in it for them?"
- "Product endorsements are becoming more common."

*[N = 3]* Organizations are "fronts" for self-interest of members.
- "Factionalism."
- "Multiple professional organizations are competing for membership, causing a narrowing of focus and appeal to self-interests."
- "Some organizations exist to promote a business model, e.g., sleep dentistry."
- "ASDA [American Society for Dental Ethics] and the ADA need to grow up on this issue of patients on licensure exams."
- "Different organizations are representing particular interests in an effort to draw membership from those seeking personal advantage at the expense of colleagues generally."

*[N = 2]* Weak leadership, tolerate unethical members, commercial interests
- "State boards have lost control of the profession."
- "Ethics has become 'enforceable up to the cost of legal defense.'"
- "Boards are not taking on the known offenders; afraid of counter-suits, underfunded."
- "Boards are overdoing the idea of recovery or reclaiming previous offenders and letting bad actors back into the profession when they have not changed."

*[N = 2]* Government: regulations and low reimbursement rates
- "FTC's [Federal Trade Commission's] preoccupation with driving down cost is destroying quality of care is an issue that is having unintended consequences."
- "Legislators always respond to appeals for 'free trade' and 'patient safety.'"

*[N = 2]* Dental school environment fosters competition.
- "Dental schools are falling behind in what they are teaching about ethics."

- "The ethics of the emerging graduates is the ethics of the future of the profession."
- "Schools may not be able to do anything about the ethics of young people (already formed in youth), but they should be more selective in admissions."
- "Young people today are going into dentistry for the money."

*[N = 2]* Mid-level providers are a question mark.
- "The effects of mid-level providers may be positive for patients and negative for dentists."

[General comment: "There are so many definitions of ethics and so many applications of principles. We need to work on what to do when there are differences." There appeared to be more concern over dentist-to-dentist ethical issues than over those involving patients.]

### Dental Leader Focus Groups
Seventeen leaders in the Oklahoma Dental Association; 9 officers of the California Dental Association (only addressed issues relating to dentists and organizations); 13 CDA Judicial Council members; 20 Ohio "Young dental leaders"

**Dentist-to-Dentist Ethical Issues**
*[N = 40]* Practicing in isolation
- "We can still afford to live in our own worlds; no need to collaborate."
- "Little real opportunity to communicate or cooperate on treatment standards."
- "Practice is in silos."
- "Patients are confused, and consequently trust in the profession is eroded."
- "Neither patients nor colleagues have a voice in quality or type of care provided."
- "Dentists can collaborate as much or as little as they want to."
- "Lack of clear and consistent standards for what constitutes good dental care."
- "Every dentist can do whatever he wants as long as he can talk enough patients into it."
- "Egos."

*[N = 18]* Lack of collegiality: view other dentists as competitors

- "Some make unjustifiable negative remarks about others' work."
- "Overtreatment comes from feeling of competitive need."

*[N = 8]* The profession does a poor job of policing itself.

- "Justifiable criticism is mistaken for unprofessional poaching, so avoided."

*[N = 5]* Unclear relations with specialties and medicine

- "Currently care for the patient is divided and allocated to individuals with specialized training or public perception of best care, including on the basis of patients' perceptions of cost/benefit calculations."
- "Fragmentation causes appearance of competition is for market share."
- "Generally, evidence is lacking to support often voiced claims of superiority of outcomes for many kinds of providers."
- "Better interprofessional communication and outcomes-based decision making are needed."

*[N = 3]* Different practice models and reimbursement systems

- "Dentists working for dentists introduces new layers of ethical complexity and responsibility."

**Dentist-to-Patient Ethical Issues**

*[N = 21]* Overtreatment

- "Overtreatment is driven by competition among dentists."
- "Advertising serves greed rather than trying to reach those most in need of dental care."
- "The new standards are money, technology, and egotism."
- "Patients and insurance companies are putting downward pressure on dentists' ability to maximize treatment offered."

*[N = 21]* Bad dental practices

- Over-diagnosis, Botox, not being honest about own bad work, fraud, cherry-picking treatment, treatment beyond competence, insurance manipulations

*[N = 16]* Commercialism: business is the new standard.

- "Patients as 'customer' rather than individual needing professional care. Dentistry is now something to 'sell'; treating teeth instead of patients."
- "Rebranding (anti-aging dentistry), smiles, brand named technologies disguises what oral health is really about."
- "Patients treat dentists as providers of commercial services rather than professionals."
- "Loss of trust, bad-mouthing, skipping payment, shopping (both dentists and patients are doing this)."
- "Patients demanding specific care based on advertising or recommendations from other dentists."
- "Conflicts between treatment priorities and patients' financial resources."
- "In the corporate model we are seeing 'diagnosis' at front desk."
- "Treating to insurance."

*[N = 11]* True market demand does not reach what dentists hope for.

- "Dentists blame government and insurers for not putting enough money into the system."
- "Dental care trends toward services beyond true oral health needs because that is where the money is. This makes dental care appear 'elective.'"

*[N = 10]* Advertising, misrepresentation, media advertising

- "Patients do not hear same story from all dentists."
- "Patients are being told that dentistry is a series of one-off transactions rather than a relationship."
- "Claims of superior or exclusive skills or services."
- "Appeal to uneducated public rather than colleagues to decide who is good dentist."
- "Getting too close to commercial organizations, advertisers, web designers, group-ons."

*[N = 8]* Patients and dentists have different views of good dentistry.

- "Dentistry is defining itself in terms of services delivered, especially at very high levels of excellence. But this is not the way patients define dentistry. They seem to define good oral health as not needing to see the dentist."

*[N = 7]* Failing to present all treatment alternatives, lack of informed consent

- "Treatment options are often tailored to maximize profit or the dentist's view of optimal oral health."
- "Dentists are trying to take treatment decisions away from patients."

*[N = 4]* Others than dentists or other dentists are influencing patient expectations; extra-professional values

*[N = 4]* Increasing specialization and defining practice in terms of techniques rather than comprehensive health outcomes causes fragmentation of both the profession and care.

*[N = 4]* Patients no longer trust dentists, weak relationship, shift to financial basis of relationship

- "Old model of dentist and patient (with dentist having recognized authority) being replaced by multiple forces competing to represent dentists' and patients' interests."
- "Patients can no longer afford to stay with a dentist long enough to build relationship because of cost factors."

*[N = 2]* Conflict between ideal care and what patients can afford

*[N = 2]* Undertreatment of those without funds

### Dentist-to-Organization Ethical Issues
*[N = 21]* Organized dentistry cannot influence the way dentistry is practiced.

- "We are aware of the problem (confusion and miscommunication leading to reduced trust), and we talk about it. But organized dentistry really cannot do anything about the problems."
- "There is no common place to discuss ethics or the alternatives to the way dentistry is trending."
- "Even in the face of strong messaging from organized dentistry and mandatory continuing education, the fact that dentists do not

depend on each other collectively for achieving best outcomes, or even financial success, means that public relations campaigns will be superficial and the potential impact of professional communication is diluted by messages from other, often commercial, sources. Organized dentistry may not be using its communication platform effectively, or it may be too focused on legal and financial aspects of dentistry."

- "Enforcement is spotty. State boards no longer involved except in most outrageous cases or cases where dentist does not put up a fight."
- "There are silos; folks are now using private definitions of what is right. There is a growing sense in American culture that 'everyone has a right to be right by his or her private standards.'"
- "It is inappropriate to comment on a colleague's work. It is even becoming inappropriate to discuss this. We lack the language and opportunities to have discussions (other than attacking others self-righteously)."
- "Organized dentistry focuses on legal and regulatory action rather than dealing directly with influential others."
- "The most questionable dentists are probably not members of organized dentistry, so we have no influence over them."
- "The ADA has become a bureaucracy that does not represent individual practitioners."
- "Organized dentistry is prevented by law from interfering in individual dentist's commercial activities."
- "The [ADA] code of ethics is aspirational and not enforceable."
- "Is it wise to have one organization attempting to speak for all dentists?"
- "Oral health no longer a standard."
- "Using political position to advance private practitioner income."

[N = 20] Benefit of organized dentistry not clear, too many organizations, fragmented participation

- "Organized dentistry could overcome the isolation of individual dentists, but it does not seem to be effective at doing so."
- "It is hard for individual dentists to resist the pressures of commercialism, advertising, politics and regulation by themselves."
- "Young practitioners learn how to practice from senior dentists."
- "We want more from organized dentistry."

[N =18] Fragmentation in understanding what it means to be a professional
- "We are not sure how to reach the cost/value point of practitioners."

- "One can be 'professional' without sharing values or activities with one's colleagues. Traditional dental professionalism competes with many other value sets."
- "Non-membership is a growing issue."
- "Educational debt must be managed."
- "We now expect organized dentistry to promote profession only, not profession and patients."
- "Dentists are getting their values from places other than their colleagues."
- "Money and technical excellence on big cases ("show-off dentistry") is becoming an independent standard."
- "HMO [health maintenance organization] practice model is inserting new values."
- "Practice is increasingly being steered by marketing values."

*[N = 13]* Benefits companies will not pay for all work dentists want to provide

*[N = 6]* Turf battles (in court), who gets to provide care, competition among groups, organized dentistry no longer single clear voice
- "Many organizations besides organized dentistry are now influencing practice."

*[N = 6]* Student debt
- "Dental schools cannot change ethical orientation in the face of what is happening in practice."
- "The young want to live the life style of their parents."
- "As a younger dentist, I resent the claims that I must be unethical just because I have a high debt load when no one has shown me any evidence that this is true of me or of my peers in general."

*[N = 4]* "Good old boys' club": no longer representing all dentists.

*[N = 4]* Corporate is a viable alternative
- "Corporate and 'institutes' are a viable alternative home for dentists drifting toward a business definition of dentistry rather than a professional one."

*[N = 3]* Online discussions, social media, unproductive

- "I do not trust or participate in online discussions because they are dominated by commercial interests and people with axes to grind."

## Patient Focus Groups

Eight-six patients in eight focus groups in San Francisco, California; rural and urban North Carolina; Cleveland, Ohio; and Oklahoma City, Oklahoma.

### First Thought That Comes to Mind Regarding Dentistry

| | |
|---|---|
| Cost | 17 |
| Issues of competence | 7 |
| Overcharge, overtreat | 6 |
| Pain, scary | 6 |
| Hassle, inconvenience, unavoidable necessity | 4 |
| Cleaning, health, professionalism, quality | 5 |
| Communication issues | 4 |

### Quality

No specific question was asked about how patients define quality of oral health care. Generally, quality seemed to mean technical outcomes and treatment in the process as expected. "Durable," "no mistakes," "preventive," "effective," "explained so I understand," "not being pressured," "nothing unnecessary."

Overall, about half have been satisfied with their dentist; those dissatisfied have moved on.

- "Good is not having to go back or to hassle the encounter."
- "I think most of the dentists have competence. It really boils down to their personality. Do they make you feel at ease?"

### Judging Competence [Criteria valued by patients]

| | |
|---|---|
| Interpersonal relationship | 18 |
| Clear explanations | 15 |
| Friendly, efficient staff | 8 |
| Appearance of office, current equipment | 7 |
| Care about pain, taking time | 4 |
| Reputation in community | 3 |
| Online references | 3 |

### Public Emblems of Quality of Little Value

| | |
|---|---|
| License on the wall is a given | 7 |
| Report card of little value | 5 |
| Too much technology | 2 |

- "I think when you are a professional you will show that, when you are examining a patient, or whatever; it'll show. You will know whether they are dedicated to their craft or are just going through the motions. The way they interact with you. You'll know whether they know what they are doing, or not."
- "I went to a dentist before and he caused the start of my problem. He first said I needed a root canal, so he shaved it all the way down to a point. The next day it broke off at the gum line, so I had no tooth left. When I first started going to him, I just didn't think he was the right one for me. I shouldn't have gone back to him. He didn't even say hello to you. I stopped going to him after that."
- "I don't think you know it until you actually go to them and see what he's like."
- "I take ratings kind of with a grain of salt."
- "It [dental license] doesn't differentiate any of them from each other because they all have it."
- "A professional testing organization would be fine for the technical aspects of what type of equipment they have, what their training is, how good their training was. This is a given. But, once you get into various mouths, everyone in here has different sensitivity."

### Finding a Dentist

| | |
|---|---|
| References from friends | 11 |
| Looking for location, convenience | 5 |
| Consult lists, shop for price, insurance | 4 |
| Avoid appearance of oversell | 3 |

- "I actually do an internet search and look on the website where they got their degree, when, what they studied. I read all of that."
- "One of the things I look at is do they work in the community for people who are in need. That ranks high. A lot of times they say if they volunteer. When you go online, you find all kinds of stuff."
- "I want to steer away from the people with the new technology and

stuff because, I mean, like, you're going to be doing fillings and root canals and things like that just like everybody else and you're going to have to charge three times as much for all your new machinery and it doesn't necessarily make you a better dentist."

- "I refused to get involved in the huge medical school, dental school system. It is so impersonal. I won't see any healthcare provider in that setting. I want them to remember me from time to time."

## Communication

| | |
|---|---|
| Could be better | 11 |
| Generally good when talking about procedures | 8 |

- "The hygienist will come in and explain what she's doing and what she found. The dentist comes in and agrees with her assessment. Then I go to the front desk."
- "Don't like the way he comes across as knowing everything but not really telling me anything."

## Paying for Care

| | |
|---|---|
| Selling, overselling | 21 |
| Generally, dentistry is too expensive | 19 |
| Cost affects when and whether care is sought | 11 |
| Postponed work because of cost | 7 |
| Medicaid coverage is inadequate for costs | 6 |
| Combine dental and medical insurance | 6 |
| Treatment offered as "Take it or leave it" | 5 |
| Private insurance is good | 4 |
| Credit, other option "bad deals" | 4 |
| Like that insurance covers prevention | 4 |
| Fail to distinguish optional from necessary | 4 |

- "This 'full amount up front and then we'll see what we can squeeze out of the insurance company' attitude makes me think they are in it for the money."
- "Way too expensive."
- "I'm missing two teeth because I couldn't pay for what I needed.... I'd still have these teeth if they'd given me a payment arrangement."
- "Under Medicaid we're usually not covered for crowns or major work or cosmetic work."

- "Cleanings and screenings—I think they should be made available to everybody as often as necessary. Anything that has to be done after that will have to be negotiated."
- "It is a put-off when they start talking about a 'perfect mouth.'"
- "Dentists charge extra if they know you have insurance."
- "Our dentist says, if you want to pay cash, I'll take some off."
- "Dental insurance makes a lot more sense than medical insurance."
- "(Even with insurance), it's still too much. From my experience, I feel like a lot of dental offices charge extra because they know it's covered."
- "They have these vouchers where if I hand them out and get referrals, I get $100 for every person I get. So, I could get 4 people to go, I could get the $400 (for a mouth guard)."
- "The only other option was to do a credit-type thing where you get a credit card and put money there and there is 37% interest, so you are paying on it beyond the year you die."
- "A good dental visit is when I don't see the dentist or he doesn't have much to say."
- "I have insurance, but I'm paying more and more out-of-pocket; it's like the dentist is trying to get paid twice."
- "Dentistry has become preventive; I don't expect to need treatment for things I am unaware of."
- "It's like going to get your oil changed, then the sales guy comes in with a list of things that 'really' need to be taken care of even though I didn't know they were a problem."
- "Is it really true that I need a cone beam every year without the dentist even looking to see if things have changed in my mouth?"
- "They do a lot of stuff that is unnecessary."
- "Several charge you interest as high as 18%."
- "I think dentists just charge as much as they think they can get. They get paid by both the insurance company and the patient. They are willing to give me a discount, so I know they are overcharging somewhere."
- "I asked for a payment plan and got no sympathy."
- "Dentists want it both ways. They sell as much as they can, so insurance picks up some and the patient gets stuck with the rest. Those without insurance, are just out of luck."
- "Just like business at the malls. They jack up the price for any one desperate enough to pay it, and then offer discounts."
- "Now I've found a good dentist. Previously I had one I felt was in it for

the money. He had a high priced office and needed to make money. He was probably 50% higher than the rest of the dentists in the area."

- "I have doubts about my dentist. He let some stuff go…. I didn't trust him and went to see someone else."
- "I think he wants to do things just because he can do them."

## Behaviors That Are Not Appreciated

| | |
|---|---|
| Excessive cost | 16 |
| Overtreating | 11 |
| Poor communication | 4 |
| Assess for the well-off | 3 |
| Self-promotion | 3 |

- "Cost of procedures."
- "Overcharging."
- "If they can turn it around and have a good practice for years, they become a millionaire they charge such high prices."
- "Dentists go into a lot of debt for schooling. I don't know if that is tied to what they charge."
- "At least cover part of the cost rather than saying you're out of luck, man."
- "I think there are a lot of goof-balls out there who are dentists."
- "Somehow he changed after he built that beautiful new office."
- "Make sure everyone has access to care."
- "Make sure they don't gouge anybody."
- "When you go to the dentist, even if you are going for your six months, every time I go in I get nervous in the chair because first I'm looking to see if they find something and then if they don't, it always feels like a little bit of a hustle to get more money from you. 'Why don't you think about whitening?' or, 'What about that tooth that's missing?' There's always something extra."
- "They have to take continuing education, right? Unfortunately, I can tell you my beautician takes more continuing education than my dentist. How do you know they actually went to those classes?"
- "Reduce the amount the dentist takes."
- "Consistency in pricing."
- "Universal healthcare should be a percentage of your gross income."
- "If there were some way to keep the dentist honest. They are in private practice so they charge whatever they want, do whatever they want."

**Response to Bad Encounters**

| | |
|---|---|
| Unaware of reporting options | 8 |
| Online and word of mouth | 5 |
| Go somewhere else | 5 |
| Confront the dentist | 5 |
| Fix the problem, complaints are useless | 4 |
| Profession and state boards cover it up | 4 |
| Report to insurance company or somebody | 3 |
| Avoid multidentist offices | 3 |
| Preserve dentist's reputation if possible | 3 |

- "The oral hygienist put me in so much pain. I told her and she started crying. The next thing I know, the dentist comes in and I can't tell you how rude she was. My friends told me that's how she is."
- "I'd talk about it at work because everyone has the same insurance. It gets around that a certain dentist sucks and people won't go to him."
- "I wish there were some sort of peer review. Four or five years ago I had a really bad crown put in and I had 4 dentists in 3 different states tell me it was a horrible crown."
- "I'd go back and if I don't get resolution to my satisfaction, I leave and find somebody else."
- "I am beginning not to trust [some] dentists. But I trust lawyers and the government even less. I hope dentists don't become like lawyers or big business retailing."
- "I'm more concerned about fixing the problem without putting more money into it."
- "Part of the question for me is the trustworthiness of any agency that monitors the healthcare professions."
- "Is it about teeth or is it about money?"
- "I would show up and ask questions."
- "I wouldn't pay."
- "Address it; fix it; change the practice; not charge you."
- "If they screw something up, they better damned well pay for it."
- "Ethical issues are likely underreported."
- "We should reduce cost by having dentists take home less money."
- "Is there a dentist's association that a patient could go to?"

## Second Opinions

| | |
|---|---|
| Yes, if did not like options offered | 8 |
| Expensive and questionable value | 5 |
| Second opinion if suspicious | 3 |
| Second opinion if large and irreversible case | 3 |

- "The first guy seemed drunk. My sister went to him anyway and they double-charged her, so I decided to get a second opinion."

## Impression of Hygienists

| | |
|---|---|
| Positive volunteered comments | 13 |
| Favor independent hygiene | 5 |

- "To me, the hygienists—they are the face of the practice. They are the ones you're going to work with."
- "The dentist is playing a smaller and smaller part in the system, just the technical stuff."
- "Keep it simple—go to the hygienist unless you need something more serious."
- "For basic cleaning it would be better to make an appointment directly with the hygienist and have it be cheaper and easier. All the dentist does is go over and look at it for 30 seconds and you have to spend however much money just for that."
- "I go to the hygienist; they have a dentist there too."

## Policy Experts Focus Group

Nine individuals representing various healthcare and patient advocacy groups, such as AARP, who interact with dentistry; one state board representative.

## First Thought That Comes to Mind Regarding Dentistry

- High-end procedures
- Patient anxiety
- Expensive
- Total health orientation
- Disconnected from the rest of the healthcare system
- Organizations engage in one-sided conversations

- "How can the profession tell the public that oral health is part of total health and then isolate itself from the rest of the healthcare system?"
- "Patients are not drawn to dentists; feel they cannot escape."

### Selecting a New Dentist
- Word of mouth
- Facebook
- Referral from previous dentist
- Major criterion is convenience

### How Is the Competency of a Dentist Established?
[The panel expressed some frustration over this question, saying that the true answer is hidden from the public.]

Licensure only establishes minimal competency, and is often unevenly enforced.

There was little interest in a "report card" or other external monitoring of continuing competence.

The best indicator is a strong personal relationship with patients.

Staff confusions and paperwork problems do not reflect well on the dentist; hassle is a bad thing; the standard should be effect on health.

Trust can be gauged by referrals, staff turnover, consistency, willingness to spend time answering questions, instinct.

Informed consent is not really practice.
- "Dentists protect each other, so they cannot be trusted to do this job. Government is no good because it cannot get the data."
- "'Top Doc' and the like is just advertising."
- "Decision useful information—patient satisfaction, what insurance is accepted, past legal actions, convenience, type of procedures, cost, outcomes, malpractice—is all hard to get because dentists practice in isolation. No transparency."
- "When I asked DC society of dentists, they would not say."
- "Checked online, but that stuff is unbelievable. Everybody can't be that good."
- "I don't think the public is listening to what individual dentists or the profession is saying about itself."
- "Dental licenses are like a driver's license (every dentist has one)."
- "Not impressed by technical jargon or talk of their training."
- "I was put off by the dentist taking a doctrinaire attitude that he should save every one of my teeth."

- "The standard should be effect on health."
- "Patients superimpose their own standards on dentists, do not accept dentist's interpretations *prima facie*. Their concern is outcomes not technique. But many dentists do not seem to understand this."

## Cost

Dentistry works on a different model from the rest of the healthcare system. The other parts are interconnected; dentistry is still largely single provider. This makes the relationship with insurance difficult.

Insurance reimbursement rates have not kept pace with inflation at the same time that dental fees have outstripped inflation.

Cost is becoming a factor in patient decisions regarding care. The well-off are consuming optional care and the poor are postponing or declining it.

Overtreatment is an issue.

Smart patients handle oversell by going to another dentist.

Criteria are being my problem taken care of with minimal hassles and surprises [?]; "All I ask is a sense that the dentist is doing the best by me."

- "Dentists are pricing patients, government safety net schemes, and even insurance companies out of the market."
- "The perception of the public and policy makers is that dentists are refusing to discuss costs and access."
- "I have been successful as a well-educated and well-connected individual in negotiating price adjustment with dentists; as a representative of groups of patients, I cannot get a hearing on this."

## Managing Unfortunate Outcomes

Say nothing, but look for alternative office. Only the confident and educated can do this.

- "Dissatisfied with technical talk about saving my teeth so I delayed payment."
- "There is no platform for discussing changes in dentistry. It is happening without control and in a haphazard fashion."
- "Patients are not agents. They have no voice."

## Treatment by Others Than Dental Practice Owner

Associates are fine as long as they are backed by presence of the head doc.

- "I go to the hygienist, not the dentist; hygienists seem to do all the work, reading x-rays, etc."

[General observation: corporations are disruptive technology; need for navigators; there is no platform for discussing changes in dentistry, it is happening without control and haphazard; IC [infection control] is not really practiced; access and outcomes are not part of the discussion; no equilibrium within the field; patient is not an agent, has no voice. (Professional facilitator remarked: "Better patients make better dentists.")]

## Practicing Dentist Survey

Administered as part of an annual mailed survey to graduates of a dental school. A total of 237 surveys were returned, 14% of which came from respondents who said they had been in practice for fewer than ten years.

**Greatest Ethical Problem Facing the Profession**

|  | Established | | Young | |
|---|---|---|---|---|
|  | # | % | # | % |
| Overtreatment, malpractice, fraud | 76 | 40 | 2 | 6 |
| Inadequate reimbursement, insurance | 40 | 21 | 11 | 35 |
| Corporate, clinics, nondentist owners | 39 | 21 | 7 | 23 |
| Not serving the poor | 17 | 9 |  |  |
| Advertising, standards, leadership | 9 | 5 |  |  |
| Debt | 7 | 4 | 11 | 35 |

- "Because of the enormous student loans, the low compensation from the dental insurance companies, and the expense of some high-tech equipment, many dentists over-diagnose and over-treat their patients. We dentists are encouraged by clinic owners, CE lecturers, and sales people to 'sell more dentistry.'"
- "We place way too much faith in latest and greatest technique or technology."
- "We are losing our soul to corporate dentistry and our associations are not addressing the loss of the solo practitioner."
- "Dentists are being pressured from multiple directions: insurance companies limiting procedures and lowering or not raising reimbursements. Expenses are increasing for employees, the many insurances required by dentists, taxes, supplies, associations, etc. Patients shop for the lowest prices and use negative online reviews as a threat. Legislative action always increases dentist expenses."
- "Dentists are turning into technicians instead of healthcare providers."

- "The lack of priority for correct use of dental floss."
- "Eliminate the moral code of self-sacrifice and teach the alternative of rational egoism."
- "Nowadays, most of our patients of all ages are grossly overweight or clinically obese. These conditions reflect a lifestyle that is hugely deleterious to overall health, and puts most of these patients on a path to having chronic heart disease, diabetes I and II, etc. All dentists and their staffs should advocate for their patients plant-based nutrition with NO EATING of dairy, or red meat."
- "Every dentist knows the 'best' way to do things. He thinks that they are correct & that every other dentist is wrong. Public goes to 3 diff dentists and gets 3 diff answers. Dentists used to be a trusted profession. Dentistry lives in the dark ages."
- "Foreign dentists pouring into the workforce and having NO ETHICAL STANDARDS!!!! They are graduating and are performing iatrogenic procedures beyond their training, and are cutthroat 'business people' performing unnecessary dentistry to line their pockets."
- "The current state of the economy both globally and locally and its negative impact on the ability to deliver optimal dental care in a private practice setting. Inflation, rising cost of supplies and salary, educational debt, etc. require higher fees and more procedures and costs to patients. How do we justify the cost of doing business in private practice?"
- "It's a challenge over a practice lifetime of forty years to maintain effective and evolving treatment plans for maturing patients and to treat three generations of patients addressing all of their dental needs and giving excellent dental care. It's unethical to milk a practice for five or ten years and then pass off all the 'problems' to a new owner."
- "The correlation of oral health to overall health is not well understood. I have enormous concern over the debt issues graduates face. Additionally, the intrusion of govt, insurance, & corporate into our noble profession is disconcerting. Integrity is being compromised and yet we wonder why. Unbelievable. People from other countries not growing up with basics of unbendable ethics of right from wrong. Get rid of the Democrats."

**What have you done personally in the last six months to make things better on the issue you identified above?**

| | Established # | Established % | Young # | Young % |
|---|---|---|---|---|
| Maintain personal standards | 36 | 23 | 2 | 6 |
| Nothing | 30 | 19 | 6 | 18 |
| Educating colleagues, students, talk about it | 23 | 15 | 2 | 6 |
| Persuade patients to my standards | 17 | 11 | 4 | 12 |
| Participate in organized dentistry | 13 | 8 | 2 | 6 |
| Eschew insurance, fight insurance | 11 | 7 | | |
| Personally quit corporate | 6 | 4 | 2 | 6 |
| Personally quit organized dentistry | 6 | 4 | | |
| More businesslike, raise fees, retire | 5 | 3 | 7 | 21 |
| Public service | 4 | 3 | 4 | 12 |
| Campaign for conservative politicians | 3 | 2 | 2 | 6 |
| Work with insurance | 2 | 2 | 2 | 6 |

- "Attempted to facilitate the education of a few hundred folks regarding concepts of individual freedom, anarchy & free market capitalism."
- "Be the best dentist I can."
- "Clear communication with patients regarding the need for the work regardless of insurance reimbursement. Declining to take patients from insurance companies that don't reimburse adequately."
- "I can't change other people, so I do my best to serve my patients and community according to my values."
- "I have chosen to continue practicing as a Solo Practitioner instead of joining a larger Group Practice, where there is less control over ethical systems. To save my practice in a highly difficult situation, I chose to let Staff go and to increase my hours. I currently work 14-19 hours/ day, Monday through Friday, and I make sure that the important systems are followed. I am exhausted, but proud."
- "I maintain my value and integrity as person, as a health care provider. Although I make less profit, I want to gain patients' trust. I spend time equally with my patients regardless of what insurance they have or how much the procedure can produce for me. My goal is to have my patients' dental health improve overtime. My reward is to see their dental health improve and have them as lifelong patients."
- "I retired, didn't want to deal with the stress anymore."

- "Keep educating my patients of the abuse (of insurance companies)."
- "Not much, other than pay my ADA, CDA and local dental society dues. One person can't do much."
- "Nothing can be done by 1 dentist."
- "Nothing. It has taken me 10 years to reach personal, financial, emotional success."
- "I offer free second opinions to patients and parents who have experienced overtreatment."
- "Paid my dues to the ADA and CDA."
- "Speaking is paying my loans."

## What should organized dentistry be doing to address the issue you identified above?

| | Established | | Young | |
|---|---|---|---|---|
| | # | % | # | % |
| Financial success of dentists, fight insurance | 41 | 23 | 11 | 47 |
| ADA, state boards not effective, no discipline | 35 | 20 | | |
| Practitioners fine; schools failing ethically | 25 | 14 | | |
| Standardize treatment, too much diversity | 18 | 10 | 3 | 14 |
| Control tuition, loan forgiveness | 13 | 7 | 5 | 21 |
| Curb corporate abuses | 12 | 7 | 3 | 13 |
| Educate the public | 11 | 6 | | |
| Access and affordable care for all, prevention | 6 | 3 | 1 | 4 |
| Continuing education | 5 | 3 | | |
| Protect dentists from suits by patients | 1 | | 1 | 4 |

- "Control the insurance companies."
- "Find a way to reconcile insurance coverage with the dental needs of the community and encouraging the public to value their dental health."
- "Social safety nets are important to have... until they begin to swallow up everything else..."
- "Making sure the dental field is not in a race to the bottom for affordable dentistry. There will come a point where reimbursements will be so low that it would not make financial sense to do clinically acceptable dentistry. Dentistry will always be practiced, but quality dentistry may fade."
- "They can't do anything."

- "Work on avenues with the insurance companies for much higher compensation for procedures so dentists can stop doing extra treatment. Dentists that do crappy quality work and over diagnose patients should have their treatment reviewed and license to practice modified. If we as dentists don't monitor our profession our reputation as a whole will be seriously affected."
- "Don't admit greedy students, limit corporate influence, get back to basics. Some of the best restorative dentistry was done in the 1960-1980s. It had an artistic approach, which allowed a bond to the subject matter... the patient."
- "Good luck on that one; organized dentistry is avoiding getting involved."
- "I am too old to worry about this."
- "Many dentists have to sacrifice patients' care to maintain their profits by spending less time, recommending unnecessary treatment."
- "It is more the responsibility of the dental school to instill a strong ethics concept in the student. Organized dentistry is providing all the ethical education necessary through the ADA CEBJA [Council on Ethics, Bylaws and Judicial Affairs] and CDA Judicial Council and local dental society newsletters and ethics committees. It's time for the dental school to step up to the plate and teach ethics not how to make the most money."
- "More oversight over training for general dentists after dental school. There needs to be some standards put in place to see that a general dentist who takes one weekend course in implant placement is not allowed to start placing implants the next day. Dentist should have minimum educational requirements to perform complex procedures."
- "Poor and elderly people need to have dental insurance in the way they have medical insurance. Patients in rural areas do not have enough dentists willing to live there."
- "Support the efforts of solo practitioners."
- "The ADA and CDA should pressure California to ease regulations. For example, the sick leave law, amalgam separator regulation is significant increase in expenses, while reimbursement fees from insurance companies do not increase. These organizations should focus on helping sole practitioners. Is it possible to organize dentists to boycott some of the dental insurance companies with poor reimbursement?"

## References

Charmaz, K. (2006). *Constructing grounded theory: A practical guide through qualitative analysis.* Los Angeles, CA: Sage Publications.

Corbin, J., & Strauss, A. (2008). *Basics of qualitative research: Techniques and procedures for developing grounded theory* (3rd ed). Los Angeles, CA: Sage Publications.

Denzin, N. K., & Lincoln, Y. S. (eds) (2003). *The landscape of qualitative research: Theories and issues* (2nd ed). Thousand Oaks, CA: Sage Publications.

# Appendix B

# Dentists' and Patients' Perspectives on Ethics

Published as Chambers, D. W. (2015). Do patients and dentists see ethics the same way? *Journal of the American College of Dentists, 82* (2), 31-47.

## Abstract

The most common approach to ethics in dentistry and bioethics generally is through principles. To be effective, principles must be interpreted in particular situations and the skill of interpretation requires many years of practice with feedback. The opinions of 91 dentists and 54 patients regarding multiple potential actions and justifications for these actions were gathered for eight dental ethics cases. The summary responses of dentists and patients have been integrated as feedback in an online ethics education exercise that individual dentists can use (see www.dental ethics.org/idea). The dataset of responses was also analyzed for general findings. It emerged that patients and dentists agree to a substantial extent on the average approaches, but differ systematically on certain of the details. Some ethical issues stimulated a narrow range of responses while others, especially those of a nonclinical nature, were regarded as ambiguous and are thus good candidates for future ethics training. A factor analysis revealed a five-dimension structure underlying dental ethics. Patients are most apt to view dentistry using a lens of oral health outcomes while practitioners prefer to stress the process or technical dimensions of practice. The largest area of difference was patients' much greater interest in dentists assuming an active role as patient oral health advocates with their colleagues.

There are troubling situations in dentistry where there is reason to follow one course of action and also reason to pursue a contrary path. This is one of the characteristics of a profession that calls for the highest levels of skill and integrity. Doing the wrong thing for the wrong reason can undo beautiful technical work and biological acumen. Deciding whether to honor a patient request (respect for autonomy) for a treatment that is of questionable value (nonmaleficence) is a problem that arises from time to time. Deciding whether to take action—and if so, what action and for what real motives— when a colleague's work is pretty regularly seen to be below the standard of care is a test of loyalty—to the profession and to the public. These are called ethical dilemmas because there is something worthwhile to be said on both sides of the matter. Other times behavior is simply wrong but tempting. It is hard to think of circumstances that would justify overtreatment, upcoding insurance claims, or permitting a hostile work environment, but it happens. Although these are not dilemmas, we might still expect to see a range of behavior supported by interpretations of particular circumstances and personal value systems. Patients bring their own moral standards to the table. Some are likely to be sensitive to and speak up about particular tough choices dentists face and overlook others. Some patients use highly personal ethical maps. Those who are not patients—including public policy makers, bloggers, and those who vigorously avoid dentists—cannot be prevented from having opinions about what is right and wrong in dentistry.

In the past few decades, the professions have addressed these issues under the heading of "principles." An ethical principle is an abstract standard for appropriate behavior. Veracity (truth telling) and justice (fair distribution of benefits and burdens) are examples. The *Belmont Report* (1979), the first comprehensive American statement of ethical policy in medicine, identified three principles: respect for persons, beneficence, and justice (National Commission for the Protection of Human Subjects of Biomedical and Behavioral Research, 1979). The field of bioethics exploded in the years following, and Tom Beauchamp and James Childress's (2009) *Principles of*

*Biomedical Ethics* has become the fundamental expression of professional principlism. Beauchamp and Childress's four cardinal principles are: (a) respect for autonomy; (b) nonmaleficence; (c) beneficence; and (d) justice. The American Dental Association added a fifth principle, veracity, which accounts for about 40% of the Code of Professional Conduct and covers mostly dentist-to-dentist issues. The American Society for Bioethics and Humanities uses a code with seven principles. The American Bar Association identifies eight. The American Medical Association Code of Ethics has nine principles.

Principles offer general guidance, but they are blunt instruments. Specific issues can often be categorized under more than one principle, and these sometimes "guide" action in contrary directions. The tension between conflicting principles is well known. Both the American Dental Association, in its *Principles of Ethics and Code of Professional Conduct*, and Beauchamp and Childress (2009) acknowledge this, and professionals are usually counseled to "use their personal judgment to reach a 'balanced' resolution." The problem is that there is no principle that determines when "balance" has been achieved (Thornton, 2005). Principles need some form of further support to finish the job (Jonsen, 1991).

The bulk of ethics training—both in dental schools and where it appears occasionally in continuing education formats—as well as codes of conduct are intended as interpretations of the principles. This is sometimes called the Ethical Syllogism (MacIntyre, 1988). It works like this: Major Premise: Beneficence consists in doing what is best for the patient. Minor Premise: If patients are only informed of treatment options that I favor based on my training, they will pick sound treatments. Conclusion: It is beneficent to steer patients in informed consent toward optimal oral health. There are no debates in dentistry over whether respect for autonomy or justice, for example, are sound ethical principles. They are. All of the discussion turns on whether specific behaviors are best interpreted as good examples of the principles. Learning to become a professional entails learning how one's colleagues interpret the principles.

Despite their open-endedness, principles are a solid place to start in ethics training for professionals. Particular problems can be examined through the lens of multiple principles to give them depth and to reduce the chance of overlooking something important. Some interpretations of specific cases are clearly wrong and others are among the several alternative acceptable options. Interpretation is necessary, but all interpretations are not equally valid. Becoming a mature ethical professional means a long period of study of a wide range of concrete cases and gradually building interpretative skill. The principles can be memorized in less than a minute; becoming an ethical professional requires a lifetime of practice.

Not all practitioners interpret ethical principles the same way. A doctrinaire insistence on the letter of the law in the kingdom of one's own office may satisfy the urge of consistency. Some dentists use a shallow grounding in ethics because they are confident that they can "just do the right thing." It would be easy to maintain these positions if patients, staff, and associates can be dismissed for not seeing things as the owner dentist does. In fact principles may not even be necessary in such cases. Being a professional means contributing to and learning from the collective wisdom of one's colleagues and other important people. Principles begin to play a useful purpose when dentists look to their colleagues and others to see whether better alternatives exist. Ethics becomes part of the language in the conversations that make it possible to grow professionally. Absent comparisons of specific ethical cases, practitioners are apt to stagnate at the level of moral maturity they had when leaving dental school or even earlier in their lives.

It may come as a surprise that there are no American journals for dental ethics. Of the more than 20 in various professional fields, there are multiple examples in medicine, nursing, law, business, clergy, education, and even the military services. This is very likely a reflection of the fact that all of these professions are practiced in public settings. Since 1998 accreditation standards for U.S. dental schools have required documented compliance with the standard that students "must be competent in the application of the principles of ethical decision making and professional responsibility" (Council on Dental Accreditation, 2013; Standard 2-20). This is managed in some schools by an hour or sometimes several hours of seminar discussion of cases. This is not enough (Bertolami, 2004).

There are several theories of moral development. James Rest (1973; Rest et al, 1999) has modified and extensively studied Lawrence Kohlberg's (1968) developmental stages model of moral reasoning. There are three levels in this characterization of ethics, each having to do with the reasons one uses in reaching moral decisions (and less so with the actions themselves). Rest identifies these levels as: (a) "pre-conventional," where the standard is to follow authority and do what is rewarded and avoid what is punished; (b) "conventional," do what your peers expect of you; and (c) "post-conventional," where abstract norms are weighted as a philosopher might. I will use the more descriptive labels: "self," "group," and "ethics," as these appear to capture where individuals orient for finding the ultimate standard for ethical decision making in various cases.

The challenge is to create a safe environment for all dentists who traditionally work in isolation to compare notes, try alternatives, and get feedback to build moral skill. We need a platform for interaction, and it needs to be pretty large, open to all, and easily available 24/7 for extended periods of time.

As a step toward creating an opportunity for dentists to engage in public interpretation of prototypical ethics cases, the American College of Dentists has created a set of eight cases for discussion. These are available in written form and will soon be available in video format. But there is a significant limitation to the effectiveness of reading about ethics. There should be some way of experimenting with options and learning what one's colleagues would do. Perhaps it would even be useful to know what a representative sample of patients thinks of these situations.

Okay, let's find out. There are two goals in this report: (a) introduce a platform for building interpretative skills in practical ethics for practitioners that can be accessed conveniently from one's office; and (b) begin to understand the norms patients and dentists hold regarding various aspects of dental practice.

## Materials and Methods

Eight cases were developed, representing a range of problematic situations that could arise in dentistry. There are existing collections of cases in various styles, but I have followed the model of the late Jim Rule in his wonderful book *Ethical Questions in Dentistry* (2004). Rule's cases are longer and more detailed than many in circulation, but they were not written to illustrate predetermined positions. Although that slows down the reader, it also reduces the chance that one will imagine unstated facts or screen out inconvenient particulars from "skeletal" cases to make them fit abstract principles or personal preferences. A little of life's messiness is necessary to be realistic. Although all the cases have multiple dimensions and interesting paths to follow, they are not all dilemmas. The goal is to involve readers in the cases, not allowing them to be theoretical commentators. The full text of the cases can be seen at www.dentalethics.org/idea. The stem theme for each case and the actions and reasons are shown here in Table B.1.

Each case is followed by from four to six potential actions, and readers are invited to indicate on a five-point Likert scale how appropriate each action would be. The scale has anchor points of "absolutely," "probably," "50:50," "doubtful," and "no way." The actions are not mutually exclusive. It might be "absolutely" appropriate to initiate two or more actions at the same time and give just a little possible credence to a third that is similar to a choice that should be avoided entirely. There is seldom exactly one response to an ethical challenge. Usually there are several appropriate things that could be done and more than one way to get it wrong. But a forced selection on behavior is important in ethical situations. Too often we mistake performing an analysis of the situation and an enumeration of relevant principles for an ethical choice. It is not. The only way others will know whether we are ethical is by watching what we do.

Each case is also accompanied by from four to six "reasons" or important considerations or ethical goals. The reasons are similarly graded on a Likert scale as "decisive," "important," "not clear," "little importance," or "irrelevant." One could think of the reasons as "justifications" or things that might be said in defense if questioned about what we had done. These reasons represent some of the goals one has in mind when taking action. Again the reasons are not mutually exclusive. Much of our action is intended to simultaneously optimize several goals and stay out of trouble everywhere that might turn up. The structure of the actions and reasons is intended to place respondents in a realistic situation rather than as an academic exercise of picking the right answer on the best theoretical grounds. Dental school may be like that, but life is not.

Norms were constructed from a sample of dentists and patients, each of whom reported what they would do and why for all eight cases. The dentist sample consisted of 91 national and section officers of the American College of Dentists, who were surveyed by mail. The patient sample was taken from the attendees of two churches in Sonoma, California, totaling 54 responses.

In addition to full descriptive tabulation of the results, t-tests were performed for differences between groups (dentists vs. patients), F-ratios were calculated for homogeneity of variances between multiple groups, a factor analysis with varimax rotation was performed to identify the latent structure in respondents' views of oral health, and correlation matrices were created to reveal associations among the variables.

This project was approved in the exempt category by the IRB at the University of the Pacific, #13-63.

## Results

Both dentists and patients were able to use the cases in the format presented. The results are summarized in Table B.1 and have been converted to feedback available in the online version of the cases. Additionally these data have been analyzed by various statistical means to reveal the structure of dentist and patient views of ethical issues in dentistry, as reported below.

## Skill Building

In the computerized version of the cases, dentist and patient norms appear on the screen as soon as the reader makes choices for the case. This provides instant feedback that takes the place of group discussion in live seminar settings. Currently the feedback is presented as a percentage of patients and percentage of dentists selecting each position on the Likert scales for each action and for each reason. Those using the online form of these cases can see how their choices would be viewed by the public and by colleagues.

Consider an example from the case on hostile workplace environment (Coach). One of the actions offered to respondents was to ignore the hygienist's complaint that a patient was making inappropriate remarks on the grounds that such matters are personal between the staff and the patient. Dentists overwhelmingly rejected this as a way of handling the matter, 86% saying "no way" and 13% saying "probably not." Any dentist working through this case who thought seriously about ducking the issue would have to be nimble in creating an excuse for why he or she is different from others in the profession. As it happens, patients see this situation the same way. Among patients, 76% said do not avoid the issue in the strongest possible terms and another 22% considered this a doubtful alternative. Any dentist still thinking that the problem should be left to sort itself out on its own now has to fabricate a justification for the public. Dentists and patients also tended to agree on the reasons various actions should or should not be taken when hostile workplace environments occur. This pattern is shown in graphic format in Figure B.1.

Patients and dentists were of a common mind that employee morale, the law, value in good interpersonal communication skills, and the dentist's sense of integrity are strong reasons for confronting the issue. Slightly less important were reasons such as abstract matters of civil liberties and the dentist's reputation in the community.

There are examples such as this throughout the cases where patients and dentists agree that certain actions and reasons are obviously correct. There are also situations that are more challenging. For example, patients and dentists often disagree regarding a dentist's responsibility for challenging colleagues who are doing faulty work. Not all issues are ones where there is near uniformity in the right action or right reason. For example, dentists are of mixed mind regarding whether to dismiss a patient who reneges on payments; the entire range from "absolutely" to "no way" being advocated by many respondents. All of these outcomes where there is no consensus can be valuable for stimulating reflection.

---

**Figure B.1. Dentist is justified in overlooking harassment of employee by patient as this is a private matter.**

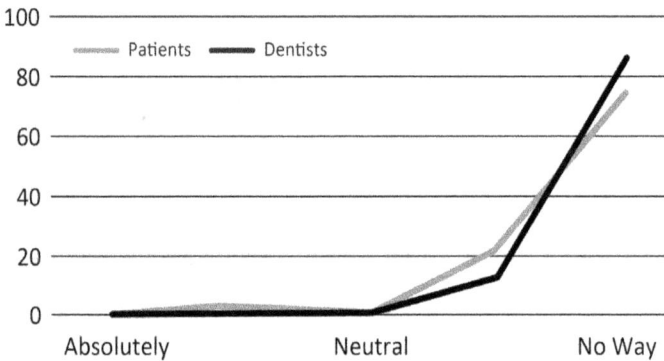

---

Principles are like a handpiece: they are a tool for doing better dentistry. Knowing about principles is like knowing about handpieces. The real result comes from repeated practice in individual situations. The eight ethics cases in this program are like the mannequin students use in preclinical technical. They are a good place to start learning.

### Understanding the Norms

This database can also be studied to learn about patients' and dentists' views of dental ethics. Are there patterns in the way the public or practitioners expect dentists to behave generally? Do the reasons given for the way dentists should act form patterns? Do patients place more or less weight on ethics and do they see particular situations the same way dentists do? Do we need continuing education courses on personnel law or on interprofessional management of patients? This is a rich dataset in which to explore such questions.

The full descriptive results are displayed in Table B.1. Patients' responses are on the top line and dentists' responses are below them in each pair. The highest score possible is 4.0, the lowest is 0.0, and the midpoint is 2.0. Means and standard deviations are shown, and symbols are used to flag statistical significance differences between groups. The symbol * indicates that the difference between patients and dentists is significant at the conventional p < .05 level; + denotes higher significance (p < .01); and # indicates significance at p < .001. The absence of a symbol means that no statistically significant difference was detected. Differences between standard deviations were also tested for significance because large ranges may indicate ambiguity or disagreement within each community of respondents. Thus it matters both where the center of opinion is on each issue (whether the peak of the curve moves right or left) and how widely spread the opinions are (how flat the curve is). The double initials in square brackets signal classifications of actions into one of five categories based on the factor analysis to be described below. Single initials ([S], [G], or [E]) are for the reasons using the relabeled Rest Three-factor Model of moral reasoning.

## Table B.1. Responses of patients and dentists to eight ethics cases.

**1. Service (Robin Hood):** Patient who has immediate need and has used current insurance eligibility requests that dentist perform work but date the insurance claim a month later so as to qualify for coverage.

| Mean | SDI | % Strong Support | % Neutral | % Strong Reject | |
|---|---|---|---|---|---|
| **Actions** | | | | | | |
| 1.41# | 1.39* | 10 | 16 | 18 | 20 | 37 | [DB] Perform the needed work and |
| .30 | .88 | 4 | 2 | 0 | 9 | 85 | submit the claims with later date |
| | | | | | | | |
| 1.60# | 1.25 | 7 | 22 | 18 | 31 | 22 | Perform the work only if Professor X |
| 2.50 | 1.29 | 30 | 23 | 24 | 18 | 8 | can pay the cash |
| | | | | | | | |
| 3.08# | .84 | 35 | 41 | 20 | 4 | 0 | [DB] Offer to perform the work at a |
| 2.52 | 1.03 | 17 | 39 | 28 | 13 | 4 | reduced rate as a public service |
| | | | | | | | |
| 2.00 | 1.23 | 13 | 18 | 42 | 11 | 16 | Make inquiries concerning other |
| 1.72 | 1.22 | 11 | 18 | 19 | 39 | 14 | dentist said to postdate claims |
| | | | | | | | |
| **Reasons** | | | | | | | |
| 2.82* | .83 | 18 | 52 | 26 | 2 | 2 | [S] Legal, contractual arrangements |
| 3.27 | 1.05 | 51 | 39 | 1 | 3 | 6 | with insurance companies |

| Mean | SDI | % Strong Support | | % Neutral | | % Strong Reject | |
|---|---|---|---|---|---|---|---|
| 3.41 | .50* | 41 | 59 | 0 | 0 | 0 | [G] Patient's oral needs and pressing |
| 3.21 | .79 | 37 | 53 | 6 | 3 | 1 | circumstances |
| 3.15 | .81 | 37 | 45 | 14 | 4 | 0 | [E] Dentist's personal values regarding |
| 1.77 | .92 | 45 | 42 | 7 | 4 | 2 | service |
| 1.93 | 1.42 | 14 | 27 | 27 | 4 | 29 | [S] Potential inaccurate dating of the |
| 3.19 | 1.71 | 26 | 19 | 6 | 9 | 40 | procedure will be detected |
| 2.62 | 1.26 | 23 | 45 | 15 | 4 | 13 | [E] Dental codes and standards in |
| 2.52 | 1.39 | 28 | 36 | 14 | 6 | 17 | the community |
| 3.66* | .47+ | 66 | 34 | 0 | 0 | 0 | Overall sense of what is right |
| 3.86 | .35 | 86 | 14 | 0 | 0 | 0 | |

**2. Third Opinion (Justifiable criticism):** Strong indications of faulty restorative work, undiagnosed periodontal problems, and overcharging the patient

| Mean | SDI | % Strong Support | | % Neutral | | % Strong Reject | |
|---|---|---|---|---|---|---|---|
| *Actions* | | | | | | | |
| 3.06 | 1.18 | 46 | 33 | 8 | 8 | 6 | Contact dentist who did the work to |
| 2.93 | 1.27 | 44 | 30 | 8 | 11 | 7 | get his or her side of the story |
| 2.32# | .96 | 11 | 34 | 32 | 23 | 0 | [JC] Lodge a formal complaint with |
| 1.44 | .93 | 2 | 8 | 35 | 40 | 15 | the dental society or dental board |
| 1.83 | 1.32 | 11 | 28 | 15 | 28 | 19 | [JC] Suggest patient return to first |
| 1.92 | 1.29 | 17 | 18 | 19 | 35 | 12 | dentist, do nothing else |
| 3.80 | .45 | 82 | 16 | 2 | 0 | 0 | Inform the patient of her present |
| 1.72 | 1.22 | 11 | 18 | 19 | 39 | 14 | condition, as you see it |
| 1.18# | 1.30# | 7 | 14 | 11 | 27 | 41 | [DB] Suggest indirectly to colleagues |
| .29 | .53 | 0 | 0 | 4 | 21 | 75 | unnamed dentist not up to par |
| *Reasons* | | | | | | | |
| 2.96* | .52* | 12 | 73 | 15 | 0 | 0 | [S] Patient's recollection of what was |
| 2.69 | .85 | 10 | 62 | 17 | 8 | 52 | done and when |
| 2.26* | 1.07 | 11 | 32 | 38 | 11 | 9 | [G] Professional code against |
| 2.64 | 1.06 | 20 | 45 | 20 | 10 | 5 | unjustifiable colleague criticism |
| 1.22 | 1.20 | 2 | 18 | 18 | 24 | 38 | [S] Dentists are independent, their |
| .92 | 1.08 | 1 | 11 | 14 | 26 | 48 | practices are their business |
| 3.78 | .42 | 78 | 22 | 0 | 0 | 0 | [E] Current health needs of the patient |
| 3.69 | .46 | 69 | 31 | 0 | 0 | 0 | |

| Mean | SDI | % Strong Support | % | Neutral | % | Strong Reject | |
|---|---|---|---|---|---|---|---|
| 1.82 | 1.17 | 5 | 27 | 32 | 18 | 18 | [S] Complexity and uncertainty of |
| 2.00 | 1.16 | 7 | 32 | 32 | 16 | 15 | interpersonal relationships |
| 1.78 | 1.16 | 2 | 28 | 30 | 20 | 20 | [S] Patient personality and motives |
| 2.05 | 1.06 | 3 | 35 | 36 | 13 | 13 | |
| 3.65 | .52 | 67 | 31 | 2 | 0 | 0 | [E] Dentists have obligation to all |
| 3.56 | .52 | 57 | 42 | 1 | 0 | 0 | patients and profession generally |

**3. Who Cares (Generalist–specialist relations):** Two periodontists in town suddenly both stop returning patients to the referring general dentist and advise patients that they all need "advanced care" that only they can provide.

| Mean | SDI | % Strong Support | % Neutral | % Strong Reject | |
|---|---|---|---|---|---|

*Actions*

| Mean | SDI | | | | | | |
|---|---|---|---|---|---|---|---|
| 1.71+ | 1.34 | 13 | 16 | 22 | 27 | 22 | Confine comments to reinforcing |
| 2.32 | 1.25 | 20 | 27 | 27 | 14 | 11 | the desirability of optimal care |
| 2.84 | .92 | 24 | 43 | 27 | 4 | 2 | Suggest that patient make an |
| 2.82 | 1.19 | 32 | 41 | 8 | 13 | 6 | appointment to be seen by specialist |
| 2.33# | 1.03 | 8 | 45 | 22 | 20 | 4 | [DB] Invite specialists to lunch, |
| 3.40 | .83 | 55 | 35 | 5 | 3 | 1 | discuss apparent change in referrals |
| 3.13# | .89+ | 42 | 33 | 21 | 4 | 0 | [DB JC] Explore generalist-specialist |
| 1.86 | 1.21 | 11 | 22 | 23 | 31 | 13 | roles with component ethics committee |

*Reasons*

| Mean | SDI | | | | | | |
|---|---|---|---|---|---|---|---|
| 2.43+ | 1.17 | 8 | 59 | 14 | 4 | 14 | [S] Patient's financial situation |
| 2.00 | 1.14 | 0 | 50 | 15 | 21 | 14 | |
| 2.67# | .97+ | 19 | 44 | 26 | 9 | 2 | [S] Implication that generalist is not |
| 3.25 | .69 | 38 | 50 | 11 | 1 | 0 | competent to maintain patient |
| 2.96 | .81 | 26 | 49 | 21 | 4 | 0 | [G] Changing trust levels between |
| .04 | .81 | 28 | 54 | 13 | 3 | 1 | patient and generalist |
| 3.57# | .57* | 61 | 35 | 4 | 0 | 0 | [S] Accuracy of informed consent so |
| 3.02 | .90 | 29 | 53 | 12 | 2 | 3 | patient understands all choices |
| 3.48* | .58+ | 52 | 44 | 4 | 0 | 0 | [E] Patient's freedom to choose the level |
| 3.16 | .79 | 32 | 59 | 4 | 2 | 2 | of care they desire |
| 3.21 | .76 | 35 | 55 | 8 | 0 | 2 | [E] Importance of optimal oral care |
| 3.37 | .62 | 41 | 57 | 1 | 0 | 1 | |

**4. Fair Payment (Patient attempts to renege on payment)**: Patient attempts to renege on part of payment for large completed treatment plan based on failure of part of it that the dentist recommended against.

| Mean | SDI | % Strong Support | % | % Neutral | % Strong Reject | |
|---|---|---|---|---|---|---|
| **Actions** | | | | | | |
| .35 | .79# | 0 | 6 | 0 | 17 | 77 | Agree to patient's suggestion to |
| .16 | .40 | 0 | 0 | 1 | 14 | 85 | cut payment |
| | | | | | | | |
| 2.06 | 1.22 | 15 | 26 | 17 | 36 | 6 | Dismiss patient through a formal |
| 1.94 | 1.16 | 8 | 26 | 29 | 25 | 12 | process and write off the bad debt |
| | | | | | | | |
| 2.88 | .96 | 26 | 48 | 16 | 8 | 2 | [JC] Refer patient to peer review |
| 2.67 | 1.13 | 28 | 33 | 22 | 14 | 3 | for adjudication of disagreement |
| | | | | | | | |
| 2.01# | 1.30+ | 14 | 27 | 20 | 23 | 16 | [DB] Negotiate compromise treatment, |
| 1.19 | 1.03 | 1 | 15 | 11 | 47 | 26 | partial, extended payments |
| **Reasons** | | | | | | |
| 2.73+ | 1.06+ | 16 | 63 | 8 | 6 | 8 | [G] Dentist's reputation in town |
| 2.26 | 1.17 | 9 | 47 | 16 | 18 | 10 | |
| | | | | | | | |
| 3.14 | .82 | 33 | 53 | 10 | 2 | 2 | [E] Get patient to accept responsibility |
| 3.35 | .73 | 43 | 52 | 1 | 2 | 1 | for both financial and health issues |
| | | | | | | | |
| 3.46+ | .58 | 50 | 46 | 4 | 0 | 0 | [S] Chart notes of options presented, |
| 3.67 | .56 | 71 | 27 | 1 | 1 | 0 | written financial arrangements |
| | | | | | | | |
| 2.49 | .86 | 2 | 60 | 30 | 2 | 6 | [S] Potential for protracted dispute and |
| 2.17 | 1.05 | 2 | 51 | 15 | 25 | 7 | lost time in the office |
| | | | | | | | |
| 3.08 | .82 | 29 | 57 | 6 | 8 | 0 | [E] Addressing patient's compromised |
| 3.02 | .74 | 22 | 65 | 9 | 3 | 1 | dental condition |
| | | | | | | | |
| 2.09 | 1.15 | 6 | 40 | 23 | 19 | 13 | [G] What other dentists might do in |
| 2.16 | 1.14 | 6 | 44 | 24 | 14 | 13 | a similar situation |

**5. Coach (Hostile work environment)**: Hygienist complains that patient ("Coach") is verbally sexually harassing her.

| Mean | SDI | % Strong Support | % | % Neutral | % Strong Reject | |
|---|---|---|---|---|---|---|
| **Actions** | | | | | | |
| 1.19 | 1.10+ | 6 | 4 | 21 | 40 | 29 | Registered letter dismissing Coach, |
| 1.06 | .82 | 1 | 4 | 18 | 54 | 23 | citing illegality of harassment |
| | | | | | | | |
| 3.20 | .95 | 46 | 36 | 12 | 4 | 2 | Talk to Coach, explain perceptions, |
| 3.37 | .74 | 48 | 45 | 2 | 4 | 0 | warn of possible termination |

| Mean | SDI | % Strong Support | % | % Neutral | % | % Strong Reject | |
|---|---|---|---|---|---|---|---|
| 2.73 | .95 | 33 | 31 | 17 | 13 | 6 | Encourage hygienist to talk with Coach, |
| 2.53 | 1.23 | 23 | 38 | 16 | 16 | 8 | help her be assertive |
| 2.40 | 1.31 | 26 | 30 | 11 | 28 | 6 | Call a staff meeting to discuss the issue |
| 2.68 | 1.26 | 32 | 31 | 17 | 12 | 8 | |
| .29 | .59* | 0 | 2 | 0 | 22 | 76 | [RA] Dentist does nothing, this is an |
| .16 | .40 | 0 | 0 | 1 | 13 | 86 | employee-customer relationship |

*Reasons*

| Mean | SDI | % Strong Support | % | % Neutral | % | % Strong Reject | |
|---|---|---|---|---|---|---|---|
| 2.70+ | 1.02 | 12 | 66 | 10 | 4 | 8 | [G] Reputation of the profession |
| 2.30 | 1.28 | 12 | 48 | 12 | 11 | 16 | in the community |
| 2.49+ | 1.20 | 16 | 47 | 22 | 2 | 13 | [R] Civil liberties and personal autonomy |
| 2.84 | 1.00 | 25 | 49 | 15 | 8 | 3 | |
| 3.18 | .44+ | 20 | 78 | 2 | 0 | 0 | [G] Employee morale |
| 3.34 | .60 | 40 | 56 | 3 | 1 | 0 | |
| 3.06+ | .85 | 31 | 51 | 14 | 2 | 2 | [S] Legal considerations |
| 3.40 | .73 | 52 | 38 | 8 | 2 | 0 | |
| 2.88 | .94 | 21 | 58 | 13 | 4 | 4 | [S] Verbal skills and confidence of |
| 3.06 | .77 | 28 | 54 | 13 | 4 | 0 | the dentist and the hygienist |
| 3.35 | .75 | 49 | 39 | 10 | 2 | 0 | [E] Dentist's personal standards of |
| 3.36 | .90 | 54 | 37 | 2 | 4 | 2 | interpersonal respect |

**6. Tooth Colored Restorations (Informed consent):** Three dentists compare different philosophies regarding treatment presentation of amalgam or composite on posterior restorations. Dr. A aggressively steers all patients toward composite; Dr. B explains both options and lets patients decide; Dr. C simply does what he thinks is best in each case without engaging the patient in the decision.

| Mean | SDI | % Strong Support | % Neutral | % Strong Reject | |
|---|---|---|---|---|---|
| *Actions* | | | | | |
| 3.33* | 1.03# | 61 | 22 | 12 | 2 | 4 | [PR] Off base to offer only composite |

| Mean | SDI | % Strong Support | % | % Neutral | % | % Strong Reject | |
|---|---|---|---|---|---|---|---|
| 3.33* | 1.03# | 61 | 22 | 12 | 2 | 4 | [PR] Off base to offer only composite |
| 3.82 | .47 | 85 | 12 | 3 | 0 | 0 | and replacing sound amalgams |
| 3.31+ | .95# | 56 | 27 | 8 | 8 | 0 | [PR] "Selling" perhaps unneeded |
| 3.82 | .47 | 85 | 12 | 3 | 0 | 0 | dentistry as "patient education" |
| .66 | .77 | 0 | 2 | 12 | 36 | 50 | [RA] Patients asked to decide when |
| .58 | .82 | 0 | 2 | 14 | 23 | 60 | not really qualified to judge |
| .60 | .96 | 2 | 4 | 8 | 23 | 63 | [RA] Carrying informed consent too far |
| .66 | .85 | 0 | 4 | 11 | 30 | 54 | |

| Mean | SDI | | | | | | |
|---|---|---|---|---|---|---|---|
| 3.08 | 1.12 | 44 | 36 | 10 | 4 | 6 | Off base to consider only dentist's values |
| 3.25 | 1.01 | 56 | 25 | 12 | 3 | 4 | |
| | | | | | | | |
| .96 | 1.22 | 8 | 4 | 10 | 31 | 47 | Informed consent is unnecessary |
| .76 | 1.16 | 7 | 3 | 8 | 23 | 59 | in such cases |

*Reasons*

| Mean | SDI | | | | | | |
|---|---|---|---|---|---|---|---|
| 3.38 | .72 | 46 | 50 | 2 | 0 | 2 | [E] Patient autonomy: patients have |
| 3.53 | .58 | 57 | 39 | 4 | 0 | 0 | ultimate say over their own care |
| | | | | | | | |
| 2.19* | .95 | 2 | 42 | 37 | 12 | 8 | [E] Dentist autonomy: dentists allowed |
| 2.72 | 1.00 | 12 | 68 | 7 | 7 | 7 | to practice as they think best |
| | | | | | | | |
| .77 | .94 | 2 | 4 | 12 | 35 | 4 | [G] Patients questioning dentist damages |
| .73 | .92 | 0 | 4 | 19 | 22 | 54 | the professional relationship |
| | | | | | | | |
| .68+ | .92* | 4 | 2 | 2 | 43 | 49 | [S] Dentists should only offer the most |
| .37 | .62 | 1 | 0 | 1 | 27 | 71 | esthetic and expensive care |
| | | | | | | | |
| 2.23 | 1.38 | 12 | 46 | 12 | 8 | 22 | [S] Dentist's comfort level talking about |
| 1.89 | 1.29 | 8 | 35 | 14 | 24 | 19 | alternatives and costs with patients |
| | | | | | | | |
| 1.60 | 1.24 | 0 | 28 | 26 | 16 | 30 | [S] Whether patient seems intelligent |
| 1.46 | 1.19 | 3 | 20 | 22 | 27 | 28 | and to value high-end care |
| | | | | | | | |
| 2.81 | 1.04 | 19 | 62 | 8 | 4 | 8 | [S] Amount of experience dentist has |
| 2.66 | .95 | 10 | 64 | 14 | 7 | 6 | with the procedures |

**7. Full Care (Pro bono work):** As a member of a local service organization that does charitable work, the dentist visits a nursing home in town and discovers substantial unmet need.

| Mean | SDI | % Strong Support | % Neutral | % Strong Reject | | | |
|---|---|---|---|---|---|---|---|

*Actions*

| Mean | SDI | | | | | | |
|---|---|---|---|---|---|---|---|
| .49 | .79 | 2 | 0 | 6 | 29 | 63 | [OH] No action—society and insurance |
| .73 | .86 | 0 | 5 | 13 | 33 | 49 | have set compensation too low |
| | | | | | | | |
| .28+ | .50+ | 0 | 0 | 2 | 23 | 74 | [OH] No action—no lasting impact, might |
| .51 | .67 | 0 | 1 | 6 | 36 | 57 | be seen as interference |
| | | | | | | | |
| 3.42+ | .66 | 49 | 45 | 4 | 2 | 0 | [OH] Work to start program that involves |
| 3.11 | .83 | 36 | 44 | 16 | 4 | 0 | other local dentists in care |
| | | | | | | | |
| 3.24# | .74 | 40 | 46 | 12 | 2 | 0 | [OH] Volunteer one day a month in |
| 2.57 | .97 | 17 | 39 | 31 | 11 | 2 | the nursing home, no matter what |

*Reasons*

| Mean | SDI | | | | | | |
|---|---|---|---|---|---|---|---|
| 2.71 | 1.08 | 16 | 61 | 12 | 2 | 10 | [G] Reputation of the profession in |
| 2.88 | .96 | 23 | 56 | 10 | 8 | 3 | the community |

| Mean | SDI | % Strong Support | % | % Neutral | % | % Strong Reject | |
|---|---|---|---|---|---|---|---|
| 3.70 | .46 | 70 | 30 | 0 | 0 | 0 | [E] Patient's oral needs |
| 3.57 | .50 | 57 | 44 | 0 | 0 | 0 | |
| 1.67 | 1.09 | 0 | 29 | 29 | 24 | 18 | [S] Each provider community and |
| 1.93 | 1.05 | 6 | 24 | 40 | 20 | 11 | funder functions independently |

**8. Who Decides? (Patient autonomy):** Patient indicates strong preference for veneers in esthetic region and a disinclination to have needed restorative and periodontal work done first.

| Mean | SDI | % Strong Support | % | % Neutral | % | % Strong Reject | |
|---|---|---|---|---|---|---|---|
| **Actions** | | | | | | | |
| 1.66# | 1.15+ | 6 | 18 | 30 | 28 | 18 | [OH] Convince patient that veneers |
| .73 | .86 | 0 | 5 | 13 | 33 | 49 | are not always the best choice here |
| 3.26# | .84 | 42 | 51 | 2 | 4 | 2 | [DB] Try to convince patient of dentist's |
| .51 | .67 | 0 | 1 | 6 | 36 | 57 | plan for long-term oral health |
| 2.70* | .82 | 13 | 53 | 25 | 9 | 0 | Suggest cleaning, replacement filling, |
| 3.11 | .83 | 36 | 44 | 16 | 4 | 0 | postpone full treatment plan |
| 1.92# | 1.13 | 8 | 23 | 37 | 19 | 13 | [OH] Say you value needs above |
| 2.57 | .97 | 17 | 39 | 31 | 11 | 2 | wants and suggest another dentist |
| 2.11# | 1.10 | 8 | 34 | 30 | 19 | 9 | Begin work while continuing to |
| 1.44 | 1.21 | 5 | 21 | 16 | 33 | 26 | educate patient during treatment |
| **Reasons** | | | | | | | |
| 2.87 | .79 | 13 | 70 | 9 | 6 | 2 | [E] Patient autonomy (right to choose |
| 2.84 | .82 | 14 | 69 | 9 | 7 | 2 | what they feel is best) |
| 3.44 | .63 | 52 | 40 | 8 | 0 | 0 | [E] Patient's comprehensive oral needs |
| 3.55 | .52 | 56 | 43 | 1 | 0 | 0 | |
| 2.75 | .57* | 4 | 67 | 27 | 2 | 0 | [E] Dentist's autonomy (right to choose |
| 2.85 | .89 | 17 | 65 | 7 | 9 | 2 | what they feel is best) |
| 2.74 | 1.00 | 15 | 56 | 21 | 0 | 8 | [S] Verbal skills and confidence of |
| 2.72 | .90 | 12 | 62 | 14 | 8 | 3 | the dentist and the hygienist |
| 1.55# | 1.14 | 4 | 14 | 41 | 16 | 25 | [S] Prospect that such a patient will |
| 2.56 | 1.08 | 14 | 54 | 15 | 11 | 7 | become a management problem |

*NB: The top line in each pair describes patients' responses; the bottom line describes dentists' responses. The means and standard deviations are shown in the first two columns of each set. Higher numbers represent greater agreement with the action or reason or larger standard deviations. Differences between patients and dentists that are significant at p < .05 are marked with a +; * is used to represent differences at p < .01; # identifies differences significant at p < .001. The numbers in italic are percentages in each group*

Figure B.2 is a graphic representation of one of the 84 elements in Table B.1, Case 3, "Who Cares", action alternative 4. It shows the percentage of respondents selecting each of the five options from strongly favorable to strongly unfavorable for taking up with the component society the issue of specialists not returning patients to the referring general practitioner. On average, patients tend to favor raising the concern at the professional level (3.13, where 2.00 is neutral) while dentists shy away from that (1.86). This difference is statistically significant at $p < .001$. Further, the standard deviation for patients is .89 compared to the statistically significantly larger standard deviation of 1.21 for dentists. Dentists are more divided in their opinions than are patients. Graphically, the differences in appropriateness of the action is clear as a shift in the two peaks on the curve. Graphically, the difference in consensus of opinion is represented by the overall flatter curve for the dentists.

**Figure B.2. Likelihood patients and dentists favor reporting dentist for gross or continuous faulty treatment.**

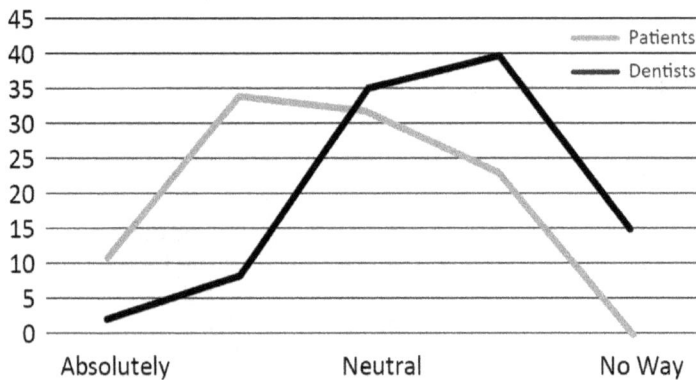

In the set of 37 possible ethical actions, the most prominent differences between patients and dentists include the following. Dentists are more apt to favor upfront payment, comprehensive treatment plans, limited informed consent, and confidential management of differences among colleagues. Patients value adjustments of payment alternatives and spacing of treatment, full informed consent, better education, active and open engagement of colleagues who are not practicing at the standard of care, and greater involvement of dentists in the general oral health needs of the community.

A striking illustration of the divergence in valued actions concerns a patient who requests veneers on teeth with questionable anatomical support. Should the dentist educate the patient regarding a long-term treatment plan based on health instead? Ninety-three percent of patients say "yes" while 93% of dentists say "no," the apparent reason being partially related to suspicions that this is an "independently minded" patient. More than half the dentists (56%) would refer such patients out of their practices, a policy endorsed by only 31% of patients. Another such example of divergent opinions regarding management of patients whose expectations differ from those of the practitioner involves renegotiating treatment and payment for a patient who is dissatisfied with the initial work performed by the dentist and not inclined to pay for it. Both patients and dentists agree strongly that letting the patient off the financial hook is inappropriate. But the typical response among patients is to explore breaking treatment plans and payments into segments. Among dentists almost 75% would look unfavorably on this action. Patients are more apt than dentists to favor referring the patient to peer review for adjudication of the disagreement.

### Agreement between Dentists and Patients

The Likert responses on each item were converted to a 4-to-0 scale and the average was taken for each item for patients and for dentists, collapsing the dataset to 37 actions and 47 reasons. The correlation between patient and dentist average scores for actions was $r = .806$. The correlation across averages for the reasons was $r = .911$. There is very high global agreement between dentists and patients in how to act and why across the eight cases studied.

### Is There One Best Answer (Issue Ambiguity)?

There was consensus on some actions and reasons and a range of responses on others. Only a dentist who was outside the tight range would need worry about these ethical issues, and by definition there will be few of them. The profession needs to turn its attention first to those issues where there is little settled opinion. Those challenges where dentists agree with each other and patients are in agreement that something else should be done are also critical and will be discussed below. How wide is the range of preferred responses?

Table B.2 presents the results of the first of several analyses intended to show the underlying structure in these data. Of the 37 action items and the 47 reason items, there were none where a single one of the five scale values was agreed by either patients or dentists. In 55% of actions and 68% of reasons, all five alternatives from "absolutely/decisive" all the way to "no way/ irrelevant" were selected by somebody. This diffuse pattern was also reflected in the modal responses. Where there was consensus, the distribution will be peaked and a large proportion of the responses will be in the mode (most commonly chosen alternative). The mode could range from a low of 20% (meaning that all five alternatives were chosen an equal number of times) to 100% (meaning that one alternative was always selected). Across all 84 items, the average modal response clustered near 50%, meaning that the most popular action or reason was favored by roughly half of the respondents. Alternatively, patients or dentists who chose the response favored by most of their peers were in disagreement with half of those in their group. Patients and dentists were equally spread on both actions and reasons. Dentists were equally spread on their choices of actions and reasons, but patients were slightly more concentrated on reasons than on actions. Items with large standard deviations tended to have larger numbers of missing values, $r = .197$. This can also be interpreted as a sign of ambiguity—respondents simply chose not to register an opinion and, presumably, would try to avoid rather than address such challenges.

---

**Table B.2. Range of reasons given for various ethical actions chosen by patients and dentists.**

|  | Actions | | Reasons | |
|---|---|---|---|---|
|  | Patients | Dentists | Patients | Dentists |
| Alternatives used | % | % | % | % |
| 1 | 0 | 0 | 0 | 0 |
| 2 | 0 | 0 | 9 | 6 |
| 3 | 11 | 16 | 15 | 6 |
| 4 | 24 | 24 | 21 | 19 |
| 5 | 65 | 59 | 55 | 68 |
| Mean modal response (%) | 46.2 | 50.1 | 52.2 | 53.5 |
| Mean SD | 1.00 | .93 | .89 | .89 |

NB: "Alternatives used" designates proportion of the five available alternatives selected by any respondent per item. For example, 5 means that at least one person chose each alternative; 3 means that two of the alternatives were not used; 1 would indicate complete unanimity. The average modal response is the percentage of respondents selecting the *commonly chosen alternative. This number would range from 20% if all five responses were chosen by an equal number of respondents to 100% in the case of unanimity. By paired-comparison t-tests, dentists tended to be more concentrated in their most preferred action than were patients (t = 1.79), but there were no differences between dentists and patients on reasons (t = .80). Reasons were more concentrated than were actions in patients' minds (t = 1.98, two group t-test), but not for dentists (t = 1.01). Mean standard deviation across items was not different across patient or dentist groups or for actions compared with reasons (F-test all under 1.75).*

The issues that drew the widest range of opinions for both patients and dentists (standard deviations above 1.25) included truthfulness in filing insurance claims, taking action regarding other dentists' questionable behavior, involving all staff in the hostile workplace matter, and extent of informed consent deemed appropriate. Providing care when the patient is making irregular payments was more of an unsettled issue for dentists than for patients.

## Matching Actions to Reasons

It is possible that there are tight connections between actions and the reasons used to justify them—each action based on a dominant reason. It is also possible that reasons support multiple actions. To explore this possibility, all correlations were calculated between actions and reasons and the average taken on a case-by-case basis. The average across all eight cases was r = .104. This means that reasons were not specific to actions. Further evidence for negligible action-reason pairing was found by locating those cases where a single reason was associated with a single action. Only 26% of the reasons motivated a single action (operationalized as a correlation significant at the p < .05 level), while 40% motivated multiple actions and 34% were not systematically associated with any action. Analyzed from the opposite perspective, 31% of the actions were significantly associated with a single reason, while 44% had multiple motivations, and 25% had none. This finding raises questions about grounding ethical analysis in principles, or at least in expecting to find that principles lead predictably to actions.

## Level of Ethical Justification

Forty-seven different reasons for ethics in dentistry is too many to work with. We need to find meaningful groupings. When psychologists, rather than philosophers, study ethics, they look to levels of reasoning or where standards are drawn from. A well-established classification system is James Rest's three categories, which I have modified slightly to emphasize the location of the standard for making ethical choice. Each of the reasons for actions in this study was assigned to one of the categories of Self, Group, or Ethical, and the results are summarized in Table B.3.

Self and Group justifications were valued to about the same extent, but Ethical reasoning was preferred or given stronger credibility. This grouping was statistically significant. There were no differences between patients and dentists on this score. The literature generally reports that individuals seldom come up with fully Ethical justifications on their own (McNeel, 1994). This study found that where such reasons are provided, they carry weight.

---

**Table B.3. Average (standard deviation) of endorsed reasons for actions classified by moral reasoning level.**

|  | Self | Group | Ethical | F | p |
|---|---|---|---|---|---|
| Total sample | 2.35 [a] | 2.53 [a] | 3.20 [b] | 7.67 | .001 |
|  | (.80) | (.71) | (.45) |  |  |
| Patients | 2.30 [a] | 2.54 [a] | 3.21 [b] | 8.77 | .001 |
|  | (.75) | (.73) | (.45) |  |  |
| Dentists | 2.39 [a] | 2.50 [a] | 3.19 [b] | 5.50 | .007 |
|  | (.89) | (.75) | (.51) |  |  |
| t-value | .34 | .11 | .10 |  |  |

NB: Types of action were identified from a factor analysis and only those actions with significant loadings were scored for each action type. In some cases, the direction of scoring was reversed based on factor loadings. The three levels of moral reasoning were categorized based on an approximation of Rest's typology. The F- and p-values on the right reflect one-way ANOVA tests across action types of moral reasoning levels. The t-values at the bottom of each column represent t-tests for differences between patients and dentists. Values having the same superscripted letter cannot be distinguished based on post hoc Duncan multiple range tests across types of actions or levels of moral reasoning. There were no significant differences between patients and dentists.

---

Self and Group justifications were valued to about the same extent, but Ethical reasoning was preferred or given stronger credibility. This grouping was statistically significant. There were no differences between patients and dentists on this score. The literature generally reports that individuals seldom come up with fully Ethical justifications on their own (McNeel, 1994). This study found that where such reasons are provided, they carry weight.

## Underlying Structure, Ethical Dimensions of Dentistry

Thirty-seven different courses of action is also too many to work with individually. It is human nature to look for patterns. One might be tempted to say, for example, some dentists are master technicians and others are born salespeople. Some are both and some are neither, but the typology still makes sense. Some office staff have names for certain kinds of patients. Every case does not fit perfectly in such systems, but we keep using them because on the whole they guide action with few surprises. There is a formal statistical procedure called factor analysis that uses the computer to identify natural dimensions in data based on how respondents group their responses. Factor analysis calls out dimension rather than clusters, so a particular item can "load" (have common properties) on several factors. Combined patient and dentist responses for all 37 actions were submitted to principle components factor analysis with a varimax rotation. Factors were retained based on analysis of scree plots, eigenvalues above 1.0, and meaningfulness of suggested interpretations. Table B.4 shows the five factors that were extracted, which together account for 57% of the variance. Only items with significant factor loadings are reported.

Table B.4 shows a very clean, five-factor structure. Most actions load on a single one of the five underlying dimensions. The most prominent factor is labeled Oral Health orientation. Items loading on this factor mention positive patient health status independent of treatment activity. The second most prominent factor (Technical Focus) selected for specific treatment, appropriateness of selected treatment, or managing workflow or financial relationships. Professional Engagement, the third factor, included items describing dentist-to-dentist relationships. The fourth factor was the classical ethical principle of Respect for Autonomy. A final dimension has been included for the sometimes mentioned practice of Paternalism. Actions loading on this factor involved behavior where the dentist alone determines what is in the patients' best interests. The same factor structure emerged when separate factor analyses were conducted for patients and for dentists.

Occasionally in such situations, a global factor emerges in a preemptive position that explains most of the variance. This was not the case here, but had that been so, it would have supported the view that there is a global construct—"being ethical"—which characterizes some dentists but not others. This analysis suggests that ethical dental practice is more nuanced and situation-specific.

## Table B.4. Factor structure among 37 actions on 8 cases, 148 combined patients and dentists.

| Factors | | Oral health | Technical focus | Professional engage-ment | Respect for autonomy | Paternalism |
|---|---|---|---|---|---|---|
| % Variance | | 17% | 16% | 9% | 8% | 7% |
| **Action** | **Case** | | | | | |
| No action–society and insurance have set compensation too low | Full care | -.813 | | | | |
| No action–no lasting impact, might be seen as interference | Full care | -.723 | | | | |
| Work to start program that involves other local dentists in care | Full care | .681 | | | | |
| Volunteer one day a month in the nursing home, no matter what | Full care | .648 | | | | |
| Convince patient that veneers are not always the best choice here | Who decides | -.614 | | | | |
| Say you value *needs* above *wants* and suggest another dentist | Who decides | .512 | | | | .527 |
| Try to convince patient of dentist's plan for long-term oral health | Who decides | -.762 | | | | |
| Perform the needed work and submit the claims with later date | Service | | -.424 | | | |
| Offer to perform the work at a reduced rate as a public service | Service | | -.526 | | | |
| Negotiate compromise treatment, partial, extended payments | Fair payment | | -.669 | | | |
| Suggest indirectly to colleagues unnamed dentist not up to par | Third opinion | | -.594 | | | |
| Invite specialists to lunch, discuss apparent change in referrals | Who cares | | .602 | | | |
| Explore GP-specialist roles with component ethics committee | Who cares | | .426 | .530 | | |

| | | | | |
|---|---|---|---|---|
| Lodge a formal complaint with the dental society or dental board | Third opinion | .701 | | |
| Suggest patient return to first dentist, do nothing else | Third opinion | -.604 | | |
| Refer patient to peer review for adjudication of disagreement | Fair payment | .681 | | |
| Dentist does nothing, this is an employee-customer relationship | Coach | | -.485 | |
| Patients asked to decide when not really qualified to judge | Tooth colored | | -.782 | |
| Carrying informed consent too far | Tooth colored | | -.811 | |
| Off base to offer only composite and replacing sound amalgams | Tooth colored | | | .760 |
| "Selling" perhaps unneeded dentistry as "patient education" | Tooth colored | | | .717 |

## Ethical Dimensions of Dentistry as Seen by Dentists and Patients

More than half the variation (57%) in the actions chosen by patients and dentists in these ethical dental situations was explained by a five-factor structure. If we know where people stand on these dimensions, we will be able to predict with some confidence how they will act when presented with ethical challenges. It would be helpful to know whether this five-factor structure is applicable to both patients and dentists independently. The answer is sketched in Table B.5.

Respect for autonomy, willingness to include others in the decision-making process, appeared as a leading ethical dimension for both patients and dentists. After that, some differences begin to emerge. Patients placed a greater salience on behavior that ensures positive oral health outcomes than did dentists. Dentists focused more on the technical aspects of dental treatment. Patients were very significantly more concerned that dentists should engage in professional interactions with colleagues on patients' behalf than were dentists.

### Table B.5. Average preferences (standard deviations) for actions of various types among patients and dentists (including only items identified in factor analysis).

| | Oral health | Technical focus | Prof. engagement | Respect for autonomy | Paternalism | F | p |
|---|---|---|---|---|---|---|---|
| Total sample | 2.80 [a] | 3.23 [a] | 2.44 [a] | 4.48 [b] | 3.10 [a] | 3.97 | .008 |
| | (1.01) | (.96) | (.67) | (.17) | (.72) | | |
| Patients | 3.37 [ab] | 2.75 [a] | 2.88 [a] | 4.48 [b] | 2.86 [a] | 2.52 | .08 |
| | (1.14) | (.84) | (.39) | (.20) | (.81) | | |
| Dentists | 2.22 [a] | 3.71 [ab] | 2.34 [a] | 4.48 [b] | 3.34 [ab] | 4.09 | .02 |
| | ( .89) | (.89) | (.62) | (.18) | (.67) | | |
| Patient-dentist difference | | | | | | | |
| $t$ | 1.72 | 1.91 | 2.34 | .02 | .80 | | |
| P | .04 | .03 | .01 | | | | |

*Higher numbers represent greater endorsement. Only items significantly loading on the identified five-factor structure were included in the calculations.*

## Ethical Dimensions of Dentistry and Levels of Ethical Reasoning

Table B.6 shows the correlation coefficients between moral reasoning level and types of actions most valued by patients and by dentists. This is a summary of the extracted five dimensions of actions and the three levels of reasons instead of the nearly 400 relationships in Table B.1. Patients favoring Self-focused, rule-based approaches over other types of ethical reasoning tended to devalue both oral health outcomes and respect for autonomy. Those with Group orientations were what might be called "casual" with regard to the way dentists preferred to run their practices. The general norm in the patient community contains ambivalent expectations. Those patients who placed a high value on understanding issues from the Ethical point of view were keen on respect for autonomy—they want to be independent moral agents.

Dentists presented a slightly different picture of the relationship between level of ethical reasoning and their structuring of ethical actions. Self-focused reasoning was associated with actions keeping practitioners out of engagement with their colleagues or the profession generally. Group thinking was associated with attention to the business of dentistry and technical performance. The dominant norm by which dentists judge each other appears to be performing technically fine treatment and running a successful practice. Higher Ethical reasoning was negatively associated with paternalism. Seeking the grounds for ethical practice in general standards was considered inconsistent with acting as one's own standard.

### Table B.6. Associations between action types and moral reasoning level.

| | Patients | | | Dentists | | |
|---|---|---|---|---|---|---|
| | Self | Group | Ethical | Self | Group | Ethical |
| Oral health | -.365+ | | | | | |
| Treatment focus | | -.302* | | | .222 | |
| Professional engagement | | | | -.312 | | |
| Respect for autonomy | -.378+ | | .269 | | | |
| Paternalism | | | | | | -.265* |

Only significant correlation coefficients are shown.
* = p < .05, + = p < .01.

## Discussion

Eight detailed cases of ethical situations that arise in and around dental practice were reviewed by 54 patients and 91 dentists. The respondents indicated their degree of agreement with multiple courses of actions and justificatory reasons in each case. This dataset was used to create an online interactive ethics learning platform where individual dentists can compare their considered actions and reasons against norms from their peers and from a sample of patients. The dataset has also been analyzed in detail to identify the underlying structure of ethics in dental practice.

Although there is substantial agreement on actions and reasons at the aggregate level (patients as a cohort and dentists as a cohort), there are patterns of particular differences that deserve further exploration. Such topics as justifiable criticism, informed consent, financial arrangements and patient responsibility, and a dentist's role in oral health beyond the purely technical tasks suggest themselves as very promising for policy discussion and education. These are areas where wide differences of opinion appear and where a range of opinions exists among dentists. The public and the profession seem to have different perspectives on the primacy of technical procedures and oral health outcomes and on how far paternalism should be carried. Another place where patients and dentists seem to be looking in different directions is on the dentists' obligation to engage colleagues or the profession as a whole on the patients' behalf.

Policy discussions, code revision, and continuing education should focus on those issues where there are material differences in the courses of action preferred by patients and dentists and where dentists exhibit a range of opinions on situations. Practical dental ethics is complex. There is little evidence in this study for grounding dental ethics in theories of ethics. There was no evidence for a general construct—"ethical dentist"—that applies across the board or for courses of actions to flow directly from principles. John Stuart Mill (1863/1920, p. 24) seems to have been correct in noting "there is no case of moral obligation in which some secondary principle is not involved." The fact that a factor structure with five dimensions emerged rather than a global "ethical/not ethical" dichotomy is consistent with the literature, including the classical Hartshorne and May (1928) study showing that children would steal a lunch but not a pencil or cheat on a test but not in a game, and various individual combinations.

It is not customary for professions to include patients or the public in the development, interpretation, or implementation of their ethics codes. Jürgen Habermas (1990) offers a helpful rule in this regard: all competent individuals who are affected by a decision should be allowed to participate in the decision. Competence in the case of individuals in need of oral health care obviously extends beyond the technical aspects of treatment, as evidenced by the content of most professional codes, and participation can certainly be representative. To the best of my knowledge, no lay individuals were involved in the development of the American Dental Association (ADA) Code and its exact shape and use are strictly controlled by the House of Delegates. By contrast, Institutional Review Boards, which are required to pass on all research involving human subjects in America, are not permitted by federal regulation to take a vote on any specific proposed project unless there is at least one lay committee member among the quorum. (See 45 Consolidated Federal Record 46.)

The level of justification or touchstone source of deciding what is right to do that was supported by the data in this analysis seems intuitively correct. The Self as standard was associated with unattractive actions for both patients and dentists. These included diminished concern for oral health outcomes, limited professional engagements, and low respect for autonomy. Accepting the norms of one's reference Group appeared to be matched with focus on technical and business aspects of practice for dentists and with some distancing from these characteristics by patients. There is a sense in which this is the public face of dentistry, with practitioners focused on aspects of delivery while patients accept this without enthusiasm and want more attention on oral health outcomes. High level of Ethical reasoning emerged as antithetical to paternalism or the imposing of one's views on others.

The five-factor structure of dental ethics issues produced by the factor analysis approach seems face valid. Oral health outcomes and technical and practice excellence should be on everyone's list as highly valued signs of the best practices and as reflections of the fundamental integrity of dentists. These concepts are present in various places in the ADA Code and the codes of specialty and other dental groups.

Paternalism (or more properly limited appeal to it) and individual members and the profession's active self-policing on behalf of patients appeared as dimensions of both patients' and dentists' ethical framework. It seems as though this matters a bit more to patients than to dentists. There is evidence suggesting that Professional Engagement, especially among the most ethical members of the profession, is a more powerful influence on the ethical character of dentistry than are enforcement actions against those who bend or break the rules (Chambers, 2014a). This is an area the profession will find fruitful to explore.

Respect for autonomy was the only ethical dimension that emerged prominently in the present dataset of ethical concerns that is also one of the five organizing principles in the ADA Principles of Ethics. But the fit is not as tight as we could hope. This is the first of the Belmont principles ("Respect for Persons"). The ADA version was changed to feature "Patient Autonomy" (Chambers, 2014b). Certainly respect is implied if not stated, but there are significant differences between patients and persons. Much of the public would not consider itself currently to be patients of record of a dentist, and some of the ethical issues studied here, such as agreement on treatment plans, care for institutionalized individuals in need of treatment, and agreement on payment and selecting and following treatment plans, are exactly about who should be considered a patient. I have long argued (Chambers, 2003; 2013) that dentists are entitled to exactly the same respect that patients and the public at large have. I would prefer the Belmont language.

Finally we must return to the beginning and see what has been learned about the role of principles in dental ethics. Philosophers have shown clearly that we can get the job of ethics done just as well without as with principles (Dancy, 2004; Hooker, 1999; Rorty, 1999). A case can be made that patients and dentists can agree with each other generally in practice without sharing a common language or appealing to principles. There was very little support in these data for a direct connection between reasons for ethical behavior and the actual actions chosen. The five-factor structure for ethics that emerged from analyzing the choices patients and dentists actually made did not match well with systems of principles derived by philosophers.

Aristotle seems to have held reservations about the usefulness of ethical principles. "If theories were sufficient of themselves to make men good, they would deserve to receive any number of handsome rewards...But it appears in fact that, although they are strong enough to encourage and stimulate the young who are already liberally minded, although they are capable of bringing a soul which is generous and enamored of nobleness under the spell of virtue, they are impotent to inspire the mass of men" (Aristotle, 1920, pp. 343-344).

Principles are useful as theoretical organizers, as the carrying cases for examples of the behavior dentists expect of each other and the public expects of dentists. But they are not the behavior itself or even possibly not the best characterization of the patterns of that behavior.

Further work is needed along these lines to clarify what will most improve oral health and how dentists can know they are on the right path. Working with cases, lots of them over a long time frame and with feedback from colleagues and the public, bids fair to serve this need.

### References

Aristotle (1920). *The Nicomachean Ethics.* J.E.C. Welldon, Trans. London, UK: Macmillan.

Beauchamp, T. L., & Childress, J. F. (2009). *Principles of biomedical ethics,* 6th ed. New York, NY: Oxford University Press.

Bertolami, C. (2004). Why our dental ethics curricula don't work. *Journal of Dental Education, 68* (4), 414-425.

Chambers, D. W. (2003). Standards. *Journal of the American College of Dentists, 70,* 61-64.

Chambers, D. W. (2013). Would someone please explain what it means to be ethical? *CDA Journal 41* (7), 493-497.

Chambers, D. W. (2014a). Computer simulation of dental professionals as a moral community. *Medicine Health Care and Philosophy, 17,* 467-476.

Chambers, D. W. (2014b). Does the ADA have a code of ethics? *CDA Journal, 42* (12), 813.

Council on Dental Accreditation (2013). *Predoctoral dental education standards.* Chicago, IL: American Dental Association.

Dancy, J. (2004). *Ethics without principles.* Oxford, UK: Oxford University Press.

Habermas, J. (1990). *Moral consciousness and communicative action.* C. Lenhart & S. W. Nicholsen, Trans., T. McCarthy, Intro. Cambridge, MA: MIT Press.

Hartshorne, H., & May, M. A. (1928). *Studies in the nature of character.* New York, NY: Macmillan.

Hooker, B. (1999). Rule-consequentialism. In H. LaFollette (Ed.), *The Blackwell guide to ethical theory* (pp. 183-204). Oxford, UK: Blackwell.

Jonsen, A. R. (1991). Casuistry as methodology in clinical ethics. *Theory and Medicine,* 295-307.

Kohlberg, L. (1968). The child as a moral philosopher. *Psychology Today, 7,* 25-30.

MacIntyre, A. (1988). *Whose justice? Which rationality?* Notre Dame, IN: University of Notre Dame Press.

McNeel, S. P. (1994). College teaching and student moral development. In J. R. Rest & D. Narváez (Eds.), *Moral development in the professions: Psychology and applied ethics* (pp. 27-49). Hillsdale, NJ: Lawrence Erlaum Associates.

Mill, J. S. (1863/1920). *Utilitarianism.* A. D. Lindsay, Intro. London, UK: J. M. Dent & Sons.

National Commission for the Protection of Human Subjects of Biomedical and Behavioral Research (1979). *The Belmont Report: Ethical principles and guidelines for the protection of human subjects in research.* Washington, DC: Department of Health, Education, and Welfare.

Rest, J. (1973). The hierarchical nature of stages of moral judgment. *Journal of Personality, 41,* 86-109.

Rest, J., Narvaez, D., Bebeau, M. J., & Thoma, S. J. (1999). *Postconventional moral thinking: A neo-Kohlbergian approach.* Mahwah, NJ: Lawrence Erlbaum Associates.

Rorty, R. (1999). Ethics without principles. In R. Rorty, *Philosophy and social hope* (pp. 72-90). London, UK: Penguin Books.

Rule, J. T. & Veatch, R. M. (2004). *Ethical questions in dentistry,* 2nd ed. Chicago, IL: Quintessence Publishing.

Thornton, T. (2005). Judgment and the role of the metaphysics of values in medical ethics. *Journal of Medical Ethics, 32* (6), 365-370.

# Appendix C

# Disciplined Licenses

Published as Chambers, D. W. (2018). Disciplined dental licenses: An empirical study. *Journal of the American College of Dentists, 85* (2), 30-39.

### Abstract

The records of 255 dentists with recent disciplined licenses for four states were read and various characteristics were coded. These were compared with 196 randomly selected records of dentists without disciplinary actions. Disciplinary actions were about evenly divided across those stemming from technical irregularities (principally diagnostic bad practice); mismanagement of patients, such as overtreatment; and drug use, DUIs, felonies, and other personal issues. Disciplinary issues were significantly underrepresented among younger dentists but overrepresented among those with multiple offices and fictitious business names. Dentists practice in communities with higher median household income, but those with disciplined licenses are more prevalent in low-income communities. Rate of discipline, sanctions, and access to records varied widely across states. Although there was a slight tendency for dentists with disciplined licenses to not be members of the American Dental Association, this may be a result of those with disciplined licenses distancing themselves from the organized profession. Complaints come from patients and law enforcement and not from dentists or benefits carriers. Dental licensure is a state issue, under the management of departments such as consumer affairs, and because a small number of bad actors damage the reputation of the entire profession, organized dentistry should engage as partners with those responsible for regulating licensure.

This project is intended to describe the mechanisms used by state departments of consumer affairs, or agencies with different names but similar responsibilities, to ensure the safety of the public with respect to licensed dentists. Although dentists are expected by their colleagues and by the public to adhere to a higher standard of care, called professionalism, they are licensed and regulated by states to conduct a business that meets minimal commercial standards for public safety. Investigation and enforcement of behavior that does not meet these standards may result in revocation or conditions placed on dentists' privilege to conduct business in the state. Licenses can be maintained only under conditions set forth in state regulations, and curbing of these privileges in proper fashion is referred to as disciplining a license. State dental boards operate as agents of executive branches of government and must, according to the most recent interpretation of the U.S. Supreme Court, function within that structure (www.acd.org/_jacd/JACD-84-2.pdf).

## Procedure

This project is empirical, in the sense of describing representative behavior that has led to disciplined licenses and their consequences. It is not meant to comment on whether these mechanisms are just or whether they function well.

Disciplined licenses were investigated in four states: California, North Carolina, Ohio, and Oklahoma. These states have participated in the American College of Dentists Gies Ethics Project in other respects, such as having had focus groups of dentists, dental leaders, and patients provide opinions about professional ethics generally.

An attempt was made to access all records of disciplinary actions arising during the 23-month period September 2015 through July 2017. In most states a list is maintained by profession of practitioners whose licenses are under investigation for possible inappropriate commercial behavior. These lists are online under the various state agencies, such as the dental board of the state. Cross-links are provided to sites where various demographic information about the licensee is given, along with further links to documents containing the accusations and actions taken against the licensee, as well as amendments and appeals. The records of disciplinary action contain the name of the practitioner, but the identities of patients are protected, usually by using initials. Such records are public and may be required by law in all states to be made available to the public as a means of facilitating the public's participation in their own safe seeking of care. This information was available online in California and North Carolina. It was not available directly to the public in Ohio or Oklahoma, but personal appeals to those in responsible positions in those states did produce what is believed to be a full record of the disciplinary actions taken there during the time period studied.

The disciplinary documents are multiple and lengthy. They contain a good deal of boilerplate, such as establishing the authority of the board to take action in specific cases and affirmations that the practitioner is a fully informed and competent participant in the process. The narrative description of the case is detailed, often containing dates and dosages of medications and technical descriptions of clinical findings and procedures. When multiple patients are involved, these descriptions can run well more than 20 pages. In situations where a court case is involved, as in public assault or DUI, the summary court ruling is incorporated. The action taken by the board is contained in a separate document from the accusation and usually follows after several months of investigation. Appeals for shortening of probationary periods may also be included in the documentation. Much of the content of the action is also standard. In the case of revoked but stayed licenses, the conditions can number more than a dozen and often occupy as many pages. Demographic information, such as year of initial licensure in the state, special permits, zip code, fictitious names, etc., are contained in the records or can be found on the web paths leading to the records.

The process for capturing data was as follows. Six months of records were retrieved and reviewed. Based on this reading a 26-item scoring sheet was created. Eight new months of records (more than 50 cases) were coded, and some adjustments were made in the scoring form. Finally, 255 records were reviewed in their entirety, some multiple times, and were read and scored. The results were entered into a database on an Excel spreadsheet for analysis.

A question arose regarding the economic level of patients treated by dentists with various types of disciplined licenses, as well as those treated by dentists who had no disciplinary actions against them. The analysis described in this paragraph was conducted only for California dentists because complete data of the type required were only available for that state. Software was used to determine the median household income of individuals living in the zip codes where dentists had their offices (www. incomebyzipcode.com). (When multiple offices were listed, one address was chosen at random using a shuffled deck of cards.) Because a comparison was to be made between dentists with disciplined licenses and those without, a mechanism was needed to sample the incomes of patients in zip codes of dentists generally. Dentists are given license numbers sequentially by date of initial licensure. For each dentist with a disciplined license, a match was found for an undisciplined dentist by advancing the identification number by one until a match was found of an undisciplined dentist actively practicing in the state. This procedure had the added advantage of matching the two samples by age since numbers are assigned sequentially by date of licensure.

The entire sample contained 255 dentists with disciplined licenses and 139 with no disciplined license.

## Types of Inappropriate Behavior

Disciplinary actions were classified as: (a) technical in nature (faulty diagnosis or treatment); (b) involving practice management (overtreatment, poor records, patient abuse, unlicensed practice); or (c) personal (impairment due to alcohol, drugs, or cognitive function and criminal activity such as tax evasion).

Table C.1. Characteristics of disciplined licenses by type of inappropriate behavior.

| Behavior | Technical | Practice Management | Personal |
|---|---|---|---|
| N | 86 | 98 | 71 |
|  | % | % | % |
| Diagnosis | 64 | 27 | 4 |
| Treatment | 65 | 25 | 4 |
| Overtreatment | 9 | 38 | 3 |
| Case management | 24 | 20 | 0 |
| Incomplete records | 42 | 26 | 3 |
| Informed consent | 27 | 16 | 1 |
| Overbilling | 7 | 39 | 6 |
| Abandonment | 0 | 6 | 1 |

| | | | |
|---|---|---|---|
| Unlicensed practice | 1 | 20 | 1 |
| Overprescribing | 0 | 13 | 7 |
| DUI | 0 | 1 | 18 |
| Drugs | 0 | 4 | 32 |
| Cognitive impairment | 0 | 0 | 17 |
| Sexual misconduct | 0 | 1 | 13 |
| Continuing education/ Paperwork | 1 | 4 | 20 |
| Other crimes | 0 | 3 | 14 |
| Deaths | 7 | 1 | 0 |
| Multiple patients | 17 | 33 | 11 |
| Court records | 0 | 18 | 38 |
| Out-of-state | 1 | 0 | 10 |
| Repeat offenders | 7 | 10 | 25 |
| American Dental Association membership | 40 | 37 | 35 |

## Technique Problems

One-third of the disciplinary cases were classified as technical, being principally matters of poorly performed dental procedures. The most prominent faulty behavior was incomplete diagnosis, including performing periodontal procedures without recording pocket depths, performing extractions with incomplete records, failing to take diagnostic radiographs, overlooking patients' medical conditions, incorrect design of implants, and performing restorative work with no characterization of the disease condition. Some technical faulty behavior involved inadequate performance of the procedure. Here, issues included removing the wrong tooth, poorly aligned implants, ill-fitting dentures, and poor technique during surgical procedures. One or both (diagnosis and treatment) were involved in all cases of misconduct classified in the technical category.

There was a single case reported of an open margin and another of incomplete root planing. The impression was of "piecemeal" care, or procedures performed out of sequence rather than of technical incompetence. In some cases it was clear that dentists just did several procedures because they seemed convenient. Much of the "incompetence" might better have been described as deviation from comprehensive patient treatment.

There were three secondary faults that often accompanied technical difficulties. These included poor case management, incomplete records, and lack of informed consent. Case management refers to sequencing and monitoring of patient progress between treatments or following surgical cases. None of the seven deaths recorded in this sample occurred in the dental office or immediately after treatment. They followed dismissal and were associated with improper case monitoring. Incomplete records were consistent with the advantageous nature of treatment planning in this category. Failure of informed consent followed the same pattern of appearing that the dentists modified procedures and treatments "on the fly."

The records are insufficient to know who registered the complaint, but the narratives in cases in the technical quality category support an impression of being patient-initiated. These appeared to be patients who were dissatisfied with both the care received and the way in which the dentist managed the complaints. Typically they involved repeated office visits and responses that were deemed below the standard for commercial transactions. In about one in six cases, a pattern was discovered either among the complaints or by investigators involving multiple patients.

There was no association between American Dental Association membership and disciplined licenses due to technical issues compared with other types of misconduct, chi-square = 1.449. Penalties for problems of a technical nature were much lighter than for cases involving practice issues or personal issues. Sixty-six percent of technical cases resulted in license revocation or stayed revocation. When the matter was for other reasons, 82% of cases resulted in revocation or stayed revocation (chi-square = 14.376, p < 0.001). In other words, technical shortcomings were not considered to be as blameworthy as other faults committed by dentists.

Figure C.1 shows disciplined licenses for technical matters by age. There are two peaks in this curve: one for practitioners in their early forties and another in the late fifties. The dashed lines represent the distribution of active dentists in the United States by age. Where the columns are above the dashed line, this represents a concentration of technical license difficulties in these age categories. Dentists under 40 years of age are marginally less likely to practice at a technical level that causes concern. Chi-square = 2.381, p = 0.080.

### Practice Management

Thirty-seven percent of the cases were classified as principally involving practice management, the most common type of disciplinary problem. Issues here included overtreatment and overbilling. Common parts of this pattern were poor case management, incomplete records, and care provided by unlicensed individuals. Less frequent, but still part of the picture, were failure to inform the patient of treatments performed, prescribing unnecessary controlled substances to patients, and patient abandonment.

Figure C.1. Technical practice difficulties by age.

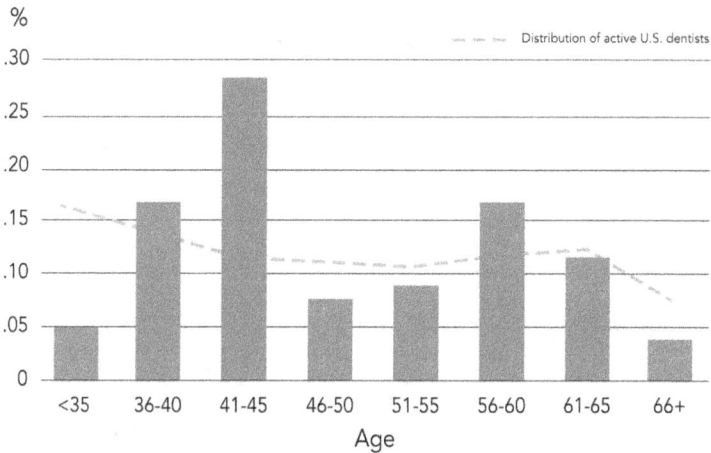

The difference between the treatment and practice management categories is a judgment call, dependent on the overall patterns of complaints in the disciplinary records. Practice management cases involved multiple appointments and featured overtreatment, overbilling, and performing work the patient had not been informed of. Although there were cases of diagnostic and treatment issues, these were not major concerns, and it appeared to be the case that three-quarters of practice management issues did not entail technically deficient dentistry. The impression was that dentists in this group were pursuing their own economic interests rather than patient oral health goals.

There was little overlap between patient management problems and general problems, such as impaired dentists. This category did, however, have a tendency for a habit or pattern, with one-third of the cases involving multiple patients and 10% of the disciplinary actions being repeat offenders.

There was no association between American Dental Association membership and engagement in practice management types of poor practice. Chi-square = 0.354, NS. However, dentists judged guilty of such poor practices were penalized by having revoked or revoked and stayed licenses almost three times as often as were those involved in technical matters. Chi-square = 12.213, p = 0.007.

Figure C.2 shows the distribution of problems with practice management categorized by age of practitioner. The most conspicuous trend is that young practitioners (under age 40) are underrepresented. Chi-square = 8.180, p = 0.004.

Figure C.2. **Practice management difficulties by age.**

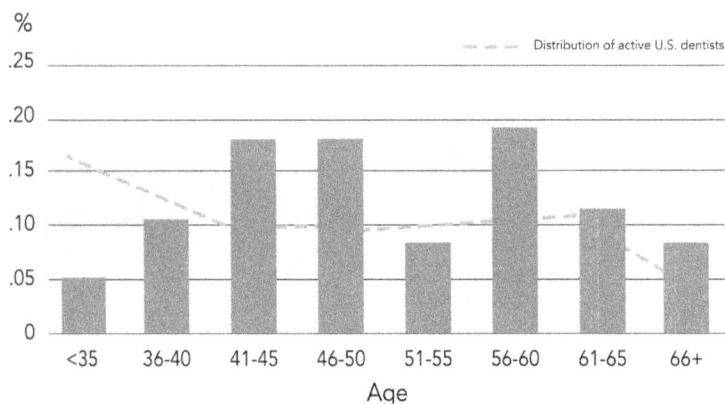

## Personal

Just over a quarter of the cases involving disciplined licenses were classified as personal issues. These generally involved problems outside the dental office. The most common problem was use of drugs by the dentist. Other common impairments included alcohol use, generally identified in DUI convictions, and cognitive challenges. Sexual misconduct was reported nine times. Other crimes included spousal abuse, tax evasion, and impersonating a state dental board officer for the purpose of harassing fellow dentists. There were two cases of Medicaid fraud. Also included in this category were "paper work" violations, such as being short on continuing education hours or filing transfer papers from other states after the deadline. Cases in the personal category were often supported by court records. There were usually multiple infractions, and one-quarter of the individuals in this category were repeat offenders for the same offense. Difficulties in this category tended to be independent of technique or practice management issues.

Dentists with life issues were marginally less likely to be American

Dental Association members, chi-square = 3.574, p = 0.06. They were also more likely to receive light penalties, chi-square = 20.478, p < 0.001. A public reprimand was more common than having the license revoked. The strongest penalty (revoked license) was, in most cases, a voluntary surrender of license taken by very senior practitioners.

Figure C.3 shows that personal difficulties leading to disciplined licenses are clearly associated with age. Older practitioners are much more likely to be impaired by using drugs and alcohol and to have committed crimes. Chi-square = 15.735, p < .001.

---

Figure C.3. **Personal difficulties by age.**

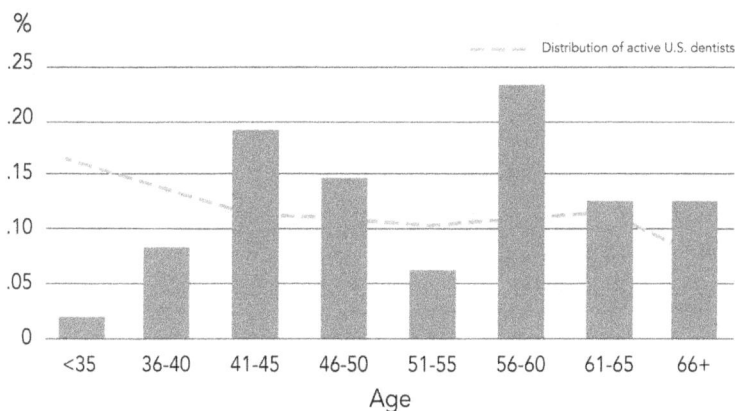

---

## Practice Environment of Dentists with Disciplined Licenses

While it is impossible to assemble a detailed picture of the circumstances surrounding the disciplining of dental licenses from public records, there are two types of information that provide some insight. The zip codes where practices are located and whether dentists have multiple offices and fictitious business names are part of the public record.

Table C.2 shows the average income of all individuals living in the zip code where California practices were located in 2015. The median household income in California was $61,818. The chart below shows that dentists provide more services to patients in locations with higher average incomes. The concentration of dentists in more affluent communities is statistically significant at p < .001 for all categories except dentists who have licenses disciplined for practice management reasons. This includes overtreatment, overbilling, and lack of comprehensive care. Poor quality technical work—

improper diagnosis or faulty treatment—was slightly more likely to be experienced by poor patients, but not as common as taking advantage of patients by misleading treatment. The differences just summarized are statistically significant by a one-way ANOVA at p < .001. Both Scheffé and Duncan multiple range tests identified the same clusters of dentist types: Practice management problems formed one group, clean practitioners and those with personal problems formed another. Dentists with disciplined licenses as a result of technical problems shared some of the characteristics of each group.

---

**Table C.2. Median household income in zip codes of dentists with various characteristics of disciplined licenses and percentage having multiple offices and fictitious business names.**

|  | N | Mean | SD | Multiple Offices | Fictitious Name |
|---|---|---|---|---|---|
| No discipline | 139 | $79,094 | $29,939 | 0.146 | 0.254 |
| Technical faults | 83 | 67,361 | 25,471 | 0.276 | 0.395 |
| Practice management | 88 | 61,924 | 24,575 | 0.392 | 0.667 |
| Personal | 51 | 80,478 | 20,717 | 0.421 | 0.421 |

This pattern was repeated with respect to having multiple offices and a fictitious business name. The historical family dentist was known by his or her personal name, had an established and long-term location, and waited for patients to come for care. Those with disciplined licenses of all types were more than twice as likely to have multiple offices and much more likely to use a fictitious business name. This was especially noticeable in the case of dentists whose licenses were disciplined for such behavior as overtreatment and overbilling. The chi-square test found that these differences were statistically significant beyond p < .001.

It was not possible to determine from the case narratives or other records which dentists were employees, associates, or independent contractors, itinerant or otherwise.

## Membership in Organized Dentistry

Dentists with disciplined licenses are somewhat less likely to be members in the tripartite structure of organized dentistry. The online directory of American Dental Association (ADA) members was searched by name (with cross-checks for state and first name) and membership was recorded. Overall 39% of dentists with disciplined licenses were members of the ADA when the data were checked. This is significantly less than the 65% current ADA membership for active dentists. Percent membership by type of disciplinary action, considering only California and North Carolina, was technical = 44%, practice management = 42%, and personal = 29%. Membership in both California and North Carolina is 67%.

There is some uncertainty in these numbers. For example, only one of the 45 dentists with North Carolina disciplined licenses was found in the ADA online membership registry. Staff at the North Carolina Dental Association performed a hand check of their records for the past five years. This search revealed that 15 of the 45 disciplined licenses were for dentists who had been members of organized dentistry during the past three years, and that four dentists listed as members of organized dentistry in North Carolina currently were not in the ADA database. It is possible that the data reported here understate the proportion of dentists with disciplined licenses who are members of organized dentistry.

Another possibility is that dentists withdraw from organized dentistry when they are under investigation or that states de-list dentists who have disciplined licenses. This would be in line with the fact that dentists who have experienced personal issues are less likely to be ADA members. Those with revoked or surrendered licenses often retire or move to other states seeking to begin a new career. As a follow-up exercise, 100 dentists from the pool of disciplined licenses were sent a customized letter containing a very short survey of attitudes toward ethics. Twelve of the 100 were returned because of a "bad address"; none of the dentists with disciplined licenses responded to the ethics survey. It is easier to defend the notion that dentists who have problems in practice pull away from organized dentistry than the alternative that organized dentistry prevents dentists from engaging in unprofessional behavior.

## Sanctions

In the table below are listed the sanctions given for each of the types of professional misconduct. Reprimand or public reprimand is a finding of misconduct with no further sanctions against the practitioner other than the fact that the public can locate and read the matter, either online or by requesting documentation of the state dental board. Nineteen percent of the cases reviewed resulted in reprimands. Suspension is seldom used (5%) and involves prohibition from practice for a stated period of time, often with no other requirement, except perhaps for court costs. In Ohio there were a number of cases of 14-day suspensions, including a case involving a death.

Stayed revocation, the most common penalty (46%), is the board's attempt to rehabilitate dentists. Dentists are prohibited from practicing during this period, which may last from one to five years. Multiple requirements are imposed, such as closing one's office and having minimal contact with patients (as in charity work or teaching). Dentists must also notify others, such as representatives of other boards, if they move to another state and must obey all laws (generally), inform the board of changes of address, and arrange for transfer of patients. Ethics courses, remedial course work, psychological evaluations and biological testing and monitoring are typically required to address specific issues. Court costs and costs of monitoring are normally included, and sometimes community service is expected. Failure to adhere to any of these requirements, especially not complying with monitoring in the case of substance abuse, can result in removing the stay and having the license permanently revoked. A revoked license means the dentist can no longer practice, absent a successful appeal for reinstatement.

---

**Table C.3. Likelihood of various sanctions by type of professional misconduct.**

|  | Reprimand % | Suspension % | Revoke-Stayed % | Revocation % |
|---|---|---|---|---|
| Technical issues | 44 | 0 | 38 | 18 |
| Practice management | 12 | 11 | 56 | 25 |
| Personal | 5 | 3 | 44 | 47 |

---

Table C.3 shows the association between type of misconduct and actions. Faulty diagnosis or treatment of the technical type most typically results in public reprimands. Practice management issues such as overtreatment, overbilling, prescribing drugs for patients, or otherwise failing to render continuous comprehensive care in the patients' best interests is most likely to result in a stayed revocation of the license. Personal issues, such as crimes or substance abuse and impairment, lead to revocation, with stays in about half of the cases. This category also includes voluntary surrender of one's license. Often older dentists or those with severe impairments retire or move to other states.

## Identifying Issues

The records do not contain sufficient information to classify or even characterize factors that initiate disciplinary inquiries. Although state dental boards say that they are "complaint driven," it is unclear where these complaints come from. The information below is anecdotal.

It is usually said that complaints come from patients. Because of limited resources, the investigative branches of the departments of consumer affairs usually focus their investigatory efforts in response to multiple complaints about a dentist. The case reports of unprofessional care of a technical or practice management nature involved descriptions of mistreatment of more than one patient in 40% of the cases. Complaints from fellow dentists and from office staff are rare to unheard of.

There are no national reports of the system for monitoring dentists against state practice acts. In 2006 the U.S. Department of Health and Human Services published a study for the medical field (aspe.hhs.gov/basic-report/state-discipline-physicians-assessing-state-medical-boards-through-case-studies). There is wide variety among the states examined. Of complaints received, 14% were not followed up because there was no jurisdiction and 65% were not followed up because of insufficient evidence. Nineteen percent were settled or dropped and 2% went to hearing. The investigator and prosecution cost of disciplining a license was generally between $50,000 and $100,000.

There are several sources of information about unprofessional conduct that come automatically to state dental boards. One involves the board's own procedures. Failure to meet continuing education hours or irregularities in applications are known immediately. There were several such cases in this dataset. Other routine sources of information about misconduct involve other governmental agencies. It is federal law that deaths must be reported to professional boards if a professional is associated with the case. There were seven such examples in this dataset. Another case of mandatory reporting is state statutes regarding felonies. This typically involves DUI convictions for repeated offenses, dispensing of drugs, and criminal matters such as aggravated assault. There were 44 such cases in this dataset. Together, about a quarter of incidents in this study would have been unavoidable knowledge to the boards.

The relationship between insurance companies and boards is unclear. Carriers have vast amounts of detailed knowledge regarding treatment and billing patterns, activities that bear on the practice management category of professional misconduct. Careful reading of the narratives left the impression that problems of this nature were initiated only by patients, disgruntled over what they regarded as unfair billing. There have been reports that insurance companies prefer to manage practice management issues themselves as commercial rather than professional matters. When patterns of inappropriate behavior are detected, carriers contact the provider and threaten to terminate the contract unless the behavior stops. There were only two cases reported here involving prosecuted Medicaid fraud, and those involved the government.

It is also unclear what the relationship is between malpractice actions and disciplined licenses. Malpractice is a civil action (a harm to a specific person) whereas licenses that are disciplined involve damage against the public. It is unknown whether carriers or courts alert dental boards of actions or whether boards feel inclined to follow up on such matters.

There is also a somewhat parallel disciplinary track involving organized dentistry. Virtually all states have a mediation mechanism for disputes between dentists and patients called peer review. This mechanism is available only to members of the tripartite structure, and the issues typically involve disputes over fees. Generally it is a condition for participation in this process that information disclosed or discovered in peer review is not available to malpractice attorneys or to state dental boards. A few states have a judiciary function through a committee of the state dental association for independently investigating and sanctioning members who have been disciplined by the state dental board. The grounds for such action are the code of professional conduct (enforceable) language in the state's ethical code. Independent fact finding and hearings are possible, and continued membership in organized dentistry may be revoked or conditioned.

### Differences Across States

There are significant differences across states in their enforcement of professional conduct. Table C.4 shows the number of disciplinary actions taken per 1,000 licensed dentists.

## Table C.4. Disciplined licenses per 1,000 active dentists.

| | Dentists | Action/year (per 1,000 dentists) |
|---|---|---|
| California | 20,150 | 5.25 |
| North Carolina | 3,241 | 6.94 |
| Ohio | 4,131 | 1.09 |
| Oklahoma | 1,306 | 1.15 |

The two states with low percentage rates of disciplined licenses are likely the result of different investigatory and enforcement standards rather than the level of dental care provided. For example, of the 12 total cases in a two-year period in Ohio and Oklahoma combined, ten of them were unavoidable by the board, including court actions, patient deaths, or board paperwork. Only two cases resulted in licenses being revoked. Neither state supports a computer verification for patients to check on the status of their provider. The records used in this study were obtained by direct contact with officers in the states. One of the officers in the board of dentistry explained that the state budget has been severely cut and that only those cases involving drugs or deaths were given priority.

Seventy percent of problems with cognitive impairment of practitioners were identified in North Carolina, a state that had only 17% of the dentists in this sample. This is most likely the result of the state's contracting with the North Carolina Caring Dental Professionals Program.

## Reflections

This report will not contain recommendations. This is a field where much is still unknown and where policies vary greatly from state to state. However, it is possible to offer a few reflections.

First, this is an understudied area. Although certain types of information are available as public record, even that is sometimes difficult to access. Cost of investigation and enforcement and litigation are chilling factors. It may also be the case that the profession is slightly reluctant to shine a light on the less exemplary aspects of dentistry.

State dental boards deserve respect and appreciation from both the public and the profession. They volunteer to engage in difficult work. The responsibility for commercially inappropriate behavior by dentists should extend to more than this small number.

Second, bad behavior is a process. The age and zip code income data combine to paint a picture of dentists who grow into inappropriate habits. It is indefensible to characterize dentists who engage in commercially inappropriate behavior as "born bad" or "bad by nature or nationality," or even as becoming bad by taking a one-time conscious decision. As one colleague who has reviewed the data remarked, "It seems to take a number of years for them to learn how to become dishonest dentists."

There seems to be support for the view that dentists "learn" either good or bad habits and perfect them over time and that practice circumstances interact with care patterns. To the extent that this is true, there is an imperative in the entire profession to interact with all its members, not just those who share similar values. Physical isolation and psychological distancing—"they are just the uncorrectable bad ones, end of story"—are not the answer. If they can learn bad habits, they can learn good ones as well.

As a third point, it may be unsound for the leadership of organized dentistry to shun the small number of unprofessional practitioners. If there were two classes of dentists—the good and the bad—the age curve for disciplined licenses would have a spike as soon as practitioners were allowed to function independently. Instead, young practitioners are underrepresented among the bad actors. The two peaks correspond with the Baby Boomer and the Gen-X generations, although this may be a confounding with stages in dental practice. The younger of these groups is concerned with practice debt (not educational debt) and the older group contains many superannuated practitioners who have extended their careers to a point that involves increasing life challenges and more limited capabilities. The fact that dentists without disciplinary actions treat populations that are almost 30% wealthier than the population at large gives them some cushion for freedom of behavior that those engaged in overtreatment, overbilling, and other shady practices do not enjoy.

In the fourth place, the reputation of dentistry, which is tarnished by some, cannot be controlled by the profession at the national level. The ADA Code of Professional Conduct applies to the voluntary members of that organization and penalties for violating the code extend only as far as discontinuing membership. Dental professionals, per the ADA Code, are urged to belong to a professional association, but there are alternatives. Licensure is not controlled by the profession, but by branches of state government charged with ensuring a level playing field between providers of all services and those they serve. This process exists at the state level, and there are notable differences across states, even in the case of dentistry. The profession must partner with a number of autonomous organizations to elevate the level of care provided to the public.

Finally, dentists are human. In any population there will be a range from the outstanding to those who are having difficulty leading the kinds of lives we all aspire to. Most of those who read this report will find it difficult to relate to the world of dentists with disciplined licenses. For that we should all be grateful. This report focuses on a very small segment of the profession, but its size and strangeness should not be an excuse to ignore it. Both patients and the dentists themselves are hurt by the behavior described in this report. Large segments of the public see this behavior and, not knowing otherwise, mark this as the way dentists behave. About one-third of the American public, according to a Gallup poll, do not trust dentists to have their (the public's) best interests at heart (news.gallup.com/poll/1654/honesty-ethics-professions.aspx). This is the lowest level of public trust of any of the health professions regularly surveyed.

The profession has more conspicuously engaged indirectly with this issue at the policy level than through direct action by individual dentists being proactively involved with their colleagues or by reporting unprofessional behavior. This is an issue for the entire profession, working with others.

# Appendix D

# Moral Priming

Previously as Chambers, D. W. (2016). Moral priming and the ACD basic rule. *Journal of the American College of Dentists, 83* (1), 38-43.

## Abstract

James Rest proposed a model of moral behavior with four components: sensitivity, reasoning, character, and courage (or action). Research has shown that moral character is a complex construct. Multiple moral self-concepts exist within each individual, and different contexts predispose various of these to become dominant in different settings. Moral priming is the practice of manipulating the environment to favor the use of appropriate moral self-concepts. A study is reported, demonstrating that dentists can be primed to express more moral views based entirely on context. The observed effect of priming was large. The American College of Dentists Rule for Moral Identity states that when there is conflict between professionalism and economic or other self-interests, professionalism takes precedence.

Morality is the pattern of actions we use to make the world better; ethics is what we say about that. Unless one is in an academic environment or making a political statement, morality is the more precious of the two. More formally, morality could be defined as the way we treat others who may or may not share our values so that we would feel comfortable exchanging places should circumstances call for that. The definition has these features: (a) there is no presumption that we have a special position based on our superior view of things; (b) we cannot be moral alone; and (c) moral opportunities are pervasive.

It is sometimes helpful to engage in ethical reflection or even justification as part of being moral. But the branch of theory known as virtue ethics (Annas, 2011; Curzer, 2014) has long made a case for the highest form of morality being semiconscious good habits. Further, it is not enough to have performed a sound ethical analysis, for example, based on principles or norms. Aiming accurately is necessary, but the act is incomplete unless we pull the trigger. Morality is about the way we act.

James Rest's Four Component Model (Rest et al, 1999) helps us find our bearings. In Rest's view, there are four characteristics of one who would be moral: (a) moral sensitivity; (b) moral reflection; (c) moral integrity; and (d) moral courage. Notice Rest's preference for the term "moral."

Moral sensitivity is realizing that one is in a situation with prominent ethical dimensions (Rest, 1986). Unless one realizes that lack of funds or insurance coverage for the most appropriate treatment leads to compromised care, for example, this may remain an economic concern and never reach the moral level. The way a situation is framed, or overlooked, determines the nature of the reflection, engagement, and action that follow. A faux form of moral sensitivity is called "moral awareness" (Reynolds, 2008). There are folks who make a career out of righteous rages against the unfairness faced by almost everyone they meet and society in general, and they are happy to point out that someone else has made a mess of things. Politicians seem to have advanced training in this practice. The difference between moral sensitivity and awareness is that the good one places the observer in the context as an agent. It is only moral sensitivity when the phrase "this is not right and someone should do something about it" is understood to mean that the speaker is among the "someones."

Moral reflection is the second of Rest's components. That is what we teach in dental schools and short courses. The customary format involves comparing alternatives against principles or norms and deciding what should be done (Beauchamp & Childress, 2009). But reflection may not always be necessary. The domain of ethical dilemmas is not the same as the domain of being a professional. Putting one's hands where they do not belong, overtreatment, insurance fraud, failing to report child abuse, and substandard care are wrong. There is no second position (or lemma) to be weighed as a plausible alternative in ethical reflection.

Moral integrity, Rest's third component, also known as moral character, is not about events in the world or about ethical theory. It is about the extent to which we are prepared to act as moral agents (Aquino & Reed, 2002). At the low end of the scale we find "moral spectators." These are often very sophisticated individuals or organizations, well-tuned to the issues of the day and capable of sustaining an extended ethical discussion at a high level. But they are more like the avid sports fan rather than an actual athlete. At the high end are moral leaders; those who make those around them better, and make a habit of it (Chambers, 2015).

Finally, moral courage refers to what it takes to act on one's moral sensitivity, reflection, and integrity. It requires both skill and commitment to *do* the right thing. Perhaps the greatest opportunity to improve the moral capacity of dentists is here. "Moral assertiveness training" might be helpful (Chambers, 2009). We need to develop and practice scripts for confronting those who are not upholding professional ideals and support systems for the many of us who would prefer not to do this alone.

An individual may possess very high levels of moral sensitivity or reflection, and so forth, yet go unnoticed as a positive force for professionalism in dentistry. Our attention would best be focused on the one or two components of morality that are our weakest, as these will usually determine the maximal moral impact we can have. A short test of Rest's Four Component Model, with automatic scoring and guidance for improvement, is part of the American College of Dentists online course for dental offices (www.dentalethics.org/pead/index-pead.htm).

This paper is about moral integrity. It would be good to have a rule to use when conflicts arise between moral behavior and other values, such as economics and personal satisfaction.

## Moral Character Is Situational

An adult's height is quite stable, but weight, not so much so. Although it is meaningful to speak of a person as being generally agreeable or cynical or good company or not, these dispositions fluctuate depending on circumstances. And the same is true for moral character. The classic study was published by Hugh Hartshorne and Mark May in 1928. Rather than using surveys— and assuming that any one administration of any survey captures one's "true moral nature"—these investigators followed boys for weeks in a variety of settings and observed how they behaved. One would sometimes cheat on a school project, but not when interacting with classmates. Another would cheat in a physically competitive game, but not in abstract games of skill. Stealing might be acceptable in the case of a friend's lunch, but not for school supplies. These patterns varied from boy to boy and were not stable within each child across time.

More contemporary research (Aquino & Reed, 2002; Welsh & Ordóñez 2014) uses questionnaires, but comes to the same conclusion: moral identity is a fuzzy concept and likely to be influenced by circumstances. Some researchers, such as Hinkley and Andersen (1996) and Aquino and his colleagues (2009), argue for multiple dimensions in an individual's moral outlook. What is "fair" depends on whether, for example, we are talking about one's self or kin and close friends or about strangers, different "others," or those deserving no respect whatsoever. Whether the dress fits is a function of who is wearing it. Others would have multiple moral standards depending on the circumstances. Throughout history, individuals such as Grotius, Jefferson, and Victor Hugo, among others, have argued that stealing is not blameworthy if compelled by necessity, such as starvation. Murder is justified on grounds of self-defense. The classic Harvard study of moral character formation during professional education and the early years in practice (Fischman et al, 2004) revealed that professionals of previous generations were quite aware that circumstances compelled them to "bend the rules" early in their careers—as long as they promised themselves that it was only until they could establish themselves financially.

Each of us has multiple moral personalities. We change them based on circumstances. It is not unusual for parents and neighbors interviewed following a mass shooting to say, "He was always such a nice boy. I can't believe he would do such a thing." Victims are usually described as having great potential. Certainly there are dominant moral characters for each of us, and that is what our reputations are built on. There are many moral or immoral personalities that would make us feel guilty or ashamed, and some we simply cannot imagine wearing. How we act in moral situations depends a lot on which of our moral characters shows up for the event. It would be good if we have a rule or some guidance regarding which of our moral selves would be most appropriate in various circumstances.

## Can Moral Character Be Influenced?

At first, it may seem a cause for concern to accept that moral character is multiple and that any of us could reasonably be expected to behave differently in different circumstances. On further reflection, this may be a blessing. We have traditionally framed character education as a matter of fundamentally remodeling others. That kind of comprehensive change has proven more than difficult, except in situations such as seminary or the military where almost total control is possible for extended periods of time. Quasi-permanent moral makeovers are possible in gang and prison culture. Certainly, it will be difficult to use moral identity traits that are not widely and conspicuously endorsed among our colleagues even if we have taken the right courses.

A more modest goal than complete moral education, but one that should not be ignored, would be to influence circumstances where agents have an opportunity to be moral. We should invite others to bring forward their better selves. Even when we pass on hoping for radical and permanent changes in character, there is something to be said for improving the moral nature of those around us here and now.

There is some research evidence that this can be accomplished predictably. If that is robustly the case, we might be able to frame a rule to serve as a general guide in dental professional situations.

In the earliest research on this topic, Mazar and colleagues (2008) paid college students serving as research subjects a small amount for each numerical puzzle they solved when given a reasonably large sample of such test sets. Subjects worked alone and turned in their answer sheets to a monitor who did not score the papers, only asking subjects how they scored themselves. Of course, there was potential for overreporting. The extent of "boosting one's score" was determined by retrieving the worksheets from a conveniently located trash receptacle subjects were instructed to use, since the worksheets had an identifying code on them. Self-promotion was not huge, but it was very widespread.

Mazar thought it would be possible to subtly influence whether an "honest" self or a "slightly self-promoting" self showed up at the desk where the payoff was given. Before beginning to solve the puzzles, some subjects are asked to engage in a neutral task such as listing books read in high school. Others are asked to write down as many of the Ten Commandments as they can recall. We learn two things from such studies. First, people cannot recall many of the Ten Commandments. Second, just trying to do so reduces cheating. The effect is called "moral priming."

Closer to the healthcare setting, priming has been demonstrated for Army medics (Leavitt et al, 2012). These individuals have two identities: military and healthcare. In this case, rather than measure cheating as the difference between actual and self-reported scores, questions were asked that reflected a disposition to treat others fairly. Ethically ambiguous decisions involved such issues as fixing the dollar amount of compensation to families of soldiers killed in combat versus saving the government money. In one condition, medics completed the ethics questionnaire wearing their uniforms, in a room decorated with military insignia. In the other, they were guided by reporting in scrubs to a room filled with medical equipment. Those primed to activate their medical moral template did in fact demonstrate more moral opinions than the same individuals who could be expected to be thinking of themselves as soldiers.

## Demonstrating Moral Priming

Modifying the circumstances to improve the chances the right sort of moral character will be activated is called moral priming. Perhaps we need not do an identity makeover on others. Perhaps it would be a worthy beginning to call out the best character that already exists in them. This would be a more plausible strategy if we could demonstrate that moral priming works in dentistry.

A moral values survey instrument is under development for use in the American College of Dentists Gies Ethics Project. This is a 48-item survey, patterned after the widely publicized Moral Factors Questionnaire developed by Jonathan Haidt (2012) and his colleagues. Embedded within the questionnaire used for this study were three additional items designed to measure pro-moral attitudes or openness to moral behavior: (a) "copayments should not be waived;" (b) "colleagues working below the standard of care should be reported when justified;" and (c) "commercialism undermines dental professionalism." Experience has shown that there is some range of opinion in the profession on these matters. The items were presented on a five-point Likert scale ranging from 1 = strongly disagree to 5 = strongly agree.

Participants in the study were regents and officers of the American College of Dentists. They completed an identical version of the Moral Factors Questionnaire survey with three embedded test items on two occasions. The first administration was during the "blue sky" session at the end of the board meeting at the annual convocation in 2015. The second administration was approximately six weeks later, and surveys were returned by mail. A code number, selected by each regent or officer, was used to match the two anonymous versions of the same form. The priming manipulation consisted of using the context of a board meeting where the future of the college and the role of the college as "the conscience of dentistry" forms a general context. The follow-up survey contained language priming respondents to assume the role of a dentist in practice. *Assume that you are completing this form as a dentist. If you are not currently in practice, try to imagine yourself about five years prior to retirement. In fact, it might be useful to recall a "typical" day in practice. How many patients did you see? Were there any that were especially challenging, technically or otherwise? Were there any staff or business issues? Did you have any contact with colleagues, either associates or others in your community? Did you do any business for "organized dentistry?"*

The outcome variable was the difference in how the three questions about moral behavior were answered in the setting primed for general moral tone among one's colleagues and the setting primed for typical individual practice. Each participant served as his or her own control. Only cases where regents and officers completed both surveys and where the identification numbers could be matched were used. There were 15 such pairs of responses. The consistency among the three items (the reliability of the test questions) had an acceptable Cronbach alpha of 0.782. This project was approved in the exempt category by the Institutional Review Board at the University of the Pacific, 16-74.

When the three moral items were rated in the context of the American College of Dentists board meeting, the average value was 3.633, where 5 = strongly agree (SD = 1.359). The same items rated in the context of private practice averaged closer to the neutral point, at 2.864 (SD = 1.495). The paired-comparison t-test value was 2.419, which is significant at $p < .05$. This is a statistically significant difference despite the small sample size. The effect size of the difference in contexts was an omega squared of 0.272. One quarter of the variation in how regents and officers responded to these moral challenges was explained by the context in which they answered the question.

This is the first evidence that dentists respond to moral situations differently based on the moral identity they bring to the situation and that the moral identity activated can be primed by varying the context. Expecting more moral behavior may bring about more of it.

## Conclusion

Years ago ecological psychologist Roger Barker (1968) famously suggested that we can better predict what others are doing if we know where they are than if we know who they are. Try it. If you know that an individual is in a dental office, there are only a few options. If I said the same person is an extrovert, a Democrat, or a morally upright individual, it would be more than a long shot to guess what they are doing right now.

It might be disappointing to some that each of us has a small repertoire of moral lenses to use in various settings. This sounds too much like situational ethics—the idea that the most right thing for an individual to do could change depending on the circumstances. Although having a few bullet-proof rules is comforting, making them fit reality is seldom straightforward. The late eighteenth century philosopher Immanuel Kant (1788/2015) tried to argue that some rules never vary across circumstances, but few academics defend this position today. White lies or hiding Anne Frank from the Nazis would be out of bounds for a purist interpretation of veracity. Justice is argued many ways depending on whose standard is used (MacIntyre, 1988). Respect for persons quickly comes down to who that person is. The American Dental Association Code, for example, only mentions "respect for patients." Most of us most of the time are strongly morally principled and, at the same time, quite adept at interpreting when circumstances call for another moral self-concept and another approach to others (Fletcher, 1966).

On the positive side, moral priming suggests a convenient and effective strategy for improving moral tone. If we adjust our moral character to match the expectations dominant in the setting, it should be simple enough to get better behavior by simply making it known that such behavior is expected. In our relations with others we can expect to get the kind of behavior we signal we are looking for. We tell each other constantly and are constantly being told what kind of moral character is appropriate for the situation.

Ethics education is assumed to involve a relatively permanent and comprehensive transformation of a person; moral priming is relatively transient and specific. We need to be cautious that the ethical language around the table in classrooms and council meetings (especially where one is away from the home environment) is likely not to travel well. There is an old question about if church were such a meaningful experience, why would people have to go every week? The answer, of course, is that the moral leaders in dentistry are not the only ones engaged in priming.

Dentistry is a complex profession. For certain there are minimal standards for economic success and personal satisfaction. Professionalism and patient service are also important. There is a requirement for legal conformity and civic responsibility, and even much to be said for status among one's colleagues. Which of these dimensions of practice speaks loudest? What moral character is expected to come forward? Dentists have a choice about who they want to be in each situation.

Here is the American College of Dentists Rule for Moral Identity: When there is conflict between professionalism and economic or other self-interests, professionalism takes precedence.

## References

Annas, J. (2011). *Intelligent virtue*. Oxford, UK: Oxford University Press.

Aquino, K., & Reed, A., II. (2002). The self-importance of moral identity. *Journal of Personality and Social Psychology, 83* (6), 1423-1440.

Aquino, K., Freeman, D., Reed, A., II, Lim, V. K. G., & Felps, W. (2009). Testing a social-cognitive model of moral behavior: The interactive influence of situations and moral identity centrality. *Journal of Personality and Social Psychology, 97* (1), 123-141.

Barker, R. G. (1968). *Ecological psychology: Concepts and methods for studying the environment of human behavior*. Stanford, CA: Stanford University Press.

Beauchamp, T. L., & Childress, J. F. (2009). *Principles of biomedical ethics* (6th ed). New York, NY: Oxford University Press.

Chambers, D. W. (2009). Assertiveness [leadership essay]. *Journal of the American College of Dentists, 76* (2), 51-59.

Chambers, D. W. (2015). Moral communities and moral leadership. *Journal of the American College of Dentists, 82* (4), 60-75.

Curzer, H. J. (2014). Patients who make terrible therapeutic choices. *Journal of the American College of Dentists, 81* (3), 41-45.

Fischman, W., Solomon, B., Greenspan, D., & Gardner, H. (2004). *Making good: How young people cope with moral dilemmas at work*. Cambridge, MA: Harvard University Press.

Fletcher, J. (1966). *Situation ethics: A new morality*. Philadelphia, PA: Westminster.

Haidt, J. (2012). *The righteous mind: Why good people are divided by politics and religion*. New York, NY: Vintage Books.

Hartshorne, H., & May, M. (1928). *Studies in the nature of character*. New York, NY: Macmillan.

Hinkley, K., & Andersen, S. W. (1996). The working self-concept in transference: Significant-other activation and self change. *Journal of Personality and Social Psychology, 71* (6), 1279-1295.

Kant, I. (1788/2015). *Critique of practical reason* (rev ed). M. Gregor, trans., A. Reath, intro. Cambridge, UK: Cambridge University Press.

Leavitt, K., Reynolds, S. J., Barnes, C. M., Schilpzand, P., & Hannah, S. T. (2012). Different hats, different obligations: Plural occupational identities and situated moral judgment. *Academy of Management Journal, 55* (6), 1316-1333.

MacIntyre, A. (1988). *Whose justice? Which rationality?* Notre Dame, IN: Notre Dame University Press.

Mazar, N., Amir, O., & Ariely, D. (2008). The dishonesty of honest people: A theory of self-concept maintenance. *Journal of Marketing Research, 45*, 633-644.

Rest, J. R. (1986). *Moral development: Advances in research and theory*. New York, NY: Praeger.

Rest, J. R., Narvaez, D., Bebeau, M., & Thoma, S. (1999). *Postconventional moral thinking: A neo-Kohlbergian approach*. Mahwah, NJ: Lawrence Erlbaum Associates.

Reynolds, S. J. (2008). Moral attentiveness: Who pays attention to the moral aspects of life? *Journal of Applied Psychology, 93* (5), 1027-1041.

Welsh, D. T., & Ordóñez, L. D. (2014). Conscience without cognition: The effects of subconscious priming on ethical behavior. *Academy of Management Journal, 57* (3), 723-742.

# Appendix E

# The Values of Dentists

Published as Chambers, D. W. (2019). Dentists' values: Actual and projected. *Journal of the American College of Dentists, 86* (1), 32-43.

## Abstract

Values represent the future worlds we strive to achieve. They play an important role in ethics by coordinating group behavior and enabling principles. An augmented version of Jonathan Haidt's Moral Foundations Questionnaire was used to assess the value structure of new and established dentists and the public on the importance of technical excellence and six value dimensions considered to be universal: caring, fairness, loyalty, authority, purity, and individuality. Although dentists scored high on caring and fairness, they also gave noticeable weight to loyalty, authority, purity, and individuality. Dentists' views of their values structure, especially those of older dentists, differed from the perceptions of the public and newer colleagues. These findings are consistent with current theory in social psychology, including the fundamental attribution error and false consensus. It is concluded that greater direct conversation between leaders in organized dentistry and others would promote clarity on the role of existing values in dentistry.

Values coordinate both individual and group behavior. Because values define what is important they keep us going in the right direction and make it easier to get along with others. Dentists who value technical excellence pay attention to ways to achieve it, they work at it, they even sacrifice to achieve it. Colleagues who value technical excellence in the same way support each other and are comfortable in each other's company. Patients who value technical excellence seek dentists who exemplify this value, and dentists are disappointed when patients do not share this value. Dentists who value community health orient less toward procedural excellence and place higher value on patient education and the adequate distribution of community resources. Dentists who value commercial success look for ways to maximize income, and patients who see oral health through a monetary lens find ways to avoid the dentist or accept only minimal treatment.

Values drive behavior and influence who we associate with. Technical definitions usually say something about "what is worth pursuing." Values are descriptions of what the best future world would look like. They are also motivational. Those who say they value caring or honesty but abuse others and distort information to gain an advantage are considered to be hypocrites. The values they claim do not match the values they live. We judge others and depend on them for the way they act and not what they say.

Values are often brought into discussions about ethics. But the relationship can be confusing. Principles have a firm place in ethical theory, but they are different from values. They are the rules for what people should do regardless of their personal values, and they tend to be black or white. "Do not lie, cheat, or steal, or tolerate any among us who do" is a famous zero-tolerance honor code at some institutions and in some professions. There is an absoluteness about principles that is comforting...in theory. Such policies have an uneven record of success (Rhode, 2018). In reality, of course, people interpret principles before they put them into practice, and the boundaries get fuzzy, especially when there are multiple and sometimes conflicting principles.

Norms are another technical term often found in discussions of ethics. Sometimes this is just a soft way of describing principles. We say of prescriptive norms, "The absolute rule is X, but people around here normally interpret that to mean roughly in the range of Y to Z." The other definition of a norm is descriptive: the average behavior in the group or the typical behavior of an individual across time and circumstances is thus-and-so. In that usage, there is no "should" attached other than the implication that if one wants to be considered to be part of the group, it would be appropriate to keep one's public behavior in the recognizable range.

Values, the focus of this paper, are personal or endorsed by a group, and they vary across a range and are dependent on local circumstances. So the speed limit on a given stretch of one's commute is 65 (the principle). The average rate of travel, all drivers and conditions taken into account, is 69 (the norm). And the speed of any particular driver may be 63 or 73 or something else (the value). The value is what the individual believes is best, all things considered, and what he or she tries to achieve. We get along on the highway because we know what we are trying to achieve and are willing to put some effort behind getting and because we have a working understanding of what others value.

We have multiple values, each has relative strength, and the mix of relevant values changes to some degree depending on the circumstances. A portfolio of values assigns probabilities to one's actions. We are more likely to act on the behavior with the strongest relevant values. It would be unusual to find a dentist who always sacrificed time and patient wishes as well as the long-range oral health of a patient to achieve perfect technical results worthy of photographing for show at a continuing education program on esthetic dentistry. But it sometimes happens. One would equally hope that it is rare to encounter dentists who subordinate everything to pumping up the bottom line. But that happens as well. Value patterns differ from one dentist to another. But trends emerge and become relatively permanent personal preferences for certain behavior patterns. We call that the value structure of a dentist or a profession. This is a convenient way to make general statements about what to expect dentists will do.

## Materials and Methods

Norms have been studied most extensively in philosophy (Wedgwood, 2006), principles more narrowly in bioethics (Beauchamp & Childress, 2009), and values primarily in social psychology (Greene, 2013). This division is recently being mended as more scholars are bridging between philosophy, social psychology, and neuroanatomy (Churchland, 2011).

There are many tools and methodologies available for studying values generally, and this report will describe one project to apply these methods to studying the value structure of dentists. Jonathan Haidt's Moral Foundations Model (2012) was used as the organizing framework here. Haidt studied what thousands upon thousands of individuals said was worth pursuing or avoiding in life. His questionnaire, the MFQ30 (yourmorals.org/haidtlab/ mft/index.php?t=questionnaires), has been used all over the world, and norms are available to make standardized comparisons (Graham et al, 2011). Haidt identified six values that characterize most of the variance in what people describe as desirable in their worlds. These are summarized in the Table E.1 below.

#### Table E.1. Value dimension of the moral foundations questionnaire.

| | |
|---|---|
| Caring | Protect others, especially the helpless, concern for other's safety and well-being, compassion and kindness |
| Fairness | Justice as the best distribution of rewards and benefits, cooperation, absence of cheating, fidelity and trustworthiness |
| Loyalty | In-group cohesion, pride and defense of distinctive features of the group, patriotism, not questioning or betraying what the group says it stands for |
| Authority | Seeing the world as hierarchically ordered, respect for those in high positions, obedience |
| Purity | Higher beliefs include order and cleanliness, avoiding unclean things and people, ritual, observance of taboos |
| Individuality | Each makes his or her own way, we keep what we earn, minimal answering to others for what we think is right |

Haidt's caring foundation is similar to the principle of beneficence in bioethics, and fairness is much like justice. A case can be made that veracity in the American Dental Association Principles of Ethics overlaps with Haidt's loyalty and authority.

A survey instrument for dentists was created for use in this study, in conjunction with researchers in Haidt's group. Items in the MFQ30 were retained, with slight word changes in some cases to better suit a professional context. An additional dimension was added comprising some questions about the value of technical excellence, as previous research as part of the American College of Dentists Gies Ethics Report showed that this is a strong dimension in dentists' self-concepts. A further addition to the survey instrument used in this research was inclusion of items asking about the values respondents projected onto others in the profession. Specifically it was asked what respondents thought new dentists would say about each of the six dimensions of the Moral Foundations value model, plus technological excellence, and what they thought established dentists would report. New dentists were defined on the questionnaire as those who were under 40 years of age or did not own a practice. Established dentists were either older than 40 or were practice owners.

A copy of the survey instrument appears in the Exhibit.

A total of 141 individuals completed the modified MFQ30 questionnaire of values. This included a sample of 118 dentists recruited from officers and fellows of the American College of Dentists, young practitioners identified by the American Student Dental Association, and faculty members in a dental school. A separate sample completed a short version of the questionnaire. These were 23 "patients," individuals who had no connection with dentistry other than being a patient, who completed the form outside the context of a dental office.

This research was approved by the Institutional Review Board at the University of the Pacific: IRB Proposal #16-74.

## Results

### Dentists' Values Generally

Figure E.1 shows the value preferences of dentists, combining across all 118 respondents. Haidt's norms for the general population are superimposed on the trend line for comparison. All values in this and other figures are "normed." This means that the reported scores have been standardized to a common scale, anchored in the average weight given to all value dimensions within each group. In other words, all value dimensions are relative within each group of respondents.

**Figure E.1. Value structure of dentists and general population.**

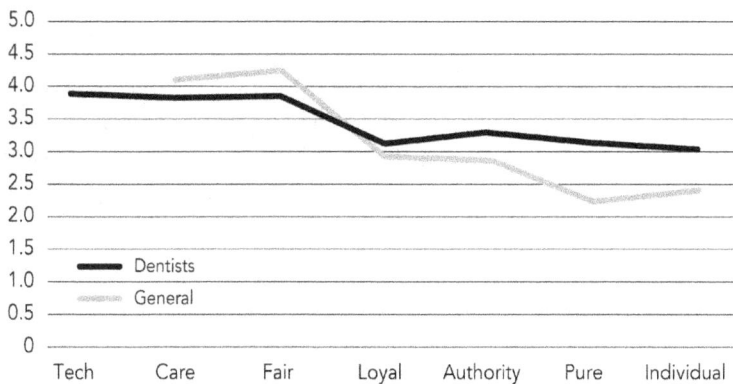

Dentists show a very balanced value structure. Importance of technical excellence is judged the value most worthy of pursuit, but is essentially even in strength with caring about others and fairness. At a slightly lower level of importance is a second cluster composed of loyalty, authority, purity, and individuality. The fact that dentists score high on loyalty and authority at the same time they value individuality will be commented on in the discussion section.

The general public, based on Haidt's norms, rank order the six value dimensions in essentially the same way dentists do. But they make larger distinctions. For example, caring and justice are relatively more important than are respect for authority, purity, and individualism. Statistical tests with t-tests were performed to confirm these differences. All differences between dentists and patients in the intensity of values (with the exception of loyalty) were significant beyond $p < .001$.

There is considerable individual variation in how both individual dentists and individual members of the public value these six dimensions of what is worth striving for. The standard deviations for both groups ranged from about 0.75 to 1.00 on a five-point scale. That means, for example, that the loyalty score, which is close to 3.0 on average for both groups, contains about 10% of respondents valuing this dimension 4.0 or higher and another 10% who value it at 2.0 or lower. There was no dimension that failed to find responses on individual items of 0.0 or 5.0 on the same item. The fairness and individuality dimensions were especially subject to wide personal swings, even within the same individual. These scales had the lowest Cronbach alpha scores for internal consistency. All other dimensions had alpha values above 0.60, which is what is generally characteristic of such surveys. Dentists responded that 3% of the fairness and 8% of the individualism questions rated a 0, while 8% and 16% respectively of the same dentists scored the same items 5. In other words, fairness and individualism are highly situation-specific. It should come as no surprise that there is great variation in individual values, even ranging to as much as a quarter of any group aligning in the extreme opposite corners. Even when there was apparent agreement on the overall importance of fairness, there was disparity on which particular cases represented fair practices and which did not.

Dentists, compared with the general public, valued being able to set their own standards (individuality) and to maintain a clean and orderly environment and avoid association with those who do not share these standards (purity). Dentists consider themselves to be both caring and fair, but seek to retain some control over how that is expressed.

## Values of New and Established Dentists

The graph in Figure E.2 contains multiple comparisons. The dark solid line represents the average responses of dentists over the age of 40 or who are practice owners. The gray solid line shows the average scores for new practitioners who are young or not practice owners. The lines cross with higher self-reports for established dentists on technical excellence, caring, and fairness and lower values for the others, when compared with new dentists. However, none of these differences was statistically significant, either by t-tests for group averages or when correlating actual respondent age on value score on an individual basis. The self-reported value structure of new and established dentists is essentially the same.

---

Figure E.2. **Values of new and established dentists.**

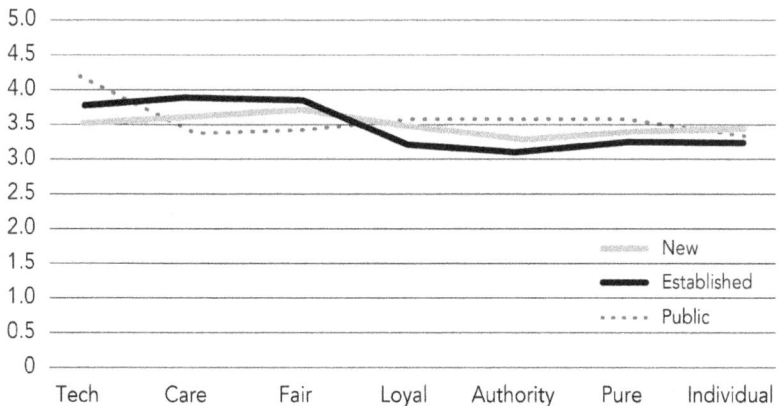

---

The third, lighter and dotted line on the graph is for data provided by 23 patients. They were asked to project the values they attributed to dentists generally (not their private practitioner). In all cases, patients projected values more nearly resembling those self-reported by the young practitioners than the self-reports of older dentists. This can be interpreted as reflecting the fact that older dentists have a self-perception of their values that differs from the way they are perceived in the public. The higher self-image on caring and fairness held by established dentists was statistically significant at p < .01. Loyalty, authority, and purity are thought by the public to better characterize dentists than established dentists believe to be true of themselves, again by a significant margin (at least p < .01). Finally, the public thinks of dentists largely in terms of their technical orientation, and significantly more so than do dentists.

## Dentists Misunderstanding Each Other

New and young dentists profess to have very similar value structures. They describe themselves in similar terms. But a question remains whether dentists believe that their colleagues share the values they espouse. It can be asked, for example, whether established dentists think new dentists share their values. An inquiry could also be made regarding what new dentists think of their age peers and their seniors. This is a question about the relative accuracy of perceiving the values of others.

To test relative perceptions of values, new dentists' values were compared with their answers to the questions regarding their feelings about the values of other young dentists and their feelings about the values of established dentists. Similar comparisons were made for established dentists, comparing what they thought of themselves relative to their younger colleagues and their age peers. The metric used to express this comparison was the difference between what dentists thought of their own values and what they thought of new or established dentists. The results for what new and established dentists thought of established practitioners is shown in Figure E.3.

Figure E.3. **Relative perception of established dentists' values by new and established dentists.**

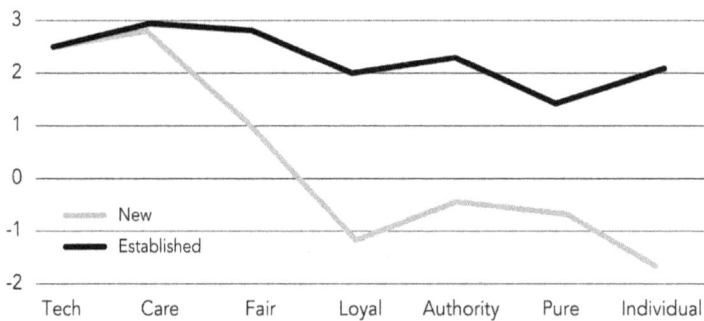

Scores above the 0-line represent positive relative self-perceptions. In this case, established dentists felt they, personally, embodied significantly more positive positions on all six values than did other established dentists. The extent of favorable comparison with colleagues was strong and highly significant. By contrast, new dentists viewed their values as being in line with those of their older colleagues. The exceptions (all statistically significant) were a personally more favorable self-perception among new dentists of caring and fairness and a disinclination to set private standards through individualization.

The graph in Figure E.4 shows what new and established dentists thought of the values of new dentists compared with their self-perceptions of these same values. Again there is general inflation of one's own values. Established dentists were generally more inclined to give themselves high values (except for purity), but not to the same extent that they overvalued their positions relative to their age peers. New dentists thought they had higher value strength for technical excellence, caring, fairness, and individualism than other new dentists.

**Figure E.4. Relative perception of new dentists' values by new and established dentists.**

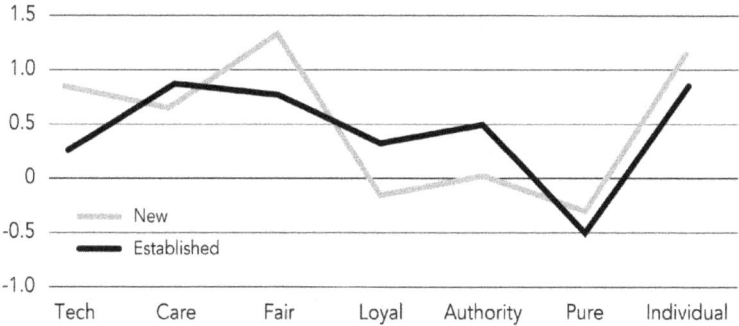

## Discussion

Values are patterns of motivation; they are generalizations about the kind of world we would prefer. As such, they are action-guiding to a greater extent than are ethical principles, which purport to describe what everyone should do all the time. Those who value the kinds of behavior associated with ethical principles will act to bring about that kind of world. Those who know the principles but do not value them will likely talk a better game than they play. Unlike principles, however, values have relative personal strength and depend on circumstances. These characteristics arguably make them more realistic carriers of the ethical code. We hold our lives together by these general patterns of desired behavior in ourselves and in others.

This study of dentists' values using a standardized instrument and a reasonably sized and diverse sample found the following.

- Dentists value technical excellence, caring, and fairness to a slightly greater extent than they value loyalty, authority, purity, and individualism.
- The same pattern is typical of the value preferences in the general population (minus technical excellence, of course), but the public puts more emphasis on caring and fairness and less on authority, purity, and individualism than do dentists.
- The value structure of new and established dentists is very similar, although the public tends to expect that dentists will behave more like the self-described values of new dentists.
- Dentists feel they have stronger personal values than they recognize among their colleagues. This is especially true for the perceptions of established dentists by their age peers.
- New dentists tend to be more accurate in their perceptions of both new and established practitioners.

## Defining Values

The finding regarding the high value placed on technical excellence is to be expected, perhaps from the nature of dentistry as a profession, but also from the findings of other research conducted as part of the American College of Dentists Gies Ethics Project. It was found there (publication forthcoming) that technical excellence is a stronger focus of dentists' attention than any other motive, including financial success. It has been argued both for dentistry and for other healthcare fields that professionals are increasingly defining themselves in terms of technical capability and less so in terms of service to the public (Sullivan, 2005).

Dentists score high on the values of caring and fairness. These values form a cluster that would be accepted by all as central to the definition of being a professional (American College of Dentists, 1999; 2000; Welie, 2004). Dentistry should be proud that so many of its members orient toward a world where these values are prominent. These will be among the first descriptors practitioners use when saying what is important in their lives.

As happy as self-reported caring and fairness are, there are a few shadows. First, the general public thinks of itself as being a bit more caring and fair than do dentists (Figure E.1), and they regard dentists as less caring and concerned with fairness than dentists see themselves as being (Figure E.2). There is also the case (Figures E.3 and E.4) that established dentists in particular see themselves as being substantially more caring and fair than they believe their colleagues are. Differences between self-perceived values and the perceptions of others are well known and have been widely studied. These effects will be discussed below. The Gallup Survey of Trust in the Professions has generally found that dentistry, at about 60% of the public agreeing with the statement that dentists have their best interests in mind, is the least trusted of the healthcare professions (news.gallup.com/poll/1654/honesty-ethics-professions.aspx).

Another part of the shadow over caring and fairness is its differential weight among the full profile of values. The public places these two values well above others in importance. By contrast, caring and fairness are more salient, but not much more so than other values, such as loyalty, authority, purity, and individualism for dentists. Dentistry is a complex profession, defined in part by commercial interests of independent practitioners who exercise some discretion over who they interact with. The value structure of dentistry is complex. It cannot be said that dentists define themselves uniquely by the values of caring and fairness, at least not to a significantly greater extent than they define themselves by other values.

It happened in the present research that while caring and fairness score high as values among dentists, relatively less value is placed here than among the public at large. Further, when asked, the public gives somewhat less weight to caring and fairness as values they associate with dentists than do dentists when describing themselves. Caring and fairness are also values that respondents on the questionnaire tended to feel better characterized themselves than their peers.

Authority and individualism are values dentists endorse more strongly than does the general public. The relationship between the dentist and patient is built on authority rather than a relationship between equals. Finding that dentists hold this value more strongly than do patients is not surprising. Individuality shows a similar pattern, and perhaps for similar reasons. Dentists practice by themselves and set their own rules. They are generally the authors of their own success. On these surveys, respondents reported significantly greater endorsement of working independently and being hesitant to share the benefits of their efforts than did the public. This was especially true of older dentists and it was the common view of both younger and older practitioners that older dentists endorse this view. In the focus groups conducted as part of the larger Gies Ethics Project, a very clear theme emerged that dentists function in isolation and independent of contact with others who might serve as a check on excessive ethical latitude. This view was shared by all groups interviewed, including dentists themselves, leaders in the profession, patients, and health policy experts.

The apparent contradiction between authority-loyalty on one hand and individualism on the other has been noted previously. In 1994, Schwartz and Shenoy reported that dentists score high on "individualism via conformity" on standardized tests. The explanation is that dentists expect to have large personal freedom in what they do in their own offices, to command respect and loyalty, and to assume that their colleagues will behave similarly. The conformity (loyalty) is not monitored or enforced by interaction or sharing of experiences, but by presumed common professional values. The value of individuality applies to dentists personally, and the value of loyalty applies collectively. The first code of ethics of the American Dental Association, for example, required price fixing as a professional courtesy (American Dental Association, 1866). Roughly 40% of the current Code of Professional Conduct describes what dentists should expect of their colleagues.

## Self-perceptions and Perception of Others' Values

The current research raises questions about the accuracy of perceived values—both one's own and the values of others. The public does not see the values structure of dentists exactly the same way the profession views itself. Established dentists in particular are more apt to feel they hold a stronger set of values as individuals than the values their colleagues hold—even when they are members of the group they are judging.

This effect is now generally recognized as part of human nature and is known as the fundamental attribution error (Jones & Harris, 1967; Ross, 1977). Publicly observable events are generally open to interpretation as to their causes. It has been discovered that there are natural patterns that distort interpretation in these cases. The basic picture is as shown in Table E.2.

---

### Table E.2. Fundamental Attribution Error Matrix.

|  | Other as Agent | Self as Agent |
| --- | --- | --- |
| Good outcome | Good luck | Talent, effort |
| Bad outcome | Deficient talent | Bad luck |

---

Sometimes we attribute the causes of situations to characteristics of the person primarily involved and sometimes we think the outcomes are principally determined by circumstances beyond anyone's control. The attribution of causes tends to follow the rule that good outcomes are the result of effort and skill if we are the agent and of luck if others are the agent. Unfortunate outcomes are usually seen coming from unavoidable circumstances if we had our hand on the project and as bungled work if others did it. This is not always a conscious and nasty rationalization. It is part of human nature. The discrepancies found in this research between projections of others' values and one's own are probably influenced to some extent by the fundamental attribution error.

A related social perception effect may also be at play here. The false consensus effect is an established bias where we overestimate the extent to which others share the values we hold. Marks and Miller (1987) and Ross and colleagues (1977) performed the original research using the following paradigm. (See also Gilovich, 1990; Krueger & Clement, 1994.) Individuals were asked to rate a behavior, such as asking money of strangers or breaking the convention of a club, in terms of (a) how likely they were to engage in the behavior, and (b) how likely they thought others were to engage in the behavior. Asking a large number of people from the same group produced both an average value score for oneself and an average value score for others. Those who were likely to engage in the behavior were more likely to exaggerate the likelihood that others would do the same. It is human nature to assume others think as we do.

The effects of fundamental attribution error and false consensus urge caution in the matter of speaking for the values of others. Research has shown the danger of allowing third parties or elite subgroups to speak on behalf of organizations when dealing with others (Flynn & Wiltermuth, 2010). Such intermediaries usually reduce the chances that diverse groups will ultimately come to understand one another's values.

Young and older dentists share similar values. The same is likely true of minorities, specialties, and others within the profession. The problem is more in the direction that assumed differences block the communication that would give the lie to believing that we are divided by imagined and exaggerated differences. The profession is too small to afford creating assumed divisions where they do not exist.

# References

American College of Dentists (1999; 2000). *Journal of the American College of Dentists, 66* (4) and *67* (1), entire issues.

American Dental Association (1866). *Transactions of the American Dental Association, Sixth Annual Meeting*. Boston, 31 July 1866.

Beauchamp, T. L., & Childress, J. F. (2009). *Principles of biomedical ethics*, 6th ed. New York, NY: Oxford University Press.

Churchland, P. S. (2011). *Braintrust: What neuroscience tells us about morality*. Princeton, NJ: Princeton University Press.

Flynn, F. J., & Wiltermuth, S. S. (2010). Who's with me? False consensus, brokerage, and ethical decision making in organizations. *Academy of Management Journal, 53* (5), 1074-1089.

Gilovich, T. (1990). Differential construal and the false consensus effect. *Journal of Personality and Social Psychology, 59,* 623-634.

Graham, J., Nosek, B. A., Haidt, J., Iyer, R., Koleva, S., & Ditto, P. H. (2011). Mapping the moral domain. *Journal of Personal and Social Psychology, 101* (2), 366-385.

Greene, J. (2013). *Moral tribes: Emotion, reason, and the gap between us and them*. New York, NY: Penguin Books.

Haidt, J. (2012). *The righteous mind: Why good people are divided by politics and religion*. New York, NY: Vintage Books.

Jones, E. E., & Harris, V. A. (1967). The attribution of attitudes. *Journal of Experimental Social Psychology, 3* (1), 1-24.

Krueger, I., Clement, R. W. (1994). The truly false consensus effect: An ineradicable and egocentric bias in social perception. *Journal of Personality and Social Psychology, 67,* 596-610.

Marks, G., & Miller, N. (1987). Ten years of research on the false-consensus effect: An empirical and theoretical review. *Psychological Bulletin, 102,* 72-90.

Rhode, D. L. (2018). *Cheating: Ethics in everyday life*. New York, NY: Oxford University Press.

Ross, I., Greene, D., & House, P. (1977). The false consensus effect: an egocentric bias in social perception and attribution processes. *Journal of Experimental Social Psychology, 13,* 279-301.

Ross, L. (1977). The intuitive psychologist and his shortcomings: Distortions in the attribution process. In Berkowitz, L. *Advances in experimental social psychology, 10* (pp. 173-220). New York, NY: Academic Press.

Schwartz, R. H., & Shenoy, S. (1994). Personality factors related to career satisfaction among general practitioners. *Journal of Dental Education, 58,* 225-228.

Sullivan, W. M. (2005). *Work and integrity: The crisis and promise of professionalism in America,* 2nd ed. San Francisco, CA; Jossey-Bass.

Wedgwood, R. (2006). *The nature of normativity.* Oxford, UK: Oxford University Press.

Welie, J. V. (2004). Is dentistry a profession? Part 1. Professionalism defined. *Journal of the Canadian Dental Association, 70* (8), 529-532.

---

# Exhibits

## *Values Inventory*
_____ Your age

When you decide whether something is right or wrong, to what extent are the following considerations relevant to your thinking? Rate each statement using this scale:

0 = Not at all relevant (this has nothing to do with judging right and wrong)
1 = Not very relevant
2 = Slightly relevant
3 = Somewhat relevant
4 = Very relevant
5 = Extremely relevant (this is one of the most important factors in judging right and wrong)

_____ Whether or not someone suffered emotionally
_____ Whether or not some people were treated differently than others
_____ Whether or not someone's action showed love for his or her country
_____ Whether or not someone showed a lack of respect for authority
_____ Whether or not someone violated standards of purity and decency
_____ Whether or not someone was good at solving complex problems
_____ Whether or not someone cared for someone weak or vulnerable
_____ Whether or not someone acted unfairly
_____ Whether or not someone did something to betray his or her group
_____ Whether or not someone conformed to the traditions of society
_____ Whether or not someone did something disgusting
_____ Whether or not someone was cruel
_____ Whether or not someone was denied his or her rights
_____ Whether or not someone showed lack of loyalty
_____ Whether or not an action caused chaos or disorder
_____ Whether or not someone acted in a way that God would approve of

**NEW STANDARD:** Indicate the extent to which you agree or disagree with the following statements

    0 = Strongly DISAGREE
    1 = Moderately disagree
    2 = Slightly disagree
    3 = Slightly agree
    4 = Moderately agree
    5 = Strongly AGREE

_____ I personally believe the technical skill of dentists is paramount
_____ I consider myself to be quite a bit more caring than others seem to be
_____ I pride myself on being fair
_____ I regard myself as being more loyal to my colleagues than others are
_____ I really respect authority
_____ One of my special characteristics is valuing purity and sanctity
_____ I consider myself as having politically conservative values

    _Remember: 0 means strongly DISAGREE and 5 means strongly AGREE_

_____ It is better to do good than to do bad
_____ It is wrong for government to redistribute wealth, no matter what good comes of it
_____ Compassion for those who are suffering is the most crucial virtue
_____ When laws are made, the number one principle is ensuring that everyone is treated fairly
_____ I am proud of my country's history
_____ Respect for authority is something all children need to learn
_____ People should not do things that are disgusting, even if no one is harmed
_____ Society works best letting individuals take responsibility for themselves, not saying what to do

An "established" dentist is roughly over 40 and owns a practice:
_____ I generally regard established dentists as holding that technical skills are paramount
_____ I generally consider established dentists to be very caring people
_____ I generally regard established dentists as being fair
_____ I generally consider established dentists as especially loyal to their colleagues
_____ I generally think that established dentists really respect authority
_____ I generally think established dentists value purity and sanctity
_____ I generally regard established dentists as having politically conservative values

_____ People who are successful in business have a right to enjoy their wealth as they see fit
_____ One of the worst things a person could do is hurt a defenseless animal
_____ Justice is the most important requirement for a society
_____ People should be loyal to their family members, even when they have done something wrong
_____ Respect for authority is too often challenged these days
_____ I would call some acts wrong on the grounds that they are unnatural

_____ It's morally wrong that rich children inherit a lot of money while poor children inherit nothing

*Remember: 0 means strongly DISAGREE and 5 means strongly AGREE*

_____ The government interferes far too much in our everyday lives
_____ It is never right for anyone to kill another human being
_____ There are too many rules that put people at a disadvantage for making small mistakes
_____ It is more important to be a team player than to express oneself
_____ As a soldier, if I disagreed with my commanding officer, I would obey anyway as that is my duty
_____ Chastity is an important and valuable virtue
_____ Government should do more to advance common good, even if it limits choices, freedoms

A "new" dentist is roughly under 40 or does not own a practice, that includes students and residents:
_____ I generally regard new dentists as holding that technical skills are paramount
_____ I generally consider new dentists to be very caring people
_____ I generally regard new dentists as being fair
_____ I generally consider new dentists as especially loyal to their colleagues
_____ I generally think that new dentists really respect authority
_____ I generally think new dentists value purity and sanctity
_____ I generally regard new dentists as having politically conservative values

*Thank you!*

## Survey for "Patients"

Please share your opinion about dentists in general. Your present personal dentist may or may not be typical, so place him or her in the background.

I am looking for your general impression. Obviously you do not know everything about every dentist any more than you know about books you have not read. I am looking for your expectations.

This project is part of a national study gathering information from dentists and others across the country for a book-length report the American College of Dentists is preparing. The survey is anonymous—so no names please—and of course, there are no "right or wrong" answers, just your personal views.

My impressions about DENTISTS IN GENERAL are that they...

5 = Always, in virtually every single case
4 = Usually
3 = Sometimes yes and sometimes no
2 = Not generally
1 = Never, this is extremely rare

5  4  3  2  1
*Always → Never*

☐ ☐ ☐ ☐ ☐  Become deeply involved when they see someone may be suffering harm

☐ ☐ ☐ ☐ ☐  Treat everyone the same, including those on Medicaid

☐ ☐ ☐ ☐ ☐  Have a strong sense of loyalty to other dentists

☐ ☐ ☐ ☐ ☐  Value respect for authority and deference to those in positions of power

☐ ☐ ☐ ☐ ☐  Prefer things neat and orderly

☐ ☐ ☐ ☐ ☐  Are politically conservative, slow to change established ways

☐ ☐ ☐ ☐ ☐  Embrace new technology as vital to the success of their practice

☐ ☐ ☐ ☐ ☐  Have one eye on the bottom line

☐ ☐ ☐ ☐ ☐  Are the most ethical of the health professionals

☐ ☐ ☐ ☐ ☐  Are primarily concerned with the overall oral health in a community

☐ ☐ ☐ ☐ ☐  Have special empathy for the weak and vulnerable

☐ ☐ ☐ ☐ ☐  Avoid giving any individuals preferential treatment

☐ ☐ ☐ ☐ ☐  Count on everyone to keep their promises

☐ ☐ ☐ ☐ ☐  Expect people to follow rules and leaders

☐ ☐ ☐ ☐ ☐  Avoid things that are disgusting, dirty

☐ ☐ ☐ ☐ ☐  Feel individuals who are successful deserve to keep what they get

☐ ☐ ☐ ☐ ☐  Take great pride in their technical skill

☐ ☐ ☐ ☐ ☐  Avoid working in prisons or nursing homes because of low reimbursement levels

☐ ☐ ☐ ☐ ☐  Do not overcharge or perform unnecessary procedures

☐ ☐ ☐ ☐ ☐  Value long-term health more than doing the best procedure the best way

# Appendix F

# The Dental Ethics Teaching Case

Published as Chambers, D. W. (2020). The Dental Ethics Teaching Case. *Journal of the American College of Dentists, 87* (1), 18-25.

## Abstract

Ethics teaching cases, dilemmas, are a staple in dental school curricula and in presentations to practitioners at meetings. They are short, hypothetical situations where various approaches might be appropriate and where the dentist is assumed to be both the independent initiator of the action and the judge of whether it is best. The use of cases for teaching works best in small groups. The goal is to teach habits of reflection-in-practice. They are seldom used to teach principles and more likely to function to explore the edges of the interpretation or application of principles. Published ethics cases in dentistry were compared with those in media, business, and nursing. Dental cases were found to be unique in being more about ambiguous matters rather than clear examples of right and wrong, more hypothetical and open to interpretations, more likely to ask that participants assume that they are the decision maker rather than the explainer of what is appropriate, and that dentists were not answerable to others for their actions.

Discussions that are centered on representative problematic incidents in practice are an important teaching tool in professional ethics. They engage learners and provide a break from didactic approaches that can seem "preachy" when talking about what people should and should not do. In dentistry teaching cases are customarily called dilemmas to emphasize the point that more than one point of view will be justifiable and that a single, completely satisfactory path forward is not expected.

This paper will discuss how teaching cases function as a method for promoting reflective ethical practice and contrast the cases used in four professions: dentistry, journalism, business, and nursing. Perhaps the types of issues taken up in teaching cases can reveal something of interest about how the professions regard the tough choices its members have to make.

## Using Teaching Cases to Build Reflective Practice

Teaching cases, whether in ethics, diagnosis, treatment planning, or other aspects of dentistry, are opportunities to reflect on situations where attention is being called to a potential problem. These are not naturally occurring ethical challenges. A group of individuals is brought together for the express purpose of considering a situation that someone with credentials in ethics has identified as a hypothetical situation where one path forward is free of regret. Reflecting on several such cases is offered as training for the general skill of making better ethical decisions.

### How Case Teaching Is Structured

Short descriptions, usually written and ranging from 25 words to three pages, describe the details of a hypothetical situation. Such descriptions allow participants to "fill in" missing detail, and one of the sources of discussion stems from the fact that participants bring something of themselves to cases. Participants are invited to assume the role of a clearly identified individual in the case ("Dr. Soandso just examined Mr. Challenge...") or to discuss generally a topic from a particular description ("Your benefits carrier just announced a change in documentation requirements for all dentists in the state..."). Learners are invited to discuss the case in small groups, with varying degree of teacher guidance and participation. Cases are chosen so that each of the most plausible actions involves both happy outcomes and disappointing consequences, for both the actor and those he or she interacts with. The goal is to find the course of action or policy that minimizes the moral regret, the ethical dis-ease in a situation that has been crafted to be problematic. Much of the work in analyzing the case is imagining particulars that fill out the brief description, uncovering implications, and linking preferred alternatives to justifications. Usually there is no attempt to reach a consensus on a course of action or a single justification that all participants will be expected to accept. Varying degrees of participation among participants is accepted.

Cases can also be used to teach by example or as illustrations of the points a presenter is trying to make in a predominantly lecture format. Particulars of situations that went conspicuously wrong are commented on and learners are invited to feel good about not behaving so badly themselves. Usually this kind of case is in the public domain, such as Dr. David Acer, who intentionally infected patients with the HIV virus, or Dr. Douglas Harrington, whose practice drew national media coverage for its awful infection control practices, or cases pulled from records of disciplinary action taken by state boards. All of these are public records and can be found on the Internet. James Rule and Mickey Bebeau's wonderful collection of biographies and analyses of great dentists is perhaps the only collection of exemplary cases (Rule & Bebeau, 2005).

Cases can be studied by individuals alone, but that is rare. The function of a case is not to learn that someone had a problem or that an expert commented on it in a certain fashion. Cases are usually discussed in small groups in order to maximize the likelihood that differences of interpretation and different value profiles will emerge.

## How Cases Teach Reflection-in-Practice

Donald Schön's research on how professionals learn to solve problems is relevant here (Schön, 1987). When faced with the need to take an action where the previously learned and habitual responses look as though they will not be satisfactory, the professional begins to reframe the problem using intellectual and actual tools particular to one's profession. The patient complains of pain in a tooth that shows no obvious signs of trauma. Problem solving is needed and will include considering several alternatives such as referred pain. Physical tests will be performed. Based on the results, new hypotheses will emerge. The process of reframing continues until it is unlikely that any further adjustments in framing seem justified...then action is taken. When processes such as this are repeated in a particular domain, the professional learns reflective skills. Case work in ethics is based on this model and is intended to teach reflection-in-practice.

In the academic setting, most cases are "given." Learners do not sense or discover that an ethical problem exists as part of their natural lives. They are told explicitly that some imagined person has a problem and it is strongly implied that reframing is expected or at least that the next few minutes will be devoted to those who wish to engage in this process. The artificiality of case learning is magnified by confining case work to previously announced times, locations, and attendance, and by instructors establishing context, even to the extent of giving a brief introduction to the topic heading, say nonmaleficence, before inviting discussion.

The size of the group working on a case is critical. When multiple participants share their perspectives, it is more likely that alternative interpretations of the situation, insight into how actions will affect others, and ways of justifying a chosen action will emerge. That is useful input for constructive reframing. The optimal size for case discussion is about four to six. A highly skilled facilitator may be able to add one or two more to the group. But beyond that number there is a danger that some will assume the role of "performed in front of their peers" and others will become "the passive audience."

Above half a dozen individuals discussing a hypothetical case, the definition of the task shifts from individuals trying out various constructions on the problem in the context of their friends to an artificial and academic task. When the group is too large for equal, open exchange of ideas, some simply become spectators. They reflect on what others are saying, not on how they would structure the matter. When the facilitator can no longer maintain active participation and begins inserting content, the process becomes academic and only a few students participate in the "guess what word the instructor wants us to say" game (Doyle & Straus, 1976).

There are two goals in a clinical case consultation involving a dental student, a faculty member, and one or more specialists: (a) what should be done for the patient's good; and (b) what can be learned by the student about how to reflect on such situations. In ethics cases, only the latter is at stake. The cases are hypothetical, or if real, they concern past events. They are also simulations or incomplete descriptions of situations. Anyone who has observed case discussions will quickly be struck by how easily participants can come to different interpretations based on plausible fabrication of missing details. Such suppositions occur in real life, but actual context is more concrete, and the assumptions can more easily be verified.

It would not be exactly right to say that cases are useful for teaching ethical principles. Overtreatment is wrong, so is fraud, and no ethics course should place that on the table for debate. Beneficence is always good, and no dental school ethics course has ever tried to prove or disprove that point. What cases are useful for is helping students recognize which are examples of principles held by the profession and which are not and how to navigate the nuances of interpretation in particular instances. The "Ethical Moment" column in the *Journal of the American Dental Association* that has been published almost monthly since 2004 has never changed the five guiding ethical touchstones or considered that there may be others. It is always about whether specific behavior fits each principle.

This is known in classical moral philosophy as the ethical syllogism (MacIntyre, 1988). Ethical principles are givens, or at least are not to be questioned in the current context. This is the major premise of the syllogism. The minor premise introduces the particulars and the circumstances. The conclusion connects the particular action with the moral character of the principle. Lying to a patient is unethical (major premise); failing to tell a patient about all the effective treatments available is a form of lying (minor premise). Therefore failure to inform the patient is unethical (conclusion). The American Dental Association (ADA) Code contains three levels. The five principles in the Principles of Ethics are the major premises. The 28 Standards of Professional Conduct and the 27 Advisory Opinions are examples of minor premises. Teaching ethics by means of cases is excellent practice for students in learning to transition between general ethical norms and particular classes of application. It should be constantly held in mind, however, that norms are not created or challenged in case discussion; only their application is, and that is an open-ended and continual process. It is also the case that minor premises can never be an exhaustive list. A dentist can conform with every Standard of Professional Conduct in the ADA Code and still be unethical. Although billing differentials are mentioned in relationship to coverage plans, there is no prohibition in the ADA Code against overbilling generally. Nor is collusion among dentists or corporations to corner a geographic market to drive up prices mentioned.

For some, there is an alternative secondary goal in using the case method with discussion in addition to building the capacity to think about complex hypothetical ethical situations that have been pointed out. Group discussion affords an opportunity for students to learn and use language that justifies their ethical intentions. Overtreatment is wrong. There is no particular reason to know which ethical principle is relevant in this case. Knowing the name of the principle cannot be counted on to change the behavior of those who overtreat. It is handy, however, to have some facility with ethics language to discuss this and to be able in public settings to connect good and bad types of behavior with commonly used terminology.

## Is "Naming That Principle" Enough?

When the justifying business overshadows doing the right thing the case method begins to wander from its original goal. Too often case discussions become an opportunity for faculty members or outside "experts" to demonstrate their insight. It is also not uncommon for a few students who are skilled verbally and politically to practice their polemic skills. When there are two or more such students in a group, others drop out, but the conversation goes on until each has sufficiently demonstrated fluency in talking about the hypothetical. Then it is agreed that "there are legitimate professional differences."

Sometimes cases are exercises in identifying particular circumstances that excuse professionals from their obligation to follow the spirit of general norms. When one hears students and faculty talk about ethical issues in the locker room or around the edges of committee meetings, the conversations are usually of a different nature. Discussion of actual ethical incidents tends to be brief, indirect, and tentative. Sometimes a principle is mentioned, but that most often is a single-word sentence.

A nursing study on teaching with the case method illustrates this point (Hofling et al, 1966). A case was discussed in class where student nurses were asked what they would do: The doctor ordered a 20 mg dose of a drug for a patient in a psychiatric ward. As described in the case, when the nurse went to the dispensary, she read the directions that 5 mg was the recommended dose, but 10 was the maximum that should be administered. Eighty percent of the nursing students said, after discussion, that they would refuse to administer the ordered dose. At the same time, in the hospital where these students did their rotations, the exact experiment was being conducted (with a placebo drug). Five percent actually refused the order.

Joshua Greene reviews the evidence that moral decisions are usually made within milliseconds of recognizing a problematic situation. It is unusual to engage in conscious reflection, and that most often happens when it is really apparent that the old ways may come up short or when we are forced into an artificial role-playing format (Greene, 2013; Haidt, 2012). In some cases, we engage in an extended rational reflection on cases that are complex or interesting, including some that we have never actually encountered or which make no practical difference to anyone we know.

Preparing an ethics lecture would be such a situation. Reflection is a separate activity from behaving in natural settings.

Ethics teaching with cases assumes the two conditions of reflection and choice of action are built into the task. In teaching situations we normally encounter reflection without action. In practice, we usually find the opposite. There is the potential in ethics teaching that reflective practice will help form our more autonomous moral habits. But the amount of ethical reflection required to shape reliable, serviceable moral habits is probably more than a few cases. There is no evidence that working through ethics cases makes a professional more ethical, other than by other measures of simulated (classroom) outcomes (Bebeau, 2006).

## Are All Professionals Ethical in the Same Way?

As part of the American College of Dentists Gies Ethics Project, surveys were sent to deans of 62 dental schools in 2015 asking them to identify the individual responsible for teaching ethics in their schools. Ten were not able to identify such a person. Fifty-seven individuals who identified as being responsible for the ethics program in dental schools completed a survey, and phone interviews were also conducted with 14 of these. The overall results are reported separately in Appendix M (Survey of Dental Ethics Education). The basic findings relative to use of case teaching are as follows: Courses in ethics have an average number of 22.8 hours, 39% of which are conducted in small groups. Thus most of ethics instruction is in the one-to-many format. The small group format may mean that a one-to-many interaction is repeated in blocks. There may also be a variety of small-group activities such as skits or group projects. Respondents reported discussing an average of 24.6 cases, one-quarter of the cases involving activities in the dental school, and that 75% of cases covered activities in practice after graduation with which students have no direct experience. Cases could have been discussed in small groups or used in a lecture format to illustrate the presenter's points.

### Sources of Professional Ethics Cases Studied

Many faculty members who teach ethics have developed their own set of cases. The most widely used collections of ethics cases are those contained in *Dental Ethics at Chairside* by David Ozar and David Sokol (with a third edition just released and available online through the American College of Dentists); *Ethical Questions in Dentistry* by Jim Rule and Robert Veatch; and the material available from the American College of Dentists at dentalethics.org. There are books on dental law and ethics by Lambden; Graskemper; Weinstein; Frey and Nichols; and Brennan, Oliver, Harvey, and Jones. There are also four texts containing cases for dental hygienists.

The standard format for such texts is to cover principles and theories of bioethics and follow with cases and expert analysis of the cases. The exception is the cases developed for use by the American College of Dentists. These are available in both text and video format and feature normative feedback from both practicing dentists and patients rather than expert analysis. A set of cases was developed by Dr. Tom Hasegawa in the 1970s that appeared in the *Texas Dental Journal.* These cases focused on which treatment might be most appropriate clinically and featured the innovation of publishing the case in one issue of the journal, followed by selected reader responses in subsequent issues. These are available at the American College of Dentists' website. Since 2004, the American Dental Association Council of Ethics, Bylaws and Judicial Affairs has published a regular "Ethical Moment" column in the *Journal of the American Dental Association* using a format of a fictitious case that is analyzed in terms of the ADA Code. Other dental journals, most notably the *Journal of the American College of Dentists* and the Academy of General Dentistry *Impact*, publish cases on an occasional basis.

Beginning with the assumption that the experts who write the books on professional ethics have an educated opinion about the nature of the problems professionals face, it would make sense to study case material to learn about the challenges thought to face the profession. It may be the case that dentists are engaged in a different set of ethical challenges than are other professionals, or at least that the problems that confront them are managed in a different context. This hypothesis was suggested by the chance review of ethics case text in several cognate disciplines.

This hypothesis was tested by analyzing the nature of ethics cases in nursing, business, and journalism, as well as in dentistry. The following sources were compared:

- Rule, J. T., & Veatch, R. M. (2004). *Ethical questions in dentistry* (2nd ed). Chicago, IL: Quintessence. [88 cases]
- Ozar, D. T., & Sokol, D. J. (1994). *Dental ethics at chairside: Professional principles and practical applications* (2nd ed). Washington, DC: Georgetown University Press. [15 cases]
- Patterson, P., & Wilkens, L. (2014). *Media ethics: Issues and cases* (8th ed). New York, NY: McGraw Hill. [61 cases]
- Lewis, P. V. (2014). *Ethics in the world of business.* Dubuque, IA: Kendall Hunt. [47 cases]

- Fry, S. T., Veatch, R. M., & Taylor, C. (2011). *Cases studies in nursing ethics*. (4th ed). Sudbury, MA: Jones & Bartlett Learning. [148 cases]

All 358 cases were read and notes were taken. In the various texts studied, cases were grouped into sections based on topic. For example, dental cases were organized by type of challenge (such as compromised patients and dentistry as a business, including honesty and third-party financing). The issues addressed in media included conflicting alliances and mass media in a democratic society. This was similar to the type of organization in business case texts, which looked at corporate social responsibility and leadership, for example. Nursing was organized around the seven principles in its code, but other topics included abortion, control of human behavior, death and dying, and the ethics of human research. No attempt was made here to classify the cases by topic since the domains covered across these professions differed so greatly.

Instead, four code categories were developed that reflected the context of the cases and the role the professional was supposed to take. The four coding categories are:

- **Type:** 1 = legitimate conflict (more than one position could be ethically defended), 2 = clearly negative example intended as a warning, 3 = clearly positive example intended as an encouragement
- **Source:** 1 = hypothetical, but with considerable level of imagined detail, 2 = real, description of a situation that has actually taken place
- **Role:** 1 = case reader is expected to take the part of one person described in the case and to choose an action, 2 = discussion, how does one feel about these issues in general
- **Authority:** 1 = reader assumes they have freedom of action and that others will be the beneficiary, or victim, of their actions, 2 = interactions with others of equal power and ethical status, 3 = participate as part of a group process

## Results

Cases were coded three times over a two-month period. The Cronbach alphas for the four scales were Type = 0.967, Source = 0.927, Role = 0.957, and Authority = 0.935. Where differences occurred, the code most frequently given was used in subsequent analysis.

Contingency tables were prepared for each of the scales, crossing profession with scale categories. This reveals that there were few cases coded as positive or negative examples. Apparently the focus of ethical teaching cases is on problematic situations rather than exposing students to behavior to be emulated or avoided. Similarly there were relatively few examples of peer and group authority, so these two categories were combined. Finally the pattern of the two dental case sets was similar, so these were combined into a single professional category.

Table F.1 shows that there were large differences across professions in the context of ethical issues featured in texts on this subject. In this table, "type" refers to whether the case was a challenge or an example, with high values representing ambiguous situations or situations where several alternatives are defensible. "Source" means whether the situation was real or made up for the sake of discussion. High values are hypothetical; low values are descriptions of situations that actually occurred. "Role" refers to whether the student was supposed to take the role of one who is expected to be the ethical actor (high value) or just to comment from an objective perspective on the case (low values). "Authority" is the degree to which the actor can count on being the final authority for the ethical resolution. A high value means that the actor is answerable only to his or her conscience; a low value means that the values of others, either on the professional team, outside authorities, or the public, must be reconciled with those of the actor.

---

Table F.1. **Characteristics of ethics teaching cases in four professions.**

|            | Type=unclear      | Source=hypoth     | Role=actor        | Authority=self    |
|------------|-------------------|-------------------|-------------------|-------------------|
| Dentistry  | 0.833 (0.400) [b] | 0.889 (0.312) [a] | 0.794 (0.406) [a] | 0.529 (0.502) [a] |
| Journalism | 0.885 (0.321) [b] | 0.475 (0.504) [b] | 0.393 (0.493) [c] | 0.328 (0.473) [c] |
| Business   | 0.383 (0.491) [c] | 0.127 (0.337) [c] | 0.617 (0.491) [b] | 0.255 (0.441) [c] |
| Nursing    | 0.987 (0.116) [a] | 0.919 (0.274) [a] | 0.351 (0.479) [d] | 0.399 (0.491) [b] |

---

The proportion of cases having the characteristic identified in the column heading is shown here, with standard deviations in parentheses. The cases considered by the professions differed significantly on all four characteristics. One-way ANOVA tests found p-values less than .001 in all cases. The superscripted letters beside the scores reflect *post hoc* tests using the Scheffé and Duncan multiple-range tests at $p = 0.05$. Professions with the same superscripted letters belong to the same groups. For example, most dental cases (53%) described situations where dentists were free to act on their own. That was so in 40% of the nursing cases, a statistically significantly smaller proposition (hence the different superscripted letter). A third group included journalism and business cases where individuals were expected to act as part of an organization or where the organization was judged to be the moral agent. These groups share a common superscript, reflecting the fact that they cannot be distinguished from each other in this respect.

Cases felt to be representative of the issues facing dentists were challenges (rather than examples of desirable or undesirable behavior) that were hypothetical and required the dentist to engage in behavior that the dentist had full authority to initiate. The summaries of the two cases below illustrate this type of case. Thirty-seven percent of the cases fit this pattern exactly.

- *Should Dr. X adjust the case presentation to Ms. Y to make it more likely that she will select the treatment the dentist feels is best for her?*
- *Should Dr. X treat patients differently if they seem to disregard their own oral health and show indications that they may not follow through on care or payment?*

Journalism cases were also challenges needing to be worked through, but they were more apt to be realistic examples rather than hypothetical, constructed cases, and they more often invited general discussion rather than independent action. Those in the media can readily become part of the public debate about how Americans choose to live. Thirty-three percent of the cases exactly matched this model format.

- *Is it right for for-profit organizations to sponsor charity events in order to get free press coverage?*
- *What does the reader think of an organization that seeks to suppress publicly available information that is not favorable to it or its sponsors?*

The business cases were particular and exemplary of what might be considered good or bad practice. Future business people were invited to consider the issues from the perspective of an active participant, but they were made aware that they could seldom act independently. Only 17% of the cases fit this typical pattern, however, and there was considerable variation in the types of cases offered.

- *A named firm engaged in selling a defective product to consumers and readers were asked to reflect on how they might have acted differently had they been part of that firm.*
- *How would the reader fit into a company that enjoys a reputation for having a culture that grows people?*

The nursing cases had yet a fourth distinctive fingerprint. The cases were clearly selected to represent hypothetical issues that combined both positive and negative aspects with unclear paths. But unlike the cases faced by dentists, nurses seldom found themselves in positions where they could act on their own authority and were usually invited to reflect on the issues generally. This was a dominant template, with 42% of cases fitting this model.

- *What does the reader think when observing patients being treated in a fashion they are uncertain is right?*
- *The hospital is considering making staffing changes that might affect the quality of care to patients in order to save money. What do you think of that?*

## Reflections

Ethics might not mean the same thing across the professions. Said differently, those asked to think about what it means to be an ethical professional are being asked to use different lenses. The differences flow from the relative power and independence of the actors in various professions. Business cases have a long tradition of being concrete and of teaching students to work through a complex set of facts. Business people work in teams, their actions affect multiple groups simultaneously, and they cannot count on being the sole or dominant judge of what is right or wrong in individual cases. Often business teaching cases contain many pages of detail about a specific firm where we know what eventually happened, and groups of students work on the cases for a term and present their critique as a group report.

Journalism is similar, although many of the outcomes involve open questions about political or philosophical standards over which the public and the industry continue to wrestle. Journalism students are invited to think about how their work affects the values of society rather than the conditions of one person at a time.

The health professions were distinct in this dataset in that readers were urged to consider situations that they had the power to make "right" or "wrong," or at least to argue for their point. Dentists and nurses function in relatively closed systems and information about what they do is protected by confidentiality standards, the inability of the public to understand what is being done, and other barriers to scrutiny. The difference between dentists and nurses was largely a matter of power within the organization. Nurses were confronted in these cases with a background issue of "distancing" or managing moral distress where, as a condition for their continued employment, they were required to engage in behavior they considered questionable. They often can have well-developed ethical views but not be free to act on them. The same would be true for staff and associate or employee dentists.

The health professions cases were also the ones dominated by hypotheticals. The cases were rich in detail but still open to personal interpretation. Because the dental cases were overwhelming theoretical, readers had the opportunity to insert personal interpretations that supported self-justified action. Only dentistry describes its ethics teaching cases as "dilemmas." A lemma is a previously worked-out small proof that can be applied in various situations. "People must have freedom of action to be responsible," "People should not be allowed to make choices that are not in their interests," and "People should be responsible for their own health" are lemmas. Often ethical arguments are shortened by invoking a lemma that justifies the chosen position of the speaker and makes the recounting of particulars unnecessary. When there is more than one lemma in a situation, it is a dilemma and there is a *prima facie* justification for any action taken (Beauchamp & Childress, 2009; Gert, 1998). By announcing in advance that ethics cases in dentistry are dilemmas, it is being suggested that dentists can be ethical despite following diverse actions. Certainly the fact that dentists practice in contexts where neither peer nor superior nor the public in general look over their shoulders is consistent with the type of cases used in ethics education.

In these respects, dentistry may play the ethics game by slightly different rules than do other professions.

## References

Beauchamp, T.L., & Childress, J. F. (2009). *Principles of biomedical ethics* (6th ed). New York, NY: Oxford University Press.

Bebeau, M. J. (2006). Designing an outcome-based ethics curriculum for professional education: Strategies and evidence of effectiveness. *Journal of Moral Education, 35,* 313-326.

Doyle, M., & Straus, D. (1976). *How to make meetings work.* New York, NY: Jove Books, Chapter 6: "How to be a good facilitator."

Fry, S.T., Veatch, R. M., & Taylor, C. (2011). *Case studies in nursing ethics.* (4th ed). Sudbury, MA: Jones & Bartlett Learning.

Gert, B. (1998). *Morality: Its nature and justification.* New York, NY: Oxford University Press.

Greene, J. (2013). *Moral tribes: Emotion, reason, and the gap between us and them.* New York, NY: Penguin Books.

Haidt, J. (2012). *The righteous mind: Why good people are divided by politics and religion.* New York, NY: Vintage Books.

Hofling, C. K., Brotzman, E., Dalrymple, S., Graves, N., & Pierce, C. M. (1966). An experimental study in nurse-physician relationships. *Journal of Nervous and Mental Disease, 143*, 171-180.

Lewis, P. V. (2014). *Ethics in the world of business.* Dubuque, IA: Kendall Hunt.

MacIntyre, A. (1988). *Whose justice? Which rationality?* Notre Dame, IN: University of Notre Dame Press.

Ozar, D. T., & Sokol, D. J. (1994). *Dental ethics at chairside: Professional principles and practical applications* (2nd ed). Washington, DC: Georgetown University Press.

Patterson, P., & Wilkens, L. (2014). *Media ethics: Issues and cases* (8th ed). New York, NY: McGraw Hill.

Rule, J. T., & Bebeau, M. J. (2005). *Dentists who care: Inspiring stories of professional commitment.* Chicago, IL: Quintessence.

Rule, J. T., & Veatch, R. M. (2004). *Ethical questions in dentistry* (2nd ed). Chicago, IL: Quintessence.

Schön, D. A. (1987). *Educating the reflective practitioner.* San Francisco, CA: Jossey-Bass.

# Appendix G

# Dentists' Knowledge of ADA Code

Published as Chambers, D. W. (2020). Dentists' Knowledge of ADA Code. *Journal of the American College of Dentists, 87* (1), 26-34.

## Abstract

Codes of ethics inform members of organizations about the expectations their colleagues have of their behavior, serve as justification for disciplinary actions, and create a positive image of the organization and its members in the public's perception. The three-part form of the American Dental Association Principles of Ethics and Code of Professional Conduct, with advisory opinions, is discussed. Knowledge of the ADA Code was tested with a multiple-choice test and an open-ended survey. It was found that knowledge of the code among ADA members was less than 50% and somewhat higher for students who had not yet been given instruction on it. This does not mean that ADA members are unethical. The research does raise some questions about the strength of the relationship between the existence of a code, knowledge of the code, and ethical behavior of organization members. Research on codes and organizations generally confirms this weak association.

Ethics codes are developed by organizations to serve, at least, these three purposes: (a) inform members of the kinds of behavior expected of them; (b) state reasons members may be dismissed or disciplined by the organization; and (c) communicate a positive image of the organization and its members to the public at large. To a lesser extent, a code can serve as the focal point for discussion among the inner circle of an organization regarding its identity.

The first two of these functions depend heavily on the code's being understood by the members of the organization. This report presents some data bearing on how familiar dentists are with the American Dental Association (ADA) Code.

## Nature of the ADA Code

The official name is the *American Dental Association Principles of Ethics and Code of Professional Conduct*. As stated in its introduction, the term "ADA Code" is used as a shorthand expression for the longer designation. There is no ADA Code of Ethics. Quoting from the introduction, "The ADA Code has three main components: The Principles of Ethics, the Code of Professional Conduct, and the Advisory Opinions."

There are five ethical principles: patient autonomy, nonmaleficence, beneficence, justice, and veracity. These were introduced in the 1990s and borrowed as a superstructure for the 80-year-old Code of Professional Conduct. The first four of these principles are the common set, referred to as the "Georgetown manta," developed in the then-emerging field of bioethics (Beauchamp & Childress, 2009). Robert Veatch, of Georgetown, served as a consultant to the group at the ADA that developed this exoskeleton. As a third of the items in the code of conduct—particularly detailed matters pertaining to fees, advertising, names of practices, announcement of specialty care, and so forth—could not easily be classified under the traditional ethical principles, an additional category, veracity, was added. The bioethics principle of autonomy or respect for persons was redefined to exclude dentists, staff, and individuals in need of oral health care who are not patients of record and is now known as "patient autonomy."

The Code of Professional Conduct enumerates 28 "specific types of conduct that are either required or prohibited" for members of the association. Such listings of expected behavior have a long history in the professions, where they were formerly known as "Codes of Professional Etiquette." They have been developed to create a common set of expectations regarding what behavior individuals in a particular profession should expect from each other. For example, the original ADA code of 1867 required that dentists consult with each other to fix common prices within communities. When the Principles of Ethics was added to the ADA Code, the Code of Professional Conduct remained essentially as it had been at the time.

The ADA Code also contains 27 Advisory Opinions. These offer guidance as to how the elements in the Code of Professional Conduct might be interpreted in specific situations. For example, the Code of Professional Conduct item on justifiable criticism expresses three obligations: (a) reporting cases of gross or continual faulty treatment to an appropriate authority; (b) informing patients of their present condition; and (c) refraining from making disparaging remarks about prior services. The Advisory Opinion is a 200-word explanation of the meaning of the term "justifiable," including the possible action of contacting the prior treating dentist to discover the conditions under which care was provided.

The numbering of elements in the ADA Code makes it easy to follow this three-part structure. Principles are indicated by a single number: 1 for patient autonomy, 2 for nonmaleficence, etc. Items in the Code of Professional Conduct are designated by an uppercase letter following the number. So justifiable criticism is the third item under the principle of justice, or 4.C. Advisory Opinions are indicated with an additional number. Recommending or performing unnecessary services being unethical is not part of the Code of Professional Conduct; it is the sixth interpretive guidance under representation of fees under the principle of veracity, or 5.B.6.

The Principles of Ethics are aspirational in the sense that the ADA suggests that these are the ethical standards for the entire profession. By distinction, the Code of Professional Conduct is enforceable. "The Code of Professional Conduct is binding on members of the ADA, and violation may result in disciplinary action." Advisory Opinions are guidance for how the ADA Council on Ethics, Bylaws and Judicial Affairs might interpret the Code of Professional Conduct in a disciplinary proceeding.

Something like this structure is repeated at the state level, although the content, wording, and interpretation may differ. Other organizations in the profession, such as ethnic, specialty, or honorary groups, also tend to have their own aspirational and enforceable ethical guidelines. It is difficult to maintain the ADA's position that the five principles it has chosen to emphasize constitute "the principles of the profession" in distinction to being the principles of the American Dental Association. Society in general has many such codes as well, including universities, the government and military services, community organizations, and commercial firms. There is potential for conflict among codes and always a trade-off between specificity of rules and their generalizability. As stated in the American Dental Association Principles of Ethics and Code of Professional Conduct, "principles can overlap each other as well as compete with each other for priority,...and the ADA Code is an evolving document and by its very nature cannot be a complete articulation of all ethical obligations."

## How Well Is the Code Understood?

The very existence of a code is of value to an organization. Being able to say to those the organization serves that there is a code guiding behavior of members has public relations value. This is especially true for enforceable codes, as this signals a willingness to self-police. There is also a sense of pride members feel in belonging to a group that publicly announces its commitment to ethical principles. The logic runs something like this: Group X stands for ethics; I am a member of X; therefore, I am ethical. Undoubtedly, this is true in fact in many cases, but it is awful logic. The better argument would be: My behavior is consistent with the ethical standards of Group X; X is seeking members who exemplify their standards; therefore, I should be invited to membership in Group X. Some organizations, such as the American College of Dentists, follow this logic. Individuals make the organization ethical. One cannot become ethical just by joining an organization.

A full understanding of how ethical codes in organizations affect the behavior of members in those organizations is still years away. One element in this understanding is almost certainly the extent to which members know the codes. The straightforward argument is that members learn codes and that knowledge affects their behavior. This is certainly a simplified view, and there are numerous contextual factors that mediate between what we know and how we behave. However, if it can be shown that members have a poor understanding of the codes, the argument that members of groups with codes are ethical by virtue of their membership is shaky.

The research reported here is intended to provide a first glimpse into how well dentists understand the ADA Code.

## The Study

A 16-question test on the ADA Code was developed and pilot tested on faculty and residents in a dental school. The test and the passages supporting the keyed answers in the ADA Code are displayed in the Exhibit to this paper. The test was administered three times. Fifty-four students at the

Oregon Health Science University took the test as part of their course on ethics, but prior to coverage of this topic. One hundred thirty-nine fellows and candidates for fellowship in the American College of Dentists completed the test as part of a workshop presentation on ethics. Twenty-three dentists of various backgrounds completed the test in a continuing education program sponsored by the University of the Pacific. An additional 16 individuals who were either Canadian dentists or American dental hygienists completed the test. All four groups were scored as part of one set and separately.

Questions were scored right or wrong based on the key described in the Exhibit. Unanswered questions were handled two ways. Where an item was left blank between previously answered items and following questions that were attempted, the item was marked wrong. Where a succession of questions at the end of the exam was left unanswered, it was assumed that the respondent ran out of time. The unanswered items were not scored and the respondent was given a score proportioned only to those items attempted to that point.

The Cronbach alpha, which reflects internal consistency of the test, was 0.582. This is satisfactory for such a short test. The overall score for 232 respondents was 46.5%. This is less than half of the questions answered correctly. As there was one correct response and three distractors for each question, the purely random score would have been 25%. A one-way ANOVA test across the four types of respondents was significant at $F = 15.100$, $p < .001$. The highest scoring group was the dental students who had not yet been exposed to the code.

## In Their Own Words

Multiple-choice tests with low scores are easy to criticize. By comparing the keyed responses with the exact language in the ADA Code in Table G.1, it should be possible to gauge whether there were trick questions. An alternative explanation is that the test did not "ask the right questions." An open-ended evaluation would have inquired about what respondents did in fact know about the ADA Code.

In order to test this possibility, one of the sessions—the one at the American College of Dentists convocation—included an open-ended question. The following instruction was given in writing: "List one element in the ADA Code of Professional Conduct that really stands out to you." Respondents were given about five minutes to complete this exercise. Table G.1 displays the responses.

## Table G.1. Elements in the ADA Code of Professional Conduct that stood out most to dentists.

*Number  Item*

**Elements in the Code of Professional Conduct**

| | |
|---|---|
| 5 | Inform patients of procedures and reasonable alternatives [1.A] |
| 4 | Keep knowledge and skills current [2.A] |
| 3 | Justifiable criticism [4.C] (plus an additional comment "Do not pass judgment") |
| 2 | Unnecessary treatment [5.B.6] |
| 2 | Charts and records [?] |
| 1 | Obliged to treat everyone |
| 1 | Announcement of services [?] |
| 1 | Provide emergency services [4.B] |
| 1 | Must refer if possible [?] |
| 1 | Announcements should bring esteem to profession [3.A] |

**Other parts of the ADA Code**

| | |
|---|---|
| 3 | Put the patient's interest first |
| 2 | Honesty, veracity, fidelity |
| 2 | Beneficence |
| 1 | Autonomy |
| 1 | First do no harm |
| 1 | Contract between the profession and the public |

The first and last items above are in the preamble of the Code. The others are principles. Respondents were instructed in writing: "Remember, patient autonomy, nonmaleficence, beneficence, justice, and veracity are principles. Do not list any of these. Only list items in the Code of Professional Conduct."

**Other comments**

| | |
|---|---|
| 2 | Dentists are encouraged to be ethical |
| 1 | Professionalism |
| 1 | Ethics and law are different |
| 1 | Evidence-based dentistry |
| 1 | Judgment |
| 1 | Communication |
| 1 | "I have never read it" |
| 1 | "I depend on my conscience" |

About half of the volunteered standout points in the ADA Code of Professional Conduct were not actually elements in the Code of Professional Conduct. Perhaps of greater concern is the fact that three-quarters of those given an opportunity to mention anything that mattered to them in the code offered nothing. To protect against the possibility that respondents may have come late or otherwise not have been in a position to respond to this item, only those forms were considered where respondents had answered the questions previous to and the questions following this item. This very large nonresponse to an open-ended question about the code is consistent with a low or nearly random response on the multiple-choice questions.

## Discussion

It is essential to recognize that this research does not support any conclusions about whether the respondents or dentists in general behave ethically. If anything, there is a bias that this sample is skewed toward the high end of ethical practitioners, as shady actors tend to avoid gatherings where ethics is likely to be a topic of conversation. What the data do challenge is the relationship between knowledge of a certain set of rules and one's reputation for professionalism. Because the American College of Dentists requires membership in the ADA, the majority of the respondents in this research were certainly bound by the ADA Code.

The ADA cannot be criticized for paying insufficient attention to getting out the word about the code. Since 2004, the association has published a feature in the *Journal of the American Dental Association* called the "Ethical Moment." This usually appears ten times per year and is usually a two-page discussion of a practice dilemma. The incidents appear to be selected because they are related to the ADA Code; or at least it is a common format for the articles to step through most or all of the sections of the code, noting the relevance of each to the case.

A long-serving member of a state dental board explained that exposure to information alone is insufficient. We learn and retain information best when there is a need to know it. He said that the kind of individual who knew every detail of the state dental practice act was the one who was defending against an action against his or her license. Dentists who are ethical or who believe they are have little incentive to memorize the details of a code, especially one filled with so many terms such as "obligation" or "duty."

Although we are not able to use the data from this study to make a strong case for knowledge of the ADA Code being linked with ethical performance, it may still be the case that the Code of Professional Conduct part of this document functions as a foundation for the association's enforcing positive ethical standards, at least among the two-thirds of dentists who belong to the ADA.

In the spring 2018 issue of the *Journal of the American College of Dentists* (Chambers, 2018) it was reported that the rate of disciplined licenses among nonmembers of the ADA is about the same as that for members. Further, there are virtually no complaints against dentists filed by their peers. This would be unexpected in light of 4.C in the ADA Code of Professional Conduct that obligates dentists to do so.

As stated in the code, Advisory Opinions are provided as interpretations of how the Council on Ethics, Bylaws and Judicial Affairs might apply the Code of Professional Conduct when disciplinary actions are taken. It has not been reported that any ADA member has been disciplined for failing to report incidents of gross or continual faulty treatment by a colleague. Although national and state judicial councils have the responsibility to propose, interpret, publicize, and apply sanctions on members who violate the codes, such sanctions are limited to privileges within the organization and do not extend to the ability to practice dentistry. Judicial bodies in organized dentistry typically apply codes after a matter has been handled by other agencies of the state, such as drug enforcement. Often dentists who have been sanctioned by the state withdraw of their own volition from organized dentistry. They occasionally will bring legal action seeking relief from the characterization of their practices as "unethical" by a group that lacks status to set standards for nonmembers.

The evidence is mixed on whether other organizations that have codes of ethics are less likely to have legal actions brought against them for violating social conventions (Bried et al, 1996; Kaptein & Schwartz, 2008). It certainly did not help in the case of Enron, which had a very strong code that can be seen online.

### References

Beauchamp, T., & Childress J. F. (2009). *Principles of biomedical ethics* (6th ed). New York, NY: Oxford University Press.

Bried, A. P., Dukerich, J. M., Brown, P. R., & Brett, J. F. (1996). What's wrong with the Treadway Commission Report? Experimental analysis of the effects of personal values and codes of conduct on fraudulent financial reporting. *Journal of Business Ethics, 15*, 183-198.

Chambers, D. W. (2018). Disciplined dental licenses: An empirical study. *Journal of the American College of Dentists, 85* (2), 30-39.

Kaptein, M., & Schwartz, M. S. (2008). The effectiveness of business codes: A critical examination of existing studies and the development of an integrated research model. *Journal of Business Ethics, 77*, 111-127.

---

# Exhibit

## *ADA Principles of Ethics and Code of Professional Conduct*

Test on the ADA Code: items, response, and documentation of the keyed response. Keyed response in italics.

%

**1. The ADA Code is a written expression of**

1   a. The aspirations of select members of the profession.

68   b. *The obligations arising from an implied contract between the dental profession and society.*

21   c. The standards required for membership in the American Dental Association.

5   d. The aspirational values of the American public for oral health.

6   [Blank]

"The ADA Code is, in effect, a written expression of the obligations arising from the implied contract between the dental profession and society." [Introduction]

**2. Because the ADA Code represents "the profession's firm guideposts," its principles are**

27   a. A comprehensive and consistent listing of the conduct of ethical dentists.

59   b. A consistent, but not entirely comprehensive, listing of the conduct of ethical dentists.

6   c. *Incomplete and sometimes conflicting suggestions for ethical conduct.*

15   d. The same as the principles in medicine, nursing, dental hygiene, and other health fields.

3   [Blank]

"By its very nature [it] cannot be complete." "Principles can overlap each other as well as compete with each other." [Introduction]

**3. The ADA Code of Professional Conduct is**

26   a. The same as (alternative name for) the Principles of Ethics.

35   b. Developed and subject to modification by the Council on Ethics, Bylaws and Judicial Affairs.

14   c. *Managed by the ADA House of Delegates and binding on all ADA members.*

17 d. The part of the ADA Code that is suggestive and open to the professional conscience of practitioners.

9 [Blank]

"All elements of the Code of Professional Conduct result from resolutions that are adopted by the ADA's House of Delegates. The Code of Professional Conduct is binding on members of the ADA." [Introduction]

## 4. The principle of autonomy (self-governance) applies to

35 a. Dentists, both in their relationship to the public and to their peers.

4 b. *Patients only.*

7 c. All individuals in need of oral health care.

51 d. Everyone.

6 [Blank]

"The dentist has a duty to respect the patient's right to self-determination." [Principle 1: Patient Autonomy]

## 5. Under the ADA Code (advisory opinion), it is NOT ethical to

2 a. Charge patients for copies of their records.

0 b. Release records to patients (they can only be released to licensed dentists).

16 c. Release records to other dentists directly (they must be requested in writing by patients).

75 d. *Withhold records of patients with significant past due balances (bad debt).*

6 [Blank]

"A dentist has the ethical obligation on request of either the patient or the patient's new dentist [to furnish copies of records]. This obligation exists whether or not the patient's account is paid in full." [Advisory Opinion 1.8.1]

## 6. Nonmaleficence is

39 a. A technical term for a reference to the Hippocratic Oath, specifically calling out not practicing below the standard of care.

1 b. A flower with large red and orange blossoms native to Central America.

0 c. A skin condition.

56 d. *Expressed as conduct that avoids inadequate training and failure to refer when appropriate, proper delegation of auxiliary personnel, not practicing while impaired, patient abandonment, and interpersonal relationships with patients that may impair judgment.*

4 [Blank]

Nonmaleficence code items: education, consultation, referral, use of auxiliaries, impaired practice, personal relations with patients, patient abandonment. [Principle 2: Nonmaleficence]

## 7. The principle of beneficence specifically FORBIDS

6 a. Entering into contractual relationships for providing care under capitated and some other contractual relationships.

72     b. *Adjusting the level of care to patients' ability to pay or mechanism of payment.*

2     c. Serving as an expert witness, if that involves testifying against a colleague.

4     d. Being compensated for endorsing products or procedures.

7     [Blank]

"The same ethical considerations apply whether the dentist engages in fee-for-service, managed care, or some other practice arrangement." [Principle 3: Beneficence]

## 8. Under beneficence, the ADA Code specifically expects dentists to perform all of these duties EXCEPT

8     a. Make the results of their research and practice experience available to all members of the profession.

19     b. Participate in organized dentistry.

61     c. *Avoid seeking public office because of inherent conflicts with the perception of esteem for the profession.*

4     d. Learn about and report suspected cases of patient abuse and neglect.

8     [Blank]

"Dentists have an obligation to use their skills and experience for the improvement of the dental health of the public and are encouraged to be leaders in their communities." [3.A]

## 9. Under the principle of justice, the ADA Code admonishes practitioners to

17     a. *Actively promote access to care.*

20     b. Enter into arrangements to share revenues with others to the extent that this promotes more patient care.

45     c. Accept all potential patients, regardless of race, sex, national origin, or nature of oral condition.

14     d. Make provisions for emergency care only for patients of record.

4     [Blank]

"Actively seek allies throughout society on specific activities that help improve access to care for all. (Dentists may not, should not, accept all patients regardless of their oral condition.)" [Principle 4: Justice]

## 10. When dentists become aware of instances of gross or continual faulty treatment by other dentists, they are obliged to

61     a. *Inform the patient of their condition and notify the appropriate local component or constituent society.*

25     b. Refrain from commenting disparagingly to anyone because the conditions of treatment may not be known.

5     c. Avoid contacting the previous dentist because of potential legal complications.

4     d. Offer to "make it right" for the patient, without questioning the previous dentists' intentions or skill, so the patient will have a good dentist.

4     [Blank]

"Dentists shall be obliged to report to the appropriate reviewing agency...instances of gross or continual faulty treatment by other dentists. Patients should be informed of their present oral health status without disparaging comment about prior services." [4.C]

**11. The ADA Code advisory opinion on amalgams states that it is unethical to remove intact amalgam restorations from patients**

34    a. *When the procedure is recommended solely by the dentist who will perform the work.*

7    b. When the procedure is requested by the patient and agreed as indicated by the dentist.

6    c. Only when it can be established that the patient is allergic to amalgam.

46    d. There is not mention of this specific matter in the ADA Code.

7    [Blank]

"When [removal of amalgam from non-allergic patients] is performed solely at the recommendation or suggestion of the dentist, [it] is improper and unethical." [5.A.1]

**12. Waiving copayment (accepting a reduced fee as payment in full for an insured procedure)**

48    a. Is unethical under all circumstances.

7    b. Is appropriate at the discretion of the practitioner.

1    c. May be appropriate if it promotes patients seeking better care and dentists providing more services.

43    d. *May be appropriate on an individual basis, provided that the insurance carrier is notified in advance and authorizes the specific case.*

1    [Blank]

"A dentist who accepts a third party payment under a copayment plan as payment in full without disclosing to the third party that the patient's payment portion will not be collected, is engaged in overbilling." [5.B.1]

**13. A dentist who recommends unnecessary services is unethical**

92    a. *PERIOD.*

0    b. If the patient waives informed consent.

0    c. If fees exceed usual, customary, and reasonable.

4    d. Only if the services are actually performed.

0    [Blank]

"A dentist who recommends and performs unnecessary dental services or procedures is engaged in unethical conduct." [5.B.6]

**14. Dentists are obliged by the ADA Code to report serious adverse patient reactions to drugs or devices to the Food and Drug Administration if**

9    a. If the drug or device is investigatory or experimental.

5    b. If the drug or device is used "off label"–for purposes other than approved by the FDA.

54    c. *In all cases.*

29    d. In no cases, there is no mention of this issue in the ADA Code.

3       [Blank]

"A dentist who suspects the occurrence of an adverse reaction to a drug or dental device has an obligation to communicate that information to the broader medical and dental community, including…the Food and Drug Administration." [5.D.1]

**15. The title "doctor" or the initials "DDS" or "DMD" are appropriate in communications with patients, but it is discouraged as misleading to the public to include any of the following EXCEPT**

14      a. Honorary distinctions by abbreviation such as FACD or MAGD (for Fellow of the American College of Dentists or Master, Academy of General Dentistry).

36      b. *Earned advanced degrees from accredited institutions, such as masters or PhD in a health field.*

7       c. Membership in professional organizations, such as "Member of the ADA."

38      d. Recognitions from institutes, academies, or continuing education programs that are not accredited by a body recognized by the U.S. Department of Education.

5       [Blank]

"A dentist may use the title Doctor or Dentist, DDS, DMD, or any additional earned, advanced academic degrees in health service areas in an announcement to the public." [5.F.3]

**16. For a dentist to ethically announce to the public credentials in a discipline not recognized as a specialty by the ADA, a general dentist must satisfy three of the following requirements. Which one is NOT required?**

20      a. Completion of a formal, full-time program of at least 12 months' duration, plus testing.

52      b. *Fees charged for involved services do not generally exceed those charged by general dentists in the area.*

10      c. It is disclosed that the dentist is a "general dentist."

15      d. It is disclosed that the ADA does not recognize this discipline as a specialty.

3       [Blank]

Specialist announcement of credentials in nonspecialty interest areas required "completion of formal, full-time advanced educational program, (graduate or postgraduate level) of at least 12 months' duration…and testing; announcement [that practice] is not recognized as a specialty area by the American Dental Association [5.H.2]; and general dentists who wish to announce the services available in their practices are permitted to announce the availability of those services…[and] state that the services are being provided by a general dentist." [5.I]

# Appendix H

# Ethical Touchstones

Published as Chambers, D. W. (2020). Ethical Touchstones. *Journal of the American College of Dentists, 87* (1), 35-40.

## Abstract

Where do dentists turn for guidance on ethical challenges? A survey was conducted using six ethical problems and five potential sources for advice on how best to proceed. Dentists overwhelmingly consult their own conscience, followed by their expectations regarding what their colleagues would approve. This is especially the case when the challenge involves the dentist's own welfare in matters such as income. Codes are much less apt to be consulted and dentists shy away from experts, such as lawyers and ethicists. This may be a function of how likely the outside advice is to be in one's interests and how easy it would be to set the advice aside if it is not welcome. Dentists do engage others who are involved in the issue to some extent.

A touchstone is what one holds tightly when making a decision. It is the place where we store our necessary supply of "becauses." One dentist says, "I do not waive copays because that would be insurance fraud, and the law is clear that this is a criminal offence." Another says, "It is not such an uncommon practice, on occasion, and some of my friends do it pretty regularly." The third says, "It is fundamentally a matter of what I believe to be right in each individual case." The touchstones here are the law, one's colleagues, and oneself. Where one looks for ethical reassurance matters for one's ethical behavior. Touchstones are the keepers of our conscience. When dentists diverge on the preferred course of action given a common problem, it is often because they are using different touchstones.

We check multiple sources for approval, some regularly and frequently, others not so often or only on special occasions. But the hierarchical profile of touchstones differs from person to person. It would be helpful to know if there are similarities from dentist to dentist in which sources of ethical guidance have priority.

If there are patterns among dentists in the touchstones they follow, this would be helpful in understanding ethics in the profession. We want to place the ethical landmarks that guide the profession in plain sight where dentists are looking for them. Do dentists pay attention to ethics experts? If the answer is "perhaps," then perhaps we need to activate additional touchstones. Before we design programs to guide dentists toward better ethical choices, we should first listen to who they are listening to. This is a report of a research study intended to provide some preliminary answers.

## Materials and Methods

Two hundred sixty-five dentists in several samples in various continuing education settings from across the country completed a short survey that asked about where they would turn for help in making ethical decisions. The survey is shown in the Exhibit at the end of this article. Six hypothetical scenarios were presented: (a) detected faulty treatment by a colleague; (b) use of an insurance reimbursement loophole; (c) sale of one's practice to a dentist with a shaky reputation; (d) dealing with a patient trying to avoid payment; (e) taking on very large and complex cases using untested procedures; and (f) treating Medicaid patients. Each of these situations has an ethical component and might be responded to differently depending on where one looks for relevant standards. Dentists were not asked, "What is the right thing to do?" in the various cases. Instead they were asked how important it would be to be square with five alternative sources of ethical guidance commonly referenced. Each touchstone was rated based on how likely the touchstone was to be consulted on a scale from 5 ("Almost in every case") to 1 ("Very rarely").

## Results

A consistent ordering of touchstones was found. One source of ethical guidance (personal convictions) was three times as likely to be consulted in cases where ethical choice was involved as was the least common touchstone (legal experts and ethicists). Personal feelings were given about twice as much weight as were codes of ethics. A statistical test (one-way ANOVA with *post hoc* contrasts) was performed that confirmed that each of the five touchstones was different from those adjacent to it at $p < 0.05$. So, for example, dentists were significantly more likely to consult their own conscience than their colleagues. They are significantly more likely to consult colleagues than to talk with others involved in the situation. They are significantly more likely to engage in conversations with those involved in the situation than to look to codes. Finally dentists are significantly less likely to look to experts than to any other source.

**Figure H.1. Where do dentists look for help in making ethical decisions?**

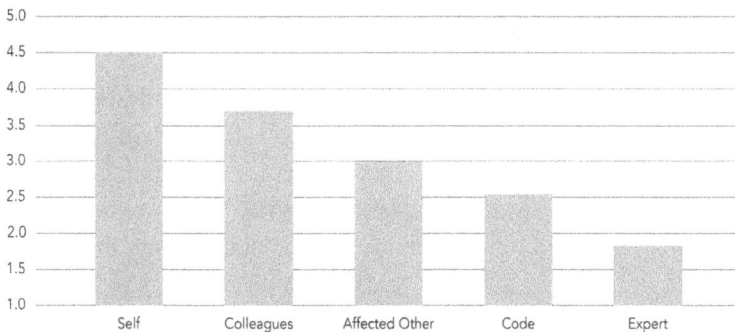

Respondents were also asked to rate each of the six challenges in terms of how important the issue was seen to be, regardless of where they would look for assistance in solving it. Some of the challenges were thought to be highly important while others were seen as mattering less one way or the other. High scores reflected those challenges where a satisfactory resolution was very important. The three challenges having to do with dentist's income (insurance, sales of practice, and big or novel treatment) were statistically significantly more apt to be considered important than were the other three. This was also confirmed by ANOVA tests with p-values below 0.05. Considering both the order of relevance of decision guidance and the type of issue together, it appears that dentists consult their own judgment on matters that affect their own well-being.

## Discussion

The results of this research are consistent with the general finding in the ethics report commissioned by the Board of Regents of the American College of Dentists. In particular, multiple focus groups across the country noted, and often with some concern, that dentists embrace personal rather than profession-wide standards for guiding their relationships with patients. It appears to be the case that many practitioners will only consider alternative touchstones that involve others if their individual standards fail to provide favorable guidance. This is consistent with the general literature on ethics, which shows that individuals who are in a position to substitute personal status or power for negotiated agreement tend to do so (Diekmann et al, 1996; Hegarty & Sims, 1978; Kabanoff, 1991). Chambers and Eng showed that dentists engage with patients and staff over disagreements by "talking others into their position" (educating the patient) while they approach conflicts with their peers by "having a conversation" (Chambers & Eng, 1994). This early research found that dentists feel they are more successful reaching agreement with patients than with colleagues.

Dentists have traditionally enjoyed an enviable position of having enormous say in how dentistry is practiced in their own offices. Such an independent ethical foundation is being called into question in recent years. Benefits carriers, government regulation, commercial consolidation, and marketing that gives greater online voice to the public are new influences. In some ways, the growing concern over ethics in dentistry is not the result of more dentists acting unethically, but appears to be due to others having more say in how dentists act.

The data in this research show that dentists give considerable weight to the standards used by their colleagues. This touchstone should not be confused with codes or the advice of ethics experts. Dentists are guided by what they see their colleagues doing and what they believe the results to be. They are also guided by what they imagine their colleagues might think of them. If a colleague seems to be thriving by advertising and offering cookie-cutter rather than customized care, that may become a standard to be emulated. If they admire a colleague who only practices at the highest level of care and works to build the profession, that will be their touchstone. If other dentists do not seem to be concerned how one practices, that touchstone drops out of consideration.

A lesson to be drawn from the prominence of the effectiveness of one's colleagues' behavior is that the critical factor is perceived success of the potential model (Bandura, 1977). A powerful tool for modifying the ethical tone of dentistry is to reward behavior that is ethical. It is a well-documented law in psychology that a sure way to encourage the wrong kind of behavior is to remain silent and let the bad actors draw reward from other sources (Skinner, 1971). If the profession does not speak out against commercial and other nonprofessional values, good dentists will drift toward imitating colleagues who get conspicuous rewards outside the profession. Many dentists are "leaders" for their colleagues. Unless the professional ones speak up, the others will lead the profession astray.

Codes of conduct, regulations, and rules imposed by business partners such as dental service organizations or benefits carriers are not often regarded as credible touchstones. Research generally shows that codes of ethics have limited effect on behavior (Bried et al, 1996; Kaptein & Schwartz, 2008). Other research shows that dentists have an imperfect understanding of the code of the American Dental Association (Appendix G). On average dentists were able to correctly answer fewer than half the questions on a short test of the code. In open-ended responses, a frequent remark was that one's own values take precedence over codes. Part of the reason for this may be the fact that codes are of necessity general. Interpretation is always necessary, and that interpretation is understandably individual. Often codes, rules, and the like only become active players in the ethics of dentistry when interpretations and justifications fail to excuse behavior chosen for other reasons. When codes are seen as enforceable standards, they become obligations or minimum standards (Appendix L).

Experts are the touchstone of last resort. It is somewhat ironic that part of the push for ethics in dentistry over the past few decades has been to highlight "experts." Their popularity may be due to their seeming stature while they are regarded as being relatively benign. Lawyers and ethicists bring in external standards. Theory from other fields such as bioethics and law are cited. We have added the teaching of ethical theory as a requirement in dental schools, dilemmas presentations at conferences, and journals that feature short, regular columns, and some states are considering mandatory continuing education hours on ethics. These are all well-intended efforts to highlight the importance of ethics. The current research suggests that practitioners are not paying as much attention to these sources as their sponsors would hope. A case might even be made that putting our attention where practitioners are not looking may be misdirecting scarce resources.

A common trend in the four touchstones discussed so far is the importance of dentists' personal control in ethics. As the options move from self-determination to like-minded friends to public positions of the profession and, finally, to outsiders with an independent claim to authority, the likelihood of using guidance from that source declines. It is possible that publicly supported sources of ethical guidance and expert advisors are resisted because they are such sound touchstones. If a colleague advises an ethical path that is "inconvenient," there is small pressure to follow a difficult path. It is always possible that consulting professional standards or the wisdom of professionals in ethics and law will turn up some credible but unwelcome advice.

That leaves one touchstone yet to consider. One strategy for addressing ethical rough spots is to engage with others who are part of the problem and thus likely to be part of the solution as well. If there is an apparent problem with the quality of work observed by one's colleague or with a patient who appears to be weaseling on payment, some dentists will start by having a conversation with the others involved. But in research on reporting of justifiable criticism, Chambers (2017) found that dentists are more apt to hint to colleagues suspected of gross or continuous faulty treatment than to discuss the situation with patients.

Engaging with others involved in ethical issues without a prior guarantee of getting the resolution one is seeking requires moral courage. Rest (Rest & Narvaez, 1994), for example, makes that an intrinsic dimension of ethics. The difference between spectator ethics and participation ethics is a willingness to get involved. In engagement we might discover that we framed the issue inaccurately or incompletely. It might turn out that a better way to get one's own ethical goals met is to negotiate with others who have their own legitimate ethical goals. To avoid engaging others because one fears the risk of being wrong is probably both mistaken and a bit unethical. One would not know until the effort is made.

## Conclusion

Dentists have a pronounced pattern for which touchstones are most important in guiding ethical behavior. The strongest of these are personal, and the weaker are theoretical and external. It is most likely that improvements in the ethical tone of the profession will come from focusing on practice rather than theory. It is most apt to come from other dentists than from outside experts.

A unique feature of this research was identifying the importance of engagement with others who are affected by our behavior. As it turns out, the major thrust of the American College of Dentists Gies Ethics Project will be a call for conversations among all concerned with making the profession more ethical, including all dentists, leaders in the profession, patients, payers, regulators, commercial interests, and policy makers. All those affected by the actions of dentists and all those whose actions affect the profession should be at the table and should be listened to. As this research demonstrates, to leave out important others would be a bit unethical.

## References

Bandura, A. (1977). *Social learning theory*. Englewood Cliffs, NJ: Prentice Hall.

Bried, A. P., Dukerich, J. M., Brown, P. R., & Brett, J. F. (1996). What's wrong with the Treadway Commission Report? Experimental analysis of the effects of personal values and codes of conduct on fraudulent financial reporting. *Journal of Business Ethics, 15*, 183-198.

Chambers, D. W. (2017). What dentists do when they recognize faulty treatment: To tattle or build moral community. *Journal of the American College of Dentists, 84* (2), 32-66.

Chambers, D. W. (2020). Dentists' knowledge of ADA Code. *Journal of the American College of Dentists, 87* (1), 26-34.

Chambers, D. W. (2020). Practice goals: Opportunities and obligations. *Journal of the American College of Dentists, 87* (1), 41-47.

Chambers, D. W., & Eng, W. R. L., Jr. (1994). Practice profile: The first twelve years. *CDA Journal, 12* (12), 25-32.

Diekmann, A., Jungbauer-Gans, M., Krassnig, H., & Lorenz, S. (1996). Social status and aggression: A field study analyzed by survival analysis. *Journal of Social Psychology, 136*, 761-768.

Hegarty, W. H., & Sims, H. P. (1978). Some determinants of unethical decision behavior: An experiment. *Journal of Applied Psychology, 63* (4), 51-457.

Kabanoff, B. (1991). Equity, equality, power, and conflict. *Academy of Management Review, 16* (2), 416-441.

Kaptein, M., & Schwartz, M. S. (2008). The effectiveness of business codes: A critical examination of existing studies and the development of an integrated research model. *Journal of Business Ethics, 77*, 111-127.

Rest, J. R., & Narvaez, D. (eds) (1994). *Moral development in the professions: Psychology and applied ethics*. Hillsdale, NY: Lawrence Erlbaum.

Skinner, B. F. (1971). *Beyond freedom and dignity*. New York, NY: Knopf.

# Exhibit

This very short survey is sponsored by the American College of Dentists as part of its three-year study of values in the dental profession. It will only take a few minutes to answer these six questions, but it will help us understand where dentists look for guidance. It is entirely anonymous and voluntary, but every opinion is worth something. No names, please.

Consider the situations below that might arise in practice. It is possible that you have already faced some of these personally. Reflect back over your professional career and your image of yourself as a professional. What have been your touchstones? How do you usually react when you recognize that there is an issue at stake?

David W. Chambers, EdM, MBA, PhD
Professor of Dental Education
University of the Pacific School of Dentistry
Director, Clinical Judgment Laboratory
Editor, American College of Dentists

5 = Almost in every case
4 = Regularly
3 = From time to time, as appropriate
2 = Seldom, on special occasions
1 = Very rarely

**A. You notice a pattern of faulty treatment in the work of one of your colleagues, or that a colleague is impaired.**

5  4  3  2  1   *[5 = always get involved; 1 = never get involved]*

☐ ☐ ☐ ☐ ☐   My overall sense of professionalism and my personal standards

☐ ☐ ☐ ☐ ☐   A trusted colleague or friend

☐ ☐ ☐ ☐ ☐   Specific resources in organized dentistry, look up Code, call hot line

☐ ☐ ☐ ☐ ☐   A professional ethicist, member of clergy, a lawyer, law enforcement

☐ ☐ ☐ ☐ ☐   Engage directly with involved others as the first step

☐ ☐ ☐ ☐ ☐   This is not a major ethical issue that I would spend time considering

**B. You discover a "possible" insurance loop hole–you think they expect you to bill at a lower rate, but it is still possible to defend billing at a higher rate.**

5  4  3  2  1   *[5 = always get involved; 1 = never get involved]*

☐ ☐ ☐ ☐ ☐   My overall sense of professionalism and my personal standards

☐ ☐ ☐ ☐ ☐   A trusted colleague or friend

☐ ☐ ☐ ☐ ☐   Specific resources in organized dentistry, look up Code, call hot line

☐ ☐ ☐ ☐ ☐   A professional ethicist, member of clergy, a lawyer, law enforcement

☐ ☐ ☐ ☐ ☐   Engage directly with involved others as the first step

☐ ☐ ☐ ☐ ☐   This is not a major ethical issue that I would spend time considering

## C. Should I sell my practice to an individual whose standards appear "shaky?"

*5  4  3  2  1   [5 = always get involved; 1 = never get involved]*

☐ ☐ ☐ ☐ ☐ My overall sense of professionalism and my personal standards

☐ ☐ ☐ ☐ ☐ A trusted colleague or friend

☐ ☐ ☐ ☐ ☐ Specific resources in organized dentistry, look up Code, call hot line

☐ ☐ ☐ ☐ ☐ A professional ethicist, member of clergy, a lawyer, law enforcement

☐ ☐ ☐ ☐ ☐ Engage directly with involved others as the first step

☐ ☐ ☐ ☐ ☐ This is not a major ethical issue that I would spend time considering

## D. A patient is delaying and trying to get out of payments while still wanting more treatment.

*5  4  3  2  1   [5 = always get involved; 1 = never get involved]*

☐ ☐ ☐ ☐ ☐ My overall sense of professionalism and my personal standards

☐ ☐ ☐ ☐ ☐ A trusted colleague or friend

☐ ☐ ☐ ☐ ☐ Specific resources in organized dentistry, look up Code, call hot line

☐ ☐ ☐ ☐ ☐ A professional ethicist, member of clergy, a lawyer, law enforcement

☐ ☐ ☐ ☐ ☐ Engage directly with involved others as the first step

☐ ☐ ☐ ☐ ☐ This is not a major ethical issue that I would spend time considering

## E. Should I get involved in treating sleep apnea, large reconstruction cases, or other emerging areas of dentistry without receiving extensive, supervised training?

*5  4  3  2  1   [5 = always get involved; 1 = never get involved]*

☐ ☐ ☐ ☐ ☐ My overall sense of professionalism and my personal standards

☐ ☐ ☐ ☐ ☐ A trusted colleague or friend

☐ ☐ ☐ ☐ ☐ Specific resources in organized dentistry, look up Code, call hot line

☐ ☐ ☐ ☐ ☐ A professional ethicist, member of clergy, a lawyer, law enforcement

☐ ☐ ☐ ☐ ☐ Engage directly with involved others as the first step

☐ ☐ ☐ ☐ ☐ This is not a major ethical issue that I would spend time considering

## F. Should I accept Medicaid patients?

*5  4  3  2  1   [5 = always get involved; 1 = never get involved]*

☐ ☐ ☐ ☐ ☐ My overall sense of professionalism and my personal standards

☐ ☐ ☐ ☐ ☐ A trusted colleague or friend

☐ ☐ ☐ ☐ ☐ Specific resources in organized dentistry, look up Code, call hot line

☐ ☐ ☐ ☐ ☐ A professional ethicist, member of clergy, a lawyer, law enforcement

☐ ☐ ☐ ☐ ☐ Engage directly with involved others as the first step

☐ ☐ ☐ ☐ ☐ This is not a major ethical issue that I would spend time considering

Thank You.

# *Appendix I*

# Moral Community Simulation

Published as Chambers, D. W. (2014). Computer simulation of dental professionals as a moral community. *Medicine Health Care and Philosophy, 17,* 467-476. Reprinted by permission of Springer.

## *Abstract*

Current empirical studies of moral behavior of healthcare professionals are almost entirely focused on self-reports, usually collected under the assumption that an ethical disposition characterizes individuals across various contexts. It is well known, however, that individuals adjust their behavior to what they see being done by those in their peer group. That presents a methodological challenge to traditional research within a community of peers because the behavior of each individual is both the result of norms and a contributor to the norms of others. Computer simulations can be used to address this methodological challenge. A Markov replicator model that runs on an Excel spreadsheet was used to investigate a community with four agent types in the dental community: devious practitioners, ethical practitioners who avoid involvement in the poor ethics of others, ethical practitioners who accept it as part of their professional responsibility to challenge colleagues who act unprofessionally, and those who enforce ethical standards. A panel of leaders in the profession independently estimated parameters for the model and criteria for a possible distribution of agent types in the community. The simulation converged on distributions of the agent types that were very similar to the expectations of the panel. The simulation suggests the following characteristics of such moral communities: The structure of such communities is robust across a wide distribution. It appears that reduction in unethical behavior is more sensitive to the way ethical practitioners interact with each other than to sanctions the enforcement community imposes on unethical practitioners and that large external interventions will be short lived.

## Computer Simulation of Dental Professionals as a Moral Community

One of the insights of the TQM (Total Quality Management) movement in the 1970s and 1980s was that the number of defects thrown off by any process is independent of the proportion of those defects that are identified or corrected (Crosby, 1979; Deming, 1986; Juran, 1988). Rework and rejection decrease the number of problems reaching consumers. Making the inspection standards tighter increases the number of found problems, but it does not make them less likely. Efforts to elevate the ethical tone of the professions have tended to focus on remediating the bad actors and raising standards generally. A wiser strategy, or at least a necessary complementary one, would be to understand the profession as a dynamic system and to make those adjustments first that promise the greatest improvements. The Japanese master of quality in the automobile industry Genichi Taguchi was fond of the analogy that no improvement in learning would necessarily follow from teachers raising the standard for a B grade from 78% to 82% (Taguchi, 1993).

The dominant theoretical framework in bioethics and professionalism is normative, and usually grounded in principles (Beauchamp & Childress, 2009). On this approach, practical problems arise when acting on one principle causes moral regret because an alternative principle must be compromised. Such problems are usually worked out by carefully defining contexts where a single agent is best served, on balance, by pursuing a certain principled course of action. These analyses are the stock in trade of bioethics. *The Principles of Ethics and Code of Professional Conduct of the American Dental Association* is explicitly organized into five sections: respect for autonomy, beneficence, nonmaleficence, justice, and veracity. The *Belmont*

*Report*, which is the foundation for Institutional Review Board (ethical committee) oversight of patient-based research in the United States, is also grounded in the principles approach.

The customary method for teaching ethics in dental schools, at least in the United States, and typical discussions of dilemmas in the literature work with the relationship between general normative principles and individuals. The principles are accepted; only their application is debated. The goal is to increase an individual's conformance with these principles. The assumption is that moral communities are enhanced by increasing the proportion of members adhering to these principles.

The prospect that appropriate behavior could be situation-specific or that individuals interpret what is ethically appropriate by (at least partial) reference to the values of their peers is discomforting to some. The early work by Hartshorne and May (1928) and subsequent work summarized by Ross and Nesbitt (2011) cast doubt on the position that ethical disposition is uniform across contexts. More recently, it is becoming clear that professionals provide a dynamic context in which they judge the professional acceptability of their behavior at the same time their behavior is part of the standard for their colleagues (Ariely, 2012; Callahan, 2004; McCabe et al, 2006).

The aim of this paper is to open a conversation about methods for exploring the dynamics of multiagent ethical situations where each agent's choice of the best response depends on the choices available to other agents and where the results of agents' action at a given time have the potential to change what is most appropriate to do in future. For example, the presence of "grey market" drugs may serve to hold down the cost of brand-name or even generic drugs to the benefit of larger numbers of low-income patients who do not purchase "grey market" drugs. The concept of "grey markets" is ethically objectionable in principle. The Harvard GoodWork Project is an example of how ethical behavior at one time changes ethical behavior at another (www.thegoodproject.org). Genetics researchers and other professionals frequently report that "bending the rules" regarding conduct and publication of research is required to establish a career, while the same individuals denounce such practices once they have achieved prominence in their fields (Fischman et al, 2004).

A commonly given explanation for cheating—in health professions schools, professional practice, and society at large—is the perception that others are also cheating (Andrews et al, 2007; Brass et al, 1998; Callahan, 2004; Fischman et al, 2004; Jones, 1991; Koerber et al, 2007; McCabe et al, 2006; Olson, 1965; Zey-Ferrell & Ferrell, 1982). That makes the empirical investigation of cheating especially difficult. It is not possible to isolate a single independent and dependent variable relationship. Diagrammatically, $X \rightarrow Y$ becomes $X \rightarrow (Y \leftrightarrow Y)$, where the arrows indicate influence. A more complete picture of moral behavior in professional communities can be gained by considering the interactions within the community as well as the effects of isolated interventions on single members (Lynch, 1996).

Research on college students, dental and medical students, and practicing physicians and dentists variously place the level of cheating at between 60% and 80% of individuals (Andrews et al, 2007; Beemsterboer et al, 2000; Fuller & Killip, 1979; McCabe, 2001; 2005; McCabe et al, 2006; McCluggage, 1960). It is risky to interpret these studies and draw meaningful comparisons across groups or over time. The literature is entirely self-report and cross-sectional. Even more problematic is the lack of standardization on the stimulus question. "Cheating" is variously defined or often left undefined in such studies. In the case of questions such as "Do you know of any incidents of cheating?" a 100% in a community response could be reported based on a single, highly published incident (Beemsterboer et al, 2000). There are no experimental or observational studies of cheating among professionals (other than where sanctioned licenses are involved) (McCluggage, 1960; Papadakos et al, 2005; Yates & James, 2010), and other than the early landmark studies by Hartshorne and May (1928) virtually no investigations that explore the way cheating in one area affects propensity to cheat in others.

The research reported here explores the ways bad professional behavior responds to the dynamics within a professional community over time. The work draws on nonlinear methods, ones that cumulatively feed back the results of early effects and do not assume that subjects are independent from each other, are common in quantum mechanics, environmental science, and increasingly so in organizational research (Blum & Merkle, 2010; Clayton & Davies, 2006; Fisher, 2009; Johnson, 2004; Waldrop, 1992).

## Method

Very simple nonlinear systems can be described using calculus. More complex ones are addressed via computer modeling (Gilbert, 2008; Gleick, 1987; Goldstein et al, 2010; Holland, 1995; Kauffman, 1995; Miller & Page, 2007; Nicolis & Prigogine, 1989; Page, 2011). The latter approach involves hypothesizing an effect for each variable on each other variable. Next, the computer calculates the total impact of all such effects taken simultaneously. The new state that emerges as a result of the first interactions alters the system, creating a new baseline which becomes their context for the next iteration. This process is repeated, and in many cases (but not all), an equilibrium is eventually reached where no further changes occur. All of the random influence that existed at the beginning of the process, largely as a result of selection bias, has been absorbed and what remains is the true but complex and continuous effect of all the variables on each other. This is the steady state of the professional community. External interventions—new ethical principles or education for individuals—will either cause a systemic realignment within the community or will eventually be "absorbed" into the equilibrium of the community.

The simulation reported here is a Markov replicator model (Dawkins, 1989; Maynard Smith, 1982; Skyrms, 2004; 2010; Sober, 2008). Markov processes continuously update the baseline as a result of information obtained in the previous stage. In a replicator model individuals are considered "carriers" of behavioral propensities (in this case cheating or devious behavior). Those moral traits that are successful in a community are passed on (replicated) in the form of increasing proportions of agents demonstrating the traits in subsequent interactions. Moral traits that are unsuccessful are subsequently found in a smaller proportion of the community. Professionals are not once and for all cheats or paragons of virtue; they can acquire or shed such characteristics depending on what is happening in the environment. One might think of an individual who has cancer, but is not a cancer. For this reason, I will speak of "agent types" rather than individuals or professionals.

Two datasets are required to populate the model: (a) the vector describing the proportion of agent types at each time, initially and after each iteration; and (b) the 4 x 4 matrix that describes the effect of encounters among each pairing of agents. The base distribution of agents is simply proportions of the four types in the population totaling to 1.0. The values in the 4 x 4 matrix drive the replicator function. Values of 1.0 represent situations where encounters have no future effect. Values below 1.0 represent comparative disadvantage and carry through in the simulation as reductions in the proportion of such agent types in the future. In standard simulations such as this, the 4 x 4 matrix of effects remains fixed and the distribution of proportions of agent types is updated at each iteration. A primary outcome of interest in this type of research is changes in proportions (dispositions to cheat, for example) as the community absorbs external influences or settles into a steady state.

Estimates of parameters for the baseline vector and the 4 x 4 matrix were determined in three ways. First, a "representative model" was created by the author, based on knowledge of the dental profession and on social psychology literature (Crant, 2000; Grant & Ashford, 2008; Parker et al, 2010). For example, in Table I.1, the top line of the 4 x 4 matrix shows projected effects on Devious dentists when they interact with the other agents in the model. Irving Goffman (1959; 1963), in his remarks on con artists, noted that their effectiveness decreases when their numbers increase because prominence erodes the public confidence in trustworthy relationships. Devious dentists are a self-limiting type because they count on the presence of a sufficient number of reputable colleagues to give them cover. Since Devious dentists do well in communities with Good-Passive practitioners, they have an interaction weight slightly above 1.0 for this type of interaction. Good dentists who are willing to speak up, however, represent a threat to Devious dentists. They can shun these practitioners, deny referrals, spread rumors, and, by the Code of the American Dental Association, are expected to report the Devious dentists to appropriate authorities. Hence, the Devious dentist gets a score less than 1.0 when these encounters occur. The worst interaction for the Devious dentist involves dealing with those who are indemnified to investigate and take action against them. This can result in the Devious dentist having to move to a different jurisdiction to continue practice, and even when exonerated, there are monetary and psychological costs in defending one's reputation.

Good-Passive dentists are so much the norm that they define the standard (1.0) for interaction within the practicing community (Epley & Dunning, 2000; Leary, 2007). By nature, they do not take an active role to create change (Tangney et al, 1996). They are aware that a few bad apples may tarnish their reputations, but are willing to accept this as a cost of practice free from other outside interference.

Effects on Good-Active dentists who are willing to speak up are slightly more noticeable, but not large because their behavior is also recognized as being close to the norm and because their speaking up is typically occasional and often indirect (Fowler & Christakis, 2010; Weber & Murnigham, 2008). There is a cost to confronting the Devious dentist. Often this is psychological, but sometimes a practitioner may tolerate marginally bad actors out of fear of legal, reputational, or other reprisal. There are also small costs in the community to the dentists who speak out if they are seen as tattle-tales, and becoming involved with enforcement authorities as witnesses in licensure disputes is at the least time consuming. The contribution of the

Good-Active dentist to the profession in general terms is recognized in this model by the tiny 1.01 weight.

---

**Table I.1. Input and output parameters for a replicator model of four agent types in a professional community–Author's representative model.**

|  | Devious Dentist | Good– Passive | Good– Active | Enforcer |
|---|---|---|---|---|
| Baseline proportions | .1% | 65% | 33.9% | 1% |

**Estimated effect of interaction matrix**

| *Result for...* | Devious Dentist | Good– Passive | Good– Active | Enforcer |
|---|---|---|---|---|
| *Interaction with* | | | | |
| Devious Dentist | .80 | 1.10 | .92 | .70 |
| Good-Passive | .97 | 1.00 | 1.00 | 1.00 |
| Good-Active | .97 | 1.01 | .98 | .99 |
| Enforcer | 1.06 | .97 | 1.04 | 1.00 |
| Result of simulation | 14.9% | 61.2% | 17.3% | 6.7% |
| Norm panel estimates | 14.2 | 64.3 | 17.8 | 3.8 |

---

Enforcement agents help the profession and protect the public, and are rewarded for doing so. Appointments to state dental boards are generally sought-after political appointments and expert witnesses in malpractice trials are well compensated. The slight negative effect on Enforcers is a reflection of their being a public symbol of flaws in the profession, their being perceived as imposing nuisance compliance, and their cost to the profession (enforcement activities are partially supported by fees candidates pay for the licensure examinations and by taxes) (Ashforth & Kreiner, 1999).

The estimated baseline proportions of the four agent types in the population are prudent "guesses," perhaps painting an overly positive picture of the profession. It will become obvious as the results are presented that such systems are robust and self-correcting concerning such initial estimates. The proportion of Enforcers is approximately accurate in empirical terms. There are about 12 dental and 24 staff officers per state on dental boards, approximately 1% of dentists. What constitutes "devious" or "active" behaviors are substantially determined by definition.

A "representative model"—a working approximation of the 4 x 4 interaction matrix—was created by the author. First approximations were based on personal knowledge of the profession, and these were adjusted when implausible outcomes emerged. Examples of implausible outcomes included more Devious than Good dentists or profiles where one or more of the agent types was missing entirely. By repetitive titration, a small band of plausible parameter values emerged and middle of these ranges was chosen. No claim is made that the representative model is the "real" descriptive mean for these interaction effects under all circumstances. (Such parameters are likely, per definition, unknowable other than for defined samples at fixed times.) The representative model does, however, provide a workable description of how dentists interact that supports meaningful exploration of system dynamics in a moral community.

The second consideration in developing a representative model for the simulation involved reasonableness of outcomes. It quickly becomes obvious that large deviations from the standard of 1.0 are implausible. They lead to outcomes where one type of agent or another becomes 100% of the community. It is obvious that all dentists cannot be Good, or Devious, or Enforcers. It is also expected that such models will converge on a steady state. A model that wanders indefinitely has no theoretical value. Operationally convergence was defined as finding no differences in any proportion of agent types at the tenth decimal point comparing iteration 40,000 with iteration 50,000.

A third approach to ensuring that the input datasets for parameters were plausible involved seeking the opinions of an outside panel of experts. All 22 regents and officers of the American College of Dentists (ACD) were invited to respond to an e-mail survey where they were asked to estimate the base distribution of agent types and the 4 x 4 encounter effect matrix. They were also asked to estimate the proportion of Good-Passive, Good-Active, Devious dentist, and Enforcer agent types in the American dental community. Nineteen individuals provided numerical estimates of these values. A definition of "deceptive dentist" was provided: "Deceptive dentists engage in actively promoting or passively allowing patients and others to believe that they are serving only the patients' best interests when in fact fully knowledgeable third parties would conclude that the deceptive dentist is gaining strategic advantage that is not being mentioned to the patient. Examples include: any amount of overtreatment, modifying treatment plans based on insurance availability, claiming unsubstantiated benefits for treatment alternatives, misrepresentation of eligibility or work done on insurance applications, and exaggeration of outcomes to patients or colleagues. An alternative definition is practice that, if known by another dentist, would be embarrassing (although perhaps not even close to being illegal) to have to explain to a formal panel of peers and the lay public. For present purposes, a Deceptive dentist is anyone who has engaged in any of the above practices twice in a month."

The aim of this research was not to estimate the proportions of dentists who can be classified by various ethical roles in the community or to provide definitive quantification of the impact of various agents in the community on each other. The goal was to demonstrate that given plausible approximations of interactions within a moral community, the internal dynamics of the community reveal dependencies that extend beyond the focal effects, that well-intended interventions may not be sustainable, that some interactions have larger impact on the entire community than others do, and that the community tends toward a stable and self-enforcing equilibrium.

The simulation runs on an Excel spreadsheet. Users are allowed to adjust ad lib both the base distribution of proportion of agent types and the 4 x 4 matrix of encounter effects. The simulation automatically performs 50,000 iterations and provides graphic display of the first 1,000 iterations. The simulation is available from the author upon request.

The research was approved as an exempt project by the IRB at the University of the Pacific, # 09-98.2.

## Results

Table I.1 displays the starting distribution of proportions, the 4 x 4 matrix of encounter effects, and stable outcomes at 50,000 iterations of the simulation based on a representative model. Following some minor shifts at the beginning, a steady state emerged where the proportions of Devious dentists and Enforcer types rose to a small, but appreciable portion of the population, and the proportion of Good-Active dentists declined. The same equilibrium was reached regardless of almost any combination of starting values in the distribution of agent types. The first 1,000 iterations in this model are displayed in Figure I.1.

Table I.2 displays average and standard deviation comparison data from the regents and officers of the ACD. There was similarity between the proportion of agent types in the dental community as estimated by the expert panel and as modeled using the representative model parameters as input for the computer simulation. For Devious dentists, the simulation estimated 15% and the panel estimated 14%; the simulation estimated 61%

Good-Passive dentists while the panel placed the number at 64%; for Good-Active dentists the estimates were 17% and 18%; for Enforcers the estimates were 7% and 4%.

---

**Figure I.1. Output of first 1,000 iterations of a replicator model containing four agent types in a professional community–Author's representative model.**

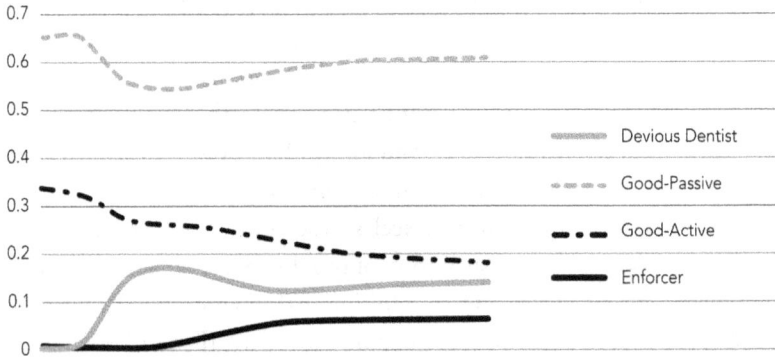

The differences between the author and the panel were slightly greater for the 16-cell matrix describing the effects of agent encounters than for the outcomes. Eleven of 16 values had the same sign (above or below 1.0 norm, representing advantage or disadvantage). A simulation was run using the values provided by the ACD panel. It quickly defaulted to a stable but unsatisfactory two-agent community (not shown) with 53% of dentists being ethical but passive and 47% of dentists being devious.

A single interaction value seemed to be responsible for the peculiar outcome in the ACD panel estimates. The average opinion of the panel was that encounters between Good-Passive practitioners and Devious colleagues would produce a huge benefit to the ethical dentist (1.388). This value was replaced by the value from the author's simulation (.97, meaning that Devious dentists undermine the public's confidence in the profession) and a new simulation was performed using all of the expert panel estimates save the modification just mentioned. The outcome values appear in Table I.2 and are graphed in Figure I.2. The graph shows wide swings in the early stages because of harmonics arising from tight interacting positive and negative feedback loops. This is a graphic display of an overly sensitive system where agents react to each other rather than their own self-interests. Ultimately the system becomes stable but with few Devious dentists, making the curve for this agent type appear as a flat line at the bottom of the graph area, and 150 Enforcers for every such questionable colleague.

**Table I.2. Input and output parameters for a replicator model of four agent types in a professional community–American College of Dentists panel perspective.**

|  | Devious Dentist | Good– Passive | Good– Active | Enforcer |
|---|---|---|---|---|
| Baseline proportions | .1% | 65% | 33.9% | 1% |

Estimated effect of interaction matrix: averages and (standard deviations)

| Result for... | Devious Dentist | Good– Passive | Good– Active | Enforcer |
|---|---|---|---|---|
| **Interaction with** |  |  |  |  |
| Devious Dentist | 1.141 | 1.240 | .959 | .931 |
|  | (.130) | (.123) | (.125) | (.294) |
| Good-Passive | 1.388* | 1.018 | 1.051 | 1.092 |
|  | (.149) | (.040) | (.096) | (.289) |
| Good-Active | .857 | 1.056 | 1.072 | .972 |
|  | (.076) | (.141) | (.136) | (.164) |
| Enforcer | .650 | .994 | 1.102 | 1.010 |
|  | (.117) | (.156) | (.197) | (.187) |
| Result of simulation | .1% | 45.5% | 34.7% | 19.7% |
|  | Devious Dentist | Good– Passive | Good– Active | Enforcer |
| Estimated proportion of agents in community | 14.237 | 64.263 | 17.842 | 3.816 |
|  | (13.36) | (16.96) | (12.45) | ( 3.43) |

* Value replaced by .971 in simulation.

The representative model developed by the author is robust, in the sense that adjustments simulating large interventions (as for example massive increases in the number of ethical dentists through education or large decreases in bad actors by heavy enforcement) are quickly "regressed out." In the base model it required 2,859 iterations to reach equilibrium of 61.2% for Good-Passive dentists. At that point, the model was "tweaked" to increase Good-Passive dentists by an unrealistic additional 20% (up to 73.4%). Operationally, this is achieved by inserting a new arbitrary base proportion vector and continuing the simulation. This might be analogous to a massive continuing education effort. The original equilibrium reestablished itself, wiping out all gains, in just 77 additional iterations. A 20% increase in Good-Active dentists is a somewhat better investment. They reach equilibrium earlier at 17.3% of the population after 1,813 iterations. The 20% bump lasted for 1,081 iterations before it entirely disappeared—about 14 times larger than the boost for Good-Passive practitioners.

**Figure I.2. Output of first 1,000 iterations of a replicator model containing four agent types in a professional community–American College of Dentists panel perspective.**

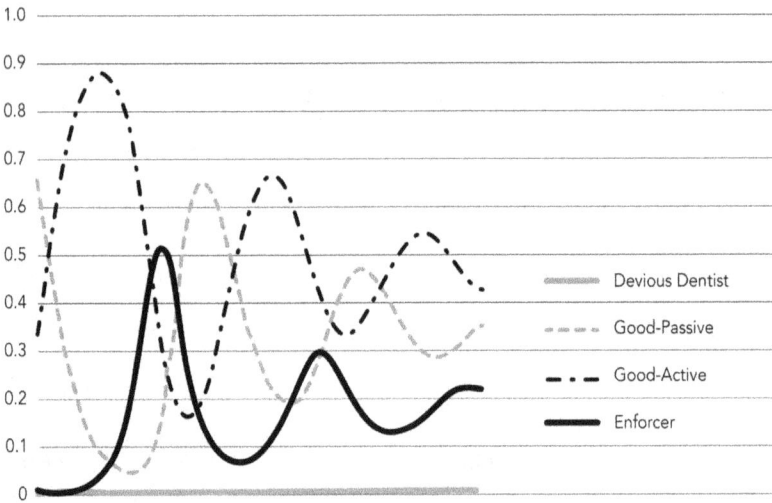

Devious dentists are insidious. If their numbers were reduced by 20% from equilibrium, they returned to regular strength in only 66 iterations. We could go to great extremes. Assume that Devious dentists are scrubbed from the system entirely. We would allow for mutations with odds of 1:1,000

and if a mutation were to appear, it would be a single dentist in a pool of 170,000 practitioners—the current number of active dental practitioners in the United States. Within an average of 862 iterations the equilibrium proportion of 15% Devious dentists would be reestablished—thus demonstrating that the system cultivates the proportion of Devious dentists it can accommodate.

The case of Enforcers is more straightforward. They are a function of the proportion of Devious dentists. Lagging Enforcers 50 iterations following Devious dentists during the first 500 periods of the simulation produced a correlation r-value of .530. Reversing the order of lag (Enforcers coming before Devious dentists) results in r = .128.

It is customary to examine the robustness of simulation models by sensitivity analysis. This is a procedure wherein each of the parameters is adjusted slightly, while holding other parameters constant, in order to gauge the extent to which various parameters play a large or small role in the model. Usually, arbitrary adjustment values are chosen, but it is possible to improve on this practice where realistic external estimates are available for how much each parameter varies in actual practice. We would like to equate, if possible, a large absolute change in a variable that fluctuates across a wide range with a small change in a variable with a restricted range, as is done with beta weights in regression analysis. The standard deviation of the estimates provided by ACD board members in Table I.2 provided such an approximation of baseline stability for each parameter.

A Bayesian approach was used for sensitivity analysis, shifting the normal density function for each parameter for an increase and a decrease of 1% and for an increase or decrease of 10% for each of the 16 values in the 4 x 4 matrix of encounter effects. Each of the 64 outcomes (an increase and a decrease of either 1% or 10% for the matrix of four agent types interacting with each of the four types of agents) was evaluated against two criteria: (a) a net deviation from the base model after 50,000 iterations amounting to more than 1% on average for each agent; and (b) elimination of one or more agent types from the model. Either outcome would be evidence of the model being hypersensitive to the involved encounter.

The model is robust for the 1% sensitivity analysis. There were no cases of eliminating an agent type, and only two of a possible 32 changes of more than 1% in agent mix (both cases involving changes in the interaction between Good-Active and Good-Passive dentists. In 25 of 32 cases, 10% variations in parameters produced cumulative changes greater than 1% in the agent mix. Thirty-two variations of 10% were available for testing.

About half of these (13) resulted in outcomes that eliminated one or more agent type.

The matrix shown in Table I.1 is arranged with interactions among ethical dentists (Good-Active and Good-Passive) clustered in the four central cells. Interactions among Devious dentists and Enforcers are displayed on the corners. This arrangement highlights the fact that relationships among ethical dentists are highly sensitive and that relationships among Devious dentists and Enforcers are slack variables (relatively insensitive to adjustments in the model). All cases of 10% adjustment involving ethical dentists led to significant changes in proportions of agent types, and 75% of such changes produced system collapse (elimination of one or more agent type). By contrast, three of eight potential adjustments among Enforcers and Devious dentists produced changes in agent type proportions and only one produced system collapse.

## Discussion

Systems of even moderate complexity may have stable levels of characteristic behaviors and these are determined primarily by details of interaction among the components of the system. Given a set of agents representative of common types encountered in a professional community and a matrix of the outcomes of interactions among these agent types, the community converges over time to equilibrium. This steady state is self-organizing and robust in the sense that external interventions are absorbed and the "wisdom of the system" (Surowiecki, 2005) reasserts itself in a relatively short period of time.

This simulation of iterative adjustments in a community based on a representative set of parameters produced a stable estimate of the proportion of various agent types that closely approximated the mean estimates made by leaders in the profession. Moreover, dynamic analysis of the model suggested that the system is stable and capable of absorbing external interventions. Demonstration of the short-term effectiveness of isolated interventions, regardless of their design rigor and statistical measures of effect, may be overly optimistic in complex systems. It is likely that systems have their own logic that controls the proportion of elements—such as devious practitioners— and that the ethical professionals that dominate the system have a substantial influence on the level of deviation tolerated.

The results of the sensitivity analysis may appear counterintuitive. The most sensitive relationships in the simulation, the ones where small changes can have the most impact, involve the ethical professionals. Because they are most numerous and because they influence others most, the level of tolerance for unethical behavior that ethical professionals agree among themselves emerged as the most powerful lever affecting ethics in the profession. The finding that the least sensitive relationship was the effect of Enforcers on Devious dentists is actually exactly what the literature would predict. Empirical studies of the deterrent effect of punishment consistently finds that whether cheating is challenged has an effect, but the magnitude of the punishment makes little difference (Gneezy & Rustichini, 2004; Jones, 1991; McCabe, 2001; McCabe et al, 2006).

Although it is certainly true that individual practitioners can enhance their understanding of ethical issues—both at a theoretical level and by seeing better ways to manage concrete ethical issues—this will not tell the whole story of ethics in the profession. Professionals who recognize that colleagues are cutting corners will respond to this as they believe their colleagues would. Several studies report that the typical response to lapses in academic integrity is to let the matter pass without comment (Andrews et al, 2007; McCabe, 2005; Trevino & Victor, 1992). This is especially true if it is perceived that others are also reluctant to engage expedient practitioners. The dominance of passive over active ethical practitioners is consistent with Schrader's research on cheating among college students: "Most students resolve dilemmas by letting the issue drop, doing nothing, by going along with the situation or with others in it, and by letting the problem resolve itself" (Schrader, 1999, page 48).

The model suggests that it would be insufficient to concentrate on the bad actors, perhaps with a view toward converting a large proportion of them through ethics training. Without changing the conditions that allow bad actors to flourish, the expectation is that their numbers would rebound to the level the system will support. The better policy would be making it easier for ethical professionals to confront their less-than-upright colleagues. The social economics of whistle-blowing are that those who speak up are not always appreciated and they bear personal costs for the benefit of the profession as a whole (Batson & Thompson, 2001; Beene & Pinto, 2009; Bok, 1980; Diamond, 2005; Giacalone, 2007; Henle, 2006; Pinto et al, 2008; Tajfel & Turner, 1986). There is a need for professions as a whole to distribute the costs and benefits more evenly.

Research on "decoupling" in organizational ethics has found that formal approaches to ethics, such as hiring an ethics officer, providing training, and promulgating codes, is more apt to engender cynicism than improved ethical climate (MacLean & Behnam, 2010). The way specific situations are handled on a day-to-day basis appears to be the driving factor in building organizational ethics (MacLean, 2008).

There are some who will find this paper offensive because a certain level of devious behavior appears to occur as an inevitable outcome of the plausible models. There are likely more who cannot accept that some level of bad behavior is inevitable. The director of the ethics think tank the Hastings Institute, David Callahan, in his *The Cheating Culture* summarizes 350 pages of examples of decay committed by "typical citizens" as well as the arrogant elite. The popularizer of behavioral economics, Dan Ariely, calls this the "fudge factor" (Ariely, 2012) and provides evidence that it is ubiquitous among ordinary individuals. The idealism of calling for general effort to achieve ethical perfection may not be as effective, ultimately, as the realism of identifying the patterns of interaction among practitioners that could be adjusted to achieve a small improvement in the ethical tone of the profession. That should probably be the first goal.

Ethics is certainly one of the fields of research where our understanding of what individuals do under controlled circumstances needs to be supplemented with a study of how we behave naturally as a group. Complexity theorist John Holland mentions something he calls the Third Harvard Law of Biology: "With a careful research plan, controlled conditions, using selected agents, complex adaptive systems do pretty much as they please" (Holland, 1995, page 96).

## Conclusion

This paper offers a demonstration of one method to begin exploring complex moral situations where others form part of the context in which agents make ethical choices and where the outcomes of an agent's ethical choices have the potential to alter the prospects that agent faces in future. It is expected, based on this modeling, that local changes in ethical behavior are possible within a range, but that the general context places limits on change. There are forces that pull behavior toward equilibrium and it is not always apparent which changes will move the equilibrium in the desired direction or whether changes that make theoretical sense in isolation will be stable.

Professional communities, like all complex systems, have their own "wisdom" that works over time to bring about a steady state. Modifying some individuals in these communities to align them with external norms may lead to disappointing results if the relationships between individuals and communities are not understood. Focus exclusively on the relationship between prototypical individuals and an ethical principle is insufficient.

## References

Andrews, K. G., Smith, L. A., Henzi, D., & Demps, E. (2007). Faculty and student perceptions of academic integrity in U.S. and Canadian dental schools. *Journal of Dental Education, 71* (8), 1027-39.

Ariely, D. (2012). *The (honest) truth about dishonesty*. New York, NY: Harper.

Ashforth, B. E., & Kreiner. G. W. (1999). "How can you do it?": Dirty work and the challenge of constructing a positive identity. *Academy of Management Review, 24* (3), 413-434.

Batson, C. D., & Thompson, E. R. (2001). Why don't moral people act morally? Motivational considerations. *Current Directions in Psychological Science, 10*, 54-7.

Beauchamp, T. L., & Childress, J. F. (2009). *Principles of biomedical ethics* (6th ed.). New York, NY: Oxford University Press.

Beemsterboer, P. L., Odom, J. G., Pate, T. D., & Haden, N. K. (2000). Issues of academic integrity in U.S. dental schools. *Journal of Dental Education, 64* (12), 833-838.

Beene, G., & Pinto, J. (2009). Resisting organization-level corruption: An interview with Sherron Watkins. *Academy of Management Learning & Education, 8* (2), 275-89.

Blum, C., & Merkle, D. (Eds). (2010). *Swarm intelligence: Introduction and applications*. Berlin, DE: Springer.

Bok, S. (1980). Whistleblowing and professional responsibilities. In D. Callahan & S. Bok (Eds.), *Ethics teaching in higher education*. New York, NY: Plenum.

Brass, D. J., Butterfield, K. D., & Skaggs, B. C. (1998). Relationships and unethical behavior: A social network perspective. *Academy of Management Review, 23*, 14-31.

Callahan, D. (2004). *The cheating culture: Why more Americans are doing wrong to get ahead*. New York, NY: Harvest Books.

Clayton, P., & Davies, P. (Eds.) (2006). *The re-emergence of emergence*. Oxford, UK: Oxford University Press.

Crant, J. M. (2000). Proactive behavior in organizations. *Journal of Management, 26*, 435-462.

Crosby, P. B. (1979). *Quality is free: The art of making quality certain*. New York, NY: New American Library.

Dawkins, R. (1989). *The selfish gene*. Oxford, UK: Oxford University Press.

Deming, W. E. (1986). *Out of crisis*. Cambridge, MA: MIT Center for Advanced Engineering Study.

Diamond, J. (2005). *Collapse: How societies choose to succeed or fail*. New York, NY: Penguin.

Epley, N., & Dunning, D. (2000). Feeling "holier than thou": Are self-serving assessments produced by errors in self- or social prediction? *Journal of Personality and Social Psychology, 79*, 861-875.

Fischman, W., Solomon, B., Greenspan, D., & Gardner, H. (2004). *Making good: How young people cope with moral dilemmas at work*. Cambridge, MA: Harvard University Press.

Fisher, L. (2009). *The perfect swarm: The science of complexity in everyday life*. New York, NY: Basic Books.

Fowler, J. H., & Christakis, N. A. (2010). Cooperative behavior cascades in human social networks. *Proceedings of the National Academy of Sciences, 107*, 1-5.

Fuller, J. L., & Killip, D. E. (1979). Do dental students cheat? *Journal of Dental Education, 43* (13), 666-669.

Giacalone, R. A. (2007). Taking the red pill to disempower unethical students: Creating ethical sentinels in business schools. *Academy of Management Learning & Education, 6* (4), 534-542.

Gilbert, N. (2008). *Agent-based models*. Thousand Oaks, CA: Sage Publications.

Gleick, J. (1987). *Chaos: Making a new science*. New York, NY: Penguin.

Gneezy, U., & Rustichini, A. (2004). Incentives, punishment, and behavior. In C. F. Camerer, G. Loewenstein, & A. Rabin (Eds.), *Advances in behavioral economics* (pp. 572-589). Princeton, NJ: Princeton University Press.

Goffman, I. (1959). *The presentation of self in everyday life*. New York, NY: Anchor.

Goffman, I. (1963). *Stigma: Notes on the management of spoiled identity*. New York, NY: Simon & Schuster.

Goldstein, J., Hazy, J. K., & Lichtenstein, B. B. (2010). *Complexity and the nexus of leadership: Leveraging nonlinear science to create ecologies of innovation*. New York, NY: Palgrave-Macmillan.

Grant, A. M., & Ashford, S. J. (2008). The dynamics of proactive equity at work. *Research in Organizational Behavior, 28*, 3-34.

Hartshorne, H., & May, M. A. (1928). *Studies in the nature of character*. New York, NY: Macmillan.

Henle, C. A. (2006). Bad apples or bad barrels? A former CEO discusses the interplay of person and situation with implications for business education. *Academy of Management Learning & Education 5*, 346-355.

Holland, J. H. (1995). *Hidden order: How adaption builds communities*. New York, NY: Basic Books.

Johnson, S. (2004). *Emergence*. New York, NY: Scribner.

Jones, T. M. (1991). Ethical decision making in individuals in organizations: An issue-contingent model. *Academy of Management Review, 16*, 366-395.

Juran, J. M. (1988). *Juran on planning for quality*. New York, NY: The Free Press.

Kauffman, S. (1995). *At home in the universe: The search for the laws of self-organization and complexity*. Oxford, UK: Oxford University Press.

Koerber, A., Botto, R. W., Pendleton, D. D., Albazzaz, M. B., Doshi, S. J., & Rinando, V. A. (2007). Enhancing ethical behavior: Views of students, administrators, and faculty. *Journal of Dental Education, 71* (2), 213-224.

Leary, M. R. (2007). Motivational and emotional aspects of the self. *Annual Review of Psychology, 58*, 317-344.

Lynch, A. (1996). *Thought contagion: How belief spreads through society*. New York, NY: Basic Books.

MacLean, T. L. (2008). Framing and organizational misconduct: A symbolic internationalist study. *Journal of Business Ethics, 78*, 3-16.

MacLean, T. L., & Behnam, M. (2010). The dangers of decoupling: The relationship between compliance programs, legitimacy perceptions, and institutionalized misconduct. *Academy of Management Journal, 53* (6), 1499-1520.

Maynard Smith, J. (1982). *Evolution and the theory of games*. Cambridge, UK: Cambridge University Press.

McCabe, D. L. (2001). Cheating: Why students do it and how we can help them stop. *American Educator*, 1-7.

McCabe, D. L. (2005). It takes a village: Academic dishonesty & educational opportunity. *Liberal Education Summer/Fall*, 26-31.

McCabe, D. L., Butterfield, K. F., & Trevino, L. K. (2006). Academic dishonesty in graduate programs: Prevalence, causes, and proposed action. *Academy of Management Learning & Education, 5* (3), 294-305.

McCluggage, R. W. (1960). The profession, ethics, and history. *Journal of Dental Education, 24* (3), 171-175.

Miller, J. H., & Page, S. E. (2007). *Complex adaptive systems: An introduction to computational models of social life*. Princeton, NJ: Princeton University Press.

Nicolis, G., & Prigogine, I. (1989). *Exploring complexity: An introduction*. New York, NY: W. H. Freeman.

Olson, M. (1965). *The logic of collective action: Public goods and the theory of groups*. Cambridge, MA: Harvard University Press.

Page, S. E. (2011). *Diversity and complexity*. Princeton, NJ: Princeton University Press.

Papadakos, M., Teheran, A., Banat, M., Knitter, T., Ratner, S., Stern, D., et al (2005). Disciplinary action by medical boards and prior behavior in medical school. *New England Journal of Medicine, 353*, 2673-2682.

Parker, S. K., Bindl, U. K., & Strauss, K. (2010) Making things happen: A model of proactive motivation. *Journal of Management, 36*, 827-856.

Pinto, J., Leana, C. R., & Pil, F. K. (2008). Corrupt organizations or organizations of corrupt individuals? Two types of organizational-level corruption. *Academy of Management Review, 33* (3), 685-709.

Ross, L., & Nisbett, R. E. (2011). *The person and the situation: Perspectives of social psychology*. London, UK: Pinter & Martin.

Schrader, D. E. (1999). Justice and caring: Progress in college students' moral reasoning development. In M. S. Katz, N. Noddings, & K. A. Strike (Eds.), *Justice and caring: The search for common ground in education* (pp. 37-55). New York, NY: Teachers College Press.

Skyrms, B. (2004). *The stag hunt and the evolution of social structure*. Cambridge, UK: Cambridge University Press.

Skyrms, B. (2010). *Signals: Evolution, learning, & information*. Oxford, UK: Oxford University Press.

Sober, E. (2008). *Evidence and evolution: The logic behind the science*. Cambridge, UK: Cambridge University Press.

Surowiecki, J. (2005). *The wisdom of crowds*. New York, NY: Anchor Books.

Taguchi, G. (1993). *Taguchi on robust technology development: Bringing quality engineering upstream*. New York, NY: ASME Press.

Tajfel, H. & Turner, J. C. (1986). The social identity theory of intergroup behavior. In Worchel & Austin (Eds.), *Psychology of intergroup relations* (2nd ed.) (pp. 7-24). Chicago, IL: Nelson-Hall Publishers.

Tangney, J. P., Miller, R. S., Flicker, L., & Barlow, D. H. (1996). Are shame, guilt, and embarrassment distinct emotions? *Journal of Personality and Social Psychology, 70*, 1256-1269.

Trevino, L. K., & Victor, B. (1992). Peer reporting of unethical behavior: A social context perspective. *Academy of Management Journal, 35* (1), 38-64.

Waldrop, M. M. (1992). *Complexity: The emerging science at the edge of order and chaos.* New York, NY: Simon & Schuster.

Weber, J. M., & Murnigham, J. K. (2008). Suckers or saviors: Consistent contributions in social dilemmas. *Journal of Personality and Social Psychology, 95,* 1340-1353.

Yates, J., & James, D. (2010). Risk factors at medical school for subsequent misconduct: Multicenter retrospective case-control study. *British Medical Journal, 340,* doi: doi.org/ 10.1136.

Zey-Ferrell, M., & Ferrell, O. C. (1982). Role set confirmation and opportunity as predictors of unethical behavior in organizations. *Human Relations, 35,* 587-604.

# Exhibit

General findings of a computer simulation of moral behavior of four types of dentists in a moral community.

1.  Because of the interaction of components, it is almost impossible to determine from inspection what the result of change in a single component will be in the entire system.

2.  Small changes in sensitive relationships in the system can cause greater disruptions in equilibrium than large changes in slack variables can.

3.  Systems are often more responsive to relationships among components than to initial proportions of the components.

4.  Core agents and their interactions establish the system capacity for less central agents. Ethical dentists determine the profession's tolerance for Devious dentists.

5.  Complex systems in equilibrium can absorb external interventions and quickly return to the previous steady state.

6.  In the base model, Good-Active dentists were driven to virtual extinction while Good-Passive dentists retained an essentially undiminished high proportion. This reflects the fact that agents playing similar roles can be substituted functionally for each other to a certain extent and under suitable circumstances.

7.  Agents that depend on others are highly responsive to changes in the proportion of those agent types. Changes in proportions of Enforcers depend more on changes in proportions of Devious dentists than vice versa.

8.  Parasite agents depend on the health of others in the system so they will flourish only if conditions are favorable to those they depend on. They cannot achieve dominance, however, because they would destroy the base on which they depend. Small proportions of Devious dentists and Enforcers are expected to always exist.

The method used here is standard for such research (Dawkins, 1989; Maynard Smith, 1982; Skyrms, 2004; 2010; Sober, 2008) and involves multiplying a four-element vector containing the proportion of each agent in the community by itself to produce a four-by-four matrix. This matrix describes the proportion of 16 different types of interactions in the community, on the assumption that interactions are random but proportional to the agents. The four-by-four matrix of proportion of encounters is multiplied by a second four-by-four matrix that describes the effect of each interaction. This multiplication produces a four-element vector of the proportion of each element, adjusted simultaneously for the double effect of impact on other agent types and for the likelihood of encountering them. The "replicator" nature of such models refers to the fact that "successful" encounters increase the proportion of agents following that strategy. The "Markov" nature of such models refers to the fact that the final vector of proportion of each agent type becomes the input vector for the subsequent iteration of the model. Input in the simulation consists of a one-time specification of the initial vector of proportion of agents and a one-time specification of the matrix of the effects of the interactions among agents.

# Appendix J

# Justifiable Criticism

Published as Chambers, D. W. (2017). What dentists do when they recognize faulty treatment: To tattle or build moral community. *Journal of the American College of Dentists, 84* (2), 32-66.

## Abstract

Justifiable criticism is the obligation to speak out in the face of gross or continuous faulty treatment. The assumption is that dentists are in the best position to recognize practices that damage patients and jeopardize the reputation of the profession and that early and positive intervention by dentists is preferable to later actions taken by lawyers and government enforcement agencies. This report summarizes five studies conducted to characterize how dentists and patients regard justifiable criticism. It is part of the American College of Dentists Gies Ethics Project, which is intended to offer perspective on the ethical dimension of dental practice. It is expected that this reflection on professional practices will open insight and discussion regarding ways to improve oral health and the professional satisfaction of dentists. This report consists of a summary report and five supplemental papers describing individual studies.

What one says about the work of one's peers requires careful judgment. This is affected by the nature of the treatment, what one knows about the circumstances, and the motives involved. Dentists X and Y may have different opinions about the appropriate treatment for the patient:

A.  Does it matter to the outcome?
    1.  X believes Y is practicing differently, but acceptably
    2.  X believes Y is practicing below the standard of care and thus endangering patients
    3.  X believes Y is practicing in a fashion that will damage the reputation of the profession

B.  Is there an information barrier?
    1.  X has sufficient understanding of the situation to form a defensible position
    2.  X needs additional information to make sense of what Y is doing
    3.  X believes there is something useful to learn from Y

C.  What motives are involved?
    1.  X sees an opportunity to increase business at the expense of Y
    2.  X sees an obligation to protect the public or the profession
    3.  X believes that all will benefit from understanding what Y is doing

There are three possible courses of action:
**Unjustifiable criticism**: A1 in combination with C1 while disregarding B
**Professional development**: A1 in combination with B and C3
**Justifiable criticism**: A2 or A3 with C2, adjusted for B

This paper will focus on justifiable criticism.

## The Profession's Obligation to the Public

Writers on the professions (Hughes, 1959) generally agree that the following characteristics set professionals apart from others who provide services to the public for financial compensation:

1.  A body of specialized knowledge and skill requiring years of preparation and continuous updating to remain current
2.  Service to the public at large, including helping the public make informed decisions by full disclosure of alternatives and their effects
3.  A substantial degree of self-determination regarding standards for education, admittance to the profession, and practice

The second and third characteristics are usually considered to be complementary. They are sometimes referred to as an "implied contract." Professional self-governance is granted by the public in exchange for service. Regulation of oral health care is inserted by third parties into this relationship, as with all other commercial activities, to the extent that the public or special interest groups in the public feel members of a profession place their own interests above those of the public at large.

Various groups within the professions create, modify, negotiate, and update standards that the public can expect of the profession generally. The ethical dimensions of professional-public relationships are the subject of the Gies Ethics Project.

The voluntary enforcement of the implied contract is a separate ethical issue from the creation of the standards. Because neither the public nor reasonable regulatory monitoring can adequately detect quality professional care, monitoring remains the responsibility of the profession. That is sometimes accomplished by standardized and invasive methods, such as insurance standards, initial licensure examination, or continuing education hour requirements and OSHA, HIPAA, and other compliance monitoring. Sometimes it is done by lawsuits initiated by staff, former partners, or patients, or by the threat of them. On very rare occasions, it is done by voluntary peer monitoring and reporting. The latter is commonly spoken of as "justifiable criticism."

## The Code of Professional Conduct

The American Dental Association Code of Professional Conduct, in the section on Justice, states: "C. Justifiable Criticism. Dentists shall be obliged to report to the appropriate reviewing agency as determined by the local component or constituent society instances of gross or continual faulty treatment by other dentists. Patients should be informed of their present oral health status without disparaging comment about prior services."

There are two positive obligations in this statement: (a) bring matters of perceived unprofessional conduct to the attention of authorized representatives of the profession; and (b) ensure that the patients are informed regarding their oral health condition. This is plain enough.

What is excluded from the statement is also important. Dentists are not expected to pass judgment on their colleagues' motives or to personally intervene to correct their behavior. Creating doubts in the patient's mind regarding the treating dentist is specifically interdicted. This is either "unjustifiable criticism" or placing the responsibility for redressing the issue on the patient. By extension, undermining a colleague's reputation within the profession by innuendo is equally prohibited, although not specifically mentioned in the code.

The moral expectation is clear: responsible perception of inappropriate treatment is to be reported in a descriptive fashion to those in the profession who have the responsibility for managing such matters. Every member of the American Dental Association is expected to observe this ethical rule as a condition for retaining association membership.

## How Do Practitioners Use this Rule?

This rule is not an ethical principle, but an element in the Code of Professional Conduct. A member of the American Dental Association can be sanctioned for not reporting a colleague who engages in gross or continuous faulty treatment, although I am unaware that this has ever happened. Nor do I know of any case where a dentist has lost a license exclusively for failing to report a colleague.

Many dentists are ambivalent about publicly commenting on the quality of their colleagues' work. The reactions range from false disparaging comments and suggestions about competence intended to "steal" patients and gossip among colleagues that cause damaged reputations, to complete silence and denial of ever having seen anything reportable. In the other direction one finds "hints that a wise person should know what to do with," to informal professional engagement in hopes of helping a colleague, to very frank discussions with warnings attached, and even reporting to the appropriate group, either within organized dentistry or through the state licensure mechanism. The latter actions initiated by dentists are believed to be fairly rare. Most disciplinary actions against dentists are initiated by staff members and patients.

## Should and Will

It does not make any sense to simultaneously endorse an ethical principle and fail to act on it. The most typical way this is done is to endorse the ethical principle in theory but add practical circumstances that excuse one from having to do anything. A dentist peer may demonstrate consistent evidence of substandard treatment, but "Who knows the circumstances?" or "You cannot believe everything patients tell you," or "My colleague certainly would not want me poking my nose in his practice." That is an automatic pass while still wearing the moral mantle. Although it has not been studied in dentistry, there is ample evidence in business that questionable practices on the part of others are tolerated as a form of "protection" for our own minor deviations. Not quite so obvious, but nevertheless a reason for avoiding calling out bad actors, is the cover they provide. If Dr. A cuts corners and engages in questionable practices, it is in his or her best interest to hide behind the cover of others who are behaving more outrageously. Certainly there is little to be gained by more transparency and an open discussion of where the line should be drawn. Why draw attention to the problem generally?

## Whistle-blowing

We know from the research that whistle-blowing is uncommon, that whistle-blowers are admired in the abstract and shunned in practice, and that few who do it once make it a habit (Greenberger et al, 1987). We also have some insight into what prompts some to alert those outside the group to inappropriate behavior of some in the group.

More common reasons for holding justifiable criticism at arm's length include the belief that becoming involved will be personally costly and is unlikely to make a difference. A prominent pattern is that A is upset by the behavior of B but believes that peers and immediate superiors will do nothing or will make an inadequate response. Repeatedly, this is given as the major reason students are unwilling to report academic dishonesty. Women often say the same about sexual abuse or even rape. The United States has a special program for undocumented persons who report gang activities, drugs, and domestic violence and assist in the prosecution of bad actors. They are given a U-visa. The program has all but dried up recently.

Similarly, potential whistle-blowers perform a simple calculation: are the social and hassle costs worth the effort? The difficulty with making this calculation is that the costs are typically personal while the benefits accrue to others generally, such as the profession or society. The government has attempted to mitigate this difficulty by offering financial rewards, a percentage of settlement damages, to promote whistle-blowing. This is a cheap trick on the part of authorities and open to abuse, such as the specialized lawyers who hunt down minor infractions of the Americans with Disabilities Act.

Yet another justification for not identifying a colleague as apparently damaging patients, even when the evidence is *prima facie* strong and there would be more to gain personally than lost by doing so, involves loyalty to the profession. The original American Dental Association Code of a century and a half ago was explicit that ethical dentists must charge comparable prices (price fixing) and the current code, in the language immediately following that quoted above, in 4.C warns: "Dentists issuing a public statement with respect to the profession shall have a reasonable basis to believe that the comments made are true." As Robert Jackall notes in his classic study of ethics in business organizations (1988), publicly noting a flaw in the behavior of a member of an organization makes one vulnerable to sacrificing the protection of the organization.

A related explanation for not becoming involved in justifiable criticism is deeply psychological. We all have images of what the world is like. For example, most dentists believe, and there is much reason to support this, that they are members of a noble profession where dentists place their patients' interest foremost. This becomes a lens through which the world is seen, and inconvenient counter examples have a diminished chance of being noticed. Further, modifying that generalization can be challenging to one's self-image. Even maintaining the generalization but carving out and explaining exceptions is an unwelcome cognitive burden.

It is plain that the normative principle of justifiable criticism is a blunt instrument for correcting problems with dentists being reluctant to take appropriate action to stop colleagues from damaging patients. If principles were enough, there would be no issue to discuss. Even among dentists who publicly endorse principles in a code, they can duck out in practice by any of several means. It is easy enough to hold that one has an obligation to take action in the face of recognized patient abuse without being required to take action. Nonmaleficence is a handy counter principle: Do no harm to others, especially one's colleagues, would trump the need to report. Principle underdetermination is another escape. "I must report gross or continuous faulty treatment." "Conceivably, the case in hand has some plausible explanation." Therefore "I both hold the principle and need not take action."

A more direct analysis could be framed in terms of costs and benefits. If a former associate breaches the terms of a noncompetitive clause in the employment contract, the senior dentist will determine whether to take action based on the chances of getting a settlement and its amount, minus the costs of pursuing the matter. If the expected reward is greater than the expected cost, the senior dentist will probably go forward. Something like this direct logic seems to be working in the case of dentists who poach others' patients and risk being a bit pushy in the eyes of patients and colleagues for the chance to increase the bottom line. This is a personal good calculation.

But this analysis fits poorly in the case of justifiable criticism. There is a personal cost in terms of time, reputation, collegial relations, and the possible embarrassment of being wrong. But there is little or no direct personal benefit. The benefit is to the patient and to the profession generally. This is what is known as a "common good" situation rather than one involving a "personal good." The individual pays a personal cost, but the reward is a fractional share of what everyone is entitled to (Fehr & Gächter, 2000). Typically the perceived share of a better reputation of dentistry generally is small and diminishing. An individual may be willing to act in a case where he or she stands to receive all or a significant share of the good coming from the action, but will be reticent to get involved where the benefit is spread evenly across many, including those who bear no personal risk and even a few bad actors. If the individual considering justifiable criticism views the cost of involvement as high or the changes of corrective action following as low, he or she will likely duck the issue. The determination of personal cost versus collective benefit is likely to dominate the decision to act or not, and this will be independent of judging the ethical nature of the previous treating dentist's actions.

It is probably unfortunate to characterize speaking up to stop gross or faulty treatment as tattling. This report will conclude that it is unwise to require whistle-blowing as an ethical obligation.

## Studies of Justifiable Criticism

The work reported here is preliminary and descriptive. The intent is to observe dentists making decisions in a context where there is probably concern that a colleague is delivering gross or continuously faulty treatment. We need to know what kinds of treatment are considered faulty, whether the relationship between the treating and reporting dentists matters, the extent to which patterns matter, and who else a reporting dentist might want to involve. There is also something to be learned from patients about their views on whether dentists manage this matter well. The goal of this project is descriptive rather than to offer suggestions about changing the kind of behavior typically encountered.

Five studies were conducted. They are summaries in this report, and each is discussed in more formal detail in a numbered appendix.

### Study #1: Dentist and Patient Perceptions
The first inquiry involved dentist and patient perceptions regarding a written exercise where a dentist is asked for a second opinion about a

case involving strong evidence of poor treatment (Chambers, 2015). The case describes failure to diagnose an abscess and periodontal involvement, incomplete information given to the patient, and an extremely high quoted fee. Respondents were asked to indicate on a scale from "Absolutely appropriate" to "No way" their inclination to engage in five alternative behaviors and to indicate from "Decisive" to "Irrelevant" how important each of seven possible reasons was in supporting their action decisions. Ninety-two dentists and 52 patients completed the survey.

Dentists and patients alike strongly agreed that the patient should be informed of his or her oral health needs because current needs are paramount and all patients should be treated equally. Both dentists and patients were more mixed in the opinions regarding involving the treating dentist and the fact that dentists operate independent businesses and that patients' personalities may be part of the consideration. Both dentists and patients were twice as likely to strongly favor giving a full explanation to the patient as they were to engage the treating dentist.

**Figure J.1. Likelihood dentists and patients favor reporting dentist for gross or continuous faulty care.**

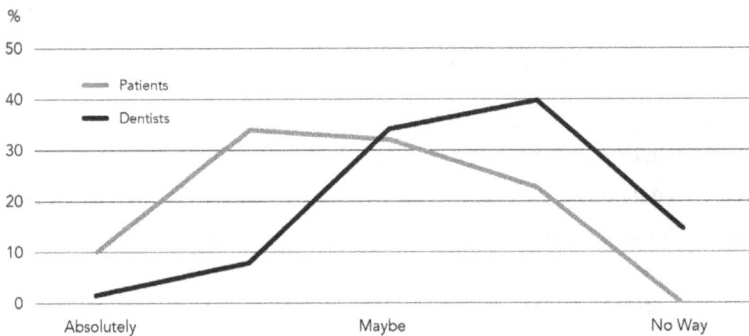

There were also significant differences between the views of dentists and patients. The most obvious discrepancy involved whether the matter should be private or more public. As shown in Figure J.1, patients were significantly more in favor of the consulting dentist lodging a formal complaint against his or her colleague. Patients were also significantly more prone to inform their friends informally of their dissatisfaction with the treating dentist than dentists were to mention anything to their colleagues. A supporting motive for dentists' reticence to become involved in such matters was their belief that there is a "code" that prohibits criticism of colleagues. The personal interpretations of their treatment carried more weight with patients than they did with dentists.

There were generally weak correlations between preferred actions and reasons offered in justification. The only statistically significant associations turned on the degree of acceptance of the professional "contract" between dentists and the public. Patients were more likely to report their dissatisfaction with the treating dentist if they believed that dentists consider each other as independent rather than part of the same profession. Dentists who placed weight on avoiding "unjustifiable" criticism were more likely to displace responsibility for resolving matters of inappropriate care on the patient. In both cases, weaker acceptance of the implied social contract for dentists taking responsibility for their colleague's performance were paired with expectations of greater public engagement.

## Study #2: Practical Exercise Involving Vignettes

Subjects, 23 dentists, were tested individually. Following informed consent, participants were shown five sets of slips of paper and told that short descriptions were written on each. Participants were instructed to assume the role of an endodontist in a community. The scenarios in the Patient set were brief descriptions of the presenting condition of various patients, all from the same Dr. X, a general practitioner in the area. For patients these ranged from "Ms. 2 presents for RCT. There is extensive reconstruction work under way, which you find Dr. X started several months ago. The approach is intriguing: it is not exactly what you would do with the case, but it might work" and "Mr. 9 presents for RCT. Two new posterior composites have been placed, and they both look well prepped and contoured" to "Mr. 3 presents for RCT. There are preparations for veneers on the upper anteriors. Many of the teeth were previously unrestored. There is also clear evidence of extensive periodontal involvement in both the maxilla and mandible. The patient reports that this has not been brought to his attention" and "Ms. 14 is being seen on a referral from Dr. X for a confirming diagnosis on treating #18. The radiographs show poorly done root canals on #3, #4, and #5. There is also a clear image of an endo file in the sinus. The patient says the work has been 'going on for many months,' but is unaware of any complications."

Participants begin the study by drawing at random any of these 14 scenarios. If they choose not to take any action, they draw another scenario from the stack. There were four kinds of alternative responsive actions available to participants. There were five responses that involved engaging the patient, ranging from [2] The patient says "Dr. X hinted that some others who are not as well trained, I mean have not had current and advanced training like he has, might raise questions. He is one of the most professional people I can imagine. He explains everything and I can tell he has my best interests at heart" to [5] The patient says "I think I need to talk to a lawyer. Every single tooth that Dr. X has worked on eventually needed a root canal. I now require my sixth root canal in three years. Are there lawyers that specialize in this sort of thing?"

Alternatively respondents might wish to communicate with Dr. X by drawing a scenario at random from among the six available. Again these covered a range from being very open and offering to share breakfast and discuss treatment philosophies to an extreme put-off where the office manager phones and says that Dr. X is too busy to discuss specific cases.

There are five scenarios describing what might happen if a professional colleague is consulted. These range from the benign "Oh, various things happen," to the rather pointed "I have my own doubts about Dr. X but haven't wanted to say anything." The final set of scenarios represented contacting "the appropriate reviewing agency as determined by the local component or constituent society." By selecting any of these slips at random the participant is imitating an act of reporting justifiable criticism.

At each choice point, before a slip was selected at random from any set, subjects were asked to report what they hoped to accomplish and what they would say to the patient, dentist, colleague, or board. Because respondents could choose whom else to involve in the case, including no one, and because the selection of scenarios was random, the path through the exercise was customized and no two subjects encountered the same overall experience. The exercise was concluded when a respondent determined to involve the board or when all 14 patient cases had been seen. At the end of the procedure, each subject was asked whether the exercise seemed realistic. All said yes, and most followed this answer with lengthy descriptions of situations they had personally encountered that were like the path through the exercise they had actually taken.

Twenty-three dentists participated in the primary study. The number of years of experience ranged from 5 to 46 and the sample included one individual who had served on a peer review committee, six specialists, and a diversity of practice sizes and sizes of communities where respondents had practiced.

The sessions were audio taped and transcribed. Subjects were given an opportunity to review and edit the transcripts. Data analysis consisted of counting choices made by respondents and patterns of paths through the exercise and of reporting verbatim comments associated with these choices.

Although 9 of 23 subjects in this study ended by referring the treating dentist for formal review, this was a conclusion that participants came to gradually rather than being based on a single instance of gross faulty treatment. Of the 139 initial visits, 42% of them resulted in no action being taken. Respondents were one and two-thirds times as likely to discuss the matter with the treating dentist as with the patient. Colleagues were almost never involved and referral for possible disciplinary action was rare, and only occurred based on an average of patient visits and repeated conversations with the treating dentist.

The overall impression is one of dentists referring their colleagues for possible action reluctantly and only following multiple examples and failed attempts to work with the treating dentist to prevent continuous faulty treatment.

There was noticeable individual variation in this general pattern of attempting to build up a constructive relationship between the consulting and treating dentist. Although no consulting dentists went to review quickly, three based their actions on three or fewer patients. The attempt to build a relationship was focused on extensive back-and-forth with the treating dentist, and occasionally with colleagues. At the opposite extreme were four consulting dentists who attempted, sometimes very briefly, to build a relationship with the treating dentist but ended by running all 14 cases by turning in the slips and doing nothing. They had resigned themselves to the treating dentist providing continuous faulty treatment but were unprepared to involve others.

Dental peers were consulted in fewer than 10% of cases, and in four of the nine where participants in the study referred the treating dentist for formal review without ever consulting the patient about his or her condition. The general pattern is that dentists consider potential incidents of continuous faulty treatment as involving primarily themselves and the treating dentist and that third parties are involved only after it has been determined that the treating-consulting relationship had failed.

## Study #3: How Dentists "See" Cases

Dentists orient toward the clinical manifestations of particular cases. It may be more difficult for them to gauge the patient's relationship to their oral condition or the attitude another dentist places on work that has been done. There may also be some difficulties associated with seeing patterns of treatment outcomes. All of these "context" factors are used to frame the meaning of a case. They are needed to judge the competence of another dentist, which is something different from spotting an instance of an open margin or a missed canal.

When a consulting dentist says, "I cannot pass judgment based on seeing just this outcome, I was not there," the dentist is correct. But that alone does not excuse the consulting dentist from placing the clinical situation in a plausible context and then verifying that interpretation. Nor does it excuse the consulting dentist from engaging both the patient and the treating dentist in a discussion so that all parties understand what is at stake. Identical presenting cases can be judged differently depending on what the patient and treating dentist believe is going on and on what has gone on before.

In the scenario exercise described as Study #2 respondents' reflections as they interpreted the case were recorded and transcribed into almost one hundred pages of text. This corpus was analyzed using the conventional techniques of qualitative research to extract major themes. Such themes were documented by verbatim quotations. This provided a picture of how subjects framed the issue of responding to a colleague's ambiguous treatment. The purpose of this research was not to count how many dentists responded in certain ways (as in Study #2) but to show how they structured such problematic situations. How did they "see" the problem of possible gross or continuous faulty treatment?

Six major themes emerged. In order to give a general view of how dentists frame cases involving ambiguous treatment by a colleague, the defining nature of each category will be presented below followed by a single illustrative quotation.

1. *Alerting the treating dentist is sufficient:* When an action was taken by the consulting dentist it was most often first and entirely a matter of alerting the treating dentist to the presence of a condition that might be considered below the standard of care.

    "I think he is aware now that I have mentioned the open margin. I trust him."

2. *Patients are informed tenuously:* Patients were often informed of the existence of a compromising condition, although that information may have been ambiguous, and consulting dentists resisted responding to patients other than regarding the technical nature of their clinical condition.

"Now I'm just going to retreat this [poorly done endo] and not say anything to the patient. If he asks me whether that is because Dr. X did not do it right, I'll just make up something about new circumstances requiring special additional care."

3. *Reframing the situation as convenient hypotheticals:* Consulting dentists reframed the presenting case as either so underdefined as to excuse involvement or by imagining additional facts that excused the need to become involved.

   "The important thing is to resolve these matters ethically, and to do the right thing. These things need to be handled right and resolved peacefully, I mean without entanglements. I'm not sure specifically what I would do."

4. *Patterns and general conclusions are avoided:* Individual cases tended to be considered separately; the dominant context was the current clinical situation and elements of comprehensive care and generalizations about the treating dentist were suppressed.

   "There's no line that separates competent from incompetent."

5. *Responsibility for corrective action rests with the patient:* The consulting dentist was seen as responsible for addressing the referral (if indicated), the treating dentist was responsible for restoring the patient to prior clinical standard, and the patient was responsible for everything else, including action against the treating dentist for general incompetence.

   "I would not report this matter myself. I would refer the patient with the complaint to PR [public relations]."

6. *There is no sense of general professional responsivity:* There was no "we" in these cases; treating dentist, consulting dentist, and patient had separate interests that were confined to individual treatment and they did not work together for a general resolution of difficulties or a general elevation of the profession.

   "If the guy doesn't respond [to my feedback], I'd just let it lie. Pretty soon something really bad will happen and then maybe somebody will do something."

A related part of this study involved asking respondents to match their preferred course of action in the case involving treatment-planned veneers on periodontally involved teeth with one of four radiographs showing poor to awful periodontal support. This was done after the respondents had chosen a course of action and was used as a test of the hypothesis that respondents will "imagine" a condition, given a general written description, that warrants their action or makes it easier to defend. In other words they assume that Dr. X behaved in such a manner to support the decision that the consulting dentist wants to make.

The correlation between action chosen and selection of radiographic image that supports that action was r = 0.512. This is a statically significant association. Fully one-quarter of the variance is in common, meaning that dentists, to a significant extent, see courses of action as much as they see an objective condition and then choose a course of action. This is consistent with the literature in the social psychology of perceptions (Bruner & Goodman, 1947).

### Study #4: Questionnaire Regarding Who and What Should Be Reported and by Whom

A survey study was used to explore the relative contribution of "severity" of gross or continuous faulty treatment and practice experience of Dr. X. Sixty-two clinical faculty members at the University of the Pacific Arthur A. Dugoni School of Dentistry reported the likelihood of reporting on each of the 12 cases in Study #2 where there was some ambiguity regarding quality of treatment. They offered these judgments with respect to the work having been performed by a colleague they had known in the community for many years, a new dentist in the community, and a candidate on an initial licensure examination.

There were differences in "reportability" of the 12 cases, and these paralleled the findings in Study #2. There were no differences in tendency to report ambiguous cases performed by new or veteran practitioners, but the same fault observed in a candidate on an initial licensure examination was slightly more likely to be actionable. The largest source of variance came from the consulting dentists themselves (respondents on the survey). The chance of reporting any incident in the set for any treating dentist ranged from 6% to 92%, depending on who observed the case. Respondents were more apt in this study to urge reporting in general than respondents were in Study #2 to say that they would be willing to make a report.

Together, observing dentist and the combination of the types of cases the observing dentist was most concerned with explained more than half of the likelihood that a case would be reported for potential disciplinary action. The type of incident itself explained only 10% of the variance and the treating dentist only 5%.

## Study #5: Patients' Perspective on Dentists' Responsibility for Maintaining Quality of Care

It is possible for dentists to agree with each other to a very significant extent while patients may be left with an inaccurate understanding or come to a different conclusion about the care received. Quite independent of whether the information they receive would make a material difference in treatment decisions, many patients use the amount and understandability of information as part of their determination of the quality of care they receive. It is a foundation of both law and ethics that patients must be provided with sufficient information to determine, as an autonomous agent when competent to do so, what is done to their bodies and whether they choose to enter into a financial arrangement. Where there are questions about the appropriateness of part of that care, the importance of information for patients increases.

Often, questionable care prompts exactly the opposite strategy— information is withheld or perhaps even shaded. It is appropriate then to inquire how patients feel about justifiable criticism.

Sixty-eight patients responded to a questionnaire that listed the 14 ambiguous incidents that have been studied from the dentists' perceptive. They were asked to imagine themselves as a patient in the office of the endodontist (consulting dentist) who, upon examination, discovered the various situations described in the 14 incidents. Patients were asked what information they expected to be given by the consulting dentist and whether they expected the consulting dentist to alert the treating dentist. Much like Study #1, there were similarities between dentists and patients imagining themselves in these situations and there were differences.

Both dentists and patients agreed substantially on which incidents presented the most danger to the patient, and they favored direct action on the part of the consulting dentist and greater involvement of the original treating dentists in these cases. In fact the correlations reflecting seriousness were highly significant at more than $r = 0.700$ and almost exactly half of dentists and patients favored direct contact with the treating dentist with a view toward explanation or correction of the issue.

But there were also differences with respect to information expected from the consulting dentist and about expectations for the relationship that exists among dentists. Dentists were twice as likely to let an incident pass without involving either the patient or the treating dentist as were patients (40% versus 20%). Both dentists and patients wanted the treating dentist involved, but with substantial differences in the extent to which patients were to be informed and involved. Dentists chose to engage patients about 40% of the time, but patients expected to be informed and to participate in decisions about correcting the problem in 80% of the cases. Although consulting dentists in Study #2 contacted both treating dentist and informed patient in about 20% of the cases, it was much more likely that a dentist was consulted and the matter closed than that the patient had the final say.

The perception of dentistry as a profession seems to differ slightly for dentists and patients. Patients in Study #5 gave the clear impression that the specialist was a member of the profession, fully responsible for the care of the patient. If there were problems that the consulting dentist could manage, he or she was expected to do so. That extended to brokering the proper relationship with the original treating dentist. Even though the specialist was not expected to render all aspects of care, and the general dentists had primary and more general responsibility in that regard, the specialist was seen as a member of the profession with the same overall responsibility for the oral health of the patient. Fully four of five patients expressed the opinion that their issues were the responsibility of the profession and they did not expect that the profession would be segmented in a manner that added to their burden.

Patients were saying, in effect, "I expect the profession to treat my oral health needs and I expect to be well enough informed to participate in that process. Further, I expect that each member of the profession will advocate on my behalf. All types of dentists share that obligation by virtue of being a dentist." Only two participants in the survey mentioned their view that dentists look out for each other more than for patients.

The pattern of responses on Study #2 is consistent with the view that many dentists consider justifiable criticism to be a matter of the relationship among dentists and that should good faith efforts in that direction prove insufficient, at least one has done one's duty. It may be recalled from Study #1 that patients were significantly more likely to expect that dentists will police their colleagues and are more willing to take their concerns to the street informally. Dentists and patients appear to have a different interpretation of the definition of dentistry and the extent to which professional responsibility can be segmented. Although these conclusions pass muster by fine-grained statistical tests, they are orders of magnitude effects that should be noticeable to all.

## Discussion

The overall picture painted by these five studies suggests that dentists do not frame the issue of justifiable criticism of colleagues' gross or continuous faulty treatment as a matter of detecting colleagues who are off base and reporting them through professional channels. The role of whistle-blower does not come naturally to dentists. Instead, a more nuanced process appears to be in play. Some dentists assume that their colleagues are practicing to professional standards regardless of evidence to the contrary; others respond to indications that there is a problem with a colleague's competence or judgment by intervening with the dentist in hopes of bringing about an improvement. Most tend to shield the patient from awareness of professional issues and regard correcting problems as the patient's responsibility. Contacting an agency in organized dentistry to report gross or continuous faulty treatment seems to occur as a last resort after personal intervention has proven unsuccessful.

### Judging Clinical Situations Rather than the Process that May Be Responsible for It

Of the three alternatives tested in the survey study, individual standards of the potentially reporting dentist account for significantly more of the variation than do either the objective nature of the mistreatment or the professional status of the treating dentist. Three-quarters of the variance was associated with personal standards of the consulting dentist. About half of this is attributable to personal opinions regarding how faulty each type of problem is and half to personal willingness to see situations as needing intervention.

Coupled with a range of personal standards for what is acceptable care and the extent to which one wishes to become involved, is an understanding that there is no bright objective line for faulty treatment that can be determined by looking at a single case out of context. Dentists are often aware that the meaning of a clinical condition depends on what has gone before, but they are reluctant to inquire about that. The preferred role is that of diagnosing a clinical condition as though it were a new presenting case.

A single bad outcome, of the type studied here, was never considered adequate evidence in itself to justify a judgment of incompetence. Almost every individual instance was regarded as treatable.

Although it will be argued shortly that the reaction of the treating dentist, and perhaps the patient, are critical to an incident eventually being reported, the sheer frequency of incidents seems to matter little.

There appears to be a personal severity buffer that allows dentists to make adjustments between fact and action. The perception study demonstrated that subjects "saw" cases as less serious if they intended not to become involved. Many participants in Study #2 were incapable of recognizing patterns of treatment, preferring to isolate the case as a unique example to be managed clinically, often by the consulting dentist. We literally shade our perception of the world to better agree with our preferred behavior habits. There is a small literature in decision science indicating that this is typical of many who are unable to combine new with existing information (Chambers, 2018).

### Involvement in a Thin Relationship

No case was referred for review without involving a consultation with Dr. X. Further, an uncooperative response from Dr. X was strongly predictive of pursuing action. The data are consistent with a four-stage hypothesis.

*First*, the case is considered clinically as a single incident that the consulting dentist can either treat or not.

*Second*, if the patient is dissatisfied with the care provided by the treating dentist, that is largely the patient's problem.

*Third*, if the consulting dentist chooses to engage the treating dentist, simply alerting him or her is considered to be the appropriate response.

*Fourth*, if the treating dentist adopts a posture of resistance to feedback, the consulting dentist either reports the treating dentist or seeks to avoid future contact.

Passing over faulty work by Dr. X necessitates no defense of one's own standards.

Attempting to bring about a reconciliation (or the assumption that this would happen) is undertaken with at least the possibility that Dr. X will see the better position of the judging dentist. When that fails, the judging dentist appeals the matter. This view is supported by the fact that colleagues are almost never consulted; the matter is kept confidential for as long as possible.

The relationship with the patient is also somewhat complex. In many cases, the dentist did inform the patient of his or her condition. But often this was indirect, as in, "What has Dr. X told you about this case?" There was a preference for distancing oneself from problematic cases. When patients asked for support, the consulting dentist most typically referred the patient back to Dr. X, often without clearly defining what the problem was and almost never with an explanation as to what might occur if the matter were not corrected. Issues of legal action were left entirely to the patient. The most typical intent in talking with patients was to determine the extent of involvement or liability of the specialist. In no case did the dentist assume the role of advocating for the patient's best interests or long-term oral health. There was no discernible pattern of dentist behavior contingent on information from the patient. Distancing or treatment per expectation were the only actions.

## Changing the Code?

The American Dental Association Code on justifiable criticism of gross or continuous faulty treatment lays out two specific requirements: (a) inform the patient of his or her current condition; and (b) report the treating dentist to the appropriate organizations. The five studies reported here suggest that that may be a difficult obligation for not a small proportion of practicing dentists. Certainly the latter is not a role most readily embrace. More to the point, this research suggests that dentists actually frame such matters differently from the way they are stated in the Code of Professional Conduct. Dentists, at least those in these current studies, ask themselves when they see unexpected treatment:

a.  Can this possibly be interpreted as within the envelope of plausible outcomes or approaches based on random distribution in typical practice?

b.  What does the patient know about this and does the patient attitude limit possible resolutions?

c.  Can I afford to ignore the problem in hopes it is a self-correcting aberration or that someone else will manage it?

d.  How does the treating dentist respond to my guidance?

e.  If the treating dentist resists my help, I will consider approaching a formal third party.

It is probably unwise to honor this code requirement in the breach or mount a campaign to increase awareness and enforcement. To my knowledge, no member of the American Dental Association has been sanctioned for failing to report gross or continuous faulty treatment by a colleague. A better strategy might be to rewrite the code. Some potential elements might be as follows.

- No patient will leave a dental office without knowledge of his or her oral condition, alternatives for addressing the problem, and an understanding of the consequences of not addressing the issue.

- Colleagues of all patients seen on referral will be informed of information given to patients during referral examinations.
- Colleagues should understand and accept each other's treatment philosophies.
- No disciplinary action (and certainly no third-party disparaging remarks) should be made without first consulting the treating dentist.
- All dentists are to some extent responsible for the care provided by their colleagues.

## Conclusion

1. Dentists prefer to manage perceived discrepancies with their colleagues confidentially so as not to have to defend their own standards to others.
2. To the extent that the public perceives the profession to be lax in self-monitoring of its avowed standards, it will seek formal regulation by outside parties to level the playing field.
3. Announcing higher standards without enforcement will lead to cynicism and fragmentation of the profession.
4. The public wants to be better informed about the decisions it is offered with regard to oral health.
5. The extent and nature of engagement with one's colleagues in maintaining standards in the profession is a personal matter among dentists and great variations exist, including some who will not engage under any circumstances.

## References

Bruner, J. S., & Goodman, C. C. (1947). Values and need as organizing factors in perception. *Journal of Abnormal and Social Psychology, 42*, 33-44.

Chambers, D. W. (2015). Do patients and dentists see ethics the same way? *Journal of the American College of Dentists, 82* (2), 31-47.

Chambers, D. W. (2018). How dentists learn by combining evidence and experience. *Journal of the California Dental Association, 46* (5), 315-325.

Fehr, E., & Gächter, S. (2000). Cooperation and punishment in public goods experiments. *American Economic Review, 90*, 980-994.

Greenberger D. B., Miceli, M. P., & Cohen, D. J. (1987). Oppositionists and group norms: The reciprocal influence of whistle-blowers and co-workers. *Journal of Business Ethics, 6* (7), 527-542.

Hughes, E. (1959). The study of occupations. In R. K. Merton, L. Bloom, & L. S. Cottrell, Jr. (Eds), *Society today*. New York, NY: Basic Books.

Jackall, R. (1988). *Moral mazes: The world of corporate managers*. Oxford, UK: Oxford University Press.

# Appendix K

# ADA News and ADA Membership

Published as Chambers, D. W. (2018). The *ADA News* and ADA membership. *Journal of the American College of Dentists, 85* (3), 38-43.

## Abstract

An organization's communications with its members can be read as partially reflecting the identity of those members. Four issues of the *ADA News* from each of the years 1975, 1985, 1995, 2005, and 2015 were coded for content. Information from the association and news about developments affecting the context of practice remained a constant feature through the period analyzed. Commercial advertisements and sales promotions to member dentists increased dramatically at the same time that letters from members and personal stories about dentists were less commonly featured. These changes parallel the steady decline in ADA membership during this same period. Several hypotheses may explain this relationship.

*The world is a looking-glass, and gives back to every man the reflection of his face. —William Makepeace Thackeray*, Vanity Fair

Membership in the American Dental Association (ADA) has declined steadily over the past half-century. As shown in Figure K.1, in the middle of the past century more than nine in ten active dentists were ADA members. Although there is some sign that the rate of decline may be abating, the rate of loss has been about 0.6% each year since 1965.

---

**Figure K.1.** Fifty-year membership trend in the American Dental Association showing members as a percentage of active dentists.

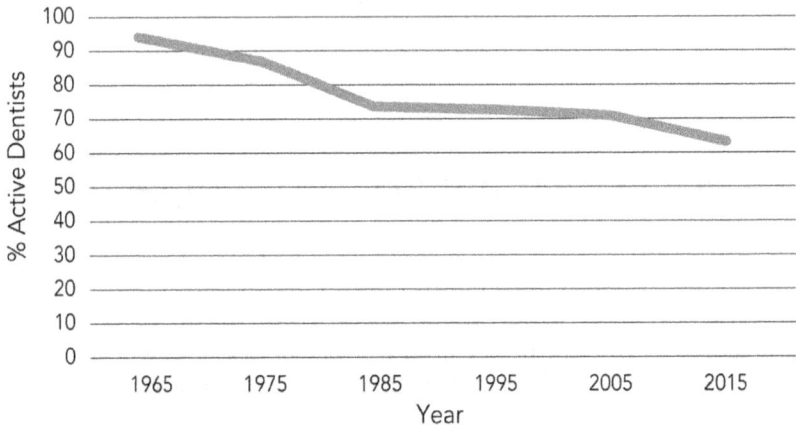

Sources: Putnam, R. D. Bowling alone: The collapse and revival of American community. New York: Simon & Schuster, 2000; and American Dental Association. National recruitment and retention report for active licensed dentists: End of year 2015. Chicago: The Association, 2016.

---

Even though the direction and regularity of this trend is clear, it must certainly reflect a variety of causes. Similar trends have been noted over the time period in many organizations. Among the health professions, medicine and dentistry show comparable losses, while nursing, veterinary medicine, and others have been less impacted. Generally, civic and fraternal organizations such as the Masons and the League of Women Voters have seen heavy losses while professions such as engineers, accountants, lawyers, and architects have remained steady (Putnam, 2000).

The general decline in "joining" was examined in Chambers (2004). It is almost certain that, in the case of dentistry, there are both general societal causes and changes in what dentists value. It is not the purpose of this study to identify the causes and give them their relative weights.

This report looks instead at how changes in one organization's (the American Dental Association's) self-image, as expressed in a publication intended to communicate with its members, interacts with membership rate.

Arguably, the *ADA News* reflects the interests of the association's members. To the extent this is true, it should be possible to "read" what the association believes its members are like or what they value by studying the content of the publication. If both membership and content in the *ADA News* changed in a systematic fashion during the past 40 years, a *prima facie* case can be made that some dentists may be leaving the association because it no longer reflects their values.

## Materials and Methods

The *ADA News* began publication twice a month in 1975 as a means of providing members with timely information regarding association activities and events of importance to practice. Originally two-tone and 12 pages in length, it became full-color, four-column grid, 11 x 14, and varied in length from 12 to 32 pages in subsequent years.

The ADA library provided digital copies of 20 back issues of the *ADA News* for examination. These consisted of two issues from March and two from August in each of the years 1975, 1985, 1995, 2005, and 2015.

The content of these issues was measured in terms of percentage of space devoted to eight different content categories. Space per item was measured using a ruler, with text and photographs being given equal weight. Because the number of pages differed across issues, space per category was converted to percentages within each issue.

Coding categories were determined by an iterative process. Eleven potential categories were identified by review of 2016 and 2017 issues (not included in the study). Approximately six months later, four 2017 issues of the *ADA News* were reviewed and each item was placed in the category demonstrating the best fit. When it was uncertain how to categorize an item, that prompted crafting tighter category definitions, consolidations, and eventually the elimination of three potential categories.

The categories retained for use are shown in Table K.1. Banners, statements of ownership, and similar material were not coded. The selection of March and August issues was partially determined by a desire to avoid heavy emphasis on the ADA annual meeting or campaign material relative to officer elections. Approximately four pages of such coverage were found in the 20 issues examined, but they were excluded from coding.

A single individual performed all the coding. The content of the 20 issues was recorded twice, separated by approximately two months. Where differences were found, the average of the two values was used.

## Results

Consistency of the coding was acceptable, with correlation between the first and second coding results across all categories and issues of r = 0.936.

The overall percentage of *ADA News* content is shown in Table K.1. Advertising and sales to members accounted for more than half of the material, and the proportion rose steadily over the years. Internal and external news was steady at about a quarter of the content. Focus on member opinions and accomplishments represented about 15% of content, but the proportion declined over the years.

Table K.1. **Coding categories for content in the *ADA News*.**

| Name | % | Definition |
| --- | --- | --- |
| Advertisements | 47 | Promotion of products or services paid for by commercial suppliers. (Announcements of meetings sponsored by other dental professional groups were not included in this category, but in the "Other News" category.) |
| *ADA News* | 15 | Association activities, announcements, information about officers and staff, statistics on practice patterns of dentists. (Policy positions of the association accompanied by descriptions of activity advocating these positions were coded as "Lobbying.") |
| Shout Outs | 8 | Personal recognition for individual dentists or organizations, announcements of new deans or significant honors from groups other than the ADA, stories of unusual personal accomplishments. |
| Other News | 8 | Information such as federal policy, scientific breakthroughs, and public health concerns, coming from sources other than the ADA, but relevant to dental practice. |
| Letters | 7 | Opinions from ADA members regarding issues of the day. Letters were further sorted into four categories: those that praised the ADA, those that raised challenges to its practices, those that praised other organizations, and those that challenged the actions or positions of others. |

| Internal Marketing | 7 | Announcement of services, materials, information, or other member benefits for which members (and others) would be charged a fee. Buyer guides and affinity cards (for which the association receives a commission) were so categorized here. Announcements of the annual meeting or other conferences sponsored by the ADA were not coded, in this or any other category. |
|---|---|---|
| Lobbying | 6 | Announcements of ADA lobbying positions, political stances and their reasons in opposition to positions taken by government, other professional organizations, or commercial organizations, such as benefits programs. |
| Awards | 2 | Announcements of winners of awards sponsored by the ADA or requests for nominations for such awards. |

Table K.2 shows the correlations between yearly ADA membership and percentage of *ADA News* content. There are two coefficients in each case because a pronounced curvilinear relationship was observed. This was due to the fact that the effects of changes were more pronounced in previous decades and appear to be stabilizing.

### Table K.2. Correlation between ADA membership as a percentage of active dentists across the years 1975 to 2015 and percentage of content in the *ADA News* by category.

| Category | Linear r-value | Best curve r-value |
|---|---|---|
| Advertisements | - 0.818*** | - 0.875*** |
| ADA News | 0.341 | 0.355 |
| Shout Outs | 0.450* | 0.513* |
| Other News | 0.408 | 0.418 |
| Letters | 0.894*** | 0.905*** |
| Internal Marketing | - 0.508* | - 0.521* |
| Lobbying | - 0.069 | - 0.228 |
| Awards | - 0.379 | - 0.383 |

NB: * = $p < 0.05$, *** = $p < 0.001$

Declining association membership is strongly associated with an increasing commercial orientation in *ADA News* content, as shown in the two panels in Figure K.2. This is apparent in more advertising space paid for by outside vendors and in the association's appeals to sell services to its own members.

---

Figure K.2. Changes in commercial content in the *ADA News* and association membership.

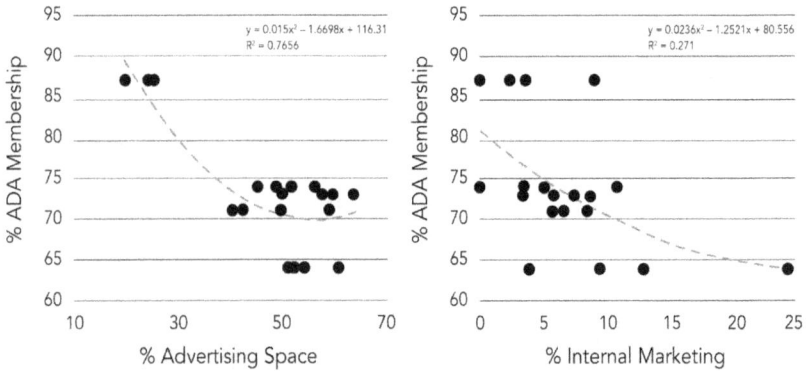

Association membership was positively correlated with two factors, both related to member participation. Opportunity to express personal opinions in the form of letters was significantly associated with high membership numbers. To a lesser, but still statistically significant, extent recognition of personal accomplishments, typically unrelated to dental practice in the form of "shout outs," was also positively related to ADA membership, as graphed in Figure K.3.

---

Figure K.3. Association between featuring individual members and membership rate on association membership.

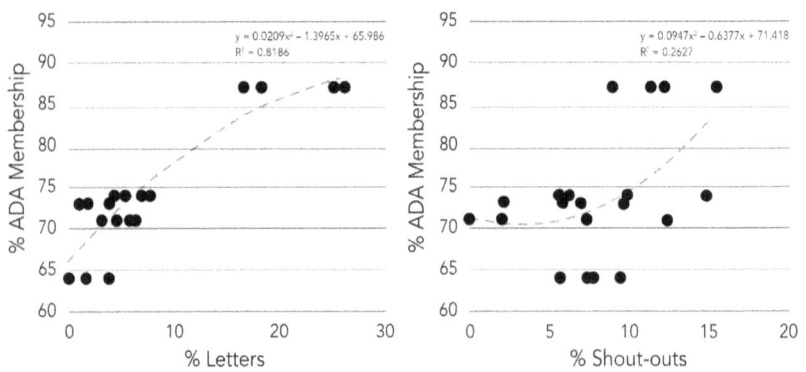

An attempt was made to further characterize the content of letters appearing in the *ADA News* by analyzing the apparent motivation of the letters. "Defender" letters were those judged to praise the ADA or criticize other organizations relative to the practice of dentistry. "Builder" letters were those that questioned positions or actions taken by the association or praised other organizations for actions thought to advance oral health. "Defender" letters constituted 55% of those published while the remaining 45% were more challenging. The graph in Figure K.4 shows an association between the attitude of letters in the *ADA News* and association membership. During times of high membership, challenging letters predominated; as membership declined, more "patriotic" letters came to predominate. Not only do the slopes for the two relationships cross each other, they are significantly different in slope at $p < 0.05$, suggesting that a strong membership base is associated with open discussion of the strengths and weaknesses of an organization relative to its context while a weaker membership is more defensive in its opinions.

**Figure K.4.** Association between ADA membership and letters classified as those defending the status quo and those challenging the profession to make improvements.

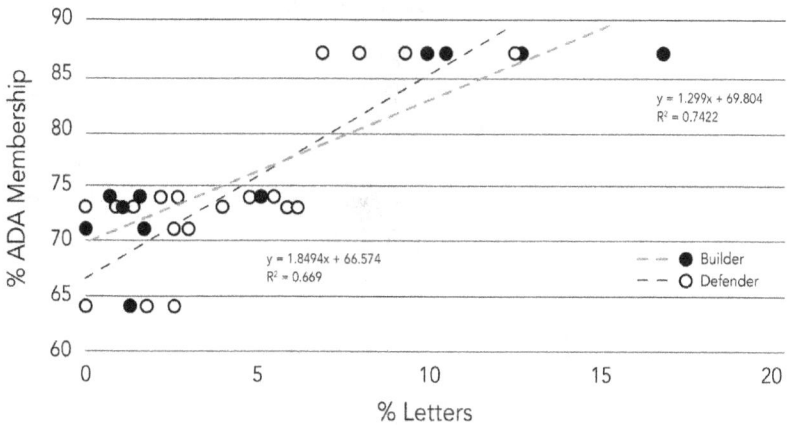

## Discussion

The official publication of an organization can be read as projecting the image those in leadership positions wish to communicate regarding who its members are and what they value. It is clear that the image of members of the American Dental Association, as reflected in its twice-monthly newsletter to its members, has changed over the past 40 years. At the same time the strength of the association, or its claim to represent the entire profession, has also changed.

The function of the *ADA News* with respect to conveying news outside the organization about matters that affect the membership and information from within the organization has remained relatively constant over the period of 1975 through 2015. The commercial emphasis of the newsletter (advertisements and offers of services from the ADA in exchange for fees paid by members) has increased from a quarter of the content to two-thirds. At the same time the content that features the opinions and personal stories of members has decreased from one-third to 10%. Both of these changes are significantly associated with declining membership in the association.

These are correlations, so it is impossible to say in a definitive fashion that a shift away from the personal voice and participation of members to a commercial orientation "caused" a decline in membership. Both trends could reflect general changes in society. Another plausible interpretation is that increased commercialism, especially a greater emphasis on drawing money from members to support the organization, represents an effort to compensate for declining membership revenues. The association's 2015-2019 strategic plan includes the following objectives: "Objective 2: Achieve a net increase of 4,000 active licensed members by the end of 2019" and "5.2: Increase member utilization of existing products and services and pursue new markets." These goals may compete against each other. To the extent that the ADA emphasizes benefits over participation it will be in competition with an increasing number of other groups, including those with commercial expertise and substantial resources, who provide specialized services for dentists. Those dentists who prioritize patient care and professional relationships over commercial success may identify less with the image of dentistry increasingly portrayed in the *ADA News*.

There is an alternative explanation for the observed association between commercial and nonpersonal characterization of the image projected by the *ADA News* and declining membership. As Robert Putnam (2000) and William Sullivan (2005) have argued, organizations are drifting toward increasing "professionalization." This is not "professionalism." As these authors use the term, it should not be mistaken for common standards of integrity and service among the members. Instead it is the use of lawyers, advertising executives, fund raisers, lobbyists, consultants, event planners, web designers, research firms, and the like—both within the organization and especially on a contract basis—to replace volunteer members in leadership positions. Such changes can become self-perpetuating when they consume increasing resources. Putnam describes this as "checkbook participation," the practice of paying non-colleagues to run an organization on behalf of the members. This explanation has the advantage of accounting for both the increased commercialization of the *ADA News* and the decreased voice given to members in terms of printing their opinions and featuring their personal accomplishments. Although not formally measured in this study, the small attention given to information from the trustees and reports from committees and councils in the *ADA News* is notable.

The opportunity for member voices in the form of letters has declined in the *ADA News* in recent years; the balance has also shifted toward a dominance of ADA-positive messages. Healthy organizations need both those who praise what is essential and those who ask how we can do better. A group that lives off its successes or publicizes past accomplishments rather than making new ones possible is unwisely investing the future of its young members (Fisher, 2009). An organization that fails to balance its attention between hunting and harvesting is doomed. Bill Bishop's *The Big Sort* (2008) is a cautionary tale of how an imbalance of the "defenders" over the "builders" leads to fragmentation rather than strength.

These results should also be considered in the context of whether the ADA represents the entire dental profession or the entire oral health profession. Membership numbers may not be the best indicator. In the 1930s and '40s, the American College of Dentists challenged the then-prevailing model of dental journalism (American College of Dentists, 1932) as being dominated by commercial interests and failing to serve the entire profession. As a result of the efforts of the college, the S.S. White Company, which published the leading journal of the field, *Dental Cosmos*, assigned ownership of its publication to the ADA, which agreed in exchange to publish a brief, periodic notification of scientific advances to be sent free of charge to all American dentists (Chambers, 2012). The current *Journal of the American Dental Association* contains a higher percentage of advertisements than did *Dental Cosmos*, and a publication for the entire profession never materialized.

The *ADA News* is one of four communication platforms used by the association. The others include the *Journal of the American Dental Association*, which is devoted to disseminating scientific information about the materials, procedures, and patient characteristics that affect clinical care; a website focused on expressing policy, services, and maintaining membership functions; and a rich range of in-person opportunities at meetings and via service on committees. As an example of "professionalization" of these platforms, the journal is now published "on behalf of" the ADA by Elsevier, Inc. These other forms of communication should be studied as has been done here in an effort to understand how communication shapes the identity of the profession and how changes in communication can best be used to strengthen it.

## References

American College of Dentists (1932). *The status of dental journalism in the United States: Report of the Commission on Journalism of the American College of Dentists, 1928-1932.* New York, NY: The College.

American Dental Association (2016). *National recruitment and retention report for active licensed dentists: End of year 2015.* Chicago, IL: The Association.

Bishop, B. (2008). *The big sort: Why the clustering of like-minded America is tearing us apart.* New York, NY: Mariner Books.

Chambers, D. W. (2004). Joining. *Journal of the American College of Dentists, 71* (1), 31-35.

Chambers, D. W. (2012). The 1932 report of the American College of Dentists Commission on Journalism: Commercialism in dental journals. *Journal of the History of Dentistry, 60* (1), 2-17.

Fisher, L. (2009). *The perfect swarm: The science of complexity in everyday life.* New York, NY: Basic Books.

Putnam, R. D. (2000). *Bowling alone: The collapse and revival of American community.* New York, NY: Simon & Schuster.

Sullivan, W. M. (2005). *Work and integrity: The crisis and promise of professionalism in America.* San Francisco, CA: Jossey-Bass.

# Appendix L

# Practice Goals:
# Opportunities and Obligations

Published as Chambers, D. W. (2020). Practice Goals: Opportunities and Obligations. *Journal of the American College of Dentists, 87* (1), 41-47.

## Abstract

Opportunities are those situations that motivate activity with little or no upper limit. Obligations are requirements to maintain a minimal threshold, with little incentive above that level. A large survey asked dentists to report their interest in learning either positive or negative information about technical advances in dentistry, economic success, professional ethics, or oral health outcomes. Dentists were most interested in technology, followed by income enhancement. Technology and income were considered to be opportunities. Ethics and oral health outcomes were regarded as obligations, with fixed standards for acceptability.

Would a dentist attend a continuing education program to learn how to adopt crummy technology or to hear about financial schemes that tend to cost practitioners money? How about signing up for a weekly newsletter that listed worthy causes needing money or offered an "Ethical Tip of the Day" intended for those who are ethical but want to attain the zenith of moral status?

Dentists value financial rewards for providing better technical quality dental care and most continue to take advantage of opportunities to make improvements in these areas. Ethics and the oral health of the public in general are also desirable values, but they seem to operate in a different way. Performance below a certain professional and public norm causes concern, perhaps even legal action. There is an obligation to remain above that level, but few dentists are heavily invested in being more ethical than necessary.

Courses and other opportunities to learn about emerging technology or the financial success of a practice often take the format of top performers showing others how they can do even better. Ethics courses frequently include many examples of the bad things others have done with the implicit message that the audience is ethical because it does not engage in these practices.

## Introduction and Hypothesis

The study of values is complex and difficult. Very little work has been done for dentistry in this area.

The literature on dentist values is thin and somewhat inconsistent. Most studies are dated and report findings from dental students, not practitioners. On standardized psychological tests, dentists often express a preference for concrete or practical thinking over abstract and theoretical framing of issues (Kirk et al, 1963; Linn, 1968; Manhold et al, 1963; More, 1961; Mozer et al, 1988; Schwartz & Shenoy, 1994). However, a few studies reported a preference for conceptual thinking among dentists (Cain et al, 1983; Heist, 1960; Silberman, 1976). There are studies reporting dentists' orientation toward economic values (Cain et al, 1983; Heist, 1960; Manhold et al, 1963; McDonald et al, 1985) and toward technical topics (Schwartz & Shenoy, 1994).

Surveys of dentists' attitudes toward ethics are rare. The 1995 study by Kress and colleagues did not actually focus on differences among dentists regarding how they would react to a common set of ethical challenges. Rather, it was a report of how dentists would rank issues facing the profession. Only the work of Chambers (2015) has reported that there is a significant range in the actions dentists would feel appropriate in specific cases, such as sexual harassment or patients attempting to control treatment sequence or skip on payment, and the reasons for their intended actions.

There are at least four problems in trying to be specific about how dentists value ethics. First, there is the matter of relative value. Ethics is only one of many potential action-guiding motives. Next is the matter of scale. Improving the strength of ethics may matter more when there are deficiencies than when one is already comfortably among one's peers. There is also the problem of social desirability in reporting. It is natural to self-report information that makes one look good. Finally, it is important to focus on the range of differences between dentists themselves, as well as on differences in types of problems presented. Why are some dentists oriented more toward ethics than their colleagues are?

The purpose of this study was to test these hypotheses.

1.  Dentists orient more toward technique and income when choosing how to act than they do toward ethics and public health outcomes.
2.  Dentists see technique and income as opportunities and ethics and oral health outcomes as obligations.
3.  There is substantial variation from dentist to dentist in how alternative values are seen.

## Materials and Methods

A method sometimes used when surveying public opinion is to ask respondents to report what they believe others like themselves would say. Besides the obvious difficulty of inferring the character of a generalized other, there will be reluctance to make honest reports, especially of suspected negative motives of one's colleagues. The following question was put to two samples totaling 196 fellows of the American College of Dentists: "Estimate the percentage of dentists who have overdiagnosed or overtreated any patients in the past three months." The average response was 24.6%. But the range of answers was from 0% to 100%, and 63% of those asked declined to answer.

The method used in this project was chosen with a view toward reducing "social desirability bias." The approach takes advantage of another well-known human characteristic known as "attention bias" (Baron, 2008; Ross & Nisbett, 2011). It is natural to orient toward, remember better, and accept as true those things that confirm our established values. Republicans watch Fox and Democrats watch CNN. The media are selected so as to maximize the number of stories or sessions of commentary that offer positive pictures viewers prefer to see and to maximize the air time describing the bad nature of those with whom one disagrees. We seek to confirm positive reports of what we like and negative reports of what we dislike. We avoid information that challenges our values.

A survey form was developed based on this connection between attention and values. Respondents were asked to imagine that they had received a stack of short journal articles from a colleague. The question was, which ones would most command interest and be read. Respondents were only given the titles of the papers and asked how likely they would be to read a paper based on the title. There were eight titles. These covered four theme areas: (a) technical characteristics of dentistry; (b) dentists' incomes; (c) ethical matters; and (d) oral health outcomes in general. There were two titles per value theme: one suggested a positive report and the other a negative read. For example, one title suggested that new and highly effective technology is being introduced at a rapid rate while the other mentioned that dentists cannot take advantage of technology because they lack the needed training.

The survey is shown in the Exhibit. A subsample of respondents also indicated their age, the size of the community in which they practiced, an estimate of the proportion of their colleagues who overtreat, and whether they identified as being general dentists, specialists, educators, or retired.

Data continue to be collected, but this paper will report on 265 dentists who took the survey in seven group settings between 2015 and 2018 in six states. The survey was administered in various settings, including events sponsored by state dental associations, the American College of Dentists, and dental schools. All surveys were completed anonymously and the project was approved by the Institutional Review Board at the University of the Pacific.

## Results

The psychometric characteristics of the survey were evaluated by traditional methods. The Cronbach alpha for internal consistency was 0.643—an acceptable value for an instrument with only eight items. Factor analysis was performed with verimax rotation. This resulted in identification of two latent factors. Twenty-six percent of the variance was attributable to a general factor characterized as preference for reading either many or few articles, regardless of their content. An additional 23% of the variance was associated with interest in either of two types of articles. Approach to technical and income topics comprised one reading pattern, while interest in ethics and oral health outcomes represented a separate pattern.

Table L.1 shows the average scores for interest in reading each of the eight articles. Scores of 3.0 indicate an even chance of reading or not reading the article. A score of 4 indicates about a two-thirds chance of reading. The standard deviations are large; every article received both scores of "must read" and "not at all interested."

---

**Table L.1. Strength of interest in reading papers in four areas of dentistry as a measure of relative value strength: means (standard deviations), with larger numbers indicating greater interest.**

**Technique Considerations**

| | | |
|---|---|---|
| 3.580 | (1.17) | Rapid introduction of new technology |
| 3.126 | (1.21) | Lack of training delays adaptation of emerging technology |

**Dentists' Income**

| | | |
|---|---|---|
| 3.419 | (1.33) | Characteristics of top income earners |
| 3.079 | (1.21) | Dentists' incomes predicted to be flat |

**Ethics**

| | | |
|---|---|---|
| 3.333 | (1.05) | Surveys show patients trust dentists |
| 3.379 | (1.14) | Dentists disagree on reporting incompetent colleagues |

**Oral Health**

| | | |
|---|---|---|
| 3.155 | (1.10) | Organized dentistry increases emphasis on population oral health outcomes |
| 3.242 | (1.08) | Fewer Americans believe they have healthy mouths |

---

Table L.2 classifies the approach to various topics in two ways. "Interest" reflects the combined weights for both papers on each of the four value dimensions. "Concern" reflects the difference between potentially positive and negative papers.

---

**Table L.2. Overall interest and level of concern in four value dimensions in dentistry: means (standard deviations).**

| | Technology | Income | Ethics | Oral Health |
|---|---|---|---|---|
| **Interest** | 6.742 | 6.498 | 6.711 | 6.392 |
| | (1.83) | (2.04) | (1.71) | (1.80) |
| **Concern** | 0.417 | 0.340 | -0.048 | -0.086 |
| | (1.510) | (1.45) | (1.36) | (1.39) |

---

Respondents said they would be slightly more inclined to read about technology and ethics than financial matters or oral health of patients. These differences were statistically significant (F = 3.701, p = 0.01), with all *post hoc* contrasts showing significant differences at p = 0.05. All of the gaps between topic groups were individually significant by the Scheffé and Duncan multiple-range tests.

However, the picture is different when considering the personal engagement in these four areas. The extent to which respondents care whether the story is likely to be positive or negative is a measure of concern with which direction the value is trending. Again there was an overall statistically significant difference (F = 15.404, p < 0.001) with all contrasts being significant.

The strength of concern is greater than the strength of interest, and the order of the topics differs. The interest in technique and income impact on respondents' practices is much stronger than concern over issues in ethics or oral health outcomes. This mirrors the result found in the factor analysis. These effects are shown in Figure L.1. The point to focus on is the difference (positive or negative) that each value exhibits from neutral. The greatest level of concern is with technology and income.

---

Figure L.1. **Level of concern (value) over dental issues.**

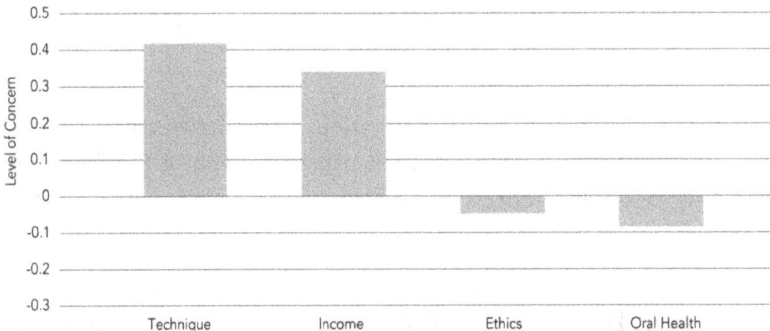

The directional measure of concern (above or below the neutral line) tells another story: the extent to which the value is seen as an opportunity or an obligation. Values above the neutral line indicate a preference for seeking positive or confirming information; values below the neutral line indicate a recognition that negative articles should be avoided. It is expected that there will be a preference for positive information, and this was observed in the cases of technology and dentists' income, as these signal areas of opportunity. It is also expected that attention to obligations—those areas where negative news is more likely than positive news—will be present, but less pronounced.

It is also expected that there will be individual differences regarding whether ethics or technology, for example, are considered to be opportunities or obligations. In Figure L.2, it is apparent that the spread on this question is normally distributed. Values to the right in the graph signal preference for positive information. Most respondents were largely neutral with regard to ethics, with slightly more avoiding the negative and thus signaling that ethics is an obligation. By contrast, although also spread, perceptions of technology show that this represents an opportunity.

## Figure L.2. Obligation or opportunity for dental issues.

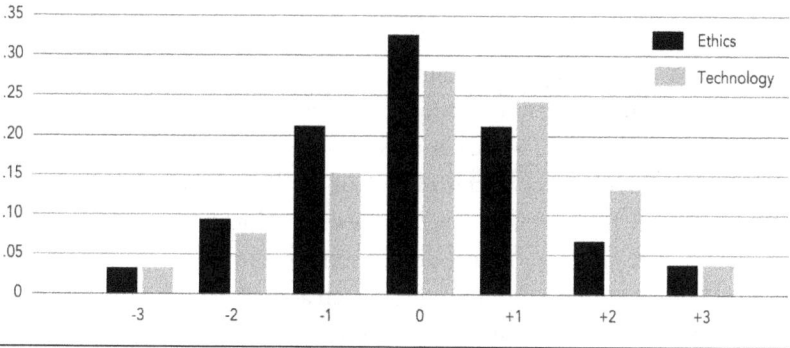

There were no significant associations for either level of interest or amount of concern over the four topic areas investigated and age of respondents, the size of the communities where they practice, their estimate of the proportion of their colleagues who overtreat, or whether they identified as general dentists, specialists, educators, or were retired. Respondents who completed the survey in a venue sponsored by the American College of Dentists were significantly more likely to report higher levels of interest in reading about all topics, other than dentists' incomes (p <0.001), but there were no differences in their expressions of concern for favorable or unfavorable reports.

## Discussion

Based on surveys of 265 dentists in seven settings it appears that dentists are more concerned about the technical and income dimensions of practice than the ethical or oral health outcome dimensions. They are more likely to favor positive reports than negative ones about the first two topics. This would be consistent with classifying the former as opportunities, where further attention promises advantages. Ethics and oral health outcomes tended slightly in the direction of obligations, where a certain level of attention is needed but "adequate." They were more concerned to avoid the negative than to seek the positive.

The ranking of value concerns across technology, income, ethics, and oral health discovered in this project very nearly matches the distribution typically seen among courses offered and state and regional dental conventions.

This separation into two types of values is consistent with a study in a previous publication (Chambers, 2015) where eight cases were presented to both dentists and patients. Dentists were asked to indicate the likelihood of their engaging in several different actions and patients were asked to state their expectations that their dentist would select various behaviors. Both reported the strength of reasons for their preferred actions. A factor analysis identified a statistically significant pattern of preferences, with dentists oriented toward the technical set of responses or toward control of actions taking place in the office while patients focused on health outcomes.

One hears cynical characterizations of dentists as being motivated by economic gain. For example, the *U.S. News & World Report* surveys have placed the profession at or near the top in terms of American JOBS and some dental schools and other groups are now creating "success" programs. The annual American Dental Education Association survey of graduating seniors has asked for years what motivated students to seek a career in the profession. The results have been stable and reflect a blend of several values. The top values in 2017 were service (94%), income expectations (90%), and "doing dentistry" (89%). If we identify "doing dentistry" with technology, these results are similar to those reported here. Improving the oral health outcomes in specific communities ranks as a low value, generally less than 25%.

The professions generally have been defined in terms of self-management, specialized knowledge and skill, and service. Increasingly service is being characterized in terms of economic transactions and skill is being replaced by control of technology. William Sullivan (2005), who led the most recent round of studies regarding the professions of medicine, nursing, engineering, law, and the clergy for the Carnegie Foundation for the Advancement of Teaching, identified emerging technology as the greatest threat to professionalism in America. It permits others to "buy into" professional status, spawning the proliferation of "soft professions" and fragmenting traditional values, especially those concerning service. It privileges success over service. Technology also favors an approach based on acute care. Oral health, by contrast, is predominantly a chronic disease.

The distinction between ethics as an opportunity or an obligation has not been considered previously in the literature. It is, however, an established concept in the psychology and management field. Frederick Herzberg (1968) noted half a century ago that some incentives, such as safe working conditions and freedom from harassment (which he called hygiene factors), affect performance only when they are lacking. Others, such as income and job challenge (which he called motivators), are of little value at the low end but kick in at higher values. There is virtually no limit to how much additional motivators can enhance performance. For the majority of Americans, oral health is in the hygiene category. It only becomes a concern when there is an acute deficit. Ethics, legal matters, and oral health outcomes may function as hygiene factors for dentists.

In October of 2014, at the American Society for Bioethics and Humanities Affinity Group on Dentistry meeting in San Diego, a report was presented on the first 18 months of operation of the American Dental Association's ethics hotline. Forty requests were received during that period, but none from recent grads. The service was not available to staff or patients. The most common concerns were: (a) determination of when the legal relationship with a patient begins (discharging or refusing treatment); (b) insurance and billing; (c) competition from former associates and associates taking patients when they leave a practice; (d) senior dentists resisting standards of care by associates; (e) delegation of duties; and (f) prescription writing for nonpatients. In almost all cases, the calling dentist was the "victim" of presumed bad ethics on the part of others. The hotline has been discontinued due to lack of use by dentists.

There have been attempts to reposition ethics as a motivator in dentistry. Jim Rule and Mickey Bebeau's book *Dentists Who Care* (2005) is an inspiring collection of stories about dentists whose lives have been dedicated to raising the standard of the profession. In the spring of 2008, the entire theme of the *Journal of the American College of Dentists* was devoted to "positive ethics." There are associations, programs, and awards for charity care, but these tend to have a focus outside the office and other than for regular interactions with patients. There is discussion about requiring courses in ethics for continuing licensure, much like radiation safety instruction for staff. One of the predictable consequences of having a disciplined license is that one will be obligated to receive ethics instruction.

One might be motivated by the opportunity to dig deeply into the intricacies of new technology or explore the fine points of a new way to finance a practice. The prospect of reading a journal article working through the details of dental ethics or the general oral health of Americans would probably strike some as an obligation more suited to others.

## References

Baron, J. (2008). *Thinking and deciding* (4th ed). Cambridge, UK: Cambridge University Press.

Cain, M. U. J., Silberman, S. L., Mahan, J. M., & Meydrech, E. F. (1983). Changes in dental students' personal needs and values. *Journal of Dental Education, 47*, 604-608.

Chambers, D. W. (2015). Do patients and dentists see ethics the same way? *Journal of the American College of Dentists, 82* (2), 31-47.

Heist, P. A. (1960). Personality characteristics of dental students. *Educational Researcher, 41*, 240-252.

Herzberg, F. (1968). One more time: How do you motivate employees? *Harvard Business Review, 46* (1), 53-62.

*Journal of the American College of Dentists* (2008). Positive Ethics [Theme issue], *75* (2), 2-48.

Kirk, B. A., Cummings, R. W., & Hackett, H. R. (1963). Personality and vocational characteristics of dental students. *Personality and Guidance Journal, 41*, 522-527.

Kress, G. C., Hasegawa, T. K., Jr., & Guo, I. Y. (1995). A survey of ethical dilemmas and practical problems encountered by practicing dentists. *Journal of the American Dental Association, 126* (11), 1554-1562.

Linn, E. L. (1968). Service to others and economic gain as professional objectives of dental students. *Journal of Dental Education, 32*, 76-81.

Manhold, J. H., Shatin, L., & Manhold, B. S. (1963). Comparison of interest, needs and selected personality factors of dental and medical students. *Journal of the American Dental Association, 63*, 601-605.

McDonald, S. P., Siler, W. M., & Isenberg, B. P. (1985). Analysis of personality traits of the contemporary dental student. *Journal of Dental Education, 49*, 579-583.

More, D. M. (1961). The dental student: Personality patterns of entering dental students. *Journal of the American College of Dentists, 29*, 1-93.

Mozer, J. E, Lloyd, C., & Puente, E. S. (1988). GB/polar personality patterns of senior dental students. *Journal of Dental Education, 52*, 452-457.

Ross, L., & Nisbett, R. E. (2011). *The person and the situation: Perspective of social psychology.* London, UK: Pinter & Martin.

Rule, J. T., & Bebeau, M. J. (2005). *Dentists who care: Inspiring stories of professional commitment.* Chicago, IL: Quintessence.

Schwartz, R. H., & Shenoy, S. (1994). Personality factors related to career satisfaction among general practitioners. *Journal of Dental Education, 58,* 225-228.

Silberman, S. L. (1976). Standardization of value profiles of dental students and dental faculty. *Journal of Dental Research, 55,* 939-950.

Sullivan, W. M. (2005). *Work and integrity: The crisis and promise of professionalism in America* (2nd ed). San Francisco, CA: Jossey-Bass.

Wanchek. T., Cook, B. J., & Valachovic, R. W. (2018). Annual ADEA survey of dental school seniors: 2017 graduating class. *Journal of Dental Education, 82* (5), 524-539.

# Exhibit

## Survey Form

This research study is part of the ACD Gies Ethics Project. It is voluntary and anonymous. DO NOT PUT YOUR NAME or any identifying information on the form. Dr. Chambers will debrief the findings from others after the forms have been collected. Questions can be referred to (209) 946-7716.

Imagine yourself in your office reflecting on the profession and your dental career. A friend has sent you a list of eight journal articles he thinks raise interesting points that affect every practicing dentist on a daily basis. PDFs of the papers were sent along as well. All of the articles appeared in respected, peer-reviewed journals with high impact factors. They are research studies, not editorials. They are about dental practices like yours. Your friend says they make strong cases backed by data. Each is about six pages long, including graphs and tables.

Because of limited time available, limit your estimates to the reading you would do now, not later.

**How typical do you think you are of the average dentist?**

| *I am an ADA member, practicing > 30 hrs/wk* | → → → ☐ ☐ ☐ ☐ ☐ | *I am a little more distant from "typical"* |
|---|---|---|

| Must read now | | Not interested | | | |
|---|---|---|---|---|---|
| 5 | 4 | 3 | 2 | 1 | *Article Title* |
| ☐ | ☐ | ☐ | ☐ | ☐ | Reasons for divergence in preferred treatment plans is caused by lack of current technical training among most dentists |
| ☐ | ☐ | ☐ | ☐ | ☐ | Organized dentistry to put greater emphasis on population oral health outcomes |
| ☐ | ☐ | ☐ | ☐ | ☐ | Dentists are divided over whether to contact colleagues when there is clear evidence of gross or continuous faulty treatment |
| ☐ | ☐ | ☐ | ☐ | ☐ | Three new factors that distinguish top earning dentists from those who are less successful |
| ☐ | ☐ | ☐ | ☐ | ☐ | New and highly effective techniques are being introduced into dentistry at fastest pace in years |
| ☐ | ☐ | ☐ | ☐ | ☐ | Steady recent decline in the proportion of American adults deemed to have healthy mouths |
| ☐ | ☐ | ☐ | ☐ | ☐ | National survey reveals public trusts their dentist to have their best interests at heart |
| ☐ | ☐ | ☐ | ☐ | ☐ | Why dentists' incomes are predicted to be flat or decline in next decade because of poor business skills |

# Appendix M

# Survey of Dental Ethics Education: 2018

Published as Chambers, D. W. (2020). Survey of Dental Ethics Education: 2018. *Journal of the American College of Dentists, 87* (1), 48-58.

## Abstract

A survey was conducted of those who have responsibility for the ethics component of dental curricula in U.S. schools. Background and training of those responsible for dental ethics education were identified, as were methods of instruction, time available for such teaching, methods used, evaluation systems, and aids and barriers to learning ethical habits. Trends in publications of scholarly articles on dental education were also surveyed. Generally, there are minimal teaching and scholarship resources and these have been declining over the past ten years. It is difficult to make the case that there is a true discipline of dental ethics.

It is widely believed that the growing edge of disciplines and professions is the university. This is where each generation of professionals is trained and where scholarship develops and innovations are tested that enhance society. Of course there are other important forces such as professional organizations, the government, industry, and the market place. But any profession that rests on a weak foundation of training and scholarship will be handicapped and eventually pay a price. The central recommendation in the *Flexner Report* on medicine, the *Gies Report* on dentistry, and the *Reed Reports* on law was the same in every case: No profession can excel without a firm educational base.

The data reported here are intended as a compendium of facts relative to teaching dental ethics in schools and to the growth of the scholarly grounded discipline of dental ethics. The formal development of learning to become ethical in general is presented in the main body of the report.

## Survey of Dental Educators

A survey was conducted in early 2016 of those individuals responsible for the dental ethics curriculum in U.S. dental schools. Previous studies of this type have focused on counting the number of clock hours and characterizing the format of formal courses in dental ethics in 1982, 1988, 2000, and 2011 (Lantz et al, 2011; Odom, 1982; 1988; Odom et al, 2000). The report by Lantz, Bebeau, and Zarkowski (2011) provided a wealth of detail about the theories and perspectives and the resources and methods used in these programs.

The focus of the present study was on those individuals who teach dental ethics (their interest and formal preparation), the integration of ethics teaching in the rest of the dental curriculum, and evidence used to evaluate the impact of these courses. A copy of the survey is attached as Exhibit A at the end of this Appendix.

Prior to e-mailing the survey, a note was sent to 62 dental school deans asking them to identify the individual on their faculty responsible for ethics instruction. With several follow-up phone calls, ten deans did not make such a person available. Of the 52 nominated individuals, 49 responded, for a return rate of 94%. Fourteen of the respondents were also interviewed by phone, either because they asked for that option on the survey or because their responses were of special interest.

## Responses

Responses are presented in descriptive format, usually percentages of responses to both structured and unstructured questions. A summary observation is offered for each question or set of related questions.

### Who Teaches Dental Ethics and Why?
*Observation: Those teaching dental ethics come from a variety of backgrounds and have sketchy training.*

Dental ethics programs in schools are primarily in the hands of dentists or dental hygienists who put themselves forward for this responsibility as a supplemental activity to their other teaching or administrative duties. None has this as a full-time responsibility, and few have formal training in ethics.

## Table M.1. Professional background of those teaching dental ethics.

| | |
|---|---|
| 57% | DDS, DMD, DH |
| 17 | Psychology, social work |
| 7 | Philosophy, bioethics |
| 7 | Law |
| 4 | Basic science |
| 4 | Divinity |
| 2 | Education |

## Table M.2. Path to teaching dental ethics, influences.

| | |
|---|---|
| 31% | Chance opportunity, asked to do it, "just fell into it" |
| 24 | Always had a personal interest in the good of the profession |
| 19 | Part of administrative responsibility, position description of dean (such as student affairs) |
| 15 | Chance to fix some of the problems seen as a practitioner |
| 11 | "I am just helping out temporarily" |

## Table M.3. Preparation for teaching dental ethics.

| | |
|---|---|
| 48% | Reading, "on-the-job training," workshops |
| 24 | Formal degree or certificate program |
| 12 | Mentors |
| 8 | Legal training |
| 8 | None |

Eighty-two percent of respondents said they began learning about ethics after accepting responsibility for the dental ethics program.

## Table M.4. Time commitment to the dental ethics program.

| | |
|---|---|
| 45% | < 10% |
| 16 | 10 – 20% |
| 10 | 20 – 30% |
| 4 | 30 – 40% |
| 10 | 40 – 50% |
| 4 | > 50% |

Average = 18%, none said they were full-time teachers of dental ethics

## Structure of Formal Instructional Program

*Observation: There is no standardized understanding of what constitutes instruction in dental ethics.*

Ethics teaching remains predominantly didactic (one-to-many format) and is spread throughout the four years of dental school. Cases involving what dentists might do in practice are a significant teaching vehicle. There is a growing trend for ethics to be part of "professionalism threads." After several decades of increasing emphasis, dental ethics is now declining as a percentage of the curriculum [Tables M.1–M.5].

---

### Table M.5. Clock hours in the formal dental ethics curriculum.

22.8 Average curriculum hours for dental ethics (about half of 1% of the typical dental curriculum)

| | |
|---|---|
| 31% | First year |
| 15 | Second year |
| 19 | Third year |
| 15 | Fourth year |
| 22 | "Thread" (not a formal part of the program) |

---

Of programs reporting formal dental ethics courses, the range was from 10 to 131 hours.

Sixty percent of programs have ethics instruction in either three or all years of their programs.

Dental students often feel that the time devoted to ethics instruction is excessive (Wanchek et al, 2018). On a list of courses, time devoted to selected areas of education and training: ethics 11% excessive, second only to biomedical sciences.

The clock hours for dental ethics in various past years were recorded from the previously published papers identified at the beginning of this section.

"Thread" approaches to teaching dental ethics are grounded on the premise that there is no identifiable formal teaching because "ethics is taught everywhere." This includes expectations for mention in oral diagnosis and treatment planning courses, natural activity in the clinic, guest speakers, and White Coat Ceremonies and class orientation programs. The nature of ethics content and consistency across students is impossible to characterize [Table M.6].

## Figure M.1. Proportion of dental schools reporting free-standing dental ethics programs.

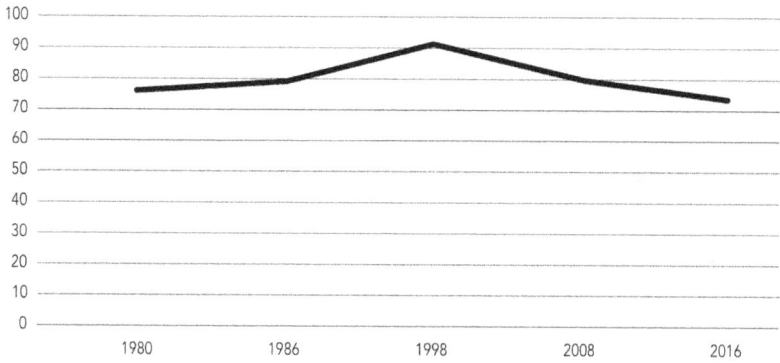

## Table M.6. Activities in formal dental ethics courses.

61%   Didactic instruction (one-to-many)

39%   Group activities

18.2   Number of cases discussed involving situations in practice

6.5   Number of cases discussed involving situations in dental school

Seventy-six percent of schools report having a Student Professionalism and Ethics Association chapter.

## Evidence of Impact of Ethics Education Programs

*Observation: There is no firm evidence that ethics education programs have an impact* [Tables M.7–M.10].

## Table M.7. How are students evaluated in dental ethics courses? [Multiple evaluation methods are used: what proportion of programs use each of these methods?]

50%   Attendance, participation

45   Multiple-choice and other exams

45   Written cases reports, analyses

19   Self-reflection

10   Student ratings of the course

5   Presentations, group skits

## Table M.8. How are students evaluated for ethics in the clinic? [Multiple evaluation methods are used]

48% No evaluation
24 "Professionalism" is part of the daily grade
5 Competency tests for ethics
5 Incident reports

## Table M.9. How does the school evaluate the level of ethical performance of students?

86% There is no system in place for such an evaluation
10 Ethics councils investigate complaints
7 "Informally"
5 Ethical rounds

## Table M.10. How does the school evaluate the ethics of its graduates?

83% No such evaluation
10 Self-report surveys

## Issues in Teaching Ethics in Dental Schools

*Observation: Students' lack of ethical knowledge or reflective skills is not considered to be a problem in the school or later in practice.* [Tables M.11–M.13]

## Table M.11. Salient characteristics affecting how dental ethics is taught and practiced in schools.

**Positive Factors**

10 Dedicated and knowledgeable speakers and facilitators
9 Support from chairs and administration
7 American College of Dentists, state organizations, American Dental Association resources
4 Student-led organizations

**Negative Factors**

9 Clinical requirements create wrong incentives for students
9 School appears to sanction commercialism
4 Clinical faculty are poor role models
3 Ethics course director does not have enough time
3 Mechanism for handling ethical violations is a mystery or does not exist

## Table M.12. What are the major ethical issues?

**In Dental Schools**

| | |
|---|---|
| 25 | Cheating on written tests |
| 14 | Pressure for clinical productivity, requirements |
| 8 | Faculty present diverse treatments for cases |
| 8 | Lack of civility, professionalism |
| 7 | One-shot initial licensure examinations |
| 6 | Showing respect for patients |
| 3 | Quality of students |
| 3 | Substance abuse |
| 3 | Educational debt |

**In Practice**

| | |
|---|---|
| 21 | Overtreatment |
| 14 | Commercialism, marketing, production |
| 14 | Serving only those who can pay going rate |
| 13 | Professionalism with respect to patients |
| 8 | Fraud, cheating |
| 6 | Low quality standards |
| 5 | Alternative practice models based on nondentist control |
| 3 | Educational debt |
| 2 | Substance abuse |

## Table M.13. Where does the responsibility lie for improving ethics in dentistry?

| | |
|---|---|
| 9 | Leadership in organized dentistry |
| 3 | Human nature of students and practitioners |
| 2 | The schools |

## The Dental Ethics Literature

*Observation: The literature in dental ethics does not reflect a distinct and cumulatively growing discipline.*

It is possible to sketch a picture of dental ethics as a discipline by summarizing the literature in this field. There are literally hundreds of case analyses where a particular situation is taken as a dilemma and interpreted from the perspective of various normative standards. There must be even more editorials inveighing against various specific abuses or urging one's colleagues to take a higher tone.

The literature of concern here includes peer-reviewed papers structured on the standards of empirical research or philosophical argumentation. A Google Scholar search was conducted on "dental ethics" and "dentistry, academic integrity." Papers judged to be part of the "discipline of dental ethics" published between 2000 and 2018 were selected. These papers are characterized below and listed as Exhibit B.

Seventy-four papers met the inclusion criterion. These fell roughly equally in three topic categories: (a) experiences teaching dental ethics—topics and method; (b) theoretical papers intended to define the boundaries and nature of dental ethics; and (c) empirical studies describing the incidence of interesting practices and questionable behaviors, especially of students.

Figure M.2 shows the trend in publications for the period 2000 to 2015 for educational method, theory, and empirical publications in dental ethics. The historical pattern is similar to that seen for clock hours of instruction in dental ethics. There was a rise in academic work on dental ethics, peaking about ten years ago and then declining. That pattern, combined with the tiny number of papers published compared with other disciplines, makes it difficult to speak of a free-standing and sustaining discipline of dental ethics.

**Figure M.2. Numbers of publications in dental ethics by topic and publication date.**

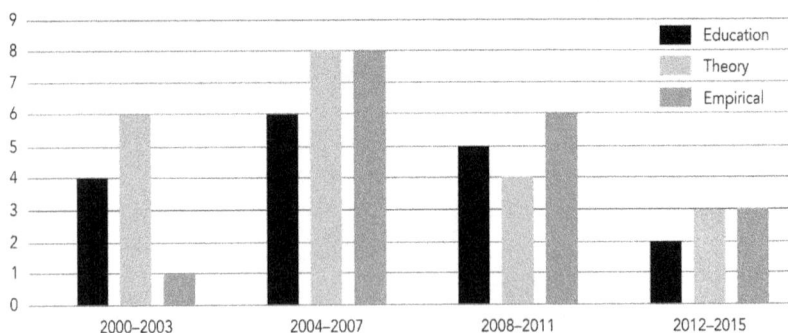

Google Scholar reports the number of citations for each paper published. Papers that described experience with various, usually innovative, methods or social issues covered in dental ethics courses were referenced by other scholars an average of 21.3 times. Articles intended to define the field of dental ethics or distinguish it from other branches of ethics or bioethics were referenced only 10.2 times on average. Reports of surveys or counts of ethical incidents were cited most often. If a paper mentioned behavior such as volunteering or presented catalogues of ethical issues identified by students, such papers were referenced by other scholars an average of 17.2 times. The literature on cheating in dental schools was more popular, being cited an average of 46.3 times per published paper. This confirms a general impression that the profession is interested in questionably ethical conduct among students.

The 74 articles studied were authored by 51 individuals or teams. There were only two cases where authors were on more than one team, most joint authorship being the result of working together at a single institution. Forty-two authors (83%) published a single paper during this period. Only one author published in each of the four time segments studied and only one author wrote in the three areas of education, theory, and empirical studies.

The list of publications in dental ethics was cross-tabulated with the survey data on teaching ethics in dental schools. Twelve cases of individuals affiliated with hygiene programs or dental schools outside the United States were set aside. Of those remaining, 25% of papers were published by individuals who teach dental ethics. Of those who teach dental ethics, only 12% have published.

## Reflections

Unlike periodontics, oral diagnosis, or care for patients with disabilities, there is no academic discipline of dental ethics. Much of the formal curricular content is borrowed from bioethics or based on personal interpretation of codes. The cadre of those who teach ethics turns over regularly and consists of those whose predominant relationship is with practice or teaching in other subjects. Evaluation of the impact of ethics instruction is often informal and there have been no rigorous studies of the effect of dental school experiences on ethics in practice. The trend in the past decade has been toward reducing the number of hours devoted to ethics and to "integrating" it into the educational program as an assumed responsibility of everyone, regardless of their training or interest in the field.

The literature in ethics is predominantly personal opinions about isolated practices about which there is concern, with a somewhat more formal genera of selected cases (dilemmas) analyzed from the perspective of normative principles. The peer-reviewed literature contributed by scholars making cumulative advances to the field is small and decreasing.

## References

Lantz, M. S., Bebeau, M. J., & Zarkowski, P. (2011). The status of ethics teaching and learning in U.S. dental schools. *Journal of Dental Education, 75* (10), 1295-1309.

Odom, J. G. (1982). Formal ethics instruction in dental education. *Journal of Dental Education, 46* (9), 553-557.

Odom, J. G. (1988). The status of dental ethics instruction. *Journal of Dental Education, 52* (6), 306-308.

Odom, J. G., Beemsterboer, P. L., Pate, T. D., & Haden, N. K. (2000). Revisiting the status of dental ethics instruction. *Journal of Dental Education, 64* (11), 772-774.

Wanchek, T., Cook, B. J., & Valachovic, R. W. (2018). Annual ADEA survey of dental school seniors: 2017 graduating class. *Journal of Dental Education, 82* (5), 524-539.

---

# Exhibit A

## *Survey Used to Collect Information from Those Who Teach Ethics in U.S. Dental Schools*

### Ethics Project: Survey of Dental Ethics Educators

Name:                          School:
E-mail address:          Phone number:

**Questions about you...**

1.  Self-describe your role in dental ethics.

2.  When did you first start thinking of yourself as being interested in ethics? Was there a specific trigger?

3.  How have you prepared yourself to teach dental ethics?

4.  In addition to your role in ethics, what else do you do—teach other subjects, practice?

5.  What proportion of your time are you acting as an ethicist? _____

6.  How do you engage in ethics outside of teaching at your school?

7.  What help do you need to be a more efficient dental ethicist?

**Questions about the ethics program at your school...**

| Curriculum | Total clock hours | Hours in small group work | # Cases for issues in practice | # Cases for issues in school |
|---|---|---|---|---|
| First year | _____ | _____ | _____ | _____ |
| Second year | _____ | _____ | _____ | _____ |
| Third year | _____ | _____ | _____ | _____ |
| Fourth year | _____ | _____ | _____ | _____ |

Is there a SPEA club? Is it active?

Changes to ethics curriculum in past five years

**Tracking Outcomes...**

How do you monitor the success of your program?

1.  Students in ethics courses

2.  Students' ethical behavior elsewhere in the school

3.  The overall ethical tone of the school

4.  Graduates once they are in practice

5.  What help and resources do you get to support your ethics program?

6.  Is there any structure or practice, outside of your teaching, in place in your school that supports or detracts from what you are doing in teaching ethics?

7.  Is there any structure or practice, outside of your teaching, in place in dental practice that supports or detracts from what you are doing in teaching ethics?

**Ethical issues facing the profession . . .**
1. List the three top ethical issues in your opinion

*In the school...*

A.


B.


C.

*In dentistry...*

A.


B.


C.


What could be done by you and the profession to address these?



**General comments...**
Please e-mail your response to me at dchamber@pacific.edu or call me at
(415) 929-6438.

Check as appropriate:

☐   There is more I would like to say. Let's set up a time for a more in-depth phone
     interview.

☐   If the survey is not clear, we can set up a phone interview or you can e-mail me
     for clarification.

☐   I am not the one you want to be talking to here. I have passed this request on to


_____at (e-mail) _____

# Exhibit B

## Bibliography of Dental Ethics Publications, 2000–2018

### Experience Teaching Dental Ethics (topics and methods)

Zarkowski, P., & Graham, B. (2001). A four-year curriculum in professional ethics and law for dental students. *Journal of the American College of Dentists, 68* (2), 22-26.

Bebeau, M. J. (2002). The Defining Issues Test and the Four Component Model: Contributions to professional education. *Journal of Moral Education, 31* (3), 271-295.

Christie, C. R., Bowen, D. M., & Paarmann, C. S. (2003). Curriculum evaluation of ethical reasoning and professional responsibility. *Journal of Dental Education, 67* (1), 55-63.

Turner, S. P., & Beemsterboer, P. L. (2003). Enhancing academic integrity: Formulating effective honor codes. *Journal of Dental Education, 67* (10), 1122-1129.

Bertolami, C. N. (2004). Why our ethics curricula don't work. *Journal of Dental Education, 68* (4), 414-425.

Beemsterboer, P. L. (2006). Developing an ethic of access to care in dentistry. *Journal of Dental Education, 70* (11), 1212-1216.

Gadbury-Amyot, C. C., Simmer-Beck, M., McCunniff, M., & Williams, K. B. (2006). Using a multifaceted approach including community-based service-learning to enrich formal ethics instruction in a dental school setting. *Journal of Dental Education, 70* (6), 652-661.

Graham, B. S. (2006). Educating dental students about oral health care access disparities. *Journal of Dental Education, 70* (11), 1208-1211.

Kacerik, M. G., Prajer, R. G., & Conrad, C. (2006). Ethics instruction in the dental hygiene curriculum. *Journal of Dental Hygiene, 80* (1), 9.

Christie, C., Bowen, D., & Paarmann, C. (2007). Effectiveness of faculty training to enhance clinical evaluation of student competence in ethical reasoning and professionalism. *Journal of Dental Education, 71* (8), 1048-1057.

Bebeau, M. J. (2009). Enhancing professionalism using ethics education as part of a dental licensure board's disciplinary action. Part 1. An evidence-based process. *Journal of the American College of Dentists, 76* (2), 38-50.

Bebeau, M. J. (2009). Enhancing professionalism using ethics education as part of a dental licensure board's disciplinary action. Part 2. Evidence of the process. *Journal of the American College of Dentists, 76* (3), 32-45.

Brondani, M. A., & Rossoff, L. P. (2010). The "hot seat" experience: A multifaceted approach to the teaching of ethics in a dental curriculum. *Journal of Dental Education, 74* (11), 1220-1229.

Kalenderian, E., Skoulas, A., Timothé, P., & Friedland, B. (2010). Integrating leadership into a practice management curriculum for dental students. *Journal of Dental Education, 74* (5), 464-471.

Chambers, D. W. (2011). Developing a self-scoring comprehensive instrument to measure Rest's Four-Component Model of moral behavior: The Moral Skills Inventory. *Journal of Dental Education, 75* (1), 23-35.

Lantz, M. S., Bebeau, M. J., & Zarkowski, P. (2011). The status of ethics teaching and learning in U.S. dental schools. *Journal of Dental Education, 75* (10), 1295-1309.

Brondani, M. A. (2012). Teaching social responsibility through community service-learning in predoctoral dental education. *Journal of Dental Education, 76* (5), 609-619.

Schwartz, B., & Bohay, R. (2012). Can patients help teach professionalism and empathy to dental students? Adding patient videos to a lecture course. *Journal of Dental Education, 76* (2), 174-184.

Donate-Bartfield, E., Lobb, W. K., & Roucka, T. M. (2014). Teaching culturally sensitive care to dental students: A multidisciplinary approach. *Journal of Dental Education, 78* (3), 454-464.

Quick, K. K. (2016). The role of self- and peer assessment in dental students' reflective practice using standardized patient encounters. *Journal of Dental Education, 80* (8), 924-929.

## What is Dental Ethics?

Beemsterboer, P. L., Odom, J. G., Pate, T. D., & Haden, N. K. (2000). Issues of academic integrity in U.S. dental schools. *Journal of Dental Education, 64* (12), 833-838.

Chaves, J. F. (2000). Assessing ethics and professionalism in dental education. *Journal of the Indiana Dental Association, 79* (1), 16-21.

Odom, J. G., Beemsterboer, P. L., Pate, T. D., & Haden, N. K. (2000). Revisiting the status of dental ethics instruction. *Journal of Dental Education, 64* (11), 772-774.

Ozar, D. T. (2000). Dental ethics as an intellectual discipline: Taking the next step. *Journal of the American College of Dentists, 67* (1), 30-34.

Chambers, D. W. (2002). The ethics of experimenting in dental practice. *Dental Clinics, 46* (1), 29-44.

Yeager, A. L. (2002). Dental ethics for the 21st century: Learning from the Charter on Medical Professionalism. *Journal of the American College of Dentists, 69* (3), 53-60.

Whitehead, A. W., & Novak, K. F. (2003). A model for assessing the ethical environment in academic dentistry. *Journal of Dental Education, 67* (10), 1113-1121.

Welie, J. V. (2004). Is dentistry a profession? Part 1. Professionalism defined. *Journal of the Canadian Dental Association, 70* (8), 529-532.

Welie, J. V. (2004). Is dentistry a profession? Part 2. The hallmarks of professionalism. *Journal of the Canadian Dental Association, 70* (9), 599-602.

Welie, J. V. (2004). Is dentistry a profession? Part 3. Future challenges. *Journal of the Canadian Dental Association, 70* (10), 675-678.

Chambers, D. W. (2006). Distributive justice. In J. V. M. Welie (Ed). *Justice in oral health care: Ethical and educational perspectives* (pp. 145-170). Milwaukee, WI: Marquette University Press.

Chambers, D. W. (2006). Moral communities. *Journal of Dental Education, 70* (11), 1226-1234.

Chambers, D. W. (2007). A primer on dental ethics: Part II-moral behavior. *Journal of the American College of Dentists, 74* (4), 38-51.

Masella, R. S. (2007). Renewing professionalism in dental education: Overcoming the market environment. *Journal of Dental Education, 71* (2), 205-216.

Patthoff, D. E. (2007). The need for dental ethicists and the promise of universal patient acceptance: Response to Richard Masella's "Renewing professionalism in dental education." *Journal of Dental Education, 71* (2), 222-226.

Lovas, J. G., Lovas, D. A., & Lovas, M. P. (2008). Mindfulness and professionalism in dentistry. *Journal of Dental Education, 72* (9), 998-1009.

Chambers, D. W. (2009). Finding our place in dental ethics. *Pennsylvania Dental Journal, 76* (3), 27-31.

Nash, D. A. (2010). Ethics, empathy, and the education of dentists. *Journal of Dental Education, 74* (6), 567-578.

Fricker, J. P., Kiley, M., Townsend, G., & Trevitt, C. (2011). Professionalism: What is it, why should we have it and how can we achieve it? *Australian Dental Journal, 56* (1), 92-96.

Ozar, D. T. (2012). Professionalism: Challenges for dentistry in the future. *Journal of Forensic Odonto-Stomatology, 30* (S1), 72-84.

Zijlstra-Shaw, S., Robinson, P. G., & Roberts, T. (2012). Assessing professionalism within dental education: The need for a definition. *European Journal of Dental Education, 16* (1), e128-e136.

Chambers, D. W. (2013). Would someone please explain what it means to be ethical? *CDA Journal, 41* (7), 493-497.

Chambers, D. W. (2015). Moral communities and moral leadership. *Journal of the American College of Dentists, 82* (4), 60-75.

Chambers, D. W. (2016). Moral priming and the ACD basic rule. *Journal of the American College of Dentists, 83* (1), 38-43.

Chambers, D. W. (2016). Is professionalism a spectator sport or a contact sport? *Journal of the American College of Dentists, 83* (4), 27-42.

Crutchield, P., Johnson, J. C., Brandt, L., & Fleming, D. (2016). The limits of deontology in dental ethics education. *International Journal of Ethics Education, 1* (2), 183-200.

Holden, A. C. L. (2016). Dentistry's social contract and the loss of professionalism. *Australian Dental Journal, 62* (1), 79-83.

## Empirical Studies of Dentists' and Students' Ethical Behavior

King, J. (2001). Consent: The patients' view—a summary of findings from a study of patients' perceptions of their consent to dental care. *British Dental Journal, 191* (7), 36-40.

Acharya, S. (2005). The ethical climate in academic dentistry in India: Faculty and student perceptions. *Journal of Dental Education, 69* (6), 671-680.

Sharp, H. M., Kuthy, R. A., & Heller, K. E. (2005). Ethical dilemmas reported by fourth-year dental students. *Journal of Dental Education, 69* (10), 1116-1122.

Zijlstra-Shaw, S., Kropmans, T. J. B., & Tams, J. (2005). Assessment of professional behaviour—a comparison of self-assessment by first year dental students and assessment by staff. *British Dental Journal, 198*, 165-171.

de Freitas, S. F. T., Kovaleski, D. F., Boing, A. F., & de Oliveira, W. F. (2006). Stages of moral development among Brazilian dental students. *Journal of Dental Education, 70* (3), 296-306.

Nath, C., Schmidt, R., & Gunel, E. (2006). Perceptions of professionalism vary most with educational rank and age. *Journal of Dental Education, 70* (8), 825-834.

Andrews, K. G., Smith, L. A., Henzi, D., & Demps, E. (2007). Faculty and student perceptions of academic integrity at U.S. and Canadian dental schools. *Journal of Dental Education, 71* (8), 1027-1039.

Ardenghi, D. M., Roth, W-M., & Pozzer-Ardenghi, L. (2007). Responsibility in dental praxis: An activity theoretical perspective. *Journal of Workplace Learning, 19* (4), 240-255.

Chambers, D. W. (2007). Small ethics. *Journal of the American College of Dentists, 74* (1), 27-35.

Boyd, M. A., Roth, K., Ralls, S. A., & Chambers, D. W. (2008). Beginning the discussion of commercialism in dentistry. *Journal of the California Dental Association, 36* (1), 57-65.

Chambers, D. W. (2008). Large ethics. *Journal of the American College of Dentists, 75* (2), 36-48.

Sharp, H. M., & Kuthy, R. A. (2008). What do dental students learn in an ethics course? An analysis of student-reported learning outcomes. *Journal of Dental Education, 72* (12), 1450-1457.

Ardenghi, D. M. (2009). Dentists' ethical practical knowledge: A critical issue for dental education. *European Journal of Dental Education, 13* (2), 69-72.

Brands, W. G., Bronkhorst, E. M., & Welie, J. V. (2010). The chasm between knowing and choosing the ethical course of action: A survey of dental students in the Netherlands. *International Dental Journal, 60* (5), 321-328.

Chambers, D. W. (2010). Dentistry from the perspective of the San Francisco phone book. *CDA Journal, 38* (11), 801-808.

Brands, W. G., Bronkhorst, M. E., & Welie, J. V. M. (2011). Professional ethics and cynicism amongst Dutch dental students. *European Journal of Dental Education, 15* (4), 205-209.

Ford, P. J., & Hughes, C. (2012). Academic integrity and plagiarism: Perceptions and experience of staff and students in a school of dentistry: A situational analysis of staff and student perspectives. *European Journal of Dental Education, 16* (1), e180-e186.

Zijlstra-Shaw, S., Roberts, T. E., & Robinson, P. G. (2013). Perceptions of professionalism in dentistry—a qualitative study. *British Dental Journal, 215*, e18.

Chambers, D. W. (2015). Do patients and dentists see ethics the same way? *Journal of the American College of Dentists, 82* (2), 31-47.

Chambers, D. W. (2017). What dentists do when they recognize faulty treatment: To tattle or build moral community. *Journal of the American College of Dentists, 84* (2), 32-66.

Chambers, D. W. (2018). Disciplined dental licenses: An empirical study. *Journal of the American College of Dentists, 85* (2), 30-39.

*Apologies are extended to authors who were not identified in the computerized search and to those whose work was judged to represent case analysis or advocacy for a specific topic or practice when the author had a different purpose in mind.*

# Appendix N

# Ethical Attribution Effect Hypothesis

Published as Chambers, D. W. (2020). Ethical Attribution Effect Hypothesis. *Journal of the American College of Dentists, 87* (1), 59-65.

## Abstract

A body of literature in social psychology on the "fundamental attribution error" has established that the motives for behavior are attributed to ourselves and to others in a complex fashion, depending on whether the behavior is viewed as positive or negative. A parallel and balanced form survey was completed by 62 dentists to test the hypotheses that personal positive moral behavior and negative performance by others are attributed to the actor's character and that negative personal outcomes and positive performance by others are attributed to circumstances. The results confirm these hypotheses. These findings suggest that professional ethics could be better strengthened by focusing on building supporting situations in the profession rather than attempting to change human nature.

Despite there being no published evidence to support this view, it is often heard that young dentists are less ethical than more established ones because of their educational debt (Chambers et al, 2002). (It is possible that dentists two or three generations before said much the same thing.) In the absence of a stable yardstick to measure these sorts of claims and without any reasonable body of data, the problem appears to be fundamentally one of perceptions. And perceptions are facts that can be measured.

When it is judged that a particular practitioner performed below standard it still remains to answer questions about why that happened. Was it because of incompetence or a weak moral foundation (characteristics of the dentist)? Or was the undesirable outcome heavily influenced or even compelled by circumstances? For example, the patient may have been uncooperative, the materials defective, or a staff member may have misidentified the patient or procedure. When we make ethical judgments, we typically go behind the behavior in an effort to understand its causes.

Sometimes we have the opportunity to resolve these "character or circumstances" problems if we can make the right kind of multiple observations. If the practitioner is associated with repeated cases of substandard work under a variety of circumstances, we feel confident in calling this a case of questionable character. By contrast, if multiple practitioners are experiencing difficulties in similar instances, we lean toward explanations in terms of circumstances.

Parallel logic applies to exemplary performance as well. If a dentist exhibits technical excellence or leadership or service across multiple situations, we attribute this to something special in the practitioner. If the quality of care in one military dental unit is consistently outstanding or the proportion of dentists in a state who support organized dentistry is routinely above the national average, we attribute that to circumstance (the program or leadership in the state) and not to individual dentists.

The theory that underlies this pattern is one of the best-established in the field of social psychology. Virtually every textbook in the field contains a discussion of what is known as the "fundamental attribution error." The original research was done by Edward Jones and Victor Harris (1967). They asked subjects to comment on the attributes of a person who had written an essay about Fidel Castro. Opinions regarding the writer changed if subjects were told that the writer could have written anything he or she wanted or if the topic had been assigned. Since then, hundreds of papers have demonstrated that we attribute different motives to others depending on how much control we think they had over their performance (Malle, 2006).

The label "fundamental attribution error" entered the field a decade later (Ross, 1977). The construct is now fairly well understood. The issue is one of interpreting the source or reason for observed behavior (character or circumstances). Two factors have influence over this interpretation: (a) who performed the act; and (b) whether the performance is regarded as positive or negative. These two factors interact as shown in Table N.1.

## Table N.1. Fundamental attribution error matrix.

|  | Self as agent | Other as agent |
| --- | --- | --- |
| Positive performance | Character | Circumstances |
| Negative performance | Circumstances | Character |

Bertram Gawronski (2004) summarized the evidence on the fundamental attribution error where respondents were asked to judge the character of others based on their moral behavior rather than their skill or values. "A common finding in this paradigm is that perceivers generally attribute immoral dispositions to immoral behaving targets even when they learned that situation factors have a strong impact on the tendency to engage in immoral behavior" (p. 201).

This line of research is suggestive, but it fails to test the full fundamental attribution error model. It leaves out attributions of one's own moral character. There have been no studies of the fundamental attribution error as it applies specifically in dentistry.

The research reported here tests two hypotheses.

1. Dentists will attribute positive moral behavior to their own ethical character and their own negative moral behavior to circumstances.
2. Dentists will attribute the positive moral behavior of others to circumstances and others' negative moral behavior to the ethical character of others.

## Materials and Methods

A survey was conducted to test multiple examples of short descriptions of moral behavior encountered in dentistry. These incidents were expressed as short phrases, such as "A student is near the bottom of the class and regularly cuts corners in some areas of patient care because..." or "Someone you have heard of keeps getting on various committees in the component society and state association due to..." These are examples of negative and positive behaviors attributable to others. Negative and positive personal incidents would include: "If you take a 'temporary' position in an office with high pay for volume and marginal quality on a quota system, it would be because of..." and "You attend a health fair screening sponsored by the local component when a friend asked you to." For each such incident, respondents were asked to indicate on a five-point scale the degree to which they felt the behavior described should be attributed to the character of the actor or to circumstances.

The items were developed in pretests with 24 potential situations. The ten incidents eventually selected were chosen because they elicited a range of attitudes regarding how ethical the behavior was thought to be. Very obviously unethical behavior and cases of exemplary conduct were excluded. Two items were retained but not scored. One dealt with justifiable criticism and the other with overtreatment. These were included in the survey as distractors and attributed to distant acquaintances.

Two versions of the survey were prepared (see Exhibit). One contained two items each for positive and negative behavior attributed to another and two positive and two negative items attributed to the person completing the survey. The second version of the form contained the same behaviors, but attribution to "self" was switched to "other" and vice versa. This was necessary to prevent bias caused by making some items more praise- or blame-worthy. Each item served as its own control.

Sixty-two dentists completed one or the other version of the survey in a continuing education setting devoted to dental topics. Ethics was not a theme in any testing situation. Thirty-two respondents completed one version of the survey. Thirty completed the survey with reversed attribution of agency. The research was approved in the exempt category by the Institutional Review Board at the University of the Pacific.

## Results

Because of the pairing of incidents, the total set of responses was balanced. So there were 62 cases with positive and negative outcomes attributed to self and other. A score of 10 indicated that an individual judged both items in that 2 x 2 cell as entirely attributable to the character of the agent and a score of 2 indicated that the behavior was attributed entirely to circumstances.

Means and standard deviations for four combinations of agent and moral behavior are shown in Table N.2. Results are displayed graphically in

Figure N.1. Table N.3 for the two-factorial ANOVA shows the results of testing for interaction.

## Table N.2. Means and standard deviations for combinations of agent and type of moral behavior.

|  | Self | Other |
|---|---|---|
| Positive | 5.660 | 3.896 |
|  | (1.512) | (2.484) |
| Negative | 3.501 | 5.313 |
|  | (1.842) | (2.012) |

## Figure N.1. Ethical attribution.

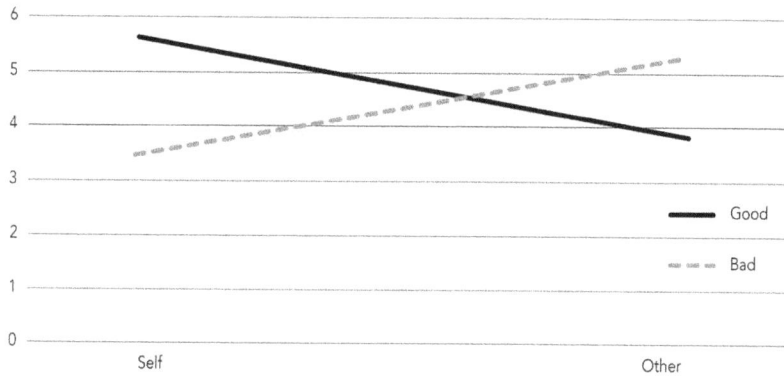

## Table N.3. The two-factor (agent and positive or negative behavior) ANOVA.

|  | MS | F | p |
|---|---|---|---|
| Self/Other | 6.974 | 1.753 | 0.187 |
| Positive/Negative | 3.271 | 0.822 | 0.365 |
| Interaction | 225.851 | 58.782 | <.001 |
| Error | 3.979 |  |  |

Considering all scored items without regard to agent or positive or negative behavior, the average score was 5.291 (SD = 1.941). A perfect balance between character and circumstances would have produced a score of 6.0. Although the overall results are near the balance point, there is a slight but statistically significant ($p < 0.01$) edge toward explanations in terms of circumstances.

Considering only those incidents where respondents answered as the moral agent, there was a strong tendency to see positive behavior as flowing from one's character and negative behavior compelled by circumstances. The t-test value for this difference was $z = 4.940$, $p < 0.001$. This difference is reflected as the vertical distance between the end points of the two lines on the left of the accompanying graph.

A similar pattern appeared on the right of the graph, but the poles are reversed. Respondents perceived positive behaviors of others as being attributed to circumstances and negative behaviors as flowing from others' character ($z = 3.423$, $p < 0.001$). This effect was stronger than for self. Personally favorable attribution of moral performance was greater for self than the attribution effect for others. This was tested by the ratio of squared t-values ($F = 2.083$, $p < 0.05$).

## Discussion

Both hypotheses were confirmed. Dentists in this study attributed positive moral behavior to their own ethical character and negative moral behavior to circumstances. At the same time they attributed the positive moral behavior of others to circumstances and negative moral behavior to the ethical character of others. The former effect was slightly but significantly stronger than the latter. Overall there was a slight, but significant, tendency to attribute moral incidents to circumstances.

The clear disordinal interaction between agent and type of behavior shown in the graph and the ANOVA results is unusual in the literature. Research on ethics that considers only whether one is the agent or is judging others, without taking into account whether the behavior is positive or negative, will draw an incorrect conclusion that there is no effect. Similarly, assessing whether positive or negative moral behavior is attributed to character or circumstances will also draw an incorrect conclusion that there is no effect. Judgments about the sources of moral behavior are complex.

This research is consistent with the previously reported literature (Bierbrauer, 1979; Miller et al, 1974; Pietromonaco & Nisbett, 1982; Sabini & Silver, 1983; Safer, 1980). It is a logical extension of social science into dentistry.

These findings are also in line with other social science findings on moral behavior. For example, Hartshorne and May (1928) found that the perception of what is acceptable behavior varies across individuals. Someone may steal from the group resources but not from a friend. And the opposite is true for others. In the current research virtually all incidents were rated by some at both ends of the scale available.

A research team led by Daniel Ariely (2009) has explored the personal side of interpreting our own behavior in the most positive light possible. A number of studies (Ariely, 2012; Mazar & Ariely, 2006; Mazar et al, 2008) have shown that it is human nature to take more credit than we deserve and to excuse ourselves for fairly routine small transgressions. For example, more Americans confess to cheating on their taxes than the number who vote in most elections (Gabor, 1994). Rhode (2018) lists several reasons given for such adjustments between what we do and the reasons we give for doing so. For example, it is thought that the good we have done that has been unrecognized needs to be balanced. We claim, perhaps correctly, that we know more about the actual circumstances of our behavior than do others. We fear that others are taking advantage of the system. We know in most cases that the cost to others to inspect and control our biased attributions is greater than what we are dealing ourselves under the table. This research demonstrates that dentists engage in typical human behavior in giving an optimistic interpretation of the motives for their own behavior.

This project is not intended to present a cynical perspective on dental ethics. It would be irresponsible to consider this study as justifying a view that dentists act unprofessionally. The question is how moral behavior is interpreted, and then what can be done to improve professionalism based on the personal interpretations of where ethics comes from.

These results do support a nontraditional position that hoping for large improvements in moral behavior as a result of telling others about morality is likely a dead letter. Most dentists believe they are already ethical. Formal ethics instruction, especially of the theoretical type, required courses in ethics for licensure or as remediation for disciplined licenses, and editorials may not be enthusiastically received by those required to listen to such messages. Suggesting that others pay more attention to their character may look promising to others. It takes a view of ethics from the right-hand side of the graph presented above. From the perspective of those being lectured to, who will position themselves on the left-hand side of the graph, this approach would not be effective.

It is not exactly correct to refer to a fundamental attribution "error" in this case. Selective attribution of the forces that drive moral behavior is a natural effect. "Circumstances" in this case does not refer to random fluctuations in the environment. Volunteering for a health fair because a colleague asks you to or promoting questionable practices on the continuing education circuit are circumstances that can be changed by professionals. This research suggests that these indirect ethical improvements have significant potential. Some of the ways more positive context would help all dentists include: peer support, clear practice standards, listening openly to colleagues, collecting accurate data on collective moral behavior, building dental skills so more of practice is successful, leadership and role models, aspirational codes, transparency, toning down the rhetoric and praise given financial success, and arrangements that are fair for all parties.

There is evidence that attention to circumstances can have a positive effect on ethics. Leavitt and colleagues (2012) measured the ethical attitudes of Army medics in two settings. In one, the medics performed an ethics task in uniform in a briefing room. They did better on a parallel task when they were in scrubs in a hospital. Chambers (2016) measured ethical attitudes at a meeting of an organization respected for its attention to ethics and again with the same individuals in their private practices. The situation that implied that ethics matters produced the most positive ethical responses.

## References

Ariely, D. (2009). *Predictably irrational: The hidden forces that shape our decisions.* New York, NY: Harper.

Ariely, D. (2012). *The (honest) truth about dishonesty: How we lie to everyone–especially ourselves.* New York, NY: Harper.

Bierbrauer, G. (1979). Why did he do it? Attribution of obedience and the phenomenon of dispositional bias. *European Journal of Social Psychology, 9,* 67-84.

Chambers, D. W. (2016). Moral priming and the ACD basic rule. *Journal of the American College of Dentists, 83* (1), 38-43.

Chambers, D. W., Budenz, A. W., Fredekind R. E., & Nadershahi N. A. (2002). Debt and practice profiles of beginning dental practitioners. *CDA Journal, 30* (12), 909-914.

Gabor, T. (1994). *Everybody does it! Crime by the public.* Toronto, ON: University of Toronto Press.

Gawronski, B. (2004). Theory-based bias correction in dispositional inference: The fundamental attribution error is dead, long live the correspondence bias. *European Review of Social Psychology, 15,* 183-217.

Hartshorne, H., & May, M. A. (1928). *Studies in deceit.* New York, NY: Macmillan.

Jones, E. E., & Harris, V. A. (1967). The attribution of attitudes. *Journal of Experimental Social Psychology, 3* (1), 1-24.

Leavitt, K., Reynolds, S. J., Barnes, C. M., Schilpzand, P., & Hannah, S. T. (2012). Different hats, different obligations: Plural occupational identities and situated moral judgment. *Academy of Management Journal, 55* (6), 1316-1333.

Malle, B. F. (2006). The actor-observer asymmetry in attribution: A (surprising) meta-analysis. *Psychological Bulletin, 132* (6), 895-919.

Mazar, N., Amir, O., & Ariely, D. (2008). The dishonesty of honest people: A theory of self-concept maintenance. *Journal of Marketing Research, 45* (6), 633-644.

Mazar, N., & Ariely, D. (2006). Dishonesty in everyday life and its policy implications. *Journal of Public Policy & Marketing, 25* (1), 117-126.

Miller, A. G., Gillen, B., Schenker, C., & Radlove, S. (1974). The prediction and perception of obedience to authority. *Journal of Personality, 42*, 23-42.

Pietromonaco, P., & Nisbett, R. E. (1982). Swimming upstream against the fundamental attribution error: Subjects' weak generalizations from the Darley and Batson study. *Social Behavior and Personality, 10*, 1-4.

Rhode, D. L. (2018). *Cheating: Ethics in everyday life.* New York, NY: Oxford University Press.

Ross, L. (1977). The intuitive psychologist and his shortcomings: Distortions in the attribution process. In Berkowitz, L., *Advances in experimental social psychology, 10* (pp. 173-220). New York, NY: Academic Press.

Sabini, J., & Silver, M. (1983). Dispositional vs. situational interpretations of Milgram's obedience experiments. *Journal of the Theory of Social Behavior, 13*, 147-154.

Safer, M. (1980). Attributing evil to the subject, not the situation: Student reactions to Milgram's film on obedience. *Personality and Social Psychology Bulletin, 6*, 205-209.

# Exhibit

## Form A

Described below are ten examples of things some dentists do sometimes. Rate each on a scale from 1 to 5 depending on whether you think the behavior is…

5 = Entirely a matter of character, it is the way the person would always act because of who they are

1 = Entirely a matter of circumstances, the situation carries great weight in cases such as this

|   All   |   |   All   |   |   |   |
| character | | circumstances | | | |
| 5 | 4 | 3 | 2 | 1 | |
| ☐ | ☐ | ☐ | ☐ | ☐ | Reason a well-respected dentist in the community reports another dentist to the state board for gross and continuous faulty treatment is because of… |
| ☐ | ☐ | ☐ | ☐ | ☐ | If it happened you promoted an innovating treatment with weak evidence but great income potential on the continuing education circuit, that would be due to… |
| ☐ | ☐ | ☐ | ☐ | ☐ | Someone you have heard of keeps getting on various committees in the component society and state association due to… |
| ☐ | ☐ | ☐ | ☐ | ☐ | If a dentist takes a "temporarily" position in an office with high pay for volume and marginal quality on a quota system, it would be because of… |
| ☐ | ☐ | ☐ | ☐ | ☐ | You attend a health fair screening sponsored by the local component when a friend asked you to |

|   All   |   |   All   |   |   |   |
| character | | circumstances | | | |
| 5 | 4 | 3 | 2 | 1 | |
| ☐ | ☐ | ☐ | ☐ | ☐ | You are near the bottom of the class and regularly cut corners in some areas of patient care because… |
| ☐ | ☐ | ☐ | ☐ | ☐ | Some dentists volunteer occasionally at the dental school to be around the best and brightest is… |
| ☐ | ☐ | ☐ | ☐ | ☐ | If someone you had heard of was performing a molar endo for the first time in years after watching a short video "course," that would be because of… |
| ☐ | ☐ | ☐ | ☐ | ☐ | Your favorite teacher suggests performing slightly more care than the patient expects based on his judgment that it is in the patient's best interests |
| ☐ | ☐ | ☐ | ☐ | ☐ | Everyone was watching as you agreed to contribute to the group's charity fund |

## Form B

Described below are ten examples of things some dentists do sometimes. Rate each on a scale from 1 to 5 depending on whether you think the behavior is...

5 = Entirely a matter of character, it is the way the person would always act because of who they are

1 = Entirely a matter of circumstances, the situation carries great weight in cases such as this

| All character | | | All circumstances | | |
|---|---|---|---|---|---|
| 5 | 4 | 3 | 2 | 1 | |
| ☐ | ☐ | ☐ | ☐ | ☐ | Reason a well-respected dentist in the community reports another dentist to the state board for gross and continuous faulty treatment is because of... |
| ☐ | ☐ | ☐ | ☐ | ☐ | A dentist who knows the evidence is weak regularly promotes an innovative treatment approach that has great income potential on the continuing education circuit due to... |
| ☐ | ☐ | ☐ | ☐ | ☐ | You find yourself getting on various committees in the component society and state association due to... |
| ☐ | ☐ | ☐ | ☐ | ☐ | If you took a "temporarily" position in an office with high pay for volume and marginal quality on a quota system it would be because of... |
| ☐ | ☐ | ☐ | ☐ | ☐ | A dentist attends a health fair screening sponsored by the local component when a friend asked him to |

| All character | | | All circumstances | | |
|---|---|---|---|---|---|
| 5 | 4 | 3 | 2 | 1 | |
| ☐ | ☐ | ☐ | ☐ | ☐ | A student near the bottom of the class regularly cuts corners in some areas of patient care because... |
| ☐ | ☐ | ☐ | ☐ | ☐ | The reason for you to volunteer occasionally at the dental school to be around the best and brightest is... |
| ☐ | ☐ | ☐ | ☐ | ☐ | If you were performing a molar endo for the first time in years after watching a short video "course," that would be because of... |
| ☐ | ☐ | ☐ | ☐ | ☐ | Your favorite teacher suggests performing slightly more care than the patient expects based on his judgment that it is in the patient's best interests |
| ☐ | ☐ | ☐ | ☐ | ☐ | Everyone was watching as a colleague agreed he would also contribute to the group's charity fund |

# References

American College of Dentists (1932). *The status of dental journalism in the United States: Report of the Commission on Journalism of the American College of Dentists 1928-1931.* Baltimore, MD: Waverly Press.

American College of Dentists, *Journal* (1999). Professional development, *66* (4), entire issue.

American College of Dentists, *Journal* (2000). Professional development, *67* (1), entire issue.

American College of Dentists, *Journal* (2012). Continued competence, *79* (3), entire issue.

American College of Dentists, *Journal* (2015). Implied contract between profession and public, *82* (3) entire issue.

American College of Dentists, *Journal* (2017a). Commercialism and journalism in dentistry: Then and now, *84* (4), entire issue.

American College of Dentists, *Journal* (2017b). Dentistry goes to court, *84* (2), entire issue.

American College of Dentists, *Journal* (2018). Technology, *85* (2), entire issue.

American Dental Association (1866). *Transactions of the American Dental Association, Sixth Annual Meeting*, Boston, 31 July 1866. Chicago, IL: The Association.

American Dental Association (2016). *National recruitment and retention report for active licenses dentists: End of year 2015.* Chicago, IL: The Association.

American Dental Association, Department of Membership Operations (various years). *National recruitment and retention for active licensed dentists.* Chicago, IL: The Association.

American Dental Association Health Policy Institute (2016). Reasons why adults do not visit the dentist more often. *ADA News*, October 3, 4.

Andrews, K. G., Smith, L. A., Henzi, D., & Demps, E. (2007). Faculty and student perceptions of academic integrity at U.S. and Canadian dental schools. *Journal of Dental Education, 71* (8), 1027-1039.

Aquino, K. (1998). The effects of ethical climate and the availability of alternatives on the use of deception during negotiation. *International Journal of Conflict Management, 9* (3), 195-217.

Arendt, H. (1963). *Eichmann in Jerusalem: A report on the banality of evil.* New York, NY: Penguin.

Ariely, D. (2009). *Predictably irrational: The hidden forces that shape our decisions.* New York, NY: Harper.

Ariely, D. (2012). *The (honest) truth about dishonesty: How we lie to everyone—especially ourselves.* New York, NY: Harper.

Aristotle (1935). The Nicomachean Ethics. In P. Wheelwright (Ed., Trans.), *Aristotle, Writings* (pp. 157-275). New York, NY: Odyssey.

Aronson, E., & Carlsmith, J. M. (1963). Effect of the severity of threat on devaluation of forbidden behavior. *Journal of Abnormal and Social Psychology, 66* (6), 584-588.

Arrow, K. J. (1951). *Social choice and individual values.* New York, NY: John Wiley & Sons.

Ashby, W. R. (1958). Requisite variety and its implications for the control of complex systems. *Cybernetica, 1* (1), 1.

Ashforth, B. E., Gioia, D. A., Robinson, S. L., & Treviño, L. K. (2008). Re-viewing organizational corruption. *Academy of Management Review, 33* (3), 670-684.

Association of Certified Fraud Examiners (2014). *Report to the nation on organizational fraud and abuse: 2014 global fraud study.* Chicago, IL: The Association.

Atran, S. (2010). *Talking to the enemy.* New York, NY: HarperCollins.

Austin, W., Lemermeyer, G., Goldberg, L., Bergum, V., & Johnson, M. S. (2005). Moral distress in healthcare practice: The situation of nurses. *HEC Forum, 17* (1), 33-48.

Axelrod, R., & Cohen, M. D. (2000). *Harnessing complexity: Organizational implications of a scientific frontier.* New York, NY: Basic Books.

Azar, O. H., Yosef, S., & Bar-Eli, M. (2013). Do customers return excessive change in a restaurant? A field experiment in dishonesty. *Journal of Economic Behavior & Organization, 93*, 219-213.

Baier, A. C. (1994). *Moral prejudices.* Cambridge, MA: Harvard University Press.

Bandura, A. (1977). *Social learning theory.* Englewood Cliffs, NJ: Prentice Hall.

Bandura, A. (1986). *Social foundations of thought and action: A social cognitive theory.* Englewood Cliffs, NJ: Prentice-Hall.

Bandura, A. (1999). Moral disengagement in the perpetuation of inhumanities. *Personality and Social Psychology Review, 3* (3), 193-209.

Baron, J. (2013). *Thinking and deciding.* Cambridge, UK: Cambridge University Press.

Baron-Cohen, S. (2011). *The science of evil: On empathy and the origins of cruelty.* New York, NY: Basic Books.

Batson, C. D. (1997). In a very different voice: Unmasking moral hypocrisy. *Journal of Personality and Social Psychology, 72* (6), 1135-1348.

Batson, C. D. (2011). What's wrong with morality? *Emotion Review, 3* (3), 230-236.

Batson, C. D., Thompson, E. R., Sueferling, G., Whitney, H., & Strongman, J. A. (1999). Moral hypocrisy: Appearing moral to oneself without being so. *Journal of Personality and Social Psychology, 77* (3), 525-537.

Baumeister, R. F., Stillwell, A. M., & Wotman, S. R. (1990). Victim and perpetrator accounts of interpersonal conflict: Autobiographical narrative about anger. *Journal of Personality and Social Psychology, 59* (5), 994-1005.

Baumeister, R. F., & Vohs, K. D. (Eds.) (2004). *Handbook of self-regulation: Research, theory, and applications.* New York, NY: The Guilford Press.

Baumna, Z. (2008). *Does ethics have a chance in a world of consumerism?* Cambridge, MA: Harvard University Press.

Bazerman, M. H., & Tenbrunsel, A. E. (2011). *Blind spots: Why we fail to do what's right and what to do about it.* Princeton, NJ: Princeton University Press.

Bazerman, M., Tenbrunsel, A. E., & Wade-Benzoni, K. (1998). Negotiating with yourself and losing: Making decisions with competing internal preferences. *Academy of Management Review, 23* (2), 225-241.

Beauchamp, T. L., & Childress, J. F. (2009). *Principles of biomedical ethics.* New York, NY: Oxford University Press.

Beazoglou, T. J., Chen, L., Lazar, V. F., Brown, L. J., Ray, S. C., Heilley, D. R., Berg, R., & Baillit, H. L. (2012). Expanded function allied dental personnel and dental practice productivity and efficiency. *Journal of Dental Education, 46* (8), 1054-1060.

Beemsterboer, P. L., Odom, J. G., Pate, T. D., & Haden, N. K. (2000). Issues of academic integrity in U.S. dental schools. *Journal of Dental Education, 64* (12), 833-838.

Benner, P., Sutphen, M., Leonard, V., & Day, L. (2010). *Educating nurses: A call for radical transformation.* San Francisco, CA: Jossey-Bass.

Bennis, W. (1989). *On becoming a leader.* Reading, MA: Addison-Wesley.

Bentham, J. (1780/1909). *An introduction to the principles of morals and legislation.* Mineola, NY: Dover.

Blackburn, S. (2001). *Being good: A short introduction to ethics.* Oxford, UK: Oxford University Press.

Block, P. (1993). *Stewardship: Choosing service over self-interest.* San Francisco, CA: Berrett-Koehler.

Bogdon, R. J. (2010). *Our own minds: Sociocultural grounds for self-consciousness.* Cambridge, MA: MIT Press.

Bok, S. (1978). *Lying: Moral choice in public and private life.* New York, NY: Vintage Books.

Boudes, T., & Laroche, H. (2009). Taking off the heat: Narrative sensemaking in post-crisis inquiry reports. *Organizational Studies, 30* (4), 377-396.

Brief, A. P., Buttram, R. T., & Dukerich, J. M. (2001). Collective corruption in the corporate world: Toward a process model. In M. E. Turner (Ed.), *Groups at work: Theory and research* (pp. 471-493). Mahwah, NJ: Lawrence Erlbaum.

Brief, A. P., Dukerich, J. M., Brown, P. R., & Brett, J. F. (1996). What's wrong with the Treadway Commission Report? Experimental analysis of the effects of personal values and codes of conduct on fraudulent financial reporting. *Journal of Business Ethics, 15* (2), 183-198.

Brounstein, M. (2000). Coaching & mentoring for dummies. New York, NY: Wiley Publishing.

Buchanan, A. E., & Brock, D. W. (1990). *Deciding for others: The ethics of surrogate decision making.* Cambridge, UK: Cambridge University Press.

Buchanan, J., & Stubblebine, W. C. (1962). Externality. *Economica, 29* (116), 371-384.

Bzdok, D., Schilbach, L., Vogeley, K., Schneider, K., Laird, A. R., Langner, R., & Eickhoff, S. B. (2012). Parsing the neural correlates of moral cognition: ALE meta-analysis on morality, theory of mind, and empathy. *Brain Structure and Function, 217* (4), 783-796.

Cain, M. U. J., Silberman, S. L., Mahan, J. M., & Meydrech, E. F. (1983). Changes in dental students' personal needs and values. *Journal of Dental Education, 47* (9), 604-608.

California Dental Association (2018). *Journal of the California Dental Association, 46* (6), entire issue.

Callahan, D. (2004). *The cheating culture: Why more Americans are doing wrong to get ahead.* New York, NY: Harvest.

Carreyrou, J. (2018). *Bad blood: Secrets and lies in a Silicon Valley startup.* New York, NY: Knopf.

Carroll, J. S. (1992). How taxpayers think about their taxes: Frames and values. In J. Slemrod (Ed.), *Why people pay taxes: Tax compliance and enforcement.* Ann Arbor, MI: University of Michigan Press.

Castiglione, B. (1507/1967). *The Book of the Courtier,* G. Bull (Trans.). New York, NY: Penguin Books.

Chahine, T (2016). *Introduction to social entrepreneurship.* Boca Raton, FL: CRC Press.

Chambers, D. W. (2001). A brief history of conflicting ideals in health care. *Journal of the American College of Dentists, 68* (3), 48-52.

Chambers, D. W. (2004a). Portfolios for determining initial licensure competency. *Journal of the American Dental Association, 135* (2), 173-184.

Chambers, D. W. (2004b). The professions. *Journal of the American College of Dentists, 71* (4), 57-65.

Chambers, D. W. (2006). Mentoring. *Journal of the American College of Dentists, 73* (2), 53-58.

Chambers, D. W. (2007a). The Hovey-Beard effect. *Journal of the American College of Dentists, 74* (3), 2-3.

Chambers, D. W. (2007b). A primer on dental ethics, Part II: Moral behavior. *Journal of the American College of Dentists, 74* (4), 38-51.

Chambers, D. W. (2009). Assertiveness. *Journal of the American College of Dentists, 76* (2), 51-59.

Chambers, D. W. (2010). Dentistry from the perspective of the San Francisco phone book. *Journal of the California Dental Association, 38* (11), 801-808.

Chambers, D. W. (2011a). Board-to-board consistency in initial dental licensure examinations. *Journal of Dental Education, 75* (10), 1310-1315.

Chambers, D. W. (2011b). Confusions in the equipoise concept and the alternative of fully informed overlapping rational decisions. *Medicine, Health Care and Philosophy, 24* (2), 133-142.

Chambers, D. W. (2011c). Developing a self-scoring comprehensive instrument to measure Rest's four-component model of moral behavior: The moral skills inventory. *Journal of Dental Education, 75* (1), 23-35.

Chambers, D. W. (2014a). Computer simulation of dental professionals as a moral community. *Medicine, Health Care and Philosophy, 17* (3), 467-476.

Chambers, D. W. (2014b). Factors driving recent changes in dentists' incomes. *Journal of the California Dental Association, 42* (5), 331-337.

Chambers, D. W. (2015a). Do patients and dentists see ethics the same way? *Journal of the American College of Dentists, 82* (2), 31-47.

Chambers, D. W. (2015b). Every pinohc should count. *Journal of the American College of Dentists, 82* (2), 2-3.

Chambers, D. W. (2016a). Are physicians really that unethical? *Journal of the California Dental Association, 44* (4), 21.

Chambers, D. W. (2016b). *Building the moral community: Radical naturalism and emergence.* Lanham, MD: Lexington Books.

Chambers, D. W. (2016c). Moral priming and the ACD basic rule. *Journal of the American College of Dentists, 83* (1), 38-43.

Chambers, D. W. (2017a). Shifting the blame. *Journal of the California Dental Association, 45* (8), 389.

Chambers, D. W. (2017b). What dentists do when they recognize faulty treatment: To tattle or build moral community. *Journal of the American College of Dentists, 84* (2), 32-66.

Chambers, D. W. (2018). Disciplined dental licenses: An empirical study. *Journal of the American College of Dentists, 85* (2), 30-39.

Chambers, D. W. (2019). The ethics of technology and innovation: Second thoughts. *Ethics in Biology, Engineering and Medicine—An International Journal, 9* (1), 49-58.

Chambers, D. W., Budenz, A. W., Fredekind, R. E., & Nadershahi, N. A. (2002). Debt and practice profiles of beginning dental practitioners. *CDA Journal, 30* (12), 909-914.

Chambers, D. W., & Eng, W. R. L., Jr. (1994). Practice profile: The first twelve years. *CDA Journal, 12* (12), 25-32.

Chambers, D. W., Hamilton, D. L., McCormick, L., & Swendeman, D. (1976). An investigation of behavior change in continuing dental education. *Journal of Dental Education, 40* (8), 546-551.

Charmaz, K. (2006). *Constructing grounded theory: A practical guide through qualitative analysis.* Los Angeles, CA: Sage Publications.

Chreim, S., Williams, B. E., & Hinings, G. R. (2007). Interlevel influences on the reconstruction of professional role identity. *Academy of Management*

Journal, 50 (6), 1515-1539.Christensen, C. M. (1997). *The innovator's dilemma: When technologies cause great firms to fall.* Boston, MA: Harvard Business Review Press.

Christensen, C. M., & Raynor, M. E. (2003). *The innovator's solution: Creating and sustaining successful growth.* Boston, MA: Harvard Business Review Press.

Chugh, D., Banajai, M. R., & Bazerman, M. (2005). Bounded ethicality as a psychological barrier to recognizing conflicts of interest. In D. A. Moore, D. M. Caine, G. Lowenstein, & M. Bazerman (Eds.), *Conflict of interest: Problems and solutions from law, medicine, and organizational settings.* Cambridge, UK: Cambridge University Press.

Churchland, P. S. 2011). *Braintrust: What neuroscience tells us about morality.* Princeton, NJ: Princeton University Press.

Cizek, G. J. (1999). Cheating on tests: *How to do it, detect it, and prevent it.* Mahwah, NJ: Lawrence Erlbaum.

Clinard, M., & Yeager, P. C. (1980). *Corporate crime.* New York, NY: Free Press.

Coase, R. (1937). The nature of the firm. *Economica, 4* (16), 386-405.

Cohen, M. D., James, G., March, J. G., & Olsen, J. P. (1972). A garbage can model of organizational choice. *Administrative Science Quarterly, 17* (1), 1-25.

Colby, A., Kohlberg, L., Speicher, B., Hewer, A., Candee, D., Gibbs, J., & Power, C. (1987). *The measurement of moral judgment.* New York, NY: Cambridge University Press.

Collins, J. (2001). *Good to great: Why some companies make the leap and others don't.* New York, NY: HarperBusiness.

Cooke, M., Irby, D. M., & O'Brien, B. C. (2010). *Educating physicians: A call for reform of medical school and residency.* San Francisco, CA: Jossey-Bass.

Corley, M. C. (2002). Nurse moral distress: A proposed theory and research agenda. *Nursing Ethics, 9* (6), 636-650.

Covey, S. R. (1990). *Principle-centered leadership.* New York, NY: Free Press.

Crilly, D., Zollo, M., & Hansen, M. T. (2012). Faking it or muddling through: Understanding decoupling in response to stakeholder pressures. *Academy of Management Journal, 55* (6), 1420-1448.

Curriden, M., & Phillips, L., Jr. (1999). *Contempt of court.* New York, NY: Anchor Books.

Damasio, A. R. (1994). *Descartes' error: Emotion, reason, and the human brain.* New York, NY: Putnam.

Damasio, A. (1999). *The feeling of what happens: Body and emotion in the making of consciousness.* San Diego, CA: Harcourt.

Daniels, N. (1985). *Just health care.* Cambridge, UK: Cambridge University Press.

Dawson, A. J. (1994). Professional codes of practice and ethical conduct. *Journal of Applied Philosophy, 11* (2), 145-153.

Decety, J. (Ed.) (2012). *Empathy: From bench to bedside.* Cambridge, MA: MIT Press.

Decety, J., & Lamm, C. (2007). The role of the right temporoparietal junction in social interaction: How low level computational processes contribute to meta-cognition. *The Neuroscientist, 13* (6), 580-593.

Decety, J., & Wheatley, T. (Eds.) (2015). *The moral brain: A multidisciplinary perspective.* Cambridge, MA: MIT Press.

de Cremer, D., van Dijk, E., & Reinders Folmer, C. P. (2009). Why leaders feel entitled to take more: Feelings of entitlement as a moral rationalization strategy. In de Cremer, D. (Ed.), *Psychological perspectives on ethical behavior and decision making* (pp. 107-119). Charlotte, NC: Information Age Publishing.

de Los Reyes, G., Jr., Kim, T. W., & Weaver, G. R. (2017). Teaching ethics in business schools: A conversation on disciplinary differences, academic provincialism, and the case for integrated pedagogy. *Academy of Management Learning & Education, 6* (2), 314-336.

Dembe, A. E., & Boden, L. I. (2000). Moral hazard: A question of morality? *New Solutions, 10* (3), 257-279.

Diekmann, A., Jungbauer-Gans, M., Krassnig, H., & Lorenz, S. (1996). Social status and aggression: A field study analyzed by survival analysis. *Journal of Social Psychology, 136* (6), 761-768.

Djulbegovic, B., Hozo, I., Beckstead, J., Tsalatsanis, A., & Pauker, S. G. (2012). Dual processing model of medical decision-making. *PLoS One,* doi: 10.1186/1472-6947-12-94.

Donaldson, T., & Dunfee, T. W. (1999). *Ties that bind: A social contracts approach to business ethics.* Boston, MA: Harvard Business School Press.

Dukerich, J. M., Kramer, R., & Parks, J. M. (1998). The dark side of organizational identification. In D. A. Whetten, & P. C. Godfrey (Eds.), *Identity in organizations: Building theory through conversations.* Thousand Oaks, CA: Sage.

Dunegan, K. J. (1996). Fines, frames, and images: Examining formulation effects on punishment decisions. *Organizational Behavior and Human Decision Processes, 68* (1), 58-67.

Dweck, C. (2006). Mindset: *The new psychology of success*. New York, NY: Ballantine.

Dworkin, G. (1972). Paternalism. *The Monist, 56* (1), 64-84.

Eubanks, V. (2017). *Automating inequality: How high-tech tools profile, police, and punish the poor.* New York, NY: St. Martin's Press.

Fast, N. J., & Chen, S. (2009). When the boss feels inadequate: Power, incompetence, and aggression. *Psychological Science, 20* (11), 1406-1413.

Fehr, E., & Gächter, S. (2000). Cooperation and punishment in public goods experiments. *American Economic Review, 90* (4), 980-994.

Fehr, E., & Schmidt, K. (1999). A theory of fairness, competition, and cooperation. *Quarterly Journal of Economics, 114* (3), 817-868.

Feige, E. L., & Cebula, R. (2011). *America's underground economy: Measuring the size, growth and detriments of income tax evasion in the U.S.* Madison, WI: University of Wisconsin-Madison.

Ferguson, N. (2013). *The great degeneration: How institutions decay and economies die.* New York, NY: Penguin.

Festinger, L. (1959). *A theory of cognitive dissonance.* Stanford, CA: Stanford University Press.

Fischman, W., Solomon, B., Greenspan, D., & Gardner, H. (2004). *Making good: How young people cope with moral dilemmas at work.* Cambridge, MA: Harvard University Press.

Fisher, R. (1971). *Basic negotiating strategy: International conflict for beginners.* London, UK: Allen Lane.

Fletcher, J. (1966). *Situation ethics: The new morality.* Philadelphia, PA: Westminster Press.

Forsberg, J., Klyop, J. S., & Landman, P. (2004). Advancing dentists' charitable dental initiatives–An American Dental Association perspective. *Journal of the American College of Dentists, 71* (1), 6-79.

Foster, C. R., Dahill, L. E., Golemon, L. A., & Tolentino, B. W. (2006). *Educating clergy: Teaching practices and pastoral imagination.* San Francisco, CA: Jossey-Bass.

Fotaki, M., & Hyde, P. (2015). Organizational blind spots: Splitting, blame and idealization in the National Health Service. *Human Relations, 68* (3), 441-462.

Fradin, G. (2007). *Moral hazard in American healthcare: Why we can't control our medical expenses.* No publisher identified.

Fraser, J., & Simkins, B. J. (Eds.) (2010). *Enterprise risk management.* New York, NY: Wiley.

Fry, S. T., Veatch, R. M., & Taylor, C. (2011). *Cases studies in nursing ethics* (4th ed). Sudbury, MA: Jones & Bartlett Learning.

Fulghum, R. (1986). *All I really need to know I learned in kindergarten.* New York, NY: Ballantine.

Fuller, J. L., & Killip, D. E. (1979). Do dental students cheat? *Journal of Dental Education, 43* (13), 666-669.

Gabor, T. (1994). *Everybody does it! Crime by the public.* Toronto, ON: University of Toronto Press.

Gabor, T., Strean, J., Singh, G., & Varis, D. (1986). Public deviance: An experimental study. *Canadian Journal of Criminology, 28* (10), 17-29.

Gawronski, B. (2004). Theory-based bias correction in dispositional inference: The fundamental attribution error is dead, long live the correspondence bias. *European Review of Social Psychology, 15,* 183-217.

Gert, B. (1998). *Morality: Its nature and justification.* New York, NY: Oxford University Press.

Geuss, R. (2001). *Public goods, private goods.* Princeton, NJ: Princeton University Press.

Gies, W. J. (1926). *Dental education in the United States and Canada: A report to the Carnegie Foundation for the Advancement of Teaching.* New York, NY: The Foundation.

Gilbert, J. (2012). *Ethics for managers: Philosophical foundations and business realities.* New York, NY: Routledge.

Gilovich, T. (1990). Differential construal and the false consensus effect. *Journal of Personality and Social Psychology, 59* (4), 623-634.

Gino, F., Ayal, S., & Ariely, D. (2009). Contagion and differentiation in unethical behavior: The effect of one bad apple on the barrel. *Psychological Science, 20* (3), 393-398.

Gino, F., Schweitzer, M. E., Mead, N. L., & Ariely, D. (2011). Unable to resist temptation: How self-control depletion promotes unethical behavior. *Organizational Behavior and Human Decision Processes, 115,* 191-203.

Glicksman, E. (2016). "What do I do?" Teaching tomorrow's doctors how to navigate the tough ethical questions ahead. *AAMC Reporter*, April.

Gneezy, U., & Rustichini, A. (2000). A fine is a price. *The Journal of Legal Studies, 29* (1) 1-17.

Goffman, E. (1959). *The presentation of self in everyday life*. New York, NY: Doubleday Anchor.

Goldstein, J., Hazy, J. K., & Lichtenstein, B. B. (2010). *Complexity and the nexus of leadership: Leveraging nonlinear science to create ecologies of innovation*. New York, NY: Palgrave.

Graham, B. S., Knight, G. W., & Graham, L. (2016). Dental student academic integrity in U.S. dental schools: Current status and recommendations for enhancement. *Journal of Dental Education, 80* (1), 5-13.

Graham, J., Nosek, B. A., Haidt, J., Iyed, R., Koleva, S., & Ditto, P. H. (2011). Mapping the moral domain. *Journal of the American Psychological Association, 101* (2), 366-385.

Graskemper, J. P. (2011). *Professional responsibility in dentistry: A practical guide to law and ethics*. New York, NY: Wiley-Blackwell.

Greene, J. D. (2008). The secret joke of Kant's soul. In W. Sinnott-Armstrong (Ed.), *Moral psychology: The neuroscience of morality* (pp. 35-79). Cambridge, MA: MIT Press.

Greene, J. (2013). *Moral tribes: Emotion, reason, and the gap between us and them*. New York, NY: Penguin.

Guay, A. H., & Lazar, V. (2012). Increasing productivity in dental practice: The role of ancillary personal. *Journal of the American College of Dentists, 79* (1), 11-17.

Gunia, B. C., Wang, L., Insead, L. H., Wang, J., & Murnighan, J. K. (2010). Contemplation and conversation: Subtle influences on moral decision making. *Academy of Management Journal, 55* (1), 13-33.

Habermas, J. (1993). *Moral consciousness and communicative action*. C. Lenhardt, & S. W. Nicholsen (Trans.). Cambridge, MA: MIT Press.

Hagger, M. S., Wood, C., Stiff, C., & Chatzisarantis, N. L. D. (2010). Ego depletion and the strength model of self-control: A meta-analysis. *Psychological Bulletin, 136* (4), 495-525.

Haidt, J. (2012). *The righteous mind: Why good people are divided by politics and religion*. New York, NY: Vintage.

Hamlin, J. K. (2013). Moral judgment and action in preverbal infants and toddlers: Evidence for an innate moral core. *Current Directions in Psychological Science, 22* (3), 186-193.

Hamric, A. B., Davis, W. S., & Childress, M. D. (2006). Moral distress in health care professionals. *Pharos, 69* (1), 16-23.

Hardin, G. (1968). The tragedy of the commons. *Science, 162* (3859), 1243-1248.

Hardin, G. (1977). *The limits of altruism: An ecologist's view of survival*. Bloomington, IN: Indiana University Press.

Hartshorne, H., & May, M. A. (1928). *Studies in deceit*. New York, NY: Macmillan.

Haski, S. (2005). *The arrogance of distance*. New York, NY: iUniverse.

Heese, J., Krishnan, R., & Moers, F. (2016). Selective regulator decoupling and organizations' strategic responses. *Academy of Management Journal, 59* (6), 2178-2204.

Hegarty, W. H., & Sims, H. P. (1978). Some determinants of unethical decision behavior: An experiment. *Journal of Applied Psychology, 63* (4), 451-457.

Heist, P. A. (1960). Personality characteristics of dental students. *Educational Record, 41*, 240-252.

Helfrich, C. D., Rose, A. J., Hartmann, C. W., van Bodegom-Vos, L., Graham, I. D., Wood, S. J. et al (2018). How the dual process model of human cognition can inform efforts to de-implement ineffective and harmful clinical practices: A preliminary model of unlearning and substitution. *Journal of Evaluation in Clinical Practice*, doi. org/10.1111/jep.12855.

Herrmann, B., Thöni, C., & Gächter, S. (2008). Antisocial punishment across societies. *Science, 319* (5868), 1362-1367.

Hersh, R. H., & Merrow, J. (2005). *Declining by degrees: Higher education at risk*. New York, NY: Palgrave.

Herzberg, F. (1968). One more time: How do you motivate employees? *Harvard Business Review, 46* (1), 53-62.

Holland, J. H. (1995). *Hidden order: How adaptation builds complexity*. New York, NY: Basic Books.

Holland, J. H. (1998). *Emergence: From chaos to order*. New York, NY: Basic Books.

Hollensbe, E. C., Khazanchi, S., & Masterson, S. S. (2008). How do I assess if my supervisor and organization are fair? Identifying the rules underlying entity-based justice perceptions. *Academy of Management Journal, 51* (6), 1099-1116.

Inglehart, M., & Bagramian, R. (2002). *Oral health-related quality of life*. Chicago, IL: Quintessence Publishing.

Jabr, F. (2019). The truth about dentistry: It's much less scientific—and more prone to gratuitous procedures—than you may think. *The Atlantic*, May.

Jackall, R. (1988). *Moral mazes: The world of corporate managers*. New York, NY: Oxford University Press.

Jasanoff, S. (2016). *The ethics of invention: Technology and the human future*. New York, NY: W. W. Norton & Company.

Jendrek, M. P. (1992). Students' reactions to academic dishonesty. *Journal of College Student Development, 33* (3), 260.

Johnson, E. A., O'Rourke, J. T., Partridge, B. S., Spalding, E. B., & Palmer, B. B. (1932). *The status of dental journalism in the United States: Report of the Commission on Journalism of the American College of Dentists 1928-1931*. New York, NY: The College.

Johnson, L., & Phillips, B. (2003). *Absolute honesty*. New York, NY: AMACOM.

Johnson, S. M. (2019). *Where teachers thrive: Organizing schools for success*. Cambridge, MA: Harvard Education Press.

Johnson, W. B., & Riley, C. R. (2004). *The elements of mentoring*. New York, NY: Palgrave Macmillan.

Jones, E. E., & Harris, V. A. (1967). The attribution of attitudes. *Journal of Experimental Social Psychology, 3* (1), 1-24.

Jordan, A. H., & Monin, B. (2008). From sucker to saint: Moralization in response to self-threat. *Philological Science, 19* (8), 809-815.

Juma, C. (2016). *Innovation and its enemies: Why people resist new technologies*. Oxford, UK: Oxford University Press.

Kabanoff, B. (1991). Equity, equality, power, and conflict. *Academy of Management Review, 16* (2), 416-441.

Kahan, D. (2000). Gentle nudges vs. hard shoves: Solving the sticky norms problem. *The University of Chicago Law Review, 67* (3), 607-643.

Kalshoven, K., Den Hartog, D. N., & De Hoogh, A. H. B. (2012). Ethical leadership and follower helping and courtesy: Moral awareness and empathetic concern as moderators. *Applied Psychology, 62* (2), 211-235.

Kant, I. (1785/1948). *Groundwork of the metaphysics of morals*. H. J. Patton (Trans). New York, NY: Harper Torchbooks.

Kaptein, M. (2010). The ethics of organizations: A longitudinal study of the U.S. working population. *Journal of Business Ethics, 92*, 601-618.

Kaptein, M. (2013). *Workplace morality: behavioral ethics in organizations*. Bingley, UK: Emerald Group.

Kaptein, M., & Schwartz, M. S. (2008). The effectiveness of business codes: A critical examination of existing studies and the development of an integrated research model. *Journal of Business Ethics, 77*, 111-127.

Katila, R., Thatchenkey, S., Christensen, M. Q., & Zenios, S. (2017). Is there a doctor in the house? Expert product users, organizational roles, and innovation. *Academy of Management Journal, 60*, (6), 2415-2437.

Keen, S. (1986). *Faces of the enemy: Reflections of the hostile imagination*. New York, NY: Harper and Row.

Kelso, J. A. S. (1995). *Dynamic patterns: The self-organization of brain and behavior*. Cambridge, MA: MIT Press.

Kern, M., & Chugh, D. (2009). Bounded ethicality: The perils of loss framing. *Psychological Science, 20* (3), 378-384.

Khan, U., & Dhar, R. (2006). Licensing effect in consumer choice. *Journal of Marketing Research, 43* (2), 259-266.

Killgore, W. D. S., Killgore, D. B., Day, L. M., Li, C., Kamimori, G. H., & Balkin, T. J. (2007). The effects of 53 hours of sleep deprivation on moral judgment. *Sleep, 30* (3), 345-352.

Kirk, B. A., Cummings, R. W., & Hackett, H. R. (1963). Personality and vocational characteristics of dental students. *Personality and Guidance Journal, 41* (6), 522-527.

Kish-Gephart, J. L., Harrison, D. A., & Treviño, L. K. (2010). Bad apples, bad cases, and bad barrels: Meta-analytic evidence about sources of unethical decisions at work. *Journal of Applied Psychology, 95* (1), 1-31.

Koster-Hale, J., Saxe, R., Dungan, J., & Young, L. L. (2012). Decoding moral judgments from neural representations of intentions. *Proceedings of the National Academy of Sciences, USA, 110* (4), 5648-5653.

Kramer, M. (2012). Dentists demonstrating professionalism: Dentists in private practice settings provide free or reduced-fee care. *Journal of the American College of Dentists, 79* (4), 72-77.

Krueger, J., & Clement, R. W. (1994). The truly false consensus effect: An ineradicable and egocentric bias in social perception. *Journal of Personality and Social Psychology, 67* (4), 596-610.

Kurzban, R. (2011). *Why everyone (else) is a hypocrite: Evolution and the modular mind.* Princeton, NJ: Princeton University Press.

Lammers, J., & Stapel, D. (2009). How power influences moral thinking. *Journal of Personality and Social Psychology, 97* (2), 279-289.

Lammers, J., Stapel, D. A., & Galinsky, A. D. (2010). Power increases hypocrisy: Moralizing in reasoning, immorality in behavior. *Psychological Science, 21* (5), 737-744.

Leavitt, K., Reynolds, S. J., Barnes, C. M., Schilpzand, P., & Hannah, S. T. (2012). Different hats, different obligations: Plural occupational identities and situated moral judgment. *Academy of Management Journal, 55* (6) 1316-1333.

Leavitt, K., & Sluss, D. M. (2015). Lying for who we are: An identity-based model of workplace dishonesty. *Academy of Management Review, 40* (4), 587-610.

LeBoeuf, R. A., Shafir, E., & Bayuk, J. B. (2009). The conflicting choices of alternating selves. *Organizational Behavior and Human Decision Process, 111* (1), 48-61.

LeDoux, J. (1996). *The emotional brain: The mysterious underpinnings of emotional life.* New York, NY: Simon & Schuster.

Levitt, S. D., & Dubner, S. J. (2005). *Freakonomics: A rogue economist explored the hidden side of everything.* New York, NY: William Morrow.

Lewin, K. (1946/2008). *Resolving social conflicts and field theory in social science.* Washington, DC: American Psychological Association.

Lewis, A. C., & Sherman, S. J. (2010). Perceived entitativity and the black-sheep effect: When will we denigrate negative ingroup members? *Journal of Social Psychology, 150* (2), 211-225.

Lewis, M., & Saarni, C. (1993). *Lying and deception in everyday life.* New York, NY: Guilford Press.

Lewis, P. V. (2014). *Ethics in the world of business.* Dubuque, IA: Kendall Hunt.

Libet, B. (2004). *Mind time—The temporal factor in consciousness.* Cambridge, MA: Harvard University Press.

Light, S., & Zahn-Waxler, C. (2012). Nature and forms of empathy in the first years of life. In J. Decety (Ed.), *Empathy: From bench to bedside* (pp. 109-130). Cambridge, MA: MIT Press.

Linn, E. L. (1968). Service to others and economic gain as professional objectives of dental students. *Journal of Dental Education, 32* (2), 76-81.

Loughran, T., McDonald, B., & Yun, H. (2008). A wolf in sheep's clothing: The use of ethics-related terms in 10-K reports. *Journal of Business Ethics, 89* (1), 39-49.

MacIntrye, A. (1981). *After virtue: A study in moral theory.* London, UK: Duckworth.

MacIntyre, A. (1988). *Whose justice? Which rationality?* Notre Dame, IN: University of Notre Dame Press.

MacLean, T. L. (2008). Framing and organizational misconduct: A symbolic interactionist study. *Journal of Business Ethics, 78,* 3-16.

Mager, R. F., & Pipe, P. (1983). *Analyzing performance problems: Or you really oughta wanta.* Atlanta, GA: CEP.

Maister, D. (1993). *Managing the professional service firm.* New York, NY: The Free Press.

Maister, D. H., Green, C. H., & Galford, R. M. (2000). *The trusted advisor.* New York, NY: Touchstone.

Malle, B. F. (2006). The actor-observer asymmetry in attribution: A (surprising) meta-analysis. *Psychological Bulletin, 132* (6), 895-919.

Manhold, J. H., Shatin, L., & Manhold, B. S. (1963). Comparison of interest, needs and selected personality factors of dental and medical students. *Journal of the American Dental Association, 63* (8), 601-605.

Marks, G., & Miller, N. (1987). Ten years of research on the false-consensus effect: An empirical and theoretical review. *Psychological Bulletin, 102* (1), 72-90.

Mayer, D. M., Kuenzi, M., & Greenbaum, R. L. (2010). Examining the link between ethical leadership and employee misconduct: The mediating role of ethical climate. *Journal of Business Ethics, 95,* 7-16.

Mayer, D. M., Kuenzi, M., Greenbaum, R., Bardes, M., & Salvador, R. (2009). How low does ethical leadership flow? Test of a trickle-down model. *Organizational Behavior and Human Decision Processes, 108* (1), 1-13.

Mayer, D. M., Nurmohamed, S., Treviño, L. K., Shapiro, D. L., & Schminke, M. (2013). Encouraging employees to report unethical conduct internally: It takes a village. *Organizational Behavior and Human Decisions Processes, 121* (1), 89-103.

Mazar, N., Amir, O., & Ariely, D. (2008). The dishonesty of honest people: A theory of self-concept maintenance. *Journal of Marketing Research, 45* (6) 633-644.

Mazar, N., & Ariely, D. (2006). Dishonesty in everyday life and its policy implications. *Journal of Public Policy & Marketing, 25* (1), 117-126.

McCabe, D. (2001). Cheating: Why students do it and how we can help them stop. *American Educator,* Winter 1-7.

McCabe, D. L. (2005). It takes a village: Academic dishonesty & educational opportunity. *Liberal Education,* Summer/Fall, 26-31.

McCabe, D. L., Butterfield, K. D., & Treviño, L. K. (2006). Academic dishonesty in graduate programs: Prevalence, causes, and proposed action. *Academy of Management Learning & Education, 5* (3), 294-305.

McCabe, D. L., Klebe, L., Treviño, L., & Butterfield, K. D. (2001). Cheating in academic institutions: A decade of research. *Ethics & Behavior, 11* (3), 219-232.

McCabe, D. L., & Treviño, L. K. (1997). Individual and contextual influences on academic dishonesty: A multicampus investigation. *Research in Higher Education, 38* (3), 379-396.

McCarthy, J., & Deady, R. (2008). Moral distress reconsidered. *Nursing Ethics, 15* (2), 254-262.

McDaniel, S. P., Siler, W. M., & Isenberg, B. P. (1985). Analysis of personality traits of the contemporary dental student. *Journal of Dental Education, 49* (8), 579-583.

Mead, N. L., Baumeister, R. F., Gino, F., Schweitzer, M. E., & Ariely, D. (2009). Too tired to tell the truth: Self-control resource depletion and dishonesty. *Journal of Experimental Social Psychology, 45* (3), 594-597.

Merrit, A. C., Effron, D. A., & Monin, B. (2010). Moral self-licensing: When being good frees us to be bad. *Social and Personality Psychology Compass, 4/5,* 344-357.

Mesmer-Magnus, J., & Viswesvaran, C. (2005). Whistleblowing in organizations: An examination of correlates of whistleblowing intentions, actions, and retaliation. *Journal of Business Ethics, 62,* 277-297.Miceli, M. P., & Near, J. P. (2002). What makes whistle-blowers effective? Three field studies. *Human Relations, 55* (4), 455-497.

Miethe, T. (1999). *Whistleblowing at work: Tough choices in exposing fraud, waste, and abuse on the job.* Boulder, CO: Westview Press.

Miller, J. H., & Page, S. E. (2007). *Complex adaptive systems: An introduction to computational models of social life.* Princeton, NJ: Princeton University Press.

Minor, W. W. (1981). The neutralization of criminal offenses. *Criminology, 18* (1), 103-120.

Moberg, D. J. (2006). Best of intentions, worst of results: grounding ethics students in the realities of organizational content. *Academy of Management Learning & Education, 5* (3), 307-316.

Monin, B., & Miller, D. T. (2001). Moral credentials and the expression of prejudice. *Journal of Personality and Social Psychology, 81* (1), 33-43.

More, D. M. (1961). The dental student: Personality patterns of entering dental students. *Journal of the American College of Dentists, 29* (1), 1-93.

Mozer, J. E., Lloyd, C., & Puente, E. S. (1988). Bi/polar personality patterns of senior dental students. *Journal of Dental Education, 52* (2), 452-457.

Muraven, M., & Baumeister, R. E. (2000). Self-regulation and depletion of limited resources. *Psychological Bulletin, 126* (2), 247-259.

Murdock, T. B., & Anderman, E. M. (2006). Motivational perspectives on student cheating: Toward an integrated model of academic dishonesty. *Educational Psychologist, 41* (3), 129-145.

Myers, K. K., & Sadaghiani, K. (2010). Millennials in the workplace: A communication perspective on Millennials' organizational relationships and performance. *Journal of Business and Psychology, 25* (2), 225-238.

Nash, J. F. (1951). Non-cooperative games. *Annals of Mathematics, 54* (2), 286-295.

Nath, C., Schmidt, R., & Gunnel, E. (2006). Perceptions of professionalism vary most with educational rank and age. *Journal of Dental Education, 70* (8), 825-834.

Nichols, T. (2017). *The death of expertise: The campaign against established knowledge and why it matters.* New York, NY: Oxford University Press.

Nuland, S. B. (1988). *Doctors: The biography of medicine*. New York, NY: Vintage.

Nussbaum, M., & Sen, A. (1993). *The quality of life*. Oxford, UK: Clarendon Press.

Ostrom, E. (1990). *Governing the commons: The evolution of institutions for collective action*. Cambridge, UK: Cambridge University Press.

Ozar, D. T., & Sokol, D. J. (1994). *Dental ethics at chairside: Professional principles and practical applications* (2nd ed). Washington, DC: Georgetown University Press.

Paharia, N., Kassam, K. S., Greene, J. D., & Bazerman, M. H. (2009). Dirty work, clean hands: The moral psychology of indirect agency. *Organizational Behavior and Human Decision Processes, 109* (2), 134-141.

Palmer, D. (2012). *Normal organizational wrongdoing: A critical analysis of theories of misconduct in and by organizations*. New York, NY: Oxford University Press.

Papadakis, M. A., Arnold, G. K., Blank, L. L., Holmboe, E. S., & Lipner, R. S. (2008). Performance during internal medicine residency training and subsequent disciplinary action by state licensure boards. *Annals of Internal Medicine, 148* (11), 869-876.

Papadakis, M. A., Hodgson, C. S., Teherani, A., & Kohatsu, N. D. (2004). Unprofessional behavior in medical school is associated with subsequent disciplinary action by a state medical board. *Academic Medicine, 79* (3), 244-249.

Papadakis, M. A., Teherani, A., Banach, M. A., Knettler, T. R., Rattner, S. L., Stern, D. T., Veloski, J. J., & Hodgson, C. S. (2005). Disciplinary action by medical boards and prior behavior in medical school. *New England Journal of Medicine, 353*, 2673-2682.

Parker, M. A. (2015). A closer look at the North Carolina Board of Dental Examiners and who can practice dentistry. *Journal of the American College of Dentists, 82* (3), 12-17.

Patterson, J., & Kim, P. (1991). *The day America told the truth: What people really believe about everything that really matters*. New York, NY: Prentice Hall.

Patterson, P., & Wilkens, L. (2014). *Media ethics: Issues and cases* (8th ed). New York, NY: McGraw Hill.

Pearce, J. M., & Dickinson, A. (1975). Pavlovian counterconditioning. *Journal of Experimental Psychology, 104* (2), 170-177.

Peltier, B. (2010). *The psychology of executive coaching: Theory and practice* (2nd ed). New York, NY; Routledge.Peters, T. J., & Waterman, R. H., Jr. (1982). *In search of excellence: Lessons from America's best-run companies*. New York, NY: Harper & Row.

Pfabigan, P. M., & Tran, U. S. (2015). Behavioral and physiological bases of attentional biases: Paradigms, participants, and stimuli. *Frontiers in Psychology, 5* (1), 5-10.

Pfeffer, J., & Sutton, R. I. (2006). *Hard facts, dangerous half-truths & total nonsense: Profiting from evidence-based management*. Boston, MA: Harvard Business Review Press.

Pinker, S. (2011). *The better angels of our nature: Why violence has declined*. New York, NY: Vintage Books.

Poundstone, W. (1992). *Prisoner's dilemma*. New York, NY: Anchor Books.

Prentice, D. A., & Miller, D. T. (1993). Pluralistic ignorance and alcohol use on campus: Some consequences of misperceiving the social norm. *Journal of Personality and Social Psychology, 64* (2), 243-256.

Puka, B. (2005). Student cheating. *Liberal Education, Summer/Fall*, 32-35.

Putnam, R. D. (2000). *Bowling alone: The collapse and revival of American community*. New York, NY: Simon & Schuster.

Rabinowitz, F. E., Colmar, G., Elgie, D., Hale, D., Niss, S., Sharp, B., & Singlitico, J. (1993). Dishonesty, indifference, or carelessness in souvenir shop transactions. *Journal of Social Psychology, 133* (1), 73-79.

Rapoport, A., Guyer, J., & Gordon, D. G. (1976). *The 2x2 game*. Ann Arbor, MI: University of Michigan Press.

Rawls, J. (1971). *A theory of justice*. Cambridge, MA: The Belknap Press.

Reay, T., Goodrick, E., Waldorff, S. B., & Casebeer, A. (2017). Getting leopards to change their spots: Co-creating a new professional role identity. *Academy of Management Journal, 60* (3), 1043-1070.

Reed, A. Z. (1921). *Training for the public profession of the law*. Carnegie Bulletin No. 15. New York, NY: The Foundation.

Reid, K., Hellyer, J. H., & Thorsteinsdottir, B. (2014). A comparison of expectations and impressions of ethical characteristics of dentists: Results of a community primary care survey. *Journal of the American Dental Association, 145* (8), 829-834.

Reiman, J. (1979). *The rich get richer and the poor get prison: Ideology, class, and criminal justice.* New York, NY: Wiley.

Rest, J. R., & Narvaez, D. (Eds.) (1994). *Moral development in the professions: Psychology and applied ethics.* Hillsdale, NJ: Lawrence Erlbaum.

Rest, J., Narvaez, D., Bebeau, M. J., & Thoma, S. J. (1999). *Postconventional moral thinking: A neo-Kohlbergian approach.* Mahwah, NJ: Lawrence Erlbaum.

Rettinger, D. A., & Kramer, Y. (2009). Situational and personal causes of student cheating. *Research in Higher Education, 50* (3), 293-313.

Revere, P. [Schissel, M. J.] (1970). *Dentistry and its victims.* New York, NY: St. Martin's Press.

Rhode, D. L. (2018). *Cheating: Ethics in everyday life.* New York, NY: Oxford University Press.

Riis, R. W. (1941). The watch repair man will gyp you if you don't watch out. *Reader's Digest, 39*, 10-12.

Rodwin, M. A. (1993). *Medicine, money & morals: Physicians' conflicts of interest.* New York, NY: Oxford University Press.

Rogers, E. M. (1995). *Diffusion of Innovations* (4th ed). New York, NY: The Free Press.

Rosenzweig, P. (2007). *The halo effect…and the eight other business delusions that deceive managers.* New York, NY: Free Press.

Rosoff, S. M., Pontell, H. N., & Tillman, R. (1998). *Profit without honor: White-collar crime and the looting of America.* Upper Saddle River, NJ: Prentice Hall.

Ross, I., Greene, D., & House, P. (1977). The false consensus effect: An egocentric bias in social perception and attribution processes. *Journal of Experimental Social Psychology, 12* (3), 279-301.

Ross, L. (1977). The intuitive psychologist and his shortcomings: Distortions in the attribution process. In L. Berkowitz, *Advances in Experimental Social Psychology, 10* (pp. 173-220). New York, NY: Academic Press.

Ross, L., & Nisbett, R. E. (2011). *The person and the situation: Perspective of social psychology.* London, UK: Pinter & Martin.

Ruedfy, N. E., Moore, C., Gino, F., & Schweitzer, M. E. (2013). The cheater's high: The unexpected affective benefits of unethical behavior. *Journal of Personality and Social Psychology, 105* (4), 531-548.

Rule, J. T., & Veatch, R. M. (2004). *Ethical questions in dentistry* (2nd ed). Chicago, IL: Quintessence.

Rushkoff, D. (1999). *Coercion.* New York, NY: Riverhead Books.

Sabini, J., & Silver, M. (1983). Dispositional vs. situational interpretations of Milgram's obedience experiments. *Journal of the Theory of Social Behavior, 13* (2), 147-154.

Satell, G. (2017). *Mapping innovation: A playbook for navigating in a disruptive age.* New York, NY: McGraw Hill.

Schaubroeck, J. M., Hannah, S. T., Avolio, B. J., Kozlowski, S. W. J., Lord, R. G., Treviño, L. K., Dimotakis, N., & Peng, A. C. (2012). Embedding ethical leadership within and across organizational levels. *Academy of Management Review, 55* (5), 1053-1078.

Schön, D. A. (1983). *The reflective practitioners: How professionals think in action.* New York, NY: Basic Books.

Schön, D. A. (1987). *Educating the reflective practitioner.* San Francisco, CA: Jossey-Bass.

Schumpeter, J. A. (1934/1983). *The theory of economic development: An inquiry into profits, capital, credit, interest, and the business cycle.* O. Redvers (Trans.). New Brunswick, NJ: Transaction Books.

Schwartz, J. M., & Begley, S. (2002). *The mind & the brain: Neuroplasticity and the power of mental force.* New York, NY: Harper Perennial.

Schwartz, R. H., & Shenoy, S. (1994). Personality factors related to career satisfaction among general practitioners. *Journal of Dental Education, 58*, 225-228.

Shafer-Landau, R., & Cuneo, T. (Eds.) (2007). *Ethical theory: An anthology.* Malden, MA: Blackwell.

Sheehan, K. H., Sheehan, D. V., White, K., Leibowitz, A., & Baldwin, D. C., Jr. (1990). A pilot study of medical student "abuse": Student perceptions of mistreatment and misconduct in medical school. *Journal of the American Medical Association, 263* (4), 533-537.

Sheppard, S. D., Macatangay, K., Colby, A., & Sullivan, W. M. (2008). *Educating engineers: Designing for the future of the field.* San Francisco, CA: Jossey-Bass.

Shu, L. L., & Gino, F. (2012). Sweeping dishonesty under the rug: How unethical actions lead to moral rules. *Journal of Personality and Social Science, 102* (6), 1164-1172.

Shulman, D. (2007). *From hire to liar: Deception in the workplace.* Ithaca, NY: ILR Press.

Siegal, L. J. (1992). *Criminality* (4th ed). St Paul, MN: West Publishing.

Silberman, C. E. (1978). *Criminal violence, criminal justice.* New York, NY: Vintage.

Silberman, S. L. (1976). Standardization of value profiles of dental students and dental faculty. *Journal of Dental Research, 55* (6), 939-950.

Sims, R. R., & Brinkmann, J. (2003). Enron ethics (or: culture matters more than codes). *Journal of Business Ethics, 45,* 243-256.

Singer, P. (2016). *Ethics in the real world: 82 brief essays on things that matter.* Princeton, NJ: Princeton University Press.

Slemrod, J., & Bakija, J. (2006). *Taxing ourselves: A citizen's guide to the great debate over tax reform.* Cambridge, MA: MIT Press.

Small, D. A., & Loewenstein, G. (2005). The devil you know: The effect of identifiability on punitiveness. *Journal of Behavioral Decision Making, 18,* 311-318.

Sober, E., & Wilson, D. S. (1998). *Unto others: The evolution and psychology of unselfish behavior.* Cambridge, MA: Harvard University Press.

Soenen, G., Melkonian, T., & Ambrose, M. L. (2017). To shift or not to shift? Determinants and consequences of phase shifting on justice judgments. *Academy of Management Journal, 60* (2), 798-817.

Sparks, S. D. (2010). Character education found to fall short in federal study. *Education Week,* October 21.

Spencer, H. (1887/1978). *The principles of ethics.* Indianapolis, IN: Liberty Fund.

Stiglitz, J. E. (2013). *The price of inequality: How today's divided society endangers our future.* New York, NY: W. W. Norton.

Sturgis, A. (1988). *The standard code of parliamentary procedure* (3rd ed). New York, NY: McGraw-Hill.

Sullivan, W. M. (2005). *Work and integrity: The crisis and promise of professionalism in America* (2nd ed). San Francisco, CA; Jossey-Bass.

Sullivan, W. M. (2018). Work and integrity: The crisis and promise of professionalism in America (excerpts). *Journal of the American College of Dentists, 85* (2), 8-21.

Sullivan, W. M., Colby, A., Wegner, J. W., Bond, L., & Shulman, L. S. (2007). *Educating lawyers: Preparing for the profession of law.* New York, NY: Wiley. Tavris,

C., & Aronson, E. (2007). *Mistakes were made (but not by me): Why we justify foolish beliefs, bad decisions, and hurtful acts.* Orlando, FL: Harcourt.

Tenbrunsel, A. E., Diekmann, K. A., Wade-Benzoni, K. A., & Bazerman M. H. (2010). The ethical mirage: A temporal explanation as to why we are not as ethical as we think we are. *Research in Organizational Behavior, 30,* 153, 156-157.

Tenbrunsel, A. E., & Messick, D. M. (2002). Ethical fading: The role of self-deception in unethical behavior. *Social Justice Research, 17* (2), 223-236.

Tetlock, P. E., Kristel, O., Elson, B., Green, M., & Lerner, J. (2000). The psychology of the unthinkable: Taboo trade-offs, forbidden base rates, and heretical counterfactual. *Journal of Personality and Social Psychology, 78* (5), 853-870.

Thagard, P. (2012). *The cognitive science of science: Explanation, discovery, and conceptual change.* Cambridge, MA: MIT Press.

Thoms, J. C. (2008). Ethical integrity in leadership and organizational moral culture. *Leadership, 4* (4), 419-442.

Thomson, J. J. (1976). Killing, letting die, and the trolley problem. *The Monist, 59* (2), 204-217.

Tillman, R., & Pontell, H. (1988). Is justice "color-blind?": Punishing Medicaid provider fraud. *Criminology, 30* (4), 547-576.

Toor, S., & Ofori, G. (2009). Ethical leadership: Examining the relationships with full range leadership model, employee outcomes, and organizational culture. *Journal of Business Ethics, 90,* 533-542.

Toulmin, S. (1950). *The place of reason in ethics.* Chicago, IL: University of Chicago Press.

Treviño, L. K., & Victor, B. (1992). Peer reporting of unethical behavior: A social context perspective. *Academy of Management Journal, 35* (1), 38-64.

Treviño, L. K., & Youngblood, S. A. (1990). Bad apples in bad barrels: A causal analysis of ethical decision making behavior. *Journal of Applied Psychology, 75* (4), 378-385.

Trivers, R. L. (2000). *Deceit and self-deception.* London, UK: Allen Lane.

Tversky, A., & Kahneman, D. (1981). The framing of decisions and the psychology of choice. *Science, 211* (4481), 453-458.

Vaughan, D. (1983). *Controlling unlawful organizational behavior: Social structure and corporate misconduct.* Chicago, IL: University of Chicago Press.

von Hipple, E. (1976). The dominant role of users in the scientific instrument innovation process. *Research Policy, 5* (3), 212-239.

Voronov, M., & Yorks, L. (2015). "Did you notice that?" Theorizing differences in the capacity to apprehend institutional contradictions. *Academy of Management Review, 40* (4), 563-586.

Vujicic, M. (2012). An analysis of dentists' incomes, 1996-2009. *Journal of the American Dental Association, 143* (5), 357-361, 452-460.

Vujicic, M. (2014). The "invisible hand" and the market for dental care. *Journal of the American Dental Association, 145* (11), 1167-1107.

Vujicic, M. (2016). Time to rethink dental "insurance." *Journal of the American Dental Association, 147* (11), 907-910.

Vujicic, M. (2017). Back to the future (supply of dentists). *Journal of the American Dental Association, 148* (5), 347-348.

Waldrop, M. M. (1992). *Complexity: The emerging science at the edge of order and chaos.* New York, NY: Simon & Schuster.

Wallace, J. D. (1996). *Ethical norms, particular cases.* Ithaca, NY: Cornell University Press.

Wallerstein, J. S., & Wyle, C. J. (1947). Our law-abiding law breakers. *Probation, 25,* 107-112, 118.

Wanchek, T., Cook, B. J., & Valachovic, R. W. (2018). Annual ADEA survey of dental school seniors: 2017 graduating class. *Journal of Dental Education, 82* (5), 524-539.

Weaver, G. R., Treviño, L. K., & Cochran, P. L. (1999). Integrated and decoupled corporate social performance: Management commitment, external pressures, and corporate ethics practices. *Academy of Management Journal, 42* (5), 539-552.

Webley, P., & Siviter, C. (2000). Why do some owners allow their dogs to foul the pavement?: The social psychology of a minor rule infraction. *Journal of Applied Social Psychology, 30* (7), 1371-1380.

Wedgwood, R. (2007). *The nature of normativity.* Oxford, UK: Clarendon Press.

Welie, J. V. (2004a). Is dentistry a profession? Part 1. Professionalism defined. *Journal of the Canadian Dental Association, 70* (8), 529-532.

Welie, J. V. (2004b). Is dentistry a profession? Part 2. The hallmarks of professionalism. *Journal of the Canadian Dental Association, 70* (9), 599-602.

Welie, J. V. (2004c). Is dentistry a profession? Part 3. Future challenges. *Journal of the Canadian Dental Association, 70* (8), 675-678.

Wiltermuth, S. S. (2011). Cheating when the spoils are split. *Organizational Behavior and Human Decision Processes, 115* (2), 157-168.

Wynia, M. K., Cummins D. S., VanGeest J. B., & Wilson, I. B. (2000). Physician manipulation of reimbursement rules for patients between a rock and a hard place. *Journal of the American Medical Association, 283* (14), 1858-1865.

York, G. (1987). *The high price of health: A patient's guide to the hazards of medical politics.* Toronto, ON: Lorimer.

Young, L., & Saxe, R. (2009). Innocent intentions: A correlation between forgiveness for accidental harm and neural activity. *Neuropsychologia, 47* (10), 2065-2072.

Yuchtman-Yaar, E., & Rahav, G. (1986). Resisting small temptations in everyday transactions. *Journal of Social Psychology, 126* (1), 23-30.

Zachary, L. J. (2000). *The mentor's guide: Facilitating effective learning relationships.* San Francisco, CA: Jossey-Bass.

# Glossary

**Academic integrity.** The polite term for the study of cheating in dental schools and other educational programs.

**Applied ethics.** The branch of philosophy concerned with justifying various specific rules of normative behavior. See also *Metaethics*.

**"Bounce off."** As an organization that once served the needs of new members settles into serving the needs of maturing members and is led by maturing members, it becomes less attractive to new members and declines in membership as potential members "bounce off," not seeing themselves reflected in the organization.

**Charity.** Behavior undertaken to benefit others out of a service motive. Often it is presumed that the value of charity is defined by the party giving it. It does not assume that the recipients of charity are moral agents in the sense of having mutual influence.

**Codes.** Statements about what is expected of members of a group, either aspirational (as goals) or enforceable (as criteria for maintaining membership in good standing).

**Content theories of ethics.** Grounding ethics in favored outcomes or, usually, behavior to be avoided regardless of circumstances. Do not kill, lie, cheat, and so forth are examples of content theories of ethics. See also *Process theory of ethics*.

**Counterconditioning.** The most effective way to reduce unwanted behavior is to reward and thus increase the likelihood of behavior that is inconsistent with undesired behavior. Punishment is not as effective because it promotes hiding the bad behavior without reducing its attraction.

**Decoupling.** An organizational practice of publicly proclaiming high ethical standards when challenged while the organization drags its feet in making corrections.

**Disciplined license.** Sanctioning by a recognized state entity in the form of restrictions, mandated corrective action (including financial penalties), suspension for a period of time, or revocation for violations of licensure statutes and regulations related to practice or to personal conduct such as civil crimes.

**Disruptive technology.** New market entry by those who can provide goods or services stripped of costly features the public does not need.

**Double messaging (hypocrisy).** Offering public praiseworthy reasons for actions that are driven by private and less laudable motives. Lack of transparency is often used to conceal true motives.

**Dual decision making.** The only ethically acceptable actions are those that a dentist and an informed patient both voluntarily agree to after full disclosure.

**Duty to punish.** Free riding can be reduced by small investments in making it unprofitable for individuals to take advantage of the common good.

**Ethical behavior.** Accepting others as moral agents and searching for the best available mutual way forward, one that neither party would change under the circumstances. Unethical behavior is denying that others are moral agents with the same privileges we enjoy or manipulating the engagement to give an unfair personal advantage, one that would not be acceptable were the roles reversed.

**Ethical hazard.** When rules are put in place to curb the unethical behavior of a few, the most likely result is that those who are ethical will absorb an extra cost of compliance while the devious actors will discover ways to get around the rules. This represents an unintended cost shift from the unethical to the ethical moral agent. A further cost is in defining a minimal standard that draws down the level of performance to the lowest acceptable level.

**Ethical substitutes.** (a) Interactions based on power, selective information, money, or political influence. Forcing others who have different values to act on one's own or a group's norms using such approaches while claiming to be "ethical" is using an ethical substitute.

**Ethical substitutes.** (b) Programs that talk about doing the good and the right without creating the conditions that promote ethical behavior substitute the appearance of ethics for its substance.

**Ethics of engagement.** Grounding of ethical behavior in the best common choice of actions among interacting ethical agents given the circumstances.

**Ethics of judgment.** Grounding ethical behavior in personal interpretation of the right and good, with an assumption that this standard applies to all others. Often there is an additional assumption that credit is earned within one's reference group and that others are unethical because their views differ.

**Ethics of justification.** Grounding ethical behavior in rational norms, principles, standards, or other general abstractions endorsed by a group.

**Externality.** Cost borne by third parties for the benefits achieved when two or more others arrange a mutually rewarding agreement.

**False consensus.** Human tendency to overestimate how many others hold the same opinions we do.

**Free riding.** Taking more than one's fair share from the common good or contributing less than one's fair share. Generally, free riding exists where the costs of detection and enforcement of abuses are greater than one's personal share of the common loss.

**Fudge.** Ethical slack individuals grant themselves in situations based on a belief that they are generally ethical.

**Fundamental attribution error.** Tendency to attribute positive ethical behavior to one's own character and negative moral performance to circumstances beyond one's control and to attribute positive ethical behavior of others to circumstances and negative behavior to their flawed character.

**Gifting.** Gifts offered to a group's members by outside interests in an effort to influence the group or a group member's behavior. Professional organizations place limits on gifting in an effort to promote a general image of high ethical standards and to limit the influence of outside organizations on their members.

**Habit.** The strengthening of a behavior pattern by repeated use without unwanted consequences. Ethical habits form over many years and may be positive, negative, or a blend. Challenged habits are more likely to be hidden than changed.

**Incommensurable norms.** Sets of norms or principles that cannot be transferred or even translated understandably from one group to another.

**Inconsistency of norms.** Fact that a given norm can be cited as justifying multiple and sometimes inconsistent acts.

**Incontinent norms.** Failure to perform consistent with one's espoused norms.

**Indeterminacy of norms.** It is logically impossible to guarantee that there will be a rational solution for ethical challenges involving more than two norms and three agents.

**Informed consent.** Uncoerced choice of a patient who has been given sufficient information to combine with personal values to reach a decision regarding care.

**Interpretation problem with norms.** Fact that norms, as generalizations, allow multiple interpretations and may justify divergent behavior.

**Justifiable criticism.** Requirement for membership in the American Dental Association to report suspected instances of gross or continual faulty treatment by another dentist to a third party that has the authority to sanction the dentist of concern.

**Know how.** [Technical knowledge] Knowing how to accomplish something of tangible high quality.

**Know that.** [Academic knowledge] Knowing the theory of something or why it comes about.

**Know whether.** [Wisdom] Understanding which things are right to do under the circumstances. Ethical behavior is knowing whether behavior is appropriate.

**Learning.** All the relatively permanent changes in behavior resulting from the learner's experiences.

**Legal.** Acting personally or expecting others to act consistent with standards that a third party is expected to enforce.

**License.** Permission granted by states to engage in commercial activity subject to minimal standards established by regulation.

**Meliorism.** The view that human nature, especially cooperative behavior in communities and organizations, can be improved over time by small steps taken in the right direction.

**Metaethics.** The branch of philosophy concerned with how we talk about ethical behavior in the abstract. See also *Applied ethics*.

**Milking.** Taking high, current rewards from an organization by deferring maintenance and investment and then skipping before the negative effects are recognized.

**Moral agent.** Anyone whose uncoerced behavior has an impact on others. Those who have no possibility of affecting our behavior are not moral agents (for us). Anyone affected by a decision who has a right to participate in the decision is a moral agent.

**Moral audience.** Moral engagements between parties take place in the context of a presumed audience. Those not directly and immediately affected nevertheless may have a stake in future transactions or may have authority to change private agreements. See also *Nested moral engagement*.

**Moral behavior.** An alternative term for behaving ethically, which emphasizes that both are patterns of behavior rather than theoretical descriptions. The term morality means actual patterns of ethical behavior.

**Moral bleaching.** Also called ethical fading, this is the practice of converting a moral misstep into a legal or economic issue and then buying off the matter without squaring the moral concern.

**Moral core.** Our deep store of moral habits, the goals or kinds of life we hope for, and the touchstones or sources of guidance on ethical matters.

**Moral distress.** The unethical practice of an organization placing members in positions where they must choose between membership benefits and acting unethically on behalf of the organization.

**Moral hazard.** The perception that risk has been mitigated increases risky behavior. This is cyclical within a group as low-risk individuals leave and increase the cost to those remaining.

**Moral negotiation.** When there is no Win-Win or Next-Best solution to a moral engagement, it is often wise to negotiate in good faith to determine whether the moral challenge can be reframed in such a fashion that it is easier to solve.

**Moral shifting.** Transferring or distancing an individual or organization from its questionably moral products or practices by selling or otherwise benefitting from the transfer.

**Nested moral engagement.** Engagements worked out between private parties to their mutual satisfaction that are still subject to review by larger, relevant communities. What is agreed to be ethical at one level may be considered unethical in the broader context.

**Next-Best moral solution.** The second-best course of action. When a moral engagement emerges where both parties cannot get all they want, a common and ethically sound strategy is that agents who have the most to lose through not cooperating should accept their second-best.

**Norms.** Community standards for behavior. Ethical norms are generalizations about behavior a group expects of its members. Descriptive norms are generalizations about how members of the group actually behave.

**Obligation.** Actions undertaken because they promise relief from negative situations. Obligation is closed at the top so that once minimally satisfied, an obligation no longer has potential to reward. See also *Opportunity* and *Supererogatory behavior*.

**Opportunity.** Actions undertaken because they promise positive reward. Opportunity is open-ended at the top. Although there may be a diminished rate of return, more is always welcome. See also *Obligation*.

**Paternalism.** Justifying acting on behalf of others, often by suppressing information or exaggerating claims, based on superior knowledge and belief that the responsibilities and values of the paternalistic actor trump the responsibility and values of those served.

**Positive-sum engagements.** In ethical engagements, it is customary that the average return to participants will be greater than would be expected by acting alone. Dentistry is a positive-sum engagement where everyone potentially benefits the more dentistry is performed.

***Post hoc* norms.** Ethical justifications that are created or publicized on request following action. This is not necessarily the reason for taking the action, but the reason given others for having taken the action.

**Power.** Capacity to force others to act against their own interests and in the interests of one holding power. An ethical substitute.

**Practice.** Performance based on custom problem solving using approaches and aiming for outcomes that are approved by one's colleagues.

**Priming.** Structuring context to create an expectation that others will act ethically, which they tend to do.

**Process theories of ethics.** Systematically searching for the most ethical behaviors by applying a chosen method, such as "the maximum good for the most people" or the Golden Rule. See also *Content theories of ethics*.

**Profession.** Classically, a community of highly educated individuals animated by a service ethic. Currently, a professional is anyone who uses native skill, special knowledge, and technology to earn prestige and high income while limiting access by others.

**Professional service firm (PSF).** Small organizations that provide customized, expert services directly to customers based on their present need.

**Relationship.** Mutually beneficial, long-term exchange of value based on trust. See also *Transaction*.

**Scope of practice.** Opportunity to engage in practices defined by state regulation.

**Self-enforcing morality.** When ethical challenges are resolved though engagement so that neither agent feels that there is a better mutual alternative given the circumstances, there is no need for external monitoring or enforcement. The use of power, expertise, deception, or coercion automatically creates the need for external enforcement and is not self-enforcing.

**Stable professional community.** Professional communities, like all complex systems, maintain a dynamic balance that includes positive and negative elements, with the proportions of each determined by how they habitually interact with each other. Every community is perfectly designed to have the proportion of good and bad actors it is willing to tolerate.

**Standard of care.** Practices a jury and case law would accept as appropriate for similarly qualified professionals.

**Supererogatory behavior.** Ethical extra credit. Behavior that is not required but admired by the community. Charity is supererogatory.

**Systemic factors.** Social conditions in groups. Individuals behave in the context of what they believe others expect of them, written and unwritten rules, and what others appear to be rewarded or sanctioned for. Although individual habits and values influence behavior, so do the social conditions in the groups we belong to.

**Teaching.** What is said or demonstrated in hopes that others might change their behavior.

**Touchstones.** Sources of ethical guidance we go to when confronted with moral choices. These may include interpretations of public standards and principles, trusted advisors, or our own conscience.

**Transaction.** One-time exchange of value governed by market considerations. See also *Relationship*.

**Unfreezing.** The first step in a change process. Understanding the factors that maintain the current situation in a state of equilibrium and building a case that change would be worth the effort.

**Unsupervised learning.** Relatively permanent changes in behavior resulting from finding reward in behavior that has not been formally presented or taught.

**Win-Win moral solutions.** Moral engagements where both parties achieve their most desired future by cooperating.